RAND McNALLY

Road Atlas 2018

WHAT'S INSIDE

Best of the Road® Trips

Our editor's six favorite road trips from our Best of the Road® collection.

Pages ii–vii

Mileage Chart

Driving distances between 90 North American cities and national parks.

Page viii

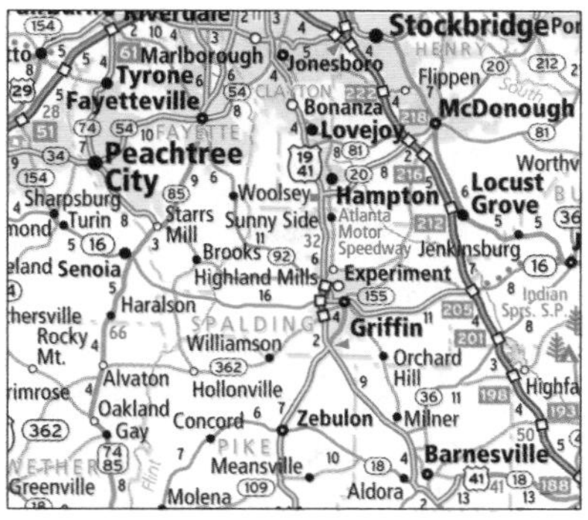

Maps

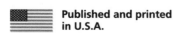

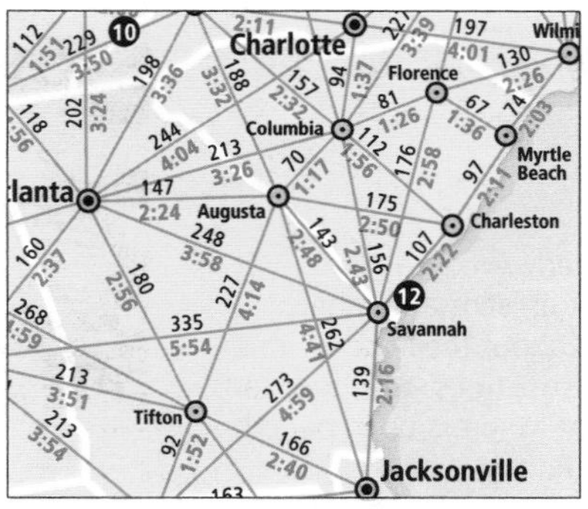

Mileage and Driving Times Map

Distances and driving times between hundreds of North American cities and national parks.

Inside back cover

If you have a comment, suggestion, or even a compliment, please visit us at randmcnally.com/contact or write to:
Rand McNally Consumer Affairs
P.O. Box 7600
Chicago, Illinois 60680-9915

Published and printed in U.S.A.

1 2 3 VE 18 17

The Sustainable Forestry Initiative® (SFI) program promotes responsible environmental behavior and sound forest management.

Printed by Quad Graphics

SUSTAINABLE FORESTRY INITIATIVE Certified Sourcing
www.sfiprogram.org
SFI-00993
This Label Applies to Text Stock Only

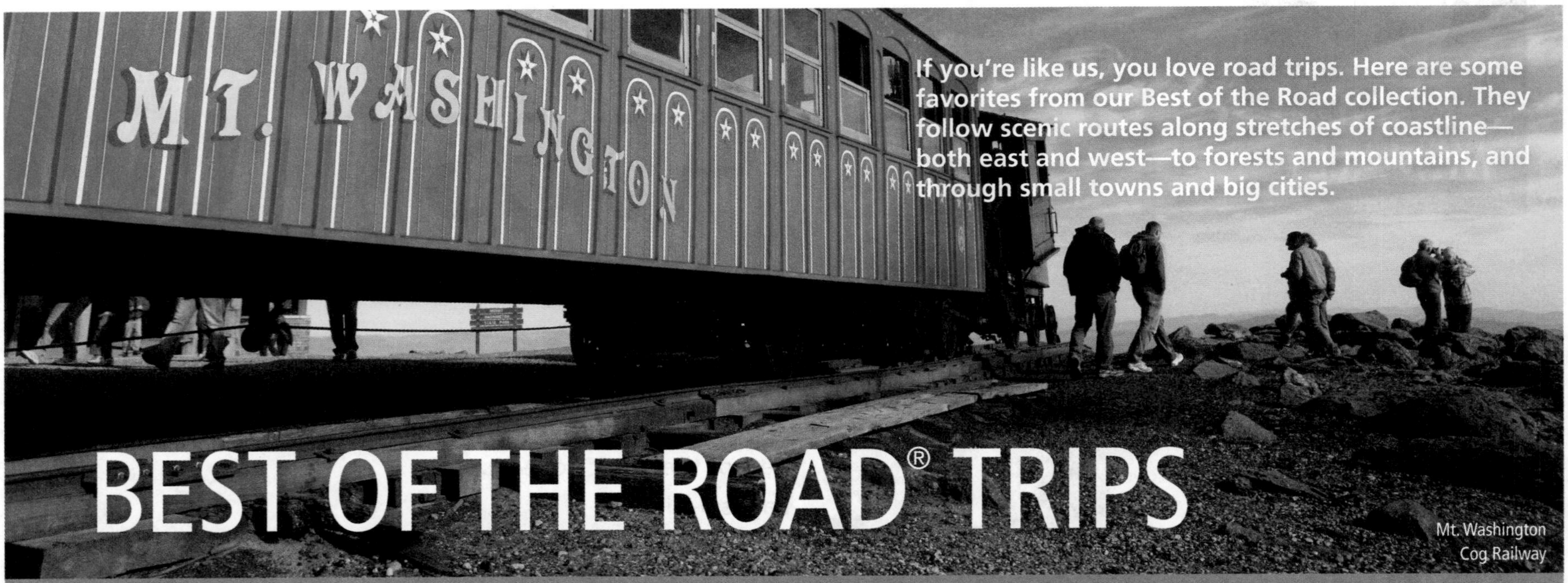

If you're like us, you love road trips. Here are some favorites from our Best of the Road collection. They follow scenic routes along stretches of coastline—both east and west—to forests and mountains, and through small towns and big cities.

BEST OF THE ROAD® TRIPS

Mt. Washington Cog Railway

Northern New England Summits & Shores

New England is rich in history and color. American heritage took root here four centuries ago, and the states of Vermont, New Hampshire, and Maine have proudly preserved much of that legacy. On this journey en route to the coast, you'll take in treasured heritage sites, museums, and landmarks.

You'll also travel through both the Green Mountain and White Mountain national forests. Both offer spectacular vistas and myriad year-round outdoor activities. Summer's hiking trails double as winter's cross-country ski, snowshoe, and snowmobile routes. And winter's slick downhill ski slopes double as summer's rugged mountain-biking terrain.

Bennington, VT

Bennington Center for the Arts Covered Bridge Museum. This full-spectrum arts center has a gallery dedicated to Vermont's iconic covered bridges, 104 of which are still operational. Explore bridge engineering, construction, and creators, and then check out the interactive map that helps you plan a tour of covered bridges, five of which are nearby. *44 Gypsy Ln., (802) 442-7158, www.thebennington.org.*

Manchester

Hildene. Robert Todd Lincoln, the only son of Abraham and Mary Todd who lived into adulthood, built this Georgian Revival mansion in 1905. It's filled with original furniture as well as presidential and Lincoln family memorabilia. The 412-acre grounds encompass a farm, gardens, trails, and woods. *1005 Hildene Rd., (802) 362-1788, www.hildene.org.*

Rutland

Norman Rockwell Museum of Vermont. Learn about the artist whose name is practically synonymous with 20th-century Americana. Displays feature more than 2,500 *Saturday Evening Post* and other magazine covers, advertisements, and paintings. *654 Rte. 4 E. (Rte.100), (877) 773-6095, www.normanrockwellvt.com.*

Waterbury

Ben & Jerry's Factory Tour. Guided half-hour tours of a Ben and Jerry's factory let you lap up the history of a beloved (and politically opinionated) brand. And yes, free ice cream samples are part of the deal. Though schedules vary, tours take place year-round and include a stop in the ice-cream and gift shop. *1281 Waterbury-Stowe Rd., (866) 258-6877, www.benjerry.com.*

Bretton Woods, NH

Mt. Washington Cog Railway. You'll channel the little engine that could during a ride on the world's second-steepest railway, a National Historic Engineering Landmark. Built in 1869, this "marvel of 19th-century technology" takes you 3 miles up the northeast's tallest peak pulled by a biodiesel locomotive or, on morning runs, a classic steam engine. *3168 Base Station Rd., 6 mi off Rte. 302, (603) 278-5404, www.thecog.com.*

Gorham

Mount Washington Auto Road. In New England, bumper stickers claiming "This Car Climbed Mount Washington" are ubiquitous. Get yours by driving to an elevation of almost 6,300 feet along this famous 7-plus-mile toll road. The route is remarkable for its curves, its views, and the fact that it's been open (weather permitting) since 1861. *Rte. 16, Pinkham Notch, (603) 466-3988, mtwashingtonautoroad.com.*

Wolfeboro

The Winnipesaukee Belle. For more than a century, Lake Winnipesaukee has been a popular cruising destination. Today, only one vessel offers relaxing waterborne tours of the 72-square-mile lake. The *Winni Belle*, a 2-story, 65-foot paddle-wheeler, makes scenic 90-minute round trips from the town docks in Wolfeboro, also known as "America's oldest summer resort." *90 N. Main St., (609) 569-3016, www.winnipesaukeebelle.com.*

Portsmouth

Strawbery Banke Museum. Early American life gets real at this 10-acre site, where artisans and other "townsfolk" in period costume go about their chores amid 42 restored and furnished historic structures. You, too, can try your hand at a craft, play games, or dress up in period clothing. The adjacent downtown Portsmouth also has a plethora of colonial buildings—many housing boutiques, restaurants, and inns. *14 Hancock St., (603) 433-1100, www.strawberybanke.org.*

Ogunquit Beach

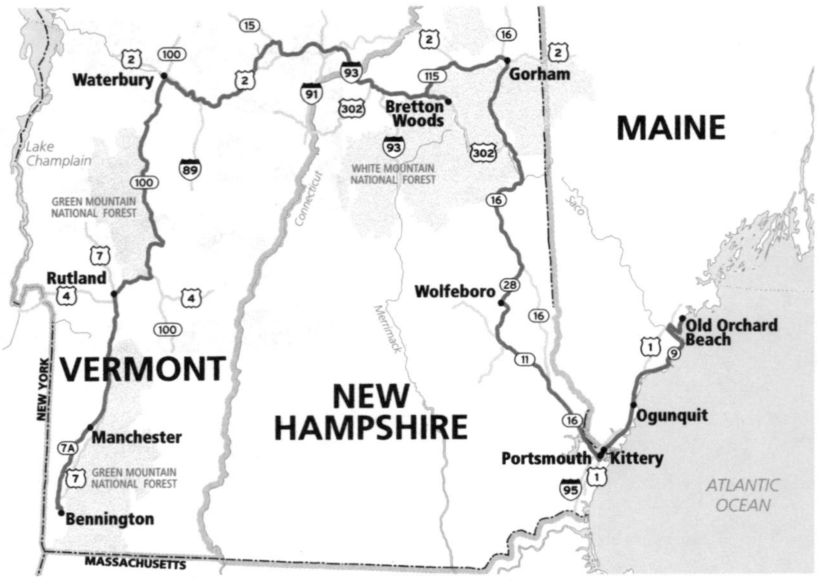

Atlas map M-2, p. 104
Distance: 425 miles point to point.

Autumn color in Vermont

Kittery, ME

Kittery Trading Post. The town of Kittery (founded in 1647) has a proud history and a truly contemporary shopping scene—one that includes several outlet malls and this rustic-looking, multilevel emporium, which has been outfitting outdoors enthusiasts since 1938. *301 U.S. 1, (888) 587-6246, www.kitterytradingpost.com.*

Ogunquit

Ogunquit Beach. This broad, gradually sloping, white-sand beach is consistently ranked one of America's 10 best. It covers 1.5 miles of oceanfront and another 3.5 miles along the Ogunquit River, behind frontal dunes. The scenic Marginal Way runs 1.5 miles along the craggy coast to Perkins Cove. *(207) 646-2939, ogunquit.org.*

Old Orchard Beach

Old Orchard Beach & Pier. In warm months, this 7-mile stretch of Maine coastline buzzes with seaside activity. At the center of the sandy beach is the Pier, a shop- and restaurant-lined boardwalk. It's all anchored by the 4-acre **Palace Playland** (207/934-2001, www.palaceplayland.com), where you can whirl, swirl, and slide on old-school amusements and new-fangled thrill rides. *(207) 934-2500, www.oldorchardbeachmaine.com.*

Blue Ridge Parkway near Asheville, NC

Inspirational Blue Ridge Parkway

Running from Virginia's Shenandoah Valley to North Carolina's Great Smoky Mountains is one of this country's greatest treasures: the Blue Ridge Parkway. This particular journey along it starts near Virginia's Shenandoah National Park, travels through several state and national forests as well as some 29 counties, and finishes near North Carolina's Great Smoky Mountains National Park.

The trip is interspersed with wonderful rock-framed tunnels and myriad scenic overlooks with elevations that vary from hundreds to thousands of feet. Just off the picturesque parkway, you'll find charming communities with general stores, folk-art marketplaces, down-home restaurants, and cultural museums. Be prepared to slow down, enjoy the views, and be inspired.

Charlottesville, VA

Monticello. The author of the Declaration of Independence, third president of the U.S., and founder of the University of Virginia put his vast knowledge of the arts and sciences to good use throughout his 5,000-acre estate. On guided tours, you'll learn that he was an agriculturalist, horticulturist, etymologist, archaeologist, paleontologist, mathematician, cryptographer, surveyor, author, lawyer, inventor, and violinist. He was also a bibliophile, whose personal collection of 6,487 books was the cornerstone of the Library of Congress. ***931 Thomas Jefferson Pkwy. (Rte. 53), (434) 984-9800, www.monticello.org.***

Grottoes

Grand Caverns. America's oldest show caves were discovered in 1804, when Bernard (Barnette) Weyer was hunting. Two years later, he opened them to curious paying guests. Civil War soldiers often explored them, and more than 200 Union and Confederate signatures remain. Tours take in popcorn, flowstone, drapery, shield, and soda-straw formations in chambers with evocative names like the Persian Palace, Dante's Inferno, and Cathedral Hall. ***5 Grand Caverns Dr., (540) 249-5705, www.grandcaverns.com.***

Monticello

Natural Bridge

Natural Bridge State Park. Before the advent of billon-dollar theme parks, an entrepreneur only had to discover a natural attraction, set up a gate, and charge admission. That's what happened here. In the 19th and 20th centuries, the 215-foot-high, 90-foot-span arch became particularly popular with Europeans and regularly appeared on Wonders of the World lists. Today the majestic formation is part of a 1,500-acre state park that includes 6 miles of trails and a visitors center. ***6477 S. Lee Hwy., (540) 291-1324, www.dcr.virginia.gov/state-parks.***

Atlas map H-10, p. 106
Distance: 450 miles point to point.

Floyd

Mabry Mill Restaurant.
The restaurant serves up barbecue pulled pork, chicken pot pie, creamed corn, and blackberry cobbler. Another plus? Breakfast is served all day. But this complex offers far more than a place to eat. It also offers a glimpse at life in the early 20th century, with a gristmill, sawmill, blacksmith shop, and the Matthews Cabin. Costumed interpreters conduct craft demonstrations, and a gift shop features Virginia crafts and foods as well as mill- and BRP-inspired souvenirs. ***Blue Ridge Pkwy., MP 176.1, (276) 952-2947, www.mabrymillrestaurant.com.***

Mount Airy, NC

Wally's Service Station. If Mount Airy seems familiar, credit actor Andy Griffith, who used aspects of his hometown to create the fictional utopia of Mayberry featured in *The Andy Griffith Show*. Today you can see show-related sites such as Floyd's City Barber Shop; the **Andy Griffith Museum** (218 Rockford St., 336/786-1604, www.andygriffithmuseum.com); and Wally's Service Station, where Gomer used to pump gas and where you can sign up for guided town tours in a vintage replica Mayberry squad car. ***625 S. Main St., (336) 789-6743, www.tourmayberry.com.***

Blowing Rock

Blowing Rock. Talk about truth in advertising. Stop at this natural attraction, and you'll understand how it and its nearby town got their names. When you stand at the precipice 3,000 feet above the Johns River Gorge, powerful gusts of wind sweep up and over the rim like invisible ocean waves. Hours are always weather permitting; call ahead before you visit. ***432 The Rock Rd., (828) 295-7111, www.theblowingrock.com.***

Tweetsie Railroad. Owing to its shrill whistle, locals gave the original East Tennessee and Western North Carolina Railroad this nickname. It stuck, becoming identified with the original steam-locomotive attraction that evolved into one of the nation's first theme parks. Today, there are several rides as well as the Deer Park zoo, gift shops, restaurants, and more. ***300 Tweetsie Railroad Ln., (828) 264-9061, tweetsie.com.***

Mabry Mill Restaurant

Valle Crucis

Original Mast General Store. Just a few miles north of Boone and the BRP is a country store that opened around 1883, when it doubled as a doctor's office and meeting place. Things haven't changed much since then. A pot-bellied stove sits in the center of the store, and racks and shelves are stocked with suspenders, birdhouses, knives, marbles and other old-time toys, cornmeal, hoes, plus a lot of things you didn't know people made any more. ***3565 Hwy. 194 S., (828) 963-6511, www.mastgeneralstore.com.***

Asheville

Biltmore Estate. Modeled after a 16th-century chateau in France's Loire Valley, George W. Vanderbilt's 250-room mansion was completed in 1895. America's largest privately owned home has more than 4 acres of floor space, 65 fireplaces, 43 bathrooms, 34 bedrooms, and 3 kitchens. You need a full day to explore the mansion, the gardens, and beyond. Note that reserving tour tickets in advance can save you a few bucks. ***1 Lodge Rd., (800) 411-3812, www.biltmore.com.***

Bahia Honda

Miami and the Keys: Destination Paradise

There are few destinations in the Lower 48 that travelers might consider exotic, but, balmy, laidback Miami and Key West definitely qualifies. With a growing Hispanic population, vivacious Miami could be considered South America's northernmost capital.

From here, you'll connect the dots via a chain of islands to arrive in Key West, a one-time hangout for pirates and drifters that has, thanks to cruise ship docks and four-star resorts, become a bit busy in recent years. But when you make the decision to search for Buffett's fictional utopia, Margaritaville, and you leap from key to shining key, you'll find there are plenty of places that remain relatively untouched, undiscovered, and ready to reveal Florida in its natural state.

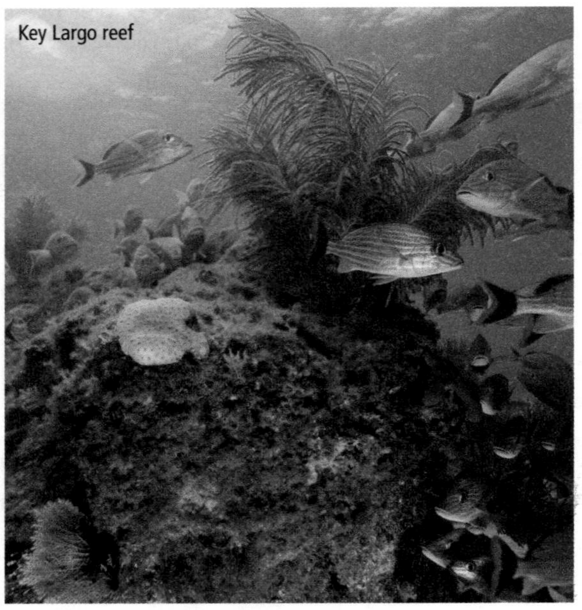
Key Largo reef

Miami

Art Deco Museum. The museum at the Miami Design Preservation League's welcome center showcases examples of Mediterranean Revival, Art Deco, and Miami Modern (MiMo) design. After viewing the exhibits, head out on either a 90-minute guided tour or a self-paced audio tour. You'll wander several blocks of South Beach while learning more about these architectural styles. ***1001 Ocean Dr., 2nd fl., (305) 531-3484, www.mdpl.org.***

News Café. Every destination has a place where locals like to hang out. In Miami Beach, it's this little café that's the perfect place to grab a bite, read the paper, and people-watch anytime—it's open 24 hours. It's also fronted by Lummus Park, a palm-lined stretch along the Atlantic that runs from 5th to 15th streets. Bordering the News Café to the north and south are classic Art Deco Historic District buildings housing classic hotels, classy boutiques, and a mix of simple and sophisticated restaurants. ***800 Ocean Dr., (305) 538-6397, www.newscafe.com.***

The Wolfsonian–Florida International University. A former storage facility, built during Miami Beach's 1920s boom, somehow seems the perfect setting for this museum's 180,000-plus items. You'll be astounded by the variety: Everything from Arts & Crafts and Art Nouveau to Art Deco and Industrial is reflected in the propaganda posters; rare books; furniture; and works in glass, ceramic, and metal. ***1001 Washington Ave., (305) 531-1001, www.wolfsonian.org.***

Key Largo

John Pennekamp Coral Reef State Park. Here's a state park with a twist: Most of it is underwater. It starts a foot off shore, flows outward 3 miles into the Florida Straits, and encompasses the only living coral barrier reef in the continental United States. Nearby dive shops can get you ready to discover this underwater world. There's also a 30,000-gallon aquarium to explore and four types of boat tours, including one aboard glass-bottom vessels that let you stay high and dry while viewing the reefs. ***102601 Overseas Hwy. (MM 102.5, Oceanside), (305) 451-1202, www.floridastateparks.org.***

Islamorada

Anne's Beach. On Lower Matecumbe Key, you can stretch out on the sand and slip your toes into turquoise water. Enjoy a swim in the calm, clear Atlantic Ocean while kiteboarders take advantage of sea breezes. See fishermen, stone crabbers, and lobster divers capture their bounties. Linger along a secluded boardwalk, walk your dog, and picnic at shaded tables among the native mangroves. ***Overseas Hwy. (MM 73.5, Oceanside), annesbeach.com.***

Marathon

Dolphin Research Center. The primary residents at this marine research and educational facility, which also helps the area's injured marine animals, include Atlantic bottlenose dolphins and California sea lions. Sign up for educational tours or, for an extra fee, enter the water and interact with dolphins (reservations required). ***58901 Overseas Hwy. (MM 59), Grassy Key, (305) 289-1121, www.dolphins.org.***

Big Pine Key

National Key Deer Refuge. Standing just about 2 feet high, key deer are miniature versions of their much larger cousins, the white-tailed deer. When their numbers were rapidly dwindling in the 1950s, they were given the protection of this 9,200-acre refuge; today, the deer population is nearly a thousand. There are walking trails, wildlife viewing areas, and a visitors center less than a mile from the intersection of U.S. 1 and CR 940. ***28950 Watson Blvd. (MM 33), (305) 872-0774, www.fws.gov/nationalkeydeer.***

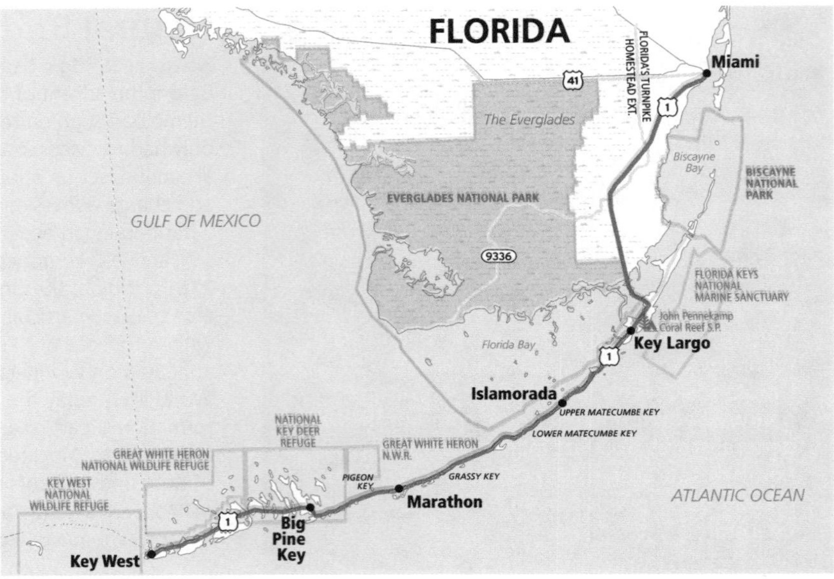

Atlas map N-13, p. 27
Distance: 185 miles point to point.

Key West

Ernest Hemingway Home and Museum. Some say it was the idyllic setting of Key West that inspired Ernest Hemingway to write classics like *For Whom the Bell Tolls* and *A Farewell to Arms* from the privacy of his second-story writing room. Today, his former home is a museum whose popularity often results in crowded tours—but it's considered a Key West must. ***907 Whitehead St., (305) 294-1136, www.hemingwayhome.com.***

Mallory Square. In a tradition dating from the 1960s, crowds gather nightly at the waterfront to watch an assortment of entertainers—tightrope walkers, jugglers of torches or chainsaws, musicians, strongmen, trained acrobatic cats—perform and to celebrate the sunset. This square is also a great place to find hand-painted T-shirts, jewelry, and other crafts. ***1 Whitehead St., www.sunsetcelebration.org.***

Southernmost Point. One of the country's most photographed landmarks, the giant yellow, red, and black, buoy-shaped monument marks the Southernmost Point in the continental United States and notes that Cuba is only 90 miles away (if you're up for a swim). ***Whitehead and South St., southernmostpointwebcam.com.***

Ernest Hemingway Home, Key West

Wisconsin shoreline

Along Lake Michigan in Wisconsin

The blue waters of Lake Michigan form the backdrop for this road trip that begins in the brewing (and Harley-Davidson) mecca of Milwaukee and ends in the Packer's capital of Green Bay. In between, the winding route hugs the lake's western shore passing through regions rich in natural beauty and towns rich in Wisconsin history.

Plan to linger awhile in Door County, the narrow peninsula that separates Green Bay from the vastness of Lake Michigan. Its small towns have colorful names like Egg Harbor, Fish Creek, and Sister Bay. Take a trolley tour to learn more about their equally colorful histories, or spend some time out on the water gazing back at the shore.

Atlas map N-13, p. 115
Distance: 213 miles point to point.

Milwaukee

Miller Brewery Tour. A guided tour traces Miller's brewing history since 1855, takes in the original storage caves, and showcases today's high-tech production lines. At the end, enjoy an ice-cold brew in the beer garden or the tasting room. ***4251 W. State St., (414) 931-2337, www.millercoors.com/breweries.***

Harley-Davidson Museum. This iconic company got its 1903 start as a small machine shop behind the Davidson family's home at 38th and Highland. Displays at this engaging museum showcase some 450 motorcycles, trace the history of the company—which is still based in Milwaukee—and its designs, and celebrate the eccentricities and creativity of the brand's aficionados. Before you leave, make sure you get your picture taken on a Harley—the perfect image to impress your friends on Facebook. ***400 W. Canal St., (414) 287-2789, www.harley-davidson.com.***

RiverWalk District. The scenic RiverWalk follows the Milwaukee River for 2 miles as it winds through the heart of the city. Lined by sidewalk cafes, restaurants, tour boats, pubs, whimsical sculptures, and trendy shops, this is one of the liveliest parts of town. ***milwaukeeriverwalkdistrict.com.***

Sturgeon Bay

Door County Maritime Museum. In addition to learning about shipbuilding and commercial fishing at this waterfront museum, you'll meet a colorful cast of characters that include hardy fishermen, ingenious shipbuilders, and stalwart lighthouse keepers. Indeed, the Baumgartner Gallery explores the history of lighthouses in Door County, which has one of the nation's greatest concentrations of them. ***120 N. Madison Ave., (920) 743-5958, www.dcmm.org.***

Carlsville

Door Peninsula Winery. The oldest and largest winery in Door County has grown into a multilevel complex that also houses a distillery and restaurant. Its tasting room gives samples of more than 45 traditional and fruit wines, which you can purchase along with every conceivable kind of wine-related accessory. The neighboring distillery makes a range of spirits from vodka and gin to single-malt whiskey. ***5806 State Hwy. 42, (920) 743-7431, store.dcwine.com/winery.***

Egg Harbor

Wood Orchard Market. Door County is famous for the market stands that sell the delectable produce of its farms, orchards, and vineyards. The Wood Orchard Market is among the best. Watch for its giant apple along State Highway 42. Inside you'll find fresh fruits, jams, and baked goods. While you shop, your kids can enjoy the property's go-cart track. ***8112 State Hwy. 42, (920) 868-2334, www.woodorchard.com.***

Door County Trolley. These bright red trolleys are a familiar sight along this region's byways, and a narrated trip on one of them lets you concentrate on the scenery instead of the road. Several themed tours are offered, from those focusing on wineries to those highlighting lighthouses. ***8030 State Hwy. 42, (920) 868-1100, www.doorcountytrolley.com.***

Fish Creek

Peninsula State Park. This 3,776-acre expanse of woods, wetlands, meadows, and dolostone cliffs is bordered by 8 miles of Green Bay shoreline. In addition to camping, swimming, boating, hiking, golfing, and biking, you can also visit one of Door County's loveliest lighthouses, Eagle Bluff. A docent-led tour gives insights into the isolated lives of those who guided ships to safety along the dangerous shoreline from 1868 until the light was automated in 1926. ***9462 Shore Rd., (920) 868-3258, dnr.wi.gov/topic/parks.***

Sister Bay

The Shoreline Charters. With 300 miles of coastline, some of Door County's best views are from the water, and this charter company offers a number of memorable boat excursions. The Lighthouse Islands Cruise travels south past clifftop mansions and alongside Peninsula State Park. The Coastline, Cliffs and Caves Cruise takes a northern route to Ellison Bay and Ellison Bluff, with glimpses of the Sister Islands bird sanctuary along the way. ***Sister Bay Marina, 10733 N. Bay Shore Dr., (920) 854-4707, www.shorelinecharters.net.***

Green Bay

Green Bay Packers Hall of Fame. Located at Lambeau Field, this hall of fame is packed with Packers artifacts and memorabilia. There's even a re-creation of legendary coach Vince Lombardi's office. You can also tour the stadium and shop for green-and-gold items in the Packers Pro Shop. ***1265 Lombardi Ave., (920) 569-7512, www.packers.com/lambeau-field.***

National Railroad Museum. With more than 70 locomotives and railroad cars, this is one of the nation's largest rail museums. Highlights include a 600-ton Union Pacific Big Boy and an exhibit on Pullman Porters that explores labor, civil rights, and railroad history. The 33-acre grounds have an 85-foot observation tower overlooking the Fox River and Green Bay. ***2285 S. Broadway, (920) 437-7623, www.nationalrrmuseum.org.***

Sturgeon Bay

Colorado River in Grand Canyon

Canyon Country

On this journey, the Grand Canyon is just one of many magnificent canyons and other natural wonders. Denver is a great place to acclimate to higher elevations and brush up on the frontier history that will unfold as you travel westward. Near the Utah border, western Colorado's majestic Rocky Mountains are replaced by glowing-red sandstone peaks and valleys. Explore them in a trio of national parks: Arches, Bryce, and Zion.

In Arizona, you'll travel along a stretch of historic Route 66, perhaps visiting the Glen Canyon National Recreation Area and Lake Powell in Page and the Lowell Observatory in Flagstaff. Then, it's on to the Grand Canyon, a place that's older than time, with views that never get old.

Denver, CO

U.S. Mint–Denver. In 1859, a year after gold was discovered in Colorado, the U.S. Government established this bastion of both gold and silver bullion. The current facility, built in 1906, stands as one of the state's most treasured institutions. Reservations are required for the free, guided, 45-minute tours. *320 W. Colfax Ave., (303) 405-4761, www.usmint.gov.*

Grand Junction

Museums of Western Colorado. Grand Junction is home to the **Museum of the West** (462 Ute Ave., 970/242-0971), where exhibits highlight 1,000 years of history—from the ancient Anasazi to old-west outlaws—and the **Cross Orchards Historic Site** (3073 F Rd., 970/434-9814), where costumed docents demonstrate pioneer life. Also affiliated with this complex is the **Dinosaur Journey Museum** (550 Jurassic Ct., 970/858-7282) in nearby Fruita. *www.museumofwesternco.com.*

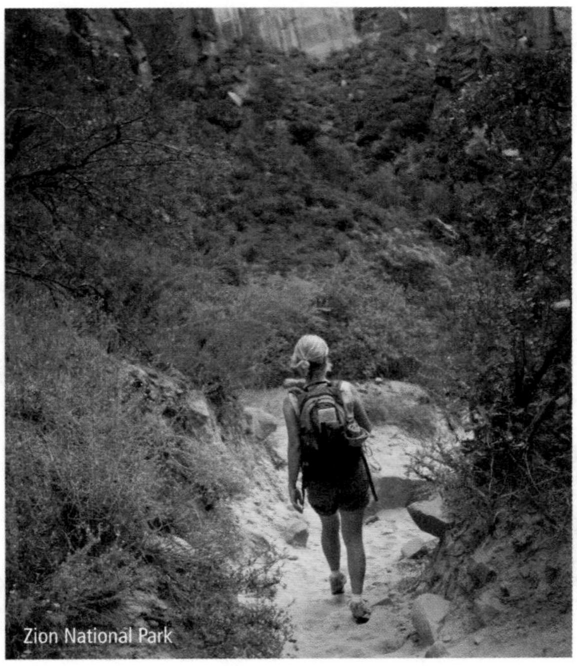

Zion National Park

Moab, UT

Arches National Park. Here, an azure sky contrasts with a crimson and gold panorama of graceful arches, spires, and fins. This park protects more than 2,000 arches, the world's largest concentration. The scenic park drive winds more than 20 miles each way. You can see plenty of awe-inspiring scenery from your car window, but be sure to get out and follow a couple short trails up to the formations. *N. Hwy. 191, (435) 719-2299, www.nps.gov/arch.*

Bryce Canyon City

Bryce Canyon National Park. Paiute lore has it that Coyote became displeased with the Legend People who lived in Bryce Canyon, turned them to stone, and left them frozen in time. Geologists have it that the fantastic spires, bridges, and hoodoos are the work of water erosion that's far from frozen in time. The limestone, shale, and sandstone continues to wear away at the rate of a foot every 50 years or so. Take in the ever-changing panorama along the 37-mile round-trip park road or one of several short trails that originate near the visitors center. *Entrance a few miles south of intersection of Hwy. 12 & Hwy. 63, (435) 834-5322, www.nps.gov/brca.*

Springdale

Zion National Park. For the past 15 million years, the North Fork of the Virgin River has been carving Zion Canyon out of the Navajo sandstone that colors its walls. The rugged high-plateau terrain is a hiker's paradise, with everything from forests of piñon and juniper pine to red rock canyons. Although you can drive the park's main highway year round, during the busy April through October season, park shuttles (mandatory) take you from the Springdale visitors center along the Zion Canyon Scenic Drive to the upper canyon. *State Rte. 9, (435) 772-3256, www.nps.gov/zion.*

Page, AZ

Glen Canyon National Recreation Area. Glen Canyon's reddish sandstone formations contrast with the sleek blue waters of 186-mile-long Lake Powell, formed when the 710-foot Glen Canyon Dam was completed in 1966. At the Carl Hayden Visitors Center, on the lake's southwestern shore, find out about trails and arrange a tour of the dam. Boating is the best way to get around; arrange guided boat or river-rafting trips through **Lake Powell Resorts & Marinas** (www.lakepowell.com). *691 Scenic View Dr., (928) 608-6200, www.nps.gov/glca.*

Flagstaff

Lowell Observatory. Founded in 1894, Lowell Observatory is where astronomer Clyde Tombaugh discovered Pluto in 1930. Its hands-on exhibit hall lets you peer through mighty telescopes, and its Steele Visitors Center has evening multimedia presentations. Guided tours take place several times daily. *1400 W. Mars Hill Rd., (928) 774-3358, lowell.edu.*

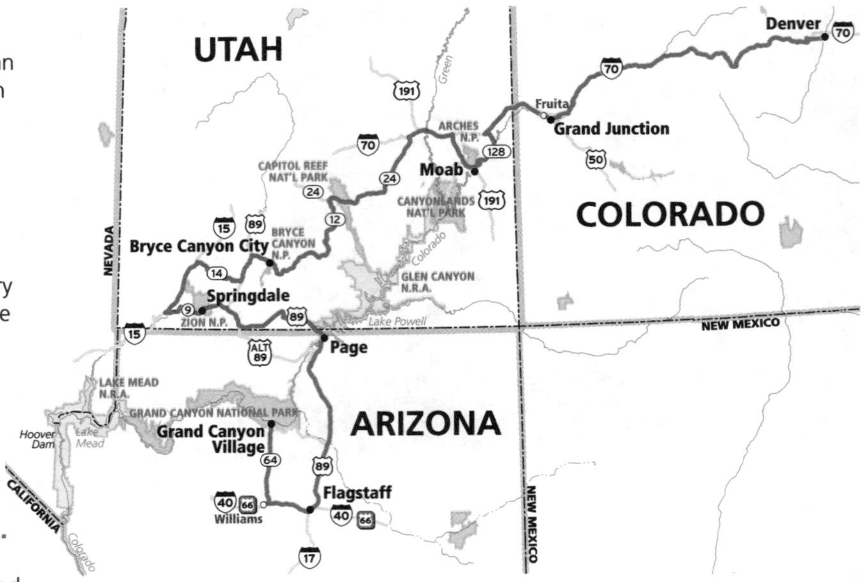

Atlas map E-13, p. 21
Distance: 1,055 miles point to point.

Grand Canyon

Grand Canyon National Park. Erosion over 5 or 6 million years carved out a natural wonder that merits its name. The Grand Canyon, a mile deep and up to 18 miles across, stretches some 277 miles. Panoramas here vary throughout each day as the golds, oranges, and blues of the exposed rock change with the sunlight. Inner canyon trails lead from the rims to the floor, where the mighty Colorado River twists and turns.

The popular South Rim has the main Mather Point visitors center and Grand Canyon Village, with its many services and amenities—including the depot for the **Grand Canyon Railway** (233 N. Grand Canyon Blvd., 800/843-8724, www.thetrain.com) out of Williams. North Rim amenities are fewer, and access is seasonal, but the views are spectacular. To see the West Rim, nearer to Las Vegas, consider a walk on the famous Skywalk. Regardless of when or where you visit, make reservations (for everything!) as far ahead as possible. *(928) 638-7888, www.nps.gov/grca.*

Delicate Arch, Arches National Park

Golden Gate Bridge, San Francisco

San Francisco and the Central Coast

California's glorious Highway 1 hugs the coast, showcasing windswept bluffs and ocean vistas at every turn. And those are just some of the intriguing sites on this trip, which starts in San Francisco and then weaves along the Central Coast through Santa Cruz, Monterey, Carmel, and Big Sur.

The route then travels inland a bit to the college community of San Luis Obispo, where you might want to set up camp to explore the Central Coast wine country. Just 100 miles south is Santa Barbara, a seaside university town favored by the rich and famous.

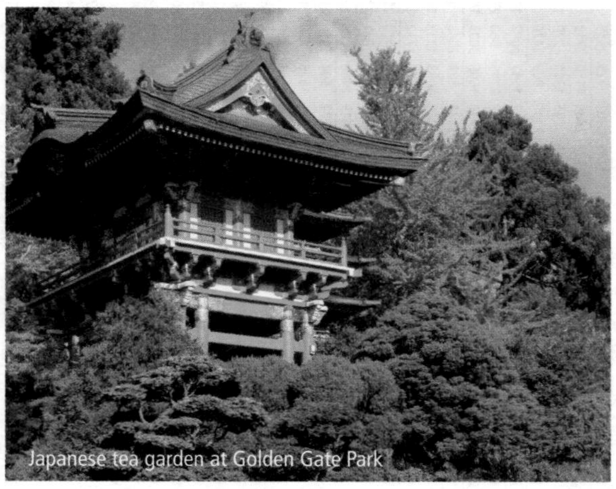

Japanese tea garden at Golden Gate Park

San Francisco

Alcatraz. Over a million people tour "The Rock," America's most renowned prison, each year. Ferries depart from Fisherman's Wharf, where you can sample clam chowder in sourdough bowls, indulge in chocolate treats at Ghirardelli Square, and visit attractions like Madame Tussauds Wax Museum. *Fort Mason, B201, (415) 561-4900, www.nps.gov/alca.*

Ferry Building. This is the epicenter of the city's epic food scene. Where else can you find organic hot dogs, zillions of mushroom varieties, locally grown lavender and heirloom tomatoes, grass-fed beef and off-the-boat Dungeness crab, pumpkin milkshakes, rose-flavored gelato, and bay views? *1 The Embarcadero, (415) 983-8030, www.ferrybuildingmarketplace.com.*

Golden Gate Park. The 1,017-acre park has trails, museums, gardens, windmills, lakes, and so much more. Join the Hippie Hill drum circle near Haight-Ashbury, enjoy house-brewed beer and thick mac and cheese at Park Chalet, or wave hello to the bison herd by Ocean Beach. *7th Ave., between Lincoln Way and Fulton St., (415) 831-5510, www.golden-gate-park.com.*

Moss Beach

Fitzgerald Marine Reserve. Low-tide pools here are rife with starfish, anemones, eels, and hermit crabs. This area is also a haven for seals and their pups. From here, pop over to Princeton-by-the-Sea and hike through the bird sanctuary to Mavericks, famous for its big-wave surf competition. End the day with a brew and a bite at nearby Half Moon Bay Brewing Company. *200 Nevada Ave., (650) 728-3584, www.fitzgeraldreserve.org.*

Santa Cruz

Santa Cruz Beach Boardwalk. This seaside amusement park offers a mix of "nostalgia" and "new." Among its more than 30 rides are two National Historic Landmarks: the 1911 Looff Carousel and the 1924 Giant Dipper coaster. Admission is free, though you'll need tickets or day passes/wristbands (a good deal!) for all rides and some attractions. *400 Beach St., (831) 423-5590, www.beachboardwalk.com.*

Natural Bridges State Beach. In addition to a photogenic sandstone arch, this park has marine-life-rich tidal pools and places to spot whales, seals, otters, and birds. There's also Monarch Grove, home to thousands of monarch butterflies from mid-October to early February. *2531 W. Cliff Dr., (831) 423-4609, www.parks.ca.gov.*

Monterey

Monterey Bay Aquarium. Located in historic shop- and restaurant-filled Cannery Row, the aquarium showcases sea otters, kelp forests, sharks, jellyfish, and a dancing school of sardines. *886 Cannery Row, (831) 648-4800, www.montereybayaquarium.org.*

Carmel

Carmel Walks. Carmel (aka Carmel-by-the-Sea) is filled with storybook buildings; inns and B&Bs; unique shops, day spas, and restaurants; and beautiful beaches. A great way to take it all in is on a two-hour guided walk. *Ocean Ave. and Lincoln St., (831) 373-2813 (info), (888) 284-8405 (tickets), carmelwalks.com.*

Big Sur

Julia Pfeiffer Burns State Park. In Big Sur's most dramatic state park an 80-foot waterfall plunges into the ocean, and trails meander along bluffs, offering peeks of migrating gray whales (in winter), sea lions, and seals. The bird-watching is great, too. *Big Sur Station #1, (831) 667-2315, www.parks.ca.gov.*

Nepenthe Restaurant. Some say the buzz surrounding this legendary restaurant surpasses the food and the service. Still, it's a requisite Big Sur stop—if only for the views and a chance to shop in its emblematic Phoenix Store. *48510 Hwy. 1, (831) 667-2345, www.nepenthebigsur.com.*

San Simeon

Hearst Castle. William Randolph Hearst's 165-room mansion—built between 1919 and 1947 through collaboration with architect Julia Morgan—contains thousands of priceless antiques and works of art. Its 127 acres of grounds are equally spectacular. *750 Hearst Castle Rd., (805) 927-2010, hearstcastle.org.*

San Luis Obispo

Mission San Luis Obispo de Tolosa. One of the original nine California missions founded by Father Junipero Serra was established in 1772. It offers free self-guided tours daily and occasional docent tours. *751 Palm St., (805) 781-8220, www.missionsanluisobispo.org.*

Atlas map NM-5, p. 12

Distance: 394 miles point to point.

Solvang

Hans Christian Andersen Museum. The Danish writer Hans Christian Andersen is honored at this small museum. Downstairs, purchase copies of some of his fairy tales at the Book Loft and then stroll cobblestone streets through the Danish-style village of Solvang, where cottages house wine-tasting rooms, shops, and restaurants. *1680 Mission Dr., (805) 688-2052, www.bookloftsolvang.com.*

Santa Barbara

Municipal Winemakers. Favorites at this shabby-chic downtown winery—one of several on Santa Barbara's Urban Wine Trail—include an old vine Blanche Chenin Blanc and several hearty reds. *22 Anacapa St., (805) 931-6864, www.municipalwinemakers.com.*

Ventura

Channel Islands National Park & Marine Sanctuary. Five of eight Channel Islands just off Ventura's coast make up the national park; the sea for 6 nautical miles surrounding them makes up the marine sanctuary. **Island Packers** (1691 Spinnaker Dr., 805/642-1393, www.islandpackers.com) ferries run to Anacapa, Santa Cruz, and Santa Rosa islands. The park's **Robert Lagomarsino Visitor Center** (1901 Spinnaker Dr., 805/658-5730, www.nps.gov/chis) has exhibits, a viewing tower, and a native plant garden.

Mileage Chart

This handy chart offers more than 2,400 mileages covering 90 North American cities and U.S. national parks. Want more mileages? Visit **randmcnally.com/MC** and type in any two cities or addresses.

	Albuquerque, NM	Amarillo, TX	Atlanta, GA	Baltimore, MD	Billings, MT	Birmingham, AL	Boise, ID	Boston, MA	Branson, MO	Brownsville, TX	Buffalo, NY	Charleston, SC	Charleston, WV	Charlotte, NC	Cheyenne, WY	Chicago, IL	Cincinnati, OH	Cleveland, OH	Columbus, OH	Dallas, TX	Denver, CO	Des Moines, IA	Detroit, MI	El Paso, TX	Fargo, ND	Grand Junction, CO	Hartford, CT	Houston, TX	Indianapolis, IN	Jackson, MS	Jacksonville, FL	Kansas City, MO	Las Vegas, NV	Little Rock, AR	Los Angeles, CA	Louisville, KY	Memphis, TN	Miami, FL	Milwaukee, WI	Minneapolis, MN	Mobile, AL	Montpelier, VT	Nashville, TN	New Orleans, LA	New York, NY	Norfolk, VA	Oklahoma City, OK	Omaha, NE	Orlando, FL	Philadelphia, PA	Phoenix, AZ	Pittsburgh, PA	Portland, ME	Portland, OR	Raleigh, NC	Rapid City, SD	Reno, NV	Saint Louis, MO	Salt Lake City, UT	San Antonio, TX	San Diego, CA	San Francisco, CA	Savannah, GA	Seattle, WA	Spokane, WA	Tampa, FL	Washington, DC	Wichita, KS
Acadia N.P., ME	2490	2206	1366	671	2507	1448	2935	283	1704	2469	728	1241	1014	1112	2198	1254	1142	911	1034	2035	2242	1570	997	2626	1900	2484	372	2115	1208	1683	1417	1692	2988	1718	3256	1249	1583	1760	1348	1667	1698	293	1370	1791	478	840	1949	1707	1559	577	2952	841	172	3360	972	2171	3154	1453	2636	2310	3317	3371	1285	3325	3045	1613	710	1884
Albuquerque, NM		284	1386	1887	998	1241	938	2219	864	990	1782	1703	1543	1626	546	1333	1387	1598	1457	647	446	983	1570	260	1318	380	2118	884	1279	1047	1636	784	572	877	786	1300	1008	1952	1354	1225	1234	2203	1219	1165	2001	1910	542	863	1730	1924	462	1641	2315	1363	1761	843	1019	1037	599	712	810	1086	1634	1438	1320	1746	1885	591
Amarillo, TX	284		1102	1602	965	957	1243	1935	580	788	1498	1419	1259	1342	515	1049	1103	1314	1173	363	424	765	1286	407	1002	607	1834	589	995	762	1352	570	857	593	1072	1016	720	1668	1132	1009	949	1919	932	881	1716	1632	256	647	1446	1640	746	1357	2031	1669	1474	714	1304	752	883	510	1097	1370	1350	1743	1505	1462	1600	382
Anchorage, AK	3672	3641	4338	4321	2660	4284	2707	4495	3788	4430	4155	4532	4111	4389	3128	3617	3914	3965	3975	4097	3227	3450	3905	3940	2935	3288	4513	4339	3804	4302	4689	3572	3424	3959	3412	3919	4093	5004	3545	3165	4486	4318	4093	4485	4428	4506	3894	3391	4782	4380	3681	4082	4443	2448	4436	2995	3026	3825	3006	4152	3532	3084	4585	2276	2387	4798	4319	3736
Atlanta, GA	1386	1102		682	1831	146	2177	1095	652	1145	894	317	502	244	1439	715	461	714	567	780	1404	902	722	1418	1361	1643	996	794	533	380	346	800	1959	515	2174	420	379	661	809	1127	328	1165	248	468	882	558	844	992	440	780	1844	684	1192	2603	408	1508	2396	555	1878	986	2138	2472	247	2649	2369	451	637	955
Baltimore, MD	1887	1602	682		1952	780	2378	400	1079	1801	372	571	361	442	1644	699	513	369	409	1368	1673	1015	524	2003	1346	1916	300	1448	584	1017	744	1068	2420	1050	2670	604	914	1082	792	1112	1003	498	703	1124	192	228	1346	1153	889	98	2349	246	496	2804	302	1616	2599	829	2081	1642	2695	2816	605	2770	2491	942	39	1260
Big Bend N.P., TX	592	470	1344	1929	1393	1201	1530	2325	973	625	1939	1661	1610	1588	938	1442	1495	1755	1614	561	838	1182	1678	325	1525	949	2226	637	1388	964	1505	988	1043	880	1128	1400	1015	1820	1525	1427	1102	2395	1226	981	2128	1912	650	1102	1598	2028	757	1794	2422	1956	1753	1190	1491	1145	1191	404	1050	1507	1558	2021	1912	1614	1892	807
Billings, MT	998	965	1831	1952		1780	620	2236	1241	1758	1786	2132	1742	1990	453	1246	1546	1596	1606	1425	551	946	1535	1257	607	662	2143	1652	1435	1688	2182	1026	971	1407	1240	1539	1477	2497	1173	838	1874	2207	1586	1868	2041	2132	1203	845	2275	2011	1210	1713	2333	891	2067	323	956	1278	552	1480	1301	1173	2078	818	540	2291	1951	1064
Birmingham, AL	1241	957	146	780	1780		2126	1177	507	1020	908	463	564	390	1386	660	464	716	569	636	1329	848	724	1274	1307	1573	1078	668	478	237	434	749	1814	370	2029	366	234	746	754	1072	258	1247	192	343	960	715	699	939	534	880	1700	748	1274	2551	555	1456	2262	501	1826	861	1994	2327	393	2597	2318	537	744	810
Boise, ID	938	1243	2177	2378	620	2126		2660	1588	1928	2214	2473	2123	2336	736	1693	1943	2020	2013	1702	830	1360	1960	1205	1227	620	2566	1930	1835	2048	2528	1372	624	1786	842	1877	1825	2844	1732	1461	2236	2636	1925	2216	2465	2525	1497	1225	2622	2435	914	2137	2761	428	2444	942	422	1622	339	1651	958	639	2418	503	425	2638	2375	1338
Boston, MA	2219	1935	1095	400	2236	1177	2660		1433	2198	453	970	744	841	1927	983	870	638	763	1764	1970	1299	724	2373	1629	2210	101	1844	937	1412	1146	1421	2714	1447	2983	978	1312	1482	1074	1396	1427	179	1099	1520	207	569	1678	1436	1288	306	2681	570	110	3086	702	1900	2881	1182	2365	2039	3046	3098	1014	3054	2774	1342	439	1613
Branson, MO	864	580	652	1079	1241	507	1588	1433		1005	995	968	755	868	851	545	601	808	668	435	806	400	784	985	816	1049	1327	602	493	432	968	209	1437	172	1651	510	274	1284	630	643	620	1417	464	597	1201	1158	323	402	1062	1138	1326	851	1529	2013	1003	920	1806	249	1288	708	1675	1950	900	2059	1780	1078	1078	292
Brownsville, TX	990	788	1145	1801	1758	1020	1928	2198	1005		1853	1459	1525	1388	1303	1474	1409	1669	1528	547	1213	1230	1673	814	1614	1370	2099	354	1379	793	1225	1036	1550	794	1630	1314	929	1538	1557	1475	821	2268	1140	700	1981	1716	738	1192	1319	1900	1259	1708	2294	2354	1556	1515	1998	1177	1589	274	1552	2010	1320	2428	2296	1329	1765	896
Buffalo, NY	1782	1498	894	372	1786	908	2214	453	995	1853		866	435	656	1478	533	434	190	326	1378	1521	849	273	1908	1180	1762	397	1499	500	1125	1037	984	2266	1061	2535	540	922	1385	630	946	1166	428	712	1248	395	569	1242	987	1184	388	2245	216	553	2639	637	1450	2433	746	1915	1654	2596	2650	909	2604	2325	1235	382	1176
Calgary, AB	1542	1511	2357	2332	541	2305	747	2615	1783	2299	2165	2542	2122	2400	998	1627	1925	1976	1985	1967	1096	1461	1915	1809	956	1154	2524	2209	1814	2239	2703	1567	1284	1958	1557	1930	2028	3018	1555	1221	2481	2380	2116	2419	2438	2516	1763	1386	2797	2390	1524	2093	2505	787	2446	865	1276	1820	869	2021	1617	1500	2620	678	424	2833	2330	1606
Charleston, SC	1703	1419	317	571	2132	463	2473	970	968	1459	866		471	207	1740	908	620	721	636	1099	1706	1199	826	1734	1557	1946	871	1105	726	697	235	1103	2276	831	2491	613	696	583	1002	1323	602	1068	549	742	768	437	1160	1293	380	668	2165	654	1066	2904	278	1811	2698	856	2180	1300	2459	2789	106	2950	2671	433	530	1272
Charleston, WV	1543	1259	502	361	1742	564	2123	744	755	1525	435	471		264	1389	491	196	250	162	1049	1355	788	352	1684	1136	1595	644	1171	312	801	642	752	2099	732	2330	244	597	990	589	902	816	813	388	908	530	403	1002	943	792	466	2005	225	840	2554	322	1410	2342	506	1829	1324	2354	2564	514	2560	2281	840	362	945
Charlotte, NC	1626	1342	244	442	1990	390	2336	841	868	1388	656	207	264		1600	769	477	514	426	1023	1566	1057	616	1662	1414	1810	742	1038	583	624	379	961	2199	754	2414	470	619	728	867	1180	571	928	407	712	641	328	1084	1151	526	539	2088	446	938	2761	168	1670	2555	714	2037	1230	2381	2712	251	2808	2528	578	398	1092
Cheyenne, WY	546	515	1439	1644	453	1386	736	1927	851	1303	1478	1740	1389	1600		960	1210	1288	1281	971	100	628	1227	807	787	340	1834	1202	1104	1316	1792	634	829	1055	1102	1144	1091	2107	1000	865	1504	1899	1192	1488	1733	1792	720	492	1885	1703	1008	1405	2024	1161	1712	298	956	888	437	1025	1162	1172	1687	1225	993	1901	1642	608
Chicago, IL	1333	1049	715	699	1246	660	1693	983	545	1474	533	908	491	769	960		289	342	354	926	1002	332	280	1455	641	1242	888	1085	181	738	1068	526	1746	650	2015	296	531	1381	90	408	917	954	469	923	787	878	792	470	1153	757	1795	459	1079	2118	816	912	1913	296	1398	1202	2080	2130	951	2063	1785	1166	697	724
Cincinnati, OH	1387	1103	461	513	1546	464	1943	870	601	1409	434	620	196	477	1210	289		248	106	934	1187	580	259	1569	937	1427	767	1055	108	686	796	584	1932	617	2172	97	482	1127	381	703	721	855	273	804	637	605	846	722	905	571	1849	288	967	2369	521	1208	2163	348	1647	1210	2196	2380	664	2363	2084	916	512	779
Cleveland, OH	1598	1314	714	369	1596	716	2020	638	808	1669	190	721	250	514	1288	342	248		142	1194	1330	659	168	1721	990	1570	562	1315	315	937	892	799	2073	868	2342	347	729	1240	434	756	973	611	525	1057	460	551	1057	797	1043	428	2060	131	736	2446	572	1260	2240	560	1725	1457	2407	2458	764	2414	2135	1091	367	992
Columbus, OH	1457	1173	567	409	1606	569	2013	763	668	1528	326	636	162	426	1281	354	106	142		1039	1261	653	191	1578	1000	1501	661	1174	176	790	812	657	2004	724	2244	206	587	1164	445	766	826	747	378	910	533	570	917	792	954	468	1920	184	859	2439	486	1270	2234	421	1718	1314	2269	2451	680	2424	2144	1007	407	851
Crater Lake N.P., OR	1307	1595	2580	2772	1033	2528	422	3054	1990	2305	2609	2866	2515	2736	1129	2086	2336	2413	2406	1976	1223	1753	2353	1473	1640	972	2959	2212	2227	2375	2931	1775	754	2178	738	2270	2235	3246	2126	1874	2562	3038	2318	2494	2858	2917	1889	1618	3025	2828	1039	2530	3156	250	2837	1351	310	2015	691	2028	858	410	2810	422	493	3041	2768	1731
Dallas, TX	647	363	780	1368	1425	636	1702	1764	435	547	1378	1099	1049	1023	971	926	934	1194	1039		880	683	1163	635	1079	1124	1665	228	873	402	992	489	1220	319	1437	836	453	1307	1010	928	589	1824	664	519	1548	1350	204	656	1086	1467	1066	1221	1861	2128	1191	1061	1668	630	1403	276	1359	1734	996	2193	1964	1102	1332	361
Denver, CO	446	424	1404	1673	551	1329	830	1970	806	1213	1521	1706	1355	1566	100	1002	1187	1330	1261	880		670	1270	707	873	243	1876	1035	1083	1226	1756	603	747	965	1015	1109	1097	2069	1042	913	1414	1942	1158	1398	1775	1758	631	534	1851	1732	908	1447	2067	1256	1678	397	1051	854	533	935	1077	1268	1651	1320	1091	1860	1671	519
Des Moines, IA	983	765	902	1015	946	848	1360	1299	400	1230	849	1199	788	1057	628	332	580	659	653	683	670		599	1124	475	909	1206	938	474	828	1253	193	1413	573	1682	586	617	1567	371	242	998	1270	656	1008	1105	1196	545	137	1339	1074	1445	777	1395	1786	1107	626	1581	354	1065	960	1747	1798	1150	1764	1484	1354	1014	391
Detroit, MI	1570	1286	722	524	1535	724	1960	724	784	1673	273	826	352	616	1227	280	259	168	191	1163	1270	599		1702	930	1508	668	1319	288	945	1002	764	2013	885	2281	361	742	1354	374	696	978	718	534	1066	613	704	1029	736	1144	583	2032	285	825	2385	677	1200	2180	533	1664	1439	2346	2397	870	2353	2075	1178	522	964
El Paso, TX	260	407	1418	2003	1257	1274	1205	2373	985	814	1908	1734	1684	1662	807	1455	1569	1721	1578	635	707	1124	1702		1370	642	2300	744	1398	1038	1619	929	718	954	796	1474	1089	1934	1497	1377	1215	2347	1300	1095	2201	1986	660	1004	1712	2102	424	1774	2455	1630	1826	1110	1166	1157	866	554	718	1175	1632	1705	1587	1728	1966	730
Fargo, ND	1318	1002	1361	1346	607	1307	1227	1629	816	1614	1180	1557	1136	1414	787	641	937	990	1000	1079	873	475	930	1370		1115	1538	1321	825	1265	1708	600	1579	988	1848	944	1054	2025	569	235	1451	1601	1116	1445	1438	1529	875	420	1807	1405	1780	1107	1726	1497	1460	550	1564	841	1160	1343	1908	1781	1609	1424	1147	1813	1344	685
Grand Canyon N.P., AZ	400	684	1786	2294	1072	1641	861	2618	1264	1390	2182	2102	1943	2025	774	1729	1786	1997	1857	1047	676	1344	1969	600	1546	433	2518	1284	1679	1446	2036	1184	275	1277	490	1699	1408	2351	1716	1586	1634	2603	1619	1565	2406	2314	942	1208	2130	2324	218	2041	2715	1286	2160	1070	722	1436	522	1112	551	788	2033	1351	1243	2146	2285	990
Grand Junction, CO	380	607	1643	1916	662	1573	620	2210	1049	1370	1762	1946	1595	1810	340	1242	1427	1570	1501	1124	243	909	1508	642	1115		2115	1279	1324	1470	1994	844	506	1207	774	1349	1340	2308	1282	1152	1657	2184	1397	1638	2014	1997	870	774	2095	1975	571	1686	2309	1046	1917	639	799	1095	283	1092	835	968	1890	1121	1002	2099	1914	759
Grt. Smoky Mts. N.P., TN	1440	1151	189	536	1806	289	2142	940	684	1310	705	333	313	190	1408	585	293	548	406	882	1375	873	561	1522	1230	1614	843	962	399	528	510	771	2010	567	2224	286	430	862	682	996	520	1015	220	633	716	485	896	964	624	637	1903	496	1042	2577	326	1479	2371	527	1852	1151	2249	2528	378	2624	2344	640	502	908
Halifax, NS	2865	2581	1742	1046	2878	1823	3306	660	2079	2844	1103	1616	1390	1488	2569	1624	1517	1286	1409	2410	2612	1940	1335	3042	2271	2854	747	2490	1583	2059	1792	2067	3358	2093	3627	1624	1958	2145	1724	2037	2073	668	1745	2166	853	1216	2324	2078	1935	952	3328	1216	550	3731	1348	2541	3524	1828	3006	2685	3688	3741	1661	3695	3416	1988	1085	2259
Hartford, CT	2118	1834	996	300	2143	1078	2566	101	1327	2099	397	871	644	742	1834	888	767	562	661	1665	1876	1206	668	2300	1538	2115		1745	834	1313	1047	1318	2619	1348	2888	877	1213	1385	980	1304	1328	198	1000	1421	108	470	1577	1345	1189	207	2580	469	197	2992	602	1808	2786	1080	2271	1940	2930	3004	915	2960	2682	1242	340	1512
Houston, TX	884	589	794	1448	1652	668	1930	1844	602	354	1499	1105	1171	1038	1202	1085	1055	1315	1174	228	1035	938	1319	744	1321	1279	1745		1021	439	871	732	1457	439	1550	960	575	1186	1163	1171	468	1914	786	347	1632	1362	437	898	965	1547	1178	1354	1940	2356	1202	1291	1904	784	1634	197	1472	1929	971	2431	2192	980	1411	595
Indianapolis, IN	1279	995	533	584	1435	478	1835	937	493	1379	500	726	312	583	1104	181	108	315	176	873	1083	474	288	1398	825	1324	834	1021		671	874	482	1828	583	2068	113	464	1198	272	591	733	921	287	818	707	720	739	613	968	643	1742	359	1034	2260	628	1100	2056	243	1541	1149	2089	2273	770	2253	1973	984	582	674
Jackson, MS	1047	762	380	1017	1688	237	2048	1412	432	793	1125	697	801	624	1316	738	686	937	790	402	1226	828	945	1038	1265	1470	1313	439	671		590	664	1620	261	1838	586	209	905	830	1040	188	1482	414	183	1198	948	603	852	683	1115	1466	971	1509	2473	789	1371	2067	491	1749	635	1759	2133	580	2537	2229	699	980	707
Jacksonville, FL	1636	1352	346	744	2182	434	2528	1146	968	1225	1037	235	642	379	1792	1068	796	892	812	992	1756	1253	1002	1619	1708	1994	1047	871	874	590		1152	2210	832	2421	772	677	349	1163	1474	403	1245	596	547	939	613	1160	1343	141	844	2050	825	1243	2954	449	1860	2748	906	2229	1066	2343	2723	135	3000	2720	198	706	1272
Kansas City, MO	784	570	800	1068	1026	749	1372	1421	209	1036	984	1103	752	961	634	526	584	799	657	489	603	193	764	929	600	844	1318	732	482	664	1152		1349	381	1616	507	451	1466	565	436	850	1405	555	844	1196	1155	348	187	1246	1127	1246	840	1518	1797	1074	704	1591	250	1073	766	1597	1808	1048	1844	1564	1252	1066	193
Key West, FL	2099	1815	809	1251	2646	905	2992	1659	1431	1688	1544	742	1149	886	2256	1534	1275	1399	1325	1455	2222	1726	1515	2082	2178	2466	1560	1334	1348	1053	507	1617	2673	1294	2884	1238	1159	162	1632	1944	866	1758	1063	1010	1446	1120	1623	1807	387	1357	2514	1332	1756	3417	956	2326	3211	1370	2693	1529	2806	3186	642	3464	3185	402	1213	1735
Las Vegas, NV	572	857	1959	2420	971	1814	624	2714	1437	1550	2266	2276	2099	2199	829	1746	1932	2073	2004	1220	747	1413	2013	718	1579	506	2619	1457	1828	1620	2210	1349		1450	270	1854	1581	2525	1786	1656	1808	2688	1792	1739	2518	2486	1112	1278	2303	2480	285	2190	2813	1022	2334	1039	447	1600	419	1272	331	569	2206	1128	1138	2319	2428	1164
Little Rock, AR	877	593	515	1050	1407	370	1786	1447	172	794	1061	831	732	754	1055	650	617	868	724	319	965	573	885	954	988	1207	1348	439	583	261	832	381	1450		1665	520	137	1147	724	815	449	1506	348	425	1230	1035	335	574	925	1150	1340	905	1543	2211	889	1093	1898	345	1488	594	1676	1963	763	2275	1948	941	1014	446
Los Angeles, CA	786	1072	2174	2670	1240	2029	842	2983	1651	1630	2535	2491	2330	2414	1102	2015	2172	2342	2244	1437	1015	1682	2281	796	1848	774	2888	1550	2068	1838	2421	1616	270	1665		2085	1794	2735	2055	1925	2014	2957	2006	1894	2787	2707	1326	1546	2515	2713	370	2428	3082	963	2548	1312	470	1821	688	1357	120	380	2422	1134	1215	2525	2670	1377
Louisville, KY	1300	1016	420	604	1539	366	1877	978	510	1314	540	613	244	470	1144	296	97	347	206	836	1109	586	361	1474	944	1349	877	960	113	586	772	507	1854	520	2085		384	1085	390	710	620	962	174	705	740	649	759	699	858	676	1762	388	1074	2310	568	1214	2104	263	1586	1111	2109	2321	658	2357	2077	872	606	701
Memphis, TN	1008	720	379	914	1477	234	1825	1312	274	929	922	696	597	619	1091	531	482	729	587	453	1097	617	742	1089	1054	1340	1213	575	464	209	677	451	1581	137	1794	384		1012	622	831	382	1369	212	394	1094	898	466	641	778	1014	1471	768	1408	2245	753	1160	2029	283	1524	727	1819	2095	626	2299	2018	779	879	577
Mexico City, DF	1392	1332	1718	2372	2301	1592	2330	2768	1548	570	2424	2029	2095	1962	1846	2017	1979	2239	2098	1090	1756	1790	2254	1124	2158	1772	2669	924	1963	1364	1796	1598	1755	1364	1839	1884	1500	2111	2100	2032	1392	2838	1710	1272	2571	2286	1282	1735	1889	2471	1469	2279	2865	2756	2126	2139	2202	1721	1991	821	1700	2218	1906	2830	2711	1905	2335	1440
Miami, FL	1952	1668	661	1082	2497	746	2844	1482	1284	1538	1385	583	990	728	2107	1381	1127	1240	1164	1307	2069	1567	1354	1934	2025	2308	1385	1186	1198	905	349	1466	2525	1147	2735	1085	1012		1475	1791	719	1587	913	861	1288	950	1476	1658	229	1180	2362	1173	1585	3260	797	2173	3063	1221	2544	1379	2656	3038	483	3315	3035	255	1044	1587
Milwaukee, WI	1354	1132	809	792	1173	754	1732	1074	630	1557	630	1002	589	867	1000	90	381	434	445	1010	1042	371	374	1497	569	1282	980	1163	272	830	1163	565	1786	724	2055	390	622	1475		336	1011	1054	564	1015	879	969	875	509	1258	849	1817	551	1176	2062	914	840	1953	379	1437	1285	2118	2170	1045	1990	1712	1260	788	763
Minneapolis, MN	1225	1009	1127	1112	838	1072	1461	1396	643	1475	946	1323	902	1180	865	408	703	756	766	928	913	242	696	1377	235	1152	1304	1171	591	1040	1474	436	1656	815	1925	710	831	1791	336		1224	1367	881	1223	1204	1295	788	372	1573	1171	1687	874	1492	1727	1227	575	1818	563	1308	1205	1986	2040	1374	1655	1377	1578	1110	634
Mobile, AL	1234	949	328	1003	1874	258	2236	1427	620	821	1166	602	816	571	1504	917	721	973	826	589	1414	998	978	1215	1451	1657	1328	468	733	188	403	850	1808	449	2014	620	382	719	1011	1224		1497	447	144	1202	887	791	1038	497	1101	1643	1000	1523	2661	737	1557	2255	645	1936	662	1936	2320	502	2727	2478	509	965	894
Montpelier, VT	2203	1919	1165	498	2207	1247	2636	179	1417	2268	428	1068	813	928	1899	954	855	611	747	1824	1942	1270	718	2347	1601	2184	198	1914	921	1482	1245	1405	2688	1506	2957	962	1369	1587	1054	1367	1497		1160	1589	306	668	1662	1408	1387	405	2666	612	220	3061	800	1871	2854	1166	2336	2096	3018	3071	1113	3025	2746	1440	538	1597
Montréal, QC	2129	1845	1218	548	2099	1299	2523	310	1342	2311	393	1118	822	980	1790	847	824	578	714	1722	1832	1163	560	2261	1496	2072	328	1884	847	1517	1294	1330	2576	1451	2845	931	1314	1646	938	1262	1549	133	1105	1640	381	717	1588	1302	1436	454	2591	603	258	2948	850	1766	2743	1092	2228	1998	2912	2960	1162	2916	2638	1490	587	1529
Nashville, TN	1219	932	248	703	1586	192	1925	1099	464	1140	712	549	388	407	1192	469	273	525	378	664	1158	656	534	1300	1116	1397	1000	786	287	414	596	555	1792	348	2006	174	212	913	564	881	447	1160		532	884	688	677	747	683	802	1682	560	1196	2357	542	1262	2151	310	1633	939	2030	2306	495	2404	2124	700	666	688
New Orleans, LA	1165	881	468	1124	1868	343	2216	1520	597	700	1248	742	908	712	1488	923	804	1057	910	519	1398	1008	1066	1095	1445	1638	1421	347	818	183	547	844	1739	425	1894	705	394	861	1015	1223	144	1589	532		1304	1026	722	1032	641	1222	1523	1090	1616	2642	878	1551	2186	675	1920	541	1816	2252	642	2716	2409	651	1087	880
New York, NY	2001	1716	882	192	2041	960	2465	207	1201	1981	395	768	530	641	1733	787	637	460	533	1548	1775	1105	613	2201	1438	2014	108	1632	707	1198	939	1196	2518	1230	2787	740	1094	1288	879	1204	1202	306	884	1304		370	1460	1245	1089	97	2463	369	304	2891	502	1708	2685	954	2170	1822	2809	2902	811	2858	2580	1138	228	1391
Norfolk, VA	1910	1632	558	228	2132	715	2525	569	1158	1716	569	437	403	328	1792	878	605	551	570	1350	1758	1196	704	1986	1529	1997	470	1362	720	948	613	1155	2486	1035	2707	649	898	950	969	1295	887	668	688	1026	370		1366	1335	755	270	2373	425	666	2962	183	1799	2744	911	2238	1557	2730	2973	481	2949	2671	808	189	1349
Oklahoma City, OK	542	256	844	1346	1203	699	1497	1678	323	738	1242	1160	1002	1084	720	792	846	1057	917	204	631	545	1029	660	875	870	1577	437	739	603	1160	348	1112	335	1326	759	466	1476	875	788	791	1662	677	722	1460	1366		452	1254	1384	1005	1100	1775	1922	1218	857	1563	496	1200	468	1351	1627	1092	1948	1710	1270	1343	158
Omaha, NE	863	647	992	1153	845	939	1225	1436	402	1192	987	1293	943	1151	492	470	722	797	792	656	534	137	736	1004	420	774	1345	898	613	852	1343	187	1278	574	1546	699	641	1658	509	372	1038	1408	747	1032	1245	1335	452		1436	1212	1325	914	1533	1650	1266	525	1445	439	930	920	1613	1662	1239	1663	1383	1445	1151	298
Orlando, FL	1730	1446	440	889	2275	534	2622	1288	1062	1319	1184	380	792	526	1885	1153	905	1043	954	1086	1851	1339	1144	1712	1807	2095	1189	965	968	683	141	1246	2303	925	2515	858	778	229	1258	1573	497	1387	683	641	1089	755	1254	1436		986	2145	975	1385	3048	597	1956	2841	999	2323	1160	2436	2816	280	3093	2814	84	849	1365
Philadelphia, PA	1924	1640	780	98	2011	880	2435	306	1138	1900	388	668	466	539	1703	757	571	428	468	1467	1732	1074	583	2102	1405	1975	207	1547	643	1115	844	1127	2480	1150	2713	676	1014	1180	849	1171	1101	405	802	1222	97	270	1384	1212	986		2387	304	402	2861	399	1675	2656	888	2140	1742	2738	2873	703	2828	2550	1040	137	1319
Phoenix, AZ	462	746	1844	2349	1210	1700	914	2681	1326	1259	2245	2165	2005	2088	1008	1795	1849	2060	1920	1066	908	1445	2032	424	1780	571	2580	1178	1742	1466	2050	1246	285	1340	370	1762	1471	2362	1817	1687	1643	2666	1682	1523	2463	2373	1005	1325	2145	2387		2104	2778	1332	2224	1305	733	1499	653	985	352	749	2091	1414	1381	2153	2348	1053
Pittsburgh, PA	1641	1357	684	246	1713	748	2137	570	851	1708	216	654	225	446	1405	459	288	131	184	1221	1447	777	285	1774	1107	1686	469	1354	359	971	825	840	2190	905	2428	388	768	1173	551	874	1000	612	560	1090	369	425	1100	914	975	304	2104		666	2563	499	1378	2357	604	1842	1495	2452	2574	697	2530	2252	1023	244	1035
Portland, ME	2315	2031	1192	496	2333	1274	2761	110	1529	2294	553	1066	840	938	2024	1079	967	736	859	1861	2067	1395	825	2455	1726	2309	197	1940	1034	1509	1243	1518	2813	1543	3082	1074	1408	1585	1176	1492	1523	220	1196	1616	304	666	1775	1533	1385	402	2778	666		3186	798	1996	2979	1279	2461	2136	3143	3196	1111	3150	2871	1438	535	1710
Portland, OR	1363	1669	2603	2804	891	2551	428	3086	2013	2354	2639	2904	2554	2761	1161	2118	2369	2446	2439	2128	1256	1786	2385	1630	1497	1046	2992	2356	2260	2473	2954	1797	1022	2211	963	2310	2245	3260	2062	1727	2661	3061	2357	2642	2891	2962	1922	1650	3048	2861	1332	2563	3186		2897	1214	578	2050	765	2076	1083	635	2844	172	351	3064	2800	1764
Québec, QC	2283	1999	1372	694	2257	1455	2681	396	1497	2472	552	1264	979	1134	1948	1004	979	735	870	1876	1991	1320	715	2416	1650	2230	427	2123	1001	1676	1440	1484	2734	1606	3003	1086	1470	1792	1096	1417	1703	259	1262	1795	524	863	1742	1457	1582	600	2745	760	275	3107	996	1921	2901	1246	2386	2152	3067	3119	1308	3074	2795	1636	733	1683
Raleigh, NC	1761	1474	408	302	2067	555	2444	702	1003	1556	637	278	322	168	1712	816	521	572	486	1191	1678	1107	677	1826	1460	1917	602	1202	628	789	449	1074	2334	889	2548	568	753	797	914	1227	737	800	542	878	502	183	1218	1266	597	399	2224	499	798	2897		1735	2690	830	2172	1397	2551	2847	322	2885	2605	648	262	1227
Rapid City, SD	843	714	1508	1616	323	1456	942	1900	920	1515	1450	1811	1410	1670	298	912	1208	1260	1270	1061	397	626	1200	1110	550	639	1808	1291	1100	1371	1860	704	1039	1093	1312	1214	1160	2173	840	575	1557	1871	1262	1551	1708	1799	857	525	1956	1675	1305	1378	1996	1214	1735		1167	959	649	1242	1372	1384	1756	1141	862	1960	1615	699
Regina, SK	1284	1253	1904	1882	472	1850	1092	2090	1321	2046	1721	2066	1674	1937	740	1151	1445	1503	1510	1510	838	1016	1441	1551	513	1080	2080	1753	1337	1805	2220	1104	1443	1525	1712	1454	1594	2570	1078	743	2009	1914	1659	1985	1994	2037	1307	927	2348	1946	1682	1619	2039	1120	2002	532	1428	1360	1024	1774	1773	1645	2117	1046	767	2360	1878	1149
Reno, NV	1019	1304	2396	2599	956	2262	422	2881	1806	1998	2433	2698	2342	2555	956	1913	2163	2240	2234	1668	1051	1581	2180	1166	1564	799	2786	1904	2056	2067	2748	1591	447	1898	470	2104	2029	3063	1953	1818	2255	2854	2151	2186	2685	2744	1563	1445	2841	2656	733	2357	2979	578	2690	1167		1844	518	1720	558	217	2644	720	793	2857	2595	1558
Saint Louis, MO	1037	752	555	829	1278	501	1622	1182	249	1177	746	856	506	714	888	296	348	560	421	630	854	354	533	1157	841	1095	1080	784	243	491	906	250	1600	345	1821	263	283	1221	379	563	645	1166	310	675	954	911	496	439	999	888	1499	604	1279	2050	830	959	1844		1326	906	1845	2061	802	2096	1817	1008	827	442
Salt Lake City, UT	599	883	1878	2081	552	1826	339	2365	1288	1589	1915	2180	1829	2037	437	1398	1647	1725	1718	1403	533	1065	1664	866	1160	283	2271	1634	1541	1749	2229	1073	419	1488	688	1586	1524	2544	1437	1308	1936	2336	1633	1920	2170	2238	1200	930	2323	2140	653	1842	2461	765	2172	649	518	1326		1311	750	735	2125	839	720	2339	2079	1042
San Antonio, TX	712	510	986	1642	1480	861	1651	2039	708	274	1654	1300	1324	1230	1025	1202	1210	1457	1314	276	935	960	1439	554	1343	1092	1940	197	1149	635	1066	766	1272	594	1357	1111	727	1379	1285	1205	662	2096	939	541	1822	1557	468	920	1160	1742	985	1495	2136	2076	1397	1242	1720	906	1311		1278	1736	1161	2150	2018	1170	1606	625
San Diego, CA	810	1097	2138	2695	1301	1994	958	3046	1675	1552	2596	2459	2354	2381	1162	2080	2196	2407	2269	1359	1077	1747	2346	718	1908	835	2930	1472	2089	1759	2343	1597	331	1676	120	2109	1819	2656	2118	1986	1936	3018	2030	1816	2809	2730	1351	1613	2436	2738	352	2452	3143	1083	2551	1372	558	1845	750	1278		501	2356	1256	1468	2447	2693	1401
San Francisco, CA	1086	1370	2472	2816	1173	2327	639	3098	1950	2010	2650	2789	2564	2712	1172	2130	2380	2458	2451	1734	1268	1798	2397	1175	1781	968	3004	1929	2273	2133	2723	1808	569	1963	380	2321	2095	3038	2170	2040	2320	3071	2306	2252	2902	2973	1627	1662	2816	2873	749	2574	3196	635	2847	1384	217	2061	735	1736	501		2720	807	874	2832	2812	1775
Sault Ste. Marie, ON	1777	1493	1040	852	1273	1014	1893	923	991	1918	514	1156	683	947	1411	471	577	496	521	1370	1428	710	347	1910	665	1692	904	1527	540	1180	1333	951	2196	1089	2465	649	972	1685	398	538	1268	740	823	1355	921	1037	1236	850	1475	911	2240	614	871	2165	1007	1118	2364	740	1848	1646	2502	2581	1201	2090	1812	1492	851	1150
Savannah, GA	1634	1350	247	605	2078	393	2418	1014	900	1320	909	106	514	251	1687	951	664	764	680	996	1651	1150	870	1632	1609	1890	915	971	770	580	135	1048	2206	763	2422	658	626	483	1045	1374	502	1113	495	642	811	481	1092	1239	280	703	2091	697	1111	2844	322	1756	2644	802	2125	1161	2356	2720		2896	2616	333	575	1202
Seattle, WA	1438	1743	2649	2770	818	2597	503	3054	2059	2428	2604	2950	2560	2808	1225	2063	2363	2414	2424	2193	1320	1764	2353	1705	1424	1121	2960	2431	2253	2537	3000	1844	1128	2275	1134	2357	2299	3315	1990	1655	2727	3025	2404	2716	2858	2949	1948	1663	3093	2828	1414	2530	3150	172	2885	1141	720	2096	839	2150	1256	807	2896		278	3109	2768	1828
Shenandoah N.P., VA	1794	1488	556	119	1951	634	2399	519	1016	1655	382	516	260	317	1650	698	474	368	389	1223	1614	1014	523	1863	1345	1855	420	1306	563	872	687	1012	2359	904	2582	506	768	1035	798	1111	886	618	558	978	320	181	1233	1155	847	217	2238	245	616	2824	263	1615	2604	768	2107	1496	2586	2842	567	2769	2490	885	82	1207
Spokane, WA	1320	1505	2369	2491	540	2318	425	2774	1780	2296	2325	2671	2281	2528	993	1785	2084	2135	2144	1964	1091	1484	2075	1587	1147	1002	2682	2192	1973	2229	2720	1564	1138	1948	1215	2077	2018	3035	1712	1377	2478	2746	2124	2409	2580	2671	1710	1383	2814	2550	1381	2252	2871	351	2605	862	793	1817	720	2018	1468	874	2616	278		2830	2490	1600
Tampa, FL	1746	1462	451	942	2291	537	2638	1342	1078	1329	1235	433	840	578	1901	1166	916	1091	1007	1102	1860	1354	1178	1728	1813	2099	1242	980	984	699	198	1252	2319	941	2525	872	779	255	1260	1578	509	1440	700	651	1138	808	1270	1445	84	1040	2153	1023	1438	3064	648	1960	2857	1008	2339	1170	2447	2832	333	3109	2830		902	1381
Thunder Bay, ON	1566	1348	1376	1288	1049	1322	1670	1298	983	1830	942	1570	1118	1382	1210	656	949	932	957	1270	1253	583	784	1718	441	1492	1305	1522	840	1361	1728	776	1996	1156	2265	957	1153	2041	585	341	1547	1121	1130	1545	1349	1473	1127	720	1822	1339	2028	1049	1246	1938	1443	913	2006	870	1648	1547	2326	2224	1613	1866	1588	1828	1286	974
Toronto, ON	1800	1516	963	472	1771	968	2194	548	1014	1919	98	964	535	756	1462	519	493	290	426	1393	1504	834	232	1932	1167	1744	490	1551	518	1186	1135	1001	2247	1120	2517	601	983	1483	609	933	1222	465	774	1306	489	669	1259	974	1284	497	2262	316	592	2620	737	1438	2414	763	1899	1669	2583	2632	1007	2588	2310	1333	482	1188
Tucson, AZ	449	735	1732	2320	1326	1588	1030	2669	1314	1145	2233	2052	1994	1975	995	1784	1836	2048	1908	952	895	1433	2020	312	1769	687	2569	1066	1728	1353	1936	1234	401	1271	485	1749	1406	2250	1805	1675	1530	2654	1617	1410	2448	2303	990	1313	2029	2383	116	2092	2766	1447	2142	1293	848	1485	776	871	407	864	1949	1529	1496	2040	2283	1040
Vancouver, BC	1574	1878	2785	2906	953	2733	638	3188	2195	2564	2740	3086	2696	2944	1372	2198	2499	2548	2560	2338	1465	1900	2487	1841	1559	1256	3094	2565	2389	2675	3136	1980	1264	2421	1275	2493	2437	3451	2125	1790	2894	2982	2540	2851	2993	3084	2083	1799	3229	2963	1550	2665	3286	313	3021	1277	890	2232	973	2286	1398	947	3032	141	413	3245	2903	1973
Washington, DC	1885	1600	637	39	1951	744	2375	439	1078	1765	382	530	362	398	1642	697	512	367	407	1332	1671	1014	522	1966	1344	1914	340	1411	582	980	706	1066	2428	1014	2670	606	879	1044	788	1110	965	538	666	1087	228	189	1343	1151	849	137	2348	244	535	2800	262	1615	2595	827	2079	1606	2693	2812	575	2768	2490	902		1258
Wichita, KS	591	382	955	1260	1064	810	1338	1613	292	896	1176	1272	945	1092	608	724	779	992	851	361	519	391	964	730	685	759	1512	595	674	707	1272	193	1164	446	1377	701	577	1587	763	634	894	1597	688	880	1391	1349	158	298	1365	1319	1053	1035	1710	1764	1227	699	1558	442	1042	625	1401	1775	1202	1828	1600	1381	1258	
Winnipeg, MB	1538	1222	1582	1570	723	1532	1345	1729	1033	1834	1403	1779	1360	1638	1006	864	1158	1214	1222	1298	1092	699	1153	1590	222	1334	1760	1541	1049	1484	1932	817	1692	1208	1965	1164	1273	2252	791	456	1721	1552	1336	1664	1659	1749	1095	640	2029	1629	2000	1331	1677	1474	1684	745	1684	1062	1277	1562	2025	1912	1829	1401	1121	2047	1568	905
Yellowstone N.P., WY	963	977	1904	2145	175	1852	418	2410	1316	1813	1960	2207	1906	2076	469	1418	1710	1772	1787	1436	563	1094	1710	1229	782	632	2315	1664	1602	1826	2256	1100	769	1519	1037	1611	1624	2569	1345	1016	2014	2381	1658	1950	2213	2314	1182	958	2356	2182	1002	1892	2506	833	2178	497	755	1356	351	1535	1098	972	2151	760	481	2356	2142	1072
Yosemite N.P., CA	989	1289	2391	2695	1129	2246	594	2979	1868	1939	2529	2708	2403	2619	1051	2012	2264	2339	2335	1636	1045	1680	2279	1104	1735	802	2888	1858	2155	2052	2642	1649	415	1870	308	2159	2009	2957	2051	1922	2239	2950	2212	2162	2802	2811	1533	1547	2735	2754	678	2457	3075	751	2762	1263	214	1899	615	1665	429	189	2639	923	967	2751	2695	1564

RAND McNALLY

Road Atlas 2018

MAPS

MAPS

Map Legend **inside front cover**

United States Overview Map **2–3**

States and Cities **4–116**

Canada Overview Map **117**

Provinces and Cities **118–127**

Mexico Overview Map and Puerto Rico **128**

INDEXES

United States Index **129–136**

Canada Index **136**

Mexico Index **136**

Quick Map References

State & Province Maps

United States

Alabama 4–5
Alaska 6
Arizona 7–9
Arkansas 10–11
California 12–19
Colorado 20–22
Connecticut 23
Delaware 24
Florida 24–27
Georgia 28–30
Hawaii 30
Idaho 31
Illinois 32–35
Indiana 35–37
Iowa 38–39
Kansas 40–41
Kentucky 42–43
Louisiana 44
Maine 45
Maryland 46–47
Massachusetts 48–49
Michigan 50–52
Minnesota 53–55
Mississippi 56
Missouri 57–59
Montana 60–61
Nebraska 62–63
Nevada 64–65
New Hampshire 65
New Jersey 66–67
New Mexico 68
New York 69–73
North Carolina 74–76
North Dakota 77
Ohio 78–81
Oklahoma 82–83
Oregon 84–85
Pennsylvania 86–90
Rhode Island 91
South Carolina 92
South Dakota 93
Tennessee 94–96
Texas 96–101
Utah 102–103
Vermont 104
Virginia 105–107
Washington 108–110
Washington, D.C. 111
West Virginia 112
Wisconsin 113–115
Wyoming 116

Canada

Alberta 118–119
British Columbia 118–119
Manitoba 121
New Brunswick 126
Newfoundland and Labrador 127
Nova Scotia 126–127
Ontario 122–123
Prince Edward Island 126–127
Québec 124–125
Saskatchewan 120–121

Selected City Maps

This list contains only 70 of more than 350 detailed city maps in the Road Atlas. To find more city maps, consult the state & province map list above and turn to the pages indicated.

Albany / Schenectady 70
Albuquerque 68
Allentown / Bethlehem 88
Atlanta & Vicinity 30
Austin 98
Bakersfield 14
Baltimore 46
Baton Rouge 44
Birmingham 5
Boston & Vicinity 48
Bridgeport / New Haven 23
Buffalo / Niagara Falls 70
Charlotte & Vicinity 76
Chicago & Vicinity 34–35
Cincinnati 80
Cleveland & Vicinity 81
Columbus 81
Dallas / Fort Worth & Vicinity 97
Dayton 80
Denver & Vicinity 22
Detroit & Vicinity 52
Fresno 15
Grand Rapids 52
Greensboro / Winston-Salem / High Point 76
Hampton Roads: Norfolk / Virginia Beach / Newport News 105
Hartford 23
Honolulu 30
Houston & Vicinity 96
Indianapolis 35
Jacksonville 26
Kansas City & Vicinity 58
Las Vegas 64, 65
Los Angeles & Vicinity 18–19
Louisville 42
Memphis & Vicinity 94
Mexico City (Ciudad de México) 128
Miami / Fort Lauderdale & Vicinity 25
Milwaukee & Vicinity 113
Minneapolis / St. Paul & Vicinity 53
Montréal 124, 125
Nashville 94
New Orleans 44
New York & Vicinity 72–73
Newark & Vicinity 66
Oklahoma City & Vicinity 82
Omaha 63
Orlando 27
Oxnard / Ventura 17
Philadelphia & Vicinity 90
Phoenix & Vicinity 7
Pittsburgh & Vicinity 90
Portland & Vicinity 85
Providence 91
Raleigh / Durham / Chapel Hill 76
Richmond / Petersburg 105
Rochester 69
Sacramento 16
St. Louis & Vicinity 57
Salt Lake City & Vicinity 103
San Antonio 101
San Diego & Vicinity 17
San Francisco Bay Area: San Francisco / Oakland / San Jose 13, 16
Seattle / Tacoma & Vicinity 110
Tampa / St. Petersburg & Vicinity 25
Toronto 122
Tucson 9
Tulsa 82
Vancouver 118
Washington & Vicinity 111
Worcester 49

National Park Maps

Acadia National Park 45
Arches National Park 103
Banff / Glacier / Kootenay & Yoho National Parks 119
Bryce Canyon National Park 103
Canyonlands National Park 103
Capitol Reef National Park 103
Colonial National Historical Park 105
Crater Lake National Park 85
Denali National Park & Preserve 6
Gettysburg National Military Park 87
Grand Canyon National Park 7
Grand Teton National Park 116
Great Smoky Mountains National Park 76
Hot Springs National Park 10
Isle Royale National Park 50
Joshua Tree National Park 14
Mammoth Cave National Park 43
Mesa Verde National Park 20
Mount Rainier National Park 110
Petrified Forest National Park 7
Rocky Mountain National Park 22
Sequoia and Kings Canyon National Parks 14
Waterton-Glacier International Peace Park 60
Yellowstone National Park 116
Yosemite National Park 12
Zion National Park 102

Photo credits: Table of contents: (t to b) ©Delpixart / istockphoto, ©Rand McNally (3); p. ii (t to b), ©Michael Dwyer / Alamy, ©Ron and Patty Thomas / istockphoto, ©David Parsons / istockphoto; p. iii (t to b) ©digidreamgrafix / istockphoto, ©Kenneth Wiedmann / istockphoto, ©cjmckendry / istockphoto; p. iv (t to b) ©Cindy Murray / istockphoto, ©Luiz Felipe Castro / Getty; p. v (t to b) ©Cindy Murray / istockphoto, ©Andrew Jalbert / istockphoto, ©Graeme Crouch / istockphoto; p. vi (t to b) ©tonda / istockphoto, ©kubrak78 / istockphoto, ©Delpixart / istockphoto; p. vii (t to b) ©Giorgio Fochesato / istockphoto, ©gregobagel / istockphoto; p. 5 ©Mobile Bay CVB; p. 7 & 9 ©Greater Phoenix CVB; p. 11 ©CJRW/Bernie Jungkind; p. 13, 16, 18, 33 & 123 ©Rand McNally; p. 15, 49, 63 71, 73, 83, 85, 97, 101, 103, 109 & 110 ©Getty Images; p. 17 ©Santa Barbara Conference & Visitors Bureau and Film Commission/J. Sinclair; p. 19 ©Huntington Beach CVB; p. 21 ©Denver Metro CVB/Ron Ruhoff; p. 22 ©Denver Metro CVB/Randy Brown; p. 25 ©St. Petersburg/Clearwater Area CVB; p. 27 ©Visit Florida; p. 29 ©GA Dept. of C&CA; p. 34 ©City of Chicago/Hedrich Blessing; p. 35 ©The Children's Museum of Indianapolis; p. 37 ©Brown County State Park; p. 39 ©IA DED Div. of Tourism; p. 41 ©Kansas Dept. of Commerce & Housing/Charlie Riedel; p. 43 ©Kentucky Tourism; p. 47 ©MD Office of Tourism Dev.; p. 51 ©Michigan DNR; p. 52 ©Robert J. Eovaldi; p.53 ©Walker Art Center; p. 55 ©MN Office of Tourism; p. 57 & 59 ©MO Div. of Tourism; p. 61 ©Travel Montana/Donnie Sexton; p. 67 ©NJ C&EGC, OT&T; p. 72 ©Photodisc; p. 75 & 76 ©NC Div of Tourism Film & Sports Dev.; p. 79 ©Ohio Tourism; p. 81 ©Warren County CVB; p. 87 ©Commonwealth Media Services; p. 89 ©GPTMC; p. 90 ©Greater Pittsburgh CVB; p. 95 ©TN Dept. Tourist Dev.; p. 96 ©Kingsport CVB; p. 99 ©State of Texas Travel CVB; p. 105 ©Virginia Tourism Corp.; p.107 ©National Park Service; p. 113 ©Kenosha Area CVB; p. 115 ©Wisconsin Dept. of Tourism; p. 125 ©J-F Bergeron/Enviro Foto/Quebec City Tourism.

For licensing information and copyright permissions, contact us at permissions@randmcnally.com

If you have a comment, suggestion, or even a compliment, please visit us at randmcnally.com/contact or write to:
Rand McNally Consumer Affairs
P.O. Box 7600
Chicago, Illinois 60680-9915

Published and printed in U.S.A.

1 2 3 VE 18 17

Capital: Washington, G-17
Land area: 3,531,905 sq. mi.

Selected National Park Service locations

- Acadia National Park C-20
- Arches National Park G-6
- Badlands National Park E-9
- Big Bend National Park L-8
- Biscayne National Park........... M-18
- Bryce Canyon National Park......... G-5
- Canyonlands National Park G-6
- Capitol Reef National Park.......... G-5
- Carlsbad Caverns National Park....... J-7
- Channel Islands National Park....... H-1
- Congaree National Park........... I-17
- Crater Lake National Park D-2
- Cuyahoga Valley National Park..... F-16
- Death Valley National Park G-3
- Denali National Park................ L-4
- Dry Tortugas National Park M-17
- Everglades National Park......... M-17
- Glacier Bay National Park.......... M-6
- Glen Canyon Nat'l Recreation Area .
- Grand Canyon National Park.......
- Grand Teton National Park ....
- Great Sand Dunes Nat'l Park & Pres..
- Great Smoky Mountains Nat'l Park..
- Guadalupe Mountains Nat'l Park ...

Population: 308,745,538
Largest city: New York, 8,175,133, E-18

Selected National Park Service locations

- laleakalā National Park. L-2
- awai'i Volcanoes National Park. L-2
- ot Springs National Park I-12
- le Royale National Park C-13
- ings Canyon National Park G-2
- ake Mead Nat'l Recreation Area H-4
- Lassen Volcanic National Park E-2
- Mammoth Cave National Park H-14
- Mesa Verde National Park H-6
- Mount Rainier National Park. B-3
- North Cascades National Park B-4
- Olympic National Park B-3
- Petrified Forest National Park I-5
- Redwood National Park D-1
- Rocky Mountain National Park F-7
- Sequoia National Park G-2
- Shenandoah National Park G-17
- Theodore Roosevelt National Park . . . D-8
- Voyageurs National Park C-12
- Waterton-Glacier Int'l Peace Park B-5
- Wind Cave National Park E-8
- Yellowstone National Park. D-6
- Yosemite National Park F-2
- Zion National Park G-5

 18-1

Alabama

Nickname: The Heart of Dixie
Capital: Montgomery, J-8
Land area: 50,645 sq. mi. (rank: 28th)
Population: 4,779,736 (rank: 23rd)
Largest city: Birmingham, 212,237, F-7

Index of places Pg. 129

Travel planning & on-the-road resources

Tourism Information
Alabama Tourism: (800) 252-2262, (334) 242-4169; www.alabama.travel

Toll Road Information
Beach Express (Baldwin Co.): (251) 968-3415; www.beachexpress.com
Montgomery Expressway (Montgomery): (334) 290-2002; www.montgomeryexpressway.com
Tuscaloosa By-Pass (Tuscaloosa): (205) 752-2003; www.tuscaloosabypass

Road Conditions & Construction
(888) 588-2848; www.dot.state.al.us, alitsweb2.dot.state.al.us/RoadConditions

(Freedom Pass)

Determining distances along roads

Highway distances (segments of one mile or less not shown):
Cumulative miles (red): the distance between red arrows
Intermediate miles (black): the distance between intersections & p

Interchanges and exit numbers
For most states, the mileage between interchanges may be determ
by subtracting one number from the other.

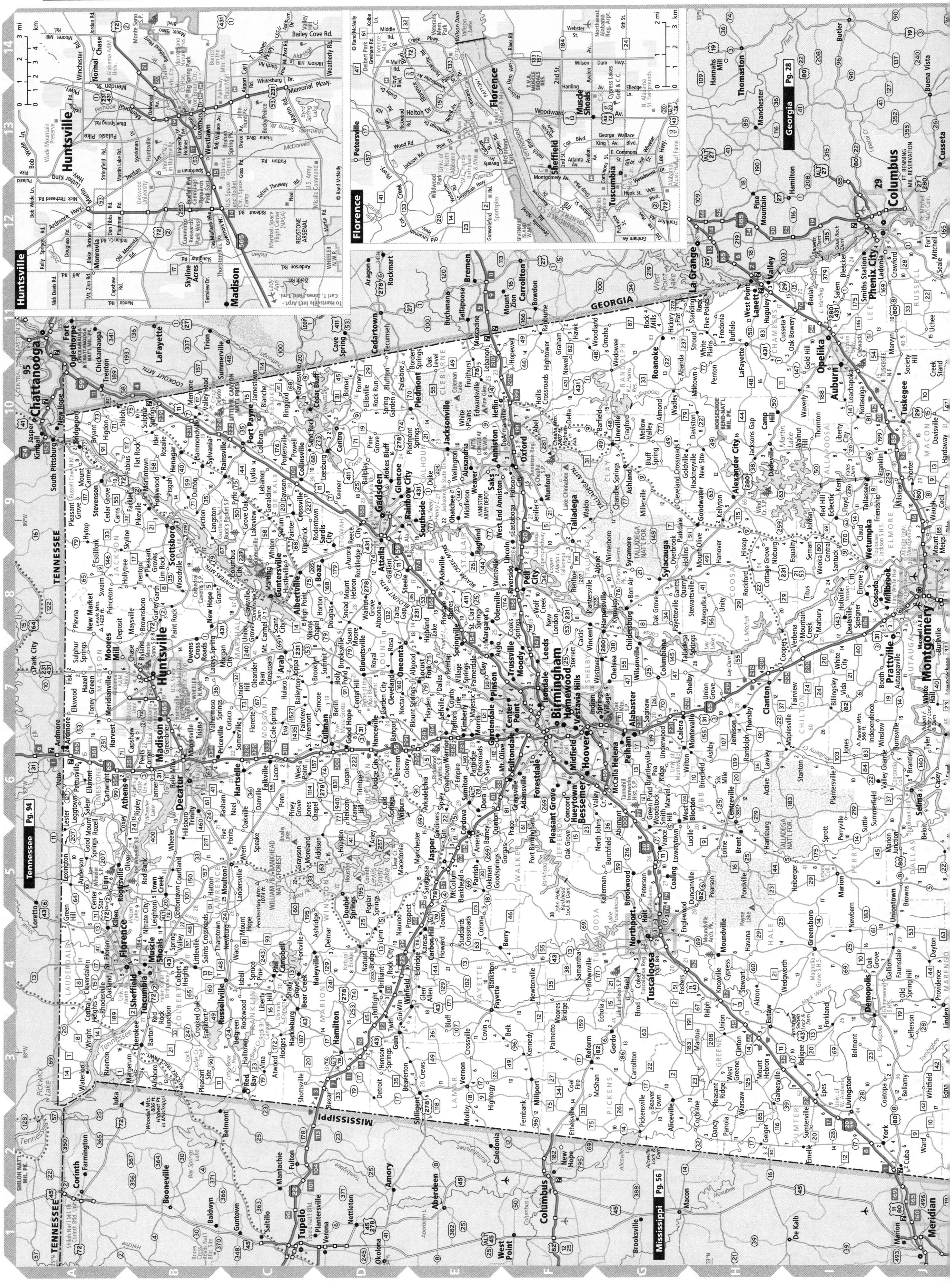

agg-Mitchell Mansion, Mobile

Mileages between cities

	Andalusia	Anniston	Auburn	Birmingham	Chattanooga, TN	Columbus, GA	Dothan	Florence	Gadsden	Grove Hill	Huntsville	Meridian, MS	Mobile	Montgomery	Selma	Tuscaloosa
Atlanta, GA	252	90	108	146	117	106	206	263	119	294	181	289	328	160	210	201
Birmingham	181	64	109		146	141	196	118	61	155	102	146	258	90	87	58
Chattanooga, TN	322	119	221	146		219	319	166	89	300	102	291	399	232	228	203
Dothan	74	207	118	196	319	99		311	252	169	294	253	196	103	148	210
Huntsville	279	104	210	102	102	243	294	64	72	254		244	356	189	188	155
Mobile	123	280	222	258	399	256	196	376	313	82	356	133		168	159	203
Montgomery	91	110	54	90	232	87	103	205	148	134	189	153	168		50	104
Tuscaloosa	194	118	159	58	203	192	210	123	118	121	155	93	203	104	75	

Total mileages through Alabama

10: 66 miles; 59: 241 miles
20: 215 miles; 65: 367 miles

More mileages at randmcnally.com/MC

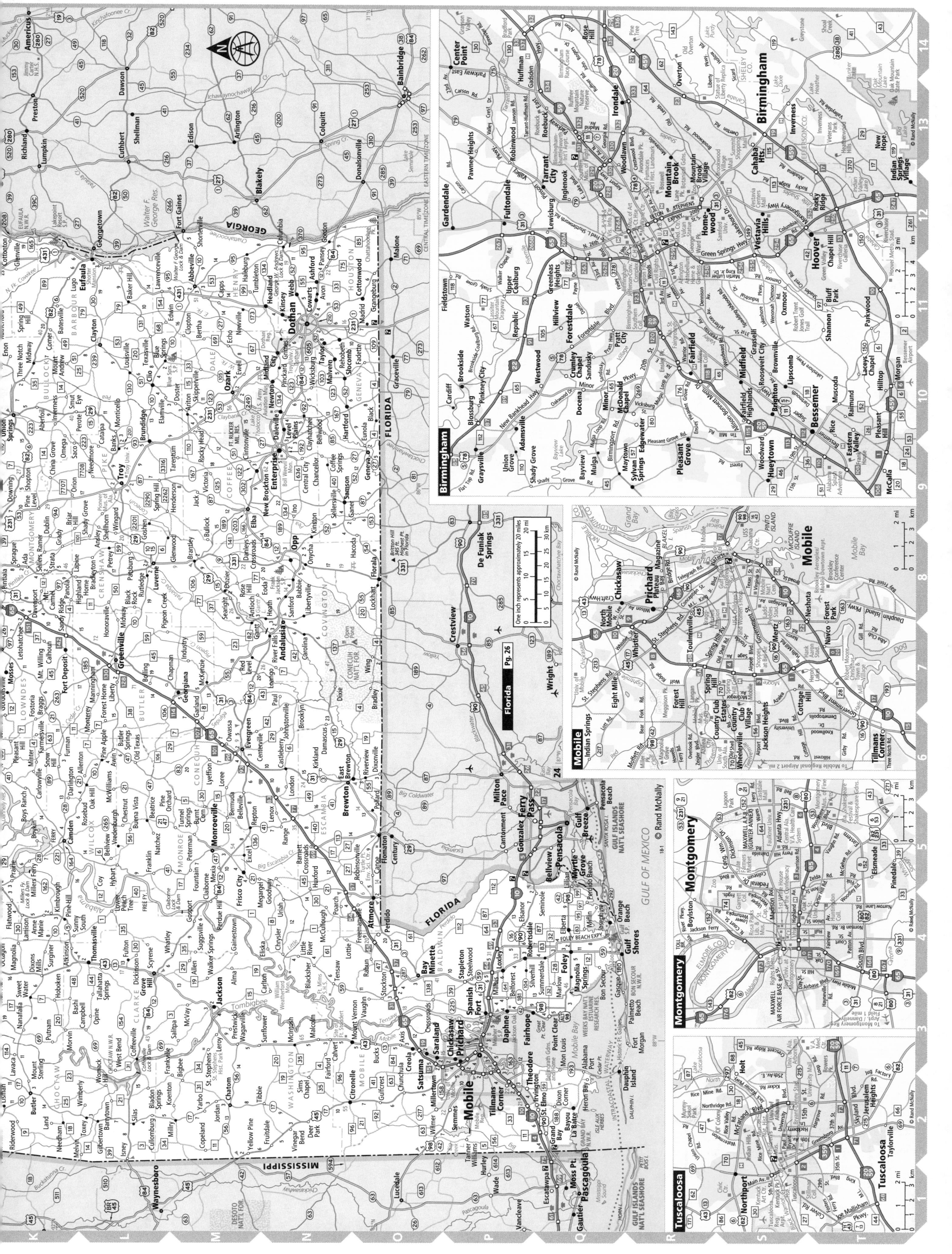

Alaska

Nickname: The Last Frontier
Capital: Juneau, H-12
Land area: 570,641 sq. mi. (rank: 1st)
Population: 710,231 (rank: 47th)
Largest city: Anchorage, 291,826, G-7

Index of places Pg. 129

Mileages between cities

	Anchorage	Denali N.P.	Fairbanks	Haines	Homer	Prince Rupert, BC	Tok	Valdez
Anchorage		236	358	756	221	1557	317	297
Fairbanks	358	122		640	578	1441	202	362
Haines	756	762	640		975	919	438	691
Homer	221	457	578	975		1776	537	277
Kenai	157	393	514	911	83	1713	473	213
Seward	126	362	483	880	168	1682	442	182
Tok	317	324	202	438	537	1240		252
Valdez	297	346	362	691	277	1493	252	

Total mileages through Alaska

① 408 miles ③ 325 miles

② 202 miles

More mileages at randmcnally.com/MC

Travel planning & on-the-road resources

Tourism Information

Alaska Tourism: www.travelalaska.com

Road Conditions & Construction

511, (907) 465-8952
www.511.alaska.gov, www.dot.state.ak.us

Toll Tunnel Information

Anton Anderson Mem. Tunnel (Whittier): (877) 611-2586;
www.dot.state.ak.us/creg/whittiertunnel

Determining Distances

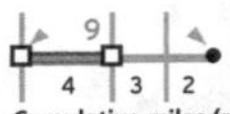

(segments one mile or less not shown)

Cumulative miles (red): the distance between red arrows

Intermediate miles (black): the distance between intersections & places

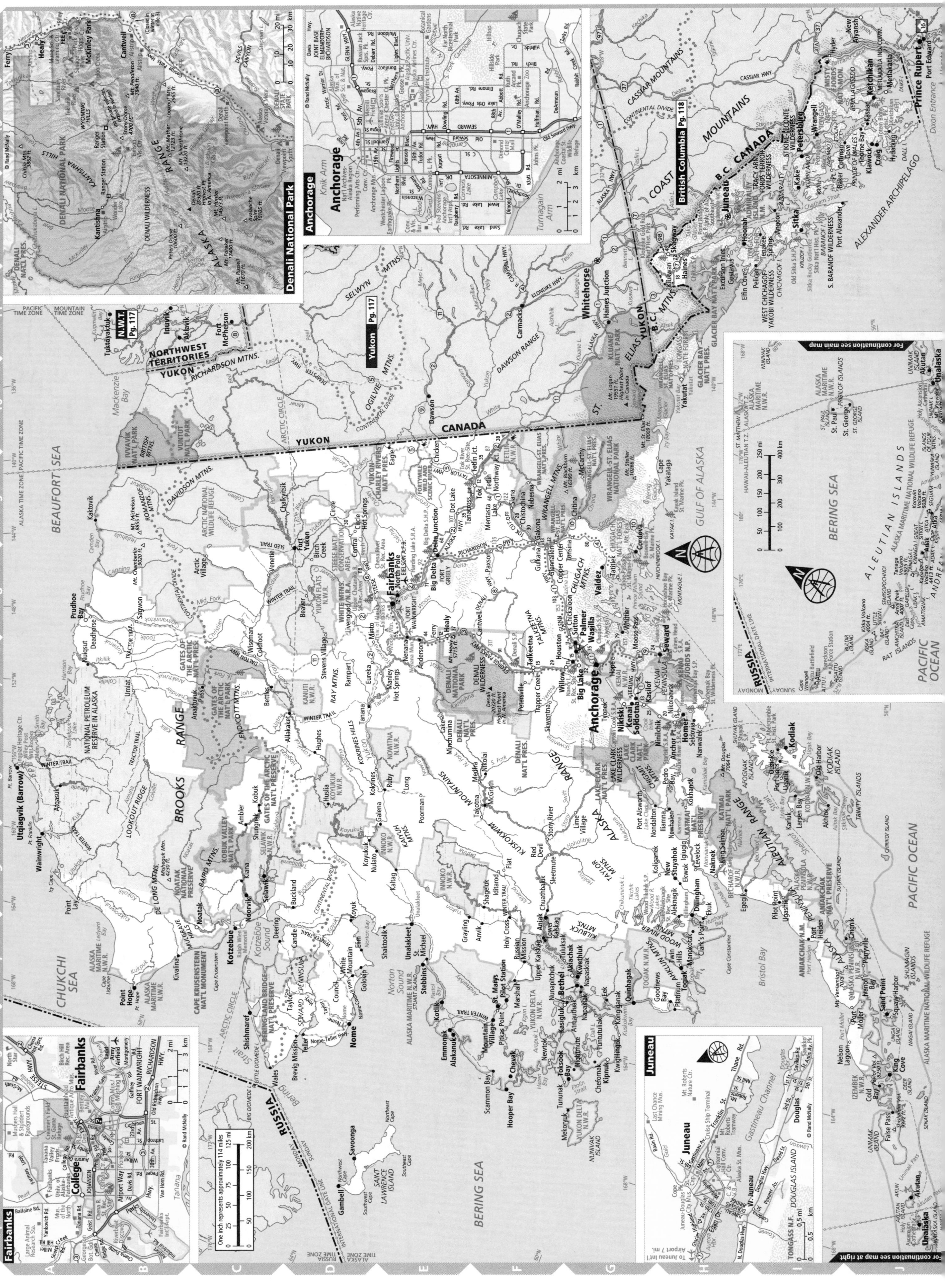

olklorica dancers

Sights to see

- Arizona Historical Society Sanguinetti House Museum, Yuma L-6
- Arizona Museum of Natural History, Mesa J-7
- Arizona Science Center, Phoenix M-3
- Arizona State Capitol, Phoenix M-1
- Heard Museum, Phoenix L-2
- Painted Desert Inn Museum, Petrified Forest N.P. L-10
- Phoenix Art Museum, Phoenix L-2
- Taliesin West, Scottsdale H-7
- Tusayan Ruin and Museum, Grand Canyon N.P. D-9
- Yavapai Observation Station, Grand Canyon N.P. D-8
- Yuma Territorial Prison State Historic Park, Yuma L-6

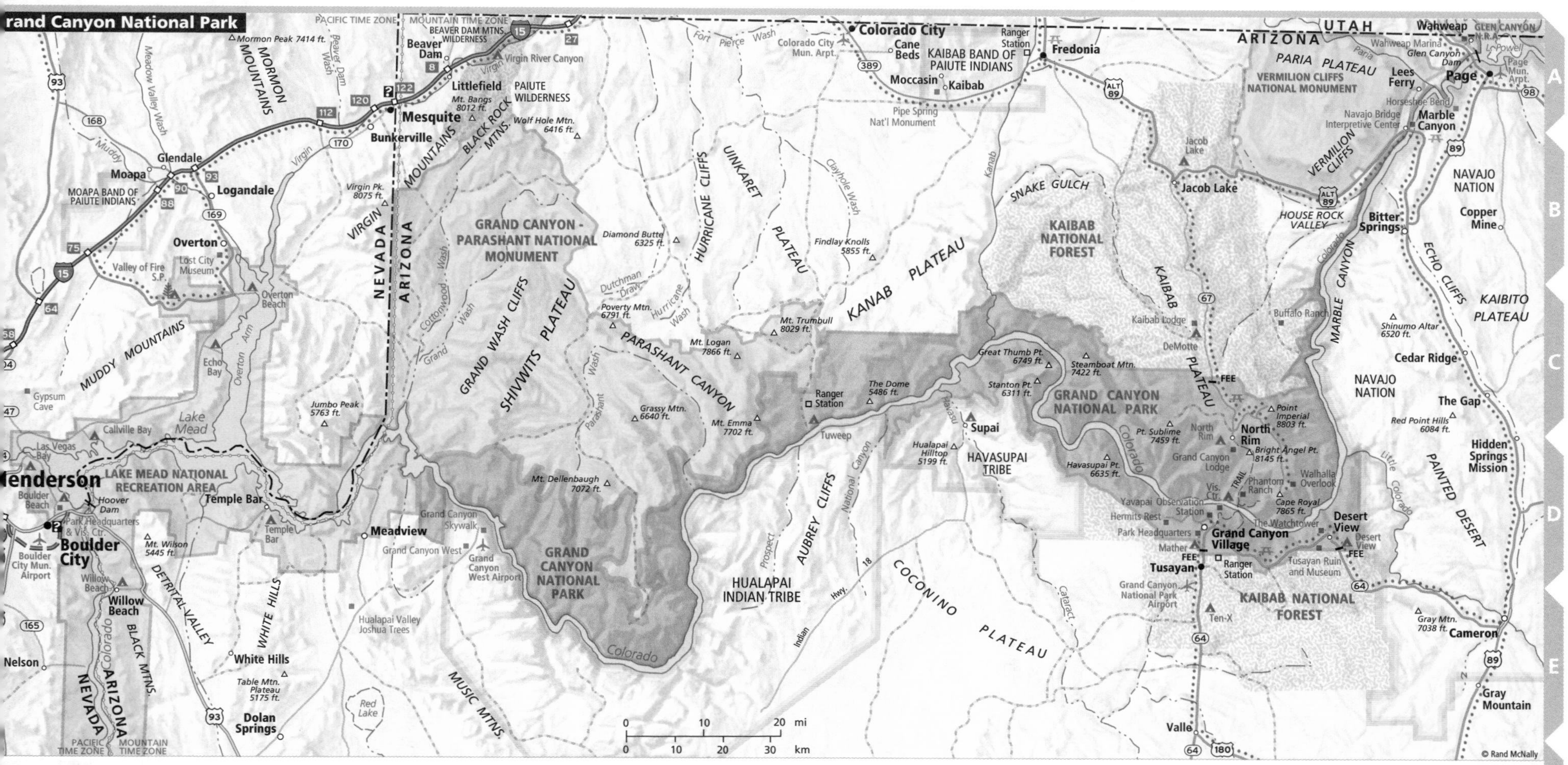

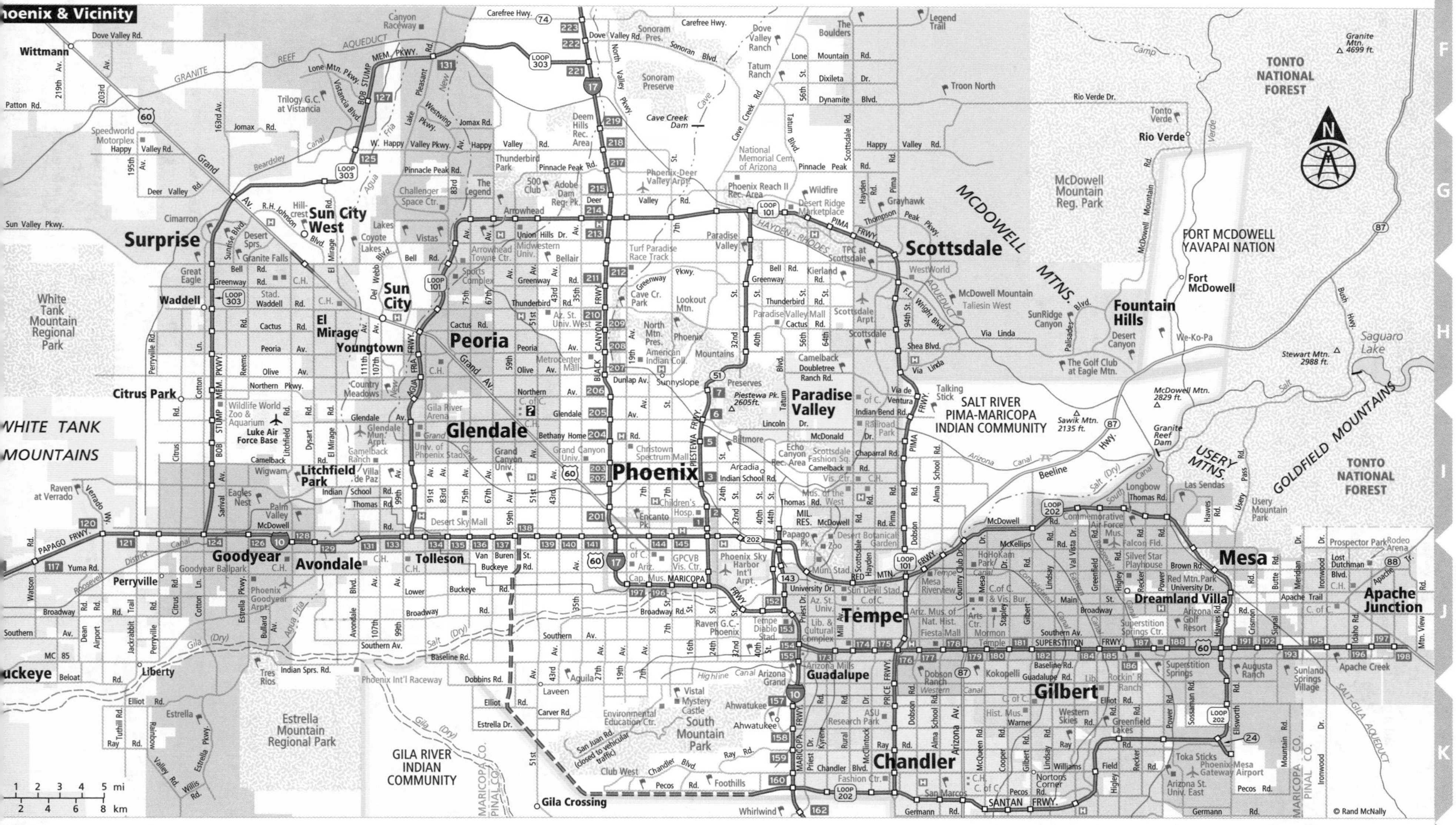

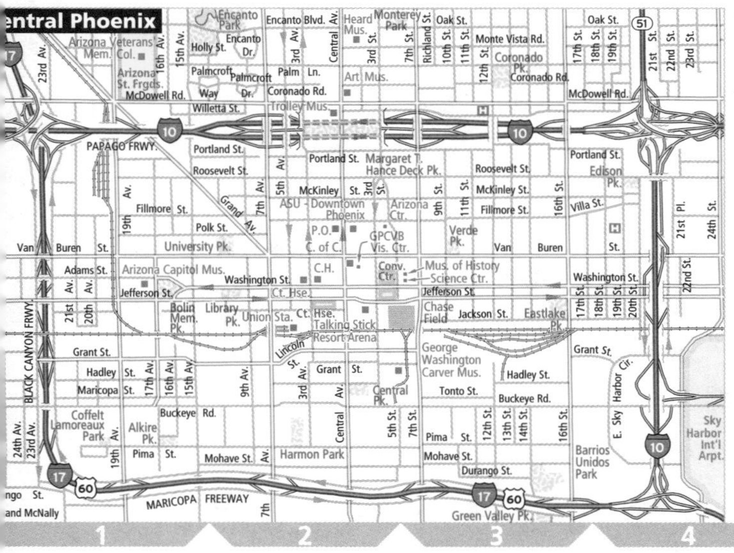

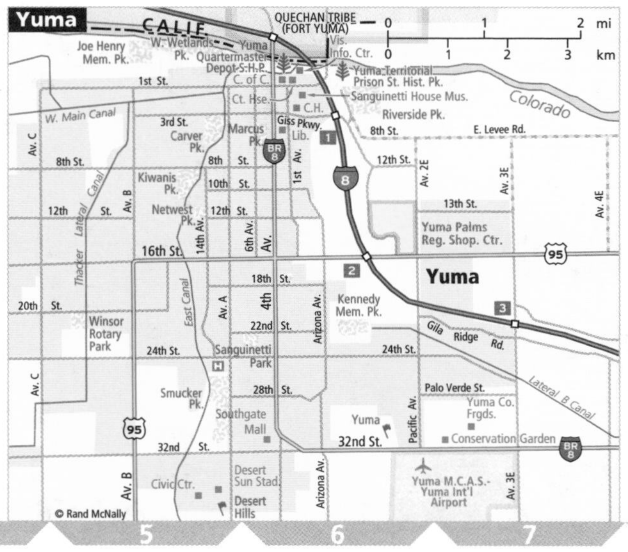

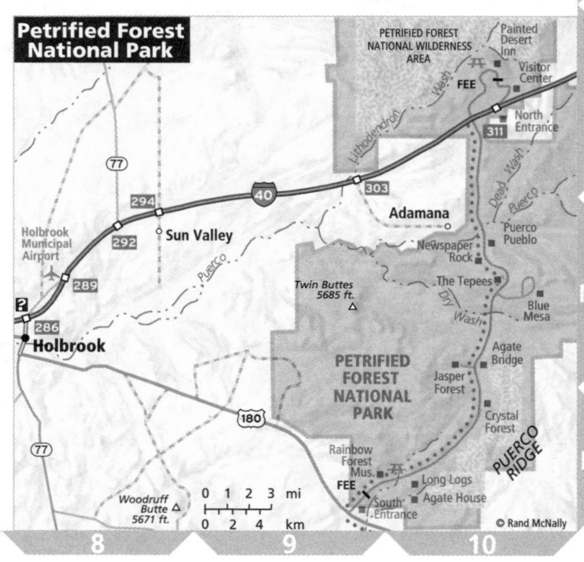

Arizona

Nickname: The Grand Canyon State
Capital: Phoenix, J-7
Land area: 113,594 sq. mi. (rank: 6th)
Population: 6,392,017 (rank: 16th)
Largest city: Phoenix, 1,445,632, J-7

Index of places Pg. 129

Travel planning & on-the-road resources

Tourism Information
Arizona Office of Tourism: (866) 275-5816, (602) 364-3700; www.arizonaguide.com

Road Conditions & Construction
511, (888) 411-7623, (888) 411-7624; www.az511.gov, www.azdot.gov

Toll Road Information
No toll roads

Determining distances along roads

Highway distances (segments of one mile or less not shown):
Cumulative miles (red): the distance between red arrows
Intermediate miles (black): the distance between intersections & place

Interchanges and exit numbers
For most states, the mileage between interchanges may be determine by subtracting one number from the other.

Creek Canyon, Sedona

Mileages between cities	Casa Grande	Chinle	Eagar	Flagstaff	Gallup, NM	Grand Canyon	Holbrook	Kingman	Lake Havasu City	Las Vegas, NV	Lordsburg, NM	Nogales	Page	Phoenix	Tucson	Yuma
Flagstaff	191	213	176		185	79	90	146	204	250	374	321	133	139	255	318
Holbrook	220	123	86	90	94	167		237	295	340	264	304	214	230	238	409
Las Vegas, NV	336	463	427	250	435	275	340	104	152		558	467	271	285	401	292
Page	324	204	301	133	255	137	214	281	340	271	499	455		275	390	453
Phoenix	48	353	226	139	324	218	230	182	198	285	268	179	275		116	181
Prescott	148	306	270	93	278	126	184	148	206	251	368	278	227	97	213	214
Tucson	66	361	238	255	333	334	238	297	314	401	156	66	390	116		236
Yuma	172	532	399	318	502	397	409	213	155	292	392	301	453	181	236	

Total mileages through Arizona

- I-8: 178 miles
- I-17: 146 miles
- I-10: 392 miles
- I-40: 359 miles

More mileages at randmcnally.com/MC

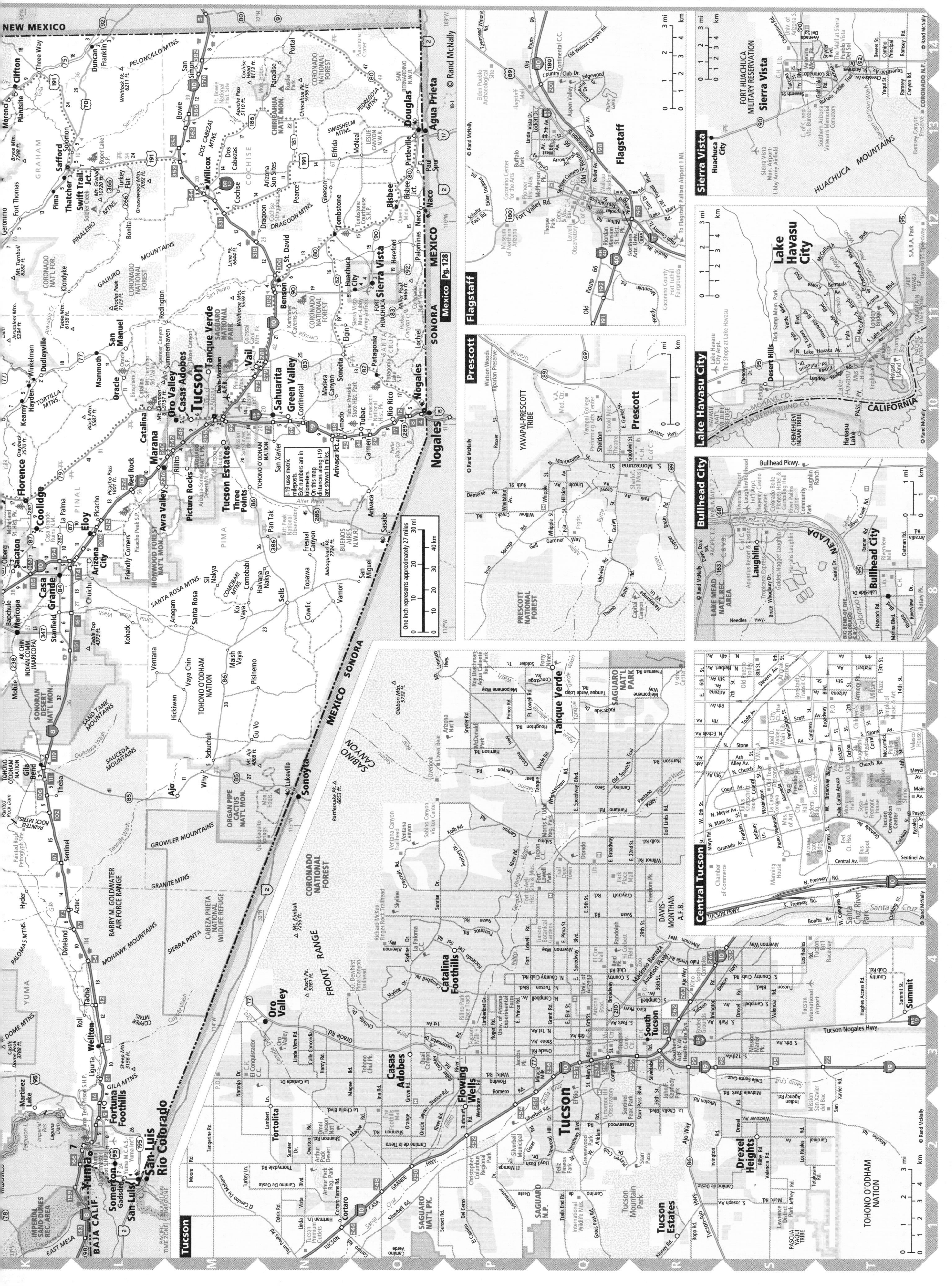

Arkansas

Nickname: The Natural State
Capital: Little Rock, G-7
Land area: 52,035 sq. mi. (rank: 27th)
Population: 2,915,918 (rank: 32nd)
Largest city: Little Rock, 193,524, G-7

Index of places Pg. 129

Travel planning & on-the-road resources

Tourism Information
Arkansas Parks & Tourism; (800) 628-8725, (501) 682-7777; www.arkansas.com

Road Conditions & Construction
(800) 245-1672, (501) 569-2374, (501) 569-2000; www.arkansashighways.com, www.idrivearkansas.com

Toll Road Information
No toll roads

Determining distances along roads

Highway distances (segments of one mile or less not shown):
Cumulative miles (red): the distance between red arrows
Intermediate miles (black): the distance between intersections & p

Interchanges and exit numbers
For most states, the mileage between interchanges may be determ
by subtracting one number from the other.

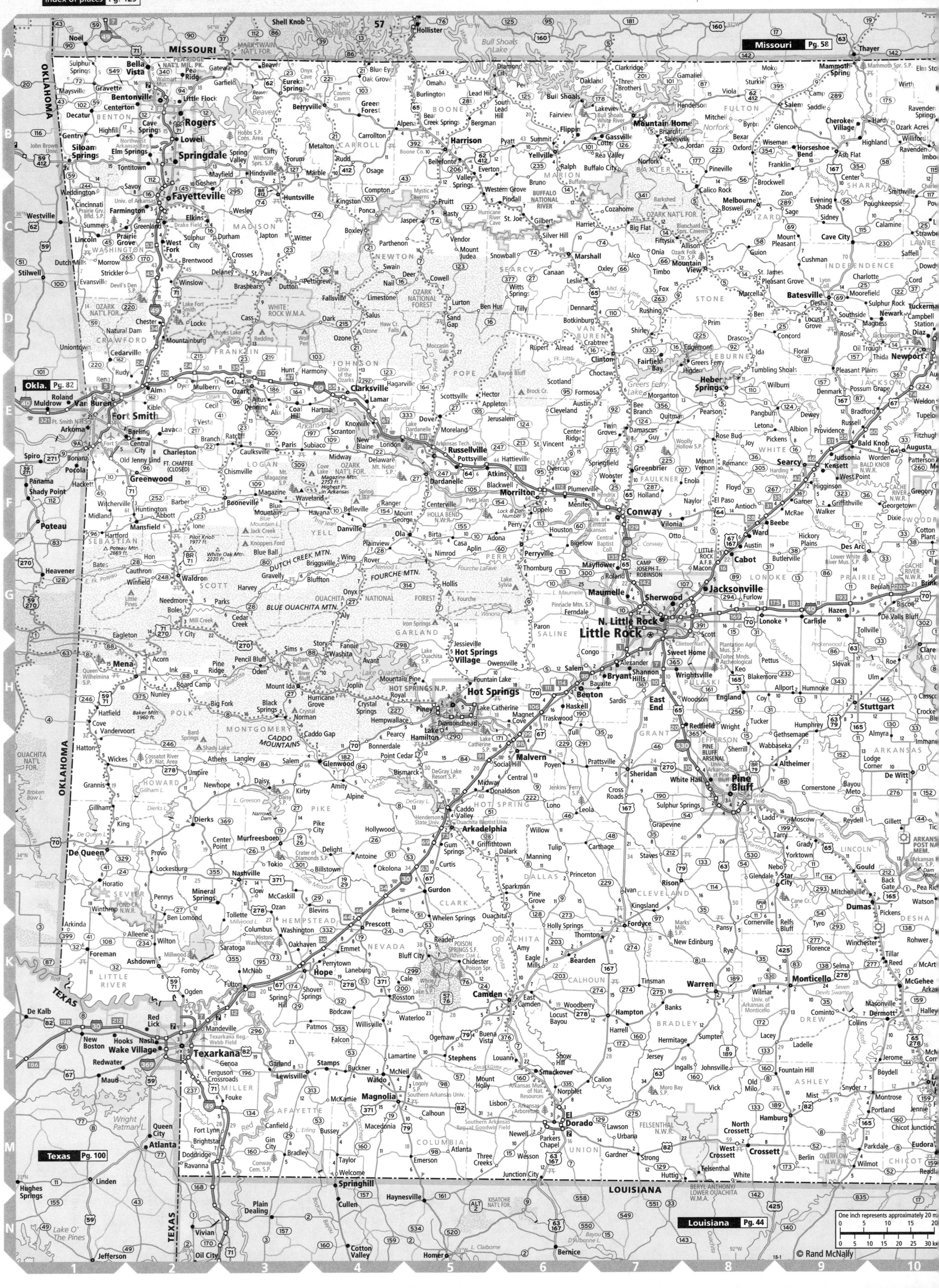

taker Point, Ozark National Forest

Mileages between cities	Batesville	Branson, MO	DeQueen	El Dorado	Fayetteville	Fort Smith	Greenville, MS	Hot Springs	Jonesboro	Little Rock	Memphis, TN	Mountain Home	Pine Bluff	Rogers	Russellville	Texarkana
El Dorado	209	287	141		304	227	109	121	245	118	250	268	91	325	190	88
Fayetteville	251	98	184	304		58	335	184	250	188	318	123	231	24	115	236
Fort Smith	219	158	130	227	58		304	130	261	158	286	187	199	81	84	182
Jonesboro	68	203	272	245	250	261	219	182		130	70	126	171	253	173	270
Little Rock	94	172	143	118	188	158	147	54	130		137	151	43	208	74	142
Memphis, TN	119	274	278	250	318	286	152	188	70	137		195	152	339	204	276
Mountain Home	78	83	287	268	123	187	298	198	126	151	195		194	126	125	287
Texarkana	234	306	54	88	236	182	198	110	270	142	276	287	152	258	209	

Total mileages through Arkansas

30 143 miles
55 72 miles
40 284 miles
65 309 miles

More mileages at randmcnally.com/MC

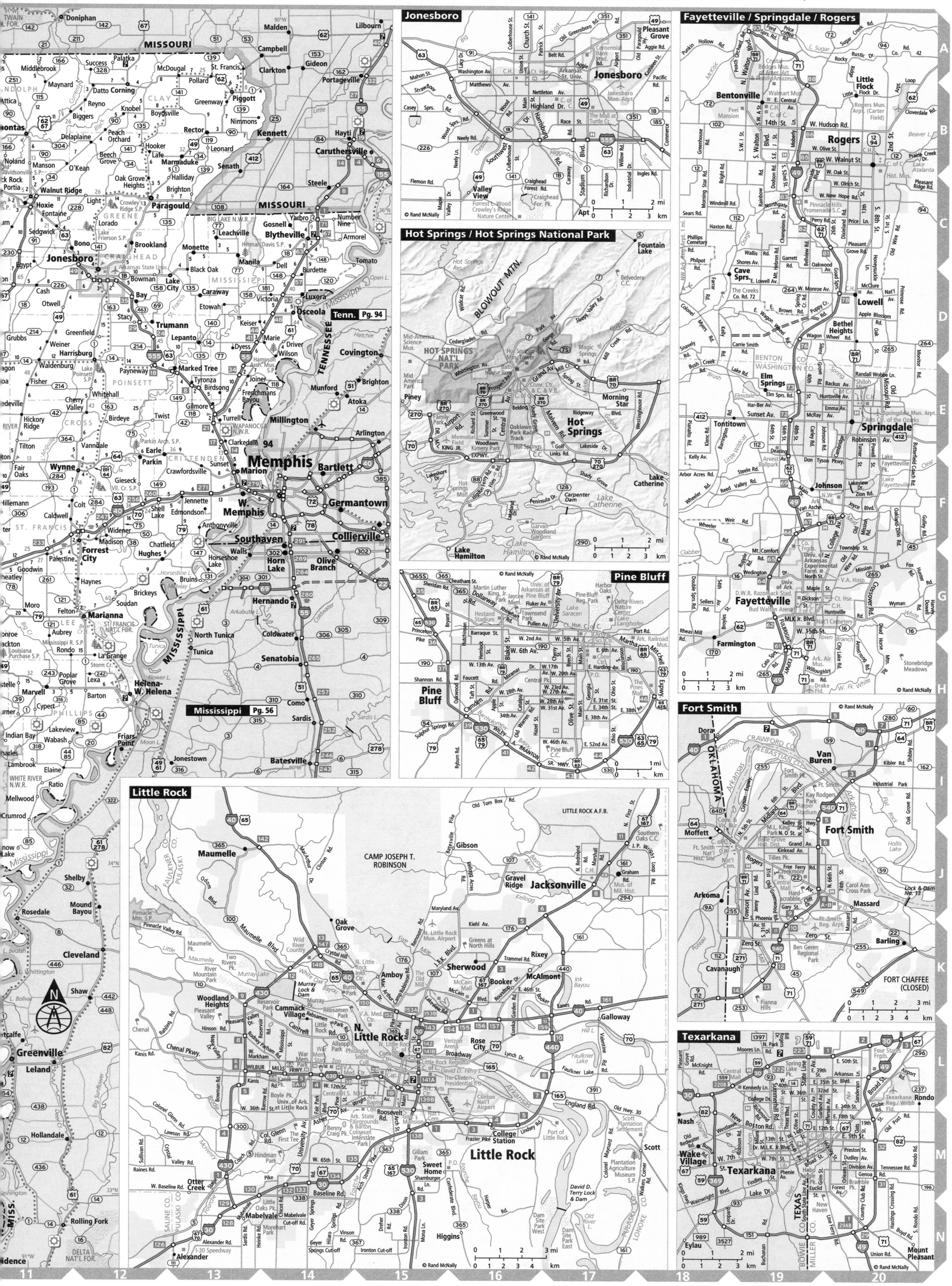

Nickname: The Golden State
Capital: Sacramento, NK-7
Land area: 155,799 sq. mi. (rank: 3rd)
Population: 37,253,956 (rank: 1st)
Largest city: Los Angeles, 3,792,621, SJ-11

Index of places Pg. 129

Travel planning & on-the-road resources

Tourism Information
California Tourism: (877) 225-4367, (916) 444-4429; www.visitcalifornia.com

Road Conditions & Construction
(800) 427-7623; www.dot.ca.gov;
Sacramento region: 511; www.sacregion511.org
San Francisco Bay area: 511; www.511.org

Toll Bridge Information *(both use FasTrak)*
Golden Gate Bridge (San Francisco Bay area): (415) 921-5858; www.goldengate.org
Bay Area Toll Authority (all other San Francisco Bay area bridges): (415) 778-6703; bata.mtc.ca.gov

Determining distances along roads

Highway distances (segments of one mile or less not shown):
Cumulative miles (red): the distance between red arrows
Intermediate miles (black): the distance between intersections & p

Interchanges and exit numbers
For most states, the mileage between interchanges may be determ by subtracting one number from the other.

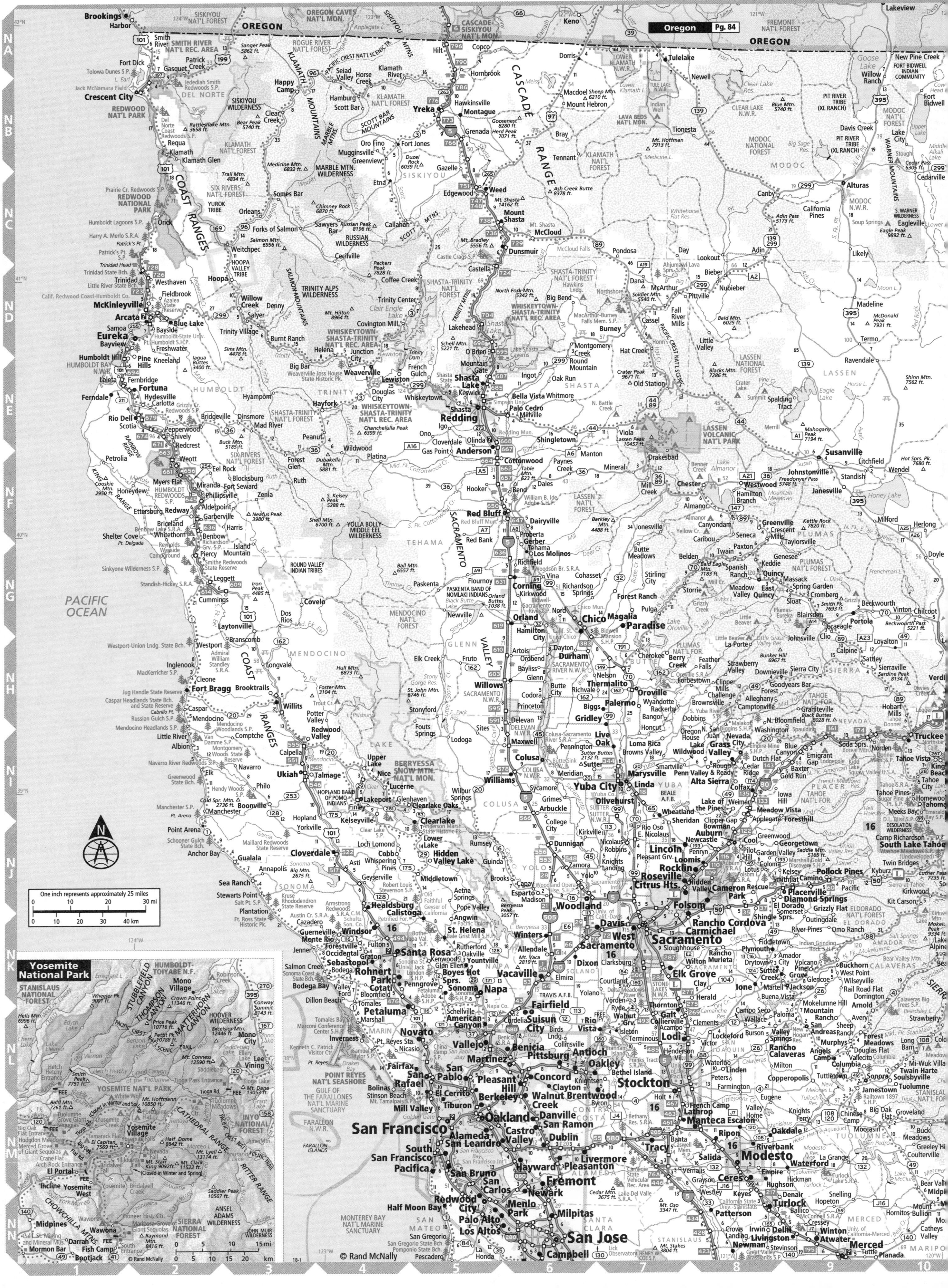

Mileages between cities

	Bishop	Crescent City	Los Angeles	Oroville	Redding	Sacramento	San Francisco	San Jose	Santa Rosa	S. Lake Tahoe	Stockton	Susanville	Ukiah	Vallejo	Yosemite N.P.	Yreka
Alturas	371	280	648	225	144	302	357	385	365	228	349	103	330	329	392	176
Bishop		614	265	326	400	269	295	290	364	176	224	286	418	328	138	454
Eureka	546	81	644	222	146	289	272	315	217	392	325	259	158	262	454	198
Redding	400	208	544	94		161	216	244	198	264	209	112	188	187	332	98
Sacramento	269	372	383	68	161		87	115	95	100	47	217	145	58	160	257
San Francisco	295	355	380	150	216	87		45	55	187	82	303	115	30	189	312
San Jose	290	396	340	178	244	115	45		96	215	74	330	156	64	182	340
S. Lake Tahoe	176	472	445	157	264	100	187	215	195		147	143	248	159	189	311

Mileages © Rand McNally

Total mileages through California

5: 797 miles 101: 791 miles
80: 199 miles

More mileages at randmcnally.com/MC

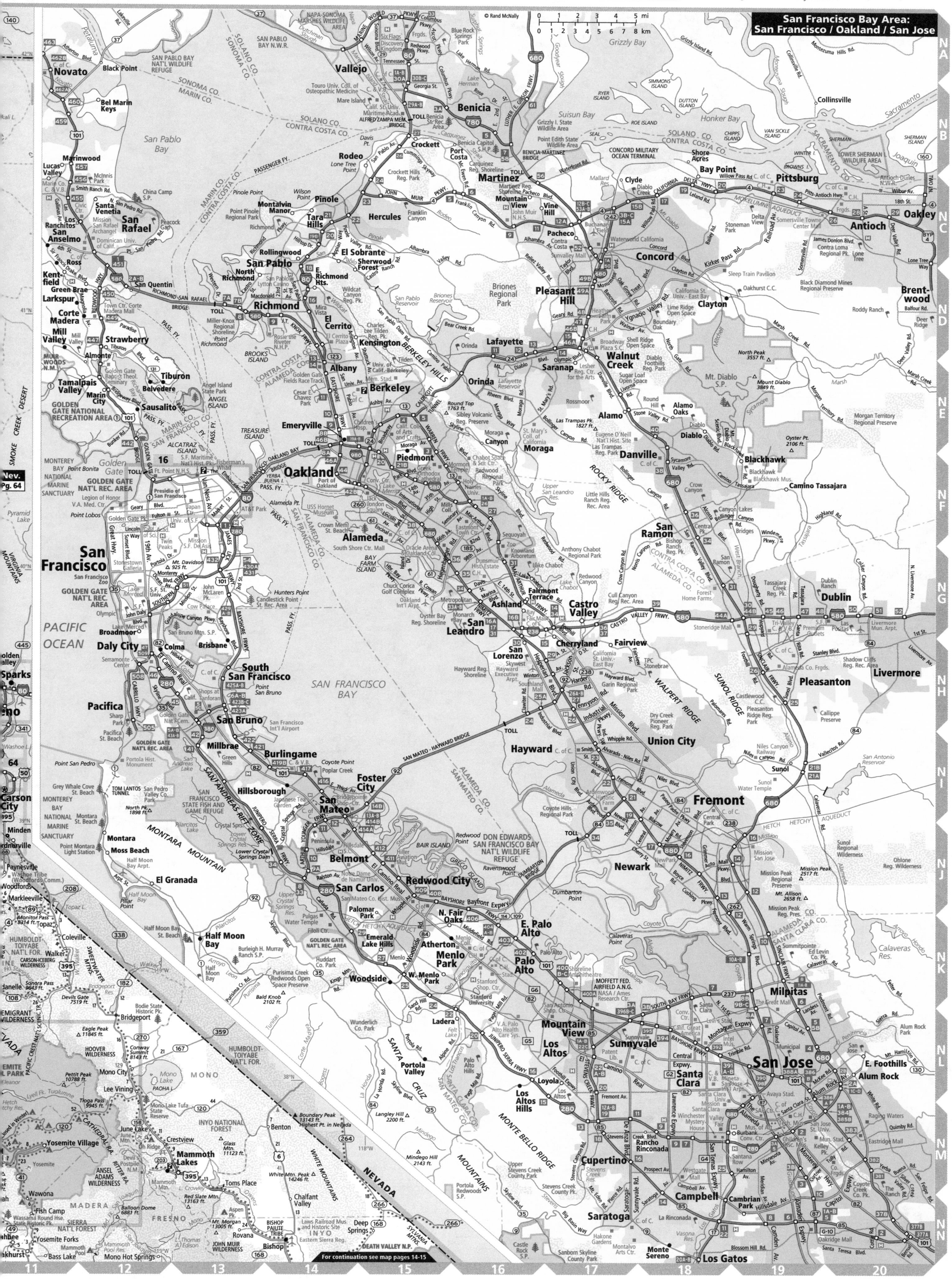

California/Southern

Nickname: The Golden State
Capital: Sacramento, NK-7
Land area: 155,799 sq. mi. (rank: 3rd)
Population: 37,253,956 (rank: 1st)
Largest city: Los Angeles, 3,792,621, SJ-11

Index of places Pg. 129

Travel planning & on-the-road resources

Tourism Information
California Tourism: (877) 225-4367, (916) 444-4429; www.visitcalifornia.com

Road Conditions & Construction
511
(800) 427-7623; www.dot.ca.gov
Los Angeles metro area: 511; www.go511.com
San Diego area: 511, (619) 661-7070; www.511sd.com

Toll Road Information
The Toll Roads of Orange Co. ***(FasTrak)***: (949) 727-4800; www.thetollroads.com
Pebble Beach Resorts (17-Mile Dr.): (800) 654-9300); www.pebblebeach.com
South Bay Expwy. (San Diego Co.) ***(FasTrak)***: (619) 661-7070; www.southbayexpressway.com

Determining distances along roads
Highway distances (segments of one mile or less not shown):
Cumulative miles (red): the distance between red arrows
Intermediate miles (black): the distance between intersections & pla
Interchanges and exit numbers
For most states, the mileage between interchanges may be determir by subtracting one number from the other.

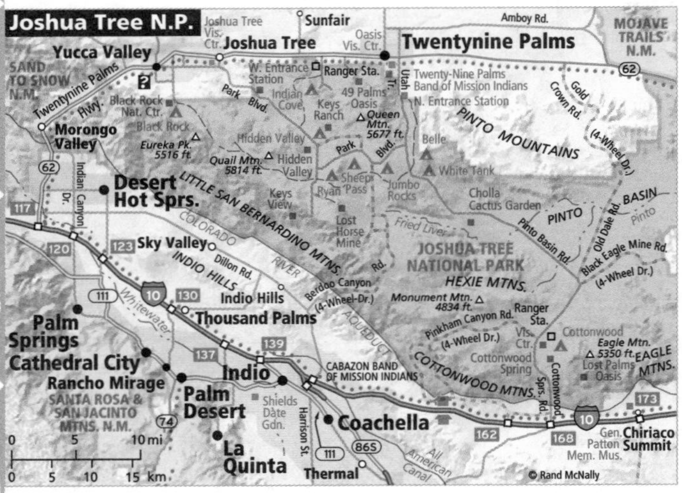

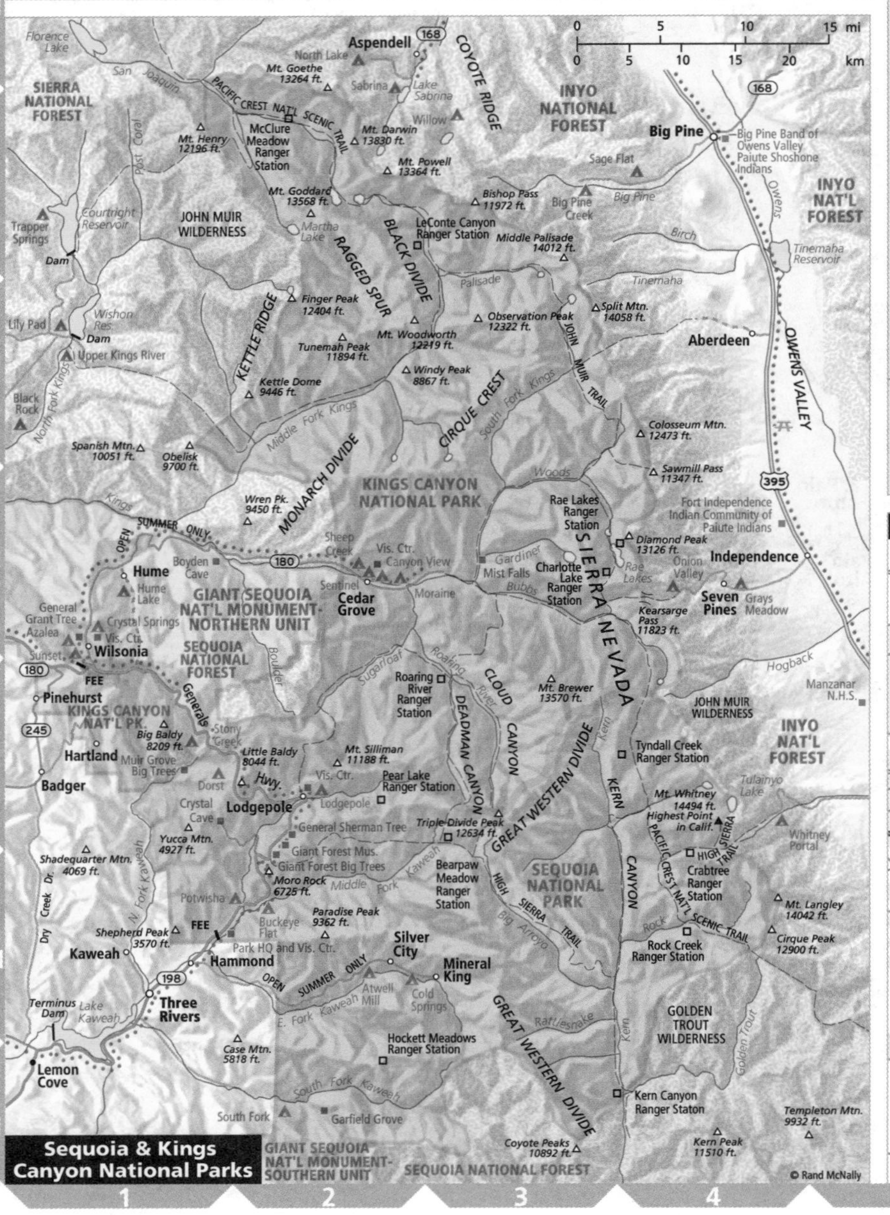

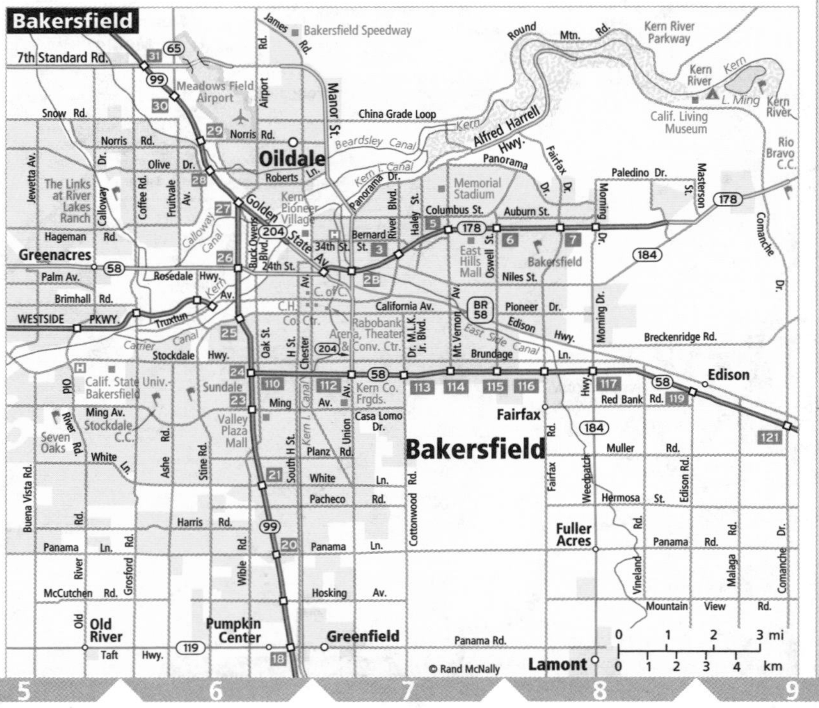

Mileages between cities	Bakersfield	Barstow	El Centro	Fresno	Las Vegas, NV	Los Angeles	Monterey	Needles	Palm Springs	Riverside	San Bernardino	San Diego	San Francisco	San Luis Obispo	Santa Barbara	Sequoia N.P.
Bakersfield		129	322	109	286	112	222	272	216	166	166	232	284	130	147	122
Fresno	109	239	429		395	218	150	381	323	271	273	339	183	130	254	77
Las Vegas, NV	286	156	312	395		270	507	110	278	234	225	331	569	415	358	410
Los Angeles	112	114	212	218	270		319	256	107	54	60	120	380	189	94	232
Monterey	222	350	530	150	507	319		494	424	372	373	439	112	142	237	226
Palm Springs	216	123	108	323	278	107	424	188		52	54	139	486	296	201	338
San Diego	232	176	113	339	331	120	439	317	139	97	106		501	313	214	352
Santa Barbara	147	203	306	254	358	94	237	345	201	148	150	214	325	94		268

Mileages © Rand McNally

Total mileages through California

- 5: 797 miles
- 15: 287 miles
- 10: 243 miles
- 40: 155 miles

More mileages at randmcnally.com/MC

For continuation see map pages 12-13

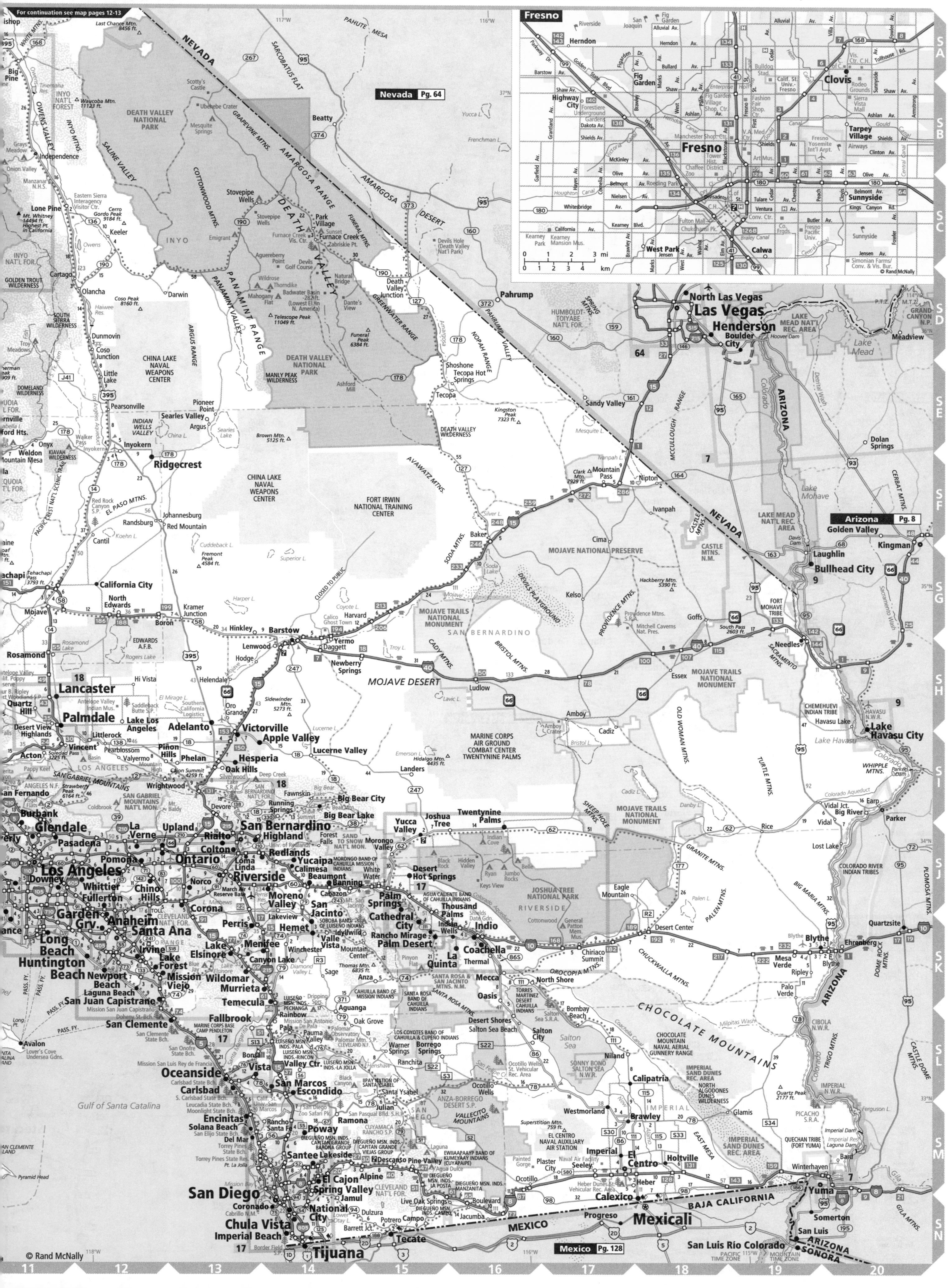

Sights to see

- California State Capitol, Sacramento I-6
- California State Railroad Museum, Sacramento H-6
- Chinatown, San Francisco C-8
- Coit Memorial Tower, San Francisco B-8
- Crocker Art Museum, Sacramento I-5
- Fisherman's Wharf, San Francisco A-7
- Ghirardelli Square, San Francisco B-7
- Golden Gate Bridge, San Francisco A-2
- Monterey Bay Aquarium, Monterey M-1
- Pier 39, San Francisco A-8
- San Francisco Cable Car Museum, San Francisco C-8
- Squaw Valley U.S.A., Olympic Valley F-8

San Francisco Fort Mason Center

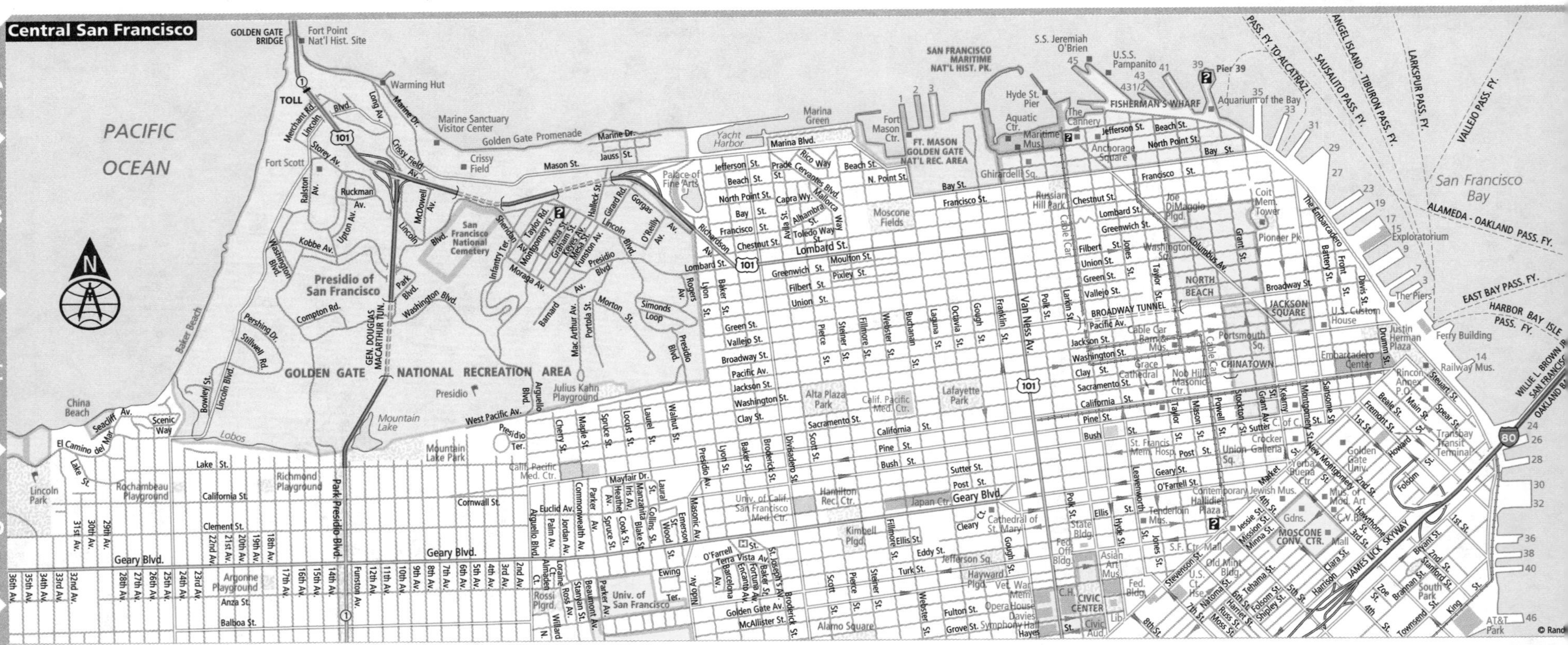

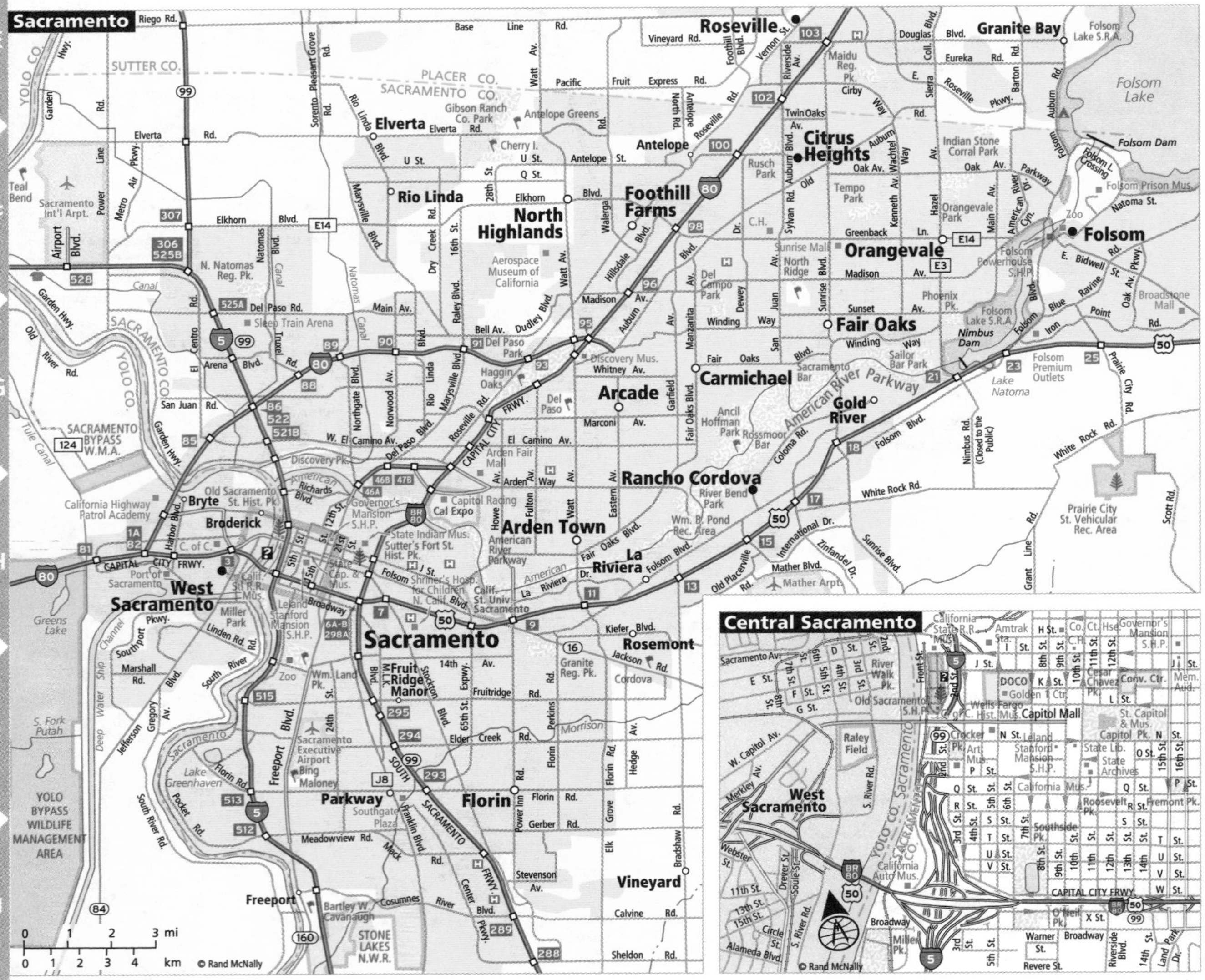

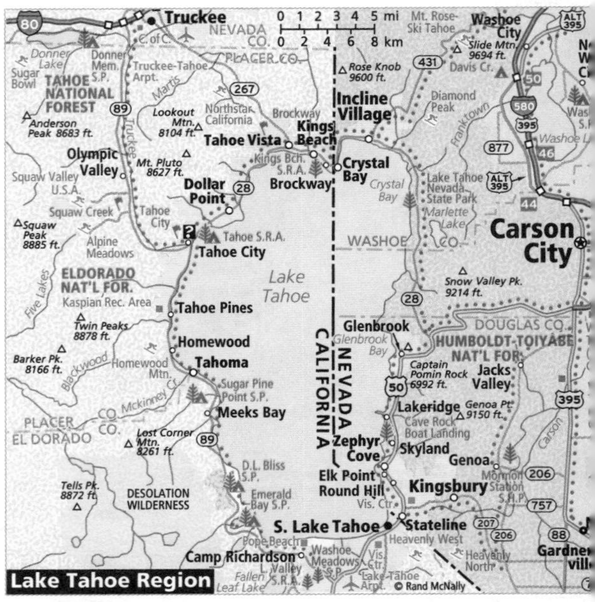

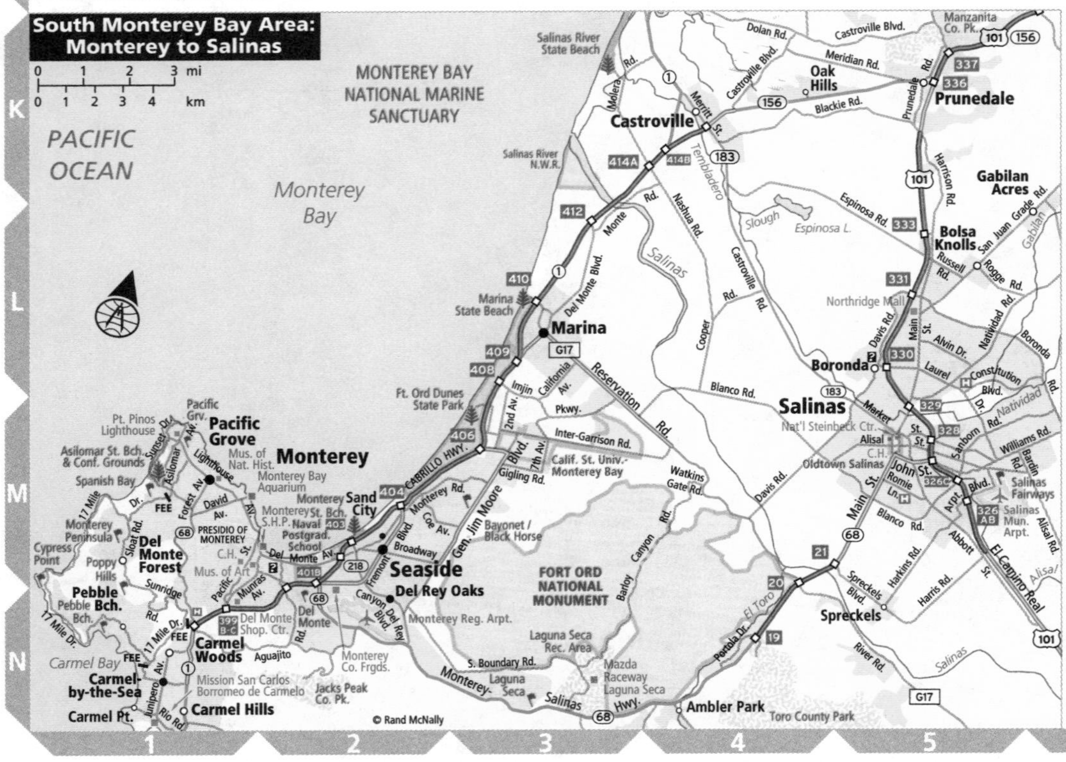

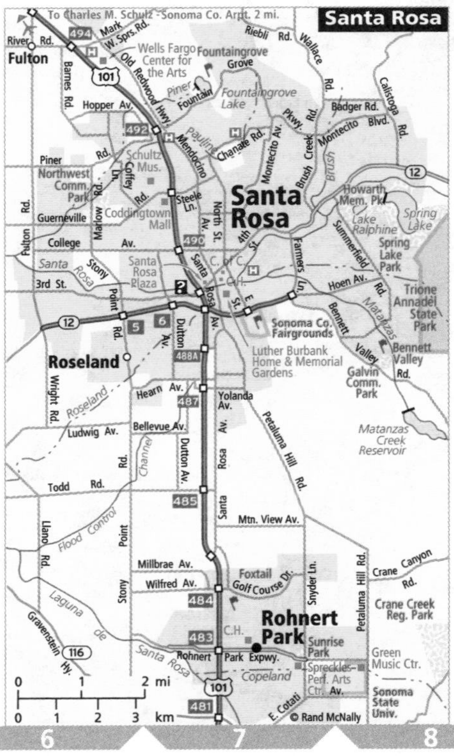

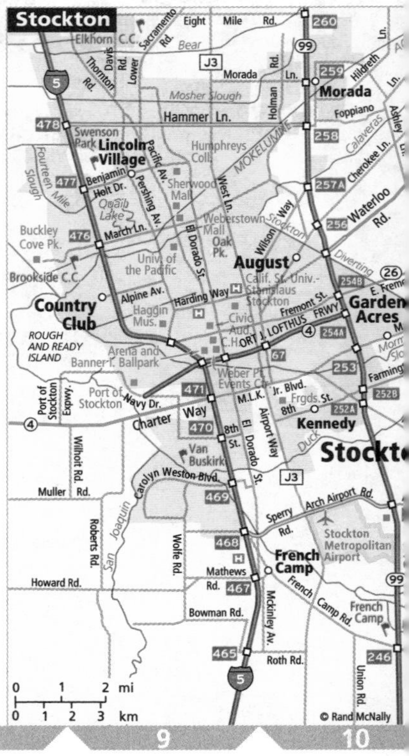

Santa Barbara harbor and coastline

Sights to see

- Balboa Park, San Diego K-10
- Birch Aquarium at Scripps Institute, San Diego G-1
- Cabrillo National Monument, San Diego K-1
- Gaslamp Quarter Historic District, San Diego M-9
- Legoland California, Carlsbad J-8
- The Living Desert Nature Preserve, Palm Desert G-10
- Museum of Contemporary Art, San Diego L-8
- Palm Springs Art Museum, Palm Springs E-7
- San Diego Air & Space Museum, San Diego K-9
- San Diego Zoo, San Diego J-3
- SeaWorld, San Diego I-1
- Stearns Wharf, Santa Barbara B-5

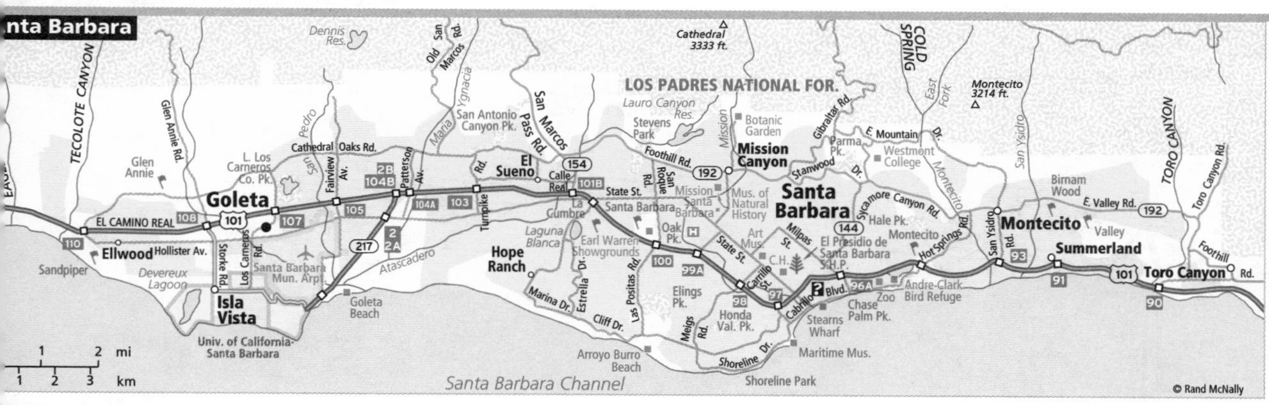

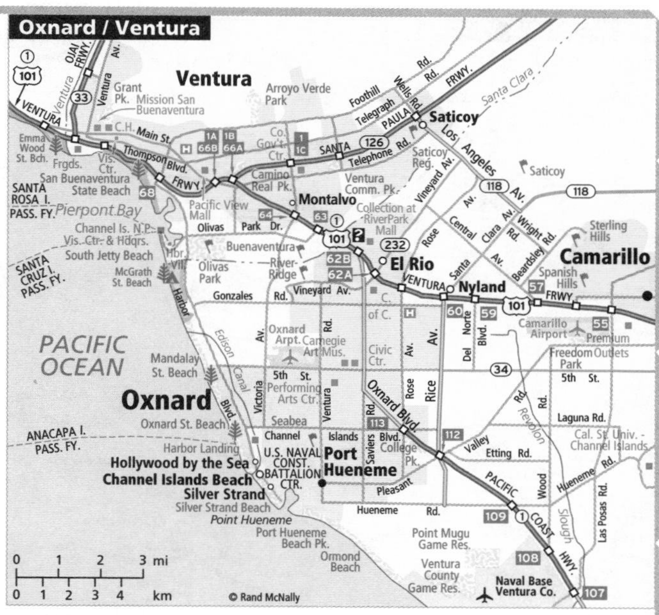

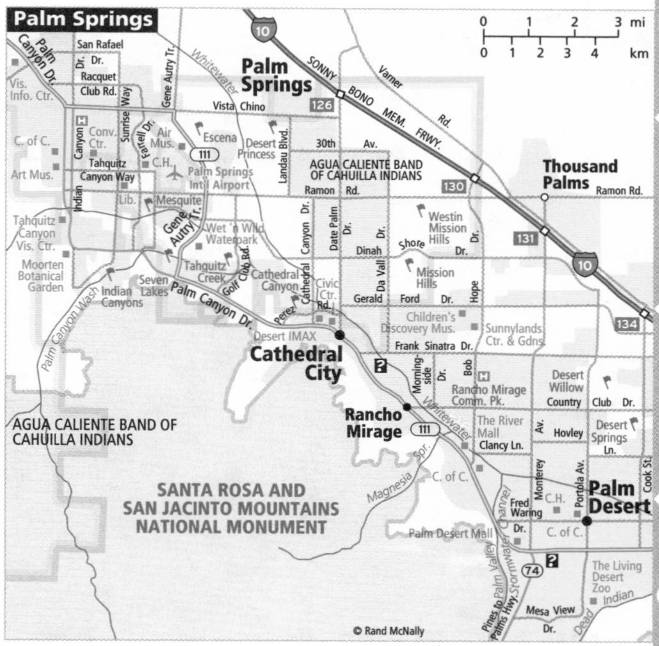

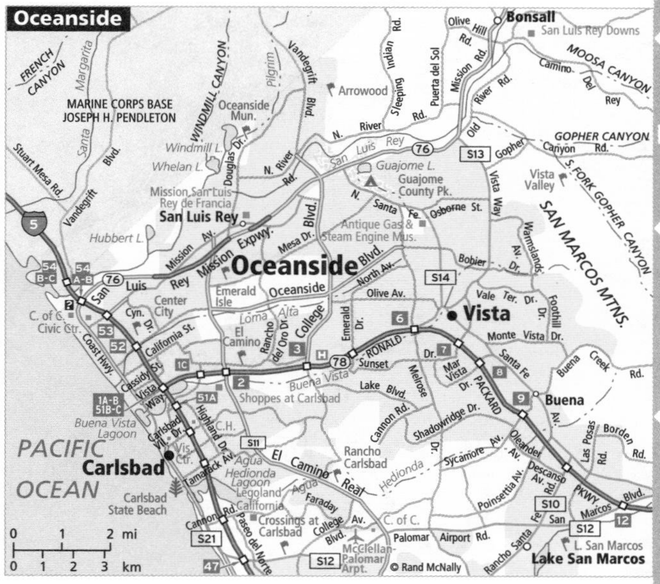

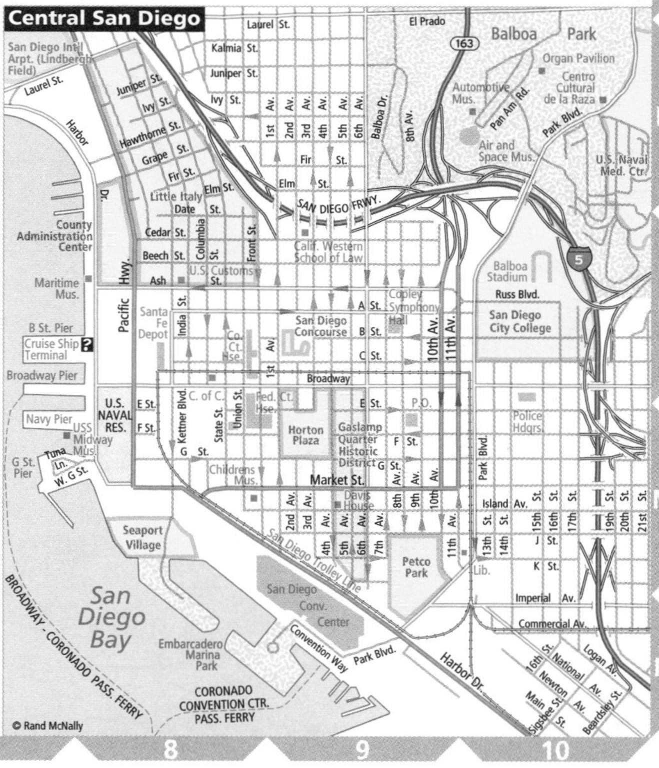

Sights to see

- Aquarium of the Pacific, Long Beach J-8
- Disneyland, Anaheim I-11
- Dodger Stadium............... E-7
- El Pueblo de Los Angeles K-2
- Getty Center............... E-4
- Hollywood Bowl............... D-6
- Huntington Library, San Marino D-8
- Japanese American National Museum K-3
- Knott's Berry Farm, Buena Park H-10
- Los Angeles County Art Museum............... E-5
- Los Angeles Maritime Museum J-7
- Los Angeles Zoo and Botanical Gardens............... D-6

Walt Disney Concert Hall

ntington Beach Pier, Huntington Beach

Sights to see

- Mission San Juan Capistrano, San Juan Capistrano . . M-14
- Old Pasadena, Pasadena D-8
- Oldest Winery in California, Rancho Cucamonga . . . D-14
- The Queen Mary, Long Beach J-8
- Richard M. Nixon Library & Birthplace, Yorba Linda H-12
- Santa Monica Pier, Santa Monica. F-4
- Universal City D-5
- Venice Boardwalk F-4
- Walt Disney Concert Hall K-1
- Warner Bros. Studio, Burbank .D-6
- Will Rogers State Historic Park, Pacific Palisades E-4

Colorado

Nickname: The Centennial State
Capital: Denver, E-13
Land area: 103,642 sq. mi. (rank: 8th)
Population: 5,029,196 (rank: 22nd)
Largest city: Denver, 600,158, E-13

Index of places Pg. 129

Travel planning & on-the-road resources

Tourism Information
Colorado Tourism Office:
(800) 265-6723; www.colorado.com

Road Conditions & Construction
511, (303) 573-7623, (303) 639-1111
www.cotrip.org

Toll Road Information
E-470 (Denver metro) *(ExpressToll)*: (888) 946-3470, (303) 537-3470; www.expresstoll.com
Northwest Parkway (Denver metro) *(GoPass)*: (303) 533-1200; www.northwestparkway.org

Determining distances along roads

Highway distances (segments of one mile or less not shown):
Cumulative miles (red): the distance between red arrows
Intermediate miles (black): the distance between intersections & pla

Interchanges and exit numbers
For most states, the mileage between interchanges may be determi by subtracting one number from the other.

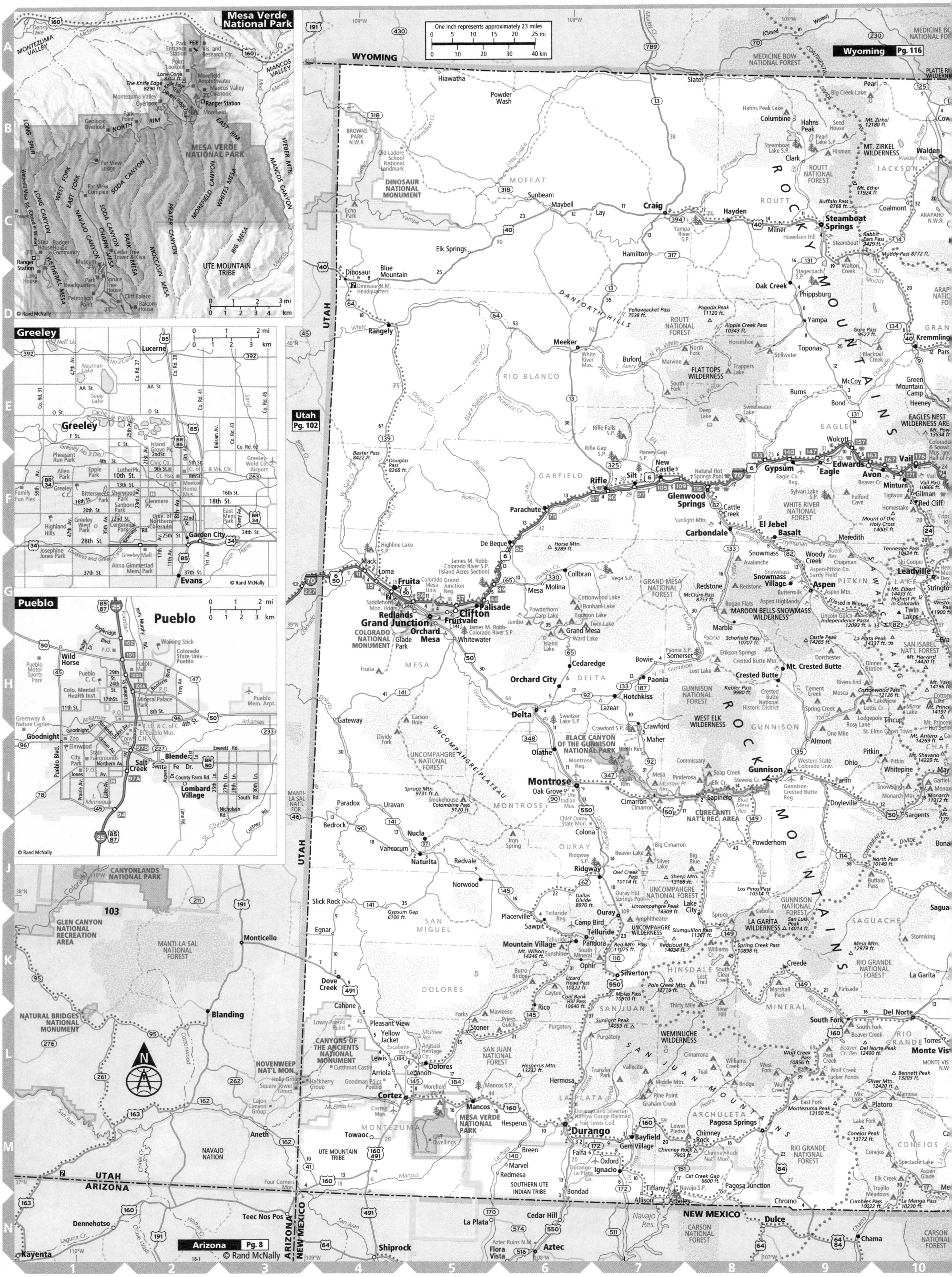

Mileages between cities

	Alamosa	Aspen	Burlington	Colorado Springs	Craig	Denver	Durango	Estes Park	Fort Collins	Grand Junction	Gunnison	Lamar	Leadville	Pueblo	Sterling	Trinidad
Burlington	311	363		151	363	166	460	222	220	408	324	108	265	189	142	230
Colorado Springs	163	155	151		264	69	313	133	133	309	166	158	121	42	194	128
Denver	234	197	166	69	197		336	64	63	243	200	208	99	112	125	198
Durango	149	246	460	313	312	336		402	396	168	142	351	253	269	458	258
Fort Collins	296	258	220	133	201	63	396	42		303	260	261	160	175	102	261
Grand Junction	247	128	408	309	151	243	168	258	303		126	448	174	287	364	370
Leadville	135	58	265	121	145	99	253	143	160	174	102	276		154	222	204
Trinidad	109	232	230	128	392	198	258	262	261	370	209	136	204	85	322	

Mileages © Rand McNally

Total mileages through Colorado

25: 300 miles
76: 185 miles
70: 451 miles
50: 467 miles

More mileages at www.randmcnally.com/MC

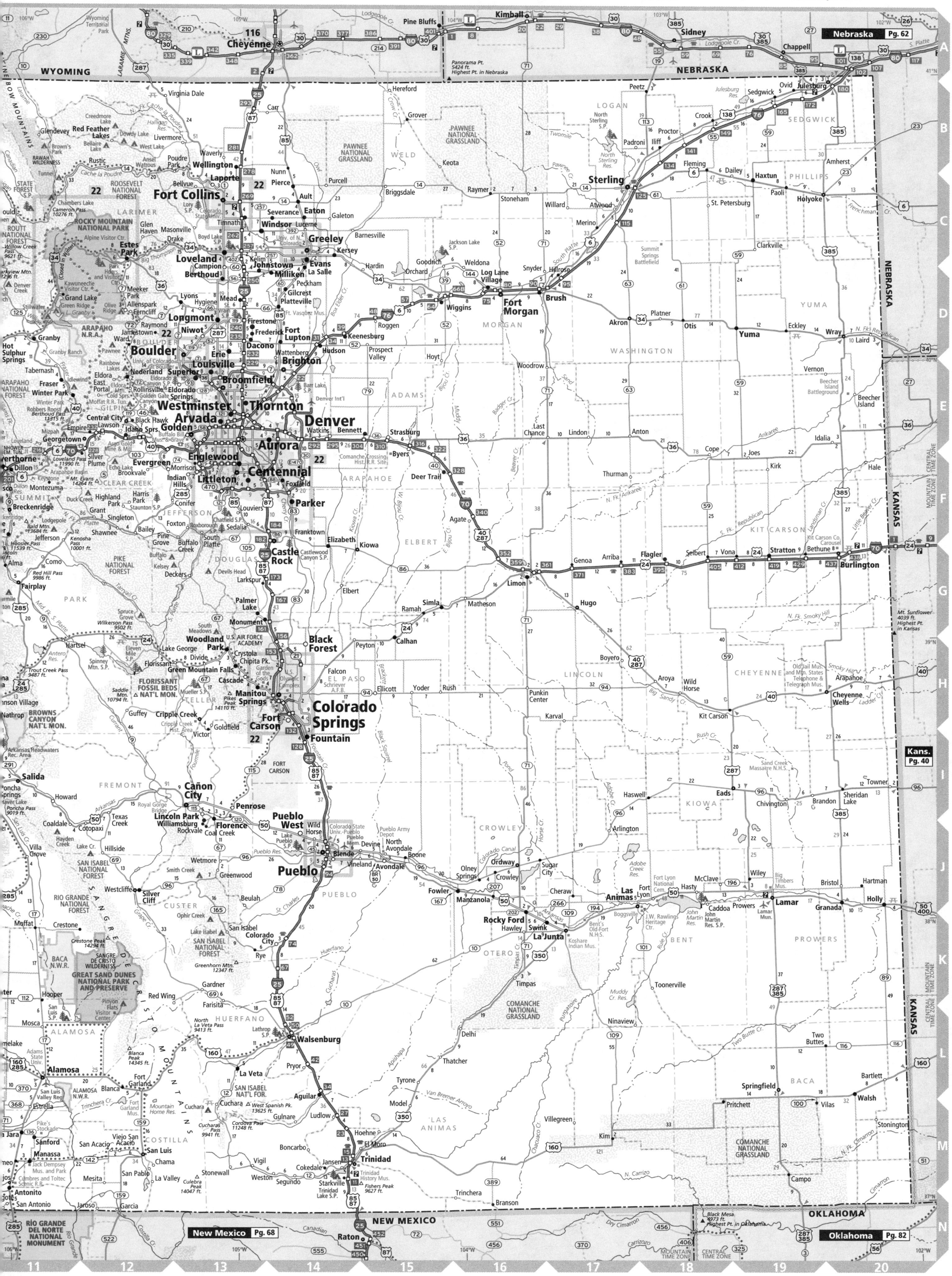

Sights to see

- Black American West Mus. & Heritage Ctr., Denver L-3
- Cave of the Winds, Colorado Springs G-1
- Colorado History Museum, Denver M-2
- Colorado State Capitol, Denver M-2
- Denver Art Museum, Denver M-2
- Denver Museum of Nature & Science, Denver I-7
- Garden of the Gods, Colorado Springs G-1
- National Center for Atmospheric Research, Boulder . . . D-4
- Old Town National Historic District, Fort Collins B-9
- ProRodeo Hall of Fame, Colorado Springs F-2
- United States Mint, Denver M-2
- World Figure Skating Hall of Fame, Colorado Springs . . I-2

The Pepsi Center, Denver

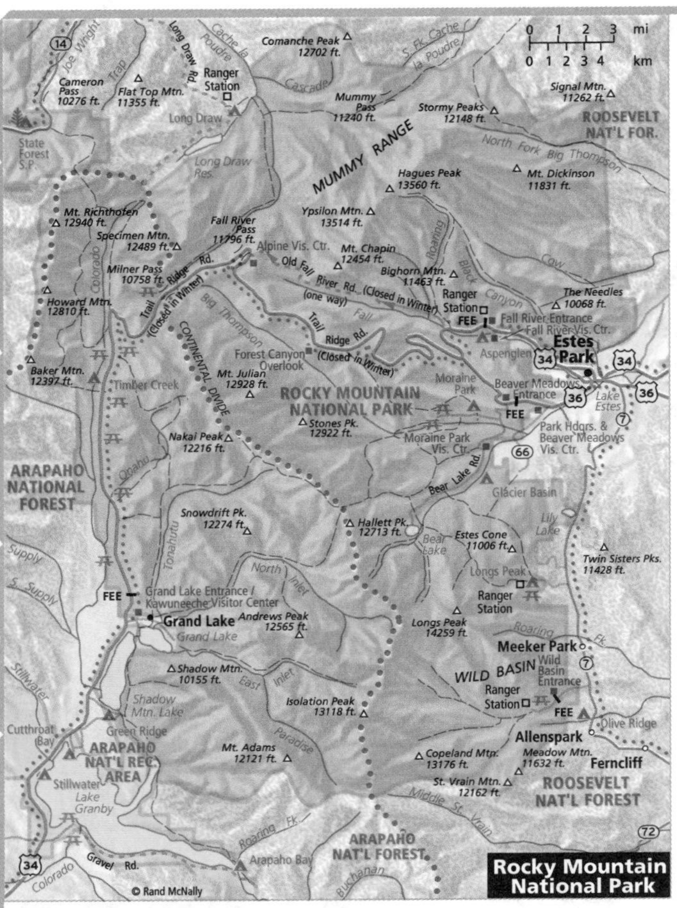

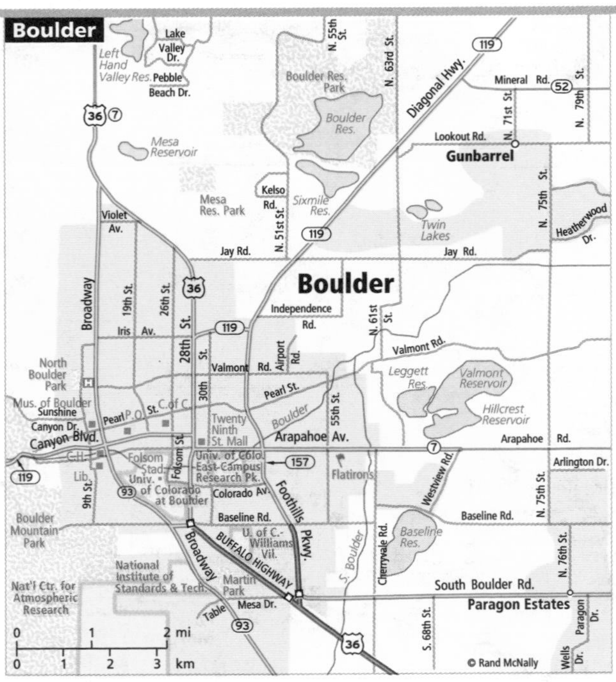

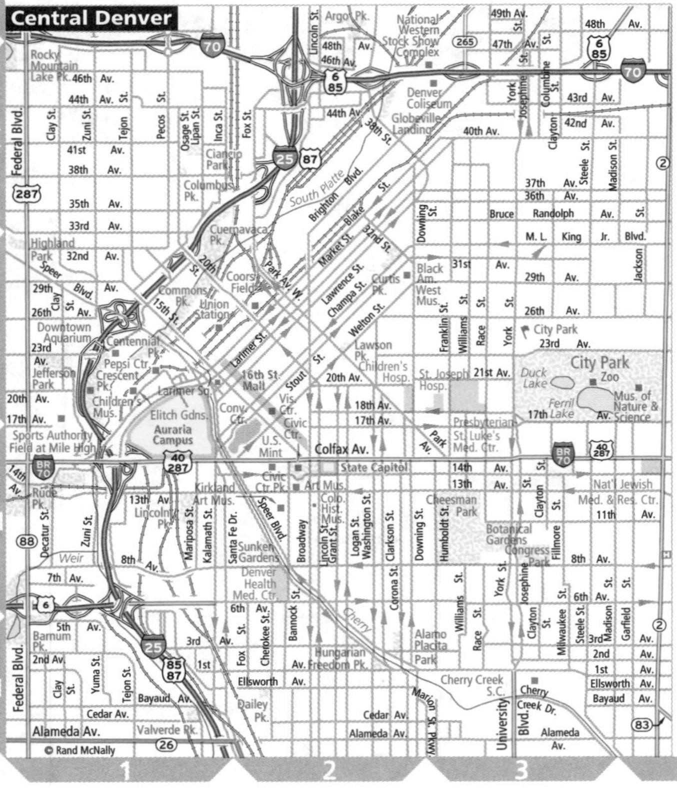

avel planning & on-the-road resources

rism Information
n. Office of Tourism:
88) 288-4748,
60) 256-2800
ww.ctvisit.com

Road Conditions & Construction
(860) 594-2000, (860) 594-2650
www.ct.gov/dot
www.i-84waterbury.com

Road Information
toll roads

Determining Distances

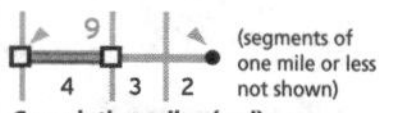

Cumulative miles (red): the distance between red arrows
Intermediate miles (black): the distance between intersections & places

Total mileages through Connecticut

84 98 miles
95 112 miles
91 58 miles
395 55 miles

More mileages at
randmcnally.com/MC

Mileages between cities	Bridgeport	Hartford	New Haven	New London	New York, NY	Putnam	Torrington	Waterbury
Bridgeport		55	18	64	54	107	50	30
Danbury	29	57	35	81	62	104	47	27
Hartford	55		38	45	108	47	26	30
New Haven	18	38		46	72	89	43	22
New London	64	45	46		118	47	79	63
Putnam	107	47	89	47	162		73	78
Torrington	50	26	43	79	109	73		20
Waterbury	30	30	22	63	89	78	20	

Mileages © Rand McNally

Nickname: The Constitution State
Capital: Hartford, C-9
Land area: 4,842 sq. mi. (rank: 48th)
Population: 3,574,097 (rank: 29th)
Largest city: Bridgeport, 144,229, H-5

Index of places Pg. 129

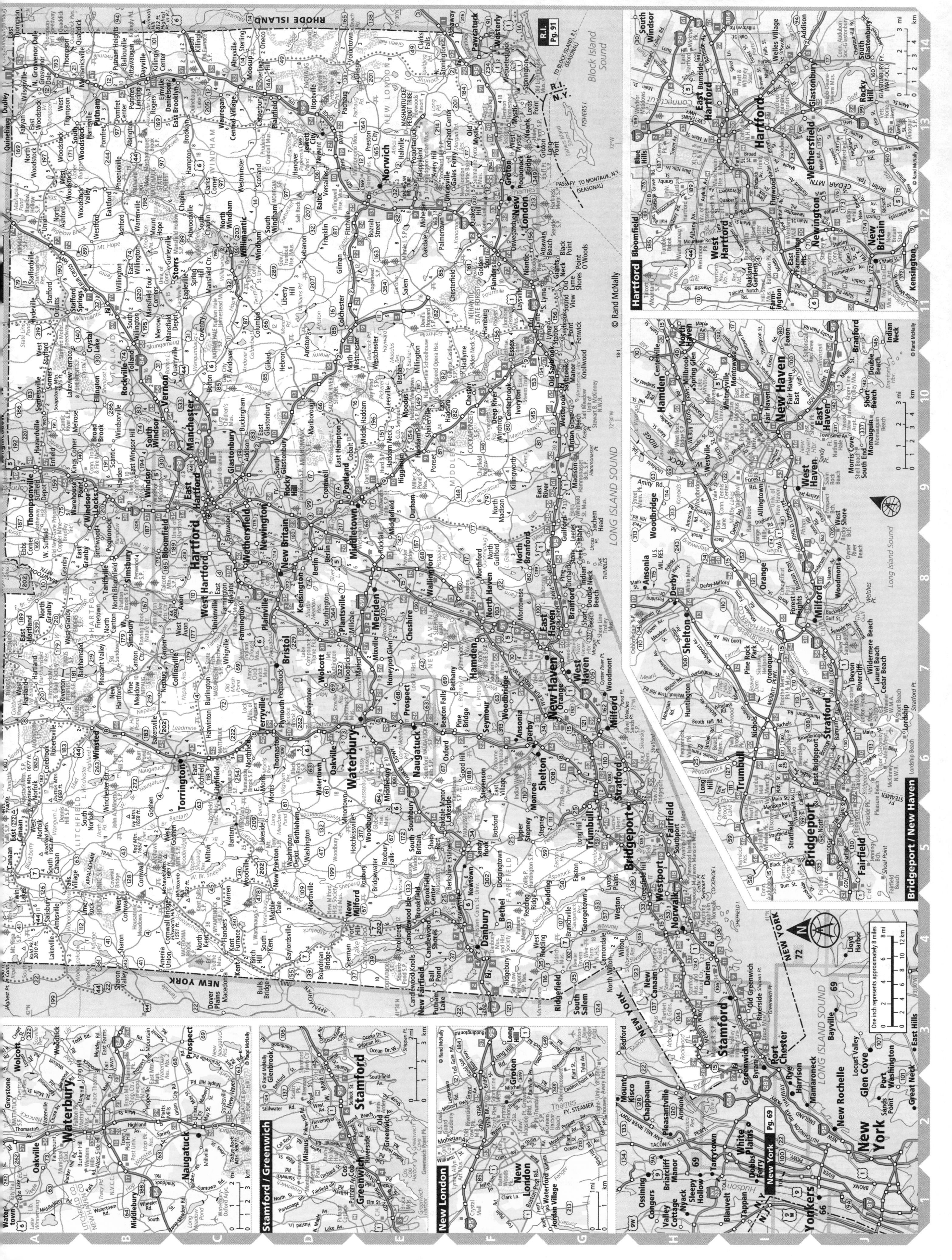

Nickname: The First State
Capital: Dover, G-2
Land area: 1,949 sq. mi. (rank: 49th)
Population: 897,934 (rank: 45th)
Largest city: Wilmington, 70,851, C-2

Index of places Pg. 129

Mileages between cities

	Dover	Georgetown	Lewes	Milford	Philadelphia, PA	Salisbury, MD	Selbyville	Wilmington
Dover		36	40	20	80	56	55	50
Georgetown	36		15	16	114	27	20	85
Lewes	40	15		21	119	43	29	90
Middletown	26	62	66	46	56	84	81	27
Millville, NJ	94	124	128	108	45	147	143	53
Newark	46	80	85	64	43	102	99	14
Selbyville	55	20	29	36	133	24		104
Wilmington	50	85	90	70	29	107	104	

Total mileages through Delaware
95: 23 miles
1: 104 miles
13: 108 miles

More mileages at randmcnally.com/MC

Travel planning & on-the-road resources

Tourism Information
Delaware Tourism: (866) 284-7483; www.visitdelaware.com

Road Conditions & Construction
(800) 652-5600, (302) 760-2080; www.deldot.gov

Toll Road Information (E-ZPa
Delaware River & Bay Authority (Del. Mem. Br. & Lewes/Cape May Ferry): (302) 571-6300; www.drba.net
Delaware Department of Transportation (all other toll roads): (888) 397-2773, (302) 678-7000; www.ezpassde.com

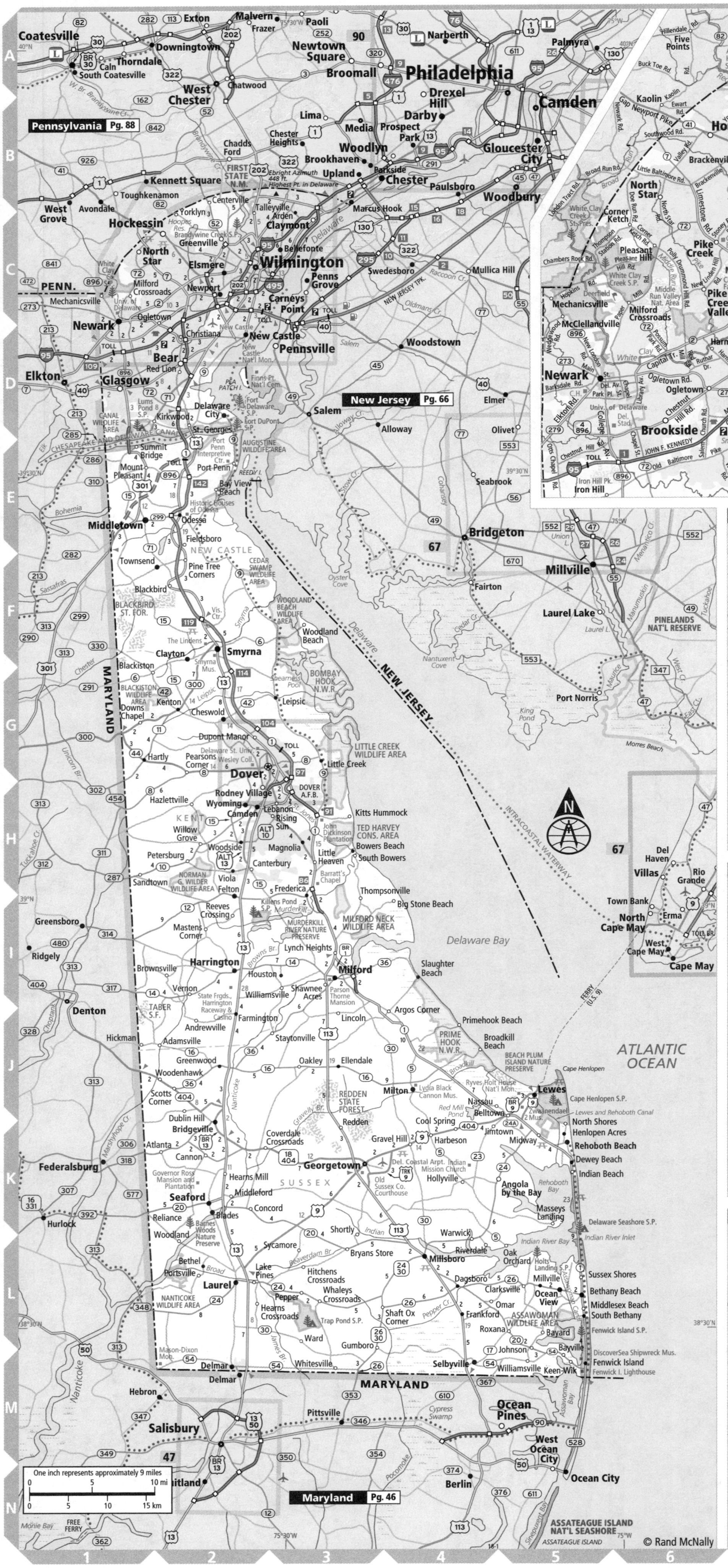

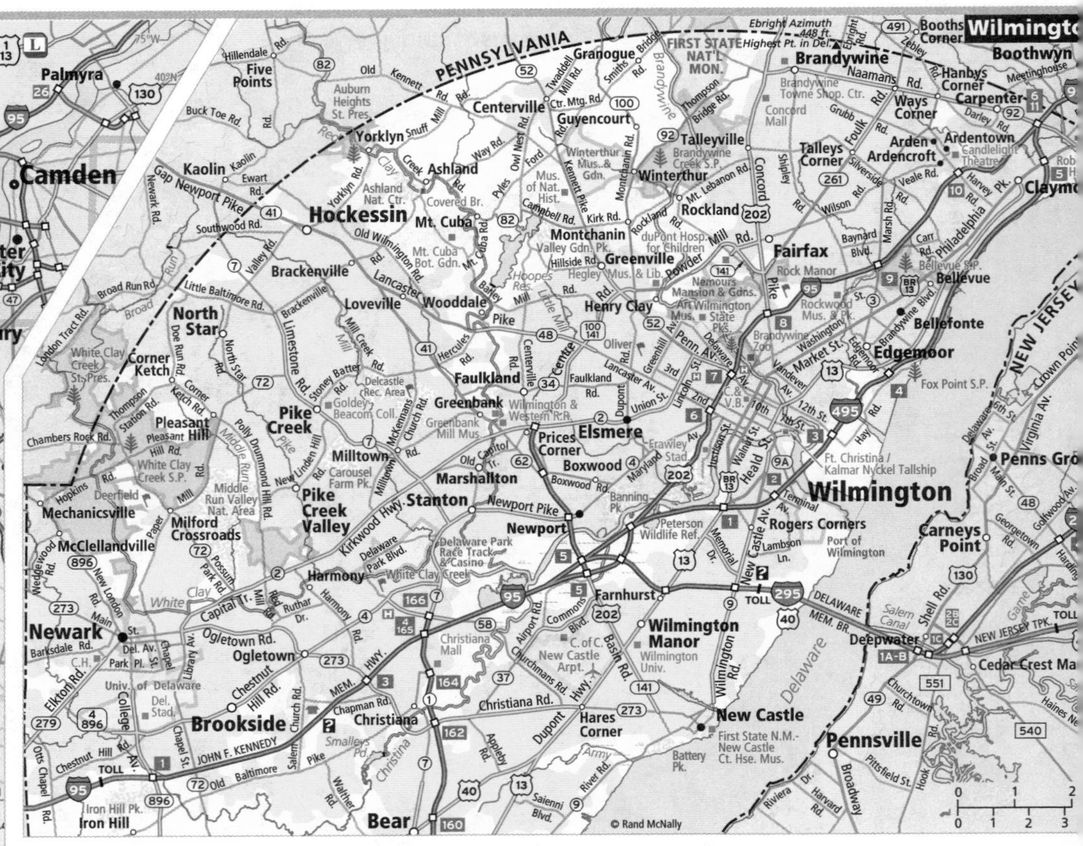

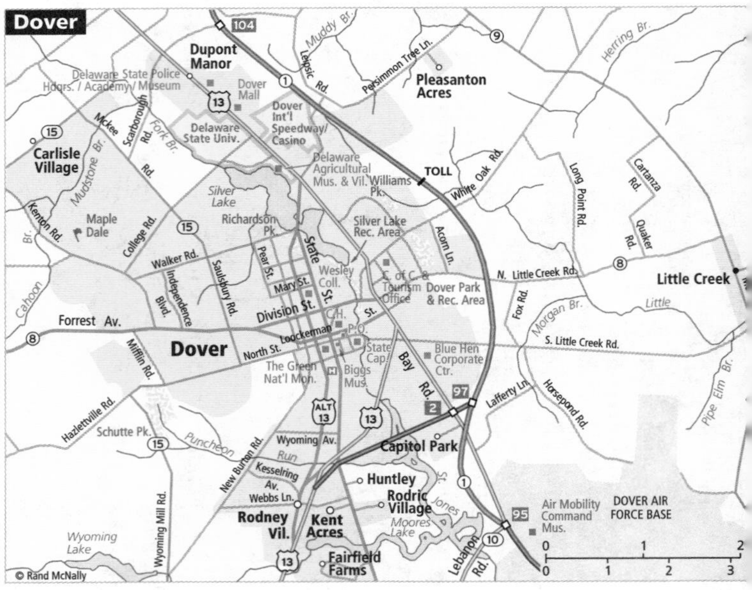

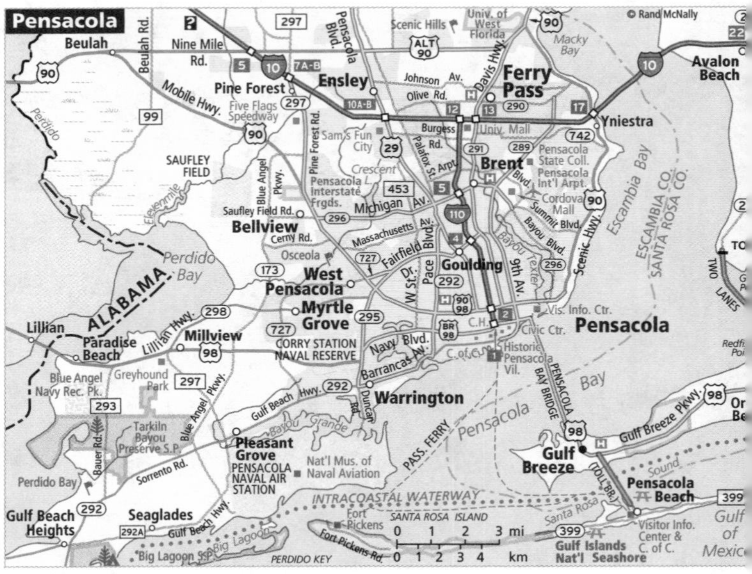

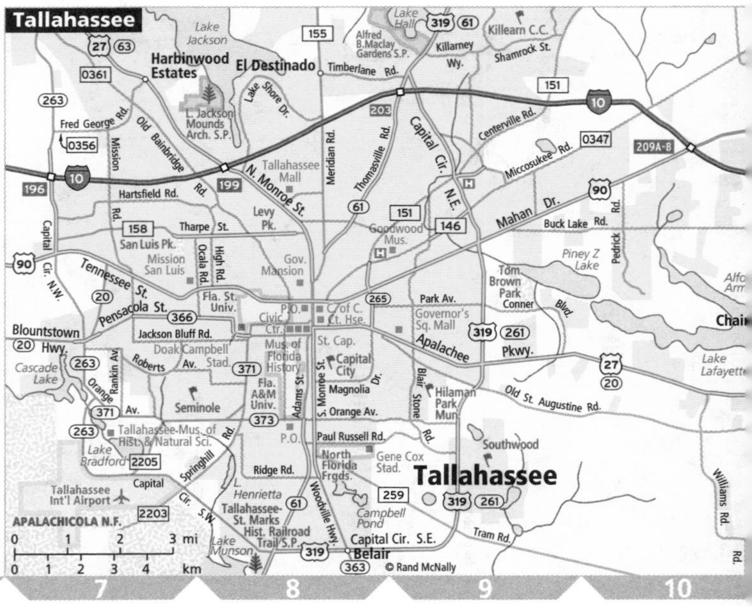

Sights to see

- Art Deco National Historic District, Miami Beach. L-9
- Busch Gardens, Tampa B-4
- Hugh Taylor Birch State Park, Fort Lauderdale. H-9
- Marie Selby Botanical Gardens, Sarasota H-3
- Miami Seaquarium, Miami M-9
- Norton Museum of Art, Palm Beach B-10
- Ringling Center for the Cultural Arts, Sarasota G-3
- Salvador Dali Museum, St. Petersburg. D-2
- St. Petersburg Museum of History, St. Petersburg D-2
- Thomas A. Edison & Henry Ford Winter Estates, Fort Myers M-2
- Vizcaya Museum and Gardens, Miami. M-8

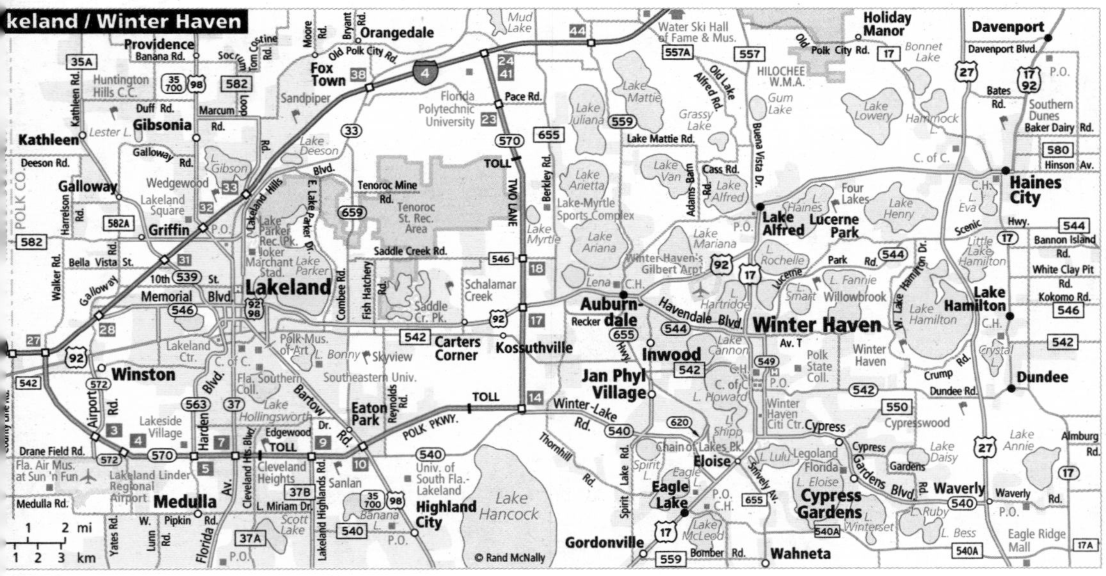

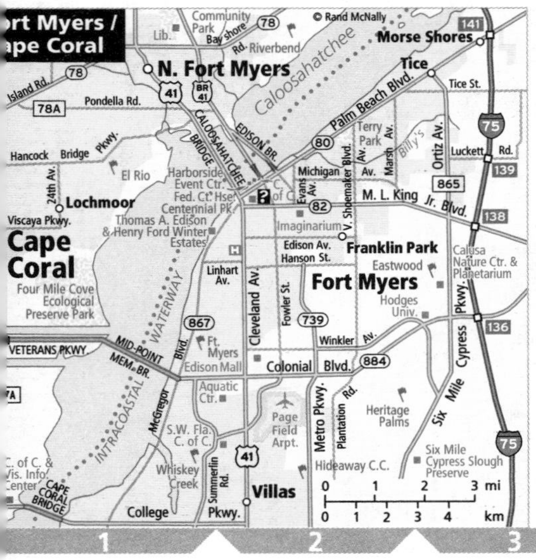

Florida

Nickname: The Sunshine State
Capital: Tallahassee, B-2
Land area: 53,625 sq. mi. (rank: 26th)
Population: 18,801,310 (rank: 4th)
Largest city: Jacksonville, 821,784, C-9

Index of places Pg. 129

Travel planning & on-the-road resources

Tourism Information
Visit Florida: (888) 735-2872, (850) 488-5607; www.visitflorida.com

Road Conditions & Construction
511
www.fl511.com, www.dot.state.fl.us

Toll Road Information
Central Florida Expressway Authority (Greater Orlando) ***(E-Pass or SunPass)***: (407) 823-7277; www.cfxway.com
Florida's Turnpike Enterprise (all other state toll routes/bridges) ***(SunPass)***: (800) 749-7453; floridasturnpike.com
Miami-Dade Expressway Authority ***(SunPass)***: (855) 277-0848; www.mdxway.com
Osceola Co. Expressway Authority ***(E-Pass)***: (407) 742-0200; www.osceolaxway.com
Tampa-Hillsborough Co. Expressway Authority ***(SunPass)***: (813) 272-6740; www.tampa-xway.com

Mileages between cities	Daytona Beach	Fort Myers	Fort Pierce	Gainesville	Jacksonville	Key West	Miami	Orlando	Panama City	Pensacola	St. Petersburg	Sarasota	Tallahassee	Tampa	Titusville	West Palm Beach
Fort Myers	225		128	254	312	279	152	171	497	589	117	80	397	130	209	124
Jacksonville	92	312	227	72		507	349	141	264	355	222	253	164	198	136	284
Key West	414	279	284	483	507		162	387	727	821	390	352	627	402	371	231
Miami	256	152	123	336	349	162		229	579	663	262	225	479	255	213	68
Orlando	54	171	110	114	141	387	229		357	451	106	132	257	84	39	159
Pensacola	442	589	549	338	355	821	663	451	102		458	511	193	459	487	594
Tallahassee	253	397	364	148	164	627	479	257	96	193	257	328		273	295	413
Tampa	137	130	151	127	198	402	255	84	373	459	23	60	273		124	202

Mileages © Rand McNally

Total mileages through Florida

- I-4: 132 miles
- I-75: 471 miles
- I-10: 362 miles
- I-95: 382 miles

More mileages at randmcnally.com/MC

Georgia

Nickname: The Peach State
Capital: Atlanta, E-4
Land area: 57,513 sq. mi. (rank: 21st)
Population: 9,687,653 (rank: 9th)
Largest city: Atlanta, 420,003, E-4

Index of places Pg. 130

Travel planning & on-the-road resources

Tourism Information
Visit Georgia: (800) 847-4842; www.exploregeorgia.org

Road Conditions & Construction
511, (888) 635-8287, (877) 694-2511, (404) 635-8000; www.511ga.org

Toll Road Information
No toll roads

Determining distances along roads

Highway distances (segments of one mile or less not shown):
Cumulative miles (red): the distance between red arrows
Intermediate miles (black): the distance between intersections & pla

Interchanges and exit numbers
For most states, the mileage between interchanges may be determi
by subtracting one number from the other.

tamaha River

Mileages between cities	Albany	Athens	Atlanta	Augusta	Bainbridge	Brunswick	Chattanooga, TN	Columbus	Gainesville	Jacksonville, FL	Macon	Rome	Savannah	Toccoa	Valdosta	Vidalia
Atlanta	182	69		148	240	275	117	106	54	346	82	70	247	94	228	172
Augusta	211	98	148		268	193	265	249	140	254	123	217	134	132	217	99
Chattanooga, TN	300	172	117	265	348	397		219	121	465	201	71	364	155	346	289
Columbus	85	171	106	249	128	258	219		161	292	98	144	249	201	173	175
Jacksonville, FL	198	310	346	254	204	66	465	292	396		270	416	135	375	121	164
Macon	106	91	82	123	163	193	201	98	132	270		152	165	143	152	90
Savannah	226	222	247	134	249	77	364	249	297	135	165	317		255	167	90
Valdosta	79	243	228	217	83	120	346	173	278	121	152	298	167	317		118

Total mileages through Georgia

- 20: 203 miles
- 85: 180 miles
- 75: 355 miles
- 95: 112 miles

More mileages at randmcnally.com/MC

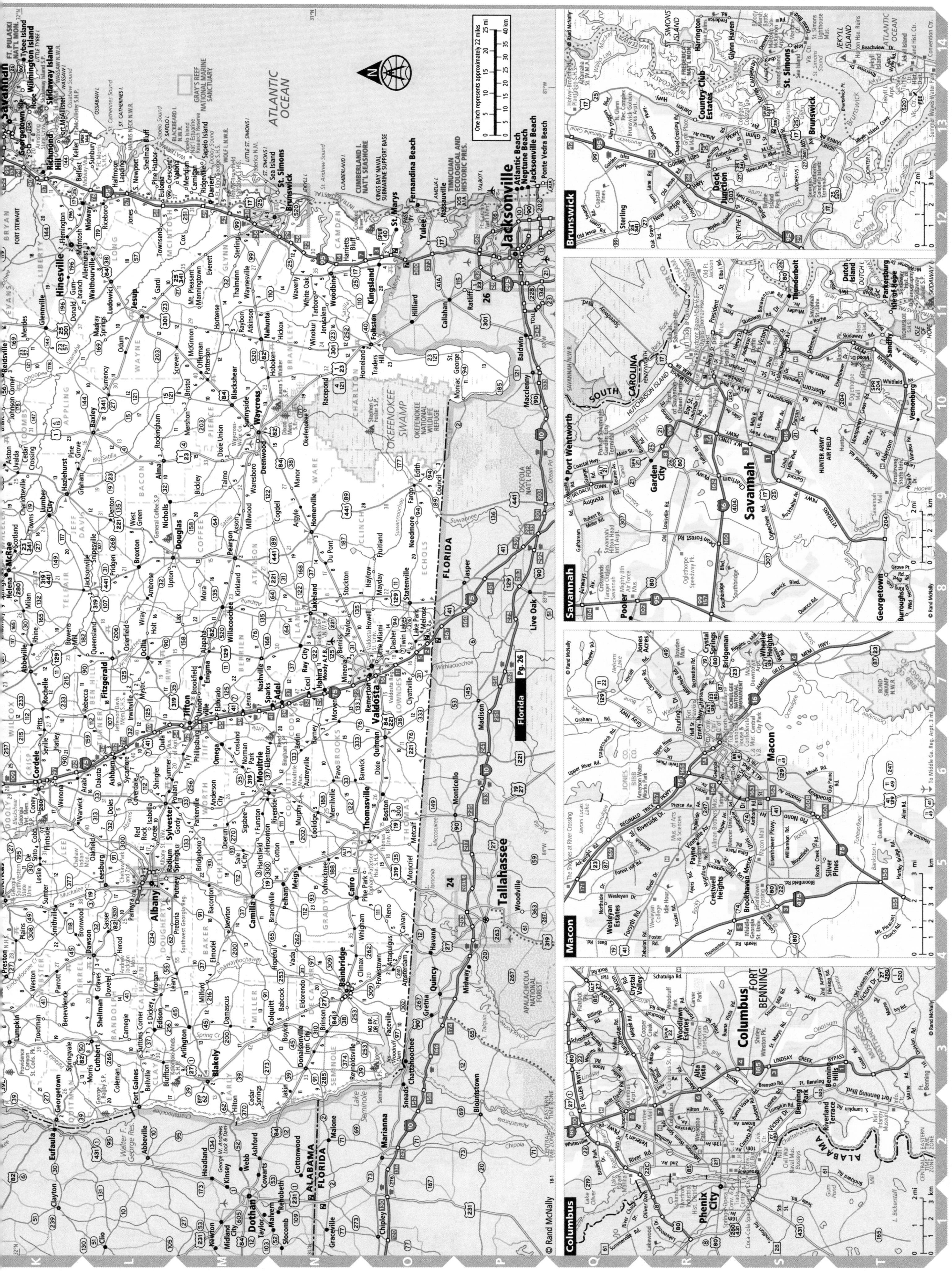

Hawaii/Georgia cities

Nickname: The Aloha State
Capital: Honolulu, N-4
Land area: 6,423 sq. mi. (rank: 47th)
Population: 1,360,301 (rank: 40th)
Largest city: Honolulu, 337,256, N-4

Index of places Pg. 130

Mileages between cities

*Via plane

	Hilo	Honolulu	Kahului	Kailua	Kailua Kona	Kapa'a	Lahaina	Wahiawā
Hilo		225*	127*	237*	74	337*	149*	236*
Honolulu	225*		108*	11	177*	116*	130*	20
Kahului	127*	108*		22*	93*	214*	22	119*
Kailua Kona	74	177*	93*	188*		283*	116*	188*
Kapa'a	337*	116*	214*	128*	283*		236*	128*
Kaunakakai	177*	68*	55*	79*	144*	174*	77*	79*
Lahaina	149*	130*	22	43*	116*	236*		141*
Wahiawā	236*	20	119*	26	188*	128*	141*	

Total mileages through Hawaii

H1 27 miles
H3 15 miles
H2 8 miles

More mileages at randmcnally.com/MC

Travel planning & on-the-road resources

Tourism Information
Hawaii Visitors & Convention Bureau:
(800) 464-2924, (808) 923-1811; www.gohawaii.com

Road Conditions & Construction
(808) 587-2220; hidaot.hawaii.gov

Toll Road Information
No toll roads

Determining Distance

(segment one mile not shown)

Cumulative miles (red): the distance between red a

Intermediate miles (black): the distance between intersections & places

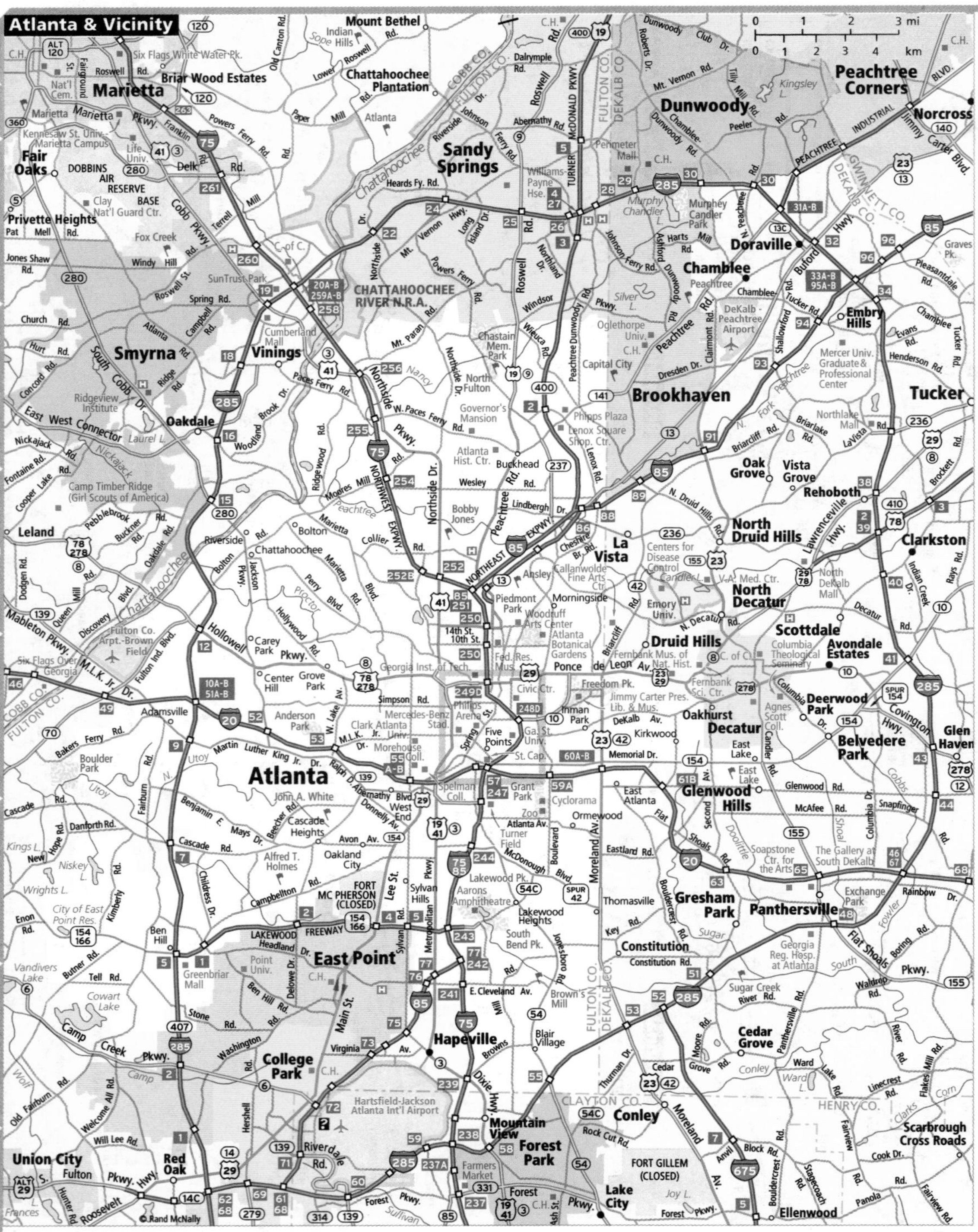

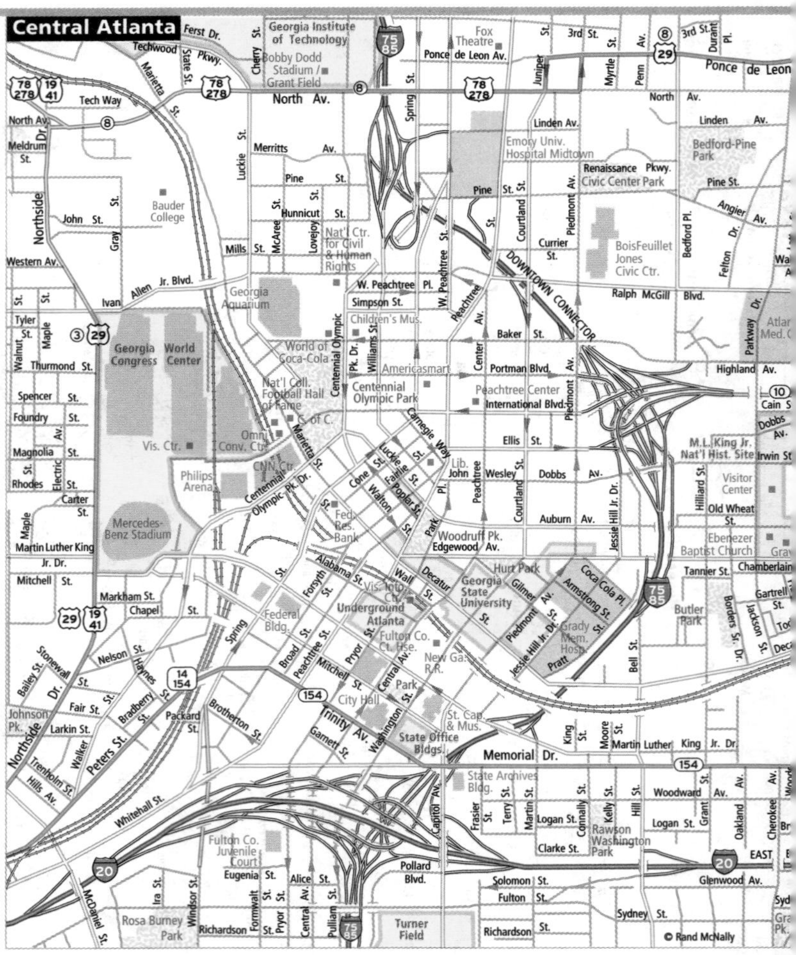

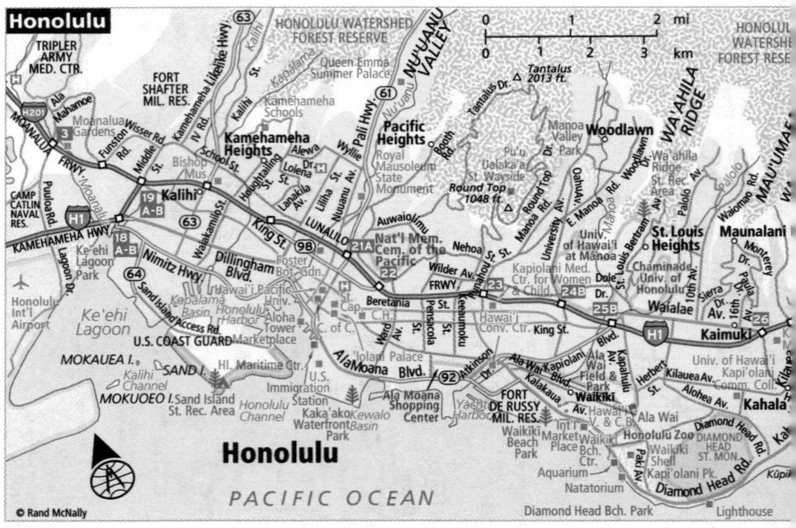

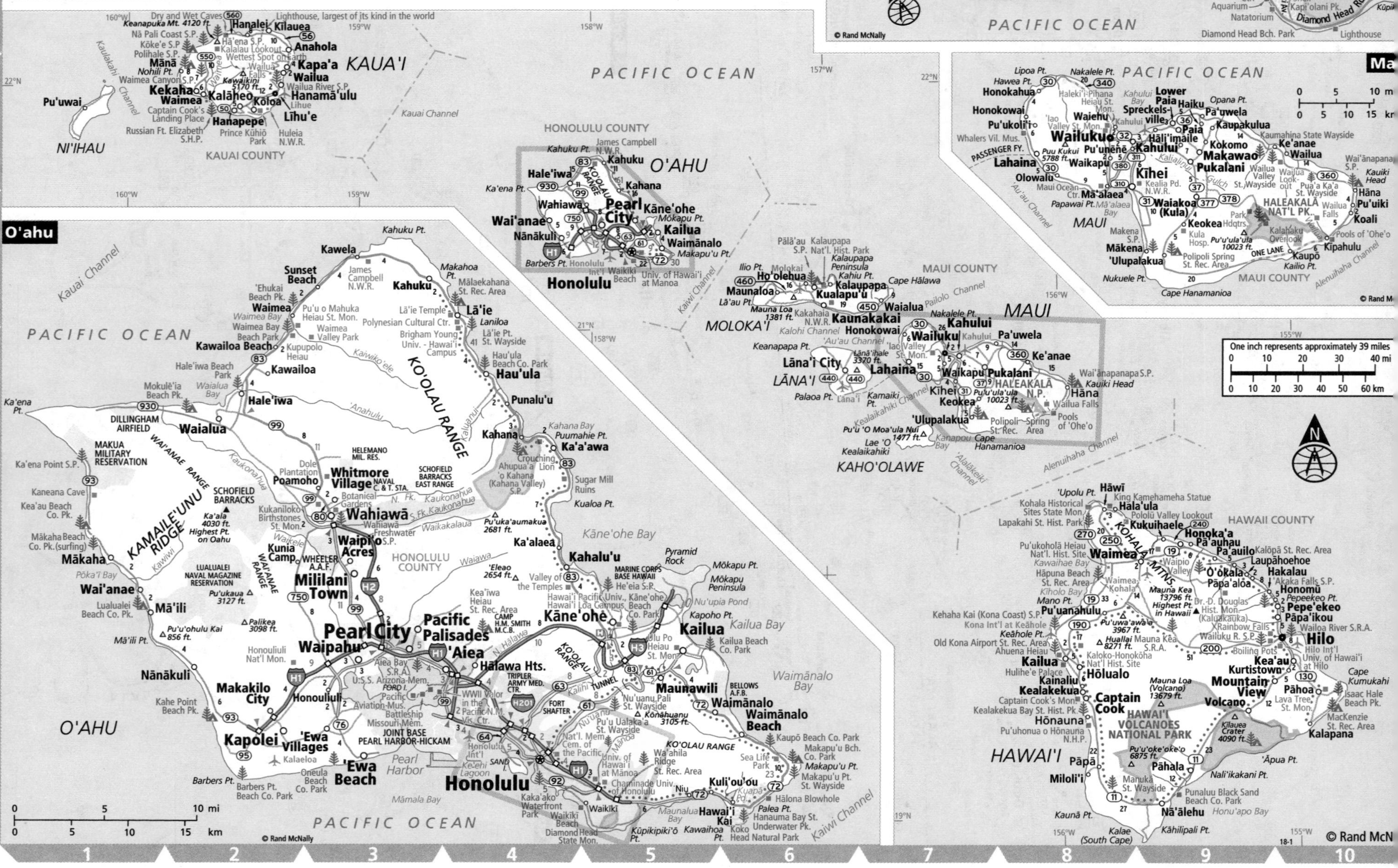

ravel planning & on-the-road resources

urism Information

ho Tourism:
00) 847-4843, (208) 334-2470; www.visitidaho.org

ad Conditions & Construction

, (888) 432-7623;
w.511.idaho.gov, www.itd.idaho.gov

Road Information

toll roads

Determining Distances

(segments of one mile or less not shown)

Cumulative miles (red): the distance between red arrows

Intermediate miles (black): the distance between intersections & places

Total mileages through Idaho

15: 196 miles	86: 63 miles
84: 276 miles	90: 74 miles

More mileages at randmcnally.com/MC

Mileages between cities

	Boise	Coeur d'Alene	Lewiston	Missoula, MT	Mountain Home	Pocatello	Salmon	Twin Falls
Boise		383	268	367	44	234	247	128
Bonners Ferry	459	76	191	212	504	573	351	589
Coeur d'Alene	383		115	166	428	525	303	513
Idaho Falls	279	478	526	312	237	49	160	159
Lewiston	268	115		214	313	504	332	398
Pocatello	234	525	504	361	191		209	114
Salmon	247	303	332	138	287	209		247
Twin Falls	128	513	398	384	85	114	247	

Mileages © Rand McNally

Nickname: The Gem State
Capital: Boise, K-2
Land area: 82,643 sq. mi. (rank: 11th)
Population: 1,567,582 (rank: 39th)
Largest city: Boise, 205,671, K-2

Index of places Pg. 130

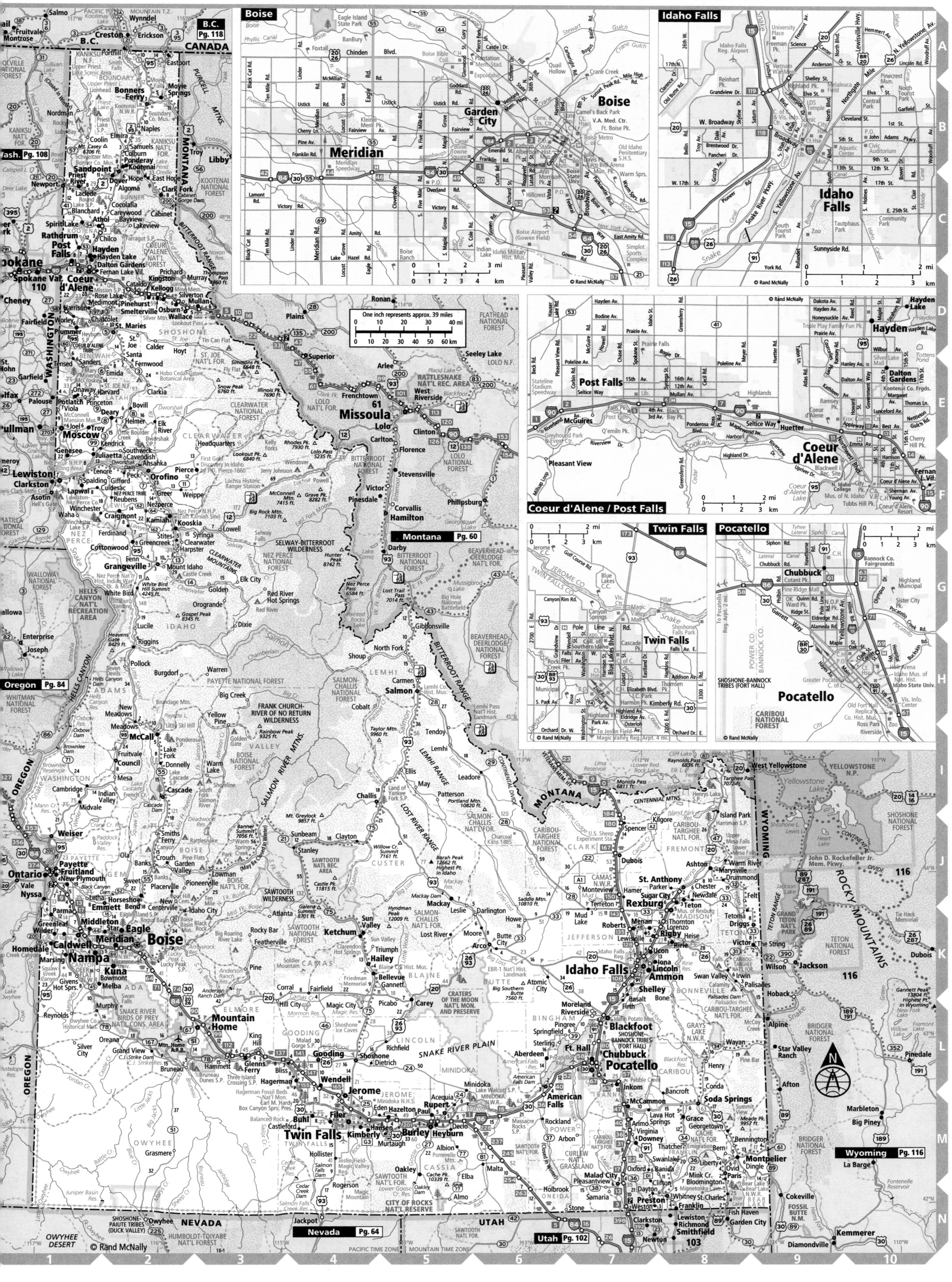

Nickname: Land of Lincoln
Capital: Springfield, J-8
Land area: 55,519 sq. mi. (rank: 24th)
Population: 12,830,632 (rank: 5th)
Largest city: Chicago, 2,695,598, C-13

Index of places Pg. 130

Travel planning & on-the-road resources

Tourism Information
Illinois Office of Tourism:
(800) 226-6632; www.enjoyillinois.com

Road Conditions & Construction
(800) 452-4368
www.gettingaroundillinois.com, www.dot.il.gov

Toll Road/Bridge Information *(all use I-Pass)*
Illinois Tollway (all other toll roads): (800) 824-7277; www.illinoistollway.com
Skyway Concession Co. (Chicago Skyway): (312) 552-7100; www.chicagoskyway.org

Determining distances along roads

Highway distances (segments of one mile or less not shown):
Cumulative miles (red): the distance between red arrows
Intermediate miles (black): the distance between intersections & places

Interchanges and exit numbers
For most states, the mileage between interchanges may be determined by subtracting one number from the other.

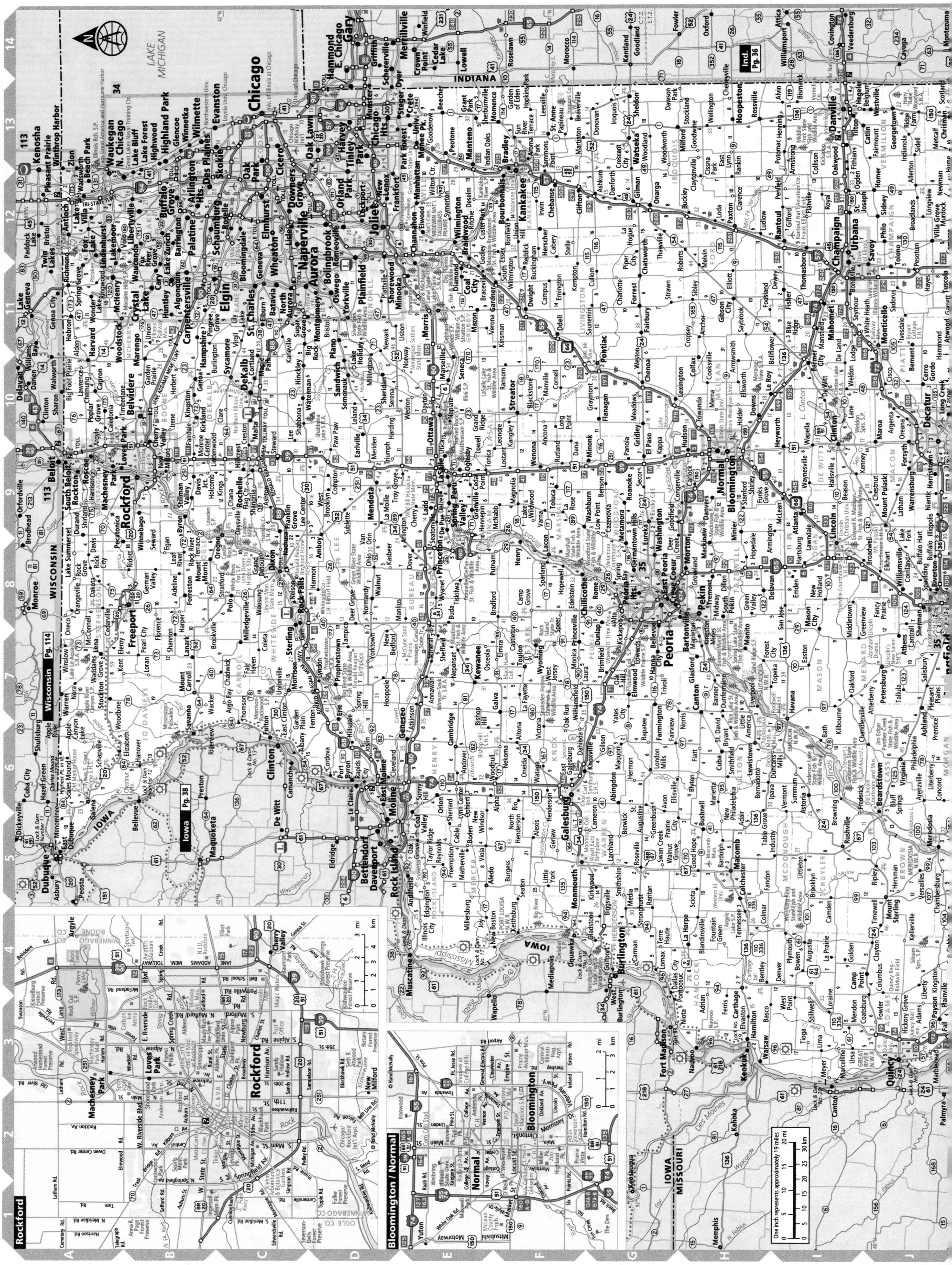

Mileages between cities

	Bloomington	Carbondale	Champaign	Chicago	Decatur	Dubuque, IA	Kankakee	Lawrenceville	Moline	Mt. Vernon	Peoria	Quincy	Rockford	St. Louis, MO	Springfield	Waukegan
Carbondale	245		200	330	176	406	272	146	332	57	240	240	379	104	170	374
Champaign	51	200		135	48	256	78	130	182	147	89	194	185	180	85	180
Chicago	132	330	135		179	177	58	247	166	277	154	309	84	296	198	38
Moline	131	332	182	166	171	75	158	307		308	93	148	120	261	164	190
Peoria	38	240	89	154	78	167	108	214	93	215		130	138	168	71	184
Rockford	132	379	185	84	180	93	139	309	120	326	138	268		294	197	73
St. Louis, MO	162	104	180	296	135	335	252	144	261	79	168	139	294		98	326
Springfield	66	170	85	198	38	238	157	153	164	138	71	112	197	98		229

Total mileages through Illinois

55 313 miles
80 164 miles
70 156 miles
90 124 miles

More mileages at randmcnally.com/MC

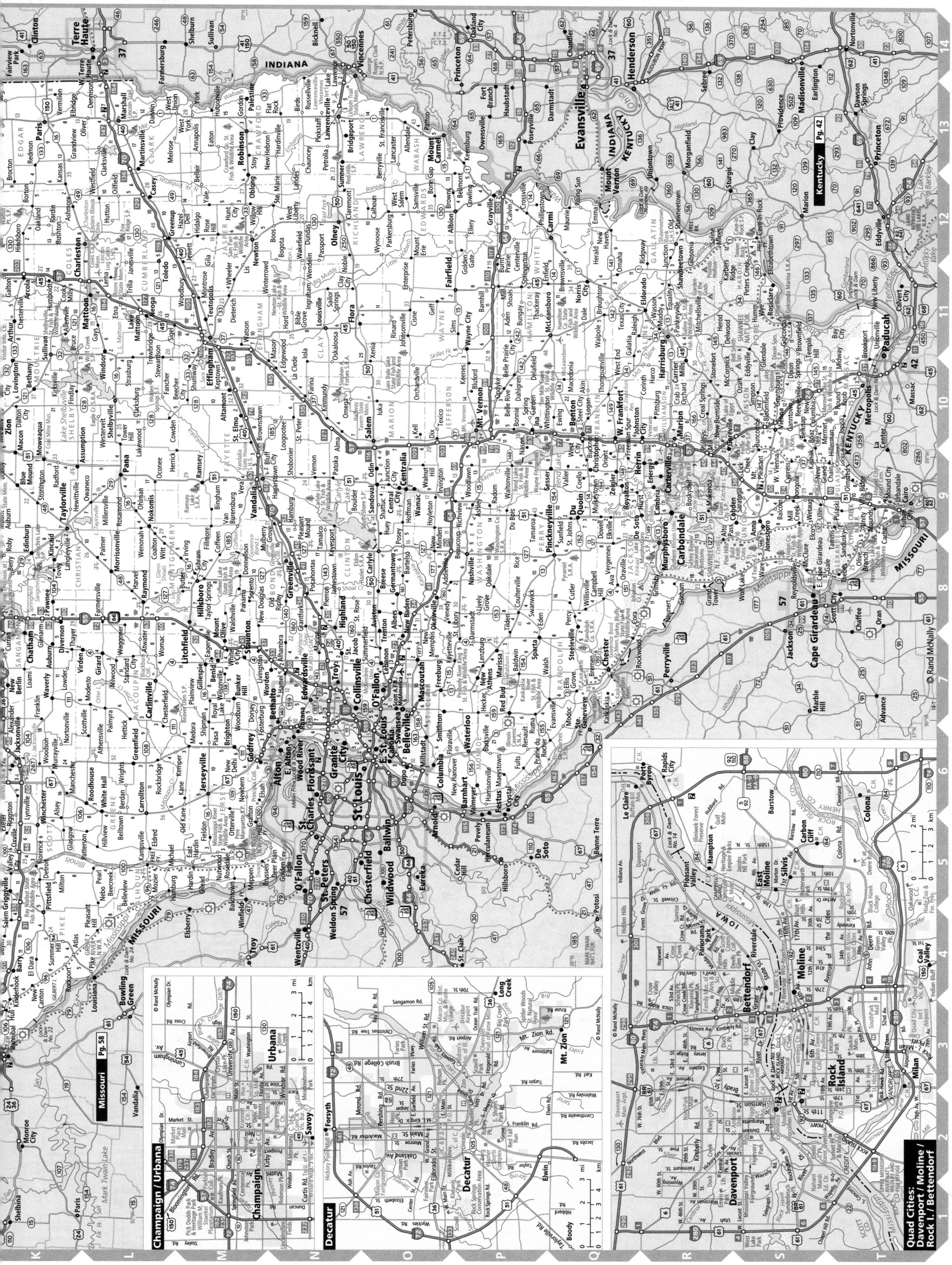

Sights to see

- Adler Planetarium G-15
- Art Institute of Chicago E-13
- Chicago Botanic Garden, Glencoe D-8
- Field Museum G-14
- Frank Lloyd Wright Home & Studio, Oak Park H-8
- John G. Shedd Aquarium G-14
- Lincoln Park Zoo H-9
- Millennium Park E-13
- Museum of Science & Industry J-10
- Navy Pier D-14
- Willis Tower E-12
- Wrigley Field G-9

Chicago Cultural Center

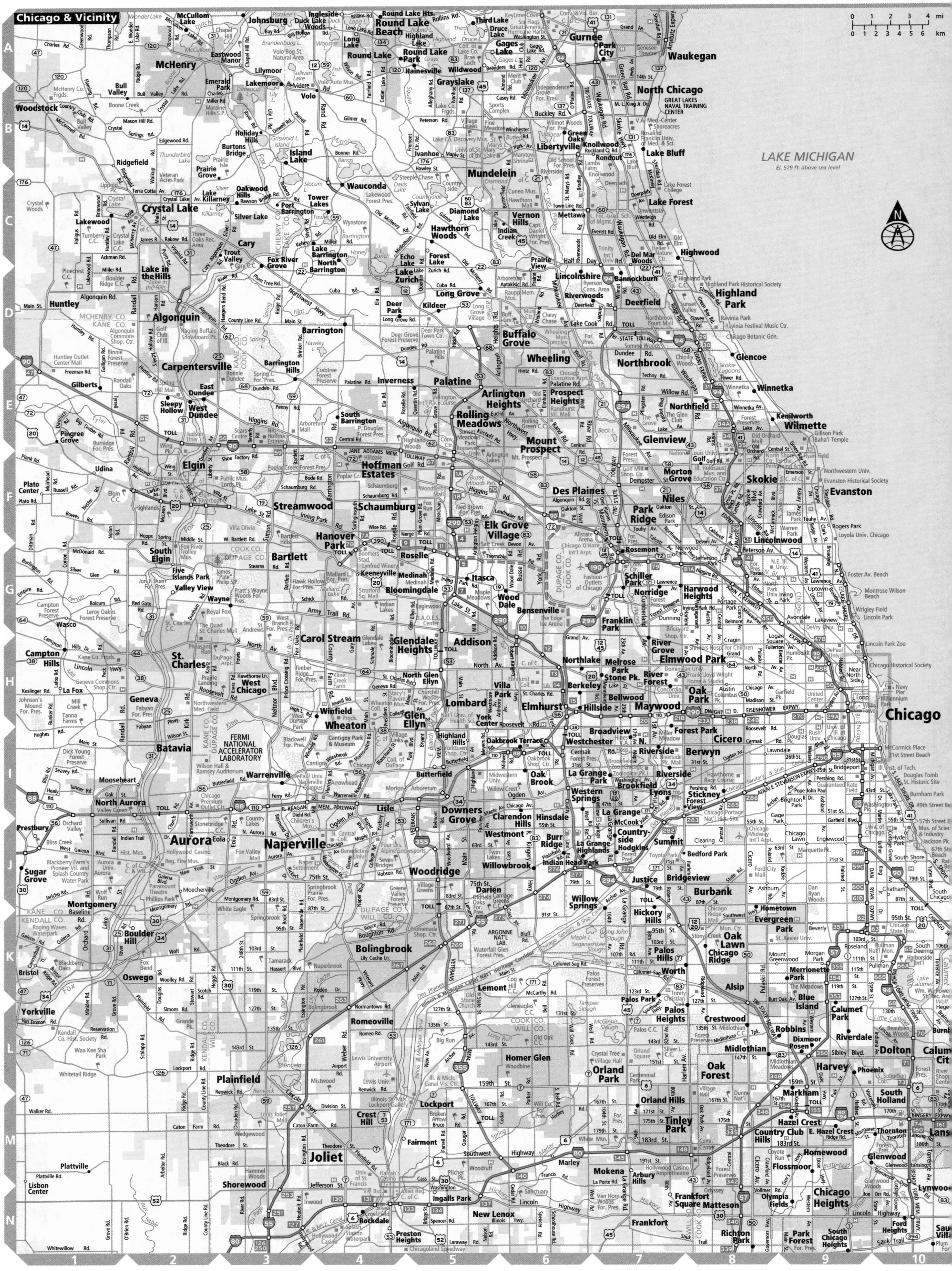

ldren's Museum of Indianapolis

Sights to see

- Abraham Lincoln Presidential Library & Museum, Springfield M-16
- Buckingham Fountain, Chicago F-13
- Children's Museum of Indianapolis, Indianapolis.... D-18
- Fort Wayne Children's Zoo, Fort Wayne L-19
- Illinois State Capitol Complex, Springfield M-16
- Indiana State Capitol, Indianapolis H-19
- Indiana State Museum, Indianapolis H-19
- Indianapolis Motor Speedway and Hall of Fame Museum, Indianapolis D-16
- NCAA Hall of Champions, Indianapolis............ H-18
- President Benjamin Harrison Home, Indianapolis F-20

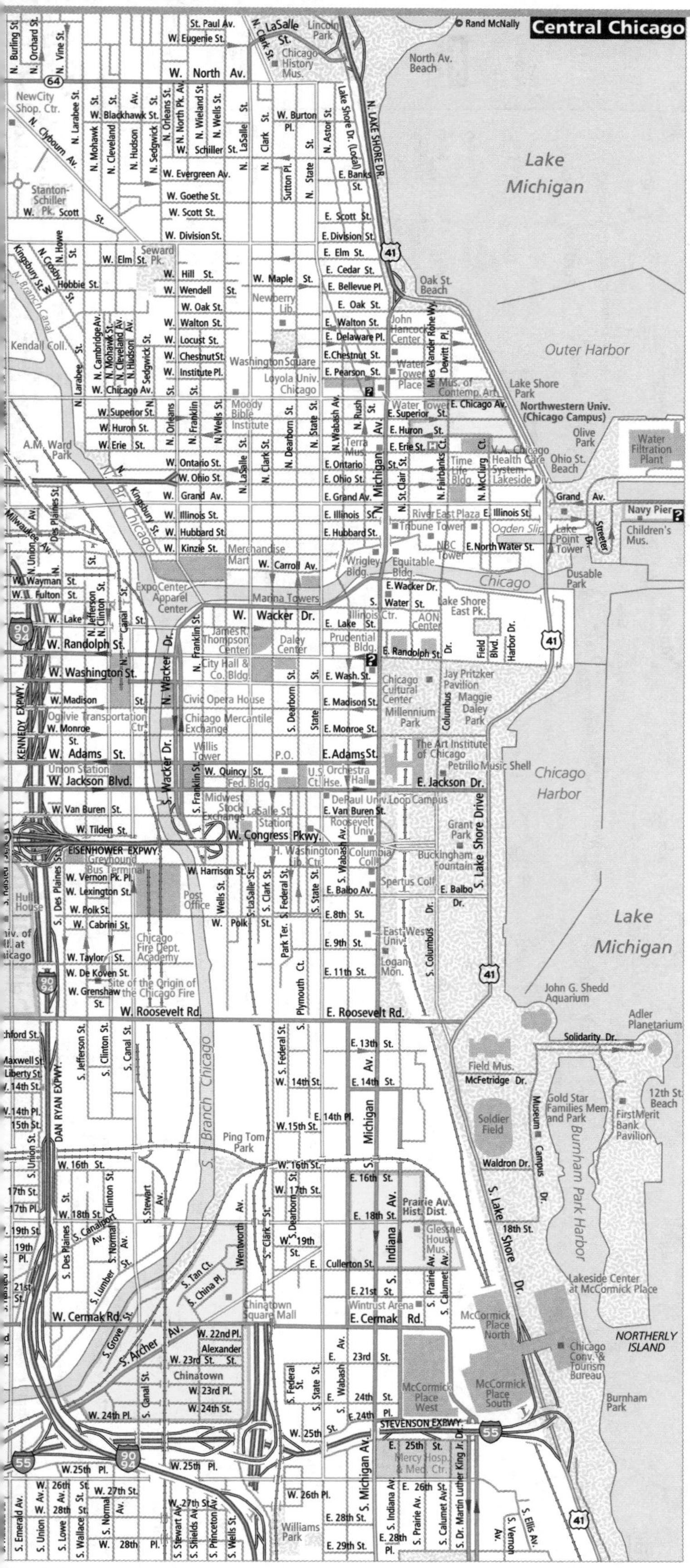

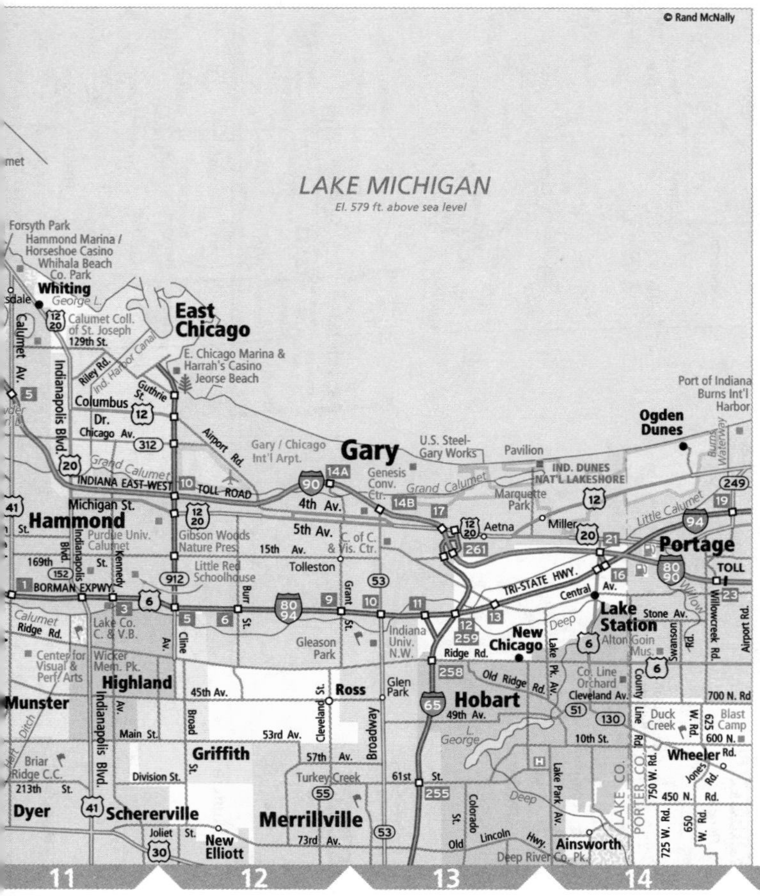

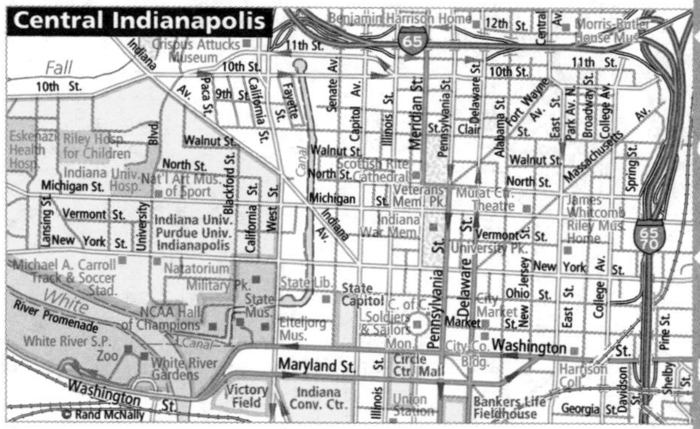

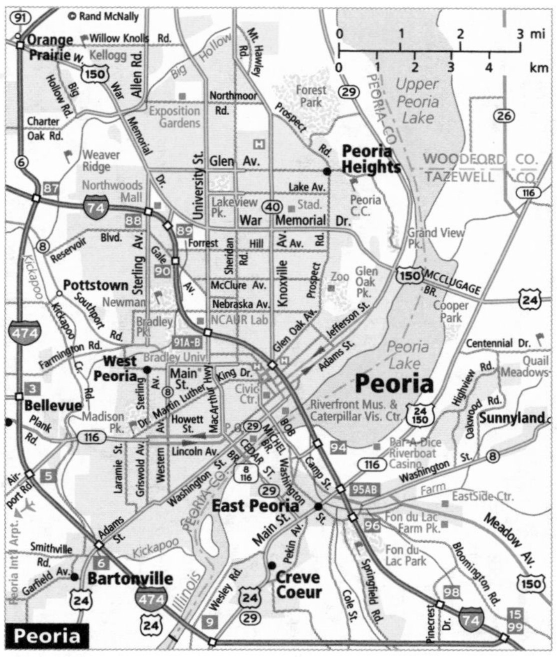

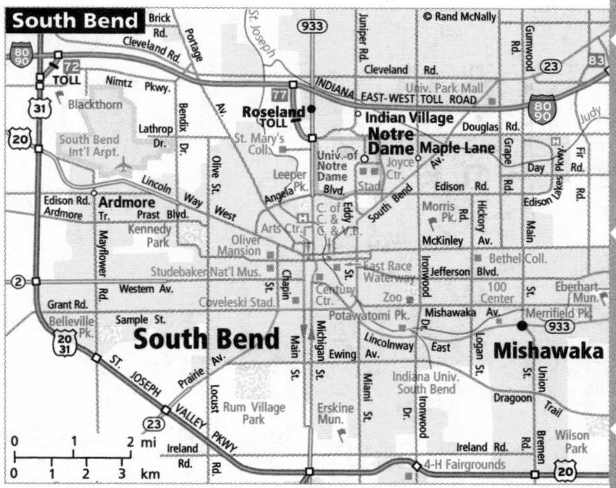

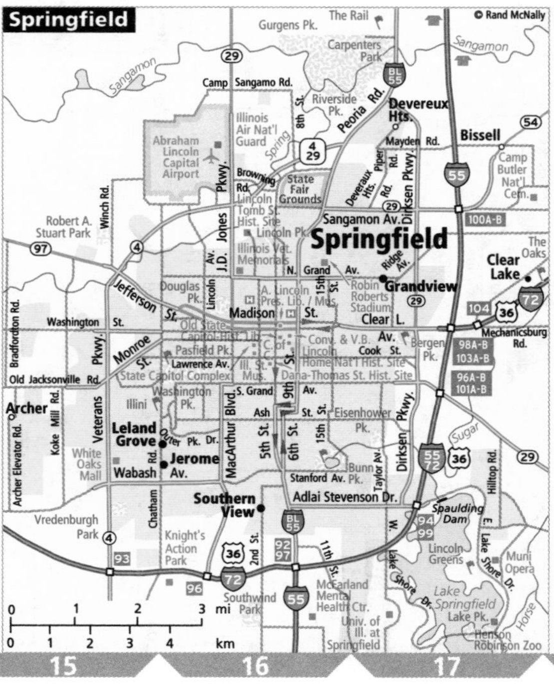

Indiana

Nickname: The Hoosier State
Capital: Indianapolis, J-9
Land area: 35,826 sq. mi. (rank: 38th)
Population: 6,483,802 (rank: 15th)
Largest city: Indianapolis, 820,445, J-9

Index of places Pg. 130

Travel planning & on-the-road resources

Tourism Information
Indiana Office of Tourism Development: (800) 677-9800; www.visitindiana.com

Road Conditions & Construction
(800) 261-7623, (866) 849-1368; www.in.gov/dot, www.in.gov/indot/2420.htm

Toll Road Information
Indiana Toll Road Concession Co. *(E-ZPass)*: (574) 675-4010; www.ezpassin.com
RiverLink (Louisville area toll bridges) *(RiverLink or E-ZPass)*: (855) 748-5465; www.riverlink.com

Determining distances along roads

Highway distances (segments of one mile or less not shown):
Cumulative miles (red): the distance between red arrows
Intermediate miles (black): the distance between intersections & pla

Interchanges and exit numbers
For most states, the mileage between interchanges may be determi
by subtracting one number from the other.

wn County State Park

Mileages between cities	Angola	Bloomington	Chicago, IL	Crawfordsville	Evansville	Fort Wayne	Gary	Greensburg	Indianapolis	Kokomo	Lafayette	Muncie	New Albany	Richmond	South Bend	Terre Haute
Evansville	347	120	289	178		309	273	202	180	234	198	244	112	255	320	109
Fort Wayne	39	178	160	162	309		132	147	129	86	117	72	238	92	89	205
Gary	135	200	30	118	273	132		203	151	127	91	196	266	222	64	164
Indianapolis	166	52	181	49	180	129	151	50		51	63	61	114	73	145	76
New Albany	276	88	296	163	112	238	266	94	114	168	178	172		184	256	146
Richmond	139	123	252	119	255	92	222	62	73	115	134	43	184		202	150
South Bend	77	195	93	135	320	89	64	183	145	87	106	143	256	202		216
Terre Haute	242	58	180	58	109	205	164	123	76	129	89	139	146	150	216	

Total mileages through Indiana

- 65: 261 miles
- 74: 172 miles
- 70: 157 miles
- 90: 156 miles

More mileages at randmcnally.com/MC

Nickname: The Hawkeye State
Capital: Des Moines, I-10
Land area: 55,857 sq. mi. (rank: 23rd)
Population: 3,046,355 (rank: 30th)
Largest city: Des Moines, 203,433, I-10

Index of places Pg. 131

Travel planning & on-the-road resources

Tourism Information
Iowa Tourism Office: (888) 472-6035, (800) 345-4692; www.traveliowa.com

Road Conditions & Construction
511, (800) 288-1047; www.511ia.org, www.iowadot.gov

Toll Road Information
No toll roads

Determining distances along roads

Highway distances (segments of one mile or less not shown):
Cumulative miles (red): the distance between red arrows
Intermediate miles (black): the distance between intersections & p

Interchanges and exit numbers
For most states, the mileage between interchanges may be determ
by subtracting one number from the other.

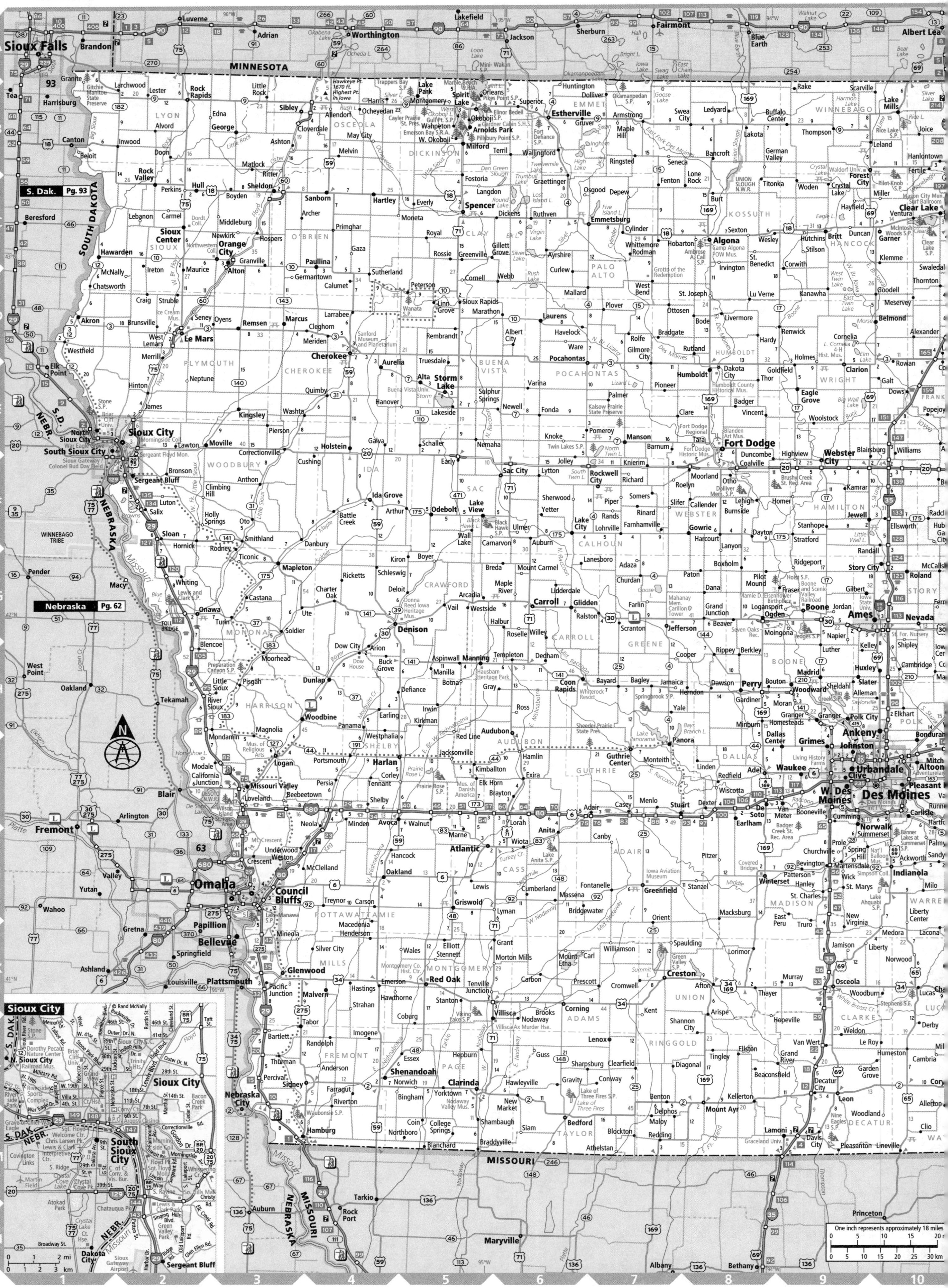

Mileages between cities

	Ames	Burlington	Cedar Rapids	Council Bluffs	Davenport	Decorah	Des Moines	Dubuque	Iowa City	Mason City	Ottumwa	Sioux City	Sioux Falls, SD	Spirit Lake	Storm Lake	Waterloo
Burlington	209		100	294	77	206	167	150	77	238	78	366	451	355	312	155
Cedar Rapids	108	100		253	82	105	126	70	28	136	110	268	357	252	212	53
Council Bluffs	160	294	253		295	328	127	327	241	246	213	94	180	176	122	253
Davenport	191	77	82	295		167	167	71	57	220	133	366	441	336	294	136
Des Moines	33	167	126	127	167	201		199	114	119	86	198	283	200	154	126
Dubuque	185	150	70	327	71	96	199		84	174	184	305	395	290	249	91
Mason City	91	238	136	246	220	88	119	174	165		203	200	222	118	135	83
Sioux City	175	366	268	94	366	304	198	305	312	200	285		85	109	78	218

Total mileages through Iowa

- 29 155 miles
- 80 303 miles
- 35 218 miles
- 218 257 miles

More mileages at randmcnally.com/MC

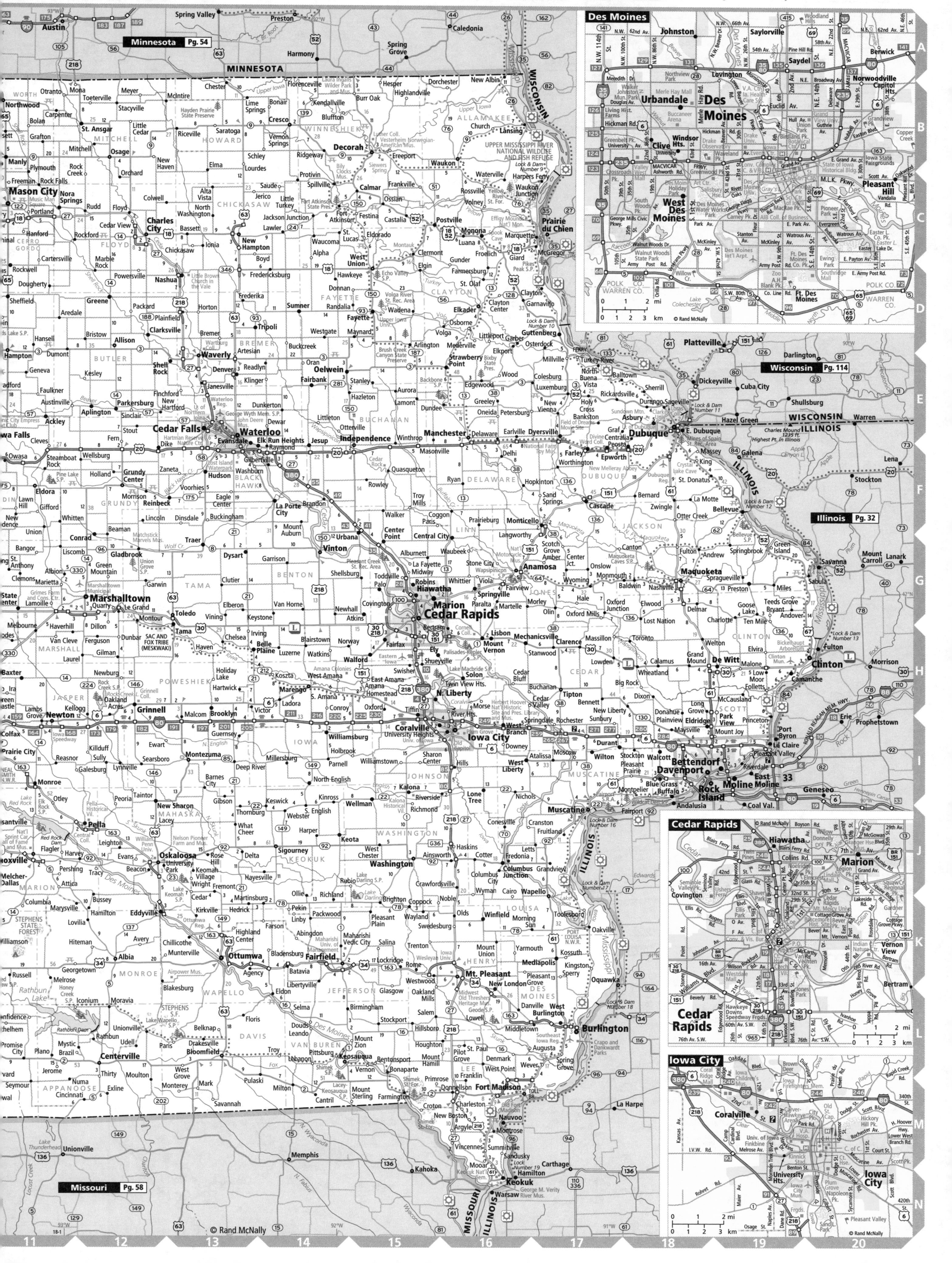

Nickname: The Sunflower State
Capital: Topeka, D-16
Land area: 81,759 sq. mi. (rank: 13th)
Population: 2,853,118 (rank: 33rd)
Largest city: Wichita, 382,368, H-13

Index of places Pg. 131

Travel planning & on-the-road resources

Tourism Information
Kansas Dept. of Wildlife, Parks & Tourism: (800) 252-6727, (785) 296-2009; www.travelks.com

Road Conditions & Construction
511, (800) 585-7623, (785) 296-3585; 511.ksdot.org, www.ksdot.org

Toll Road Information
Kansas Turnpike Authority (*K-TAG*): (800) 873-5824, (316) 682-4537; www.ksturnpike.com

Determining distances along roads

Highway distances (segments of one mile or less not shown):
Cumulative miles (red): the distance between red arrows
Intermediate miles (black): the distance between intersections & plac

Interchanges and exit numbers
For most states, the mileage between interchanges may be determir by subtracting one number from the other.

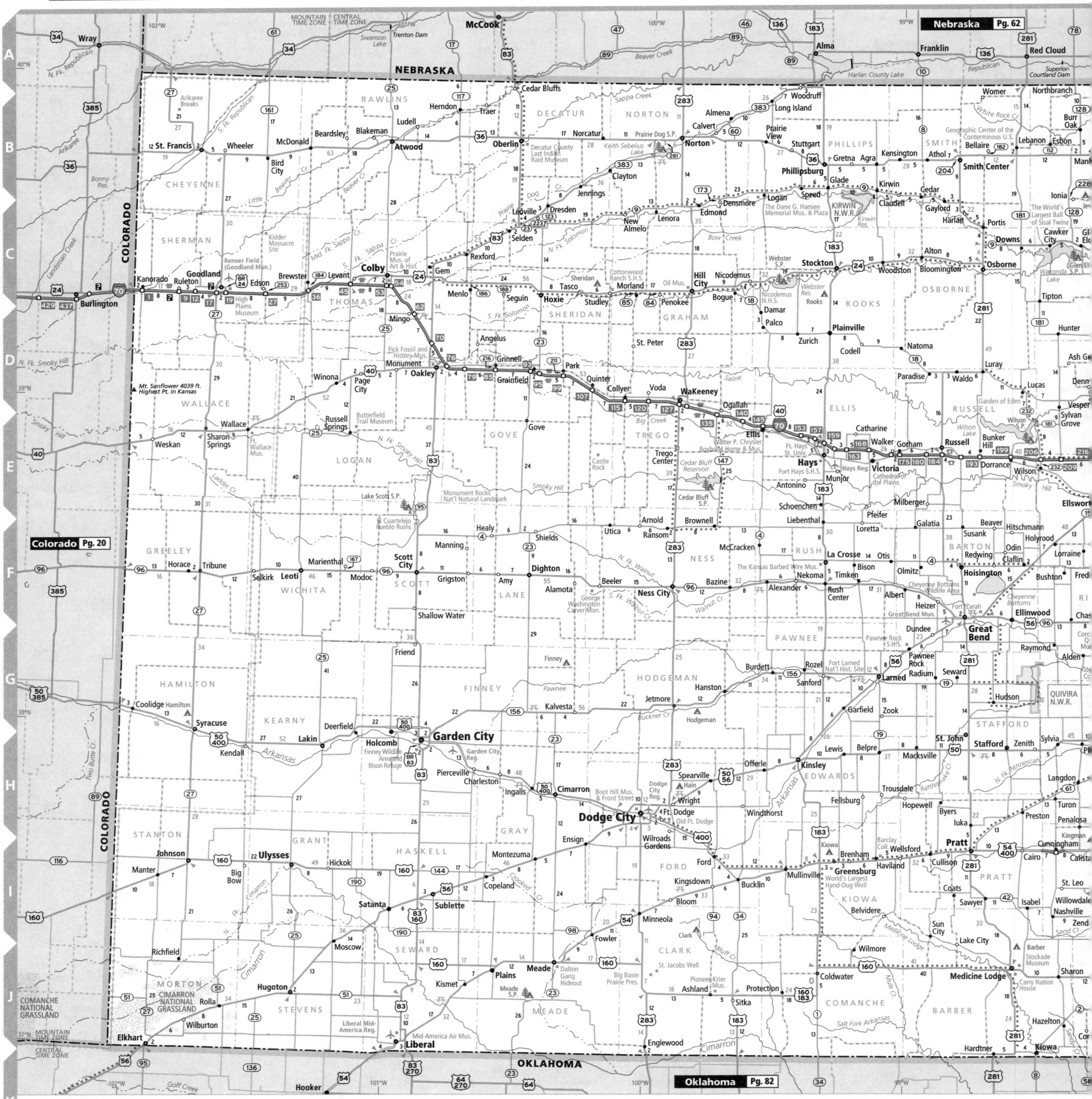

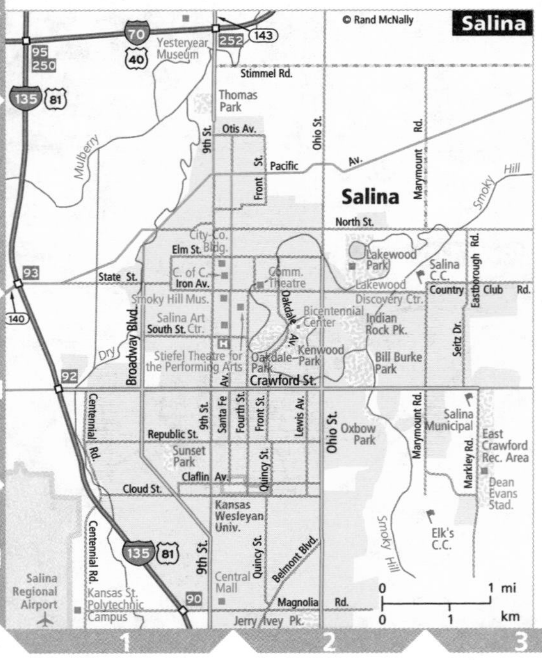

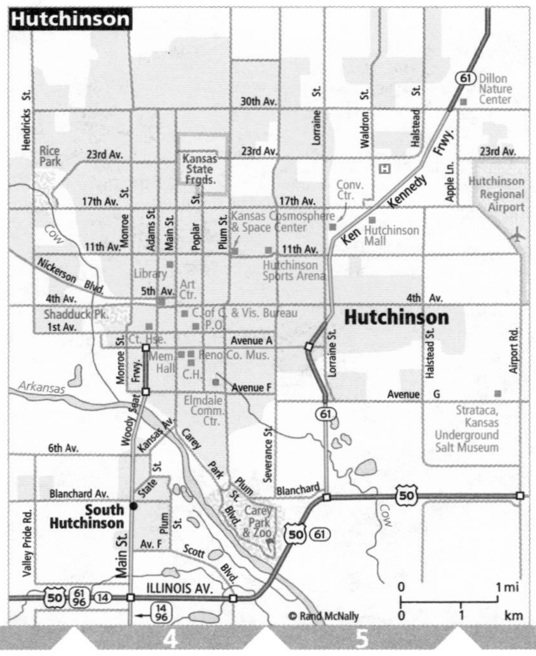

Monument Rocks

Mileages between cities	Arkansas City	Atchison	Coffeyville	Dodge City	Emporia	Fort Scott	Goodland	Hays	Hutchinson	Joplin, MO	Kansas City	Liberal	Manhattan	Salina	Topeka	Wichita
Dodge City	212	323	288		240	304	192	104	122	337	333	82	227	164	273	154
Goodland	384	395	455	192	349	472		144	268	505	406	209	299	235	344	323
Joplin, MO	150	196	65	337	177	60	505	366	233		154	395	252	274	196	183
Kansas City	228	58	172	333	109	94	406	266	220	154		406	117	173	62	196
Salina	151	160	224	164	117	238	235	96	65	274	173	246	65		109	90
Smith Center	266	213	338	195	231	342	175	91	155	387	263	277	150	117	206	205
Topeka	170	55	155	273	58	136	344	204	162	196	62	349	56	109		137
Wichita	61	188	134	154	85	149	323	183	51	183	196	212	130	90	137	

Total mileages through Kansas

35 235 miles | 56 464 miles
70 424 miles | 81 220 miles

More mileages at randmcnally.com/MC

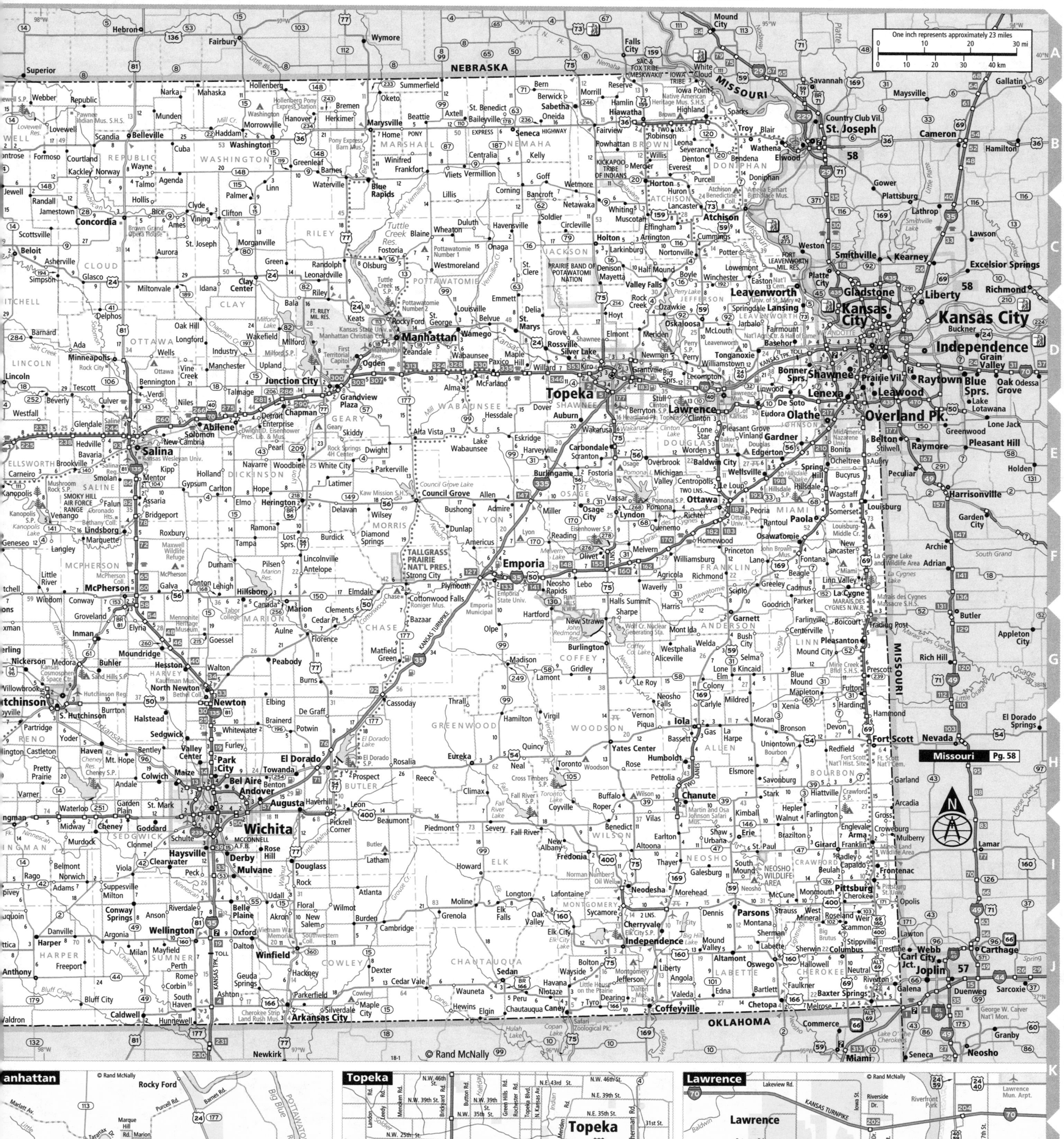

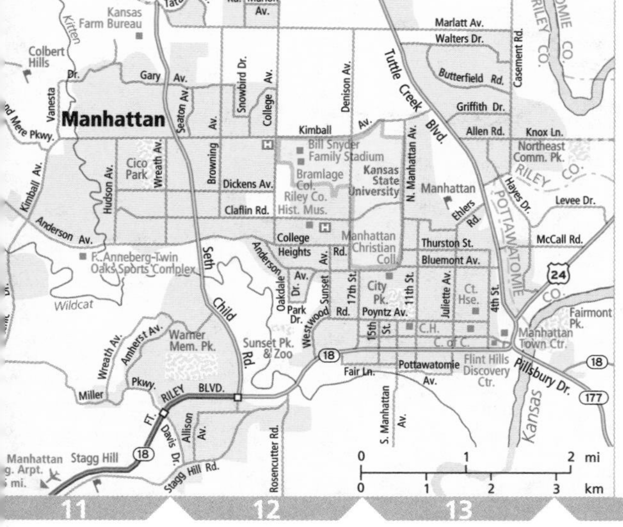

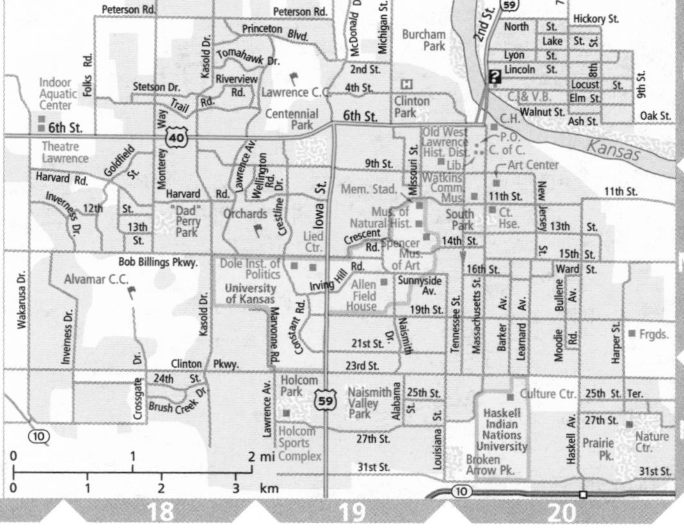

Kentucky

Nickname: The Bluegrass State
Capital: Frankfort, G-11
Land area: 39,486 sq. mi. (rank: 37th)
Population: 4,339,367 (rank: 26th)
Largest city: Louisville, 597,337, G-8

Index of places Pg. 131

Travel planning & on-the-road resources

Tourism Information
Kentucky Department of Travel & Tourism: (800) 225-8747; www.kentuckytourism.com

Road Conditions & Construction
511, (866) 737-3767; www.511.ky.gov, transportation.ky.gov

Toll Road Information
RiverLink (Louisville area toll bridges) *(RiverLink or E-ZPass)*: (855) 748-5465; www.riverlink.com

Determining distances along roads

Highway distances (segments of one mile or less not shown):
Cumulative miles (red): the distance between red arrows
Intermediate miles (black): the distance between intersections & places

Interchanges and exit numbers
For most states, the mileage between interchanges may be determined by subtracting one number from the other.

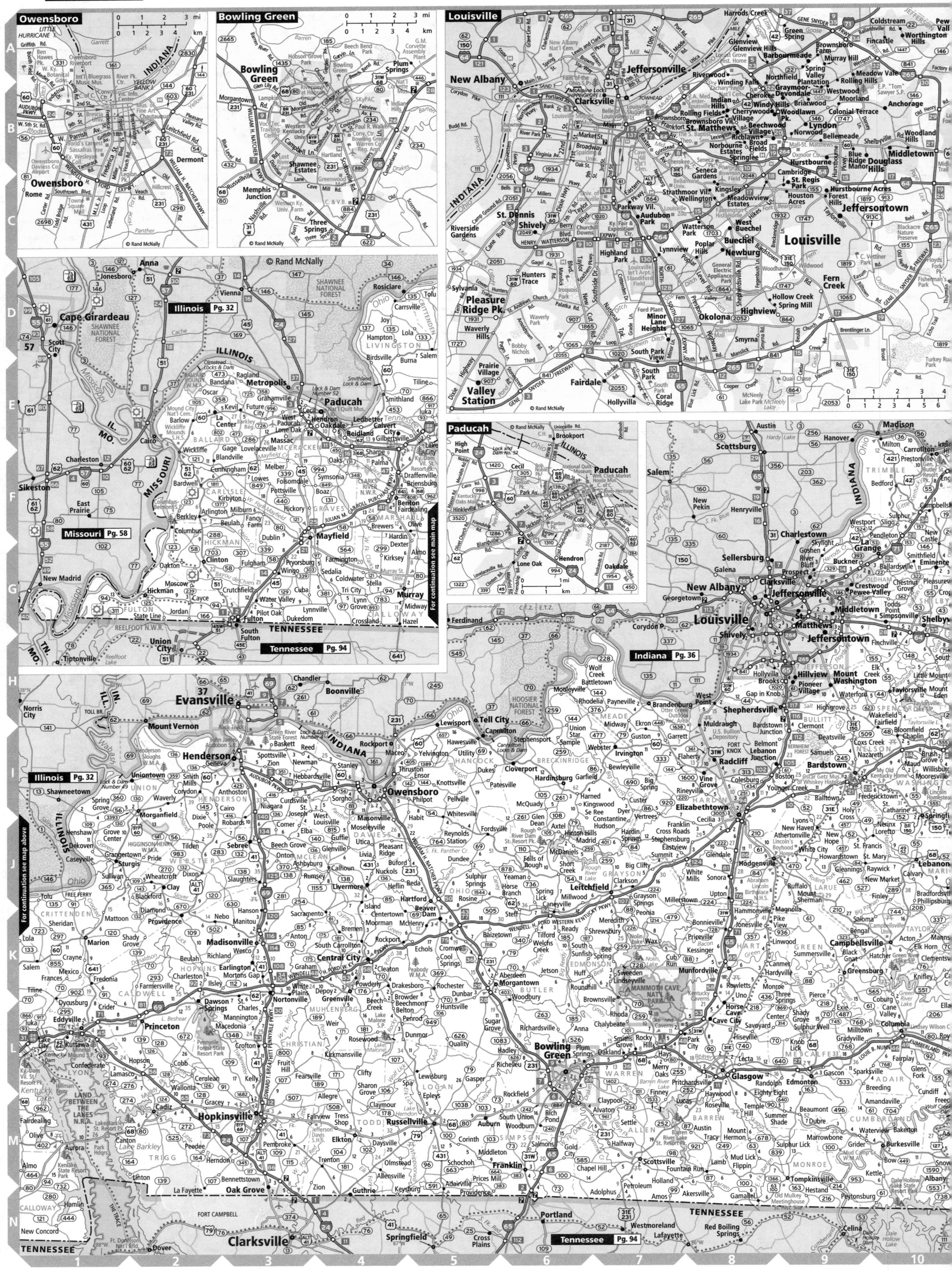

Churchill Downs, Louisville

Mileages between cities	Ashland	Bowling Green	Cave City	Covington	Elizabethtown	Frankfort	Hopkinsville	Lexington	Louisville	Mayfield	Maysville	Middlesboro	Owensboro	Paducah	Pikeville	Somerset
Ashland		269	242	138	202	140	325	117	187	383	76	227	294	372	96	175
Bowling Green	269		31	209	70	147	64	151	113	160	216	198	71	151	265	109
Covington	138	209	181		140	78	265	81	97	322	59	208	203	312	216	157
Lexington	117	151	124	81	84	29	207		76	266	63	130	177	256	140	78
Louisville	187	113	85	97	44	50	170	76		227	133	203	106	216	211	124
Middlesboro	227	198	176	208	182	157	265	130	203	363	191		275	353	125	88
Owensboro	294	71	108	203	94	159	96	177	106	154	242	275		143	318	187
Paducah	372	151	186	312	172	250	72	256	216	24	319	353	143		396	265

Total mileages through Kentucky

- 64: 185 miles
- 71: 97 miles
- 65: 137 miles
- 75: 192 miles

More mileages at randmcnally.com/MC

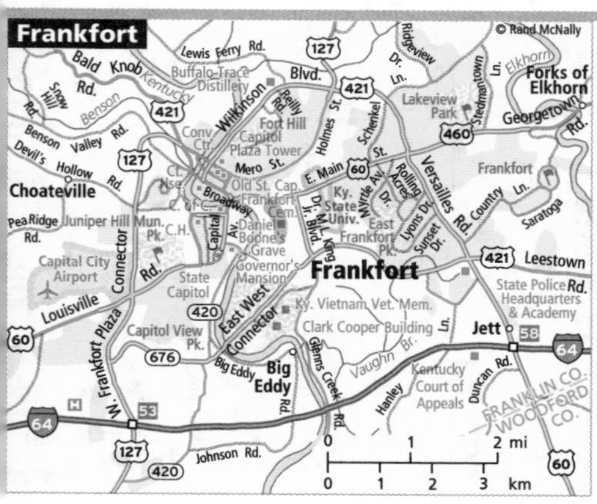

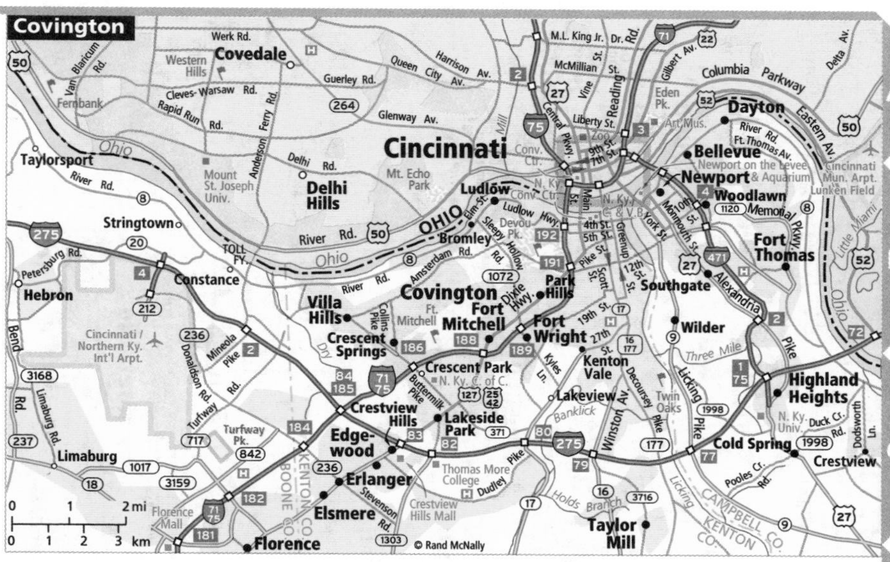

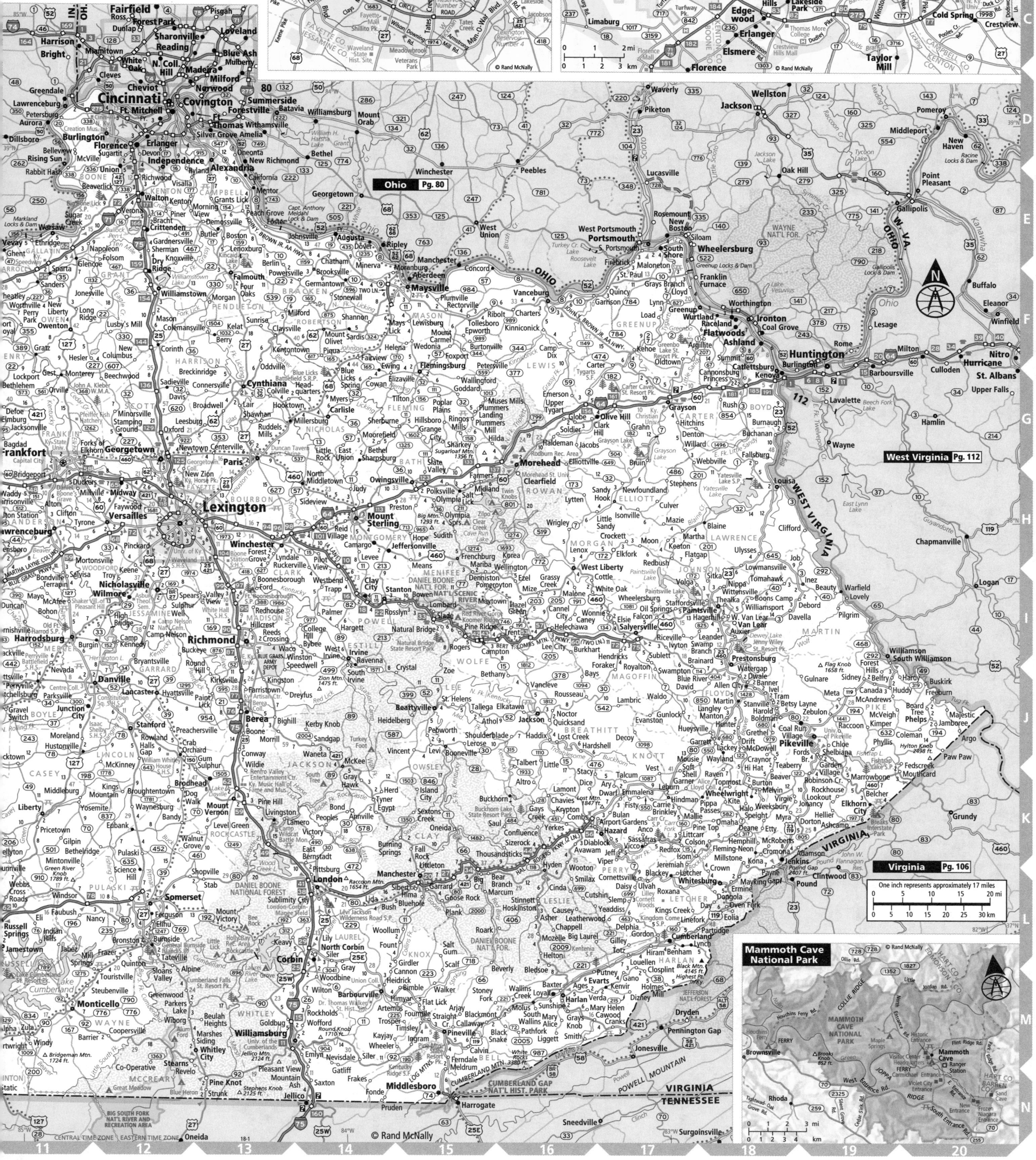

Louisiana

Nickname: The Pelican State
Capital: Baton Rouge, G-7
Land area: 43,204 sq. mi. (rank: 33rd)
Population: 4,533,372 (rank: 25th)
Largest city: New Orleans, 343,829, H-9

Index of places Pg. 131

Mileages between cities	Baton Rouge	Beaumont, TX	Houma	Lake Charles	Monroe	New Orleans	Shreveport	Vicksburg, MS
Alexandria	125	155	190	97	95	218	123	147
Baton Rouge		183	85	124	186	79	250	157
Gulfport, MS	134	318	131	258	276	78	375	201
Lafayette	55	133	102	73	182	134	211	212
Lake Charles	124	60	177		190	203	184	243
New Orleans	79	262	56	203	281		340	207
Shreveport	250	206	314	184	98	340		171
Vicksburg, MS	157	301	234	243	74	207	171	

Total mileages through Louisiana

I-10: 274 miles
I-20: 190 miles
I-49: 208 miles
I-55: 66 miles

More mileages at randmcnally.com/MC

Travel planning & on-the-road resources

Tourism Information
Louisiana Office of Tourism: (800) 994-8626, (800) 677-4082; www.louisianatravel.com

Road Conditions & Construction
511, (877) 452-3683; www.511la.org, www.dotd.la.gov

Toll Bridges
Lake Ponchartrain Causeway (*TollTag*): (504) 835-3118; www.thecauseway.us
Louisiana Dept. of Trans. & Development (La. Hwy. 1 Bridge) (*GeauxPass*): (866) 662-8987; www.geauxpass.com

ravel planning & on-the-road resources

urism Information
aine Office of Tourism: (888) 624-6345; www.visitmaine.com

ad Conditions & Construction
1, (207) 624-3000, (800) 675-7453; ww.511maine.gov, www.maine.gov/mdot

ll Road Information
aine Turnpike Authority (*E-ZPass*): 877) 682-9433, (207) 871-7771; www.maineturnpike.com

Determining Distances
(segments of one mile or less not shown)

Cumulative miles (red): the distance between red arrows

Intermediate miles (black): the distance between intersections & places

Total mileages through Maine

95: 299 miles
2: 273 miles
1: 527 miles
201: 164 miles

More mileages at randmcnally.com/MC

Mileages between cities	Auburn	Bangor	Bar Harbor	Eastport	Houlton	Millinocket	Portland	Rangeley
Bangor	107		47	120	118	72	128	120
Eastport	226	120	118		115	125	247	242
Houlton	225	118	167	115		69	246	238
Madawaska	326	219	267	218	102	170	347	339
Portland	35	128	174	247	246	181		118
Portsmouth, NH	81	180	225	301	298	231	51	165
Rangeley	84	120	165	242	238	153	118	
Waterville	53	55	101	174	173	107	75	77

Nickname: The Pine Tree State
Capital: Augusta, F-4
Land area: 30,843 sq. mi. (rank: 39th)
Population: 1,328,361 (rank: 41st)
Largest city: Portland, 66,194, H-3

Index of places Pg. 131

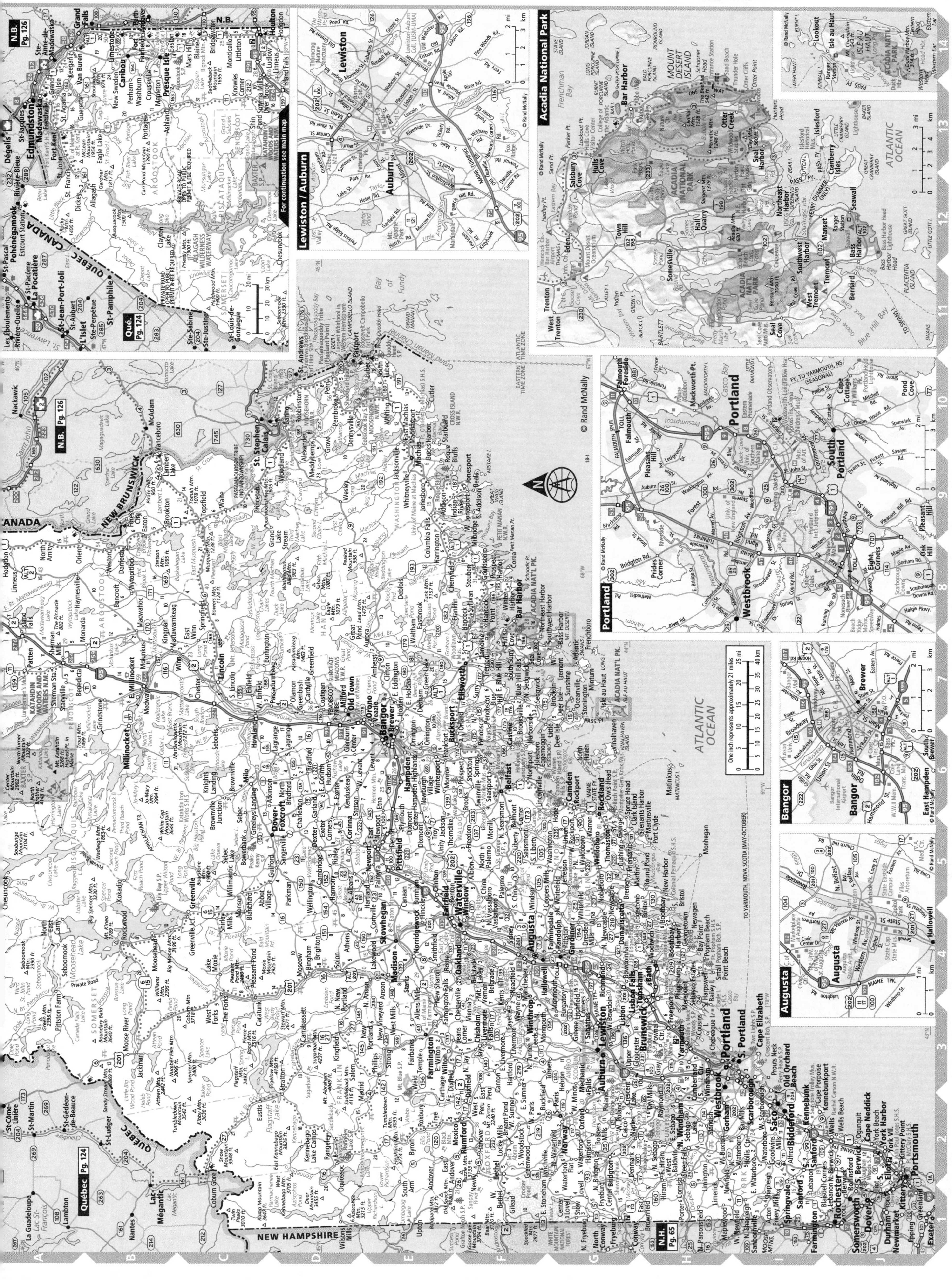

Maryland

Nickname: The Old Line State
Capital: Annapolis, E-14
Land area: 9,707 sq. mi. (rank: 42nd)
Population: 5,773,552 (rank: 19th)
Largest city: Baltimore, 620,961, C-13

Index of places Pg. 131

Travel planning & on-the-road resources

Tourism Information
Maryland Office of Tourism: (866) 639-3526; visitmaryland.org

Road Conditions & Construction
511, (855) 466-3511,
In Maryland: (800) 543-2515;
www.md511.org, www.roads.maryland.gov

Toll Road Information
Maryland Transportation Authority (*E-ZPass*):
(866) 713-1596, In Maryland: (410) 537-1000;
www.mdta.maryland.gov

Determining distances along roads

Highway distances (segments of one mile or less not shown):
Cumulative miles (red): the distance between red arrows
Intermediate miles (black): the distance between intersections & places

Interchanges and exit numbers
For most states, the mileage between interchanges may be determined by subtracting one number from the other.

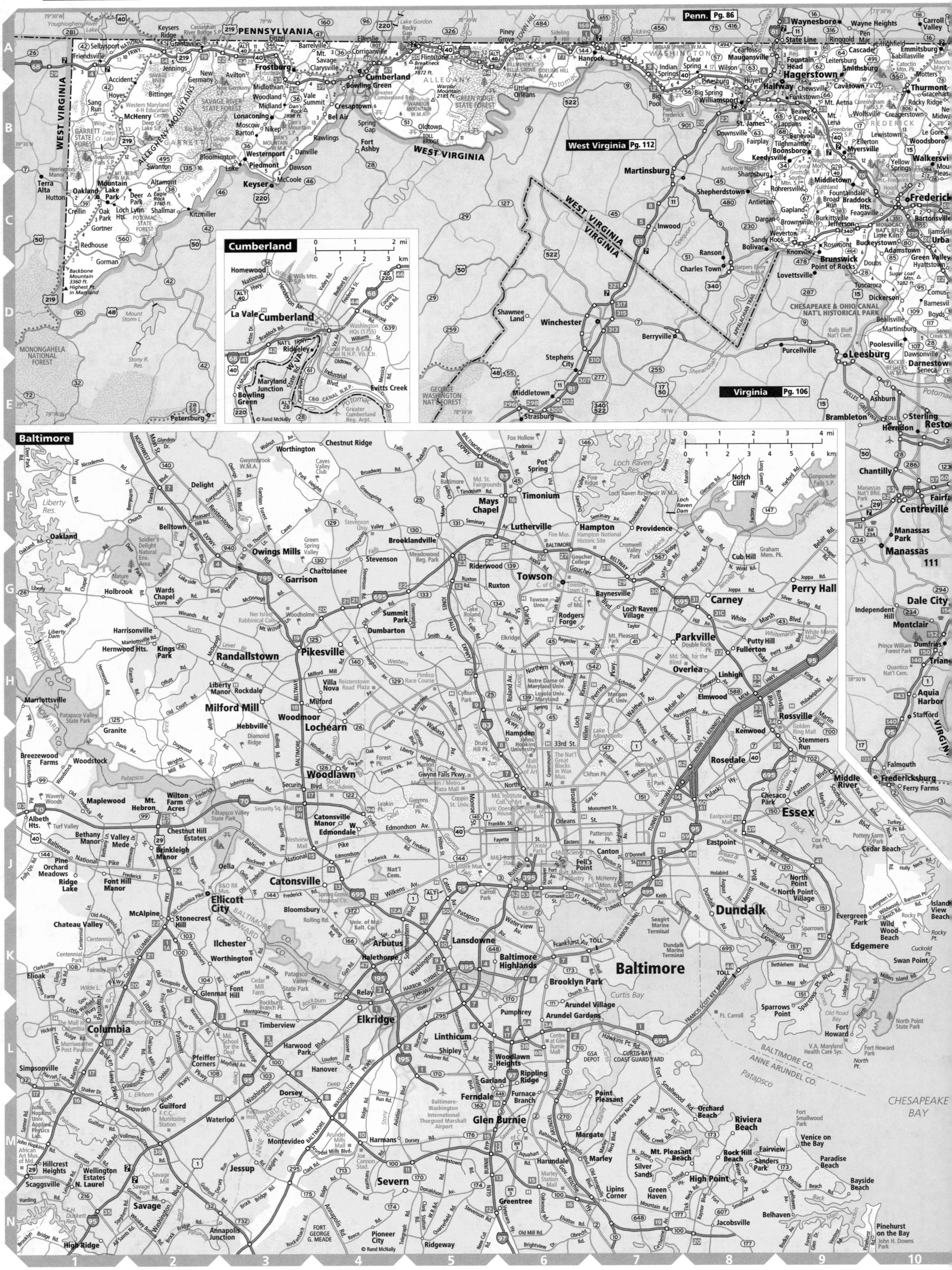

Chesapeake Bay Maritime Museum

Mileages between cities	Aberdeen	Annapolis	Baltimore	Cambridge	Chestertown	Cumberland	Frederick	Hagerstown	Lexington Park	Ocean City	Pocomoke City	Rockville	St. Charles	Salisbury	Washington, DC	Wilmington, DE
Aberdeen		58	31	113	65	171	83	107	122	134	152	74	90	122	70	42
Annapolis	58		28	57	47	157	68	93	73	108	120	42	41	89	30	96
Baltimore	31	28		84	73	136	47	72	93	136	146	42	59	116	39	70
Cumberland	171	157	136	212	203		88	67	200	263	275	116	166	244	134	209
Hagerstown	107	93	72	149	139	67	25		136	200	212	52	102	180	70	145
Lexington Park	122	73	93	127	118	200	113	136		178	190	84	37	159	67	161
Salisbury	122	89	116	32	78	244	156	180	159	29	26	130	128		118	107
Washington, DC	70	30	39	86	76	134	48	70	67	139	148	19	30	118		109

Mileages © Rand McNally

Total mileages through Maryland

68 81 miles
81 12 miles
70 94 miles
95 110 miles

More mileages at randmcnally.com/MC

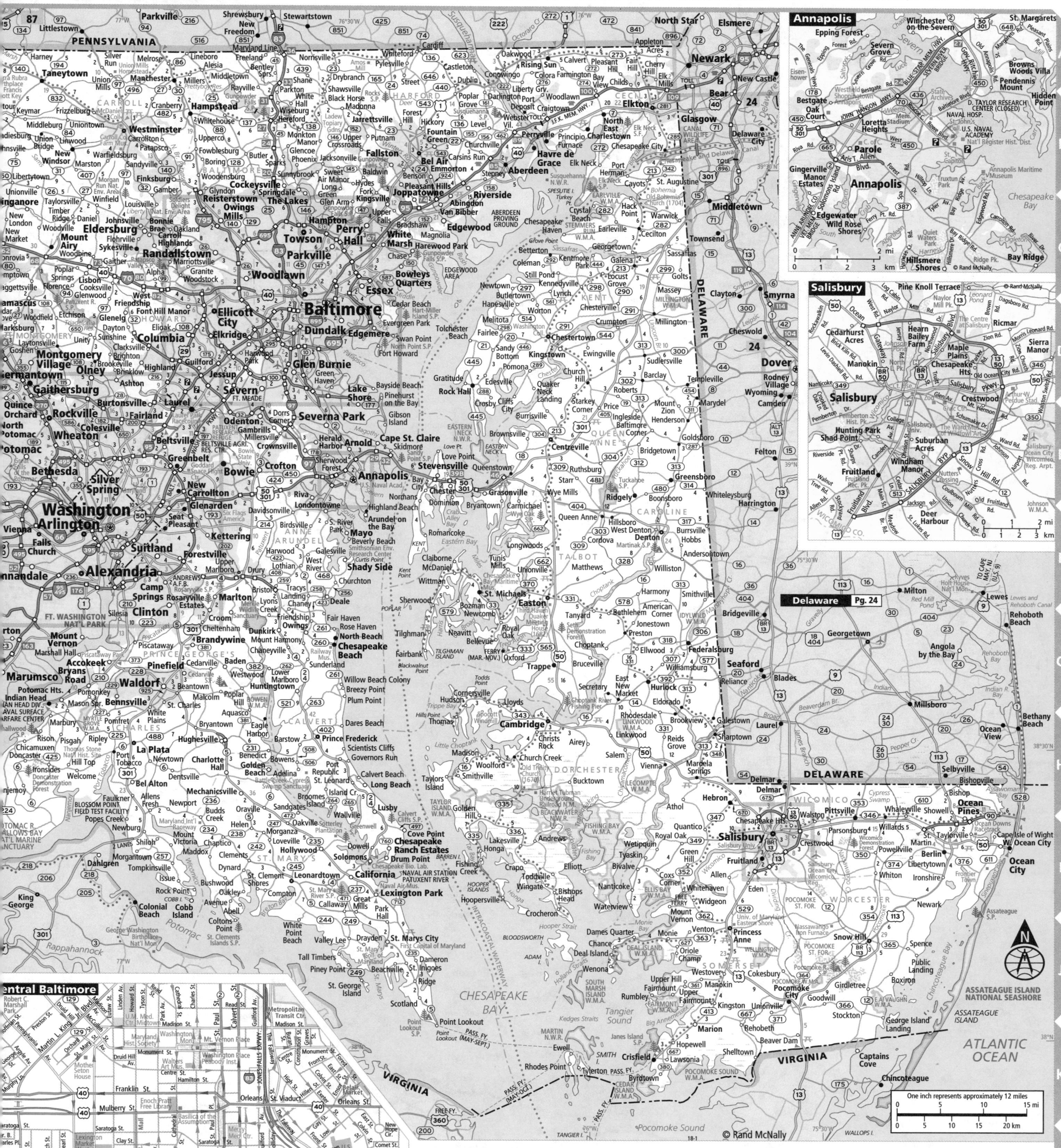

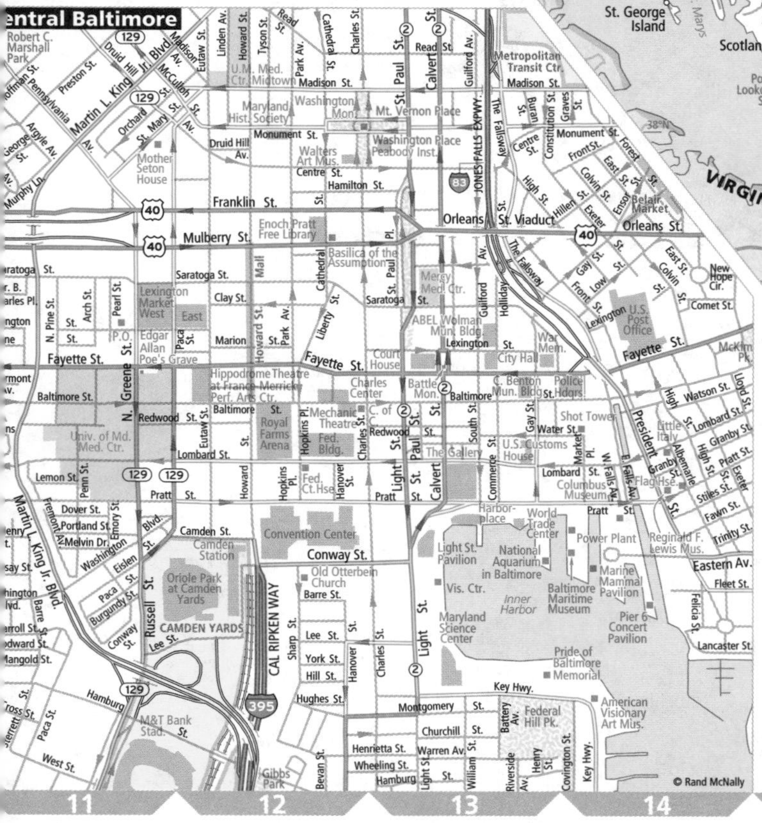

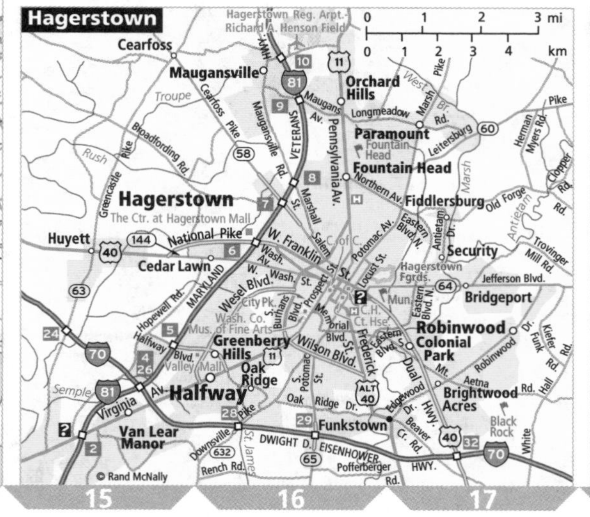

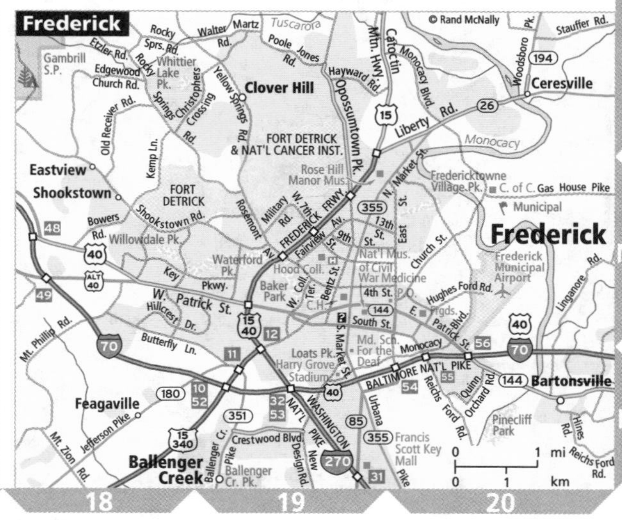

Massachusetts

Nickname: The Bay State
Capital: Boston, E-14
Land area: 7,800 sq. mi. (rank: 45th)
Population: 6,547,629 (rank: 14th)
Largest city: Boston, 617,594, E-14

Index of places Pg. 131

Travel planning & on-the-road resources

Tourism Information
Massachusetts Office of Travel & Tourism: (800) 227-6277, (617) 973-8500; www.massvacation.com

Toll Road Information
Massachusetts Department of Transportation *(E-ZPass):* (877) 623-6846, (857) 368-4636; www.massdot.state.ma.us/highway

Road Conditions & Construction 511
511, Metro Boston: (617) 986-5511, Central: (508) 499-5511, Western: (413) 754-5511; www.mass511.com, www.mhd.state.ma.us

Determining distances along roads
Highway distances (segments of one mile or less not shown): Cumulative miles (red): the distance between red arrows; Intermediate miles (black): the distance between intersections & places
Interchanges and exit numbers: For most states, the mileage between interchanges may be determined by subtracting one number from the other.

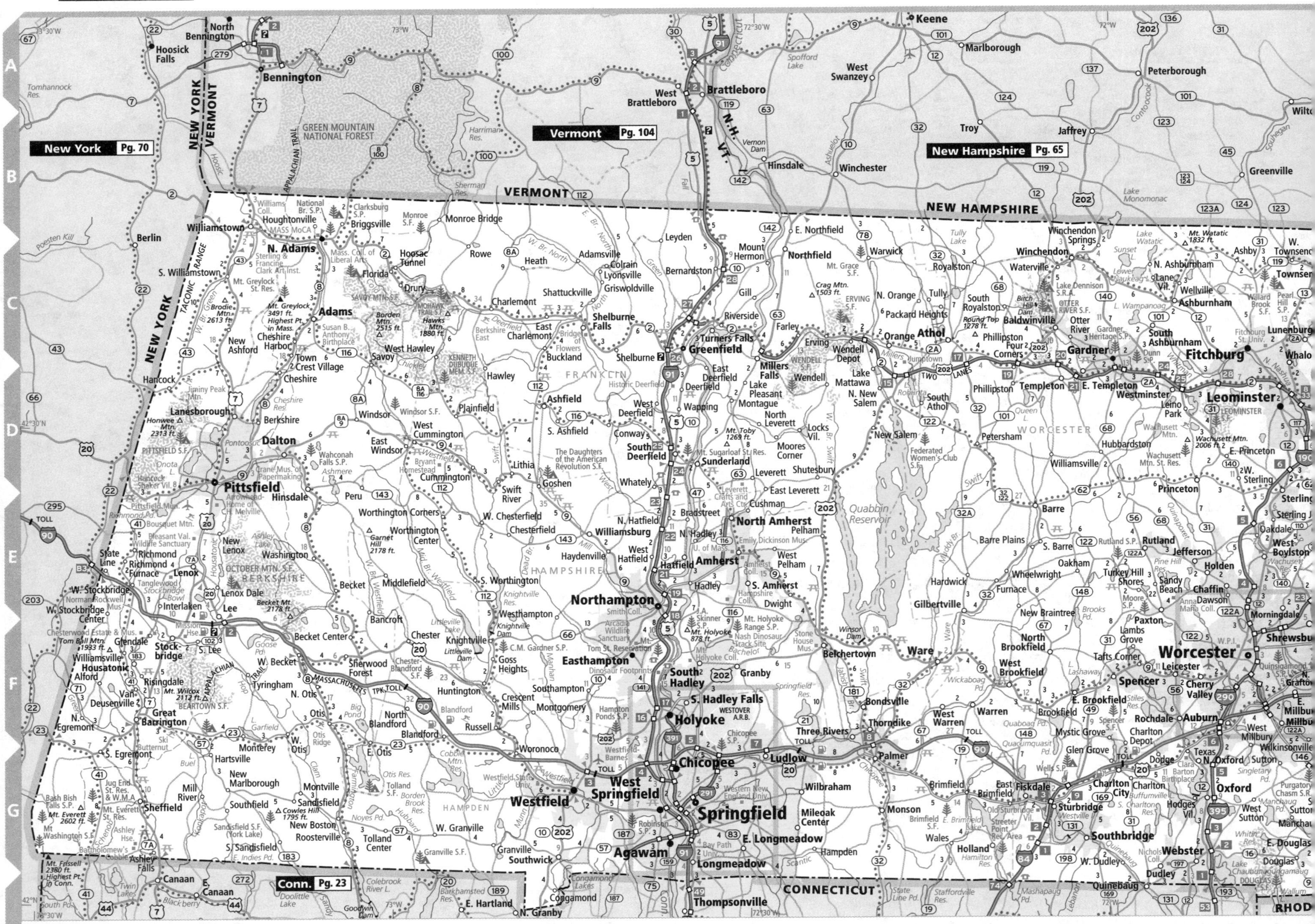

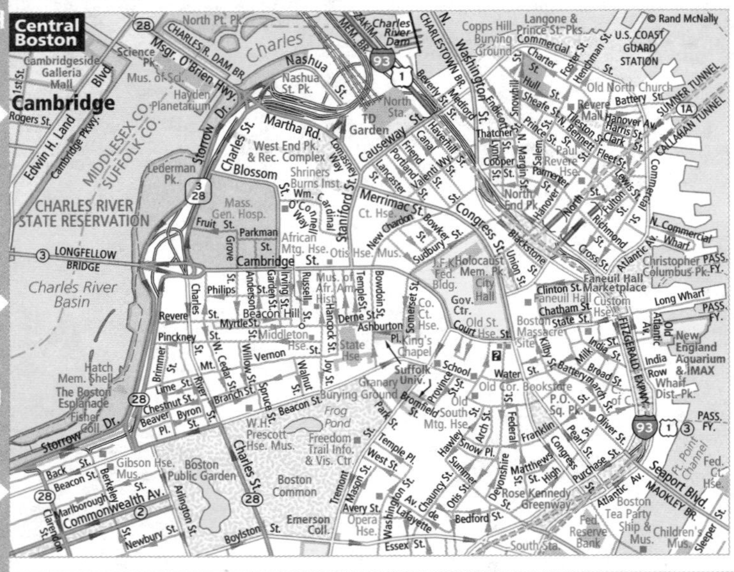

ape Cod

Mileages between cities	Boston	Brockton	Falmouth	Fitchburg	Gloucester	Greenfield	Lowell	Nantucket	New Bedford	North Adams	Pittsfield	Plymouth	Providence, RI	Provincetown	Springfield	Worcester
Boston		24	76	47	39	94	29	101*	58	157	136	40	50	116	90	43
Gloucester	39	63	114	74		120	47	140*	97	157	169	78	90	154	122	75
Lowell	29	50	102	32	47	78		130*	84	115	139	69	69	145	92	41
New Bedford	58	37	40	94	97	148	84	77*		182	161	37	31	91	114	71
Pittsfield	136	150	189	124	169	79	139	226*	161	22		167	130	240	51	98
Provincetown	116	106	69	162	154	208	145	78*	91	262	240	77	119		194	146
Springfield	90	103	143	77	122	38	92	180*	114	73	51	121	83	194		51
Worcester	43	56	96	26	75	72	41	133*	71	120	98	74	40	146	51	

*Via ferry

Total mileages through Massachusetts

90: 136 miles
91: 55 miles
93: 47 miles
95: 92 miles

More mileages at randmcnally.com/MC

Michigan

Nickname: The Great Lake State
Capital: Lansing, Q-9
Land area: 56,539 sq. mi. (rank: 22nd)
Population: 9,883,640 (rank: 8th)
Largest city: Detroit, 713,777, R-12

Index of places Pg. 131

Travel planning & on-the-road resources

Tourism Information
Travel Michigan:
(888) 784-7328; www.michigan.org

Road Conditions & Construction
(800) 381-8477, (517) 373-2090;
www.michigan.gov/drive

International Toll Bridge/Tunnel Information
Ambassador Bridge (Detroit): (800) 462-7434; www.ambassadorbridge.com
Detroit-Windsor Tunnel (***NEXPRESS***): (313) 567-4422 ext. 200, (519) 258-7424 ext. 200; www.dwtunnel.com
International Bridge Administration (Sault Ste. Marie): (906) 635-5255, (705) 942-4345; www.saultbridge.com
Michigan Department of Transportation: Blue Water Bridge (Port Huron): (810) 984-3131; www.michigan.gov/mdot

Michigan Toll Bridge/Tunnel Information
Mackinac Bridge Authority (***Mac Pass***): (906) 643-7600; www.mackinacbridge.org

Porcupine Mountains

Mileages between cities	Alpena	Chicago, IL	Detroit	Grand Rapids	Houghton	Ironwood	Kalamazoo	Ludington	Mackinaw City	Menominee	Muskegon	Port Huron	Saginaw	Sault Ste. Marie	Toledo, OH	Traverse City
Ann Arbor	227	240	43	132	538	584	98	228	272	473	172	102	86	329	51	238
Detroit	244	280		157	553	599	140	252	290	488	197	62	102	345	59	255
Flint	178	271	68	113	489	534	130	186	224	423	152	66	37	280	107	188
Grand Rapids	249	177	157		502	552	50	97	236	438	41	180	115	292	185	140
Ironwood	405	403	599	552	109		544	319	311	195	586	600	499	307	636	413
Kalamazoo	298	145	140	50	556	544		146	287	408	91	197	161	344	150	190
Lansing	228	216	90	68	494	539	75	162	228	429	107	122	88	284	118	180
Mackinaw City	94	412	290	236	266	311	287	218		200	251	290	188	56	327	102

Total mileages through Michigan

69 199 miles
94 275 miles
75 396 miles
96 192 miles

More mileages at randmcnally.com/MC

Sights to see

- Cranbrook Art Museum, Bloomfield Hills G-5
- Detroit Zoo, Royal Oak H-6
- Edsel & Eleanor Ford House, Grosse Pointe Shores I-9
- Frederik Meijer Gardens, Grand Rapids. A-3
- Gerald R. Ford Museum, Grand Rapids B-2
- Gerald R. Ford Presidential Library, Ann Arbor B-10
- Henry Ford Museum, Dearborn K-5
- Motown Historical Museum, Detroit J-7
- New Detroit Science Center, Detroit J-7
- Renaissance Center, Detroit N-10
- Sloan Museum, Flint B-6
- University of Michigan, Ann Arbor B-9

Detroit Institute of Art

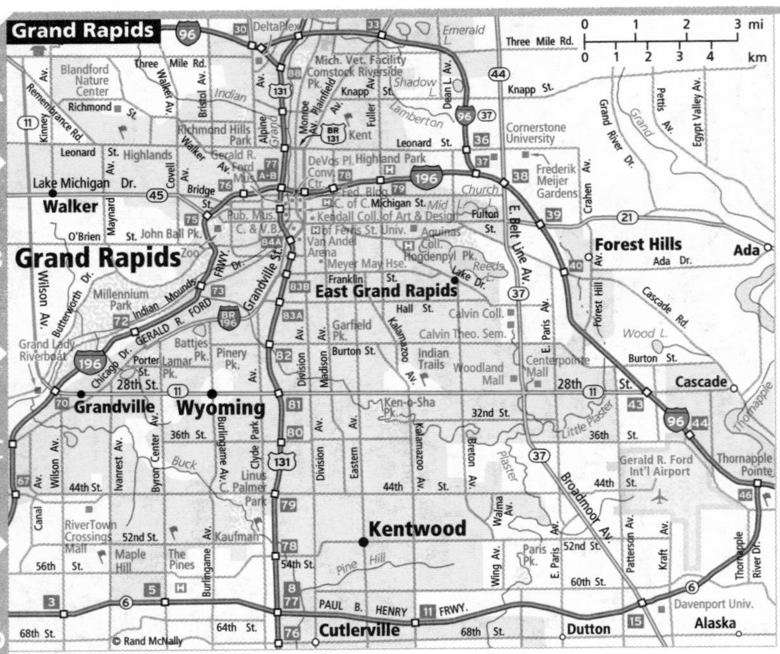

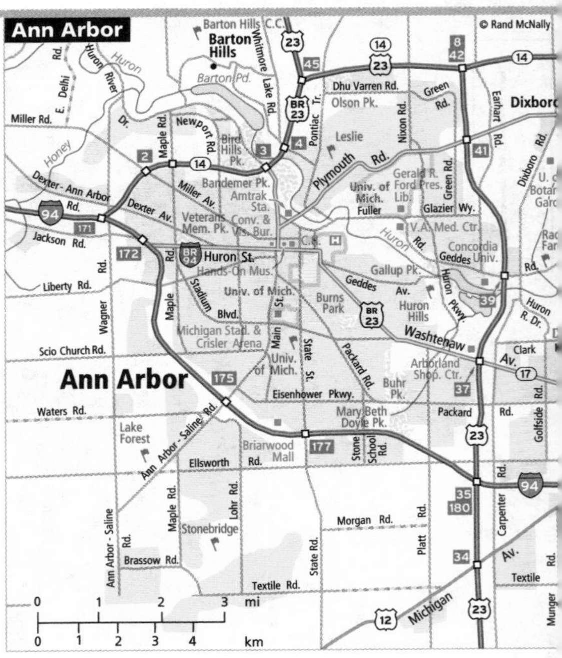

Walker Art Center, Minneapolis

Sights to see

- Bell Museum of Natural History, Minneapolis L-4
- Cathedral of St. Paul, St. Paul.................... M-7
- Frederick R. Weisman Art Museum, Minneapolis..... M-4
- Mall of America, Bloomington..................... I-5
- Mill City Museum, Minneapolis L-3
- Minneapolis Institute of the Arts, Minneapolis N-2
- Minneapolis Sculpture Garden, Minneapolis M-1
- Minnesota History Center, Minneapolis M-7
- Minnesota State Capitol, St. Paul.................... L-7
- Ordway Center for the Performing Arts, St. Paul..... M-7
- Science Museum of Minnesota, St. Paul M-7
- Walker Art Center, Minneapolis.................... M-1

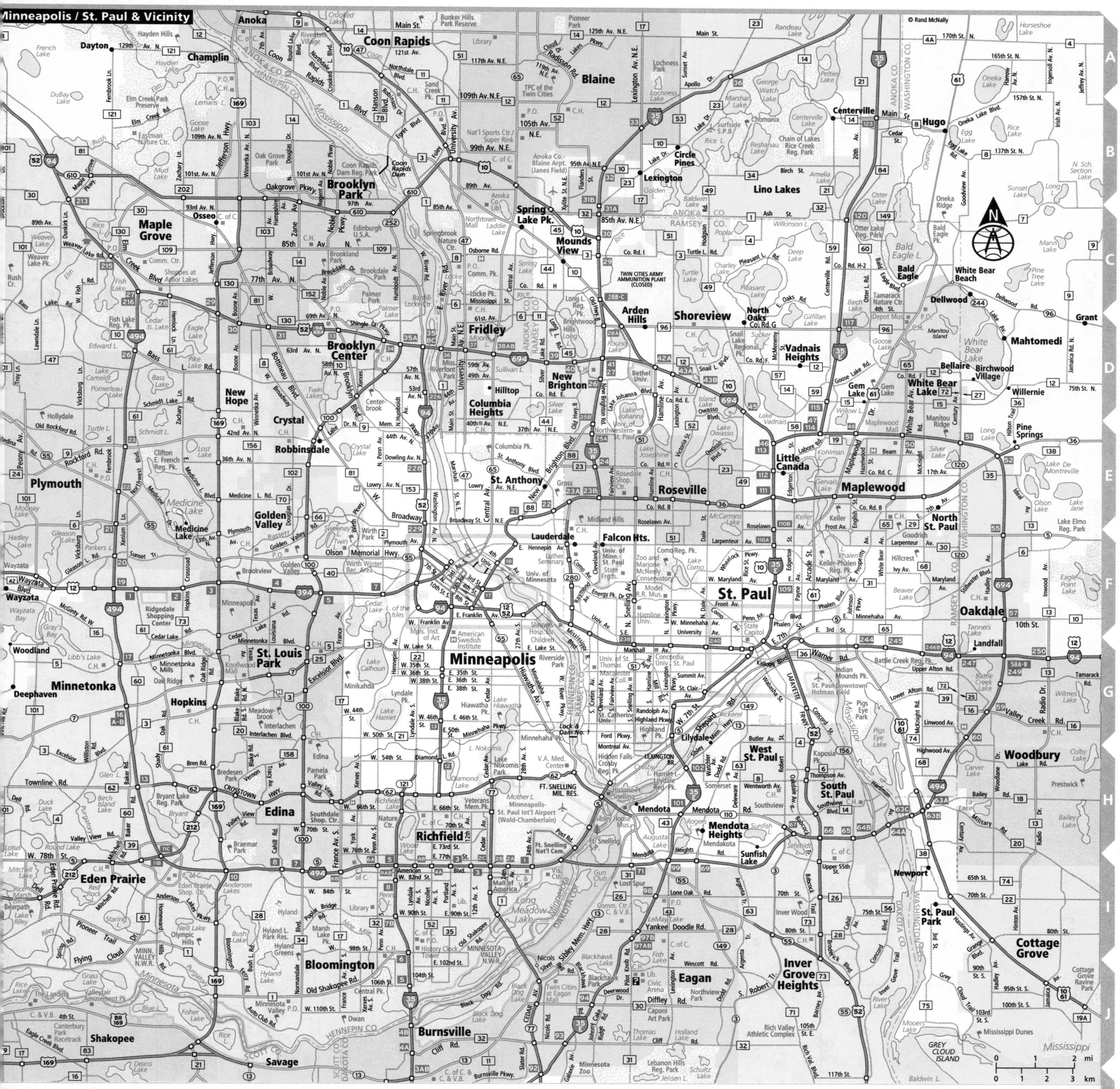

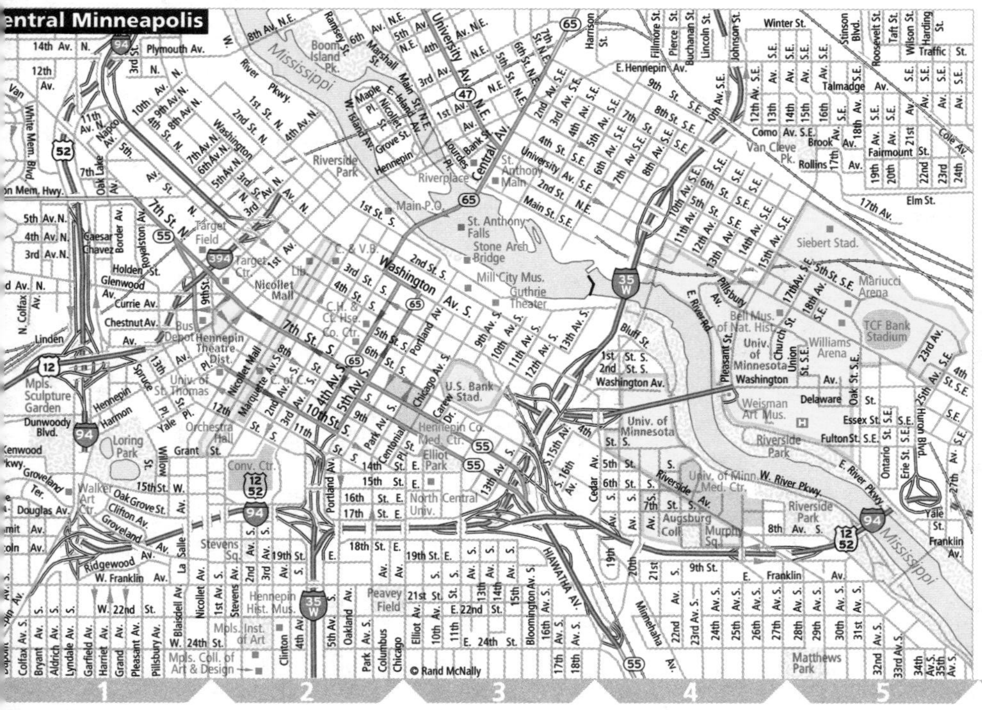

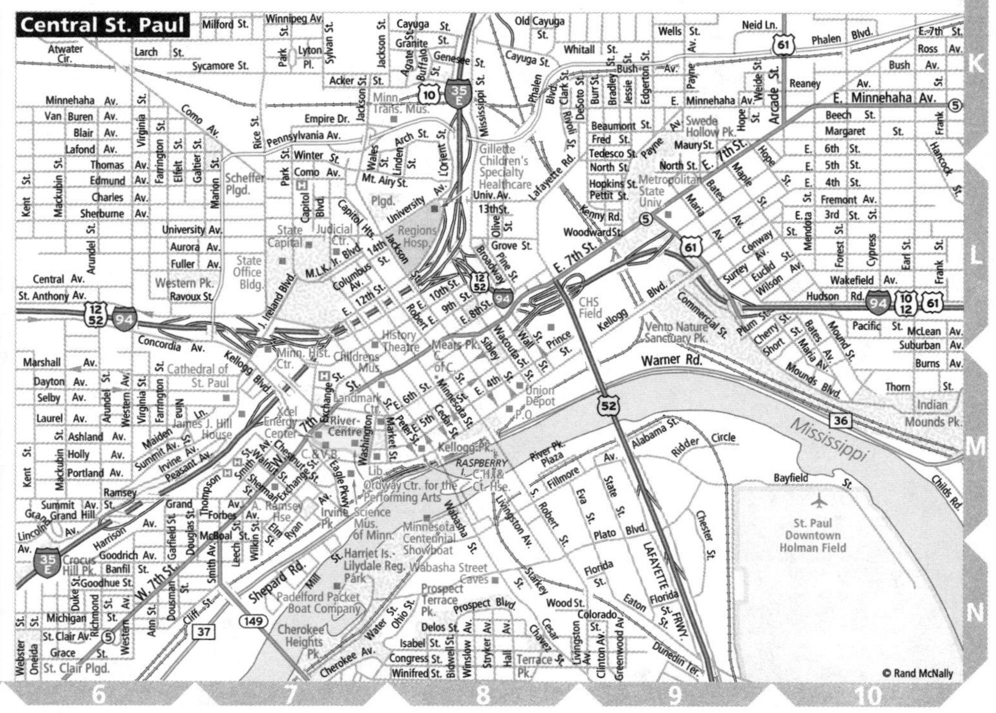

Minnesota

Nickname: The North Star State
Capital: St. Paul, O-10
Land area: 79,627 sq. mi. (rank: 14th)
Population: 5,303,925 (rank: 21st)
Largest city: Minneapolis, 382,578, O-9

Index of places Pg. 132

Travel planning & on-the-road resources

Tourism Information
Explore Minnesota Tourism: (888) 847-4866, (651) 296-5029, (651) 757-1845; www.exploreminnesota.com

Road Conditions & Construction
511, (651) 296-3000, In MN: (800) 657-3774; www.511mn.org, www.dot.state.mn.us

Toll Road Information
No toll roads

Determining distances along roads

Highway distances (segments of one mile or less not shown):
Cumulative miles (red): the distance between red arrows
Intermediate miles (black): the distance between intersections & places

Interchanges and exit numbers
For most states, the mileage between interchanges may be determined by subtracting one number from the other.

Duluth Harbor

Mileages between cities

	Albert Lea	Bemidji	Brainerd	Duluth	Grand Forks, ND	Grand Marais	Hibbing	International Falls	Mankato	Marshall	Minneapolis	Moorhead	Rochester	St. Cloud	Sioux Falls, SD	Willmar
Bemidji	316		97	151	114	259	105	112	290	258	222	135	306	151	380	188
Duluth	247	151	113		266	110	76	162	233	273	152	250	226	141	390	204
Minneapolis	96	222	130	152	314	262	208	293	80	153		233	86	65	236	93
Moorhead	328	135	136	250	82	361	212	249	303	206	233		321	170	244	172
Rochester	62	306	213	226	401	338	280	366	86	194	86	321		153	236	178
St. Cloud	160	151	63	141	251	253	173	251	135	130	65	170	153		220	62
St. Paul	98	230	137	149	325	260	204	290	87	159	9	243	78	75	241	102
Sioux Falls, SD	176	380	281	390	319	500	456	494	155	91	236	244	236	220		158

Mileages © Rand McNally

Total mileages through Minnesota

35 260 miles — 94 260 miles

90 276 miles — 2 255 miles

More mileages at randmcnally.com/MC

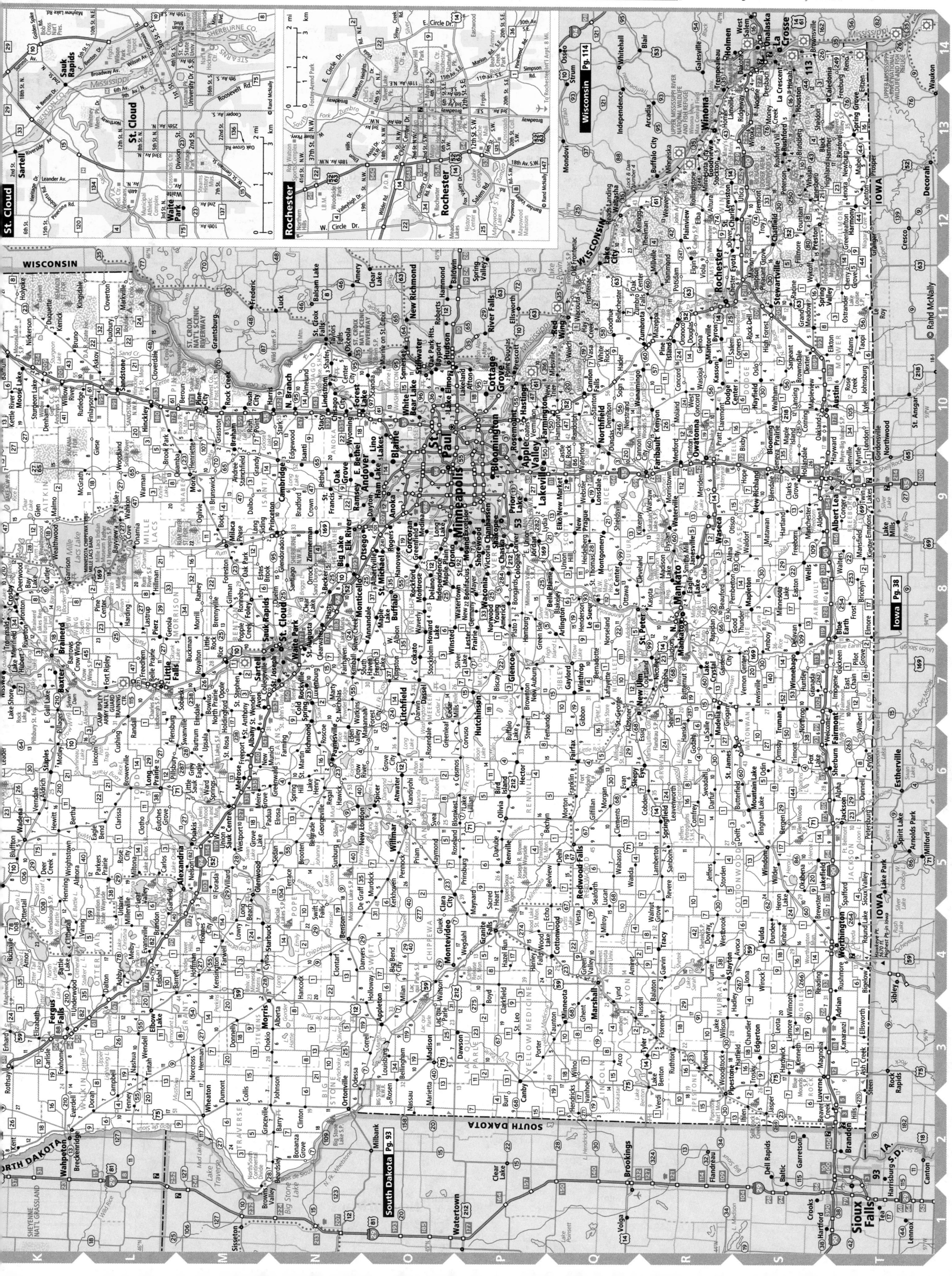

Mississippi

Nickname: The Magnolia State
Capital: Jackson, H-6
Land area: 46,923 sq. mi. (rank: 31st)
Population: 2,967,297 (rank: 31st)
Largest city: Jackson, 173,514, H-6

Index of places Pg. 132

Mileages between cities

	Batesville	Biloxi	Hattiesburg	Jackson	Memphis, TN	Natchez	Tupelo	Vicksburg
Biloxi	320		80	172	379	228	315	214
Greenville	112	293	210	121	152	152	177	91
Jackson	149	172	89		209	103	190	44
Memphis, TN	61	379	297	209		304	105	245
Meridian	176	172	89	91	234	194	142	134
New Orleans, LA	335	90	109	183	394	171	340	207
Tupelo	74	315	232	190	105	283		225
Vicksburg	188	214	131	44	245	70	225	

Total mileages through Mississippi

10: 77 miles
55: 290 miles
20: 169 miles
59: 172 miles

More mileages at randmcnally.com/MC

Travel planning & on-the-road resources

Tourism Information

Visit Mississippi:
(866) 733-6477, (601) 359-3297; www.visitmississippi.org

Road Conditions & Construction

511, (601) 359-7001;
www.mdot.ms.gov, www.mdottraffic.com

Toll Road Information

No toll roads

Determining Distances

(segments of one mile or le not shown)
Cumulative miles (red): the distance between red arrows
Intermediate miles (black): the distance between intersections & places

Sights to see

- Andy Williams Moon River Theatre, Branson M-8
- Anheuser-Busch Brewery, St. Louis . . . I-7
- Bass Pro Shops® Outdoor World®, Springfield C-3
- Dolly Parton's Dixie Stampede, Branson M-9
- Gateway Arch, St. Louis L-4
- Laumeier Sculpture Park, St. Louis . . J-4
- Magic House, Kirkwood I-4
- Missouri Botanical Garden, St. Louis . . I-6
- Shoji Tabuchi Theatre, Branson L-7
- St. Louis Art Museum, St. Louis H-6
- St. Louis Science Center, St. Louis . . . H-6
- St. Louis Zoo, St. Louis H-6
- Shepherd of the Hills, Branson K-6
- White Water, Branson M-7

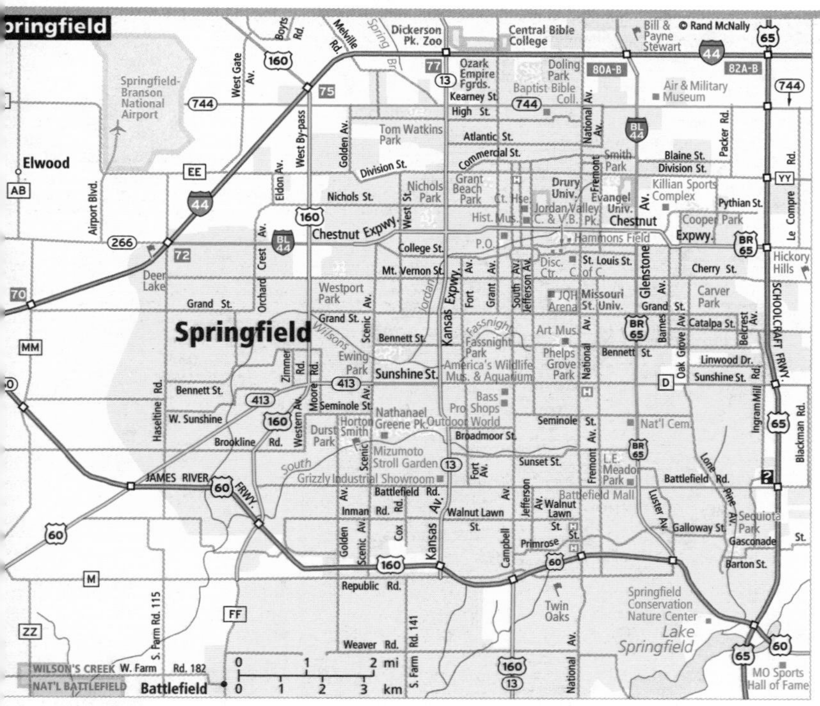

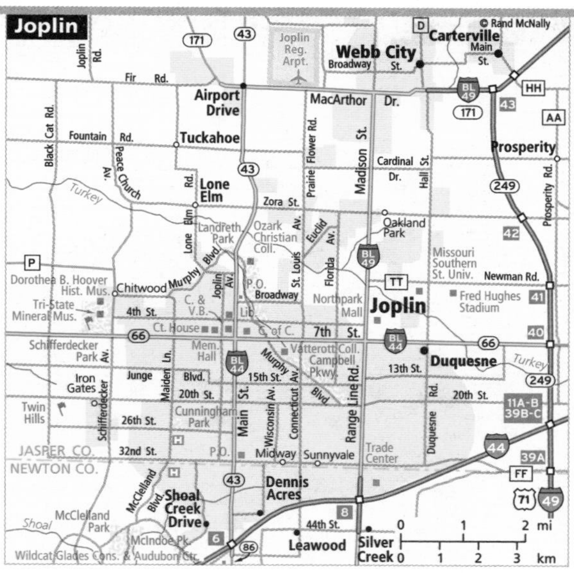

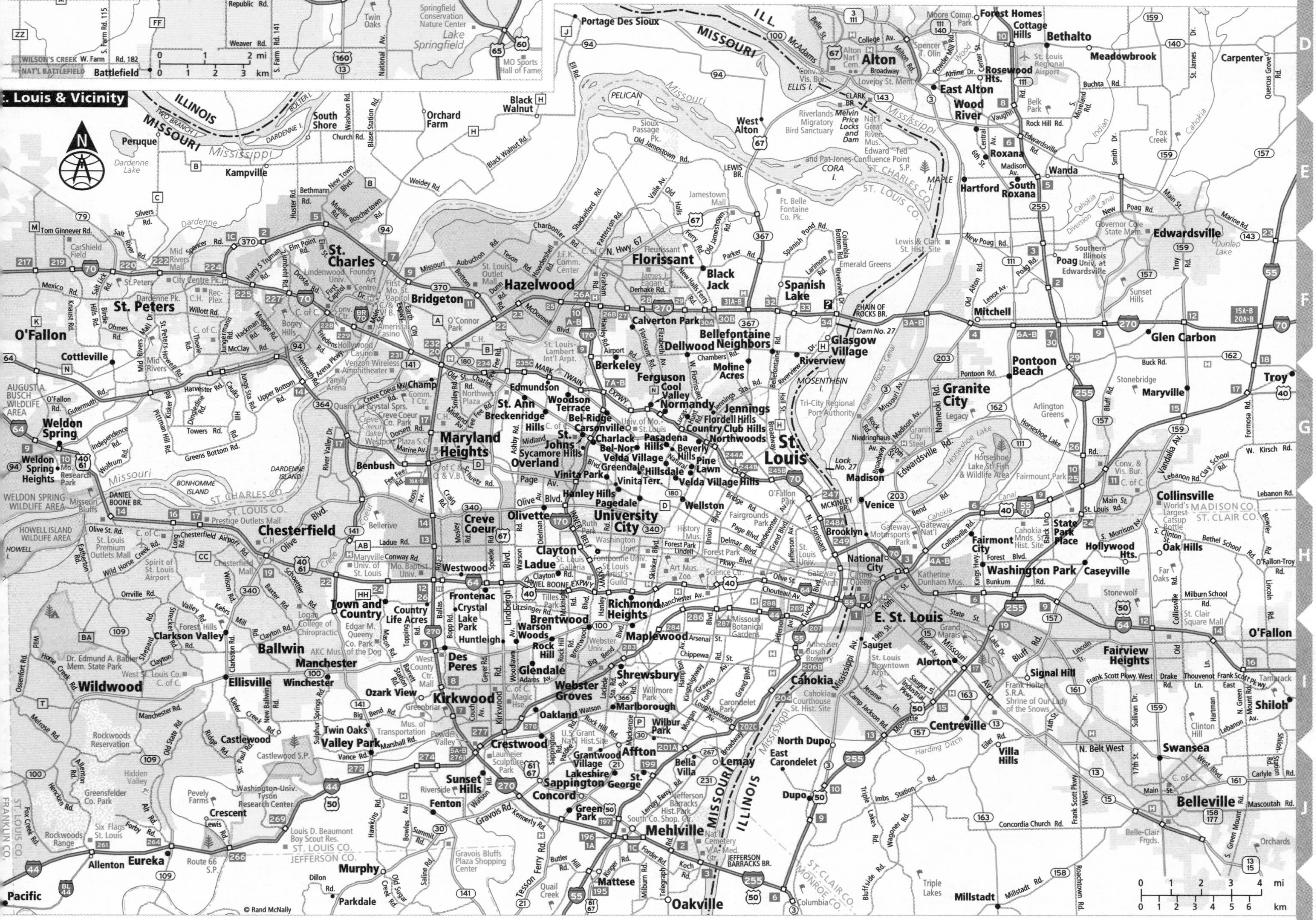

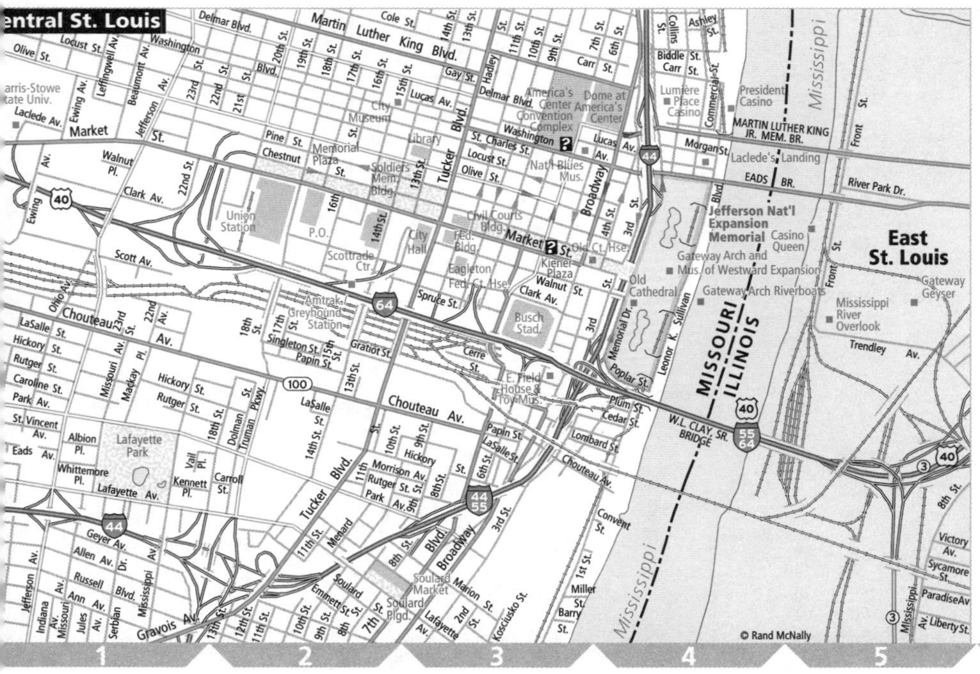

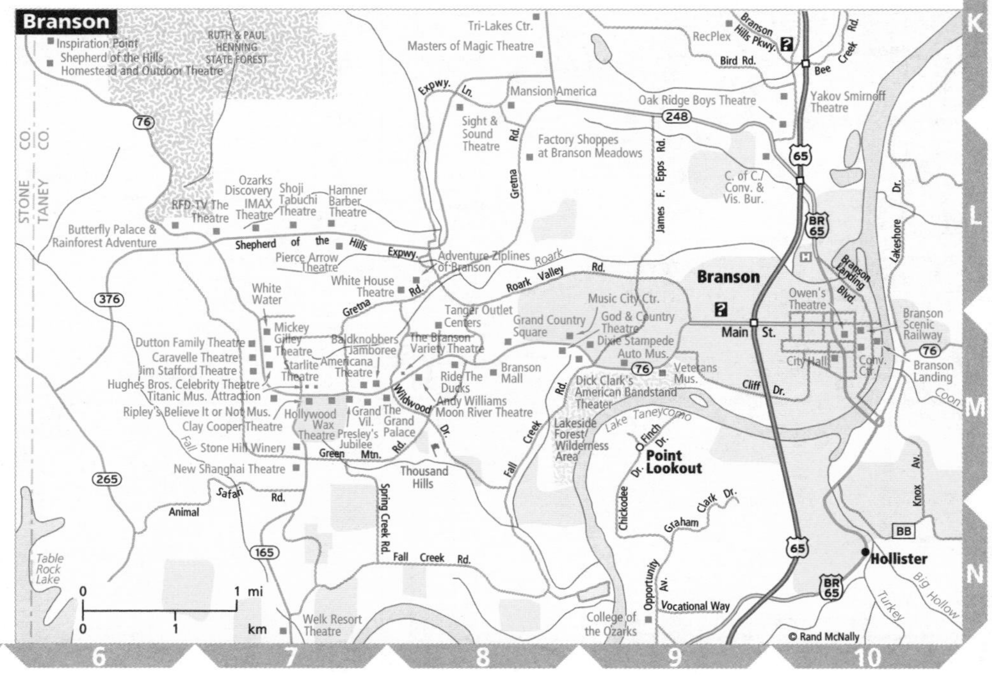

Nickname: The Show Me State
Capital: Jefferson City, G-14
Land area: 68,741 sq. mi. (rank: 18th)
Population: 5,988,927 (rank: 18th)
Largest city: Kansas City, 459,787, F-9

Index of places Pg. 132

Travel planning & on-the-road resources

Tourism Information
Missouri Division of Tourism: (573) 751-4133; www.visitmo.com

Road Conditions & Construction
(888) 275-6636, (573) 751-2551; www.modot.org

Toll Road Information
No toll roads

Determining distances along roads

Highway distances (segments of one mile or less not shown):
Cumulative miles (red): the distance between red arrows
Intermediate miles (black): the distance between intersections & places

Interchanges and exit numbers
For most states, the mileage between interchanges may be determined by subtracting one number from the other.

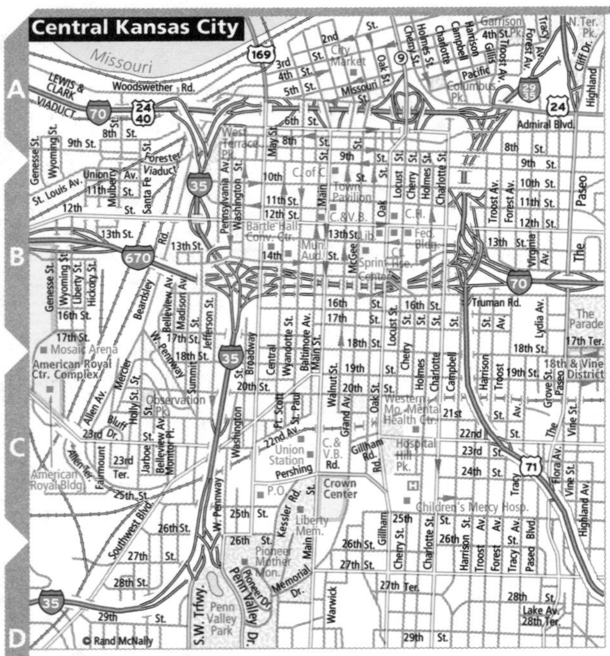

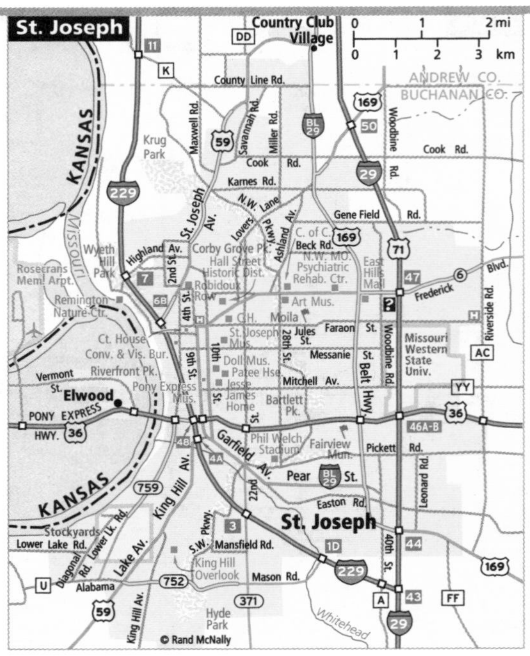

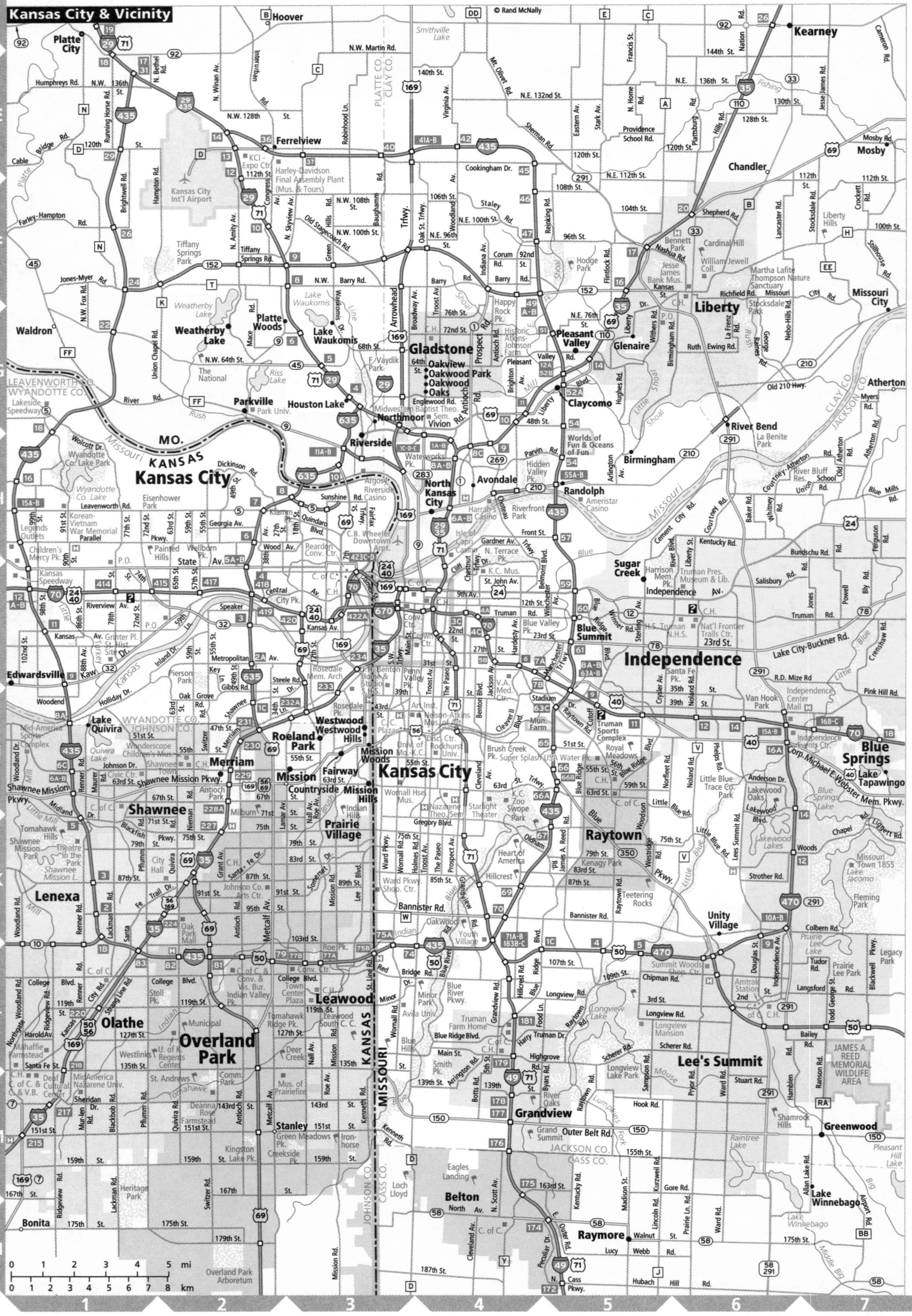

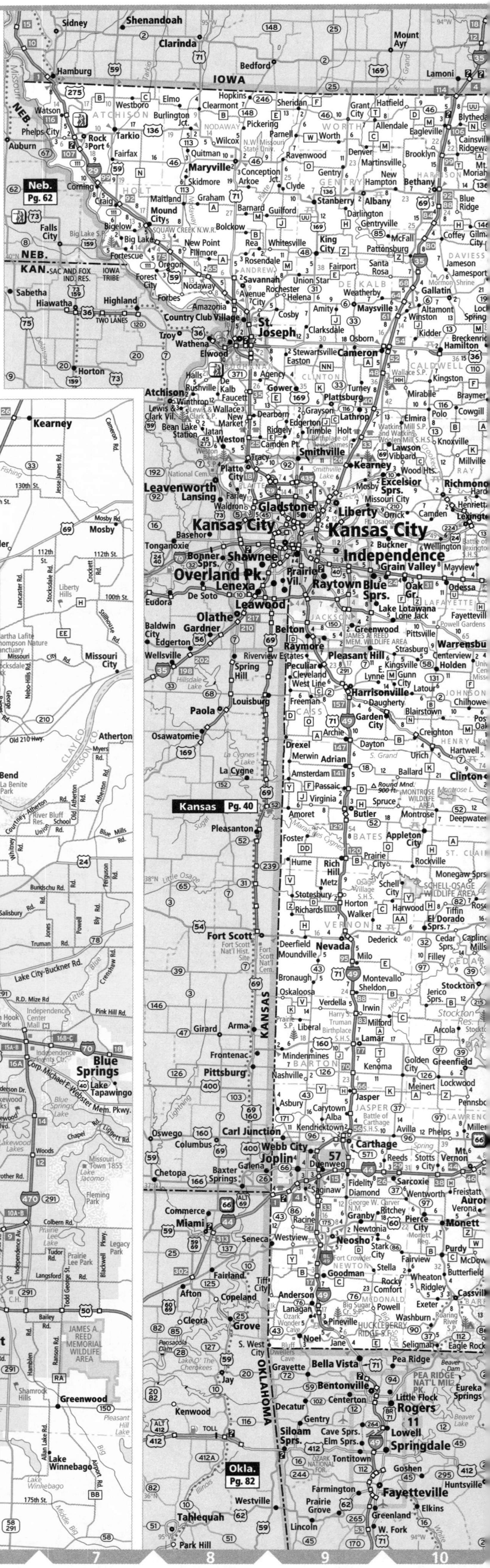

elson-Atkins Museum of Art, Kansas City

Mileages between cities	Branson	Cape Girardeau	Columbia	Hannibal	Hayti	Jefferson City	Joplin	Kansas City	Kirksville	Maryville	Osage Beach	Poplar Bluff	Rolla	St. Louis	Springfield	West Plains
Cape Girardeau	295		225	218	80	216	336	348	313	445	218	82	158	114	270	182
Columbia	205	225		97	301	32	236	124	91	222	76	261	93	126	168	191
Joplin	109	336	236	312	319	206		157	312	243	161	256	178	282	70	176
Kansas City	209	348	124	209	424	156	157		157	93	164	356	219	250	166	275
Poplar Bluff	215	82	261	255	62	223	256	356	350	457	224		147	151	191	98
St. Joseph	270	405	182	191	481	214	203	53	141	43	222	416	276	308	225	336
St. Louis	249	114	126	120	192	124	282	250	217	347	164	151	104		213	202
Springfield	42	270	168	242	253	136	70	166	259	266	91	191	108	213		108

Total mileages through Missouri

- I-35: 115 miles
- I-55: 210 miles
- I-44: 290 miles
- I-70: 252 miles

More mileages at randmcnally.com/MC

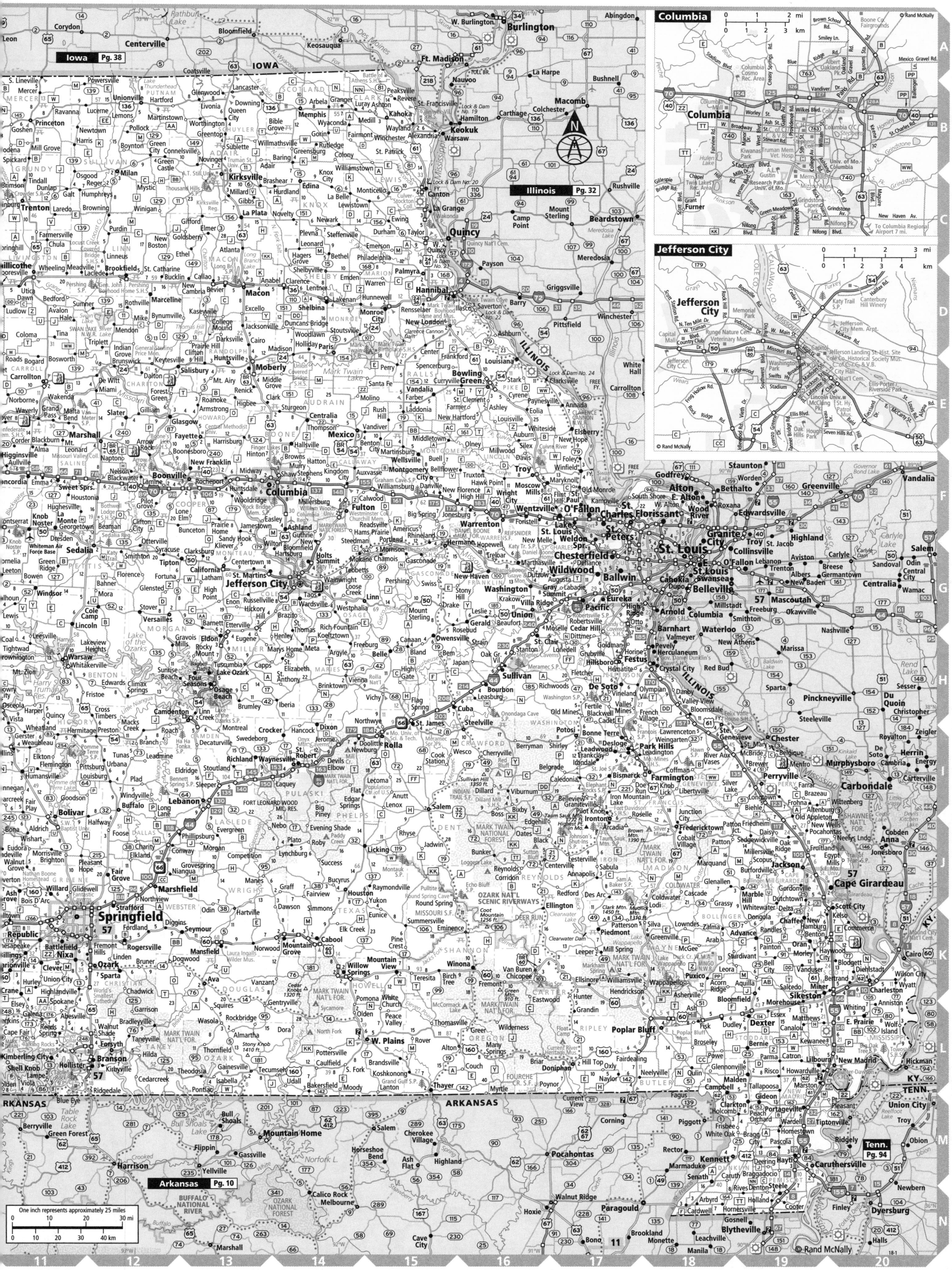

Nickname: The Treasure State
Capital: Helena, G-7
Land area: 145,546 sq. mi. (rank: 4th)
Population: 989,415 (rank: 44th)
Largest city: Billings, 104,170, I-13

Index of places Pg. 132

Travel planning & on-the-road resources

Tourism Information
Montana Office of Tourism: (800) 847-4868; www.visitmt.com

Road Conditions & Construction
511, (800) 226-7623, (406) 444-6200; www.mdt511.com, www.mdt.mt.gov

Toll Road Information
No toll roads

Determining distances along roads

Highway distances (segments of one mile or less not shown):
Cumulative miles (red): the distance between red arrows
Intermediate miles (black): the distance between intersections & places

Interchanges and exit numbers
For most states, the mileage between interchanges may be determined by subtracting one number from the other.

St. Mary Lake in Glacier N.P.

Mileages between cities

	Belle Fourche, SD	Billings	Bozeman	Butte	Dillon	Glasgow	Great Falls	Havre	Kalispell	Lewistown	Libby	Miles City	Missoula	St. Mary	Sidney	West Yellowstone
Billings	261		143	223	256	276	218	247	451	125	536	144	343	375	269	232
Butte	486	223	82		54	425	154	267	224	244	309	367	120	269	494	149
Great Falls	481	218	186	154	219	271		113	224	106	312	317	166	158	375	264
Helena	500	238	98	66	132	360	90	202	193	193	281	383	113	205	463	177
Kalispell	711	451	308	224	278	419	224	261		330	88	593	121	82	558	371
Miles City	174	144	285	367	399	195	317	333	593	211	678		487	473	126	375
Missoula	606	343	202	120	172	437	166	280	121	272	191	487		203	614	267
Sidney	298	269	411	494	524	140	375	298	558	270	646	126	614	490		501

Mileages © Rand McNally

Total mileages through Montana

15: 396 miles
94: 249 miles
90: 552 miles

More mileages at randmcnally.com/MC

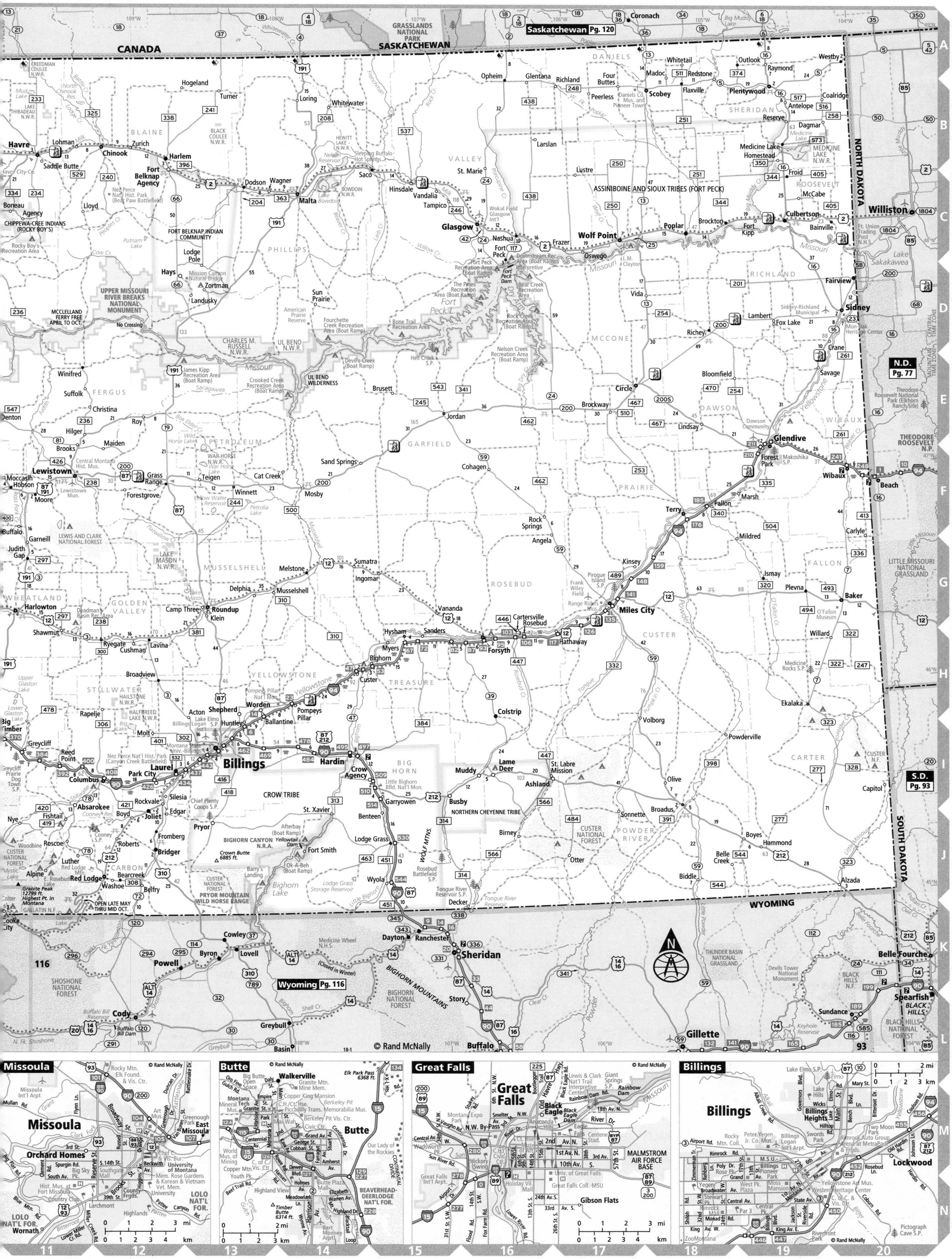

Nebraska

Nickname: The Cornhusker State
Capital: Lincoln, K-17
Land area: 76,824 sq. mi. (rank: 15th)
Population: 1,826,341 (rank: 38th)
Largest city: Omaha, 408,958, J-19

Index of places Pg. 132

Travel planning & on-the-road resources

Tourism Information
Nebraska Tourism: (888) 444-1867, (402) 471-3796; www.visitnebraska.com

Road Conditions & Construction
511, (800) 906-9069; www.511.nebraska.gov, www.dor.state.ne.us

Toll Road Information
No toll roads

Determining distances along roads

Highway distances (segments of one mile or less not shown):
Cumulative miles (red): the distance between red arrows
Intermediate miles (black): the distance between intersections & places

Interchanges and exit numbers
For most states, the mileage between interchanges may be determined by subtracting one number from the other.

Replica covered wagons

Mileages between cities	Beatrice	Chadron	Columbus	Falls City	Grand Island	Kearney	Lincoln	McCook	Norfolk	North Platte	Ogallala	Omaha	O'Neill	Scottsbluff	Sioux City, IA	Valentine
Grand Island	131	326	64	196		50	93	152	105	145	194	147	112	323	187	210
Lincoln	41	450	79	102	93	129		232	124	224	274	55	208	402	151	304
Norfolk	162	322	45	218	105	155	124	259		250	300	109	75	417	82	186
North Platte	262	229	210	327	145	99	224	67	250		53	276	189	182	373	129
Omaha	95	431	83	104	147	181	55	283	109	276	325		184	458	97	294
Scottsbluff	440	99	388	505	323	277	402	245	417	182	129	458	322		467	216
Sidney	381	131	329	445	263	218	343	186	369	122	71	394	311	77	492	251
Valentine	342	137	230	406	210	195	304	197	186	129	182	294	111	216	236	

Mileages © Rand McNally

Total mileages through Nebraska

- 80: 455 miles
- 83: 226 miles
- 81: 219 miles
- 20: 436 miles

More mileages at randmcnally.com/MC

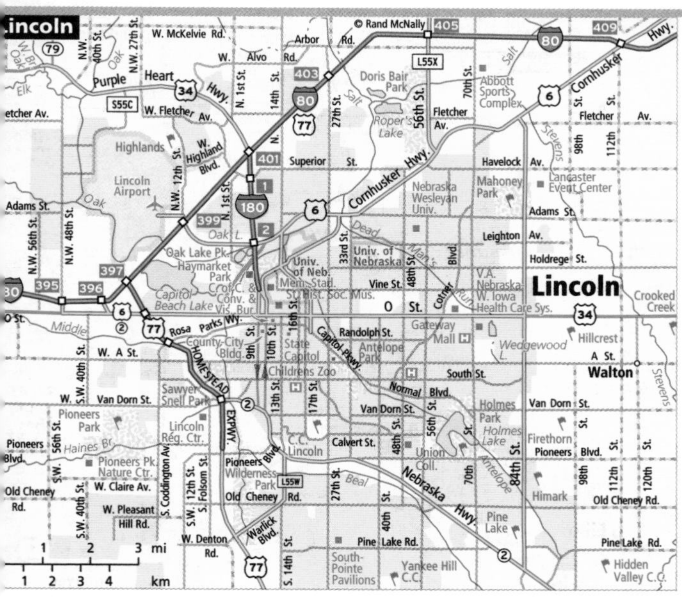

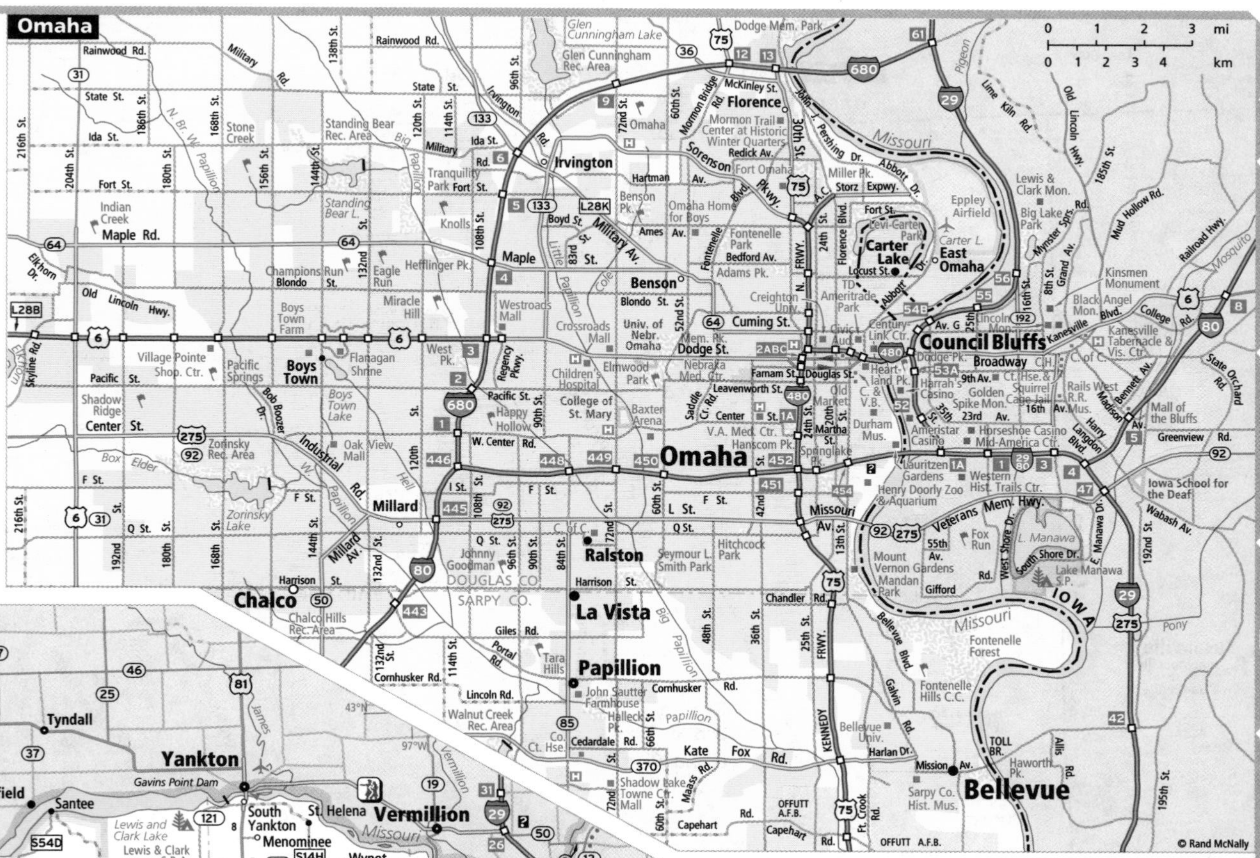

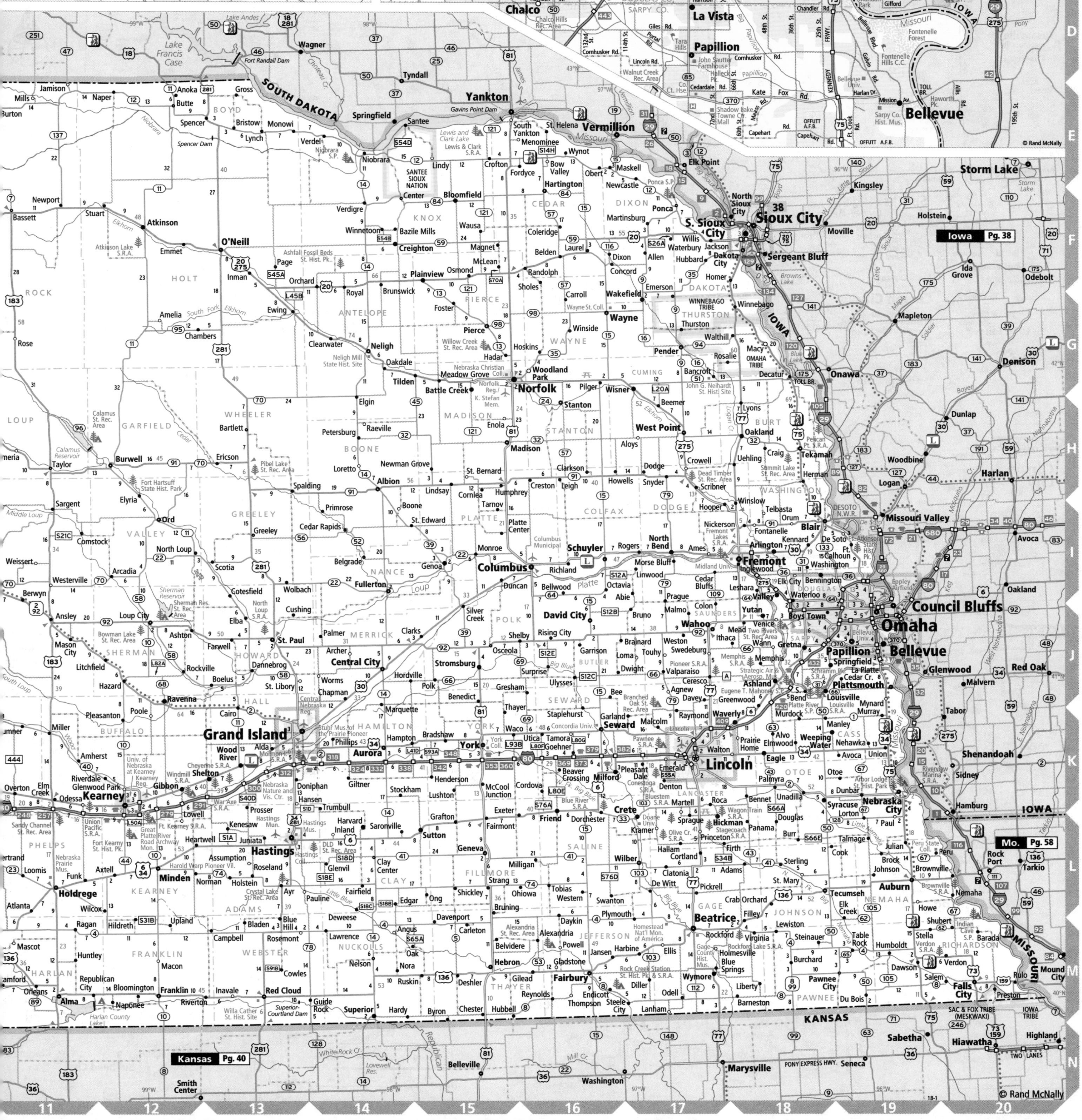

Nevada

Nickname: The Silver State
Capital: Carson City, F-2
Land area: 109,781 sq. mi. (rank: 7th)
Population: 2,700,551 (rank: 35th)
Largest city: Las Vegas, 583,756, L-8

Index of places Pg. 132

Mileages between cities

	Carson City	Elko	Ely	Jackpot	Las Vegas	Reno	Tonopah	Winnemucca
Elko	304		188	117	429	288	252	125
Ely	319	188		205	241	319	167	271
Las Vegas	435	429	241	446		447	210	472
Reno	32	288	319	405	447		237	163
S. Lake Tahoe, CA	27	332	347	450	451	60	237	208
Tonopah	225	252	167	373	210	237		261
West Wendover	414	109	120	125	361	397	288	232
Winnemucca	179	125	271	240	472	163	261	

Total mileages through Nevada

15: 124 miles
6: 307 miles
80: 411 miles
95: 652 miles

More mileages at
randmcnally.com/MC

Travel planning & on-the-road resources

Tourism Information
Nevada Commission on Tourism:
(800) 638-2328, (775) 687-4322; www.travelnevada.com

Road Conditions & Construction
511, (877) 687-6237, (775) 888-7000;
www.nevadadot.com, www.nvroads.com

Toll Road Information
No toll roads

Determining Distances
(segments of one mile or not shown)
Cumulative miles (red): the distance between red arrows
Intermediate miles (black): the distance between intersections & places

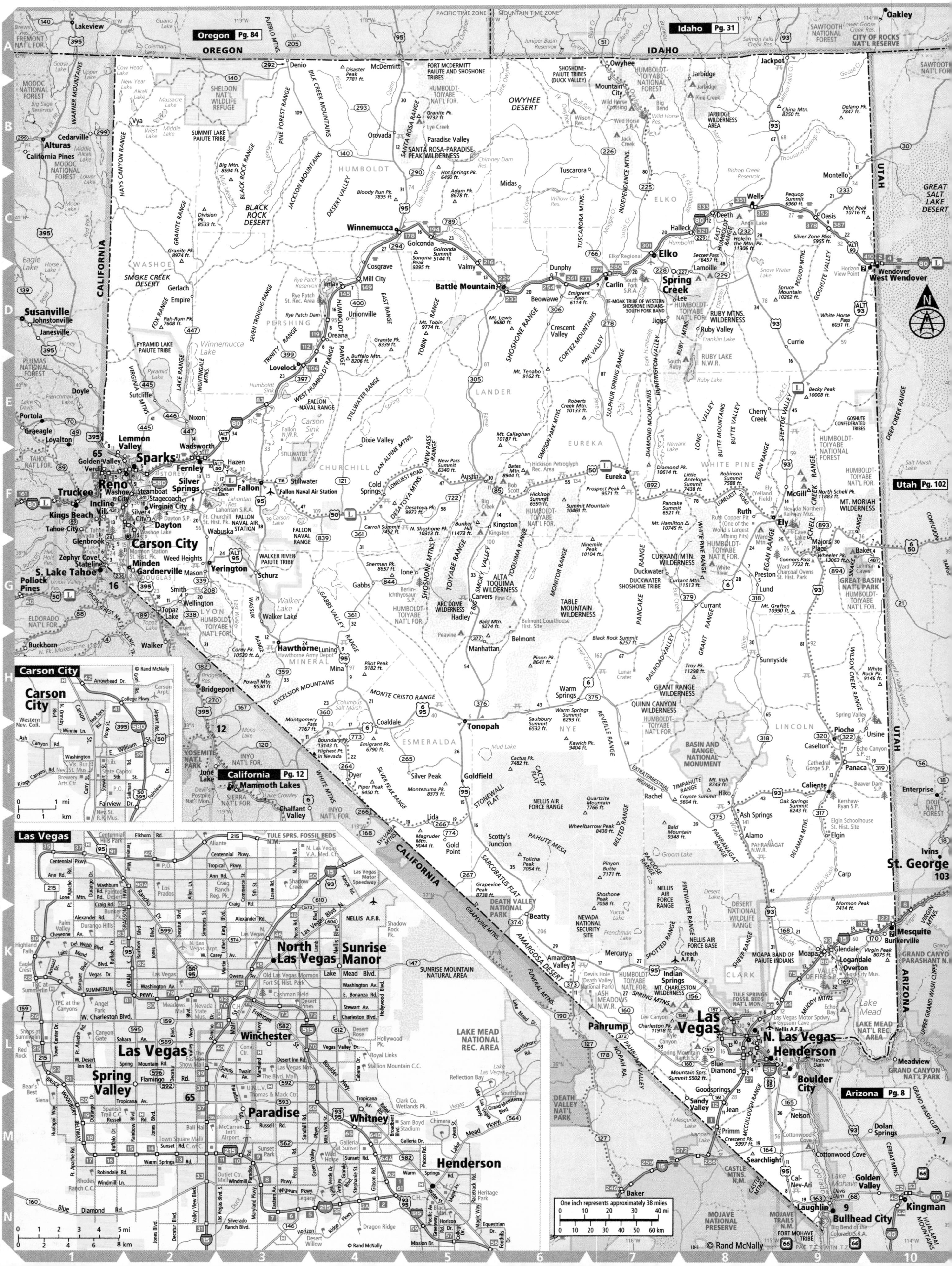

ravel planning & on-the-road resources

rism Information

w Hampshire Division of Travel & Tourism:
03) 271-2665; www.visitnh.com

ad Conditions & Construction

, (603) 271-6862; www.nhtmc.com, www.nh.gov/dot

Road Information

(E-ZPass)

eau of Turnpikes: (603) 485-3806;
ww.nh.gov/dot/org/operations/turnpikes

Total mileages through New Hampshire

- I-89: 61 miles
- I-95: 16 miles
- I-93: 132 miles
- US 2: 36 miles

More mileages at randmcnally.com/MC

Mileages between cities

	Colebrook	Concord	Conway	Keene	Laconia	Littleton	Nashua	Portsmouth
Berlin	49	115	40	168	97	42	151	117
Concord	137		77	51	27	87	36	44
Keene	181	51	130		80	136	50	99
Lebanon	128	57	88	64	58	82	89	111
Littleton	56	87	54	136	66		121	129
Manchester	155	18	95	55	45	105	18	43
Nashua	172	36	113	50	63	121		54
Portsmouth	180	44	77	99	57	129	54	

New Hampshire

Nickname: The Granite State
Capital: Concord, K-7
Land area: 8,953 sq. mi. (rank: 44th)
Population: 1,316,470 (rank: 42nd)
Largest city: Manchester, 109,565, L-7

Index of places Pg. 132

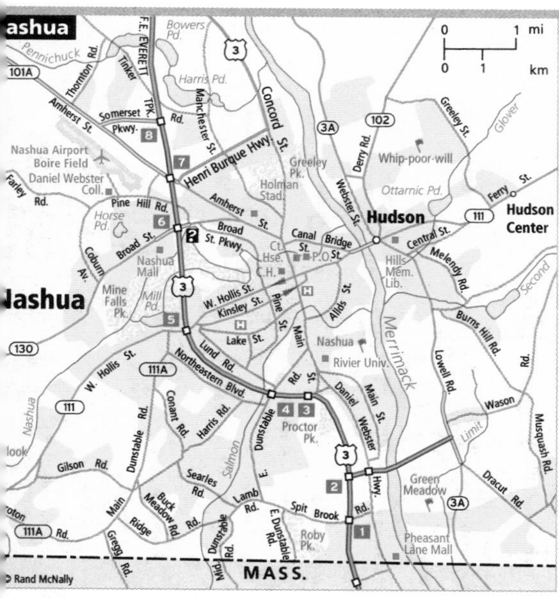

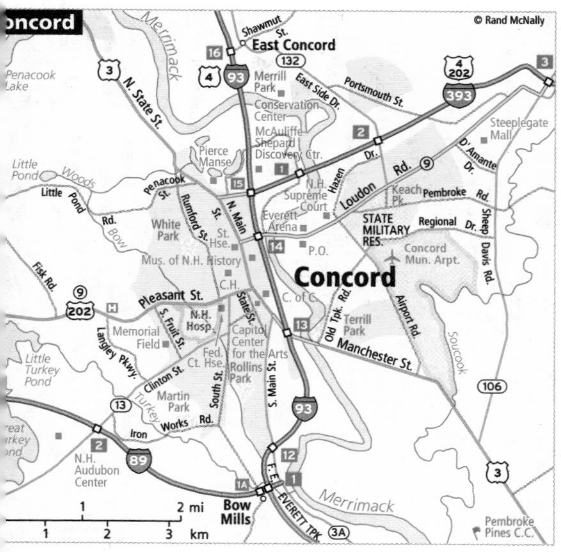

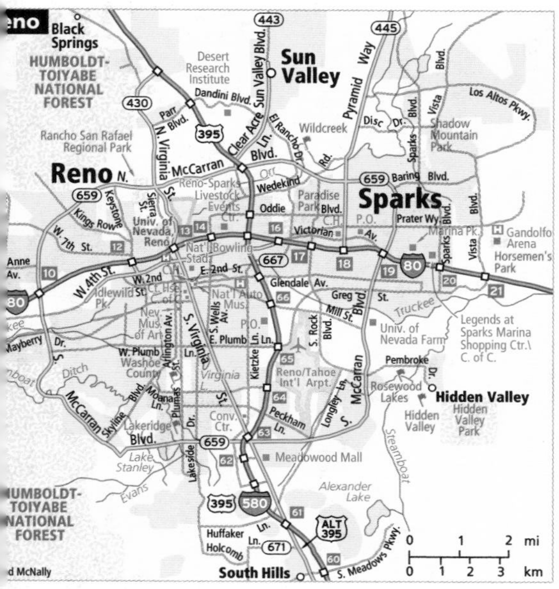

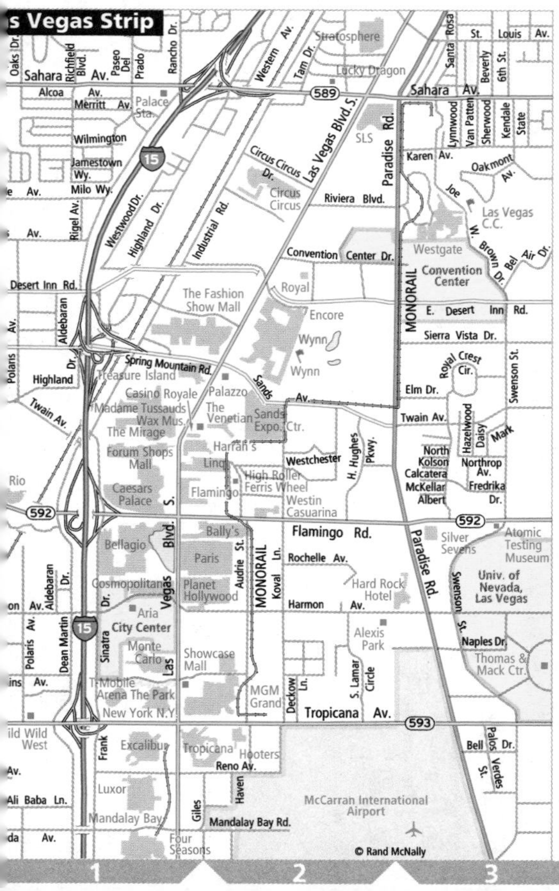

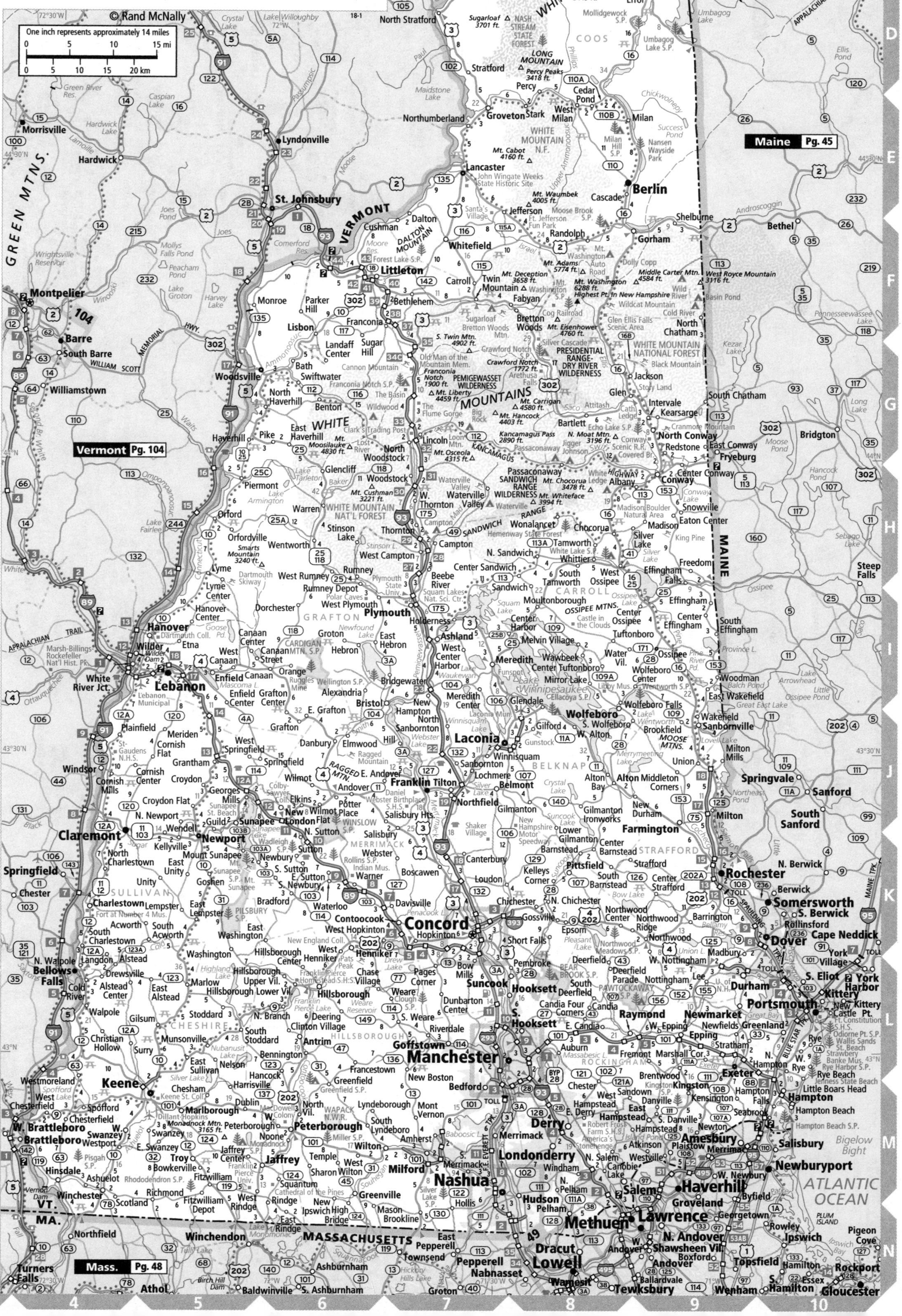

New Jersey

Nickname: The Garden State
Capital: Trenton, J-8
Land area: 7,354 sq. mi. (rank: 46th)
Population: 8,791,894 (rank: 11th)
Largest city: Newark, 277,140, F-12

Index of places Pg. 132

Travel planning & on-the-road resources

Tourism Information
New Jersey Travel & Tourism: (609) 599-6540; www.visitnj.org

Toll Road Information: *(all use E-ZPass)*
New Jersey Turnpike Authority (N.J. Turnpike, Garden St. Pkwy.): (732) 750-5300; www.state.nj.us/turnpike
South Jersey Transportation Authority (Atlantic City Expressway): (609) 965-6060; www.sjta.com

Road Conditions & Construction
511, (866) 511-6538; www.511nj.org, www.state.nj.us/transportation

Toll Bridge/Tunnel Information: *(all use E-ZPass)*
Burlington County Bridge Commission: (856) 829-1900, (609) 387-1480; www.bcbridges.org
Del. River & Bay Auth. (Del. Mem. Br., Cape May/Lewes Fy.): (302) 571-6300; www.drba.net
Del. River Port Auth. (Philadelphia area bridges): (877) 567-3772, (856) 968-2000; www.drpa.org
Del. River Joint Toll Br. Commission (other Del. River bridges): (800) 363-0049; www.drjtbc.org
Port Auth. of N.Y. & N.J. (NYC area inter-state bridges & tunnels): (800) 221-9903; www.panynj.gov

ardwalk at Atlantic City

Mileages between cities

	Atlantic City	Camden	Cape May	Jersey City	Long Branch	Newark	New Brunswick	New York, NY	Paterson	Phillipsburg	Port Jervis, NY	Princeton	Toms River	Trenton	Vineland	Wilmington, DE
Atlantic City		58	47	120	82	115	94	126	129	138	182	99	52	90	36	82
Camden	58		88	86	76	80	61	96	94	80	143	45	55	34	36	31
Cape May	47	88		151	114	147	126	157	161	170	214	131	84	121	48	98
Newark	115	80	147	6	43		25	10	15	58	74	41	63	55	114	112
New Brunswick	94	61	126	30	34	25		36	39	48	92	16	43	26	95	93
Phillipsburg	138	80	170	64	81	58	48	68	67		74	54	101	54	118	95
Port Jervis, NY	182	143	214	89	110	74	92	95	73	74		94	130	122	180	158
Trenton	90	34	121	61	52	55	26	66	69	54	122	11	47		69	61

Total mileages through New Jersey

- 78: 68 miles
- 95: 98 miles
- 80: 68 miles

More mileages at randmcnally.com/MC

Nickname: Land of Enchantment
Capital: Santa Fe, D-6
Land area: 121,298 sq. mi. (rank: 5th)
Population: 2,059,179 (rank: 36th)
Largest city: Albuquerque, 545,852, E-4

Index of places Pg. 133

Mileages between cities

	Albuquerque	Carlsbad	Clayton	Gallup	Las Cruces	Socorro	Taos	Tucumcari
Albuquerque		277	270	137	222	78	128	173
Carlsbad	277		374	412	206	241	336	263
Clayton	270	374		407	415	347	163	111
Clovis	219	180	168	356	292	248	246	83
Farmington	180	455	418	121	404	258	202	354
Las Cruces	222	206	415	338		146	351	303
Roswell	199	76	293	336	184	165	260	182
Santa Fe	58	268	215	197	282	136	68	166

Total mileages through New Mexico

I-10: 164 miles; I-40: 374 miles; I-25: 462 miles

More mileages at randmcnally.com/MC

Travel planning & on-the-road resources

Tourism Information
New Mexico Tourism Department: (505) 827-7400; www.newmexico.org

Road Conditions & Construction
511, (800) 432-4269, (505) 827-5100; www.nmroads.com, www.dot.state.nm.us

Toll Road Information
No toll roads

Determining Distance
(segme… one mi… not sho…)
Cumulative miles (red): the distance between red …
Intermediate miles (black): the distance between intersections & places

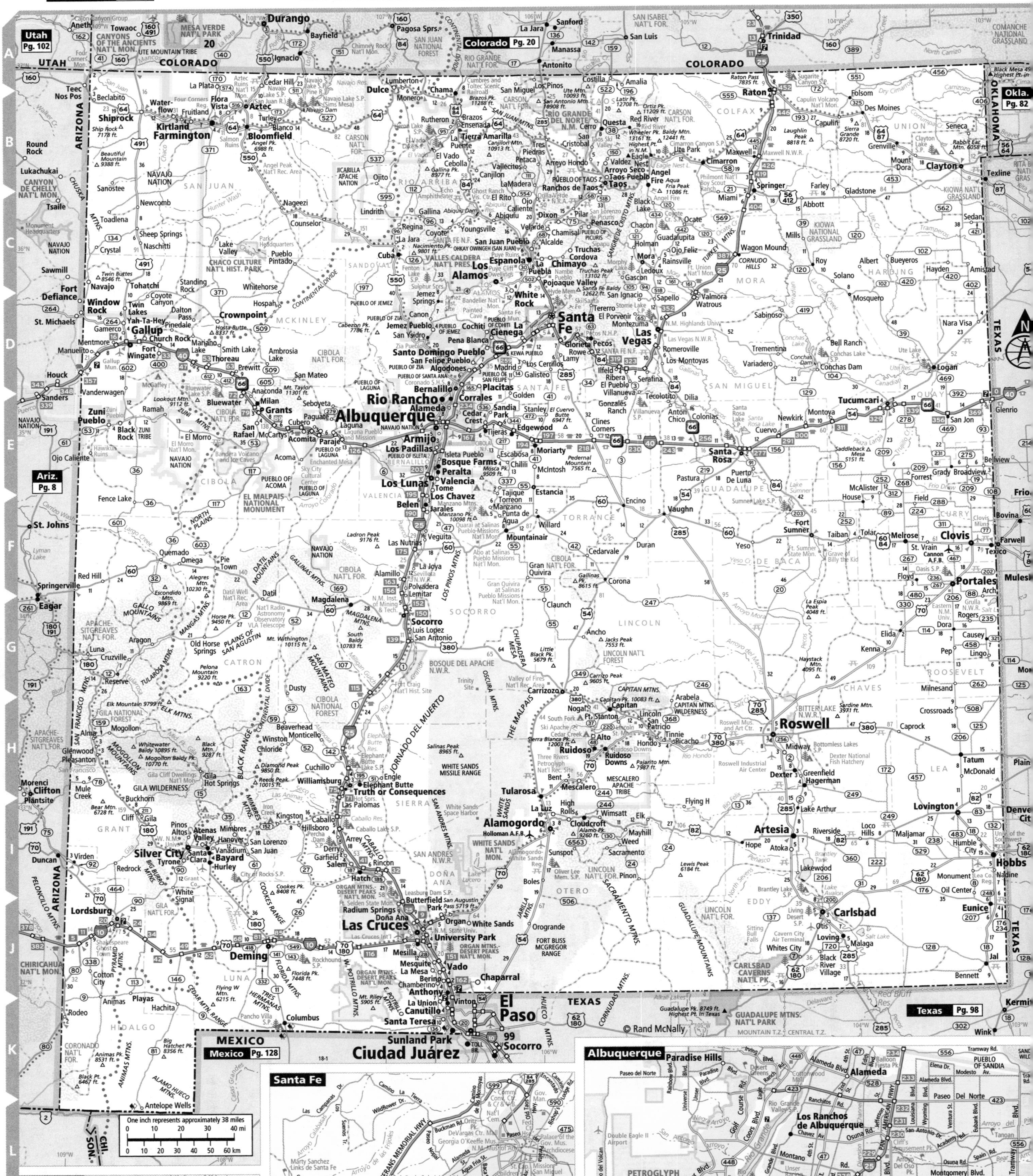

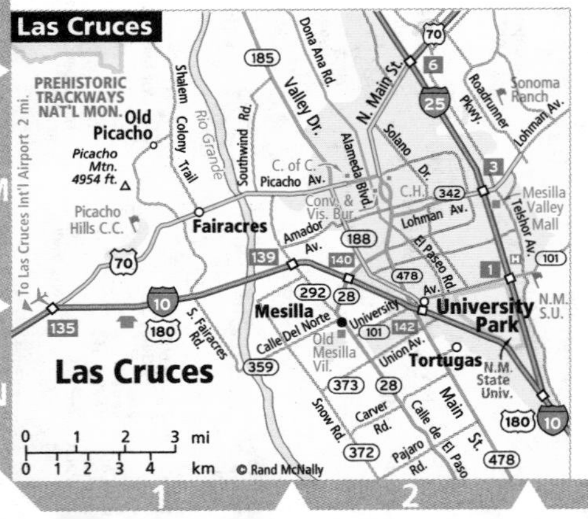

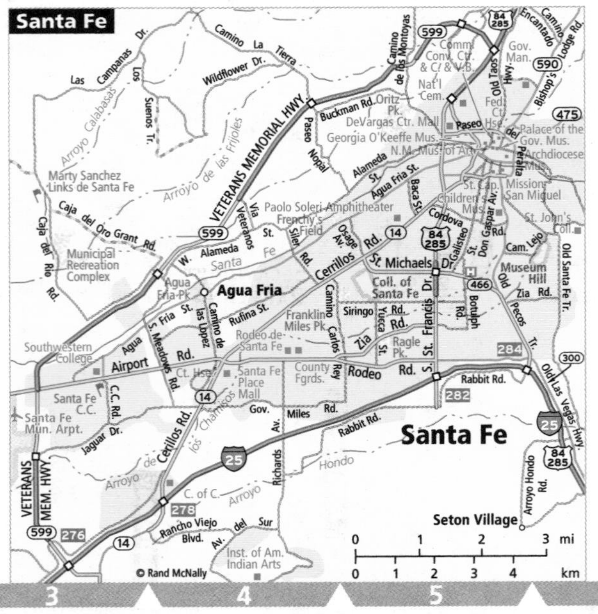

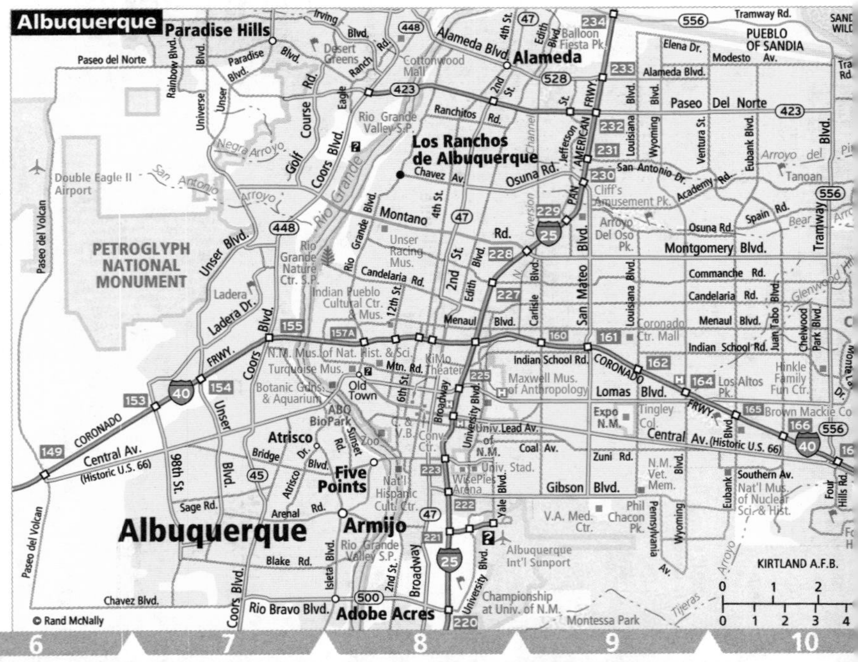

Travel planning & on-the-road resources

Tourism Information
N.Y. State Division of Tourism: (800) 225-5697; www.iloveny.com

Toll Road Info
see next page for listings

Road Conditions & Construction
511, (888) 465-1169; www.511ny.org, www.dot.ny.gov
Thruway: (800) 847-8929; www.thruway.ny.gov

Determining Distances
(segments of one mile or less not shown)
Cumulative miles (red): the distance between red arrows
Intermediate miles (black): the distance between intersections & places

Total mileages through New York
84: 72 miles
95: 24 miles
87: 334 miles
495: 66 miles

More mileages at randmcnally.com/MC

Mileages between cities

	Albany	Buffalo	Hempstead	Newburgh	New York	Poughkeepsie	Riverhead	White Plains
Albany		289	167	87	156	75	219	138
Buffalo	289		423	361	395	362	471	394
Hempstead	167	423		78	12	92	59	34
Kingston	55	339	116	37	106	19	168	87
Montauk	260	513	97	172	107	184	42	126
Newburgh	87	361	78		72	19	130	49
New York	156	395	12	72		84	66	26
Poughkeepsie	75	362	92	19	84		143	60

New York/Southern

Nickname: The Empire State
Capital: Albany, NK-19
Land area: 47,126 sq. mi. (rank: 30th)
Population: 19,378,102 (rank: 3rd)
Largest city: New York, 8,175,133, SF-6

Index of places Pg. 133

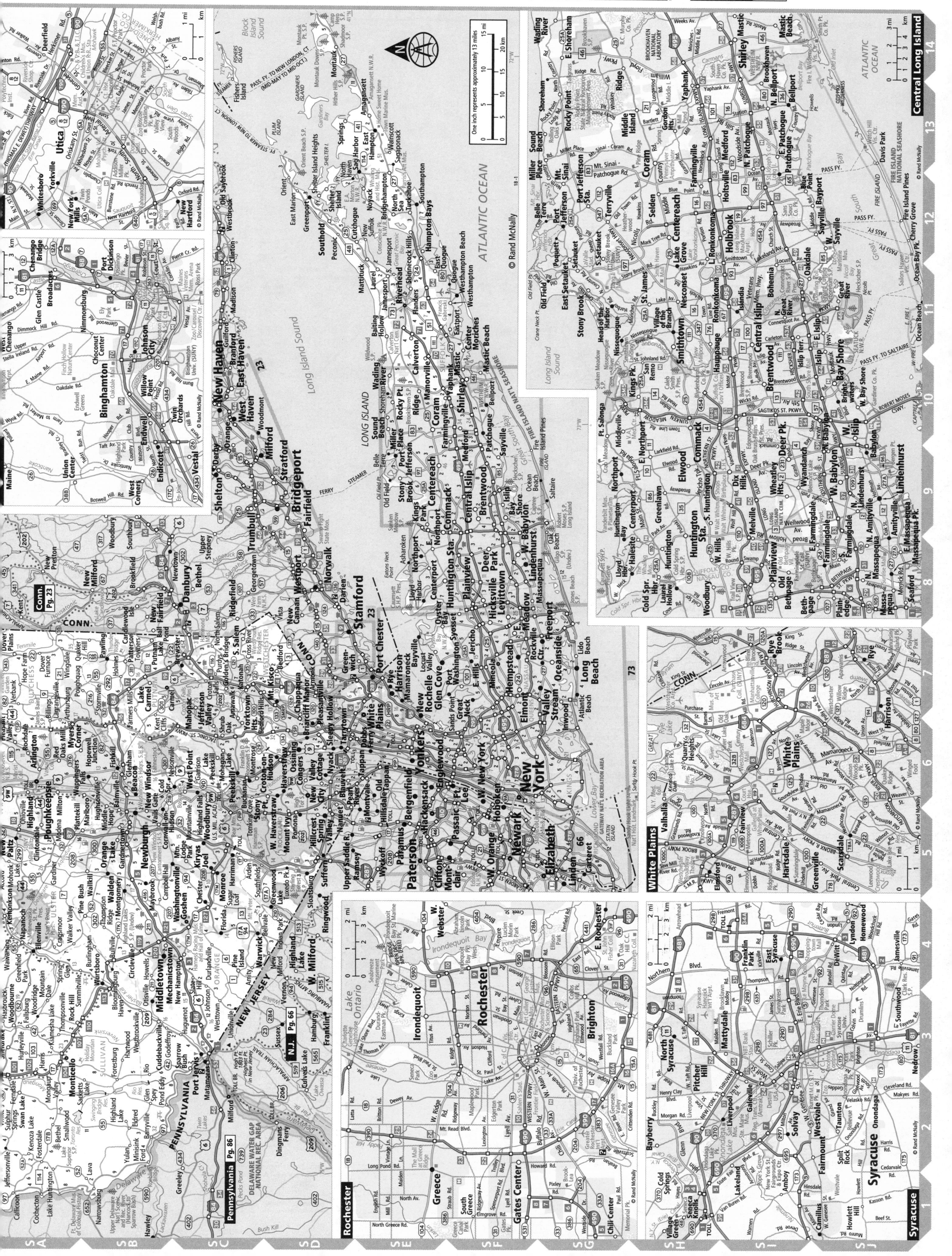

Nickname: The Empire State
Capital: Albany, NK-19
Land area: 47,126 sq. mi. (rank: 30th)
Population: 19,378,102 (rank: 3rd)
Largest city: New York, 8,175,133, SF-6

Index of places Pg. 133

Travel planning & on-the-road resources

Tourism Information
New York State Division of Tourism: (800) 225-5697; www.iloveny.com

Road Conditions & Construction
511, (888) 465-1169; www.511ny.org, www.dot.ny.gov
Thruway: (800) 847-8929; www.thruway.ny.gov

Toll Road Information: *(all use E-ZPass)*
MTA (N.Y. City in-state bridges & tunnels): (877) 690-5116, N.Y. only: 511 & say "Bridges & tunnels"; www.mta.info/bandt
New York State Bridge Authority (Hudson River bridges): (845) 691-7245; www.nysba.state.ny.us
New York State Thruway Authority: (518) 436-2805; www.thruway.ny.gov

International Toll Bridge Information:
Buffalo & Ft. Erie Public Br. Auth. (Peace Br.) *(E-ZPass)*: (716) 884-6744; www.peacebridge.com
Niagara Falls Bridge Comm. *(E-ZPass or ExpressPass)*: (716) 285-6322; www.niagarafallsbridges.com
Ogdensburg Br. & Port Auth.: (315) 393-4080; www.ogdensport.com
Seaway Int'l Bridge Corp. *(Seaway Transit Card)*: (613) 932-6601; www.sibc.
Thousand Islands Br. Auth. (Alexandria Bay): (315) 482-2501; www.tibridge.c

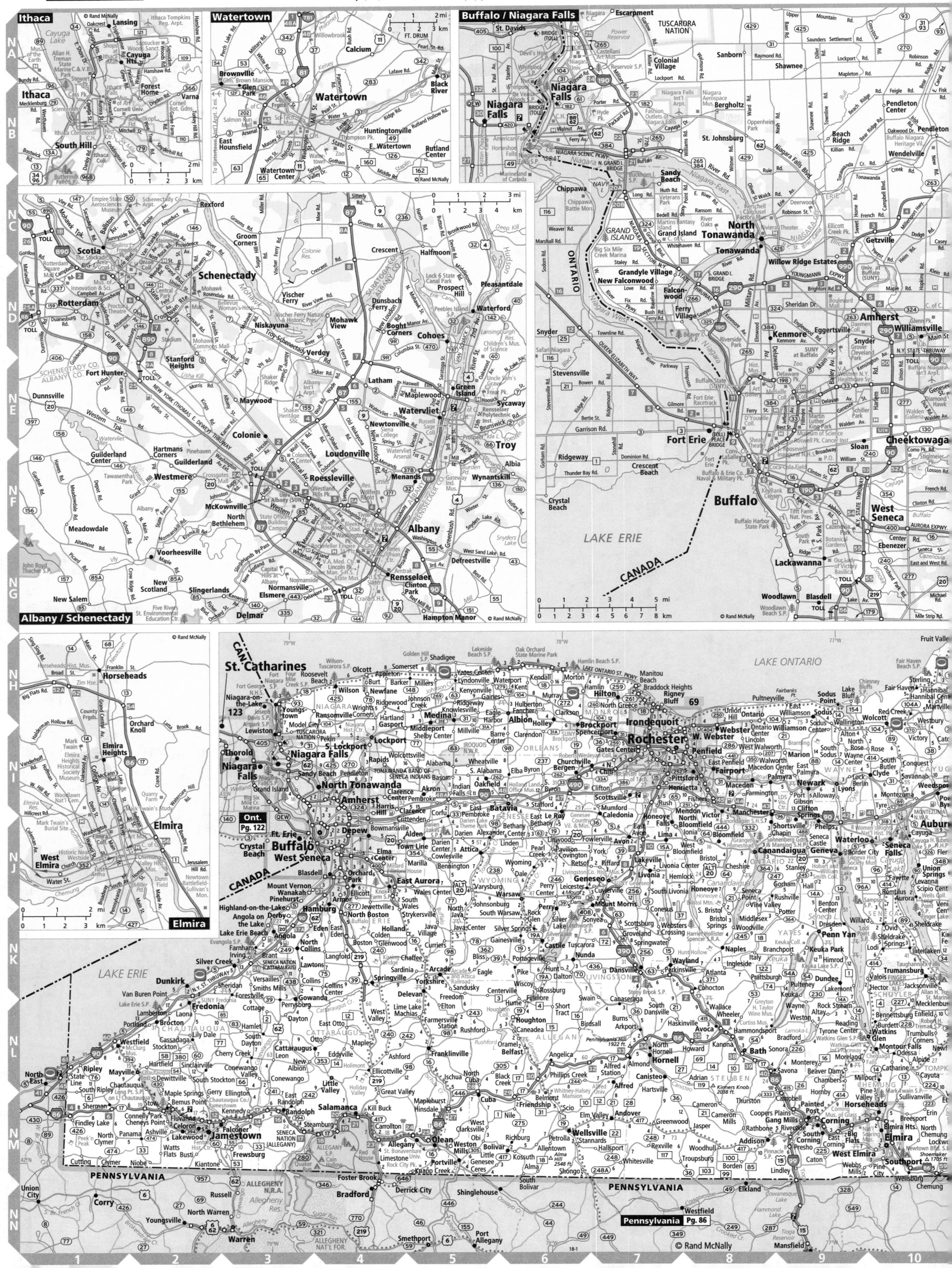

Niagara Falls

Mileages between cities	Albany	Binghamton	Buffalo	Elmira	Glens Falls	Jamestown	Kingston	Lake Placid	Massena	New York	Niagara Falls	Plattsburgh	Rochester	Syracuse	Utica	Watertown
Albany		140	289	195	53	356	55	140	217	156	302	160	226	145	94	175
Binghamton	140		222	56	179	218	130	266	231	176	235	287	159	73	89	143
Buffalo	289	222		148	313	71	339	337	305	395	21	373	73	150	198	212
Jamestown	356	218	71	163	395		349	404	370	392	92	436	139	214	263	278
Plattsburgh	160	287	373	342	110	436	214	50	82	317	384		308	227	183	165
Rochester	226	159	73	120	248	139	277	275	242	332	87	308		86	135	149
Syracuse	145	73	150	90	160	214	195	195	159	246	162	227	86		53	70
Watertown	175	143	212	160	179	278	226	125	89	316	225	165	149	70	80	

Total mileages through New York

- 81: 184 miles
- 86: 176 miles
- 87: 334 miles
- 90: 385 miles

More mileages at randmcnally.com/MC

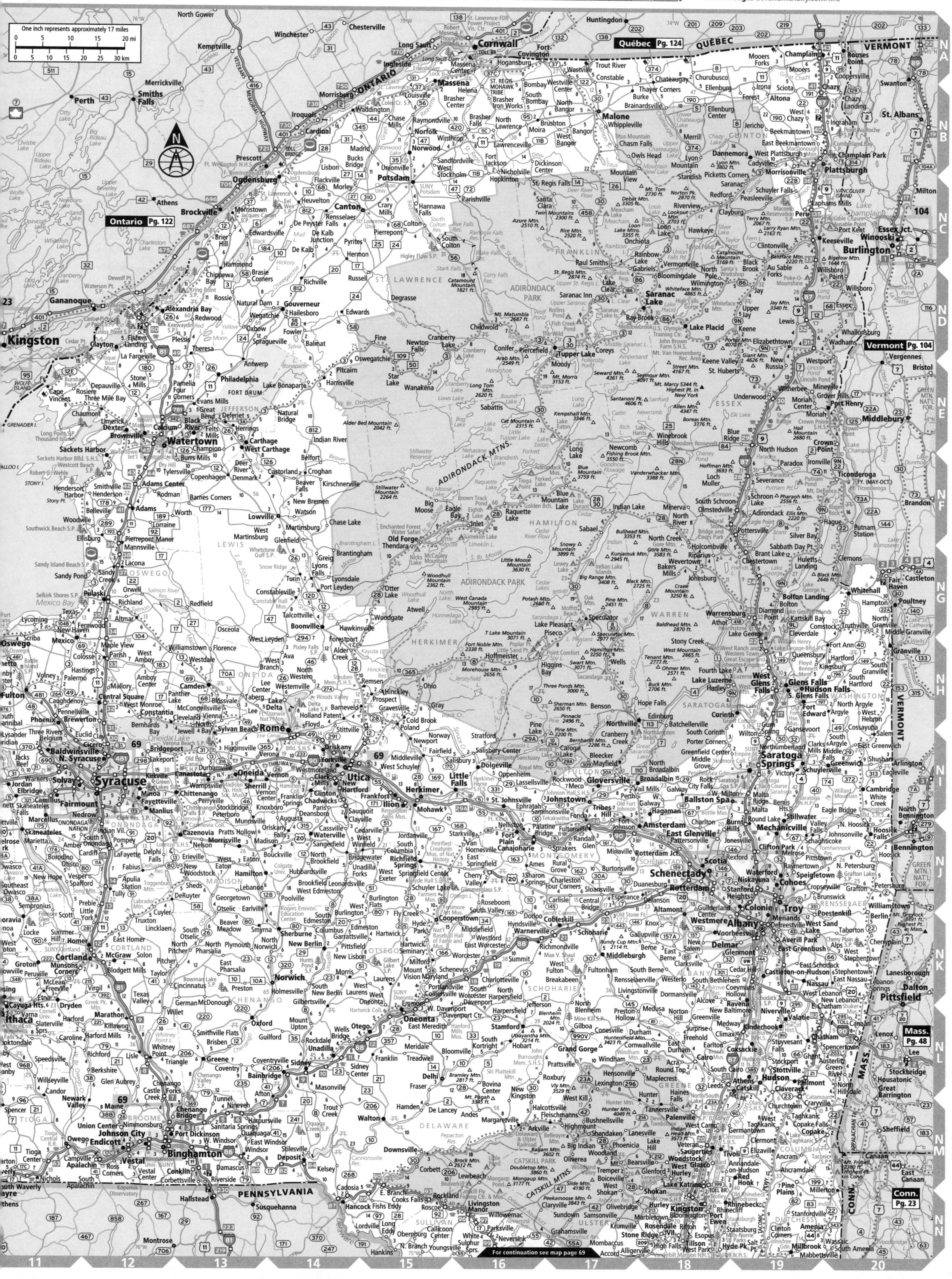

Ellis Island Museum

Sights to see

- American Museum of Natural History A-4
- Battery Park I-1
- Bronx Zoo E-12
- Brooklyn Bridge H-2
- Carnegie Hall C-4
- Central Park B-4
- Chrysler Building D-4
- Coney Island L-10
- Ellis Island I-9
- Empire State Building D-3
- Greenwich Village H-10
- Grand Central Terminal D-4

Sights to see

- Guggenheim Museum A-5
- Intrepid Sea-Air Space Museum C-2
- Lincoln Center B-3
- Madison Square Garden D-2
- Metropolitan Museum of Art B-5
- National September 11 Memorial H-1
- New York Stock Exchange and Wall Street H-1
- Rockefeller Center C-4
- Staten Island Ferry .... I-2 and J-8
- Statue of Liberty I-9
- Times Square D-3
- Yankee Stadium E-11

Nickname: The Tar Heel State
Capital: Raleigh, E-12
Land area: 48,618 sq. mi. (rank: 29th)
Population: 9,535,483 (rank: 10th)
Largest city: Charlotte, 731,424, F-5

Travel planning & on-the-road resources

Tourism Information
North Carolina Travel & Tourism: (800) 847-4862; www.visitnc.com

Road Conditions & Construction
511, (877) 511-4662; www.ncdot.gov/travel/511, www.ncdot.gov

Toll Road Information (NC Quick Pass)
North Carolina Turnpike Authority: (877) 769-7277; www.ncdot.gov/turnpike

Determining distances along roads

Highway distances (segments of one mile or less not shown):
Cumulative miles (red): the distance between red arrows
Intermediate miles (black): the distance between intersections & plac

Interchanges and exit numbers
For most states, the mileage between interchanges may be determin by subtracting one number from the other.

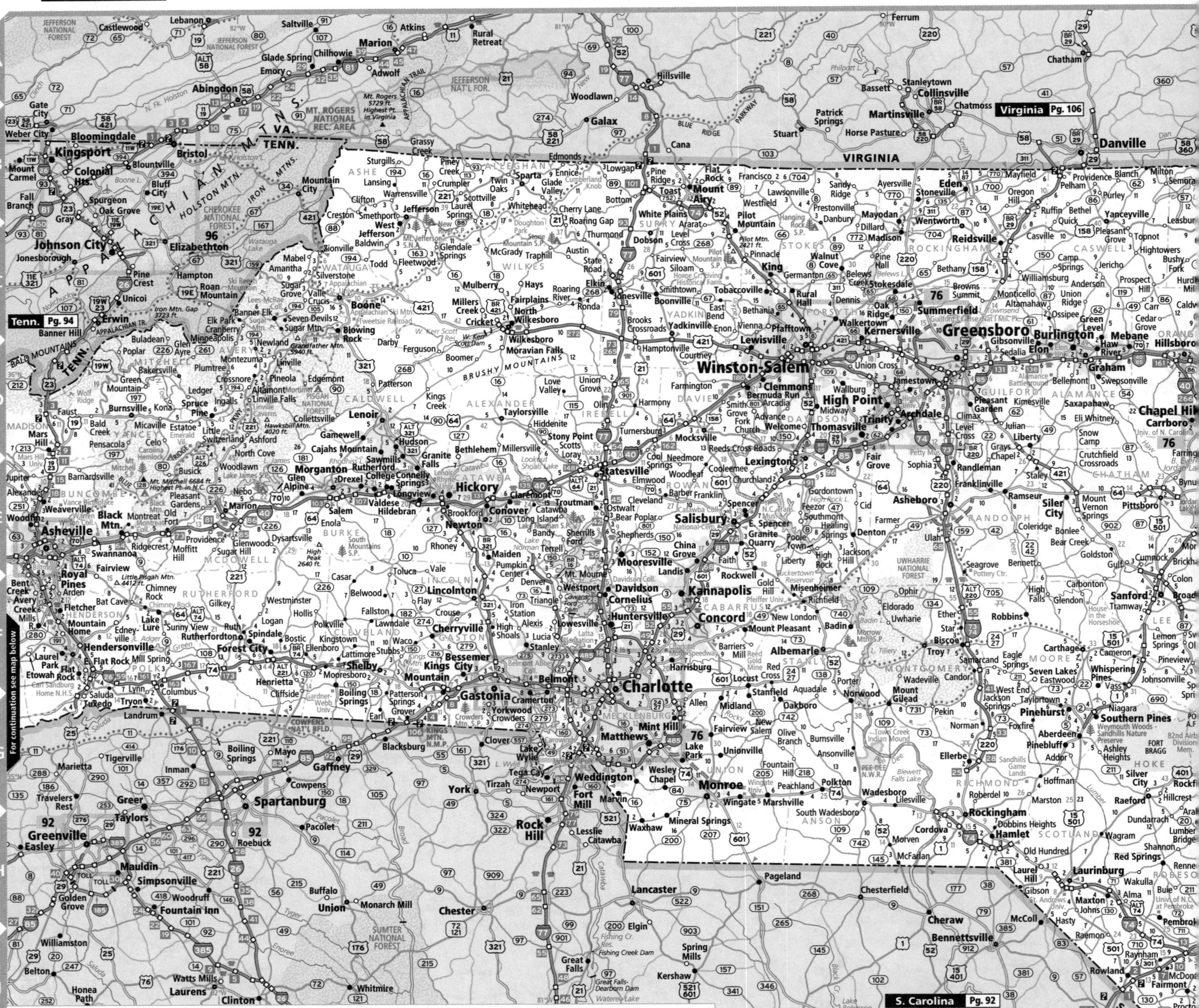

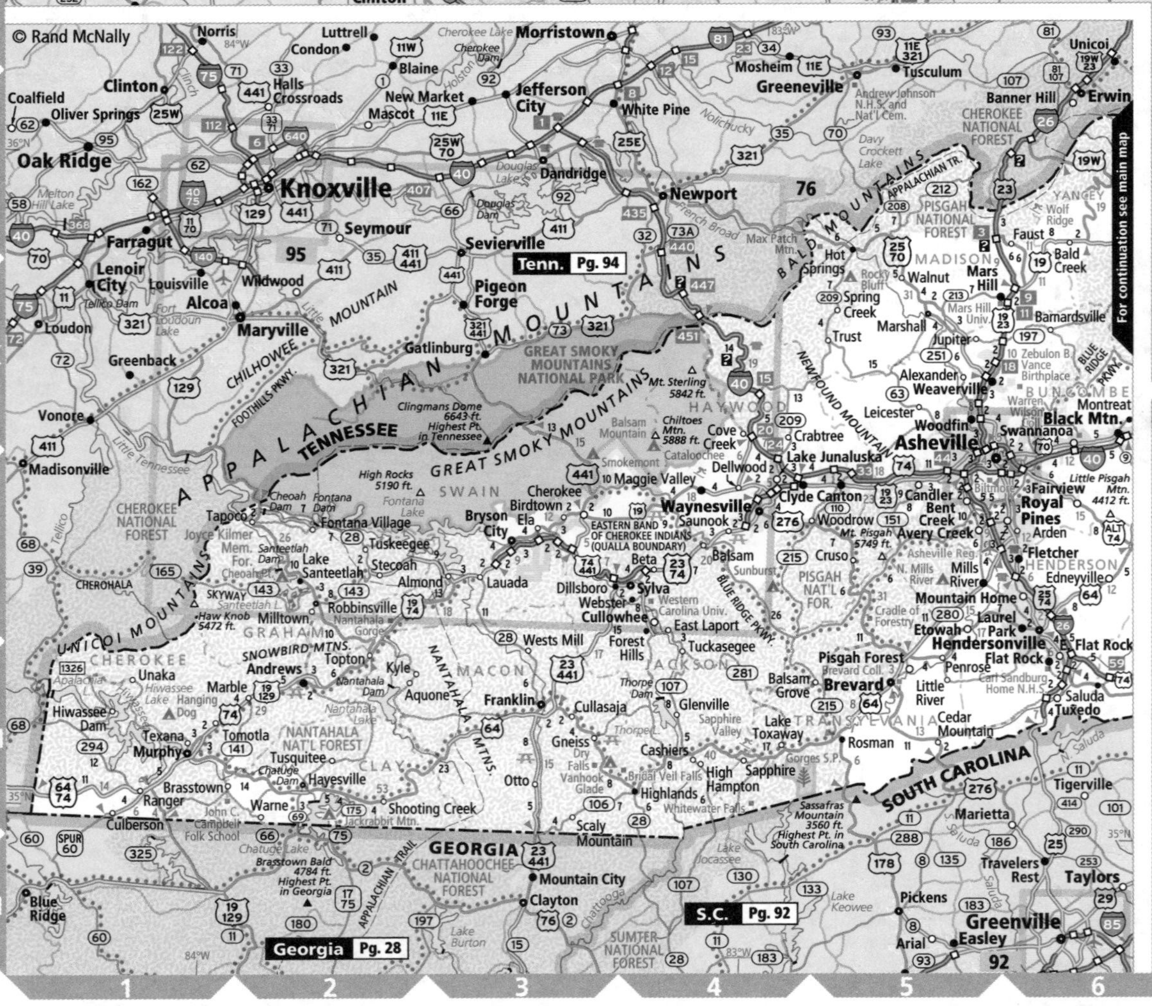

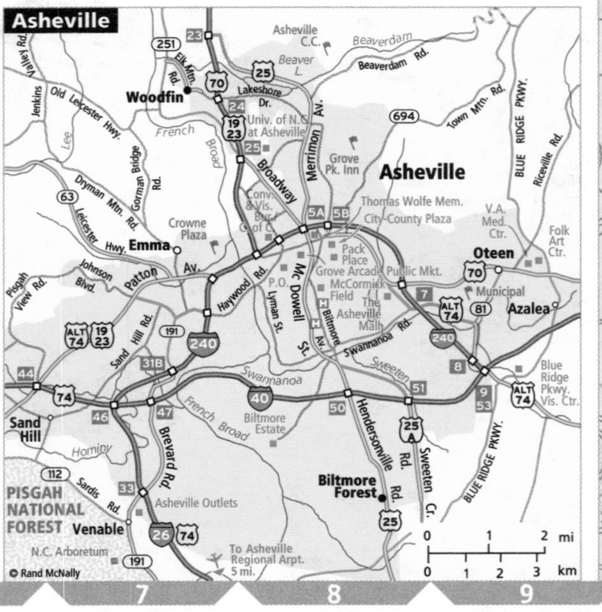

Mileages between cities

	Asheville	Boone	Charlotte	Durham	Elizabeth City	Greensboro	Hickory	Morehead City	Murphy	Nags Head	New Bern	Raleigh	Roanoke Rapids	Rockingham	Wilmington	Winston-Salem
Asheville		94	128	224	412	172	77	393	110	444	358	251	308	200	327	145
Charlotte	128	100		144	332	93	57	313	223	364	278	168	231	71	197	77
Elizabeth City	412	354	332	185		241	338	152	520	56	119	164	97	259	208	269
Fayetteville	261	202	137	89	203	94	189	138	369	234	130	63	127	64	89	119
Greensboro	172	113	93	53	241		98	223	279	271	188	80	138	83	207	29
Greenville	332	273	250	101	97	156	258	79	440	129	44	82	86	176	116	188
Raleigh	251	192	168	22	164	80	177	146	358	195	111		89	98	130	107
Wilmington	327	319	197	156	208	207	259	91	428	230	90	130	178	127		236

Total mileages through North Carolina

- 40: 419 miles
- 77: 102 miles
- 85: 233 miles
- 95: 182 miles

More mileages at randmcnally.com/MC

Sights to see

- Discovery Place, Charlotte H-4
- Duke Homestead State Historic Site & Tobacco Museum, Durham F-9
- Historic Bethabara Park, Winston-Salem A-1
- Mint Museum of Art, Charlotte H-5
- Morehead Planetarium & Science Center, Chapel Hill . . H-8
- North Carolina Museum of History, Raleigh I-12
- North Carolina Museum of Life & Science, Durham . . F-10
- North Carolina State Capitol, Raleigh I-13
- North Carolina State University, Raleigh I-13
- Old Salem, Winston-Salem B-2
- Reynolda House, Winston-Salem B-1

Old Salem, Winston-Salem

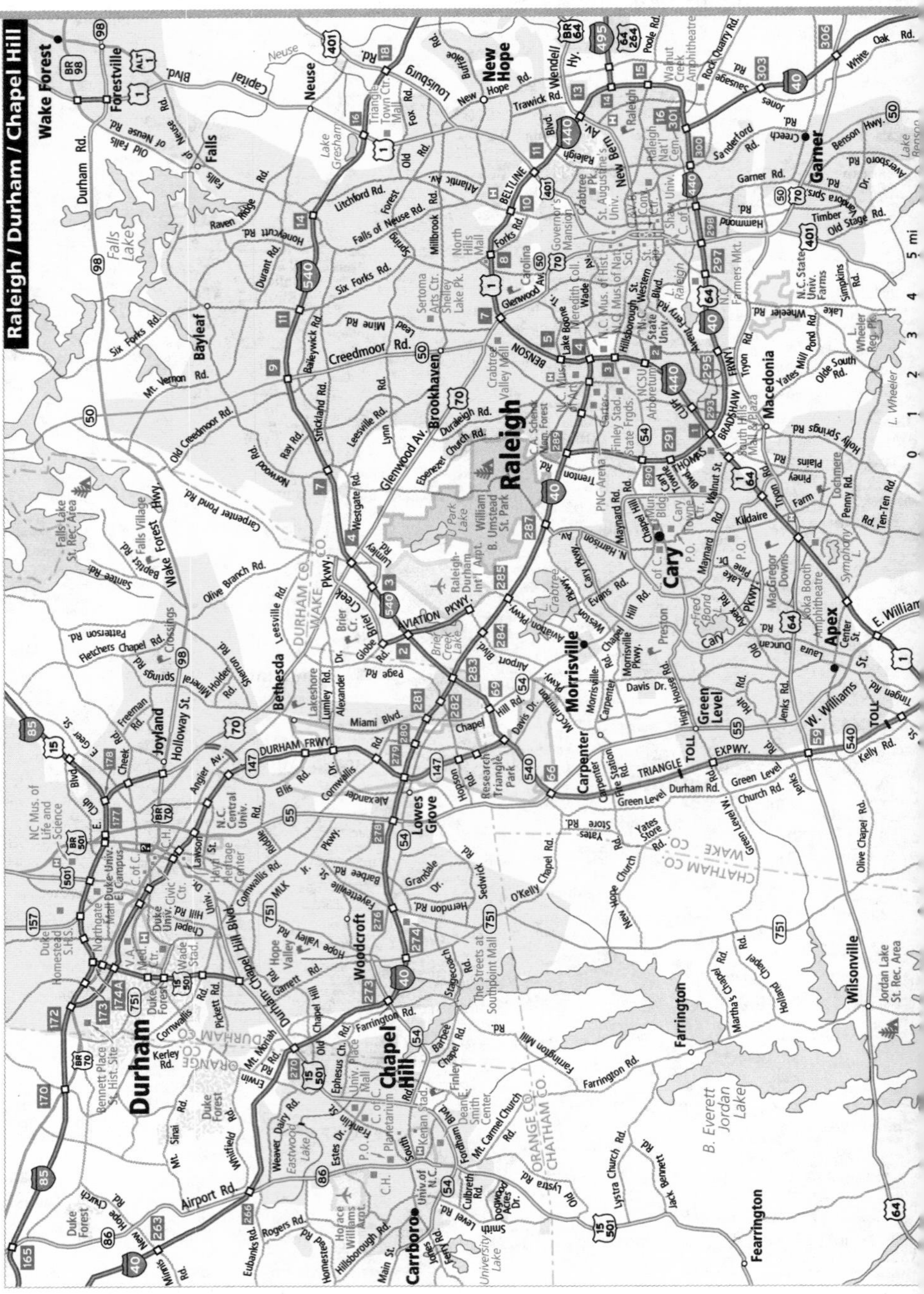

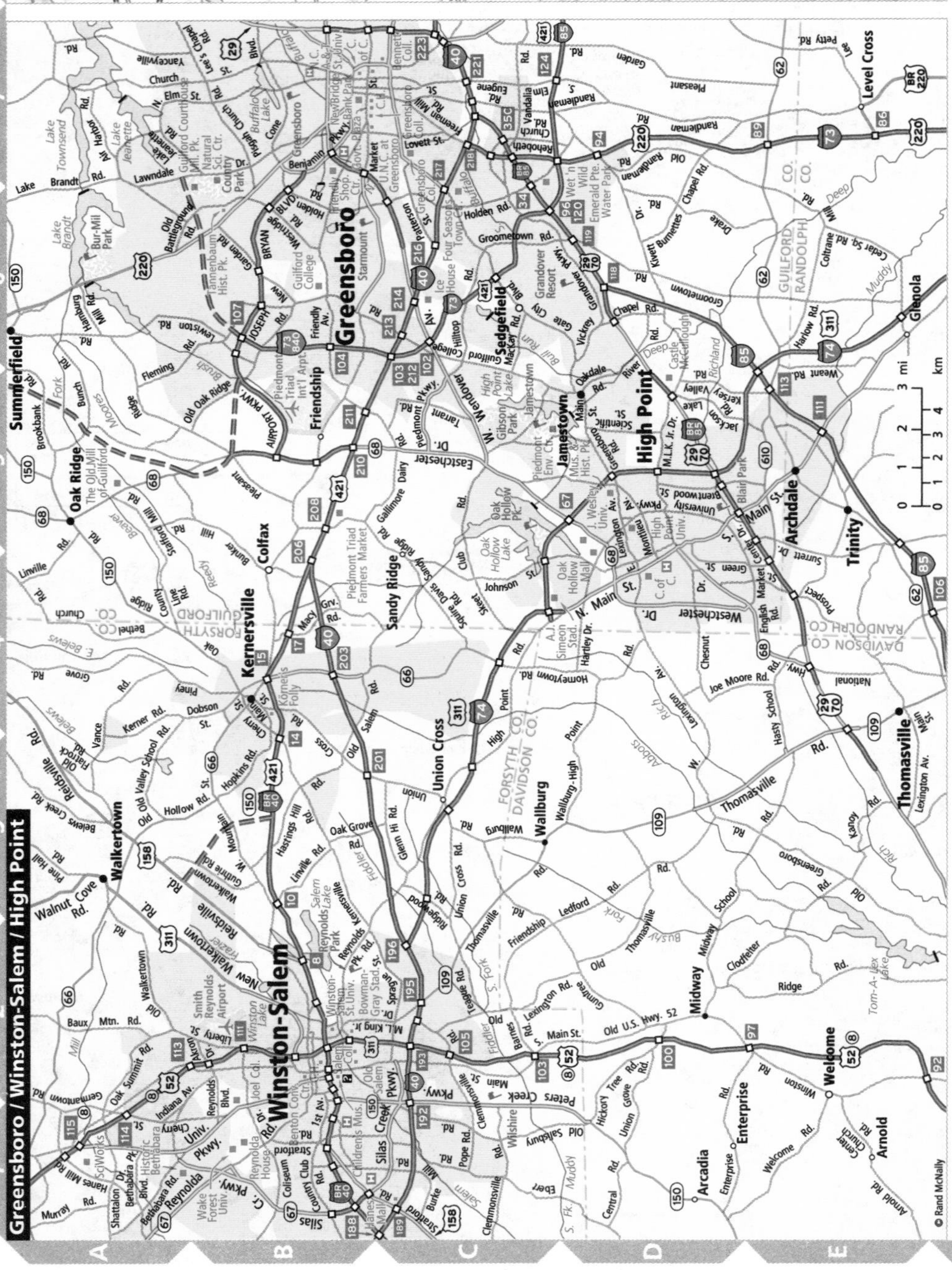

ravel planning & on-the-road resources

rism Information

rth Dakota Tourism:
00) 435-5663, (701) 328-2525; www.ndtourism.com

d Conditions & Construction

, (855) 637-6237;
w.dot.nd.gov, www.dot.nd.gov/travel-info-v2

Road Information

toll roads

Determining Distances

(segments of one mile or less not shown)

Cumulative miles (red): the distance between red arrows

Intermediate miles (black): the distance between intersections & places

Total mileages through North Dakota

I-29: 218 miles | US 2: 359 miles
I-94: 352 miles | US 83: 265 miles

More mileages at randmcnally.com/MC

Mileages between cities

	Bismarck	Bowman	Fargo	Garrison	Grand Forks	Jamestown	Williston	Winnipeg, MB
Bismarck		174	195	75	272	102	228	413
Devils Lake	180	354	165	167	89	99	245	230
Dickinson	97	78	292	149	368	198	132	509
Fargo	195	368		266	80	94	422	222
Grand Forks	272	444	80	256		171	334	146
Minot	110	260	268	47	210	170	124	299
Wahpeton	243	416	54	315	131	142	470	273
Williston	228	170	422	144	334	293		424

North Dakota

Nickname: The Peace Garden State
Capital: Bismarck, H-7
Land area: 69,000 sq. mi. (rank: 17th)
Population: 672,591 (rank: 48th)
Largest city: Fargo, 105,549, H-13

Index of places Pg. 133

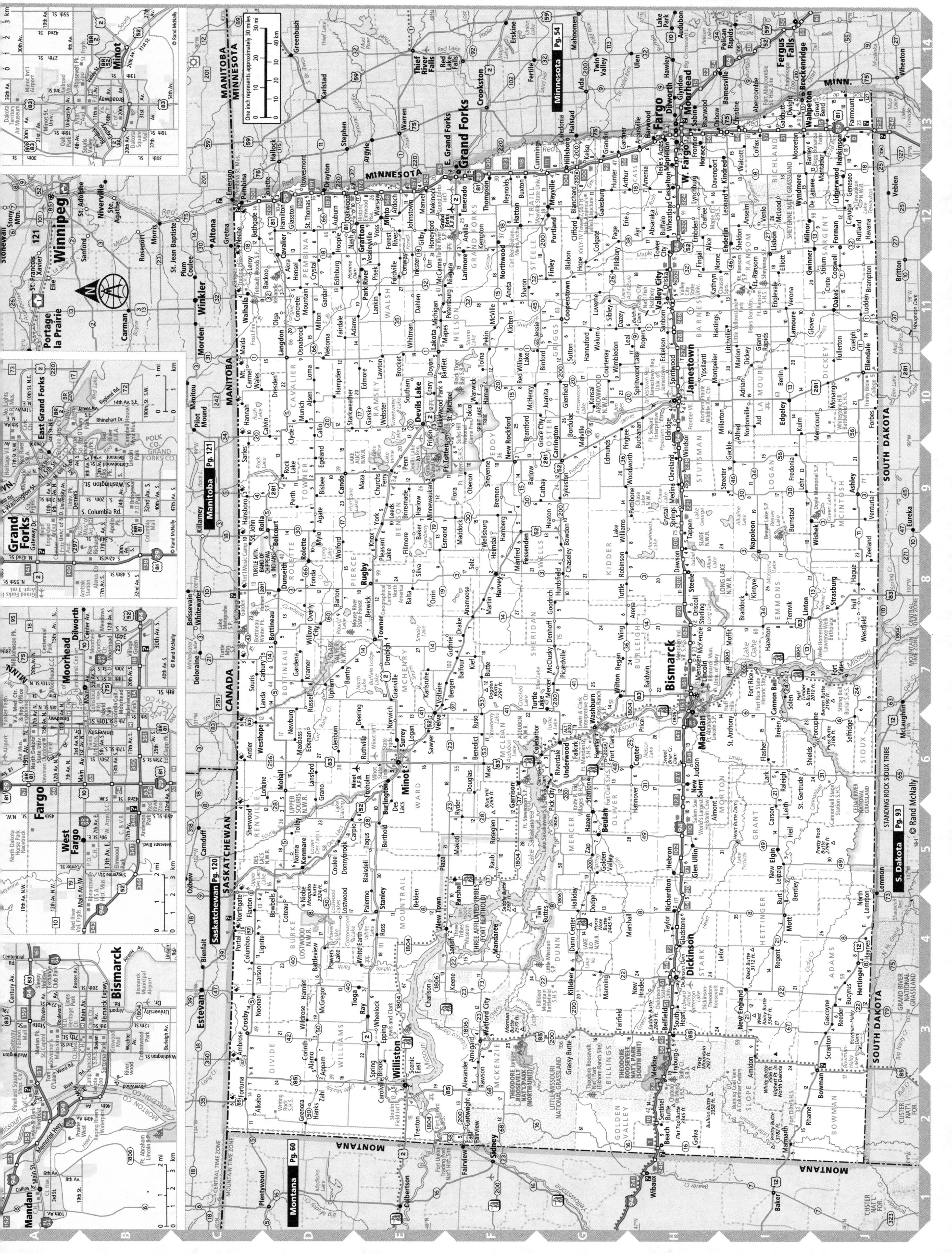

Nickname: The Buckeye State
Capital: Columbus, SB-9
Land area: 40,861 sq. mi. (rank: 35th)
Population: 11,536,504 (rank: 7th)
Largest city: Columbus, 787,033, SB-9

Index of places Pg. 133

Travel planning & on-the-road resources

Tourism Information
Tourism Ohio:
(800) 282-5393; www.discoverohio.com

Toll Road Information
Ohio Turnpike and Infrastructure Commission
(E-ZPass): (888) 876-7453, (440) 234-2081;
www.ohioturnpike.org

Road Conditions & Construction
(614) 466-7170;
www.dot.state.oh.us, www.buckeyetraffic.org;
Cincinnati metro area: 511;
www.ohgo.com/dashboard/cincinnati
Ohio Turnpike: (440) 234-2030, (440) 234-2081;
www.ohioturnpike.org

Determining distances along roads
Highway distances (segments of one mile or less not shown):
Cumulative miles (red): the distance between red arrows
Intermediate miles (black): the distance between intersections & plac
Interchanges and exit numbers
For most states, the mileage between interchanges may be determin
by subtracting one number from the other.

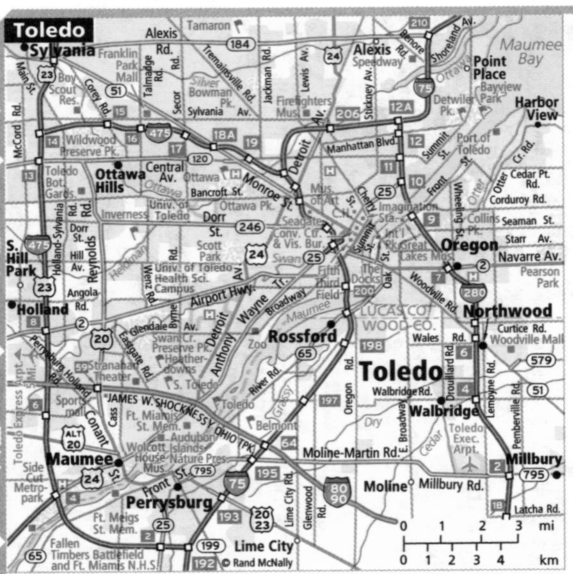

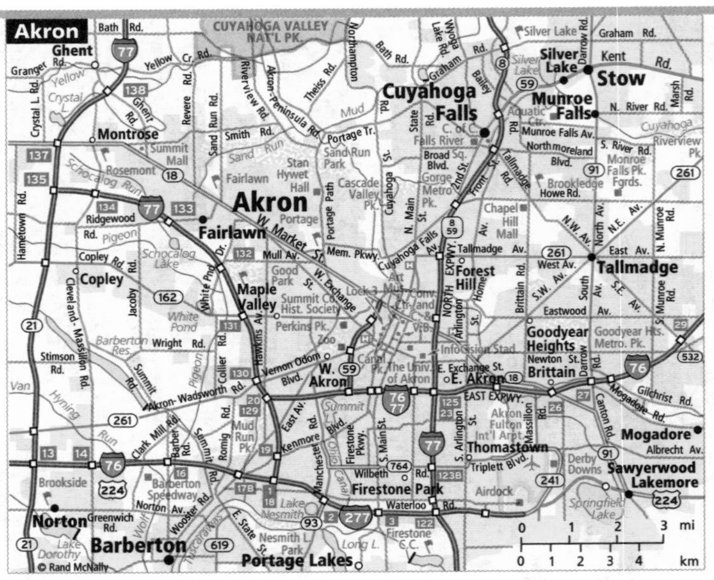

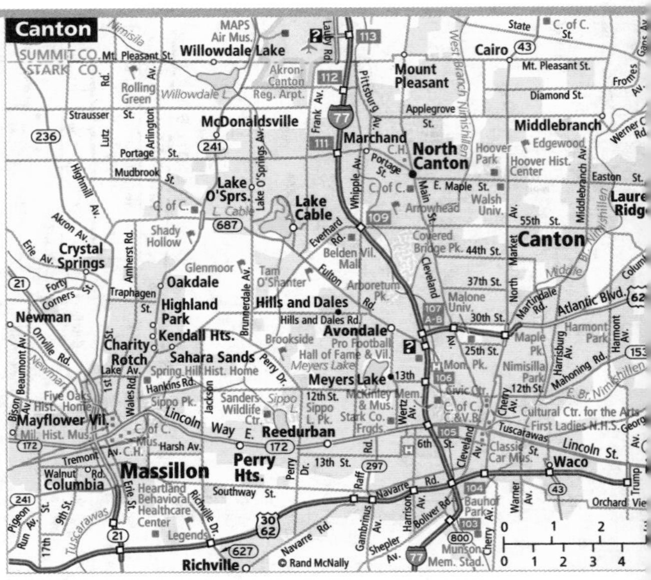

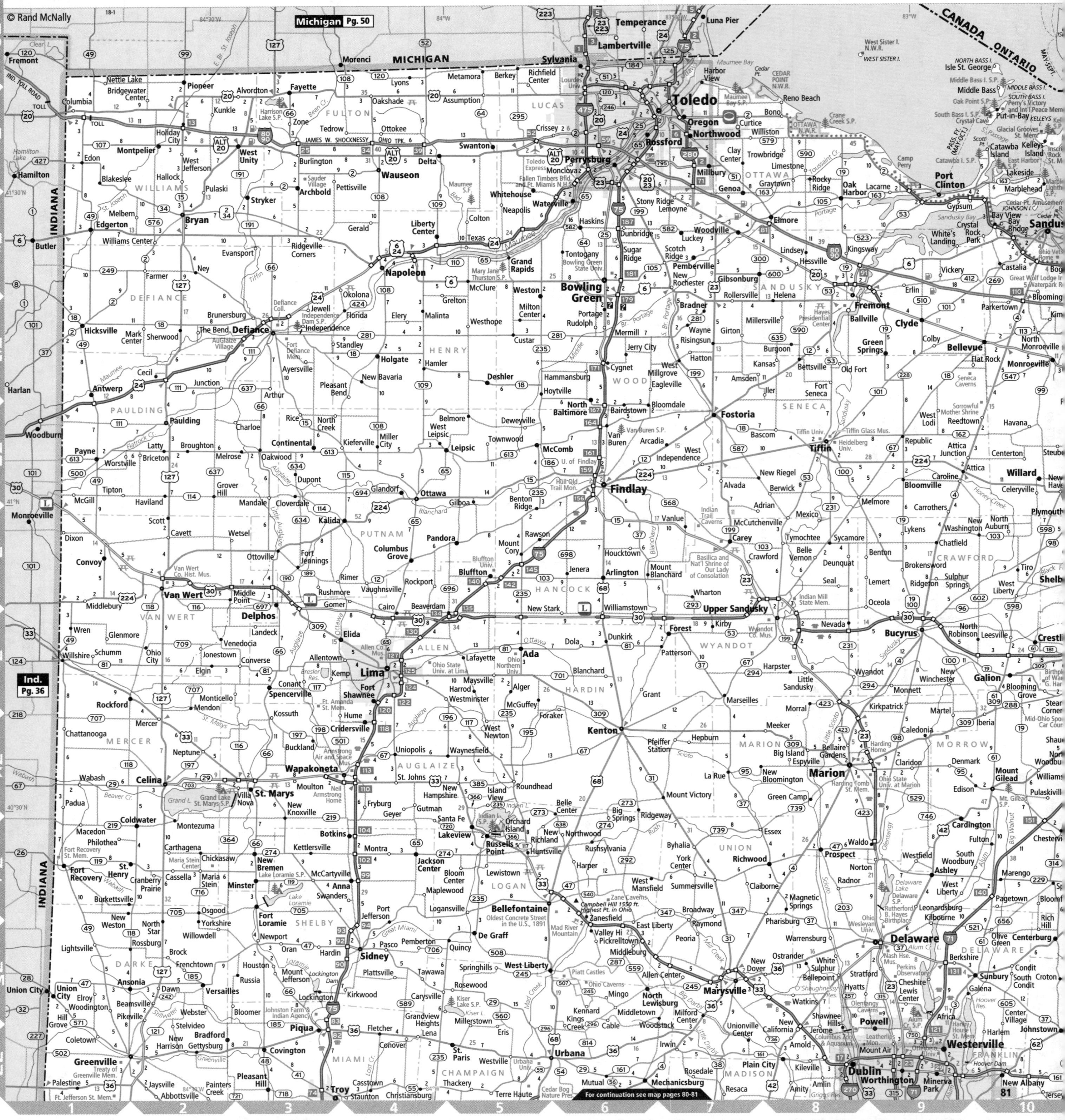

uyahoga Valley Railroad

Mileages between cities

	Akron	Ashtabula	Canton	Cincinnati	Cleveland	Columbus	Coshocton	Findlay	Lima	Mansfield	New Philadelphia	Pittsburgh, PA	Sandusky	Steubenville	Toledo	Youngstown
Akron		81	20	232	39	124	80	132	154	62	47	107	85	82	133	48
Cleveland	39	58	58	248		142	102	121	156	80	85	131	62	124	111	72
Columbus	124	194	126	106	142		71	96	91	66	118	184	112	150	142	172
Defiance	180	214	185	169	157	135	177	51	44	123	190	274	98	246	57	214
Lima	154	216	156	124	156	91	134	34		94	162	261	96	217	77	202
Mansfield	62	132	64	172	80	66	62	72	94		67	170	53	124	99	110
Toledo	133	171	152	200	111	142	152	44	77	99	179	228	58	221		169
Youngstown	48	57	57	279	72	172	117	180	202	110	84	67	122	66	169	

Mileages © Rand McNally

Total mileages through Ohio

71: 248 miles
80: 237 miles
75: 211 miles
90: 245 miles

More mileages at randmcnally.com/MC

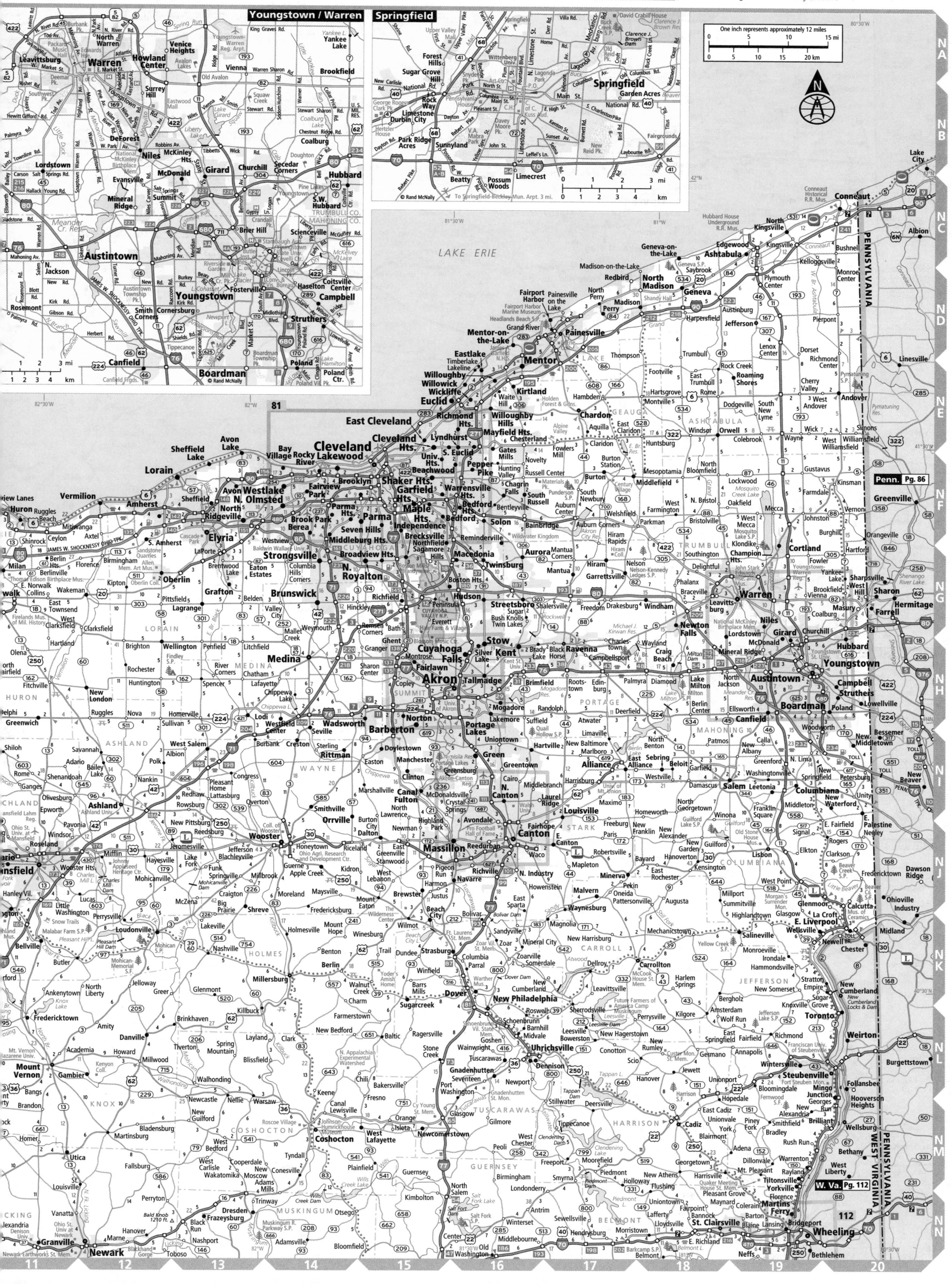

Nickname: The Buckeye State
Capital: Columbus, SB-9
Land area: 40,861 sq. mi. (rank: 35th)
Population: 11,536,504 (rank: 7th)
Largest city: Columbus, 787,033, SB-9

Index of places Pg. 133

Travel planning & on-the-road resources

Tourism Information
Tourism Ohio:
(800) 282-5393; www.discoverohio.com

Toll Road Information
Ohio Turnpike and Infrastructure Commission
(E-ZPass): (888) 876-7453, (440) 234-2081;
www.ohioturnpike.org

Road Conditions & Construction
(614) 466-7170;
www.dot.state.oh.us, www.buckeyetraffic.org;
Cincinnati metro area: 511;
www.ohgo.com/dashboard/cincinnati
Ohio Turnpike: (440) 234-2030, (440) 234-2081;
www.ohioturnpike.org

Determining distances along roads
Highway distances (segments of one mile or less not shown):
Cumulative miles (red): the distance between red arrows
Intermediate miles (black): the distance between intersections & places
Interchanges and exit numbers
For most states, the mileage between interchanges may be determined by subtracting one number from the other.

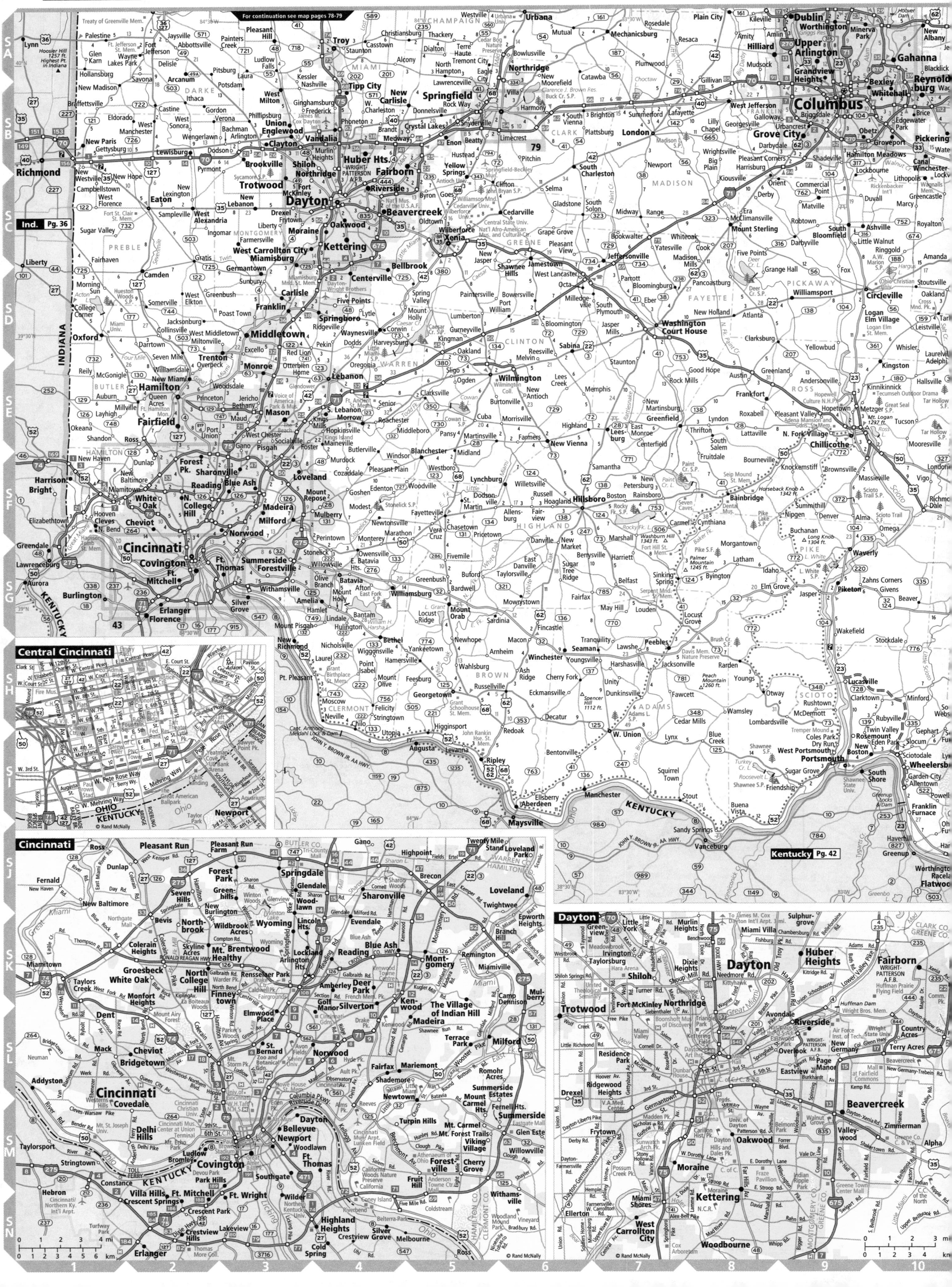

Mileages between cities	Athens	Cambridge	Chillicothe	Cincinnati	Cleveland	Columbus	Dayton	Gallipolis	Huntington, WV	Lancaster	Marietta	Maysville, KY	Portsmouth	Wheeling, WV	Wilmington	Zanesville
Cincinnati	160	183	106		248	106	50	153	148	133	210	61	110	230	51	158
Columbus	74	79	47	106	142		71	106	137	30	124	112	91	126	62	55
Dayton	134	149	77	50	212	71		137	168	101	195	108	122	197	34	126
Gallipolis	42	114	60	153	235	106	137		39	86	66	111	55	162	112	94
Marietta	44	48	104	210	164	124	195	66	106	82		165	128	90	156	69
Portsmouth	81	162	44	110	233	91	122	55	46	80	128	52		210	79	138
Springfield	118	123	69	77	185	45	27	129	160	74	168	102	114	171	38	99
Zanesville	52	24	94	158	145	55	126	94	134	45	69	164	138	72	114	

Total mileages through Ohio

- 70: 226 miles
- 75: 211 miles
- 71: 248 miles
- 77: 160 miles

More mileages at randmcnally.com/MC

Oklahoma

Nickname: The Sooner State
Capital: Oklahoma City, F-13
Land area: 68,595 sq. mi. (rank: 19th)
Population: 3,751,351 (rank: 28th)
Largest city: Oklahoma City, 579,999, F-13

Index of places Pg. 134

Travel planning & on-the-road resources

Tourism Information
Oklahoma Tourism & Recreation Department: (800) 652-6552; www.travelok.com

Road Conditions & Construction
(844) 465-4997; www.okroads.org, www.okladot.state.ok.us

Toll Road Information
Oklahoma Turnpike Authority (*PIKEPASS*): (405) 425-3600; www.pikepass.com

Determining distances along roads

Highway distances (segments of one mile or less not shown):
Cumulative miles (red): the distance between red arrows
Intermediate miles (black): the distance between intersections & plac

Interchanges and exit numbers
For most states, the mileage between interchanges may be determine by subtracting one number from the other.

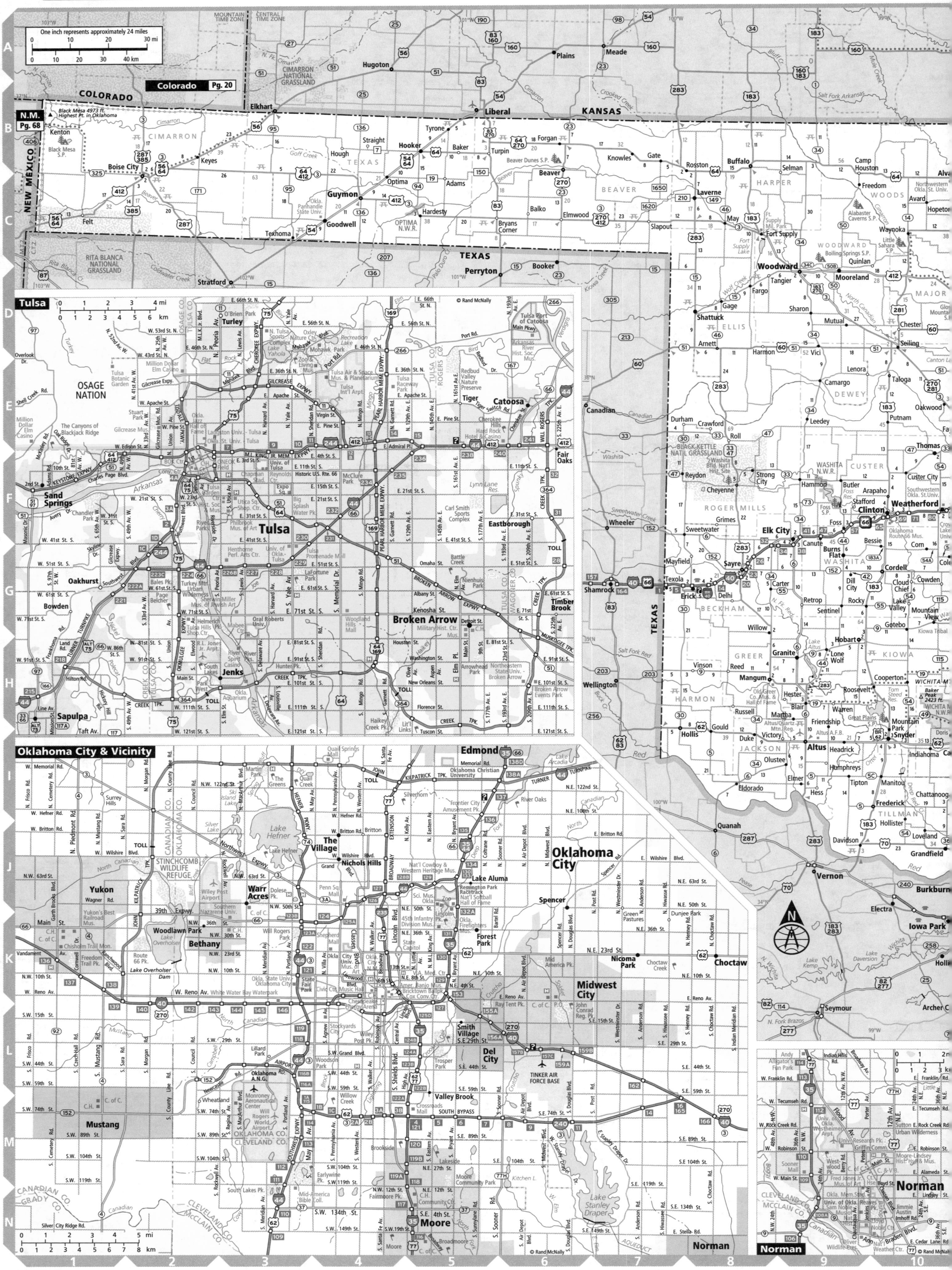

Mileages between cities	Ardmore	Bartlesville	Dallas, TX	Elk City	Enid	Ft. Smith, AR	Guymon	Joplin, MO	Lawton	McAlester	Muskogee	Oklahoma City	Ponca City	Tulsa	Wichita Falls, TX	Woodward
Ardmore		246	109	208	195	223	360	312	99	116	180	97	200	201	86	236
Elk City	208	260	303		148	292	184	327	108	240	249	112	216	215	143	77
Enid	195	134	302	148		232	211	227	142	204	164	99	67	114	196	87
Guymon	360	344	459	184	211	443		438	294	391	375	263	278	326	317	124
Idabel	149	248	171	352	316	136	504	295	245	116	180	240	293	203	238	380
Muskogee	180	91	236	249	164	70	375	117	218	65		137	142	50	272	251
Oklahoma City	97	149	204	112	99	180	263	216	86	128	137		105	104	140	139
Tulsa	201	45	258	215	114	118	326	113	191	91	50	104	91		244	202

Total mileages through Oklahoma

- 35: 236 miles
- 40: 331 miles
- 44: 329 miles
- 75: 227 miles

More mileages at randmcnally.com/MC

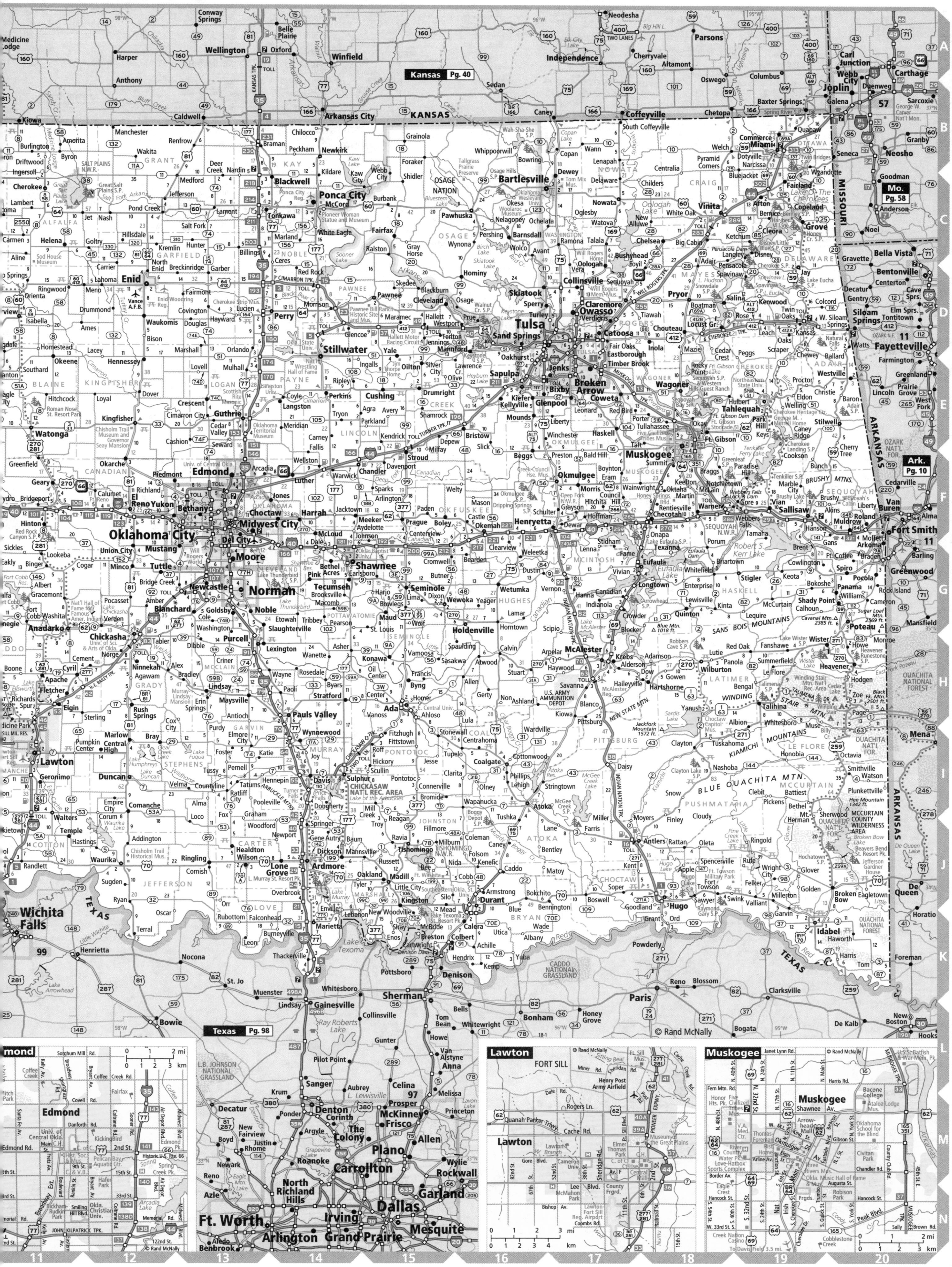

Oregon

Nickname: The Beaver State
Capital: Salem, E-4
Land area: 95,988 sq. mi. (rank: 10th)
Population: 3,831,074 (rank: 27th)
Largest city: Portland, 583,776, C-5

Index of places Pg. 134

Travel planning & on-the-road resources

Tourism Information
Travel Oregon: (800) 547-7842; www.traveloregon.com

Road Conditions & Construction
511, (800) 977-6368, (888) 275-6368; www.oregon.gov/odot, www.tripcheck.com

Toll Bridge Information
Bridge of the Gods (Cascade Locks): (541) 374-8619; portofcascadelocks.org/bridge-of-the-gods/
Hood River Bridge (*BreezeBy*): (541) 386-1645; www.portofhoodriver.com/bridge/index.php

Determining distances along roads

Highway distances (segments of one mile or less not shown):
Cumulative miles (red): the distance between red arrows
Intermediate miles (black): the distance between intersections & plac

Interchanges and exit numbers
For most states, the mileage between interchanges may be determin
by subtracting one number from the other.

Mileages between cities	Astoria	Bend	Brookings	Burns	Coos Bay	Crater Lake N.P.	Eugene	Government Camp	John Day	Lakeview	Medford	Ontario	Pendleton	Portland	Salem	The Dalles
Bend	250		287	130	228	107	115	106	151	175	172	260	242	161	131	129
Corvallis	166	127	280	257	132	187	47	126	260	284	210	387	290	82	37	165
Eugene	193	115	234	245	109	142		154	249	241	166	375	318	110	66	193
McDermitt, NV	525	277	525	147	505	356	392	380	218	222	400	187	354	436	408	405
Medford	356	172	125	305	169	74	166	317	328	171		432	481	273	228	356
Ontario	464	260	547	130	488	367	375	354	131	269	432		167	374	420	291
Pendleton	298	242	550	196	428	349	318	188	126	335	481	167		208	254	125
Portland	96	161	342	281	220	250	110	55	265	336	273	374	208		47	83

Total mileages through Oregon

5: 308 miles; 84: 375 miles; 82: 11 miles; 101: 348 miles

More mileages at randmcnally.com/MC

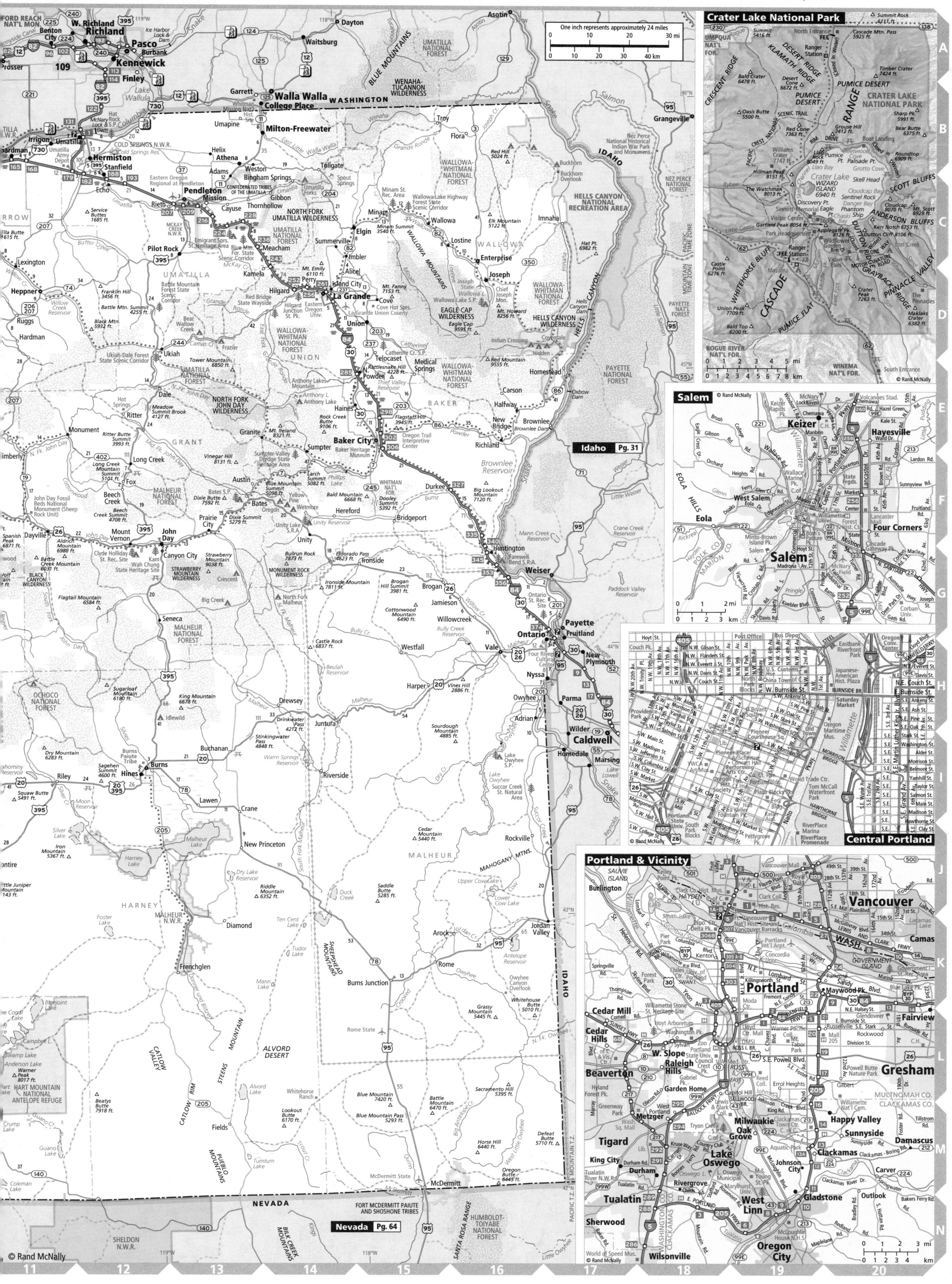

Nickname: The Keystone State
Capital: Harrisburg, EN-4
Land area: 44,743 sq. mi. (rank: 32nd)
Population: 12,702,379 (rank: 6th)
Largest city: Philadelphia, 1,526,006, EP-12

Index of places Pg. 134

Travel planning & on-the-road resources

Tourism Information
Tourism Office: (800) 847-4872; www.visitpa.com

Road Conditions & Construction
511, (888) 783-6783; www.511pa.com; www.dot.state.pa.us

Toll Road Information
Pennsylvania Turnpike Commission *(E-ZPass)*: (800) 331-3414; www.paturnpike.com

Determining distances along roads

Highway distances (segments of one mile or less not shown):
Cumulative miles (red): the distance between red arrows
Intermediate miles (black): the distance between intersections & pla

Interchanges and exit numbers
For most states, the mileage between interchanges may be determi by subtracting one number from the other.

Brady's Bend, East Brady

Mileages between cities

	Altoona	Chambersburg	Cumberland, MD	Du Bois	Erie	Galeton	Harrisburg	Johnstown	Kittanning	Meadville	New Castle	Philadelphia	Pittsburgh	State College	Uniontown	Warren
Altoona		90	66	71	202	135	134	46	79	165	127	234	96	41	112	130
Chambersburg	90		87	153	282	215	54	94	160	246	206	157	160	101	149	218
Erie	202	282	232	148		159	297	177	123	41	88	419	127	208	184	66
Johnstown	46	94	70	77	177	179	137		53	141	102	238	67	85	80	135
New Castle	127	206	156	110	88	197	250	102	48	52		350	52	171	108	120
Pittsburgh	96	160	111	101	127	200	203	67	42	91	52	304		135	51	148
State College	41	101	106	61	208	100	87	85	120	173	171	193	135		152	119
Williamsport	100	132	166	110	257	72	83	146	168	220	219	176	196	63	212	171

Total mileages through Pennsylvania

- 70: 168 miles
- 79: 183 miles
- 80: 311 miles
- 90: 46 miles

More mileages at randmcnally.com/MC

Md. Pg. 46
West Virginia Pg. 112

Nickname: The Keystone State
Capital: Harrisburg, EN-4
Land area: 44,743 sq. mi. (rank: 32nd)
Population: 12,702,379 (rank: 6th)
Largest city: Philadelphia, 1,526,006, EP-12

Index of places Pg. 134

Travel planning & on-the-road resources

Tourism Information
Tourism Office: (800) 847-4872; www.visitpa.com

Road Conditions & Construction
511, (888) 783-6783; www.511pa.com; www.dot.state.pa.us

Toll Road Information
Pennsylvania Turnpike Commission (***E-ZPass***): (800) 331-3414; www.paturnpike.com

Determining distances along roads

Highway distances (segments of one mile or less not shown):
Cumulative miles (red): the distance between red arrows
Intermediate miles (black): the distance between intersections & plac

Interchanges and exit numbers
For most states, the mileage between interchanges may be determin
by subtracting one number from the other.

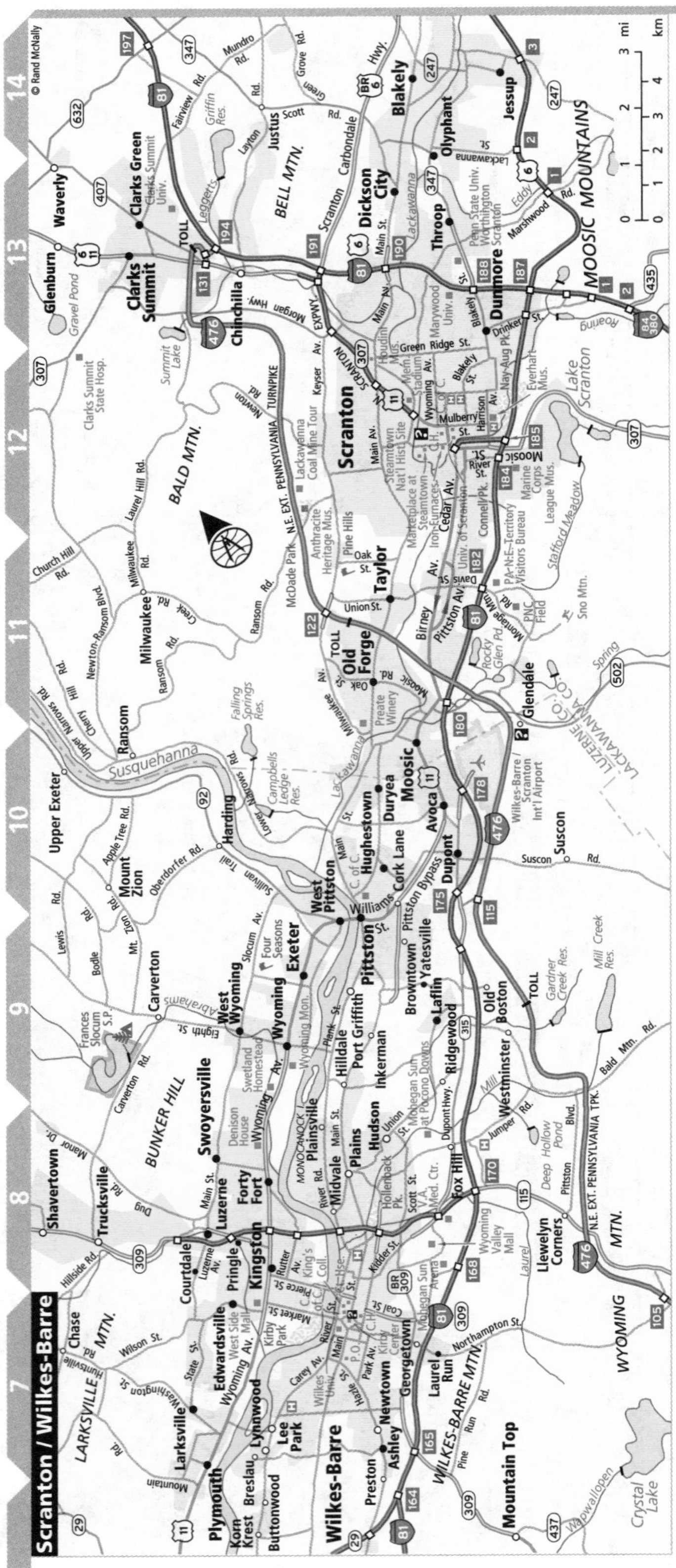

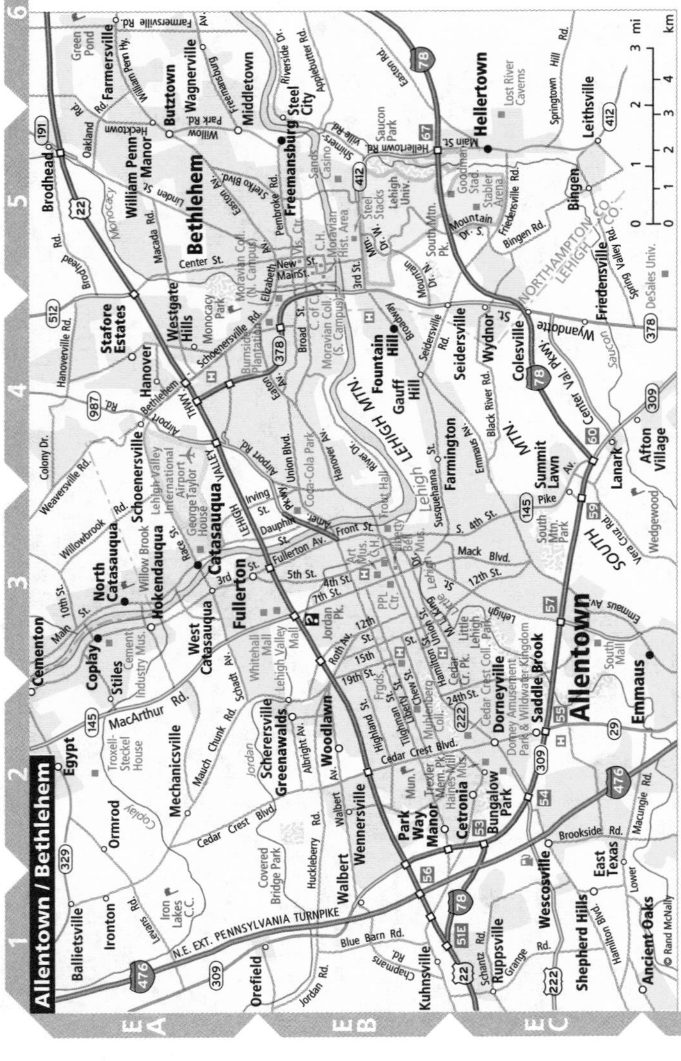

...erry rides on the Delaware River

Mileages between cities

	Allentown	Gettysburg	Harrisburg	Lancaster	Mansfield	Philadelphia	Pittsburgh	Port Jervis, NY	Scranton	State College	Stroudsburg	Towanda	Trenton, NJ	Wilkes Barre	Williamsport	York
Allentown		121	81	67	177	62	282	81	74	175	40	126	75	60	127	92
Chambersburg	132	25	54	91	182	157	160	227	171	101	170	188	177	154	132	74
Harrisburg	81	38		39	133	107	203	176	120	87	119	139	127	104	83	26
Philadelphia	62	138	107	78	226		304	140	124	193	100	175	32	109	176	101
Reading	37	96	64	34	175	62	261	118	100	150	76	152	82	86	126	56
Scranton	74	160	120	132	102	124	279	59		150	46	64	137	16	101	146
State College	175	129	87	126	107	193	135	205	150		162	134	213	132	63	118
Williamsport	127	126	83	123	50	176	196	157	101	63	113	67	189	84		115

Total mileages through Pennsylvania

- 76: 350 miles
- 80: 311 miles
- 81: 232 miles
- 95: 51 miles

More mileages at randmcnally.com/MC

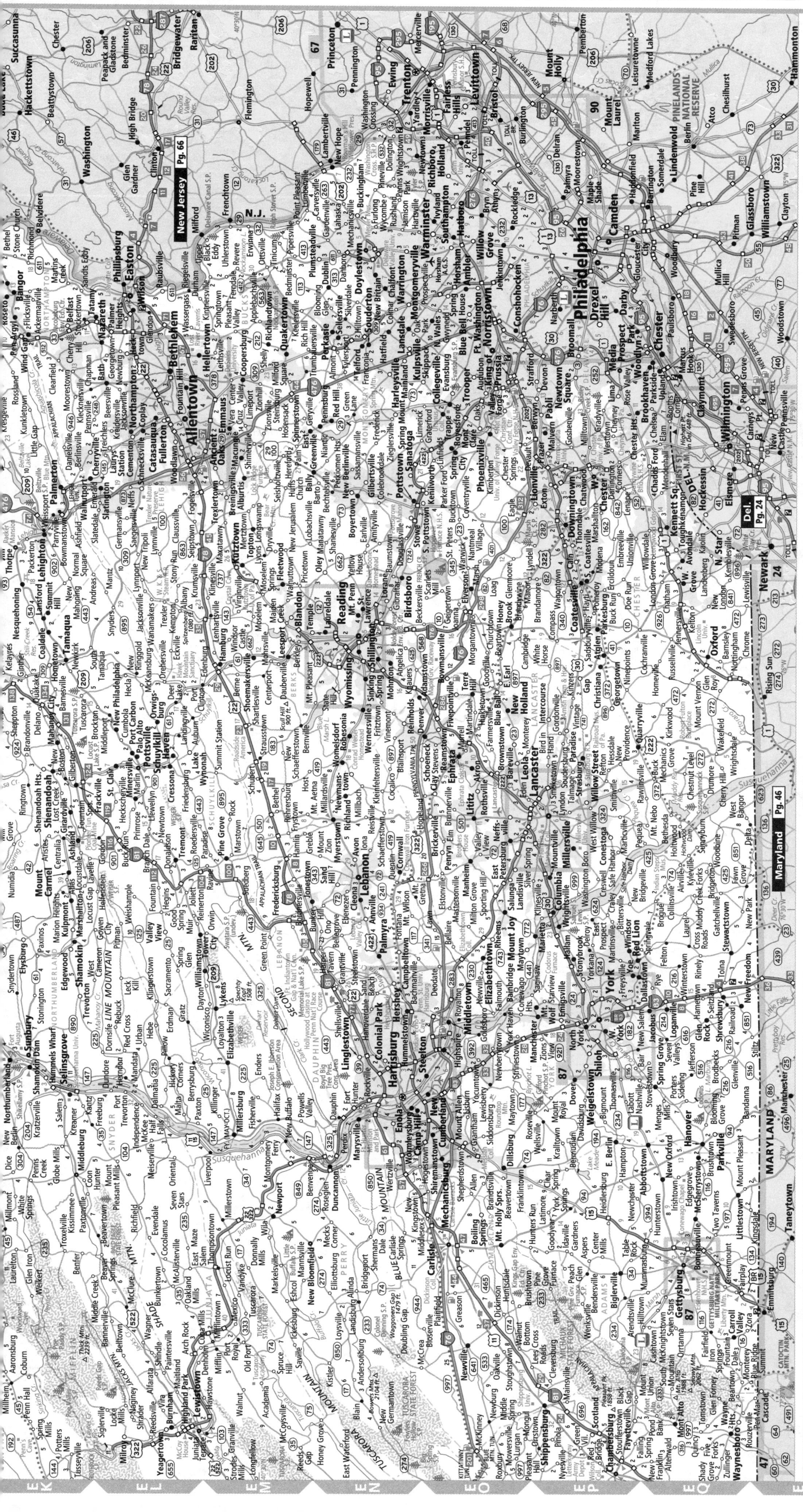

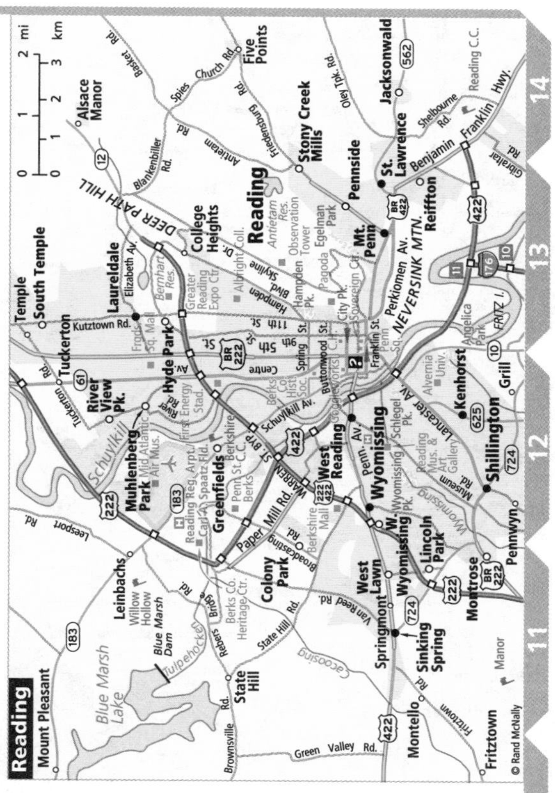

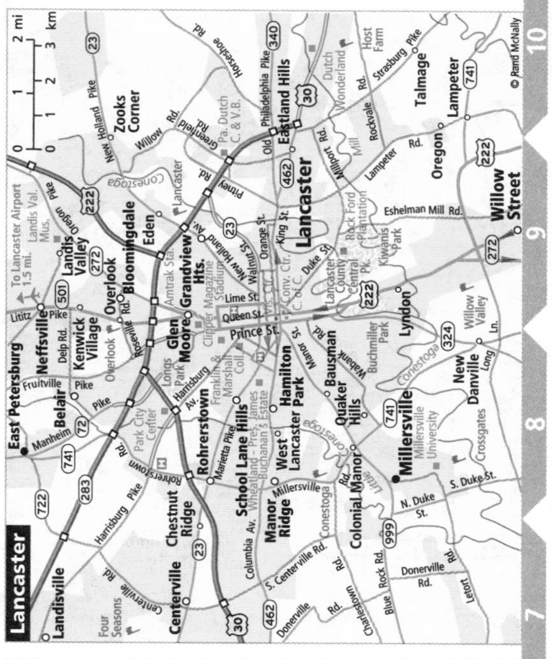

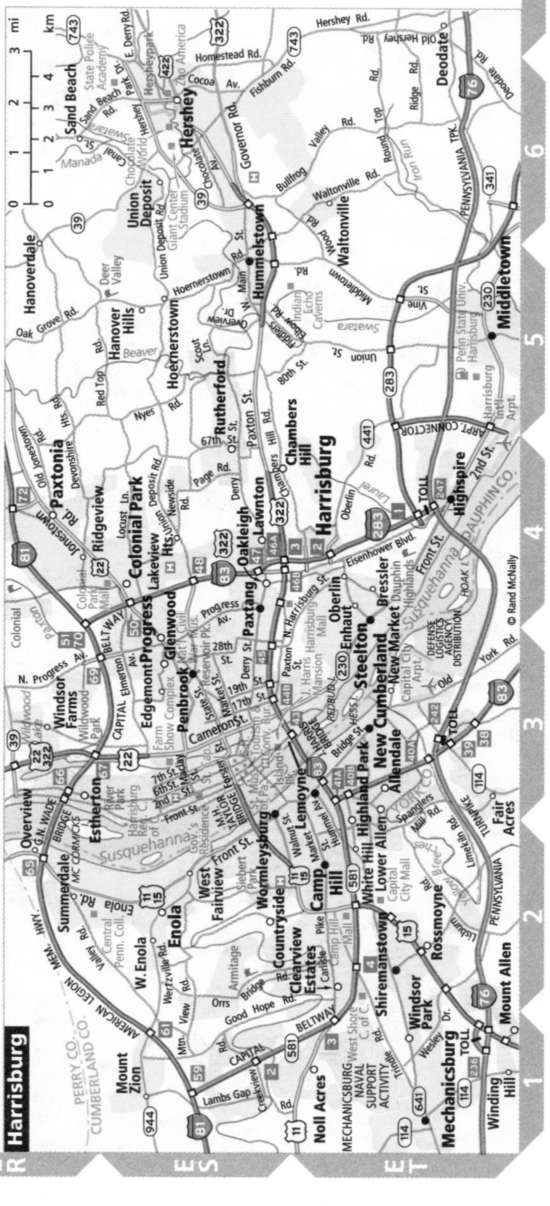

Sights to see

- Adventure Aquarium, Camden E-5
- The Andy Warhol Museum, Pittsburgh L-2
- Betsy Ross House, Philadelphia F-10
- Carnegie Science Center, Pittsburgh L-1
- Duquesne Incline, Pittsburgh M-1
- Franklin Institute Science Museum, Philadelphia F-6
- Independence Hall, Philadelphia G-9
- Liberty Bell, Philadelphia G-9
- National Constitution Center, Philadelphia F-9
- Philadelphia Museum of Art, Philadelphia E-4
- Point State Park, Pittsburgh M-1
- The Strip District, Pittsburgh L-3

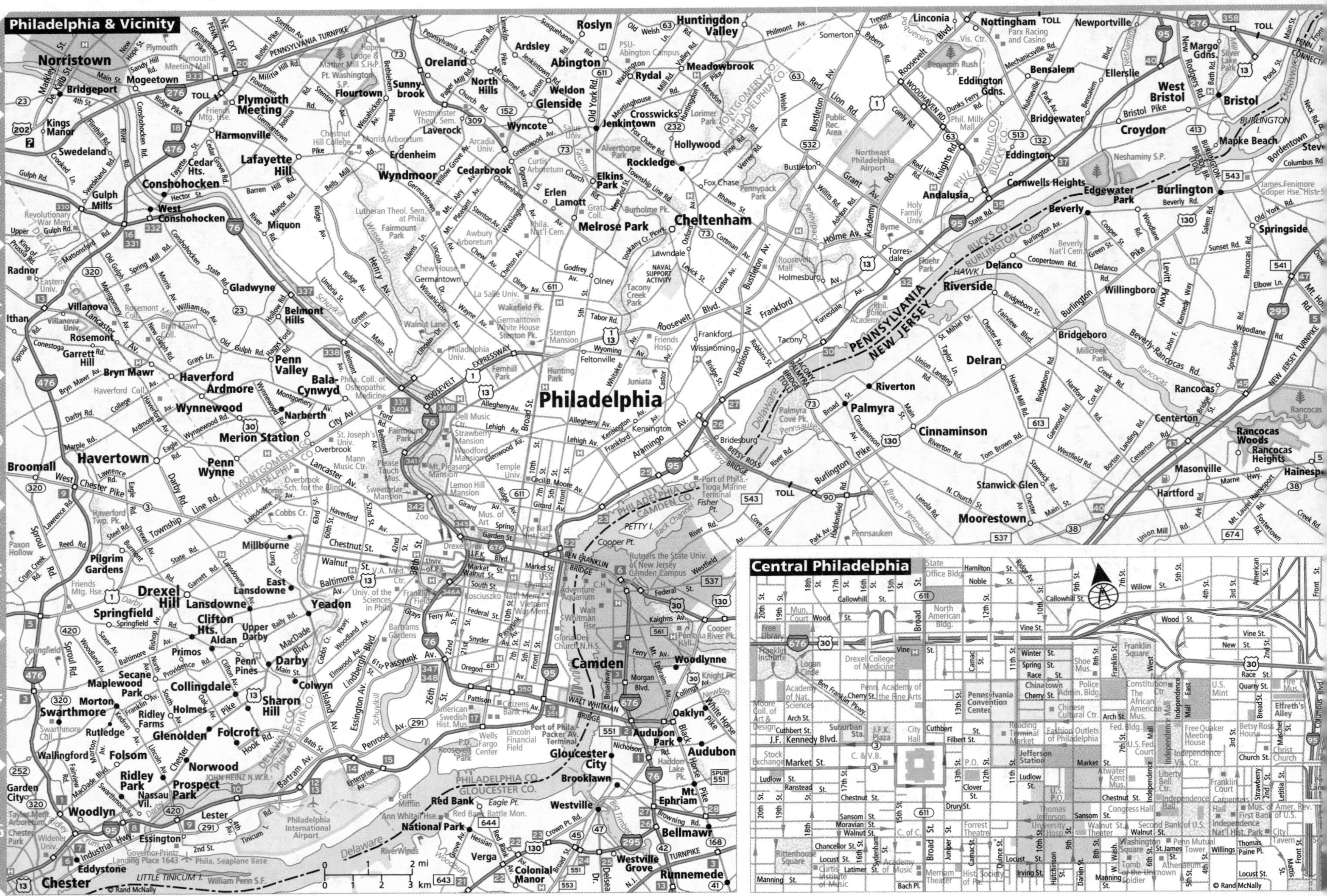

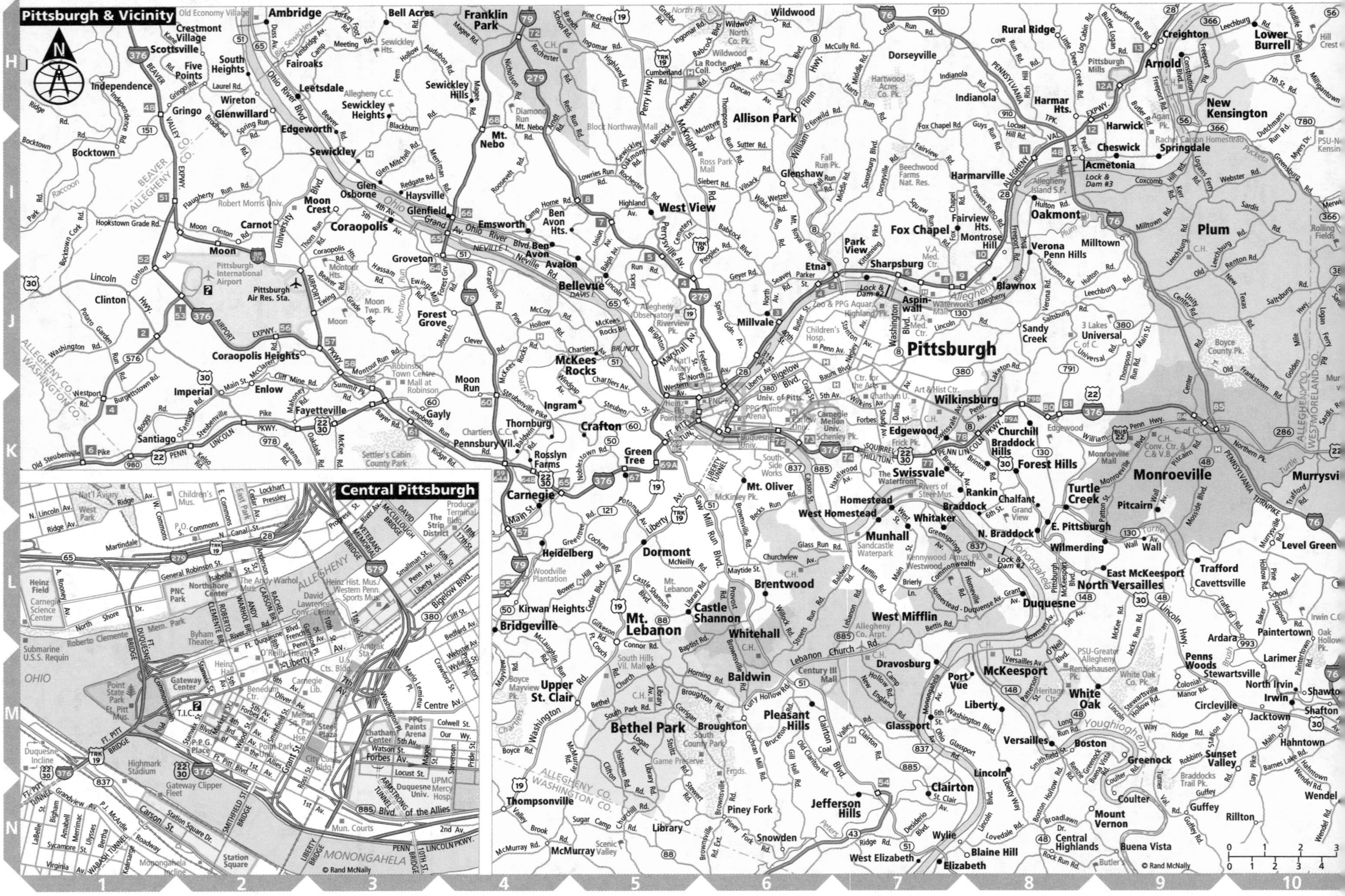

ravel planning & on-the-road resources

urism Information
ode Island Tourism Division:
401) 278-9100;
www.visitrhodeisland.com

Toll Bridge Info (*EZ-Pass*)
Rhode Island Turnpike & Bridge Authority:
(401) 423-0800;
www.ritba.org

ad Conditions & Construction
1, (888) 401-4511, (401) 222-2450;
ww.dot.ri.gov/travel

511

Determining Distances
9; 4 | 3 | 2 (segments of one mile or less not shown)
Cumulative miles (red): the distance between red arrows
Intermediate miles (black): the distance between intersections & places

Total mileages through Rhode Island
95: 42 miles
6: 31 miles
1: 60 miles
More mileages at randmcnally.com/MC

Mileages between cities

	Fall River, MA	Kingston	Newport	Providence	Warwick	Westerly	Woonsocket	Worcester, MA
Chepachet	35	41	45	19	23	54	13	37
Fall River, MA		35	20	16	25	58	31	56
Newport	20	16		33	26	39	47	72
Providence	16	29	33		10	42	14	40
Warwick	25	23	26	10		37	24	50
Westerly	58	23	39	42	37		56	82
Woonsocket	31	43	47	14	24	56		27
Worcester, MA	56	68	72	40	50	82	27	

Nickname: The Ocean State
Capital: Providence, D-6
Land area: 1,034 sq. mi. (rank: 50th)
Population: 1,052,567 (rank: 43rd)
Largest city: Providence, 178,042, D-6

Index of places Pg. 134

South Carolina

Nickname: The Palmetto State
Capital: Columbia, D-7
Land area: 30,061 sq. mi. (rank: 40th)
Population: 4,625,364 (rank: 24th)
Largest city: Columbia, 129,272, D-7

Index of places Pg. 134

Mileages between cities

	Anderson	Augusta, GA	Charleston	Charlotte, NC	Columbia	Hilton Head I.	Myrtle Beach	Spartanburg
Augusta, GA	92		175	160	72	151	216	120
Charleston	238	175		207	112	104	95	201
Charlotte, NC	128	160	207		93	253	176	72
Columbia	117	72	112	93		158	148	93
Florence	206	148	130	104	81	177	67	169
Myrtle Beach	273	216	95	176	148	200		237
Savannah, GA	282	134	106	251	156	34	202	246
Spartanburg	60	120	201	72	93	247	237	

Total mileages through South Carolina

20: 142 miles
85: 106 miles
26: 221 miles
95: 199 miles

More mileages at randmcnally.com/MC

Travel planning & on-the-road resources

Tourism Information

South Carolina Department of Parks, Recreation & Tourism:
(803) 734-1700; www.discoversouthcarolina.com

Road Conditions & Construction

511,
(877) 511-4672,
(855) 467-2368;
www.511sc.org, www.dot.state.sc.us

Toll Road Information *(all use Palmetto Pass)*

Cross Island Pkwy. (Hilton Head I.):
(843) 342-6718; www.crossislandparkway.o
Southern Connector (Greenville Co.):
(864) 527-2143; www.southernconnector.c

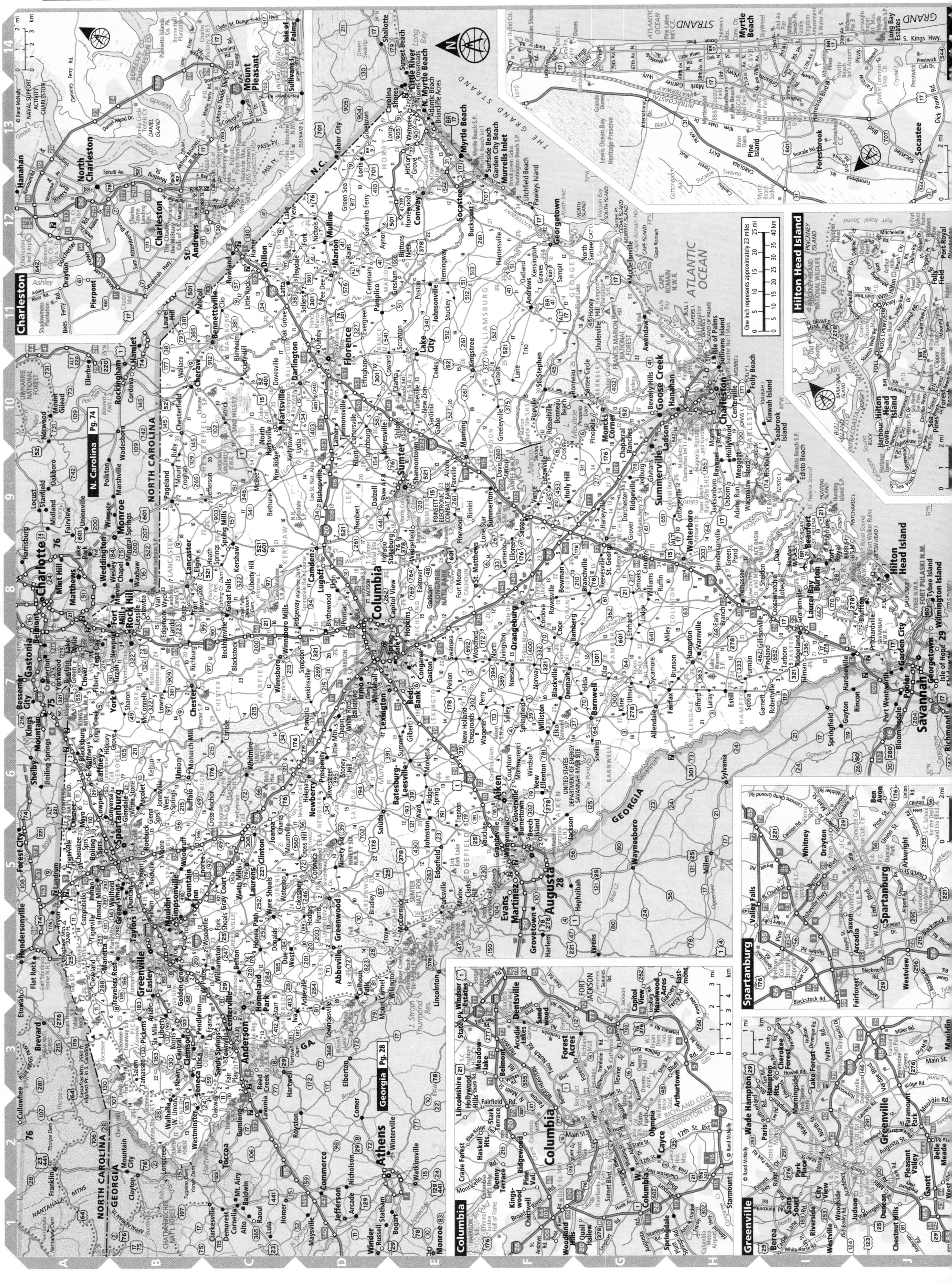

South Dakota

Nickname: The Mount Rushmore State
Capital: Pierre, D-7
Land area: 75,811 sq. mi. (rank: 16th)
Population: 814,180 (rank: 46th)
Largest city: Sioux Falls, 153,888, F-13

Index of places Pg. 134

ravel planning & on-the-road resources

rism Information
th Dakota Department of Tourism: (800) 732-5682;
ww.travelsd.com, www.travelsouthdakota.com

d Conditions & Construction
511, (866) 697-3511;
w.sddot.com, www.safetravelusa.com/sd

Road Information
toll roads

Determining Distances
(segments of one mile or less not shown)

Cumulative miles (red): the distance between red arrows
Intermediate miles (black): the distance between intersections & places

Total mileages through South Dakota

29: 253 miles
90: 413 miles
12: 317 miles
83: 242 miles

More mileages at randmcnally.com/MC

Mileages between cities

	Aberdeen	Mobridge	Pierre	Pine Ridge	Rapid City	Sioux Falls	Watertown	Yankton
Aberdeen		100	160	360	333	203	96	236
Belle Fourche	312	212	206	172	60	403	362	421
Mobridge	100		108	308	243	303	196	332
Pierre	160	108		200	173	224	188	242
Rapid City	333	243	173	111		347	403	365
Sioux City, IA	285	384	305	358	428	85	184	63
Sioux Falls	203	303	224	356	347		103	81
Watertown	96	196	188	415	403	103		155

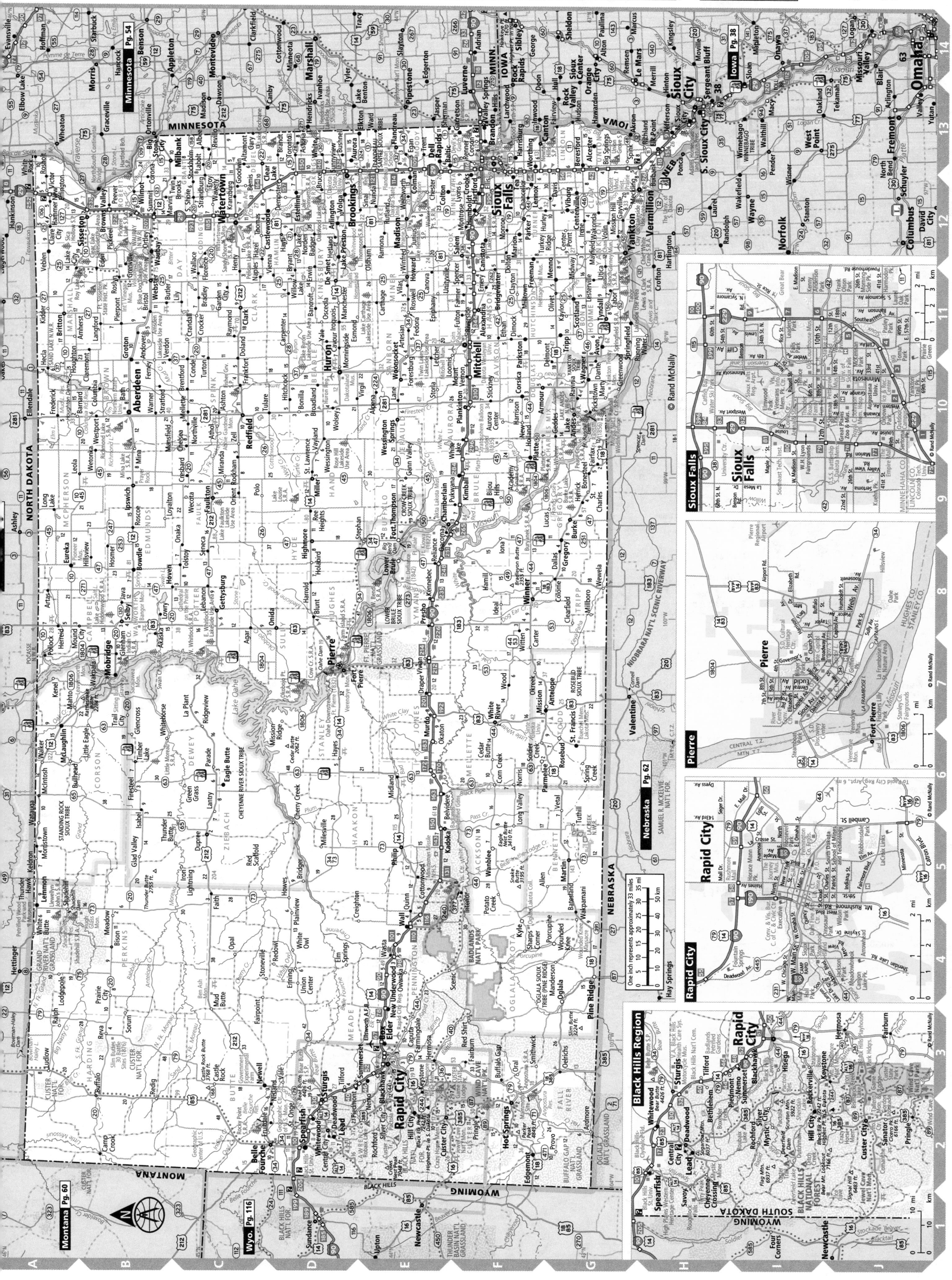

Nickname: The Volunteer State
Capital: Nashville, C-11
Land area: 41,235 sq. mi. (rank: 34th)
Population: 6,346,105 (rank: 17th)
Largest city: Memphis, 646,889, G-2

Index of places Pg. 134

Travel planning & on-the-road resources

Tourism Information
Tennessee Department of Tourist Development: (615) 741-2159; www.tnvacation.com

Road Conditions & Construction
511, (877) 244-0065; www.tn511.com, www.tdot.state.tn.us

Toll Road Information
No toll roads

Determining distances along roads

Highway distances (segments of one mile or less not shown):
Cumulative miles (red): the distance between red arrows
Intermediate miles (black): the distance between intersections & places

Interchanges and exit numbers
For most states, the mileage between interchanges may be determined by subtracting one number from the other.

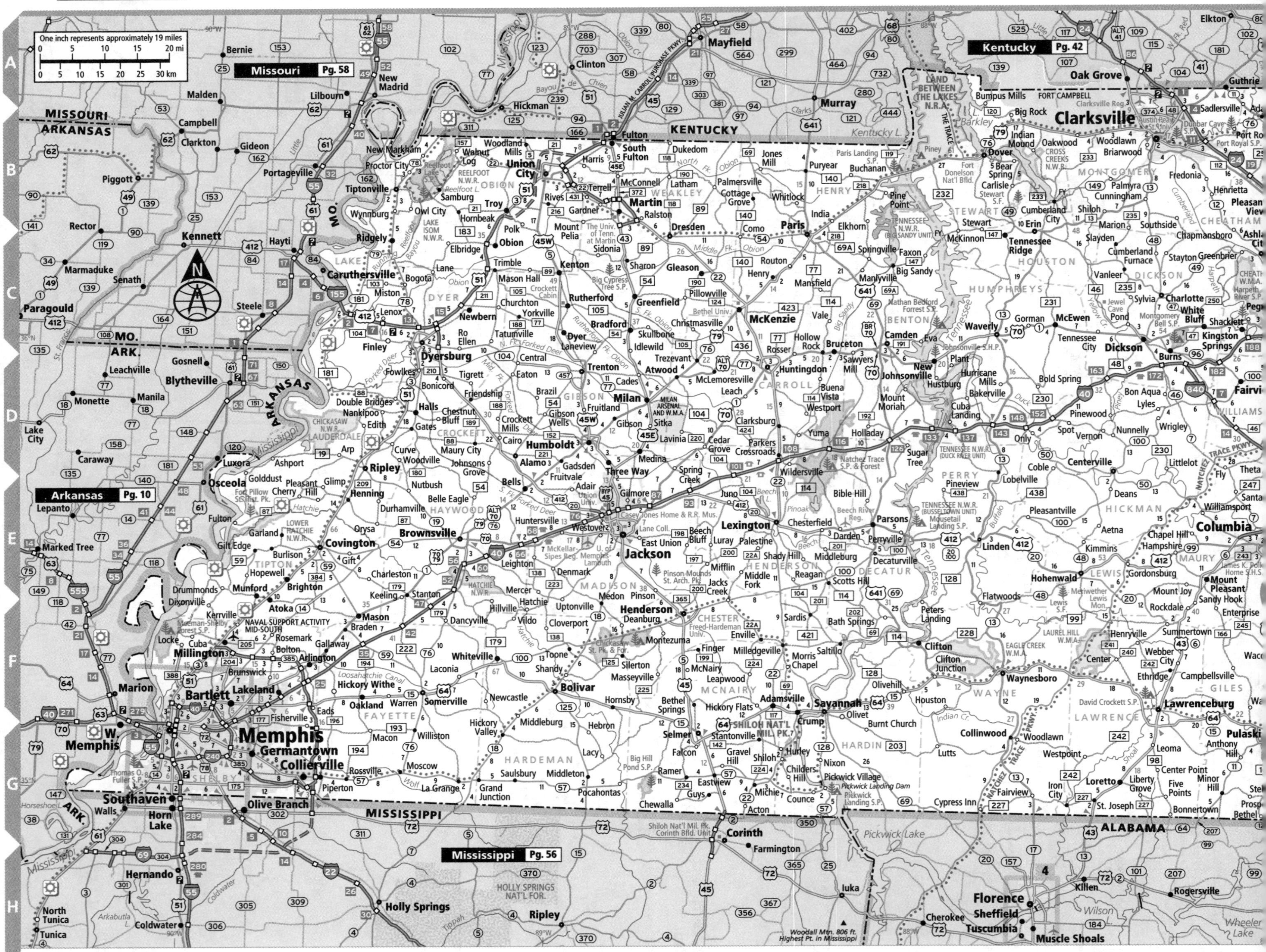

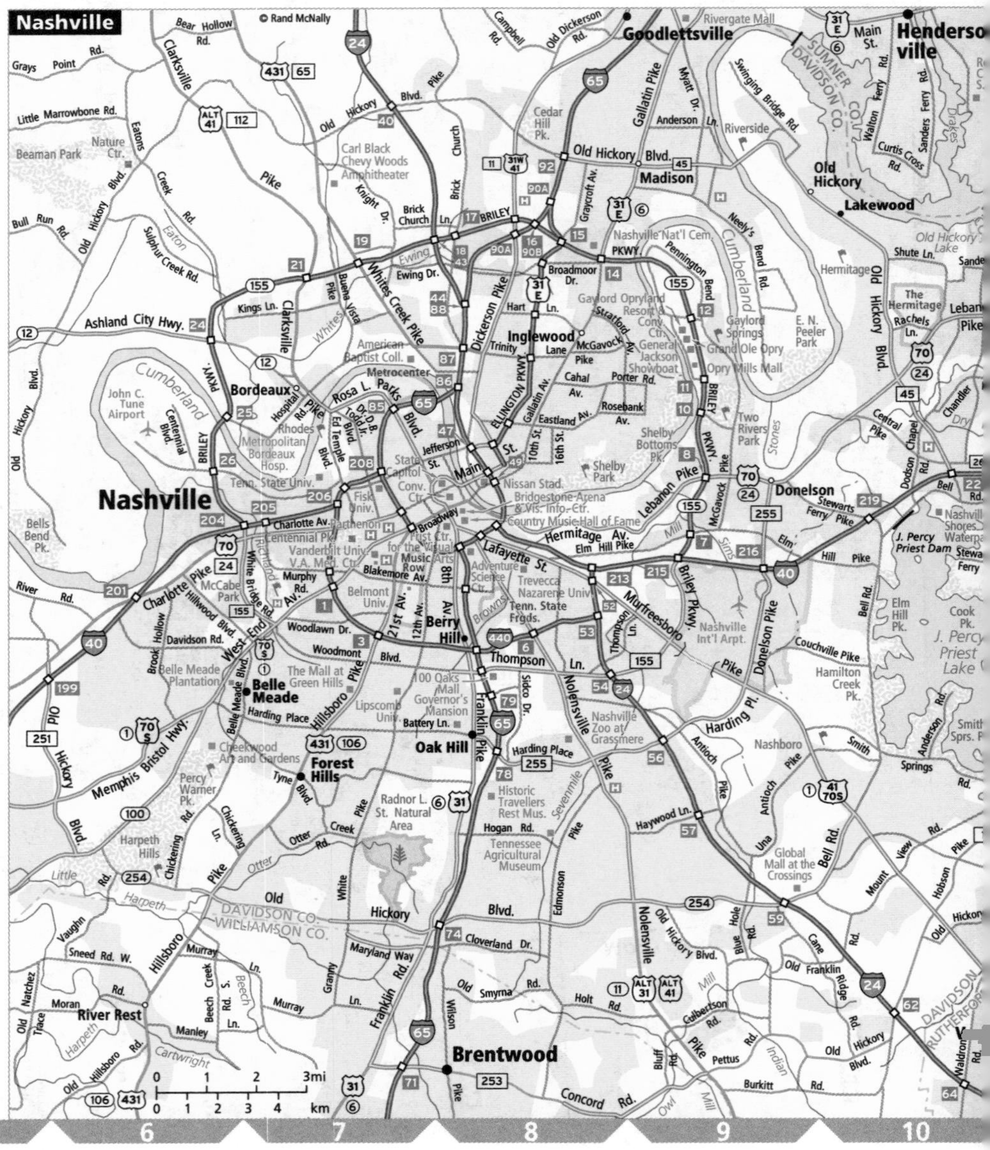

Mileages between cities	Atlanta, GA	Bristol	Chattanooga	Clarksville	Cookeville	Dyersburg	Fayetteville	Gatlinburg	Jackson	Johnson City	Knoxville	Memphis	Morristown	Nashville	Oak Ridge	Union City
Chattanooga	117	223		177	98	303	94	151	260	215	110	314	158	131	108	311
Clarksville	293	337	177		125	173	136	265	123	329	224	201	271	47	207	138
Dyersburg	418	463	303	173	252		229	392	47	455	351	76	398	172	334	34
Fayetteville	211	317	94	136	109	229		246	167	308	204	243	252	90	189	224
Johnson City	256	24	215	329	206	455	308	106	412		104	495	65	283	128	463
Knoxville	202	113	110	224	102	351	204	41	308	104		390	48	179	24	358
Memphis	380	502	314	201	291	76	243	431	87	495	390		437	212	373	113
Nashville	249	292	131	47	80	172	90	220	129	283	179	212	226		162	168

Mileages © Rand McNally

Total mileages through Tennessee

- 40: 455 miles
- 65: 121 miles
- 75: 161 miles
- 81: 76 miles

More mileages at randmcnally.com/MC

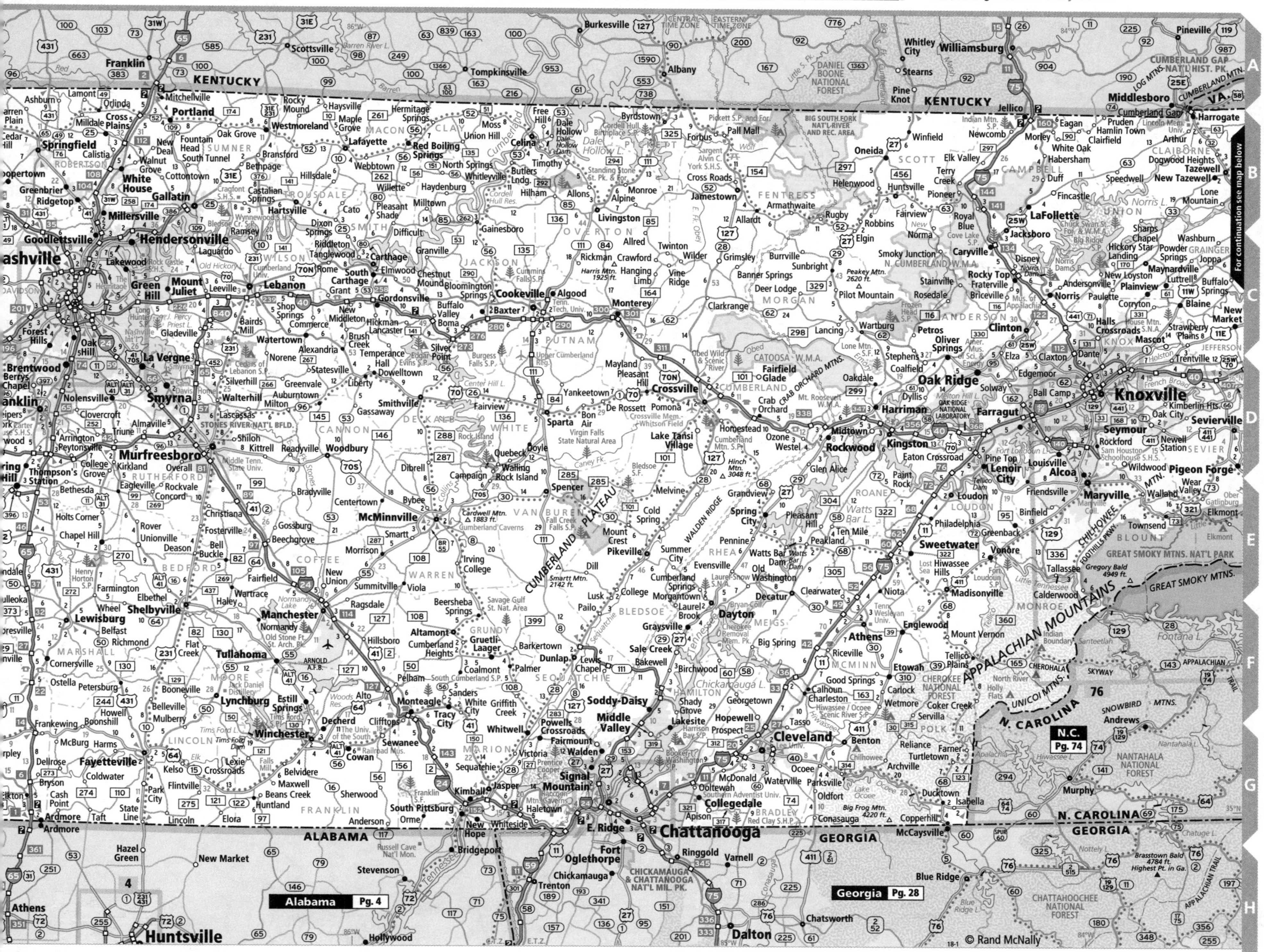

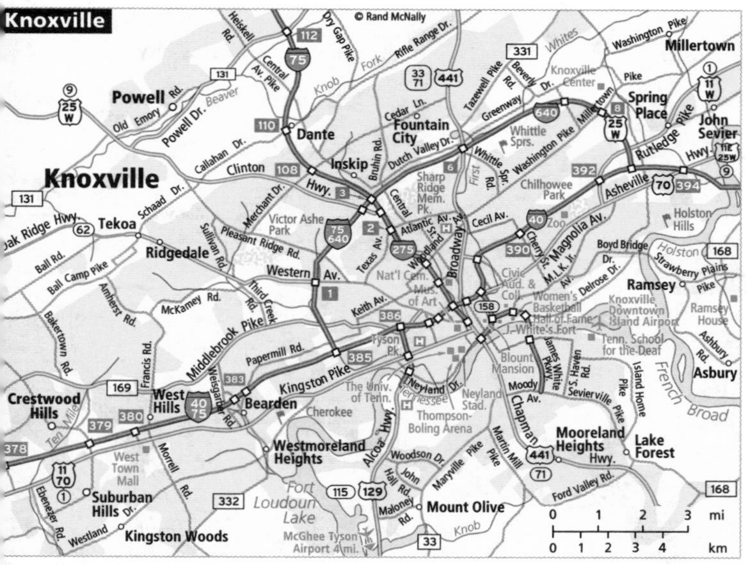

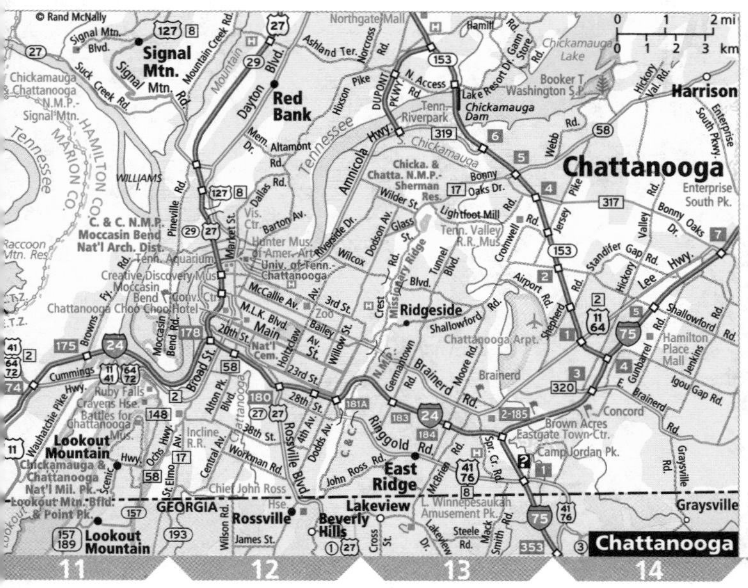

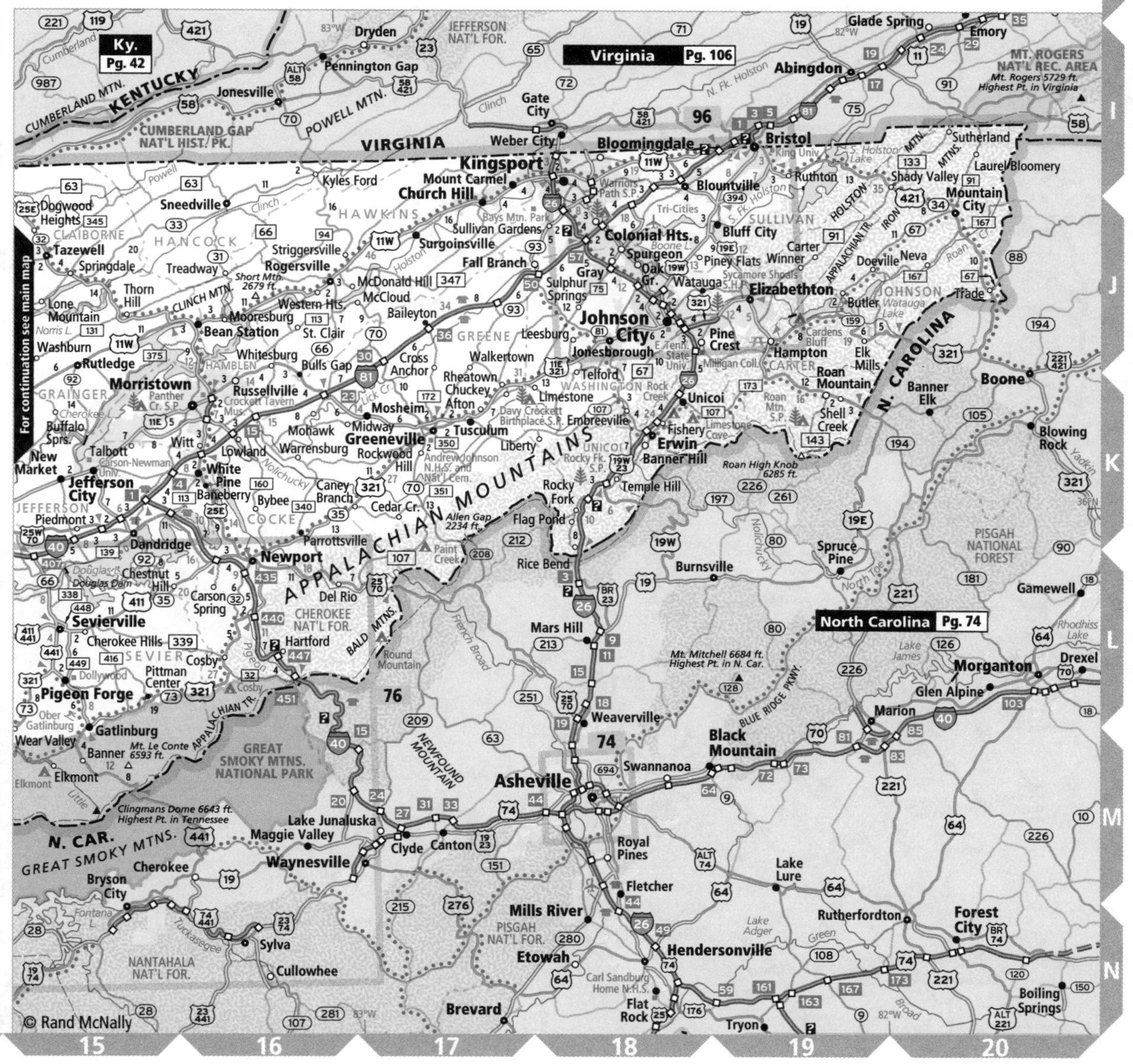

Sights to see

- Appalachian Caverns, Blountville K-3
- Battleship USS Texas, La Porte D-9
- Bayou Place, Houston K-8
- Bristol Caverns, Bristol J-6
- Bristol Motor Speedway, Bristol K-4
- Contemporary Arts Museum, Houston E-5
- Houston Fire Museum, Houston E-5
- Houston Zoo, Houston E-5
- Museum of Natural Science, Houston E-5
- Rocky Mount Museum, Piney Flats L-3
- Space Center Houston, Houston G-8
- Wortham Theatre Center, Houston K-8

Church Circle, Kingsport

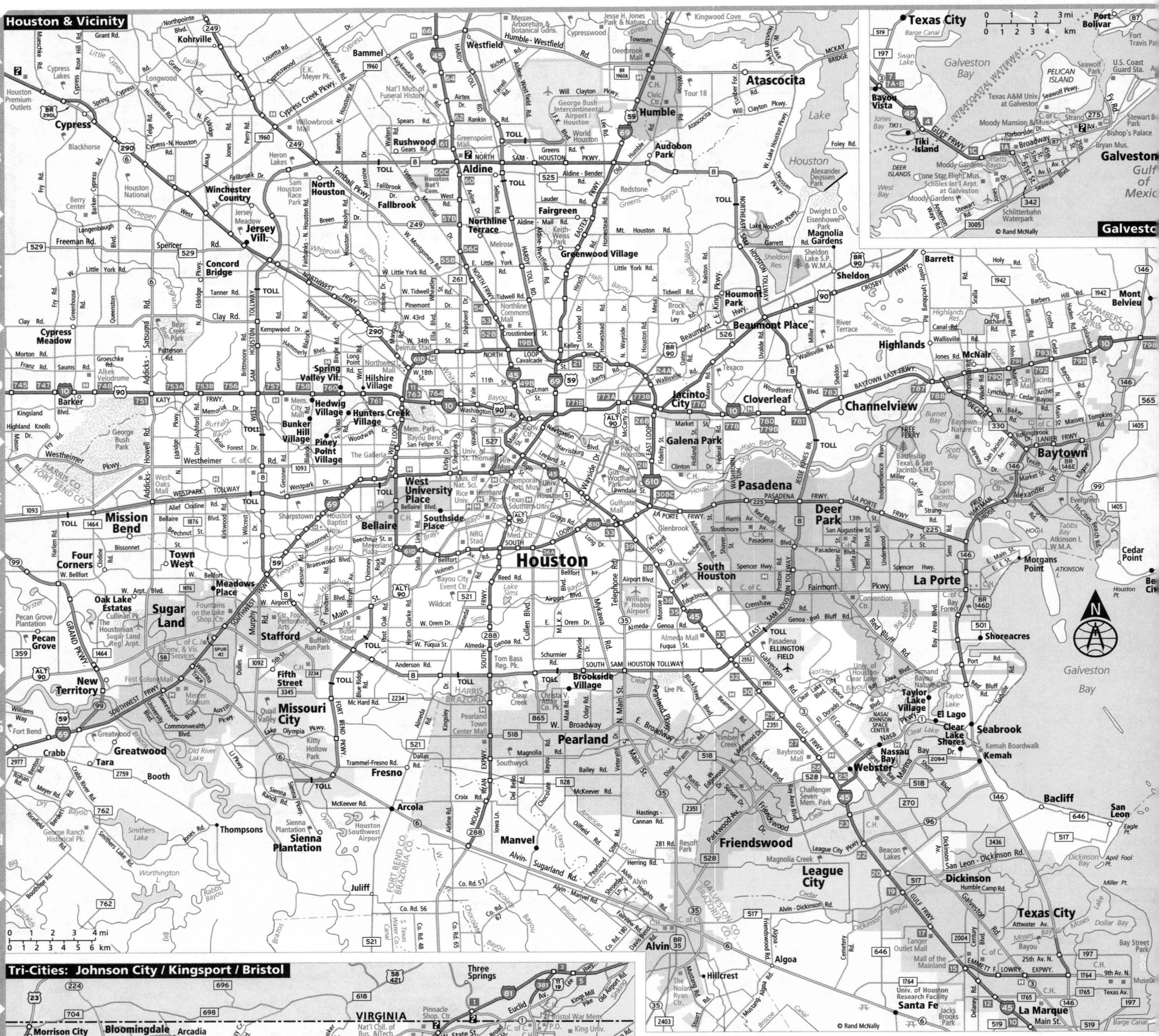

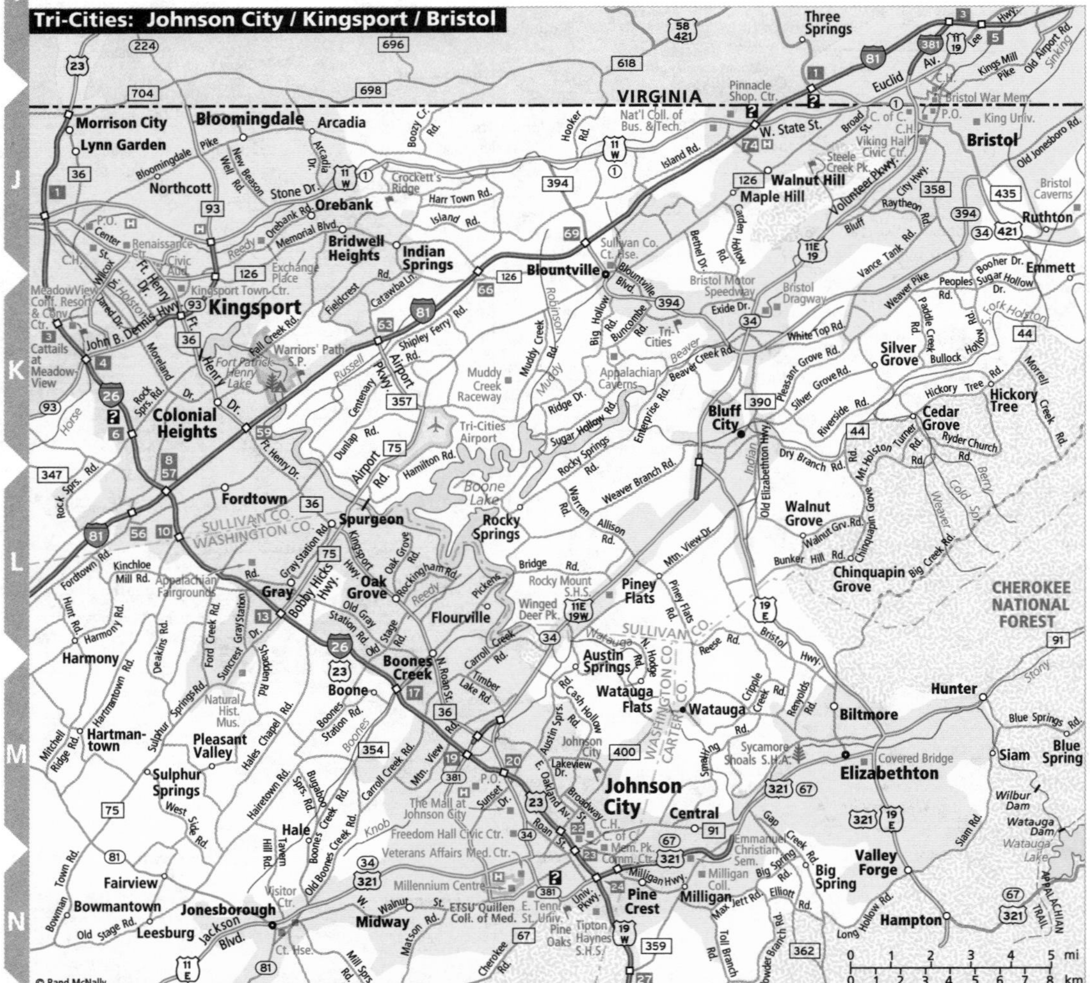

Sights to see

- Dallas Museum of Art, Dallas B-2
- Dallas Zoo, Dallas H-10
- Fair Park, Dallas G-11
- Fort Worth Zoo, Fort Worth H-4
- Louis Tussaud's Palace of Wax & Ripley's Believe It or Not!, Grand Prairie G-8
- Old City Park, Dallas C-3
- Six Flags over Texas, Arlington H-7
- The Sixth Floor Museum at Dealey Plaza, Dallas B-1
- Stockyards Historic District, Fort Worth G-4
- Sundance Square, Fort Worth E-1
- Texas Civil War Museum, Fort Worth G-2

Nickname: The Lone Star State
Capital: Austin, EK-5
Land area: 261,231 sq. mi. (rank: 2nd)
Population: 25,145,561 (rank: 2nd)
Largest city: Houston, 2,099,451, EL-10

Index of places Pg. 135

Travel planning & on-the-road resources

Tourism Information
Texas Tourism:
(800) 452-9292; www.traveltex.com

Road Conditions & Construction
(800) 452-9292, (512) 463-8588;
www.txdot.gov, www.drivetexas.org

Toll Road Information

(continued on p. 100)

Cameron County Reg. Mobility Auth. (TX 550) ***(TxTag)***: (956) 621-5571; www.ccrma.org
Harris County Toll Road Authority (Houston area) ***(EZTAG or TxTag)***: (281) 875-3279; www.hctra.org
North Texas Tollway Authority (Dallas Metroplex) ***(TollTag or TxTag)***: (972) 818-6882; www.ntta.org
Texas Department of Transportation (all other toll roads in Texas) ***(TxTag)***: (888) 468-9824; www.txtag.org

Determining distances
(segments of one mile or less not shown)
Cumulative miles (red): the distance between red arrows
Intermediate miles (black): the distance between intersections & places

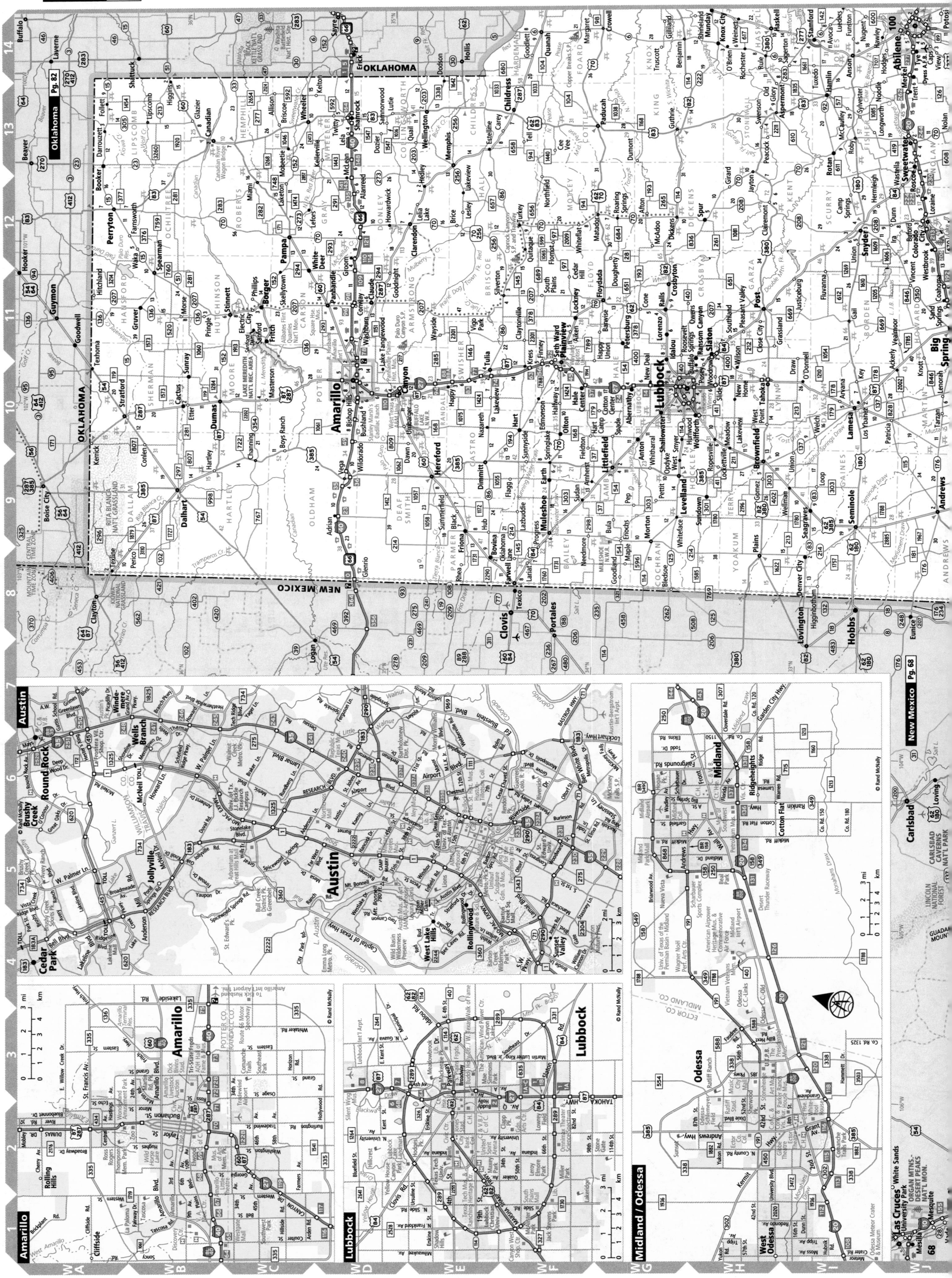

ig Bend National Park

Mileages between cities	Abilene	Amarillo	Big Bend N.P.	Big Spring	Childress	Clovis, NM	Dallas	Eagle Pass	El Paso	Fort Stockton	Lubbock	Odessa	Perryton	San Angelo	San Antonio	Van Horn
Abilene		268	380	108	155	267	179	304	454	255	163	168	306	88	250	332
Amarillo	268		470	226	112	104	363	510	407	344	120	258	115	318	510	423
Del Rio	241	454	242	240	383	425	426	56	428	184	333	258	534	154	151	303
El Paso	454	407	325	346	482	301	635	484		240	343	284	516	404	554	121
Lubbock	163	120	349	106	141	103	345	390	343	224		138	240	194	390	302
Odessa	168	258	210	61	279	204	352	314	284	85	138		377	132	352	164
San Angelo	88	318	290	86	226	296	269	212	404	162	194	132	377		213	282
San Antonio	250	510	404	299	408	493	276	143	554	315	390	352	556	213		434

Total mileages through Texas

10 881 miles
40 177 miles
20 636 miles

More mileages at randmcnally.com/MC

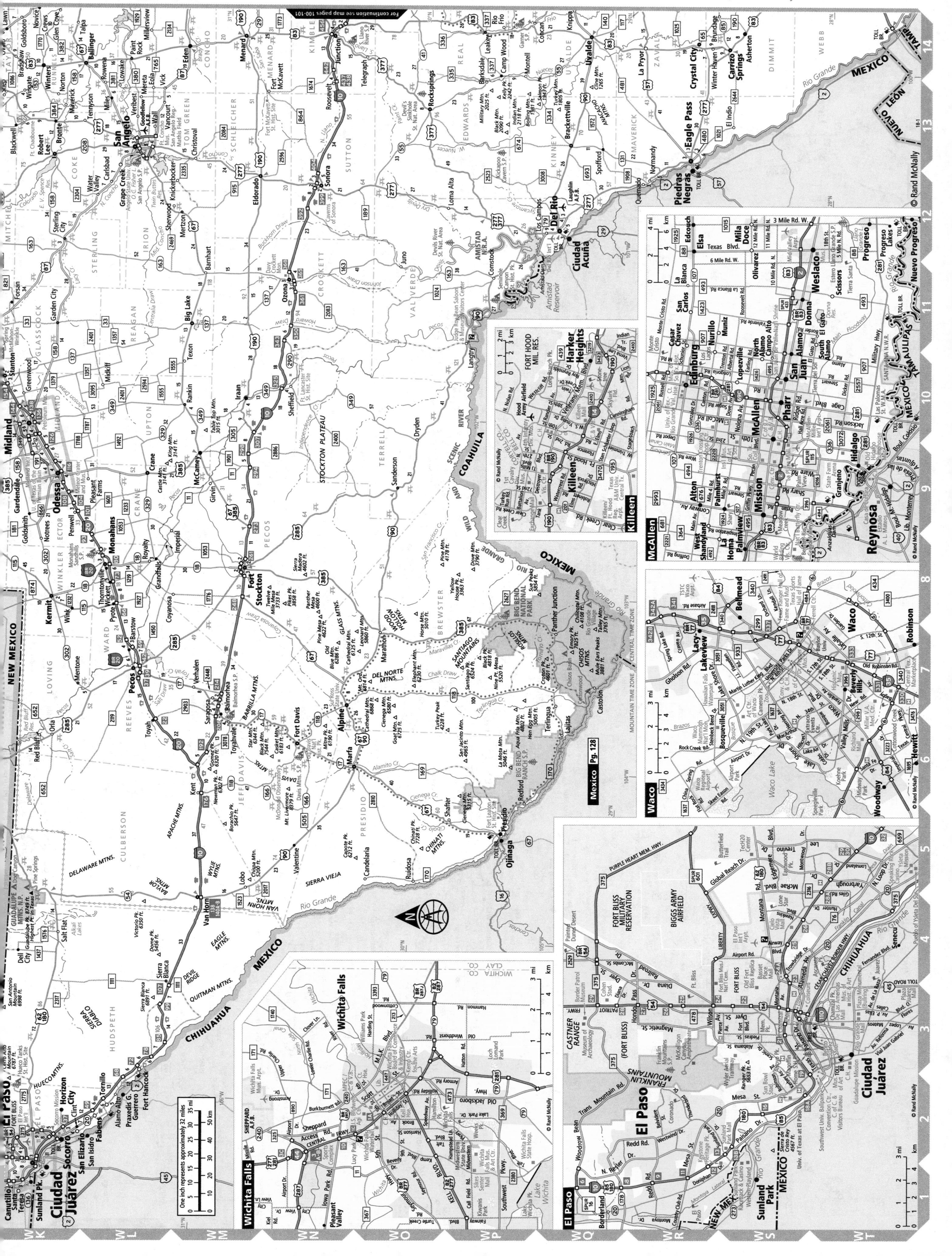

Nickname: The Lone Star State
Capital: Austin, EK-5
Land area: 261,231 sq. mi. (rank: 2nd)
Population: 25,145,561 (rank: 2nd)
Largest city: Houston, 2,099,451, EL-10

Index of places Pg. 135

Travel planning & on-the-road resources

Tourism Information

Texas Tourism:
(800) 452-9292; www.traveltex.com

Road Conditions & Construction

(800) 452-9292, (512) 463-8588;
www.txdot.gov, www.drivetexas.org

Toll Road Information

(list continued from p. 98)

Central Texas Regional Mobility Authority (Austin area) *(TxTag)*:
(512) 996-9778; www.mobilityauthority.com
Fort Bend County Toll Road Authority (Houston area) *(EZTAG or TxTag)*: (855) 999-2024; www.fbctra.com
North East Regional Mobility Authority (TX 49) *(TxTag)*: (903) 630-7447; www.netrma.org
SH 130 Concession Co. (TX 130) *(TxTag)*: (512) 371-4800; mysh130.com
Texas Department of Transportation (all other toll roads in Texas) *(TxTag)*: (888) 468-9824; www.txtag.org

Determining distances

(segments o one mile or l not shown)
Cumulative miles (red): the distance between red arrows
Intermediate miles (black): the distance between intersections & places

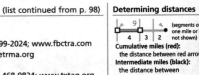

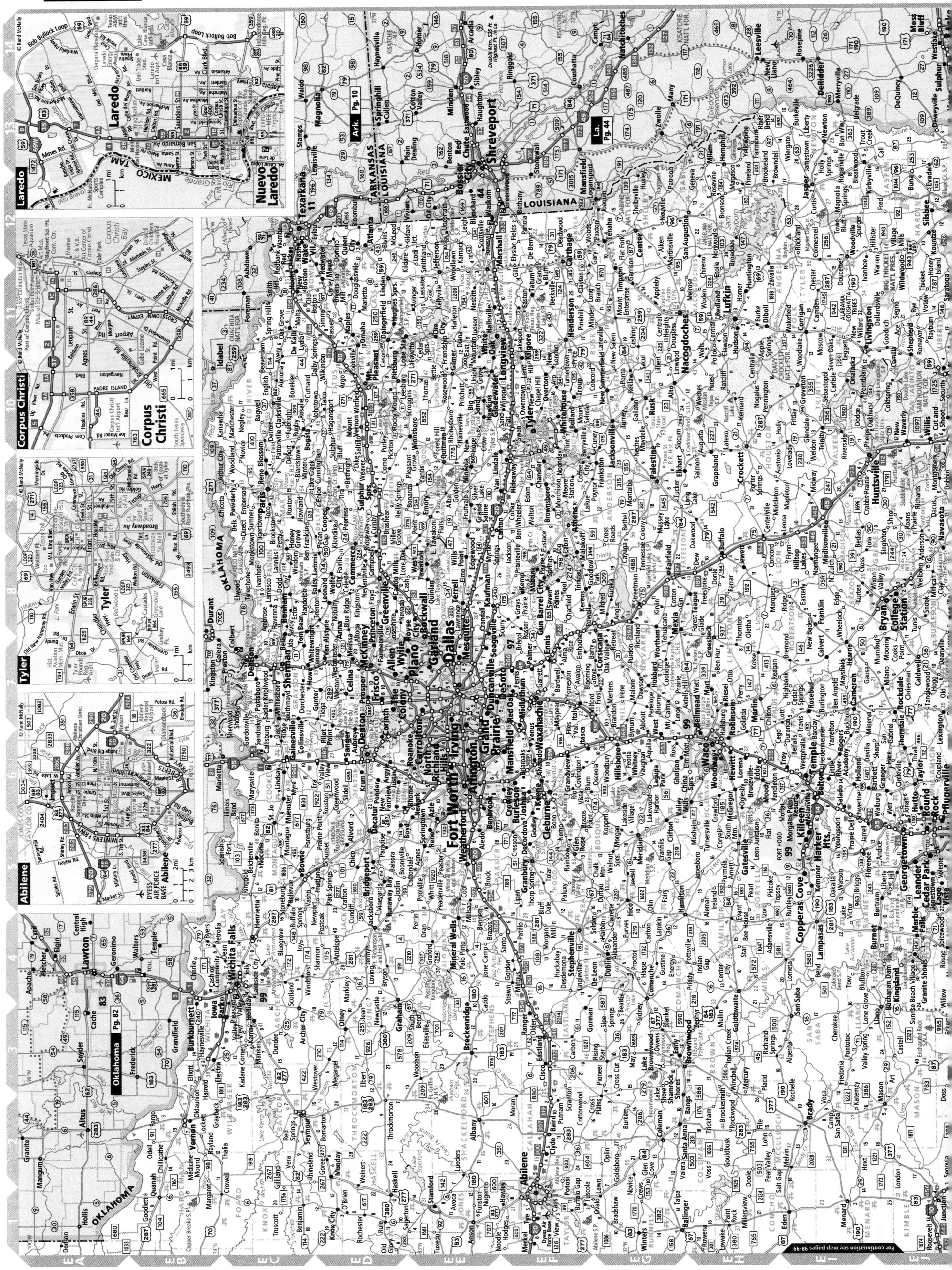

amo, San Antonio

Mileages between cities	Abilene	Austin	Beaumont	Brownsville	Dallas	Houston	Laredo	Lufkin	Paris	San Angelo	San Antonio	Shreveport, LA	Texarkana	Tyler	Waco	Wichita Falls
Abilene		221	449	524	179	377	396	363	285	88	250	368	358	280	183	151
Austin	221		242	353	193	157	237	224	296	208	81	325	366	224	99	299
Brownsville	524	353	439		547	354	204	473	622	491	274	596	650	530	435	614
Corpus Christi	387	217	292	156	410	207	138	328	496	355	138	449	504	392	316	477
Dallas	179	193	282	547		228	428	183	106	269	276	187	177	100	96	139
Houston	377	157	85	354	228		348	118	299	368	197	242	295	199	184	375
San Antonio	250	81	280	274	276	197	154	314	380	213		406	451	309	180	341
Shreveport, LA	368	325	206	596	187	242	565	120	154	455	406		72	98	226	324

Total mileages through Texas

- I-10: 881 miles
- I-20: 636 miles
- I-30: 223 miles
- I-35: 504 miles

More mileages at randmcnally.com/MC

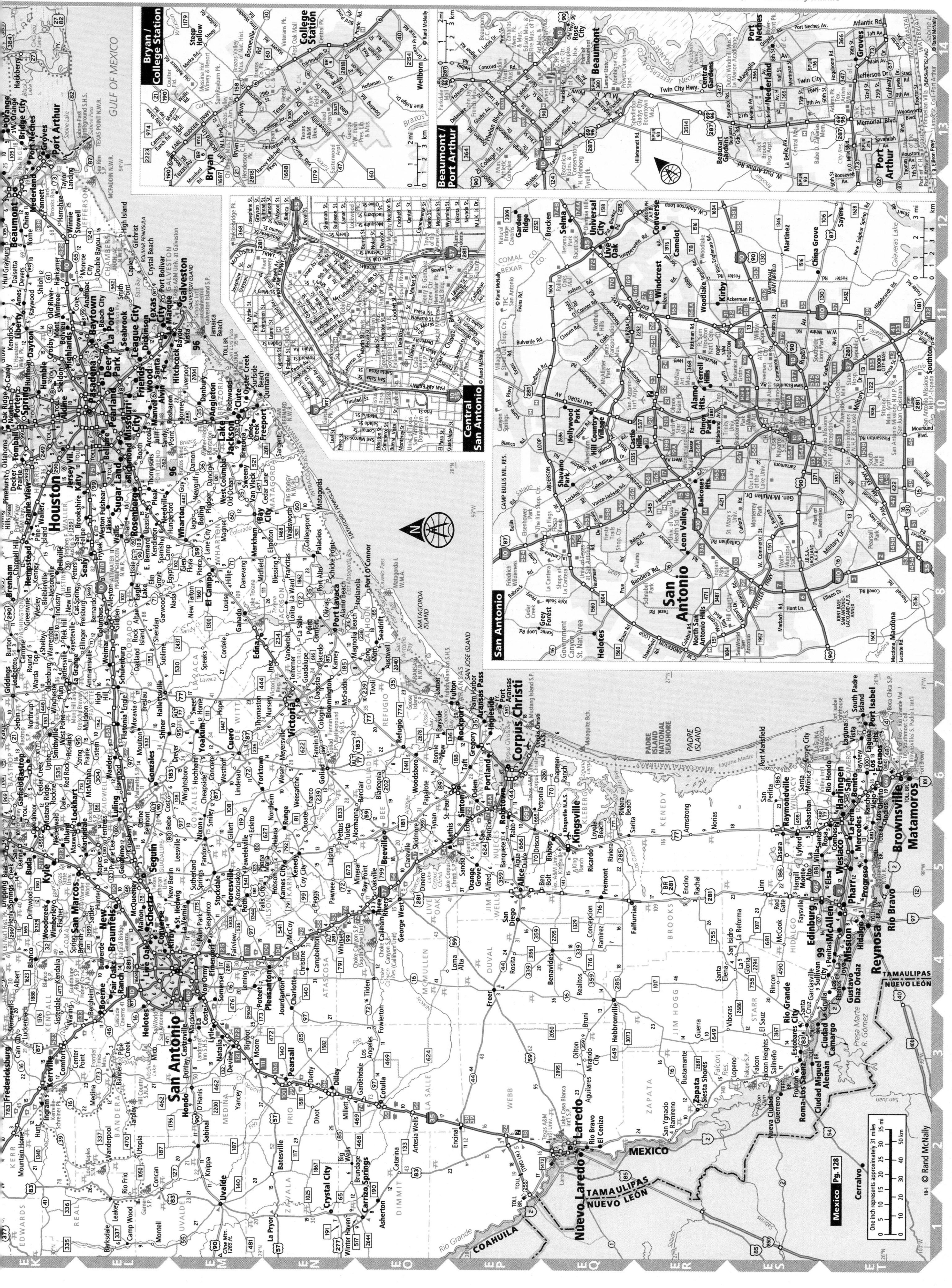

Nickname: The Beehive State
Capital: Salt Lake City, D-8
Land area: 82,169 sq. mi. (rank: 12th)
Population: 2,763,885 (rank: 34th)
Largest city: Salt Lake City, 186,440, D-8

Index of places Pg. 135

Travel planning & on-the-road resources

Tourism Information
Utah Office of Tourism: (800) 200-1160, (800) 882-4386, (801) 538-1900; www.visitutah.com

Road Conditions & Construction
511, (866) 511-8824, (801) 887-3700; www.udot.utah.gov, www.utahcommuterlink.com

Toll Road Information *(ExpressCard)*
Adams Av. Pkwy., Inc. (Washington Terrace): (801) 475-1909; www.adamsavenueparkway.com

Determining distances along roads

Highway distances (segments of one mile or less not shown):
Cumulative miles (red): the distance between red arrows
Intermediate miles (black): the distance between intersections & plac

Interchanges and exit numbers
For most states, the mileage between interchanges may be determin by subtracting one number from the other.

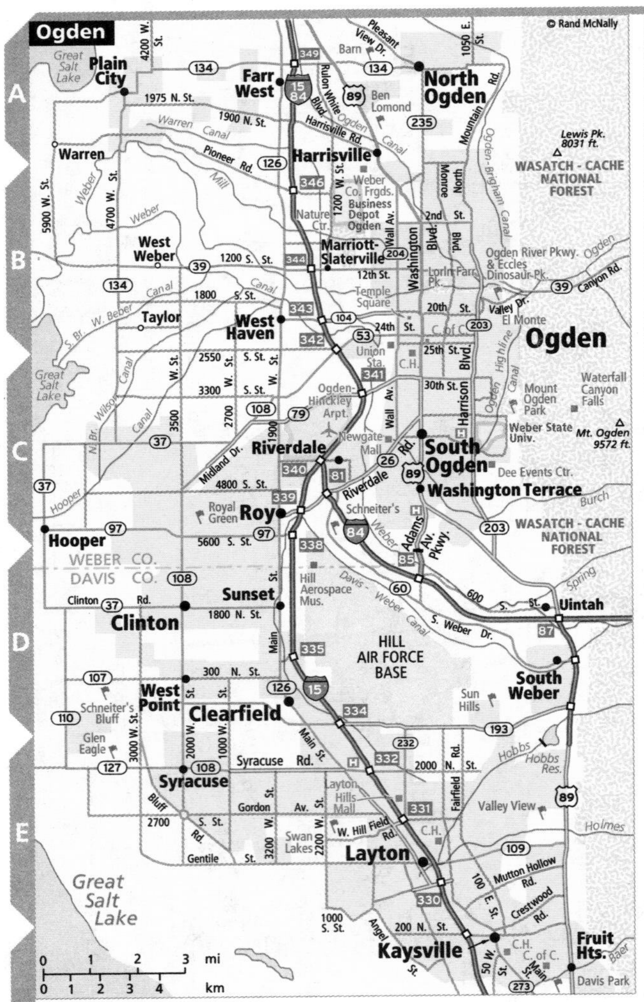

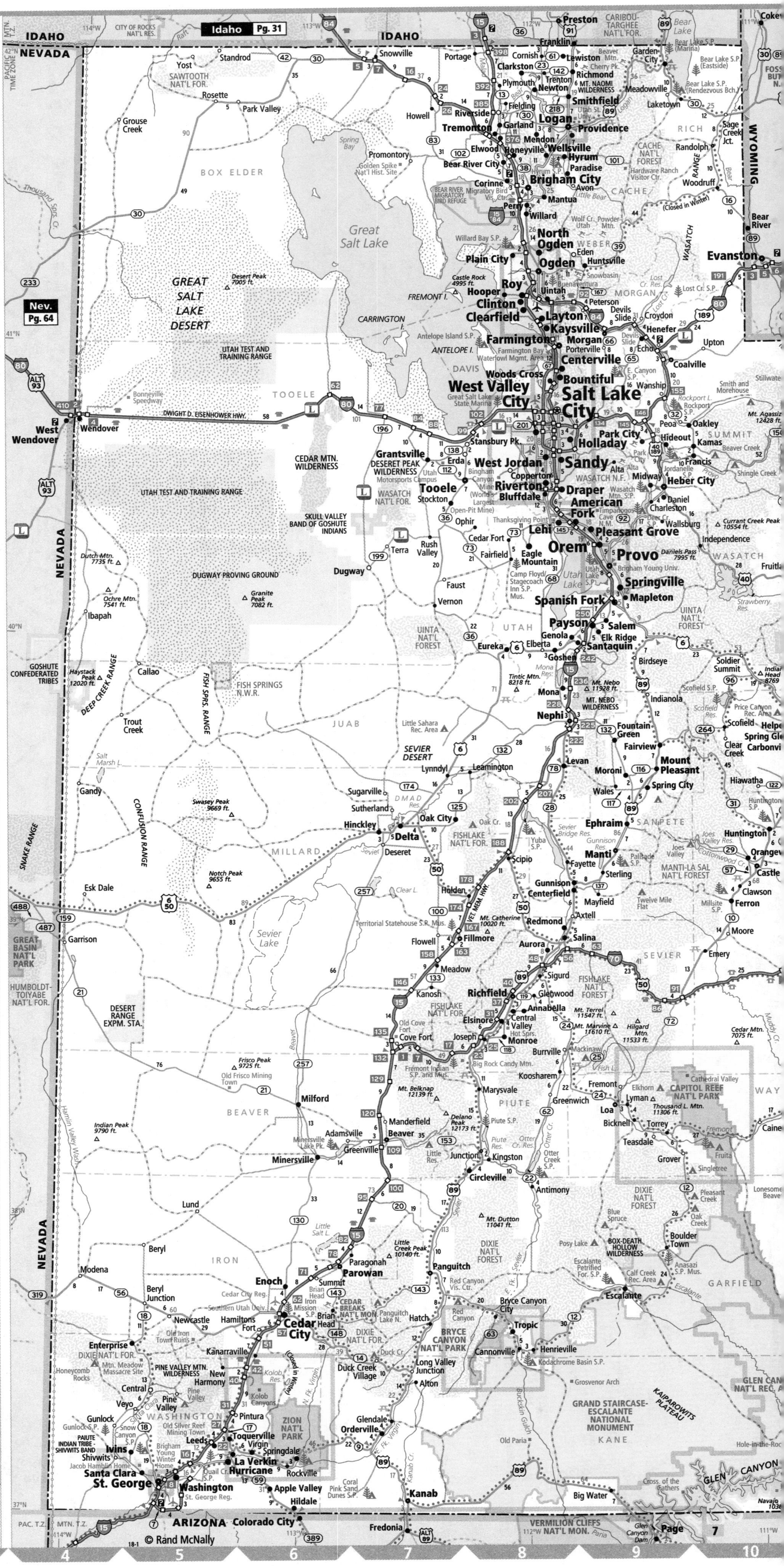

Mileages between cities	Blanding	Cedar City	Grand Jct., CO	Las Vegas, NV	Logan	Moab	Ogden	Page, AZ	Park City	Price	Provo	Richfield	St. George	Salt Lake City	Vernal	Wendover
Grand Junction, CO	186	335		506	363	112	319	380	286	164	240	224	389	283	140	401
Logan	388	330	363	499		313	46	457	113	199	124	239	385	82	252	199
Moab	74	287	112	456	313		269	268	238	115	190	174	341	234	207	352
Richfield	249	114	224	282	239	174	194	219	166	121	115		169	159	232	270
St. George	415	55	389	117	385	341	341	154	308	286	261	169		304	401	333
Salt Lake City	308	250	283	419	82	234	37	377	30	119	43	159	304		172	121
Vernal	281	345	140	514	252	207	207	450	145	112	154	232	401	172		291
Wendover	426	317	401	361	199	352	154	503	150	237	161	270	333	121	291	

Total mileages through Utah

- I-15: 401 miles
- I-80: 196 miles
- I-70: 232 miles
- I-84: 119 miles

More mileages at randmcnally.com/MC

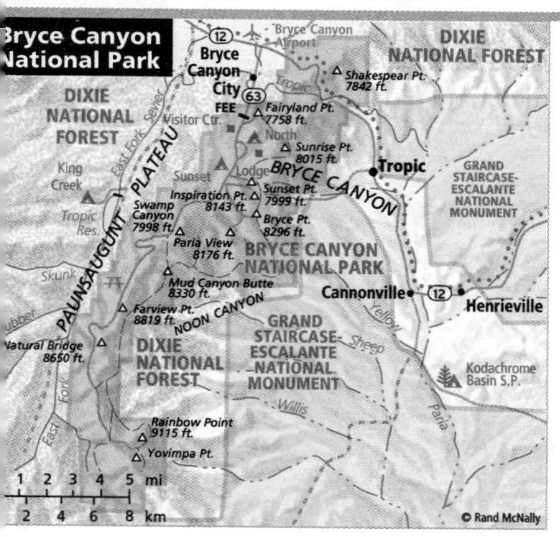

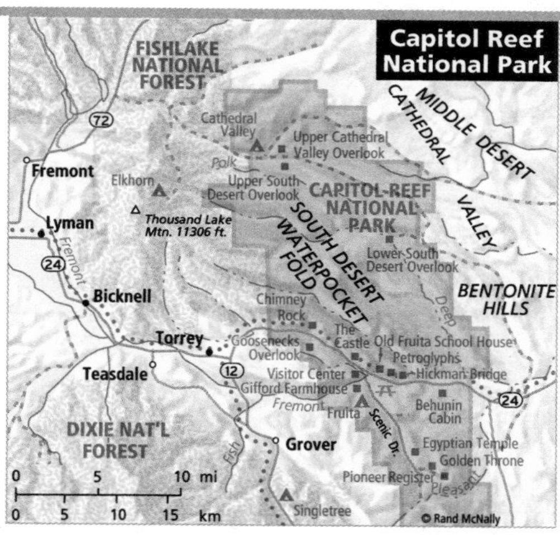

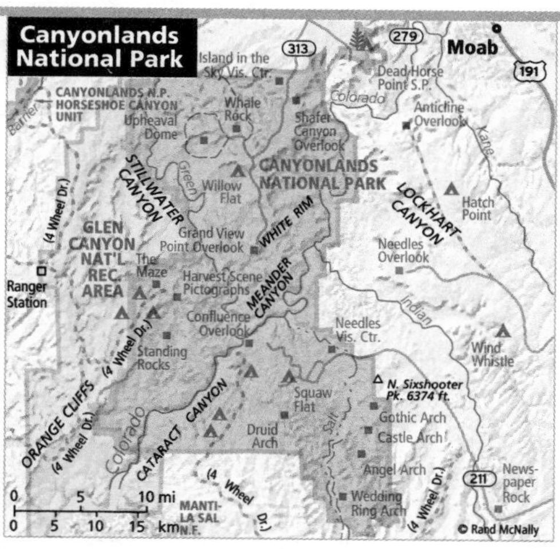

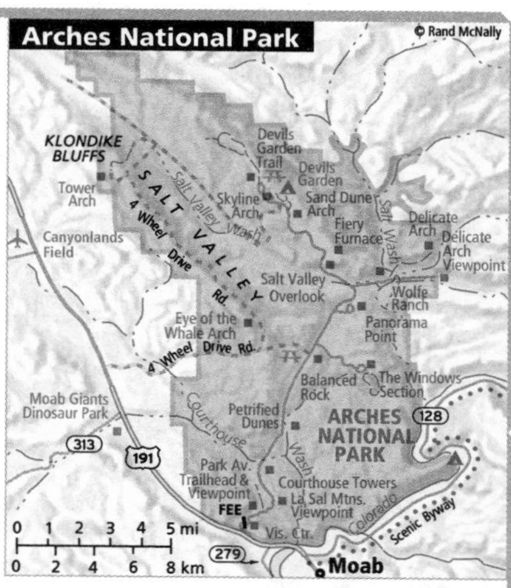

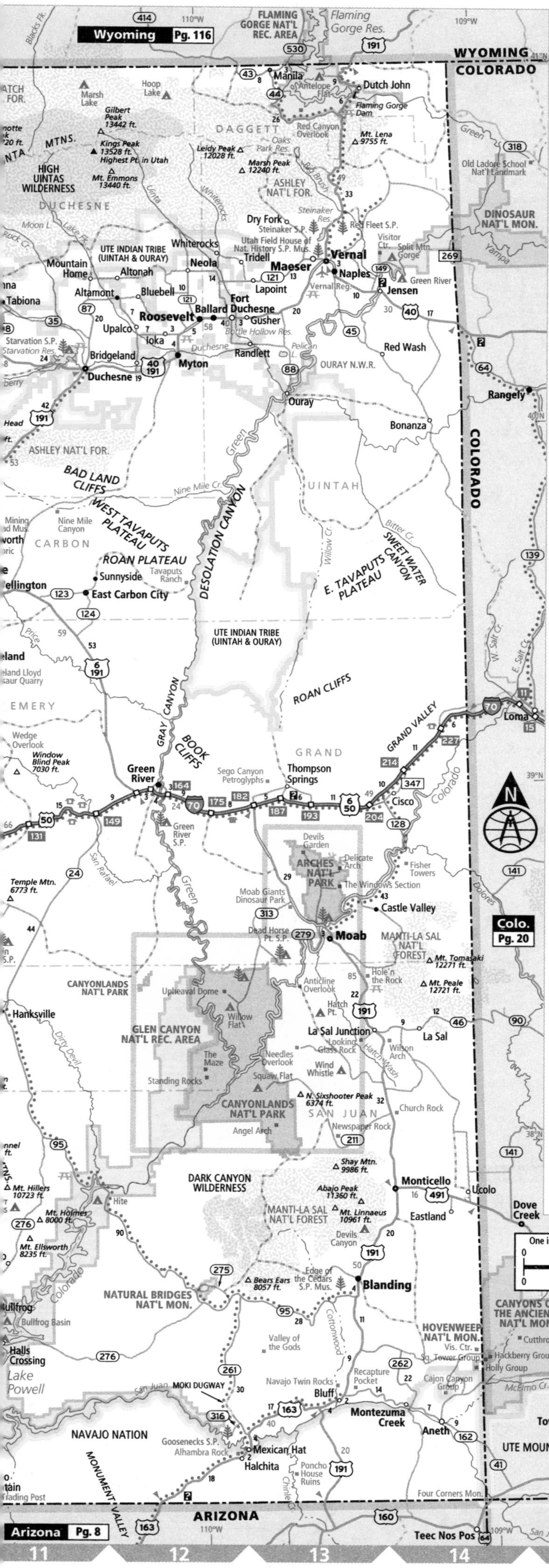

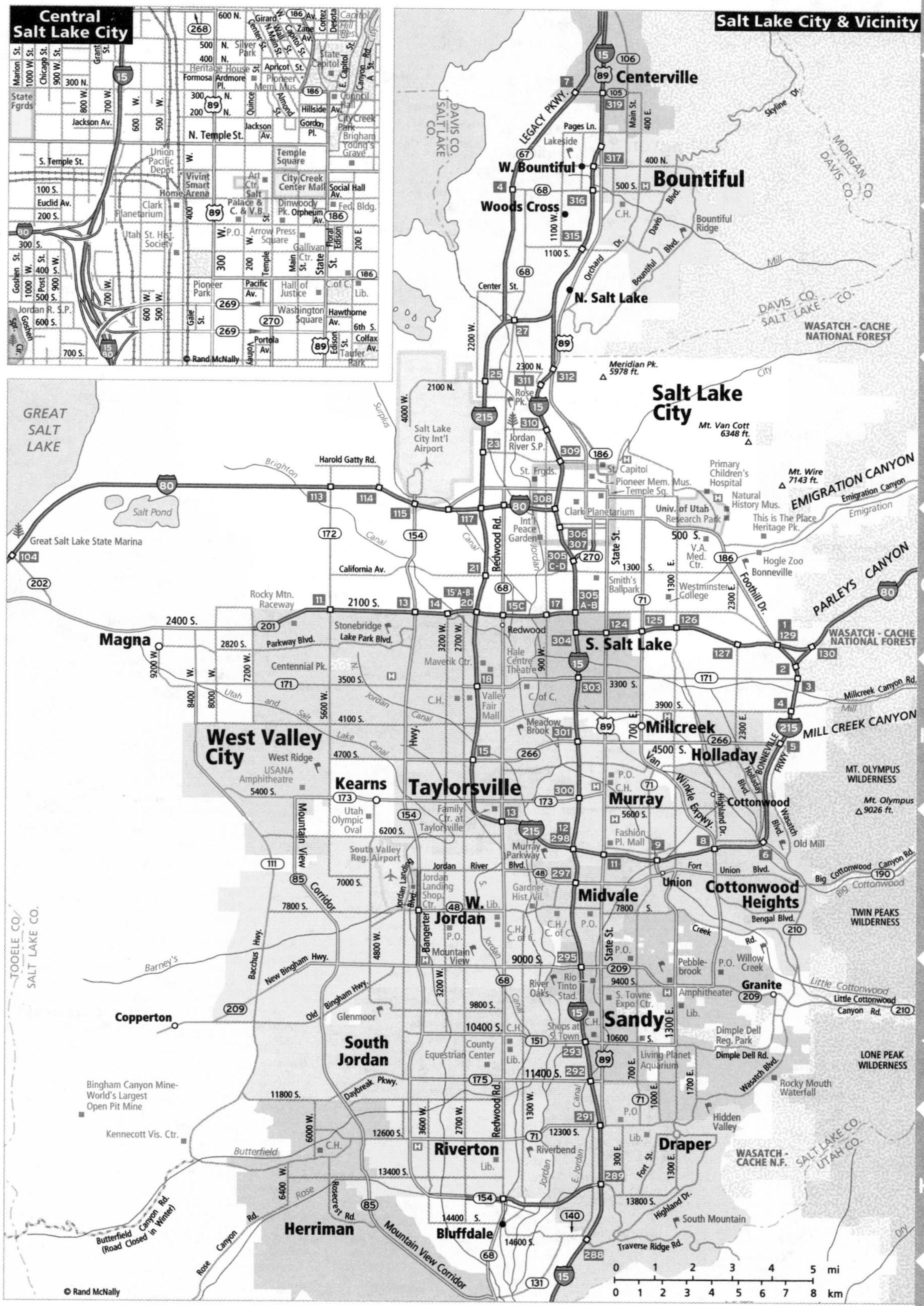

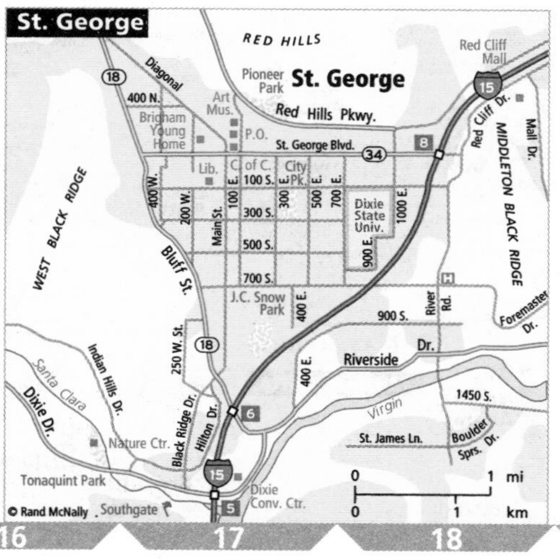

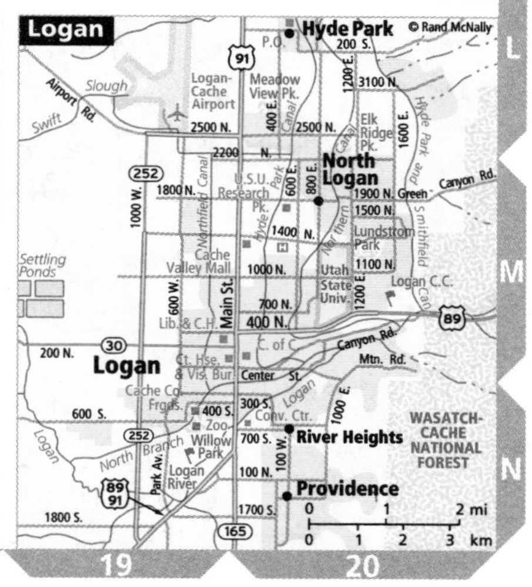

Vermont

Nickname: The Green Mountain State
Capital: Montpelier, E-5
Land area: 9,217 sq. mi. (rank: 43rd)
Population: 625,741 (rank: 49th)
Largest city: Burlington, 42,417, D-2

Index of places Pg. 135

Mileages between cities

	Albany, NY	Brattleboro	Burlington	Montpelier	Newport	Rutland	St. Johnsbury	White River Jct.
Albany, NY		78	151	156	230	90	187	128
Brattleboro	78		151	115	164	73	121	62
Burlington	151	151		39	76	67	75	90
Montpelier	156	115	39		78	66	37	54
Newport	230	164	76	78		147	43	102
Rutland	90	73	67	66	147		105	45
St. Johnsbury	187	121	75	37	43	105		60
White River Jct.	128	62	90	54	102	45	60	

Total mileages through Vermont

89: 130 miles
93: 11 miles
91: 177 miles
4: 64 miles

More mileages at randmcnally.com/MC

Travel planning & on-the-road resources

Tourism Information

Vermont Department of Tourism and Marketing:
(800) 837-6668, (802) 828-3237; www.vermontvacation.com

Road Conditions & Construction

511; www.511vt.com, www.aot.state.vt.us

Toll Road Information

No toll roads

Determining Distance

(segment... one mile... not show...)
Cumulative miles (red): the distance between red a...
Intermediate miles (black): the distance between intersections & places

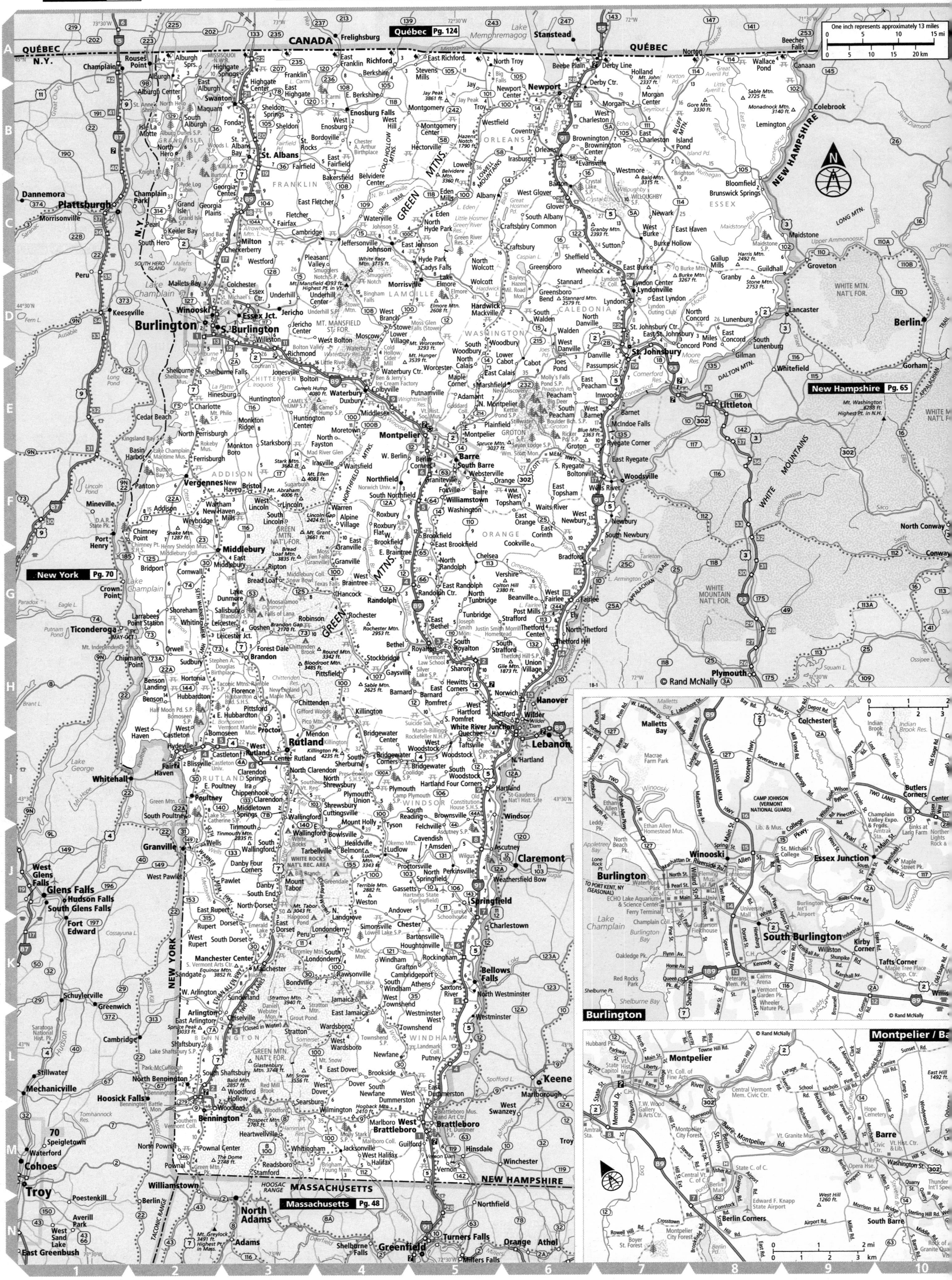

Sights to see

- Agecroft Hall and Gardens, Richmond C-7
- Children's Museum of Virginia, Portsmouth M-6
- Chrysler Museum of Art, Norfolk L-6
- Colonial Williamsburg, Williamsburg F-2
- Edgar Allan Poe Museum, Richmond C-8
- First Landing State Park, Virginia Beach L-9
- Hermitage Foundation Museum, Norfolk L-6
- Historic Jamestowne, Williamsburg G-1
- Nauticus, Norfolk L-6
- Ocean Breeze Waterpark, Virginia Beach M-10
- Old Cape Henry Lighthouse, Virginia Beach K-9
- Three Lakes Nature Center & Aquarium, Richmond ... B-8

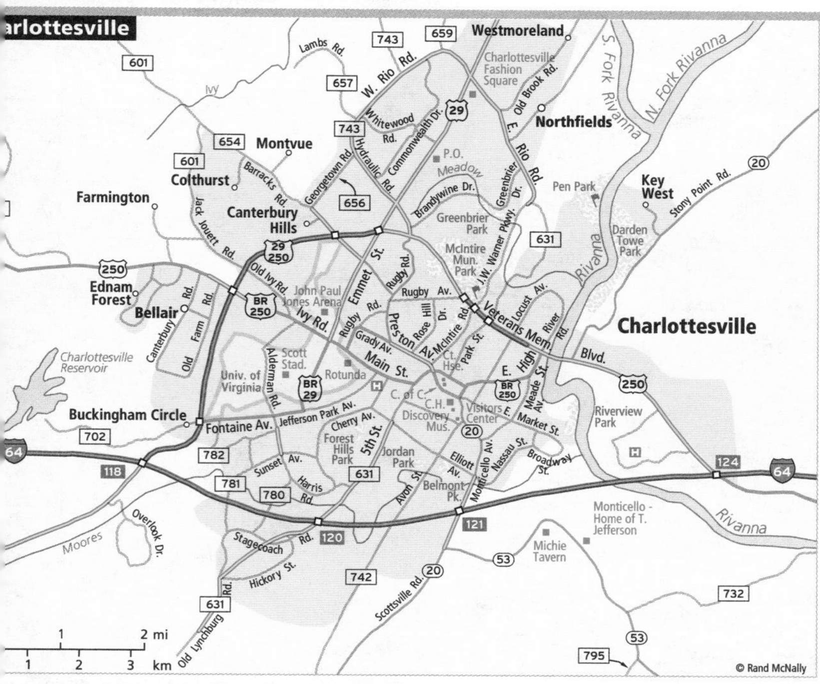

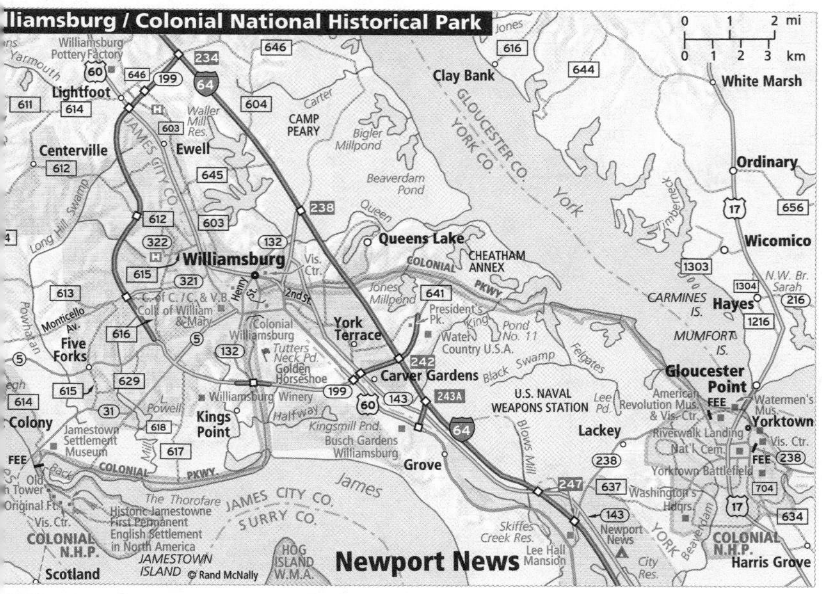

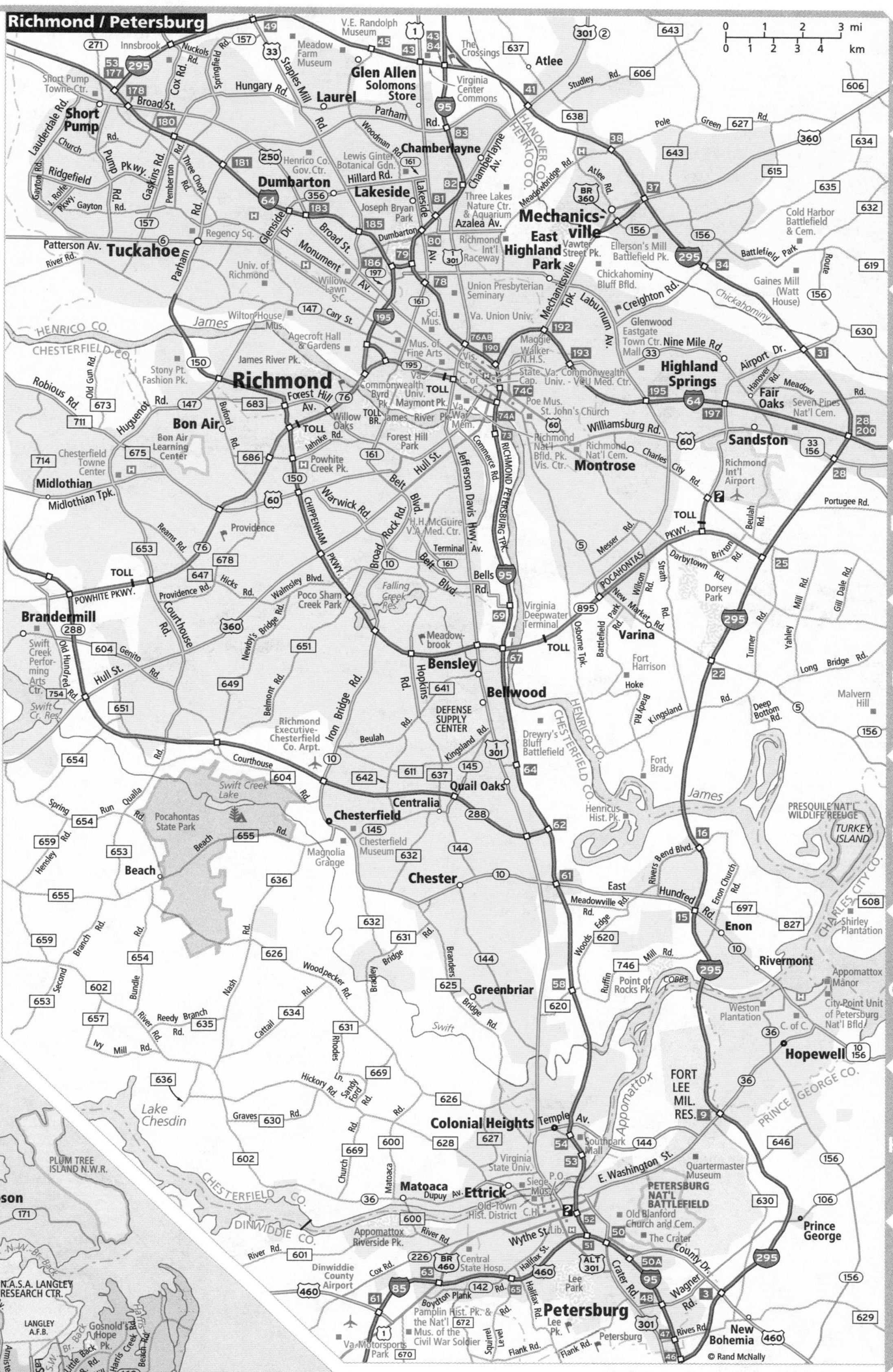

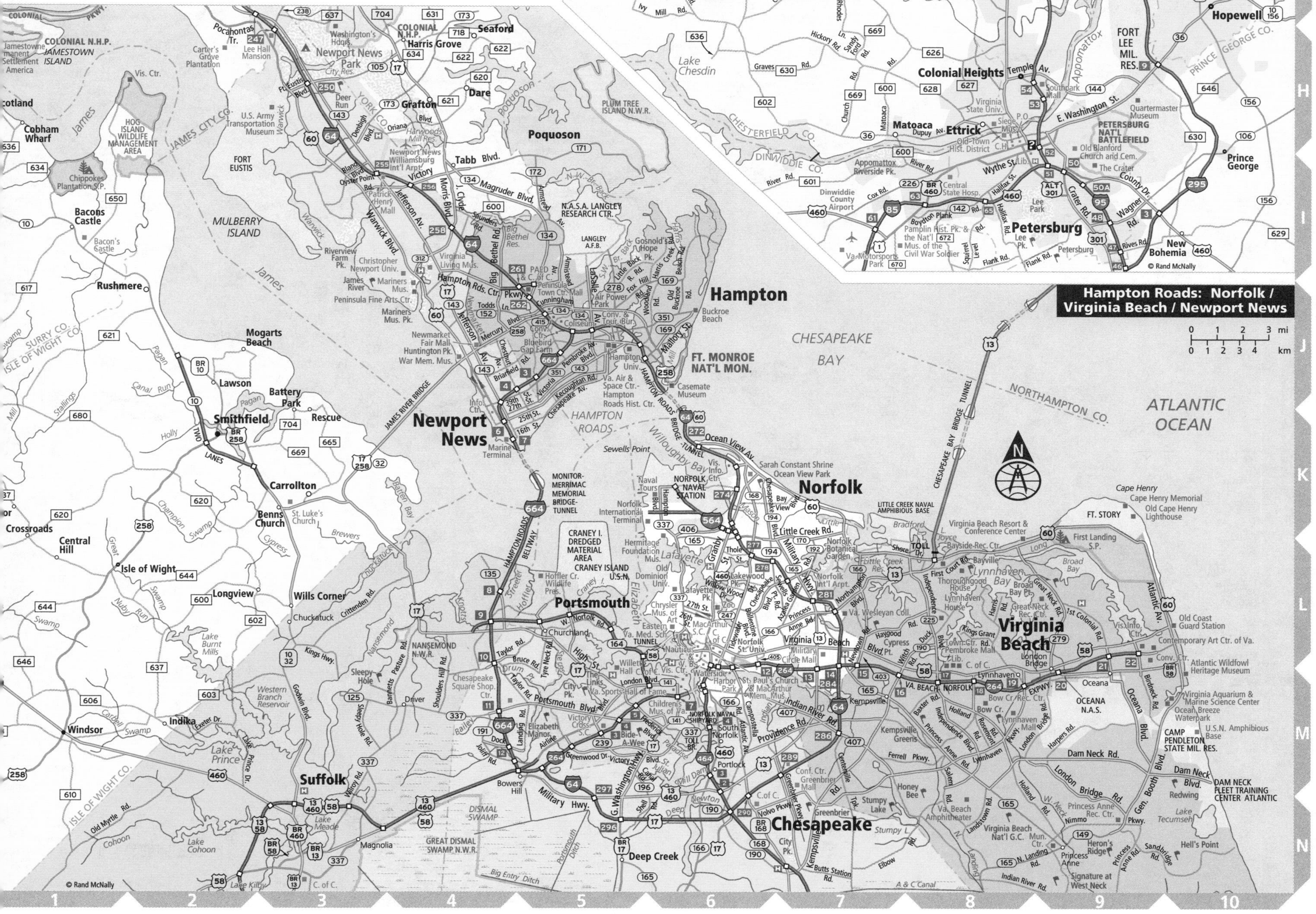

Virginia

Nickname: Old Dominion
Capital: Richmond, J-14
Land area: 39,490 sq. mi. (rank: 36th)
Population: 8,001,024 (rank: 12th)
Largest city: Virginia Beach, 437,994, L-18

Index of places Pg. 135

Travel planning & on-the-road resources

Tourism Information
Virginia Tourism:
(800) 847-4882; www.virginia.org

Road Conditions & Construction
511, (866) 695-1182, (800) 367-7623; www.511virginia.org, www.virginiadot.org/travel

Toll Road Information (all use E-ZPass)
Chesapeake Expwy. (VA 168, in Chesapeake): (757) 204-0010; www.chesapeakeexpressway.com
Dulles Greenway: (703) 707-8870; www.dullesgreenway.com
Metro. Wash. Airports Authority (Dulles Toll Rd.): (877) 762-7824; www.dullestollroad.com
Pocahontas Pkwy. (Richmond): (866) 428-6339; www.pocahontas895.com
Richmond Metro. Trans. Auth. (toll rds. within Richmond): (804) 523-3300; www.rmaonline.org
Virginia Dept. of Transportation (all others): www.virginiadot.org/travel/faq-toll.asp

Toll Bridge/Tunnel Info. (all use E-Z
Chesapeake Bay Bridge-Tunnel: (757) 331-2960; www.cbbt.com
Elizabeth River Tunnels (Hampton (855) 378-7623; www.driveert.co
S. Norfolk Jordan Bridge: (855) 690-7652; www.snjb.net

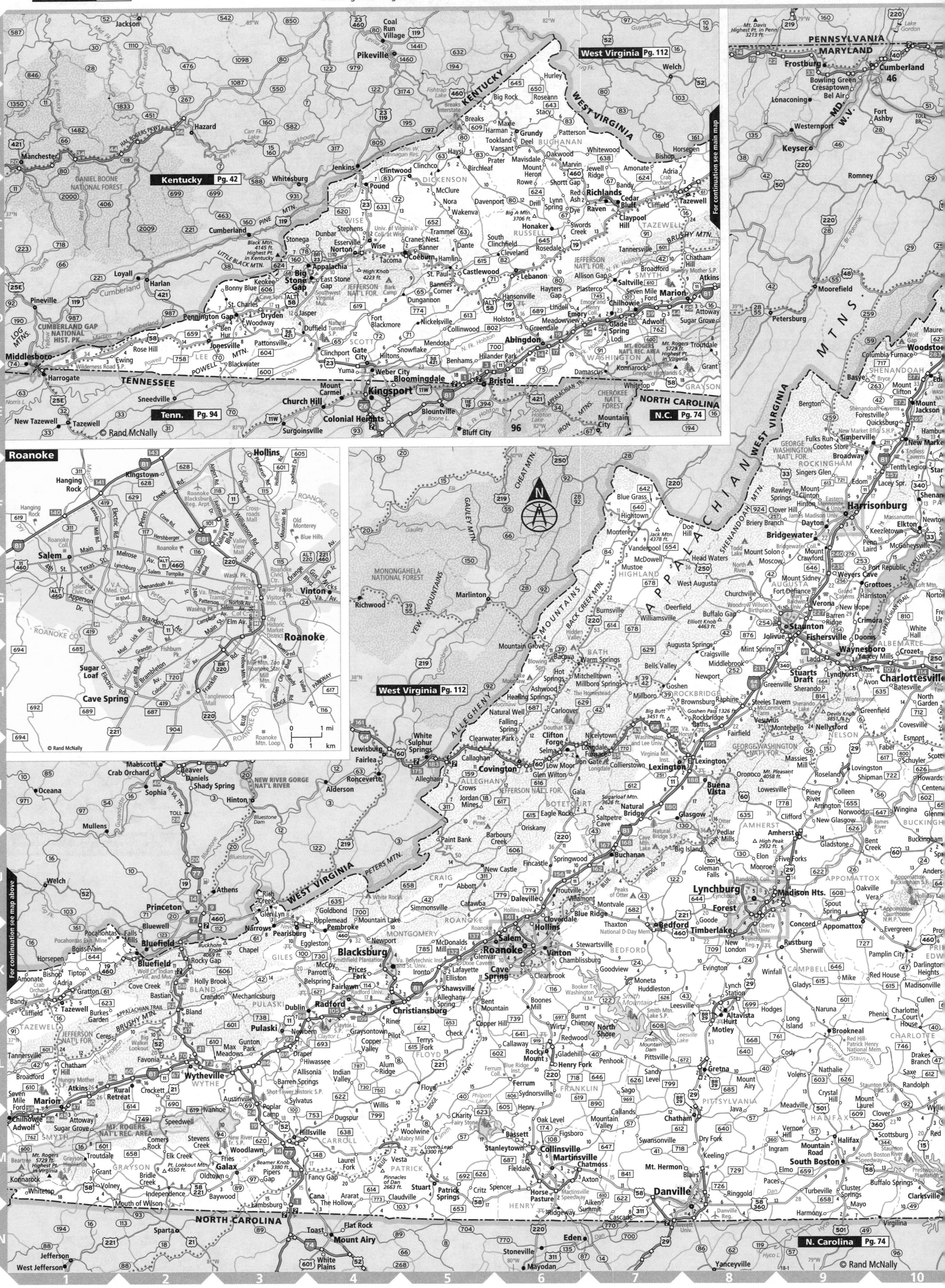

ld ponies on Assateague Island

Mileages between cities	Bristol	Chincoteague	Danville	Emporia	Fredericksburg	Harrisonburg	Lynchburg	Manassas	Norfolk	Richmond	Roanoke	Virginia Beach	Washington, DC	Williamsburg	Winchester	Wytheville
Bristol		510	192	341	323	242	200	347	407	321	145	423	377	370	310	67
Charlottesville	253	260	131	136	66	61	65	81	157	71	117	174	116	121	128	183
Danville	192	300		115	197	163	68	215	191	144	89	206	247	199	230	124
Norfolk	407	104	191	78	139	216	189	177		91	276	17	189	41	222	340
Richmond	321	190	144	66	56	130	114	96	91		187	105	107	50	135	253
Roanoke	145	378	89	176	192	111	53	214	276	187		292	241	238	178	77
Washington, DC	377	168	247	174	53	132	182	32	189	107	241	205		153	76	307
Winchester	310	244	230	200	83	68	164	54	222	135	178	236	76	181		244

Total mileages through Virginia

64 298 miles
85 69 miles
81 325 miles
95 179 miles

More mileages at randmcnally.com/MC

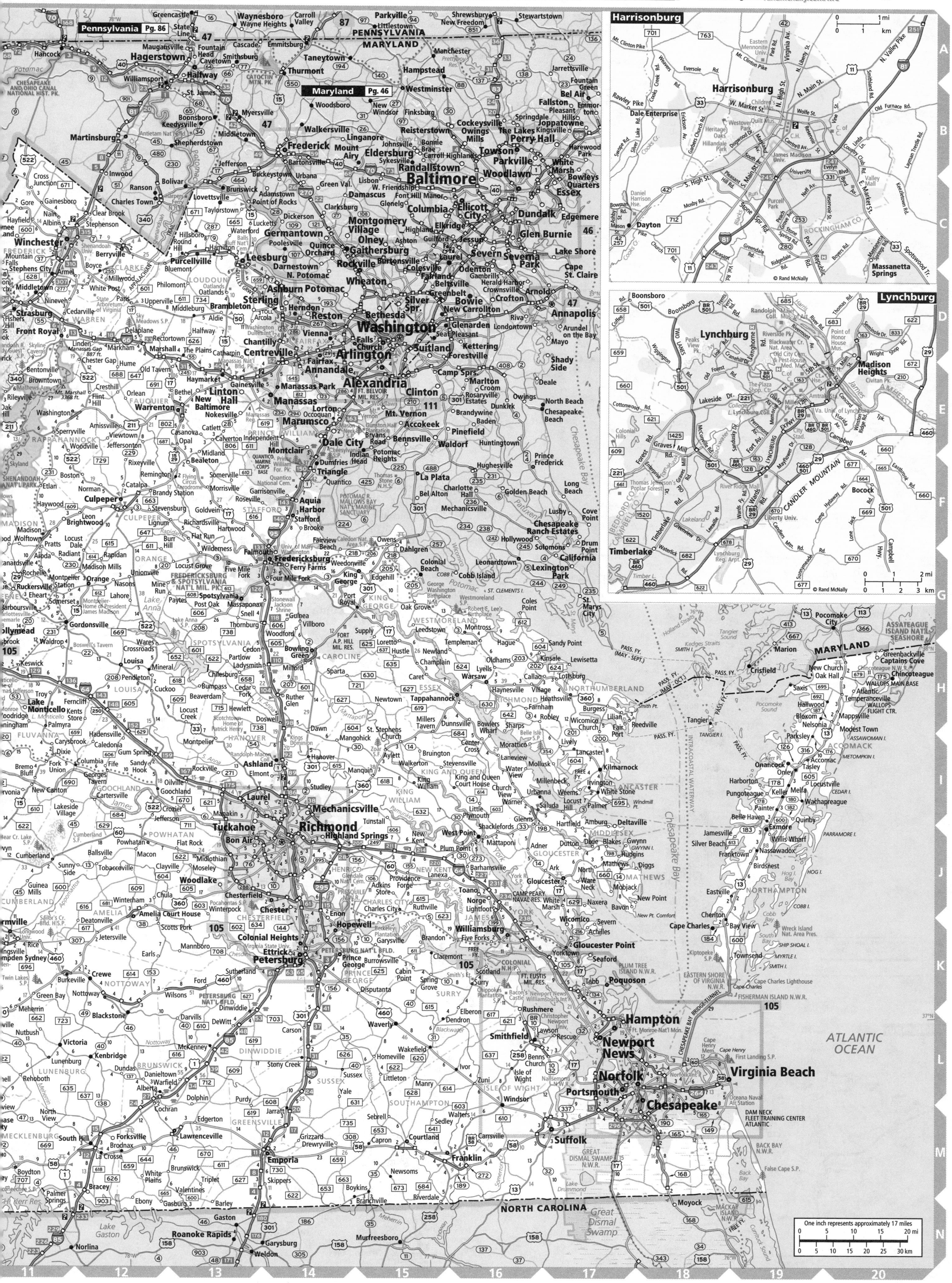

Washington

Nickname: The Evergreen State
Capital: Olympia, H-6
Land area: 66,455 sq. mi. (rank: 20th)
Population: 6,724,540 (rank: 13th)
Largest city: Seattle, 608,660, F-7

Index of places Pg. 135

Travel planning & on-the-road resources

Tourism Information
Washington Tourism: (800) 544-1800; www.experiencewa.com

Road Conditions & Construction
511, (800) 695-7623; www.wsdot.wa.gov/traffic
(Good to Go!)

Toll Bridge Information
Wash. St. Dept. of Trans. (Tacoma Narrows Br., SR 520 Br.): (866) 936-8246; www.wsdot.wa.gov/tolling

Determining distances along roads

Highway distances (segments of one mile or less not shown):
Cumulative miles (red): the distance between red arrows
Intermediate miles (black): the distance between intersections & pl

Interchanges and exit numbers
For most states, the mileage between interchanges may be determ by subtracting one number from the other.

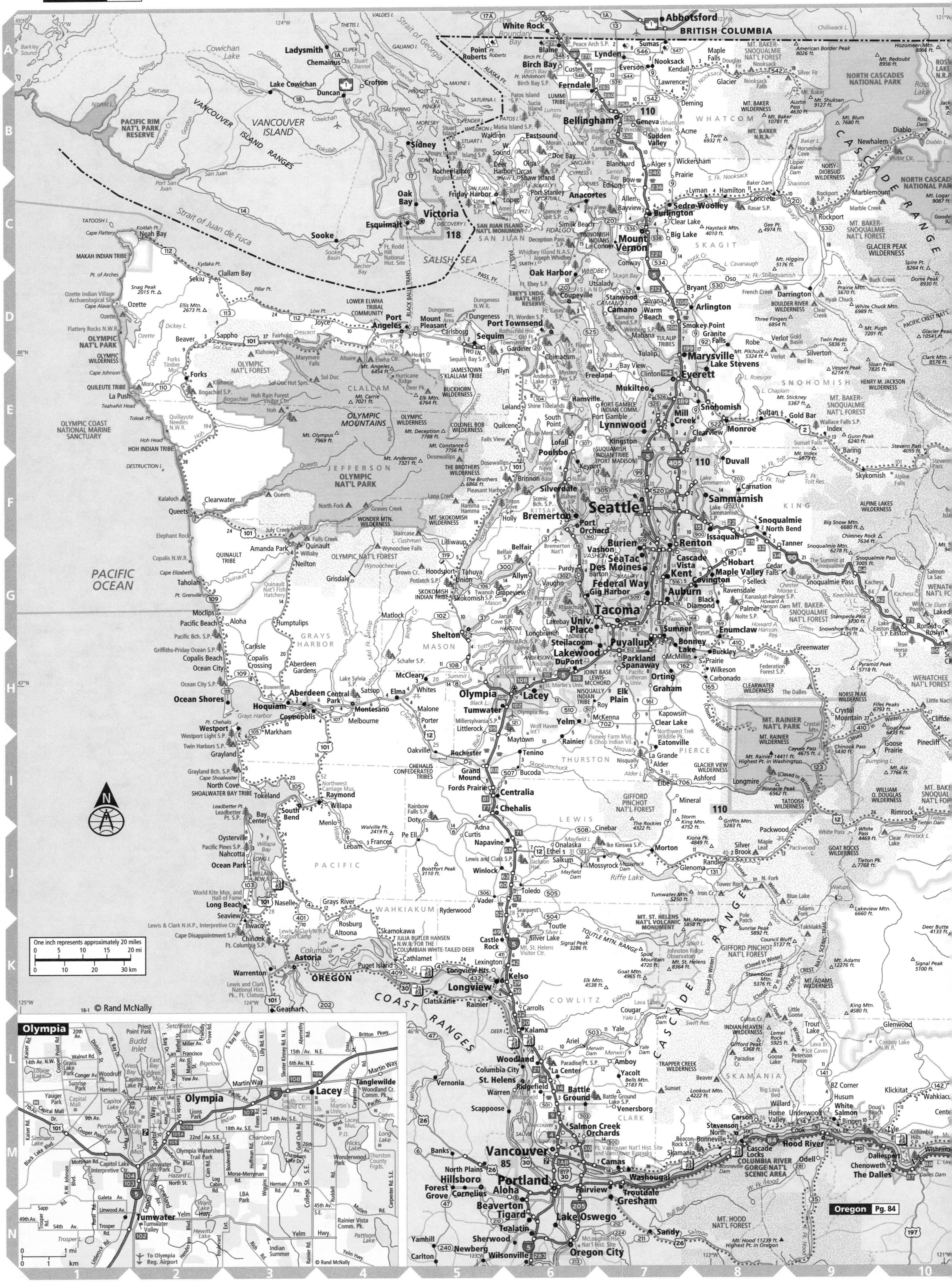

Mileages between cities	Aberdeen	Bellingham	Colville	Kennewick	Longview	Olympia	Omak	Port Angeles	Portland, OR	Seattle	Spokane	Tacoma	The Dalles, OR	Vancouver, BC	Wenatchee	Yakima
Bellingham	198		317	306	216	149	201	118	261	89	361	121	326	52	182	224
Kennewick	312	306	209		254	263	189	340	213	223	138	235	130	359	132	82
Lewiston, ID	402	396	173	124	381	353	237	431	339	313	102	325	256	449	228	204
Portland, OR	141	261	422	213	48	113	377	228		172	351	141	83	313	291	185
Seattle	108	89	350	223	127	60	236	83	172		278	32	249	141	148	141
Spokane	367	361	71	138	386	319	139	396	351	278		291	268	413	169	201
Tacoma	77	121	362	235	96	28	248	106	141	32	291		217	174	160	153
Yakima	230	224	272	82	166	181	192	259	185	141	201	153	102	276	106	

Total mileages through Washington

- 5: 277 miles
- 90: 297 miles
- 82: 133 miles
- 101: 373 miles

More mileages at randmcnally.com/MC

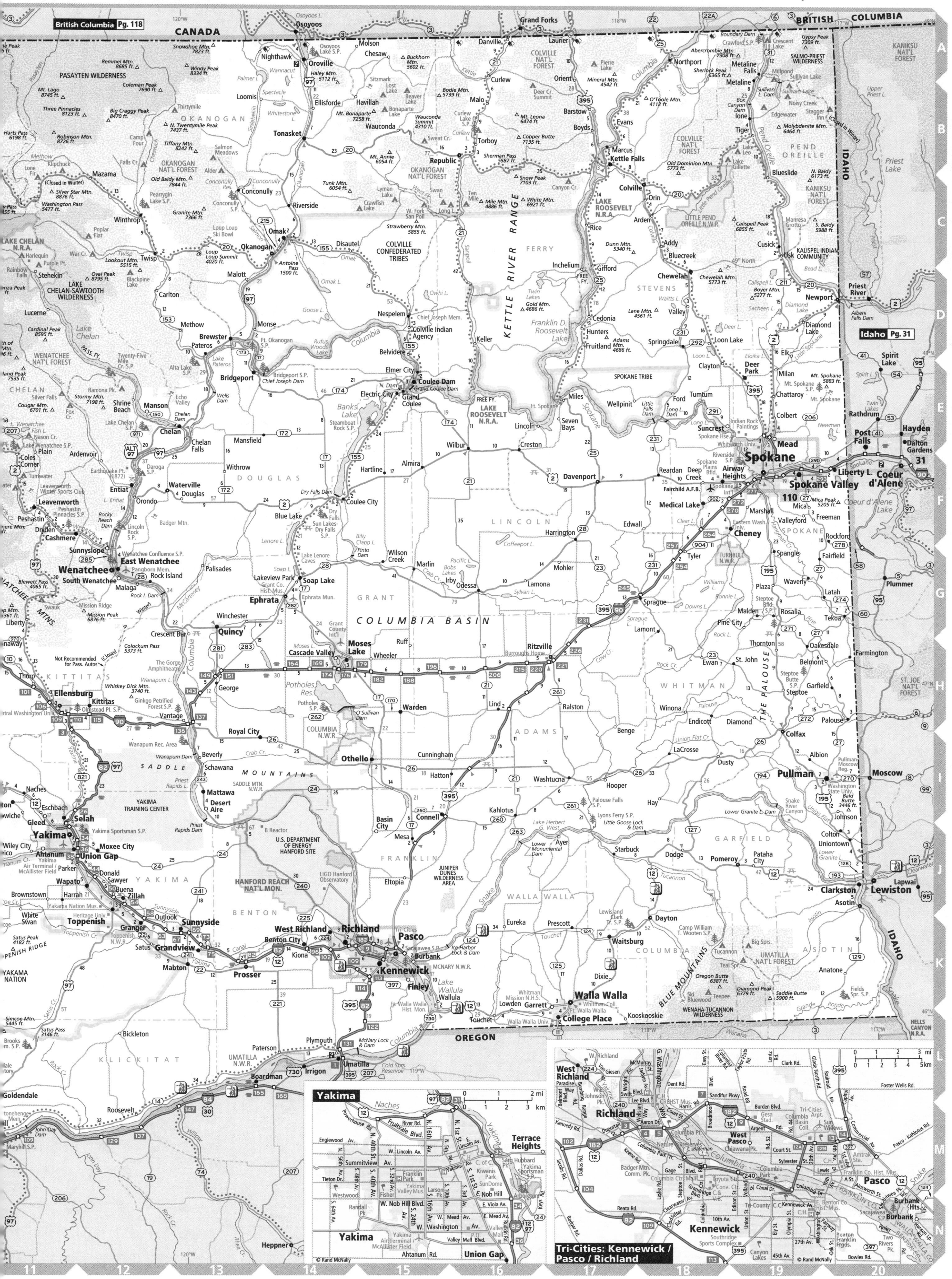

Sights to see

- Frye Art Museum, Seattle J-3
- Klondike Gold Rush National Historical Park, Seattle . . K-2
- Museum of Glass, Tacoma. L-6
- Museum of Pop Culture, Seattle H-1
- Nordic Heritage Museum, Seattle C-7
- Pacific Science Center, Seattle. H-1
- Pike Place Market, Seattle J-2
- Point Defiance Zoo & Aquarium, Tacoma. K-5
- Seattle Aquarium, Seattle. J-1
- Space Needle, Seattle H-1
- Washington State History Museum, Tacoma L-6
- Woodland Park Zoo, Seattle. C-7

Elliott Bay, Seattle

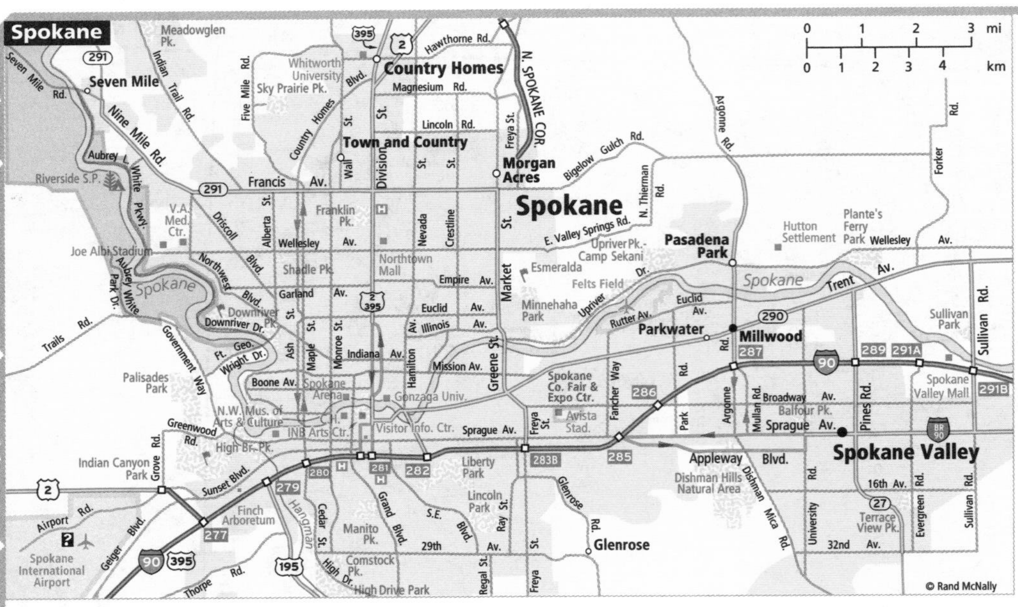

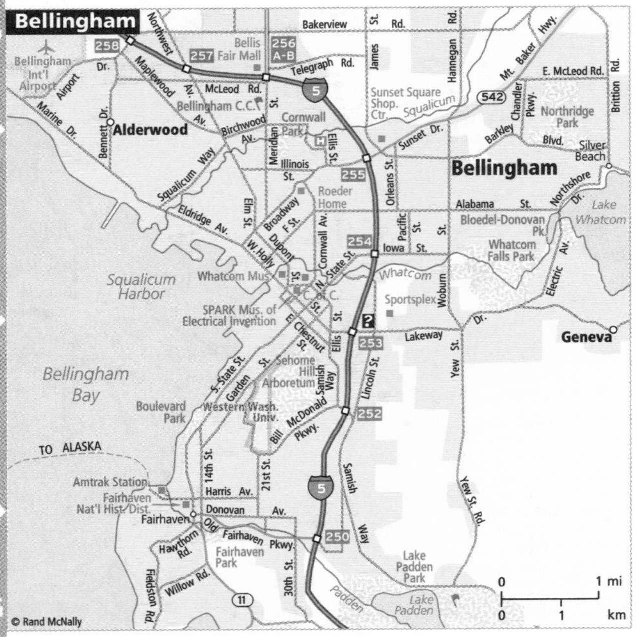

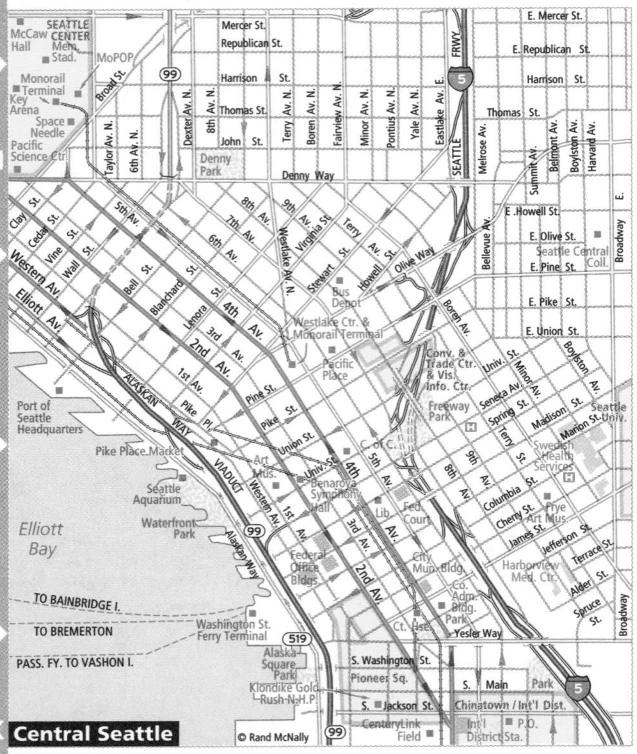

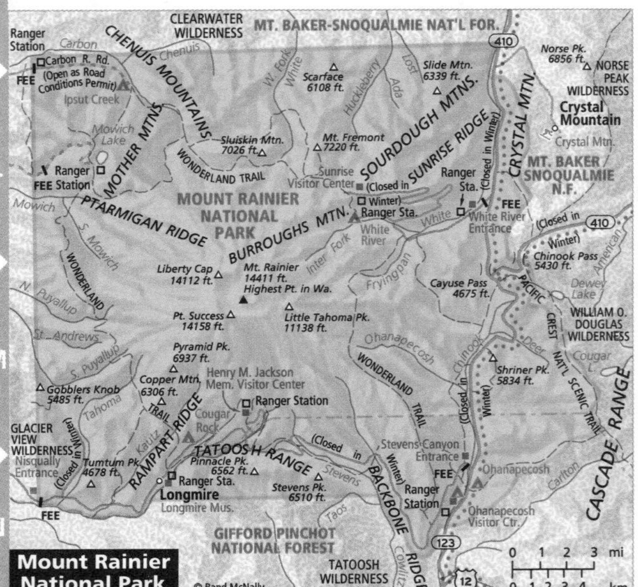

n-the-road resources

rism Information
tination DC:
)0) 422-8644, (202) 789-7000; www.washington.org

d Conditions & Construction
, (202) 737-4404, (202) 673-6813; ddot.dc.gov

Road Information
toll roads in District of Columbia
Maryland or Virginia pages for toll road information

Land area: 61 sq. mi. | Population: 601,723

Sights to see

- Arlington National Cemetery, Arlington, VA N-1
- Frederick Douglass National Historic Site .. G-7
- John F. Kennedy Center for the Performing Arts L-3
- Martin Luther King Jr. Memorial M-4
- National African American Museum .. L-6
- National Arboretum F-7
- National Mall M-7
- National Zoological Park F-6
- The Pentagon, Arlington, VA G-6
- The Supreme Court of the United States M-9
- United States Botanic Garden M-8
- The White House K-5
- Wolf Trap National Park for the Performing Arts, Vienna, VA E-2

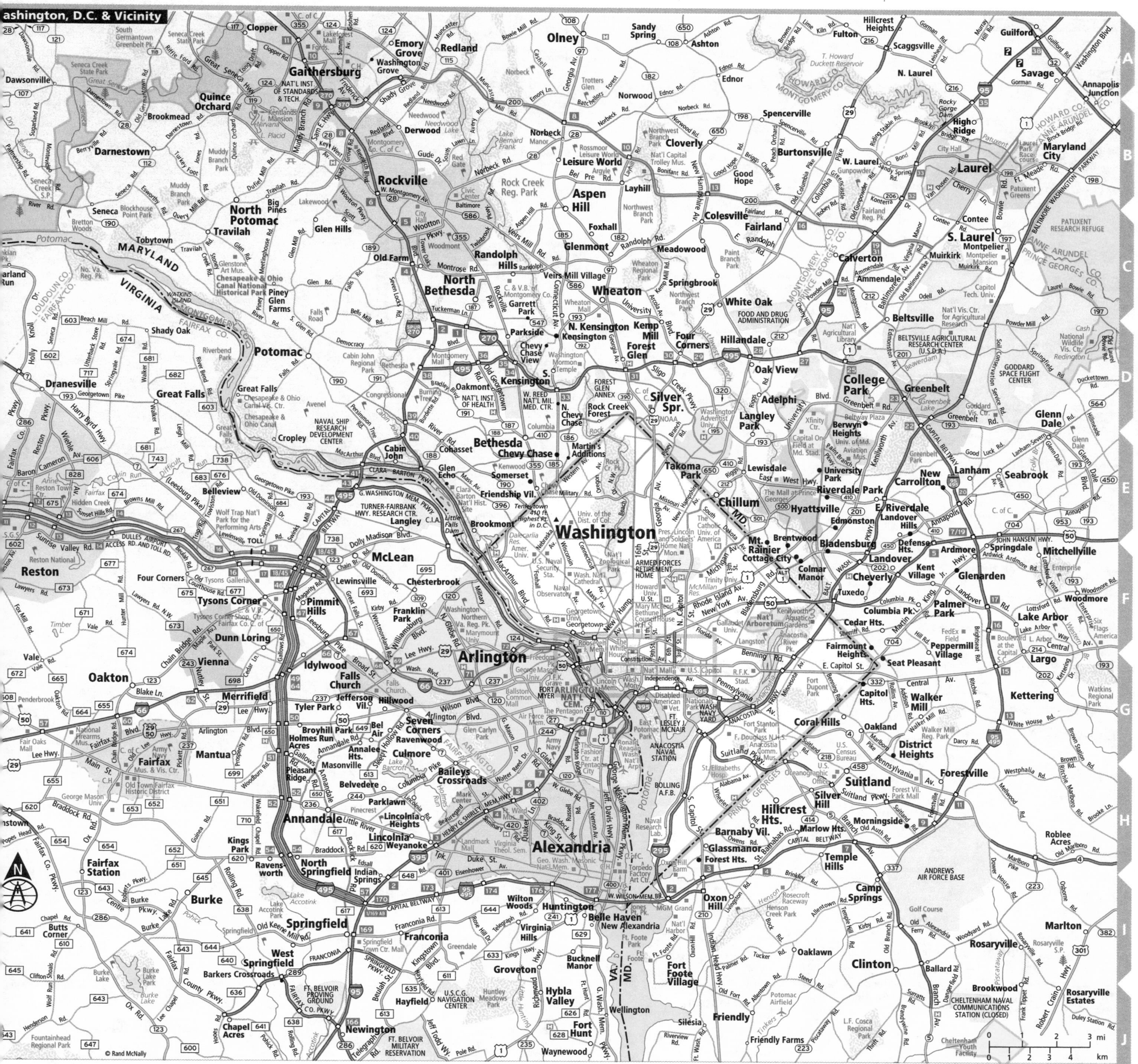

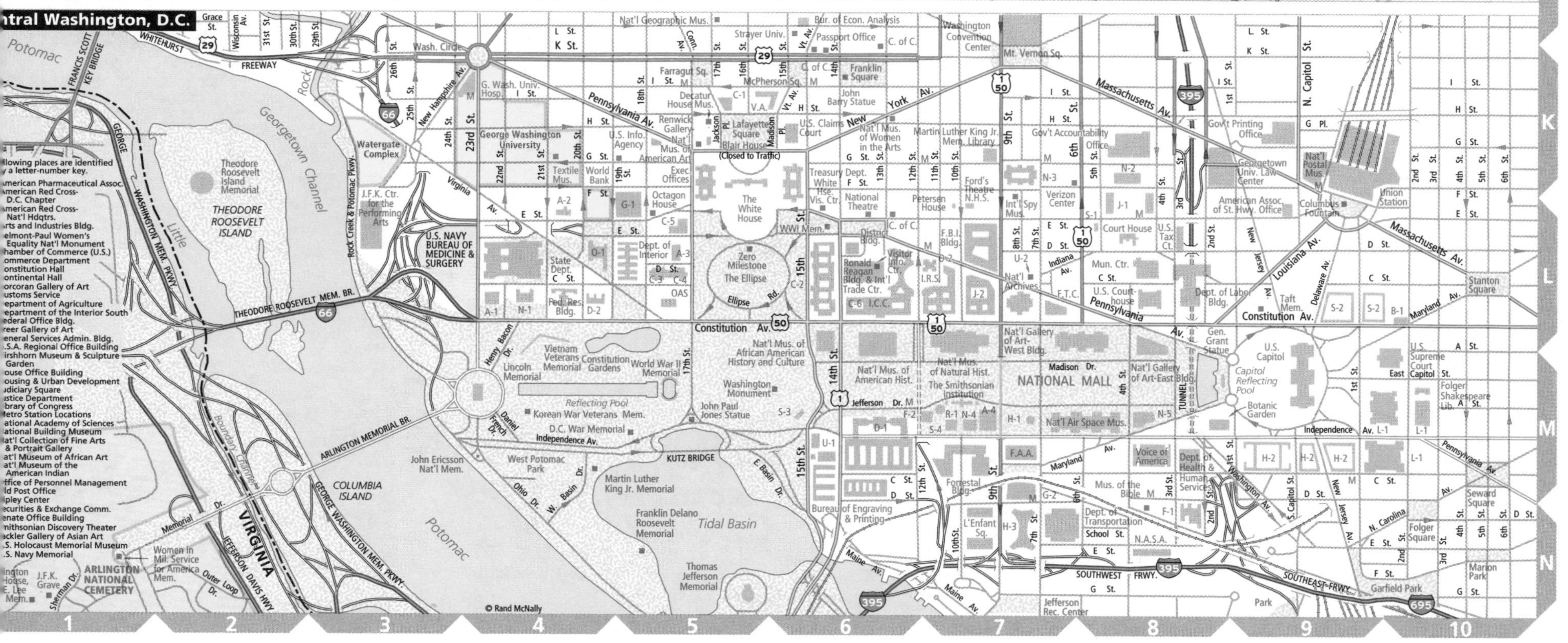

West Virginia

Nickname: The Mountain State
Capital: Charleston, J-3
Land area: 24,038 sq. mi. (rank: 41st)
Population: 1,852,994 (rank: 37th)
Largest city: Charleston, 51,400, J-3

Index of places Pg. 135

Mileages between cities

	Bluefield	Charleston	Clarksburg	Cumberland, MD	Martinsburg	Petersburg	Wheeling	Wh. Sulphur Sprs.
Beckley	50	59	136	239	267	184	236	59
Charleston	106		123	225	304	193	177	120
Cumberland, MD	288	225	109		79	66	155	194
Huntington	158	51	174	276	355	244	228	172
Morgantown	218	154	38	73	151	103	78	187
Parkersburg	183	76	72	181	259	172	104	198
Wheeling	283	177	114	155	225	179		262
White Sulphur Sprs.	79	120	155	194	208	125	262	

Total mileages through West Virginia

64: 189 miles
77: 187 miles
70: 14 miles
79: 161 miles

More mileages at randmcnally.com/MC

Travel planning & on-the-road resources

Tourism Information
West Virginia Division of Tourism:
(800) 225-5982, (304) 558-2200; www.wvtourism.com, gotowv.com

Road Conditions & Construction
511, (877) 982-7623; www.wv511.org, www.transportation.wv.gov

Toll Road Information (E-ZPass)
W.V. Parkways Authority: (304) 926-1900; www.transportation.wv.gov/turnpike

arborPark promenade, Kenosha

Sights to see

- Angel Museum, Beloit N-6
- Betty Brinn Children's Museum, Milwaukee L-3
- Golden Rondelle Theatre, Racine J-10
- Harley Davidson Museum, Milwaukee M-2
- Henry Maier Festival Park, Milwaukee M-4
- J.M. Kohler Arts Center, Sheboygan F-10
- Kenosha History Center, Kenosha L-10
- Miller Brewery, Milwaukee E-5
- Milwaukee Art Museum & War Mem., Milwaukee L-4
- Milwaukee Public Museum, Milwaukee L-2
- Mitchell Park Horticultural Conservatory, Milwaukee F-6
- Petit National Ice Center, Milwaukee F-4

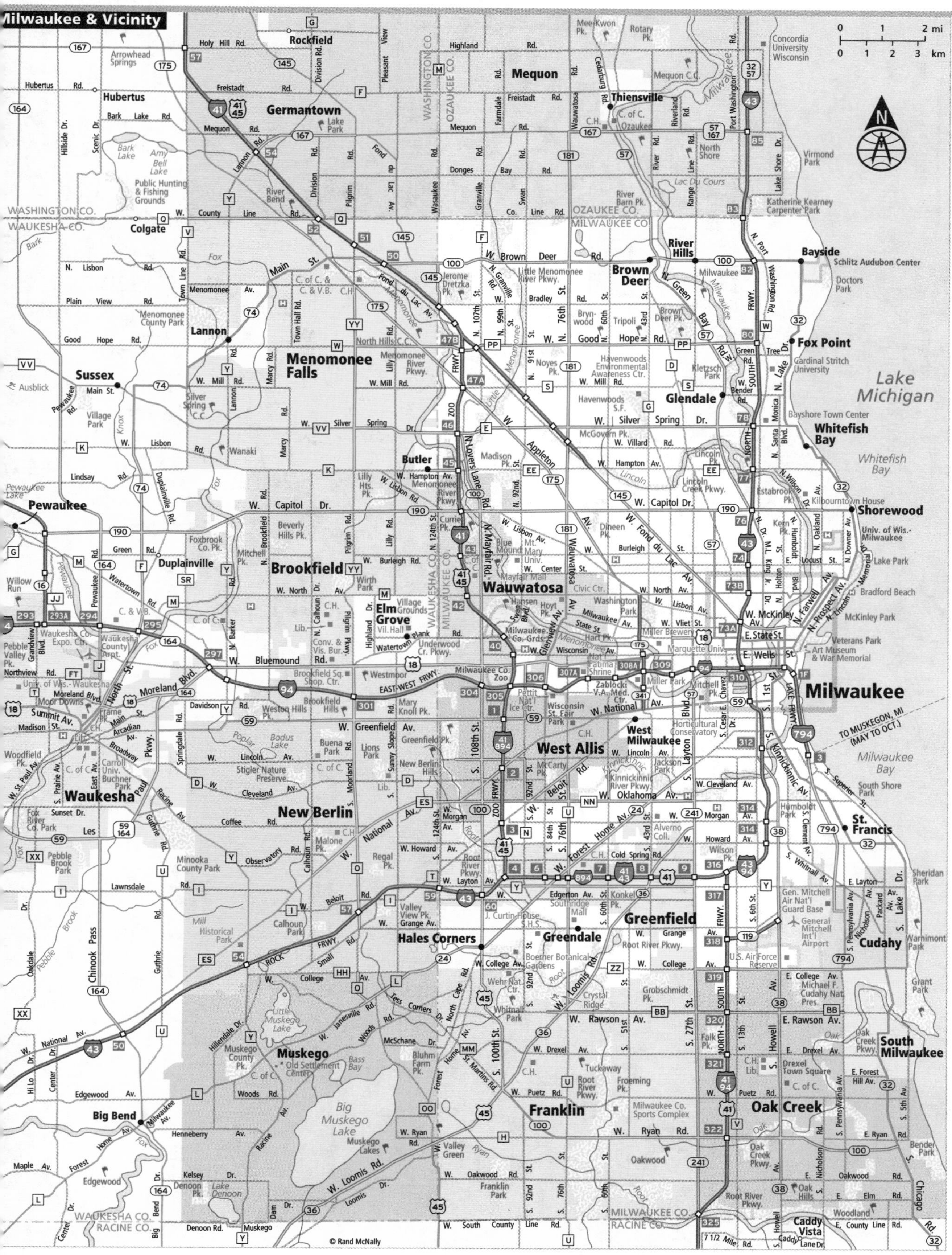

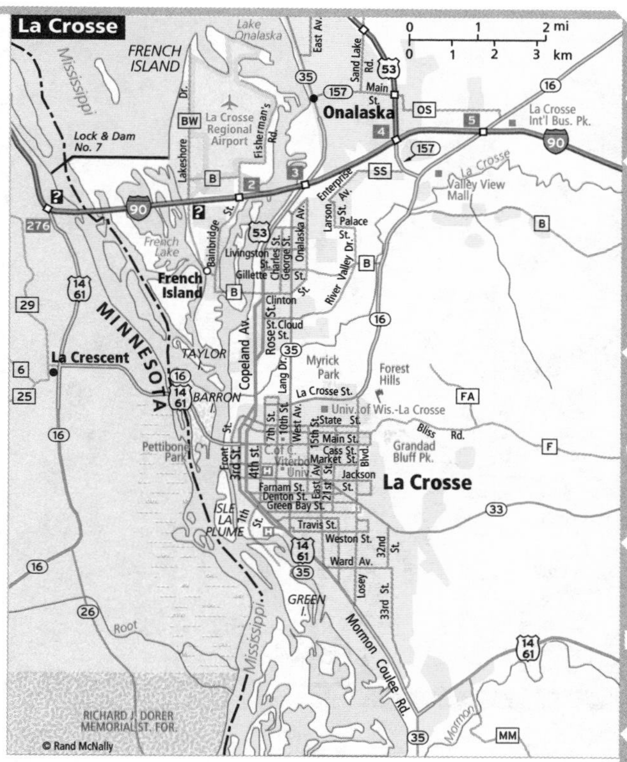

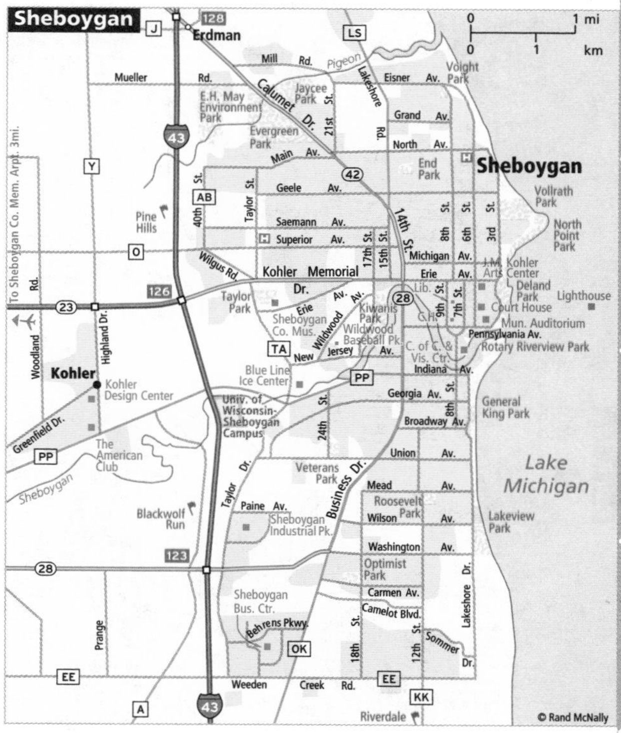

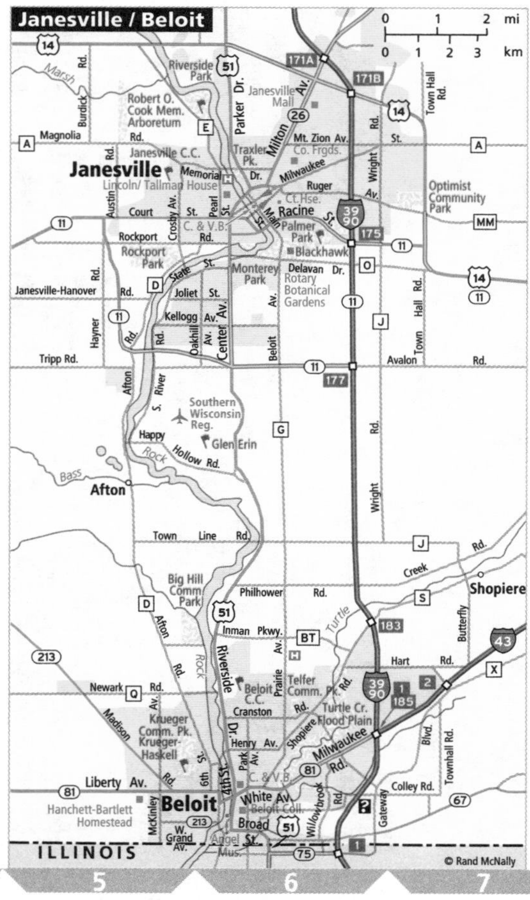

Nickname: The Badger State
Capital: Madison, N-9
Land area: 54,158 sq. mi. (rank: 25th)
Population: 5,686,986 (rank: 20th)
Largest city: Milwaukee, 594,833, N-13

Index of places Pg. 136

Travel planning & on-the-road resources

Tourism Information
Wisconsin Department of Tourism: (800) 432-8747, (608) 266-2161; www.travelwisconsin.com

Road Conditions & Construction
511, (866) 511-9472; www.511wi.gov

Toll Road Information
No toll roads

Determining distances along roads

Highway distances (segments of one mile or less not shown):
Cumulative miles (red): the distance between red arrows
Intermediate miles (black): the distance between intersections & places

Interchanges and exit numbers
For most states, the mileage between interchanges may be determined by subtracting one number from the other.

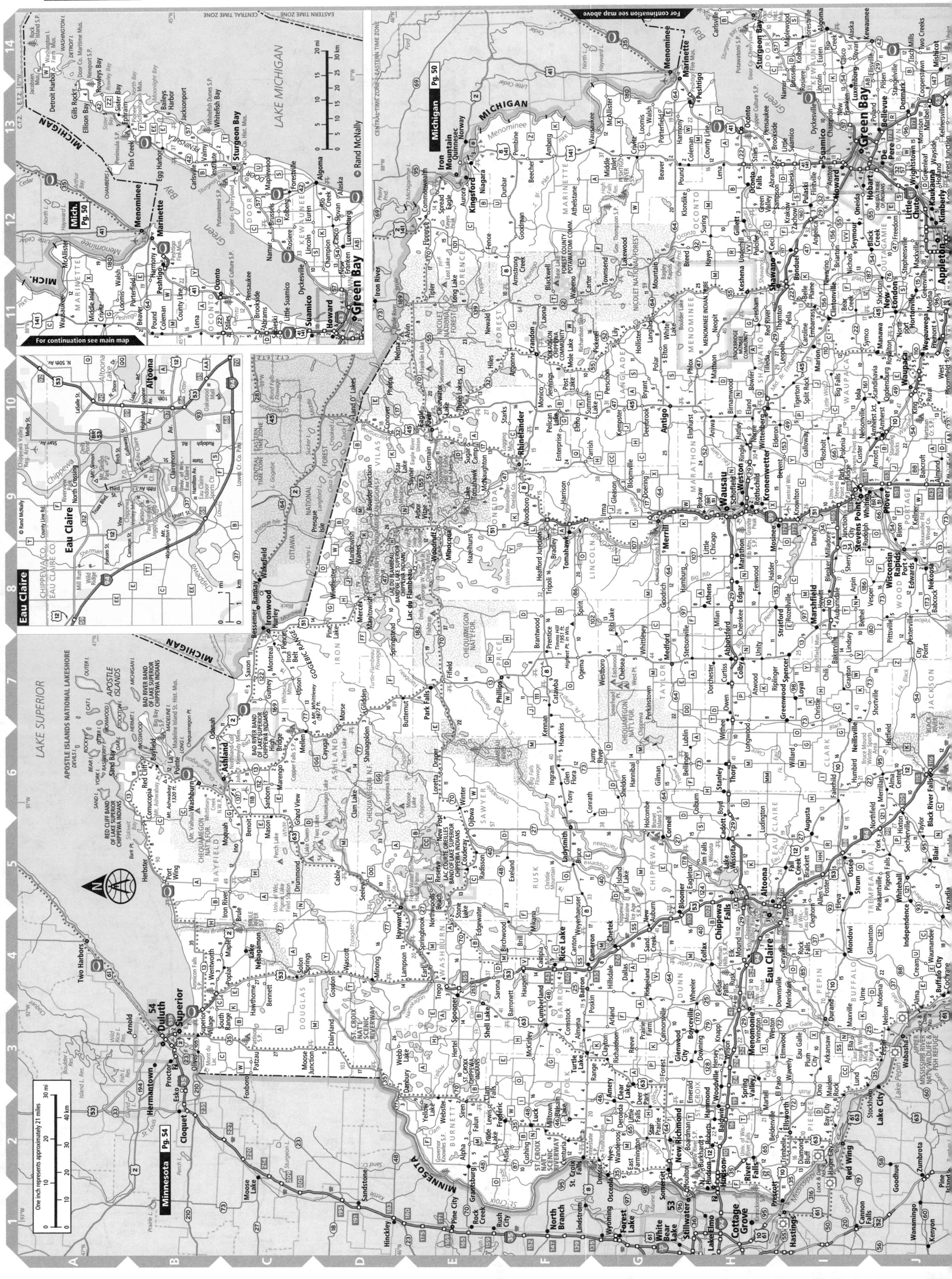

Mileages between cities

	Beloit	Chicago, IL	Dubuque, IA	Eau Claire	Green Bay	Hayward	La Crosse	Madison	Milwaukee	Oshkosh	Rhinelander	Sheboygan	Sturgeon Bay	Superior	Wausau	Wisconsin Dells
Chicago, IL	96		177	315	206	420	281	146	90	175	338	145	245	462	281	195
Eau Claire	223	315	192		192	106	86	177	243	181	155	228	237	149	98	124
Green Bay	184	206	233	192		283	203	138	116	52	136	64	44	326	96	132
La Crosse	188	281	119	86	203	190		143	209	153	214	195	248	233	170	90
Madison	54	146	93	177	138	282	143		78	87	200	117	185	325	143	57
Milwaukee	74	90	171	243	116	348	209	78		86	244	54	155	390	187	123
Superior	370	462	339	149	326	70	233	325	390	332	182	388	370		232	271
Wausau	189	281	239	98	96	• 189	170	143	187	103	59	158	141	232		112

Total mileages through Wisconsin

- 39: 182 miles
- 90: 189 miles
- 43: 192 miles
- 94: 341 miles

More mileages at randmcnally.com/MC

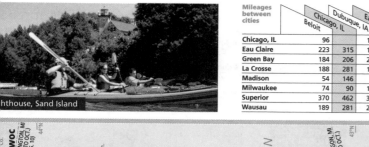

Wyoming

Nickname: The Equality State
Capital: Cheyenne, M-9
Land area: 97,093 sq. mi. (rank: 9th)
Population: 563,626 (rank: 50th)
Largest city: Cheyenne, 59,466, M-9

Index of places Pg. 136

Mileages between cities

	Casper	Cheyenne	Cody	Evanston	Gillette	Laramie	Sheridan	Spearfish, SD
Casper		178	213	325	126	147	148	219
Cheyenne	178		392	357	244	49	324	290
Cody	213	392		376	250	363	148	344
Jackson	283	432	177	190	411	383	325	504
Riverton	119	272	138	238	248	222	213	341
Rock Springs	225	257	278	100	351	207	373	444
Sheridan	148	324	148	473	103	294		196
Spearfish, SD	219	290	344	544	93	296	196	

Total mileages through Wyoming

25: 301 miles
90: 209 miles
80: 403 miles
20: 505 miles

More mileages at randmcnally.com/MC

Travel planning & on-the-road resources

Tourism Information

Wyoming Office of Tourism: (800) 225-5996, (307) 777-7777; www.wyomingtourism.org

Road Conditions & Construction

511, (888) 996-7623; www.wyoroad.info

Toll Road Information

No toll roads

Determining Distance

(segmen one mile not show

Cumulative miles (red): the distance between red a…

Intermediate miles (black): the distance between intersections & places

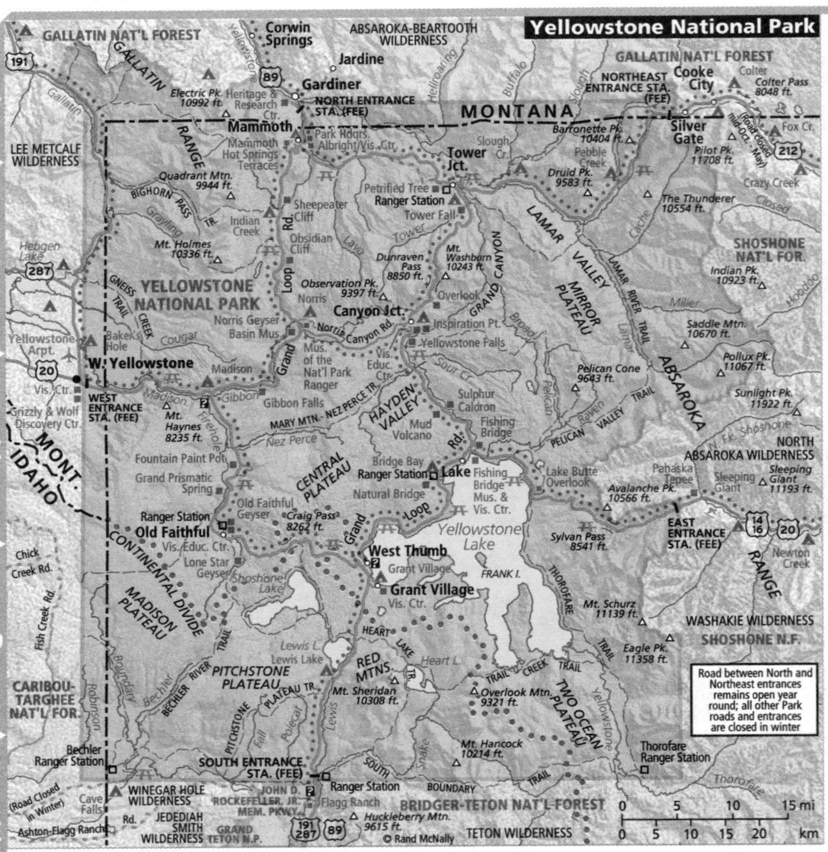

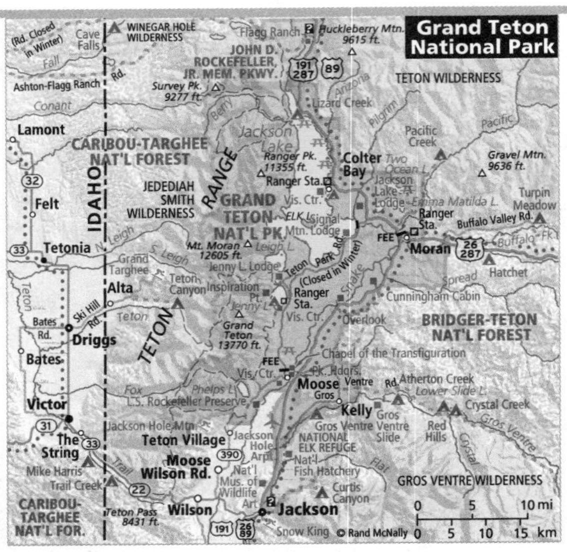

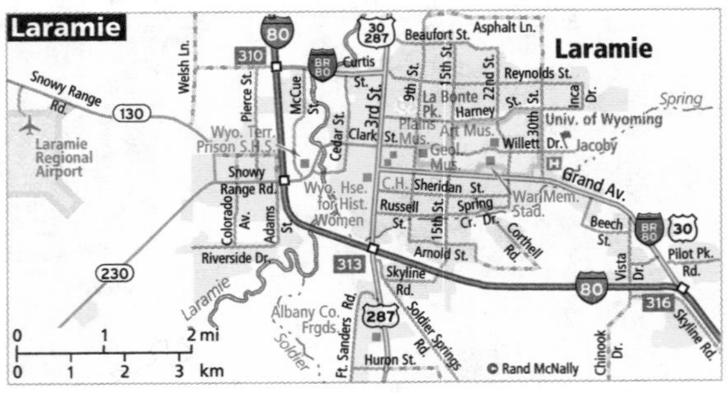

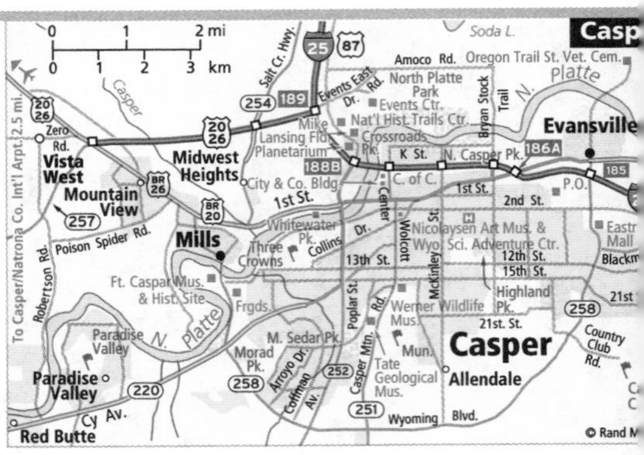

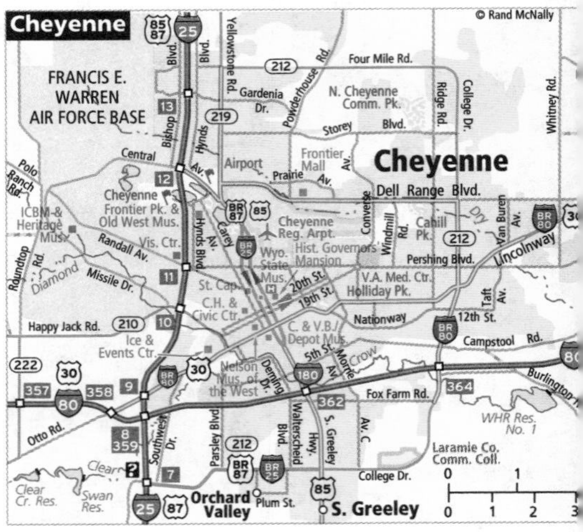

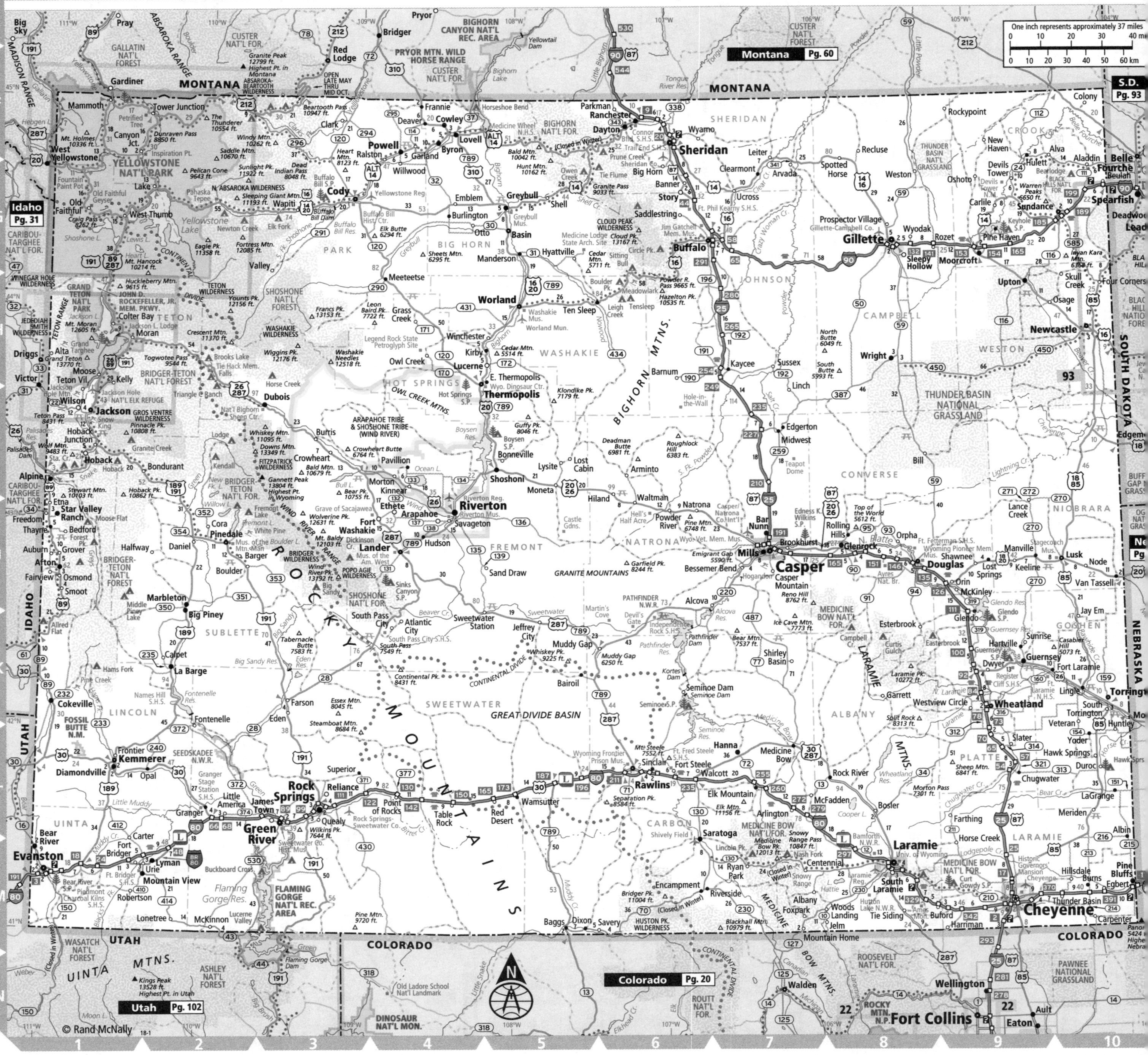

Capital: Ottawa, I-10
Land area: 3,511,023 sq. mi.
Population: 33,476,688
Largest city: Toronto, 2,615,060, I-10

Index of places Pg. 136

Selected National Park locations

- Banff National Park G-3
- Cape Breton Highlands Nat'l Park. . G-13
- Fundy National Park. H-12
- Glacier National Park G-3
- Gros Morne National Park F-13
- Jasper National Park. F-3
- Kejimkujik National Park H-12
- Kluane National Park & Reserve C-2
- Kootenay National Park. G-3
- Mount Revelstoke National Park. . . . G-3
- Parc National de la Maurice. H-11
- Prince Albert National Park F-5
- Prince Edward Island Nat'l Park. . . . H-12
- Pukaskwa National Park. H-8
- Riding Mountain National Park. H-6
- St. Lawrence Islands National Park . . I-10

Aéroport . . . . Airport
Arrondissement. . . . . District
Baie . . . . Bay
Barrage . . . . Dam
Basilique. . . . . Basilica
Bibliothèque . . . . Library
. . . Woods
Cap. . . . . Cape
Centre de recherches . . . . Research centre (or center)
Centre des congrès . . . . Convention centre (or center)
Chemin. . . . . Road
. . . Channel
Chutes . . . . Falls
Débarquement . . . . Landing
Détroit . . . . Strait
Fleuve. . . . . . Major river (that flows to the sea)
Hippodrome . . . . Race track
Hôtel de Ville. . . . . City or town hall
. . . Parliament building
Île . . . . Island
Jardin . . . . Garden
Jardin botanique. . . . . Botanical garden
Jardin zoologique . . Zoological garden (or Zoo)
Lac . . . . Lake
Lieu historique . . . . Historic site
Lieu historique national . . National historic site
Lieu natal. . . . . Birthplace
Mont . . . . Mountain
Musée. . . . . Museum
Oratoire . . . . Oratory
Parc. . . . . Park
Parc marin . . . . Marine park
Parc national. . . . . National park (or provincial park in Québec)
Pont . . . . Bridge
Promenade . . . . Boulevard
Réserve faunique . . . . Wildlife reserve
Réserve indienne. . . . . Indian reserve (or Reservation)
Rivière . . . . River
Rue . . . . Street
Stade . . . . Stadium
Tribunal . . . . Court house
Université. . . . . University

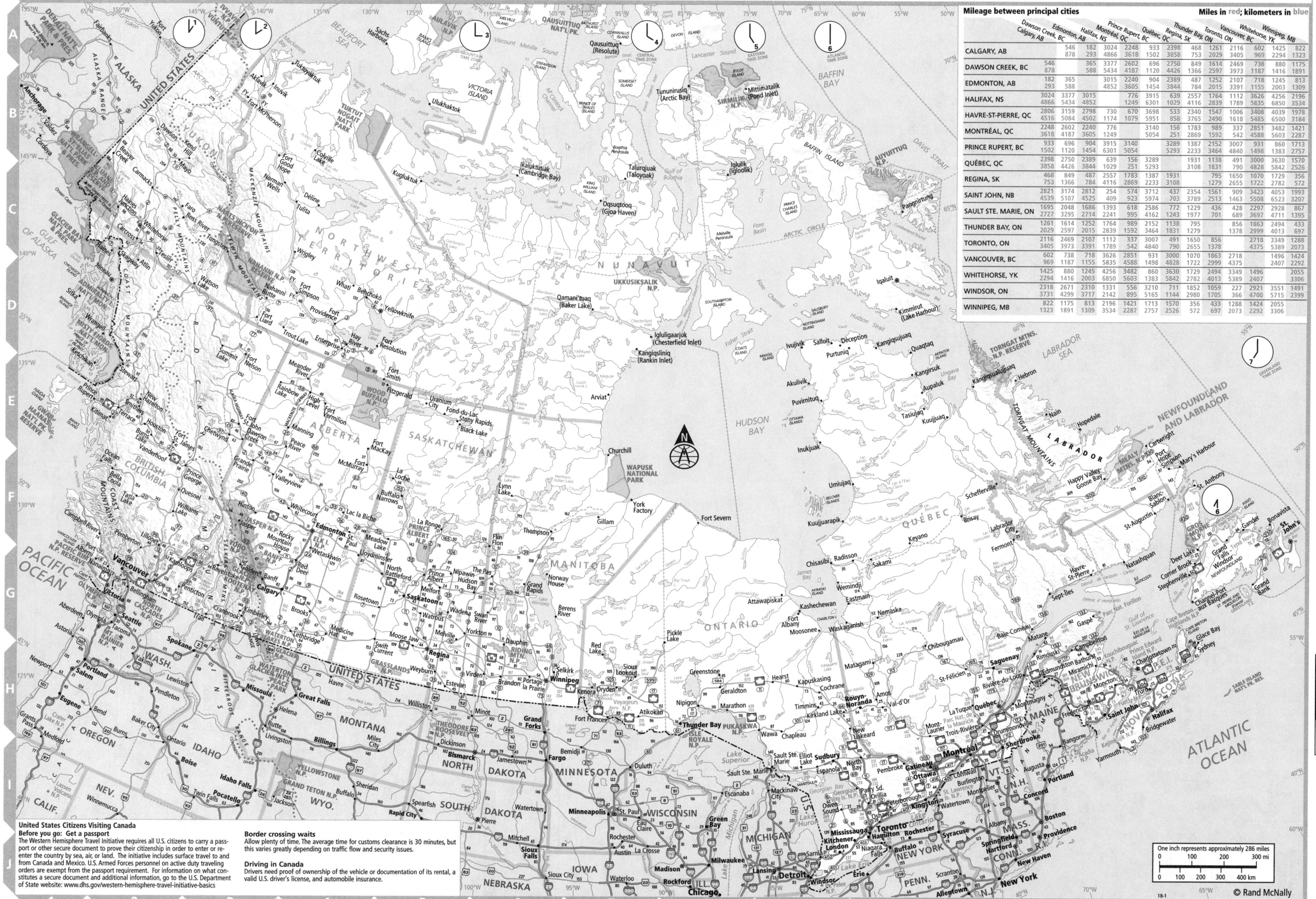

Mileage between principal cities

Miles in red; kilometers in blue

	Calgary, AB	Dawson Creek, BC	Edmonton, AB	Halifax, NS	Montréal, QC	Prince Rupert, BC	Québec, QC	Regina, SK	Thunder Bay, ON	Toronto, ON	Vancouver, BC	Whitehorse, YK	Winnipeg, MB
CALGARY, AB		546 / 878	182 / 293	3024 / 4866	2248 / 3618	933 / 1502	2398 / 3858	468 / 753	1261 / 2029	2116 / 3405	602 / 969	1425 / 2294	822 / 1323
DAWSON CREEK, BC	546 / 878		365 / 588	3377 / 5434	2602 / 4187	696 / 1120	2750 / 4426	849 / 1366	1614 / 2597	2469 / 3973	738 / 1187	880 / 1416	1175 / 1891
EDMONTON, AB	182 / 293	365 / 588		3015 / 4852	2240 / 3605	904 / 1454	2389 / 3844	487 / 784	1252 / 2015	2107 / 3391	718 / 1155	1245 / 2003	813 / 1309
HALIFAX, NS	3024 / 4866	3377 / 5434	3015 / 4852		776 / 1249	3915 / 6301	639 / 1029	2557 / 4116	1764 / 2839	1112 / 1789	3626 / 5835	4256 / 6850	2196 / 3534
HAVRE-ST-PIERRE, QC	2806 / 4516	3159 / 5084	2798 / 4502	730 / 1174	670 / 1079	3698 / 5951	533 / 858	2340 / 3765	1547 / 2490	1006 / 1618	3408 / 5485	4039 / 6500	1978 / 3184
MONTRÉAL, QC	2248 / 3618	2602 / 4187	2240 / 3605	776 / 1249		3140 / 5054	156 / 251	1783 / 2869	989 / 1592	337 / 542	2851 / 4588	3482 / 5603	1421 / 2287
PRINCE RUPERT, BC	933 / 1502	696 / 1120	904 / 1454	3915 / 6301	3140 / 5054		3289 / 5293	1387 / 2233	2152 / 3464	3007 / 4840	931 / 1498	860 / 1383	1713 / 2757
QUÉBEC, QC	2398 / 3858	2750 / 4426	2389 / 3844	639 / 1029	156 / 251	3289 / 5293		1931 / 3108	1138 / 1831	491 / 790	3000 / 4828	3630 / 5842	1570 / 2526
REGINA, SK	468 / 753	849 / 1366	487 / 784	2557 / 4116	1783 / 2869	1387 / 2233	1931 / 3108		795 / 1279	1650 / 2655	1070 / 1722	1729 / 2782	356 / 572
SAINT JOHN, NB	2821 / 4539	3174 / 5107	2812 / 4525	254 / 409	574 / 923	3712 / 5974	437 / 703	2354 / 3789	1561 / 2513	909 / 1463	3423 / 5508	4053 / 6523	1993 / 3207
SAULT STE. MARIE, ON	1695 / 2727	2048 / 3295	1686 / 2714	1393 / 2241	618 / 995	2586 / 4162	772 / 1243	1229 / 1977	436 / 701	428 / 689	2297 / 3697	2928 / 4711	867 / 1395
THUNDER BAY, ON	1261 / 2029	1614 / 2597	1252 / 2015	1764 / 2839	989 / 1592	2152 / 3464	1138 / 1831	795 / 1279		856 / 1378	1863 / 2999	2494 / 4013	433 / 697
TORONTO, ON	2116 / 3405	2469 / 3973	2107 / 3391	1112 / 1789	337 / 542	3007 / 4840	491 / 790	1650 / 2655	856 / 1378		2718 / 4375	3349 / 5389	1288 / 2073
VANCOUVER, BC	602 / 969	738 / 1187	718 / 1155	3626 / 5835	2851 / 4588	931 / 1498	3000 / 4828	1070 / 1722	1863 / 2999	2718 / 4375		1496 / 2407	1424 / 2292
WHITEHORSE, YK	1425 / 2294	880 / 1416	1245 / 2003	4256 / 6850	3482 / 5603	860 / 1383	3630 / 5842	1729 / 2782	2494 / 4013	3349 / 5389	1496 / 2407		2055 / 3306
WINDSOR, ON	2318 / 3731	2671 / 4299	2310 / 3717	1331 / 2142	556 / 895	3210 / 5165	711 / 1144	1852 / 2980	1059 / 1705	227 / 366	2921 / 4700	3551 / 5715	1491 / 2399
WINNIPEG, MB	822 / 1323	1175 / 1891	813 / 1309	2196 / 3534	1421 / 2287	1713 / 2757	1570 / 2526	356 / 572	433 / 697	1288 / 2073	1424 / 2292	2055 / 3306	

United States Citizens Visiting Canada

Before you go: Get a passport
The Western Hemisphere Travel Initiative requires all U.S. citizens to carry a passport or other secure document to prove their citizenship in order to enter or re-enter the country by sea, air, or land. The initiative includes surface travel to and from Canada and Mexico. U.S. Armed Forces personnel on active duty traveling orders are exempt from the passport requirement. For information on what constitutes a secure document and information on getting a passport, go to the U.S. Department of State website: www.dhs.gov/western-hemisphere-travel-initiative-basics

Border crossing waits
Allow plenty of time. The average time for customs clearance is 30 minutes, but this varies greatly depending on traffic flow and security issues.

Driving in Canada
Drivers need proof of ownership of the vehicle or documentation of its rental, a valid U.S. driver's license, and automobile insurance.

One inch represents approximately 286 miles

British Columbia
Capital: Victoria, M-7
Land area: 357,216 sq. mi. (rank: 4th)
Population: 4,400,057 (rank: 3rd)
Largest city: Vancouver, 603,502, L-7

Index of places Pg. 136

Mileages between cities	Banff, AB	Dawson Creek	Jasper, AB	Port Hardy	Prince Rupert	Vancouver	Victoria	Williams Lake
Banff, AB		503	178	808*	855	524	578*	483
Cranbrook	173	638	312	806*	989	521	575*	553
Dawson Creek	503		326	1022*	696	738	791*	399
Kamloops	307	576	275	502*	769	217	271*	177
Kelowna	299	671	376	526*	865	242	295*	272
Prince George	408	250	231	772*	447	488	542*	149
Prince Rupert	855	696	677	307*		931	985*	592
Vancouver	524	738	492	285*	931		72*	339

*Via ferry

Mileages © Rand McNally

Total mileages through British Columbia
1: 538 miles
16: 658 miles
More mileages at randmcnally.com/MC

Travel planning & on-the-road resources

Tourism Information
Destination British Columbia:
(604) 660-2861; www.hellobc.com

Road Conditions & Construction
(800) 550-4997; www.drivebc.ca

Toll Bridges
TransLink (Golden Ears Bridge, Vancouver) *(QuickPass, TreO)*:
(877) 299-0599; www.translink.ca
Transportation Investment Corp.: (Port Mann Bridge, Vancouver) *(TreO)*:
(604) 516-8736; www.treo.ca

ravel planning & on-the-road resources

rism Information
vel Alberta: (800) 252-3782; www.travelalberta.us

d Conditions & Construction
7) 262-4997; www.ama.ab.ca

Road Information
toll roads

Determining Distances
(segments of one mile or less not shown)

Cumulative miles (red), km (blue): the distance between red arrows
Intermediate miles (black): the distance between intersections & places

Total mileages through Alberta

1: 332 miles
16: 397 miles

More mileages at randmcnally.com/MC

Mileages between cities

	Calgary	Dawson Creek, BC	Edmonton	Fort McMurray	Grande Prairie	Jasper	Lethbridge	Red Deer
Banff	78	503	260	544	423	178	217	167
Calgary		546	182	465	463	256	139	89
Grande Prairie	463	82	283	467		246	602	376
Edmonton	182	365		281	283	226	321	95
Lethbridage	139	684	321	604	602	395		227
Medicine Hat	178	724	360	563	641	434	102	267
Peace River	480	146	299	421	123	354	618	392
Vermilion	299	481	120	321	399	342	338	211

Alberta
Capital: Edmonton, E-16
Land area: 248,000 sq. mi. (rank: 6th)
Population: 3,645,257 (rank: 4th)
Largest city: Calgary, 1,096,833, I-16

Index of places Pg. 136

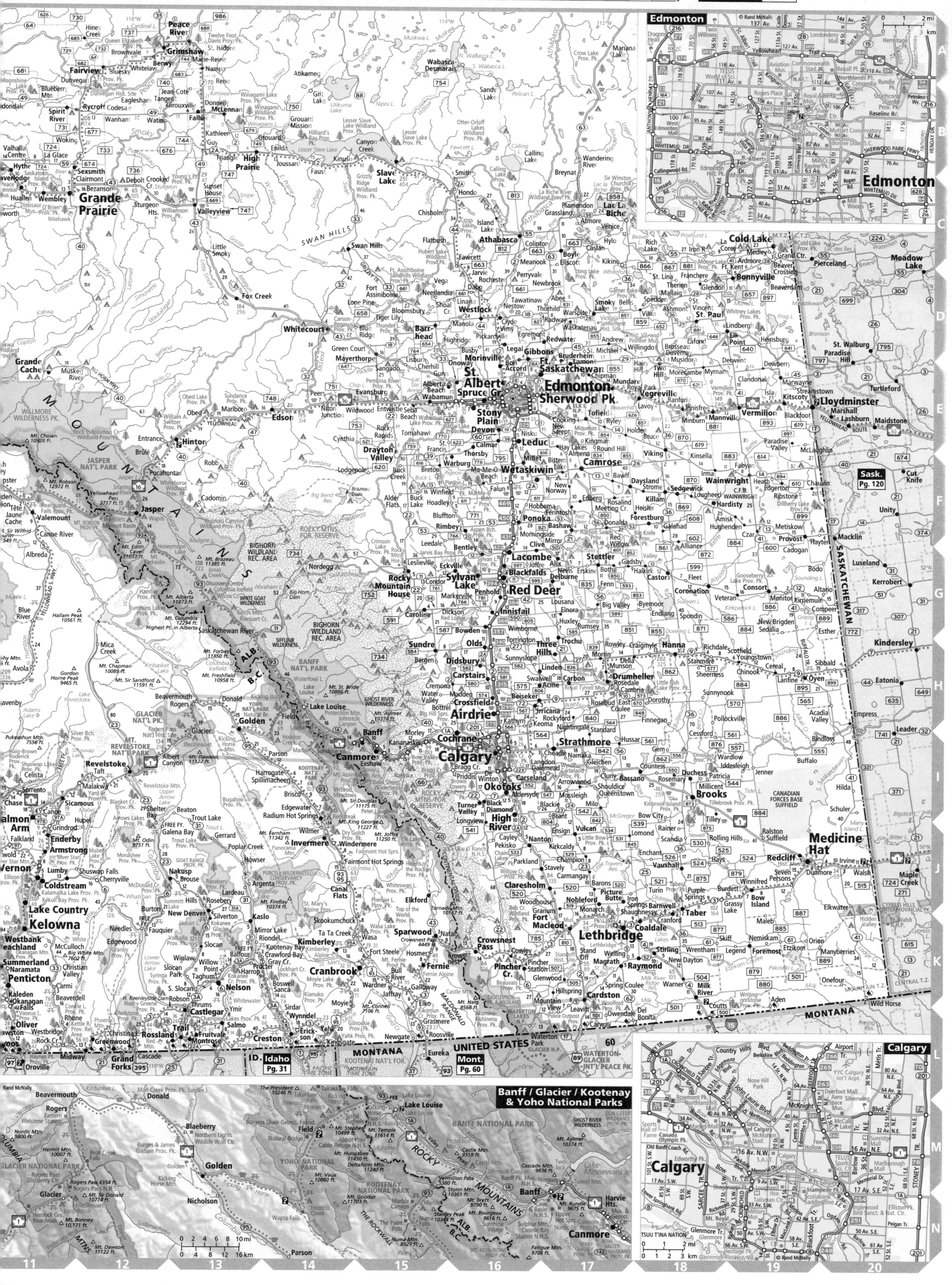

Saskatchewan
Capital: Regina, K-8
Land area: 228,445 sq. mi. (rank: 7th)
Population: 1,033,381 (rank: 6th)
Largest city: Saskatoon, 222,189, G-6

Index of places Pg. 136

Mileages between cities

	La Loche	La Ronge	Medicine Hat, AB	N. Battleford	Prince Albert	Regina	Saskatoon	Yorkton
Estevan	668	498	391	371	350	125	285	159
Lloydminster	331	347	289	85	214	331	171	375
Meadow Lake	217	232	370	98	162	343	183	388
Prince Albert	318	148	365	129		225	88	233
Regina	543	373	289	246	225		160	116
Saskatoon	379	236	277	86	88	160		205
Swift Current	505	403	139	190	255	151	167	266
Yorkton	551	382	405	290	233	116	205	

Mileages © Rand McNally

Total mileages through Saskatchewan
1: 413 miles
16: 437 miles
More mileages at randmcnally.com/MC

Travel planning & on-the-road resources

Tourism Information
Tourism Saskatchewan: (877) 237-2273, (306) 787-2300; www.sasktourism.com, www.tourismsaskatchewan.com

Road Conditions & Construction
In Saskatchewan only: (888) 335-7623, Saskatoon area: (306) 933-8333, Regina area: (306) 787-7623; www.saskatchewan.ca/residents/transportation/highways/highway-hotline

Toll Road Info
No toll roads

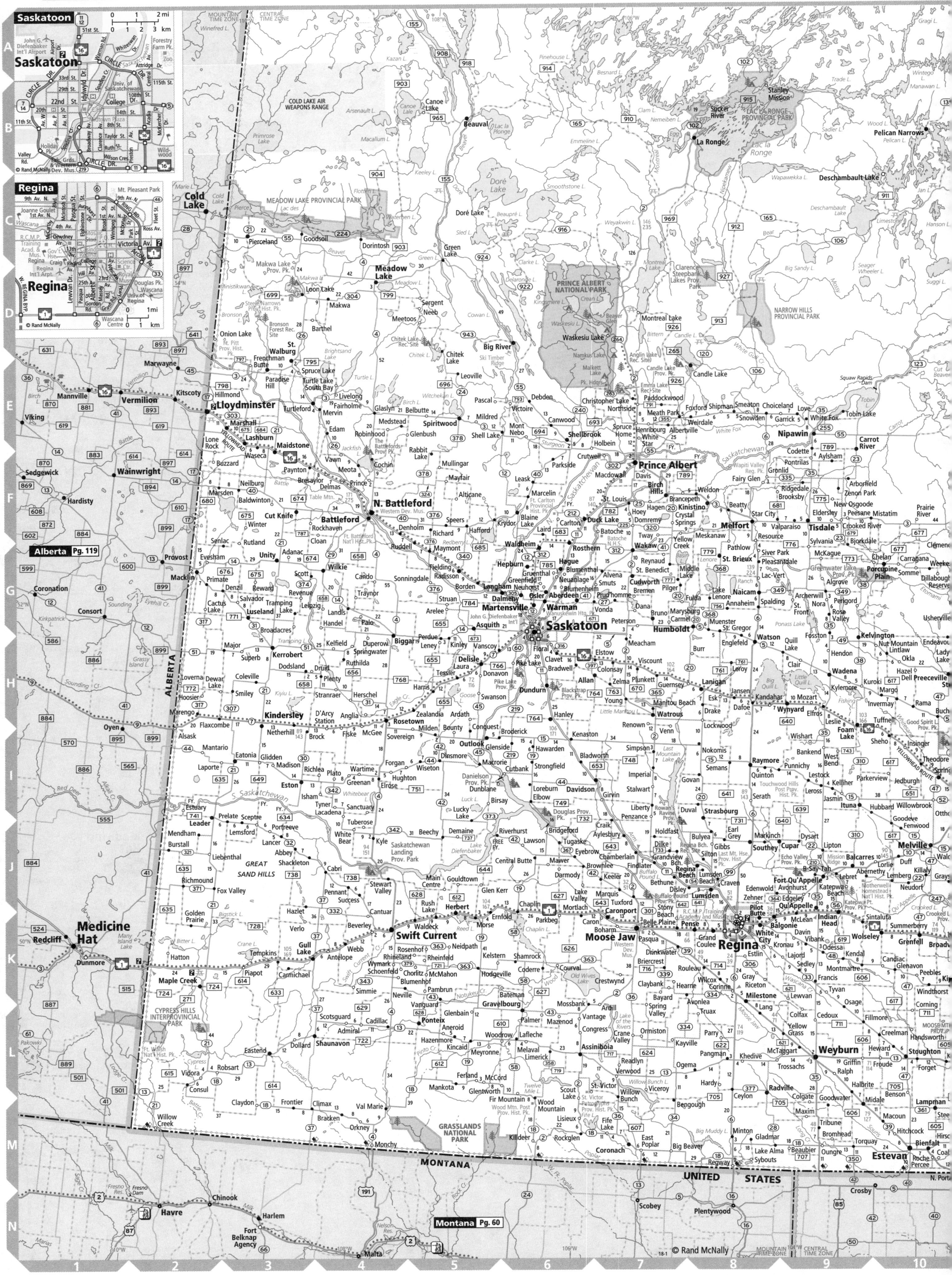

vel planning & on-the-road resources

n Information

Manitoba: (800) 665-0040, (204) 927-7800;
.travelmanitoba.com

Conditions & Construction

77) 627-6237, (204) 945-3704;
nanitoba.ca/roadinfo

511

ad Information

roads

Determining Distances

(segments of one mile or less not shown)

Cumulative miles (red), km (blue): the distance between red arrows

Intermediate miles (black): the distance between intersections & places

Total mileages through Manitoba

1 306 miles

16 166 miles

More mileages at
randmcnally.com/MC

Mileages between cities	Ashern	Brandon	Dauphin	Flin Flon	Grand Rapids	Pine Falls	Thompson	Winnipeg
Brandon	200		104	444	355	217	558	134
Dauphin	127	104		342	282	267	485	198
Flin Flon	368	444	342		255	546	244	483
Morden	184	129	216	552	338	167	542	87
Portage la Prairie	119	80	144	485	274	136	477	53
Swan River	233	208	106	236	211	372	385	303
Virden	245	47	148	419	399	262	568	178
Winnipeg	114	134	198	483	269	81	472	

Manitoba

Capital: Winnipeg, L-17
Land area: 213,729 sq. mi. (rank: 8th)
Population: 1,208,268 (rank: 5th)
Largest city: Winnipeg, 663,617, L-17

Index of places Pg. 136

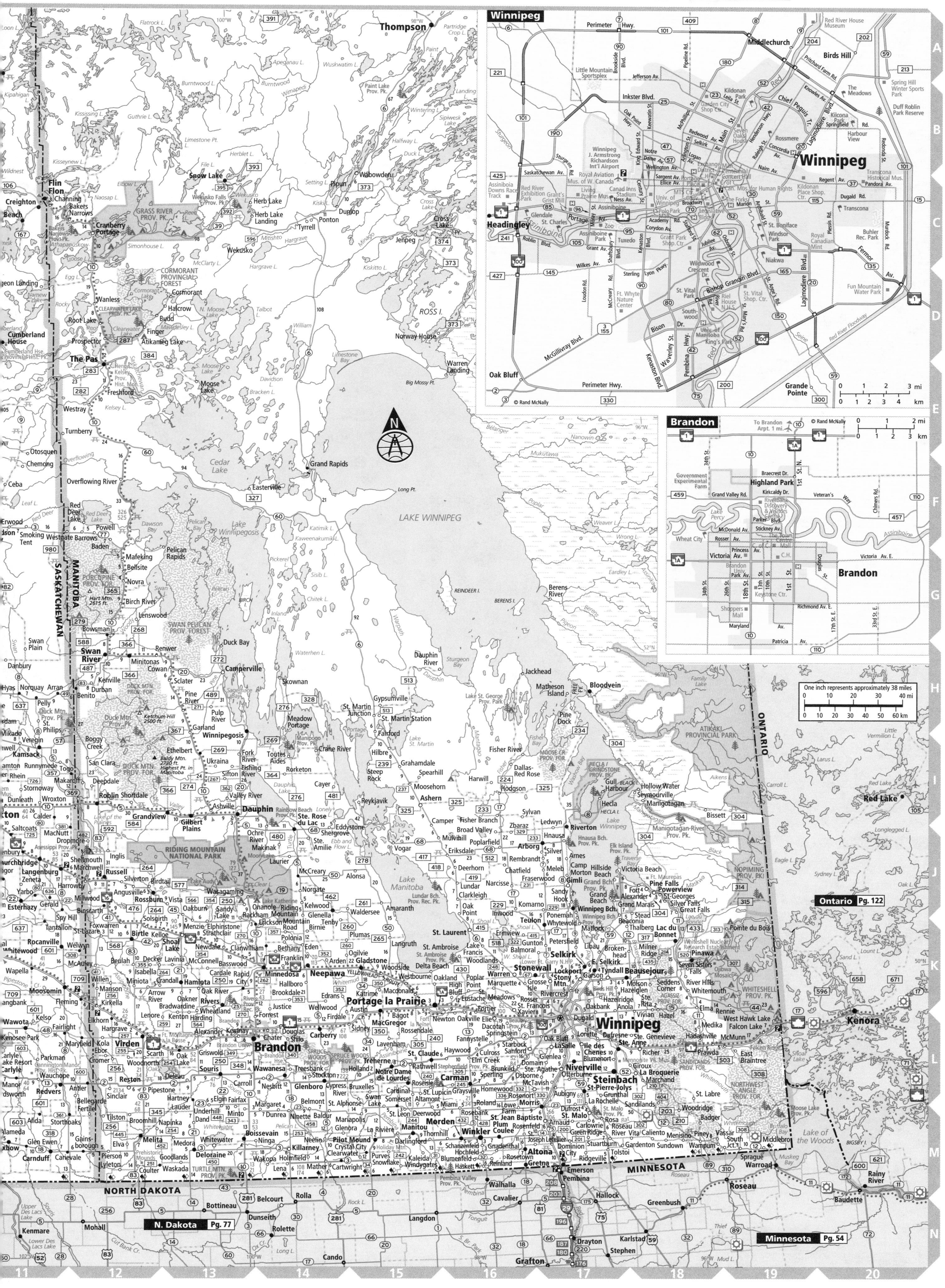

Capital: Toronto, I-10
Land area: 354,342 sq. mi. (rank: 5th)
Population: 12,851,821 (rank: 1st)
Largest city: Toronto, 2,615,060, I-10

Glossary of common French terms found on these maps: pg. 117

Index of places Pg. 136

Travel planning & on-the-road resources

Tourism Information
Ontario Travel: (800) 668-2746; www.ontariotravel.net

Road Conditions & Construction
511, (800) 268-4686, Toronto area: (416) 235-4686; www.mto.gov.on.ca/english/traveller

Toll Road Information:
407 ETR (Toronto): (888) 407-0407; www.407etr.com

Ontario–Michigan Toll Bridge Information
Ambassador Bridge (Detroit): (800) 462-7434; www.ambassadorbridge.com
Federal Bridge Corp. (Blue Water Bridge, Sarnia): (866) 422-6346; www.bluewaterbridge.ca
Detroit-Windsor Tunnel ***(NEXPRESS)***: (313) 567-4422 ext. 200, (519) 258-7424 ext. 200; www.dwtunnel.com
International Bridge Administration (Sault Ste. Marie): (705) 942-4345, (906) 635-5255; www.saultbridge.com

Ontario–New York Toll Bridge Informat
Buffalo & Ft. Erie Public Br. Authority (Peace Bridge) ***(E-ZPass)***: (716) 884-6744; www.peacebridge.com
Niagara Falls Bridge Commission: ***(E-ZPass or ExpressPass)*** (716) 285-6322 www.niagarafallsbridges.com
For St. Lawrence River crossings, see New York, p.

Mileages between cities

	Bracebridge	Hamilton	Kenora	Kingston	Montréal, QC	Niagara Falls	Ottawa	Owen Sound	Pembroke	Sarnia	Sault Ste. Marie	Sudbury	Thunder Bay	Timmins	Toronto	Windsor
Kingston	223	204	1285		180	243	120	269	154	335	555	369	983	509	161	381
London	213	81	1255	274	450	127	360	143	360	68	525	339	953	535	121	116
Niagara Falls	185	47	1227	243	419		329	163	328	188	497	311	925	507	83	233
Ottawa	237	290	1207	120	124	329		338	91	421	494	300	905	445	247	467
Sudbury	153	272	925	369	424	311	300	238	209	401	195		623	182	242	446
Thunder Bay	767	886	303	983	989	925	905	852	814	1015	436	623		517	856	1060
Toronto	116	44	1158	161	337	83	247	118	246	182	428	242	856	438		227
Windsor	319	187	1361	381	556	233	467	259	466	96	631	445	1059	641	227	

Total mileages through Ontario

(69) & (400) & (QEW) 323 miles (401) 513 miles

(17) & (417) 1358 miles

More mileages at randmcnally.com/MC

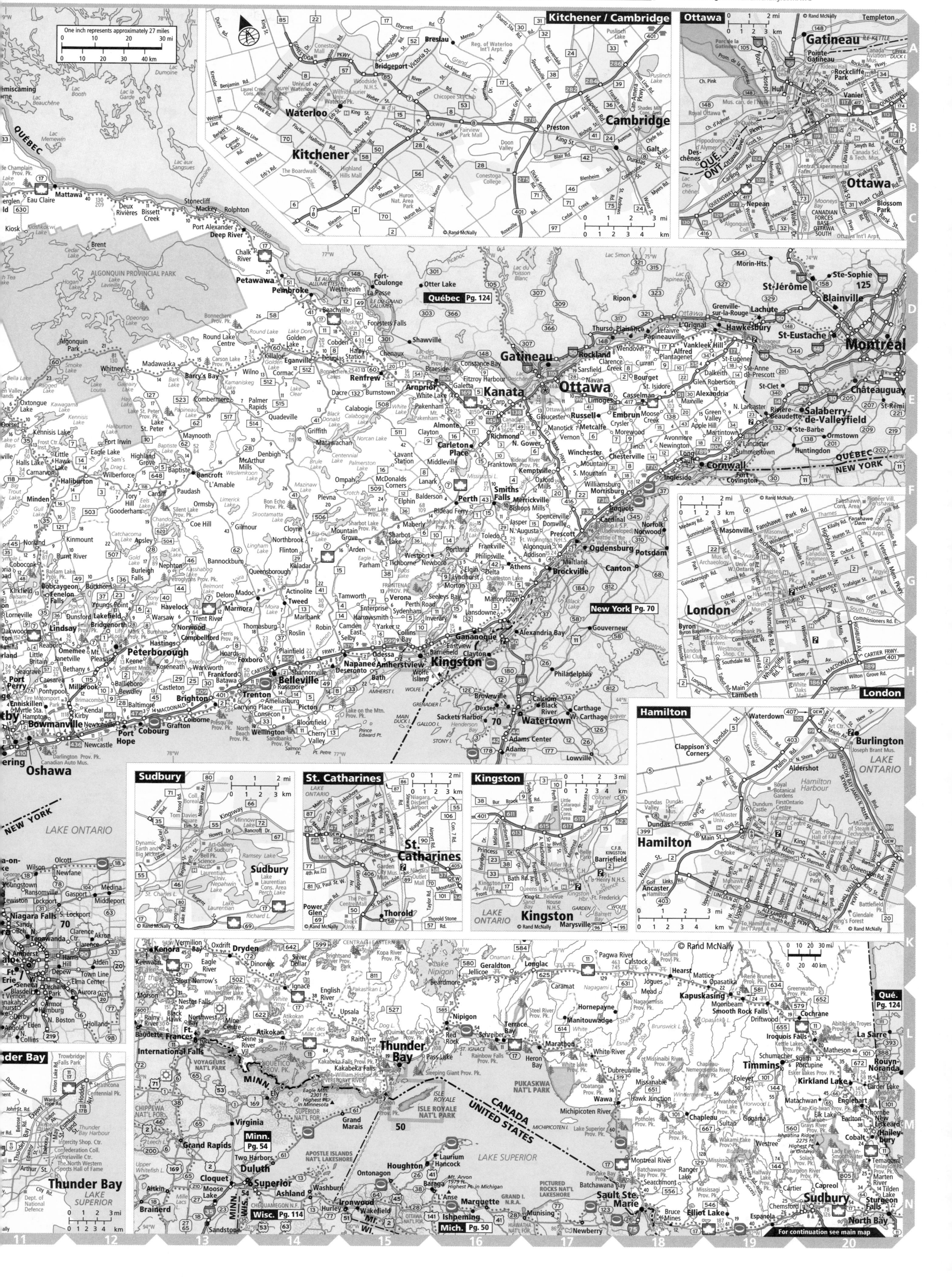

Capital: Québec, J-11
Land area: 527,079 sq. mi. (rank: 2nd)
Population: 7,903,001 (rank: 2nd)
Largest city: Montréal, 1,649,519, M-8

Glossary of common French terms found on these maps: pg. 117
Index of places Pg. 136

Travel planning & on-the-road resources

Tourism Information
Tourisme Québec: (877) 266-5687, (514) 873-2015; www.bonjourquebec.com

Road Conditions & Construction
511, (888) 355-0511; www.quebec511.gouv.qc.ca/en

Toll Road Information
Concession A25 (Pont Olivier-Charbonneau, Montréal) ***(A25 Smart Link)***:
(855) 766-8225, (514) 766-8225; www.a25.com
A30Express (near Montréal) ***(A30 Express)***:
(855) 783-3030, (514) 782-0800; www.a30express.com

Determining distances along roads
Highway distances (segments of one mile or less not shown):
Cumulative miles (red): the distance between red arrows
Cumulative kilometers (blue): the distance between red arrows
Intermediate miles (black): the distance between intersections &

Comparative distance: 1 mile = 1.609 kilometers 1 kilometer = 0.621 mi

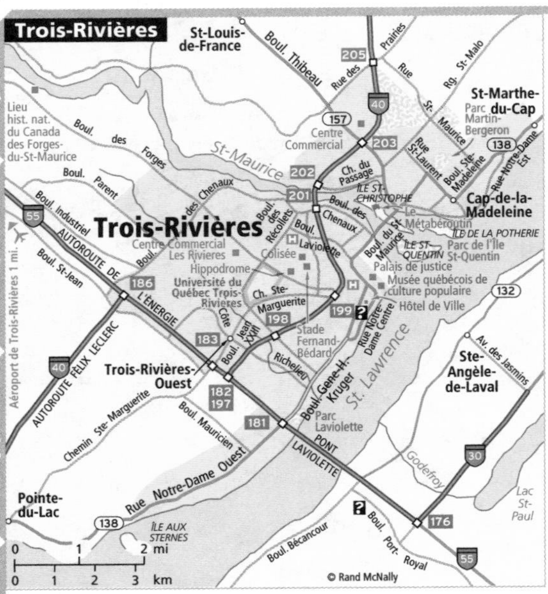

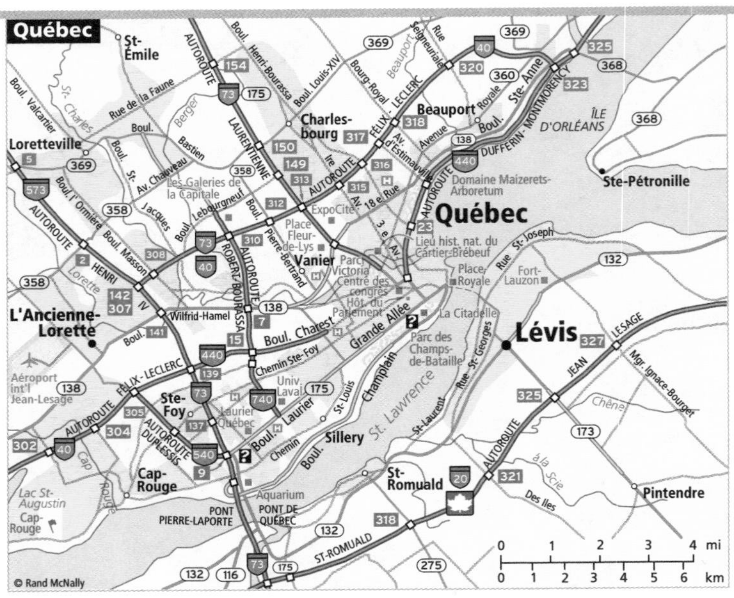

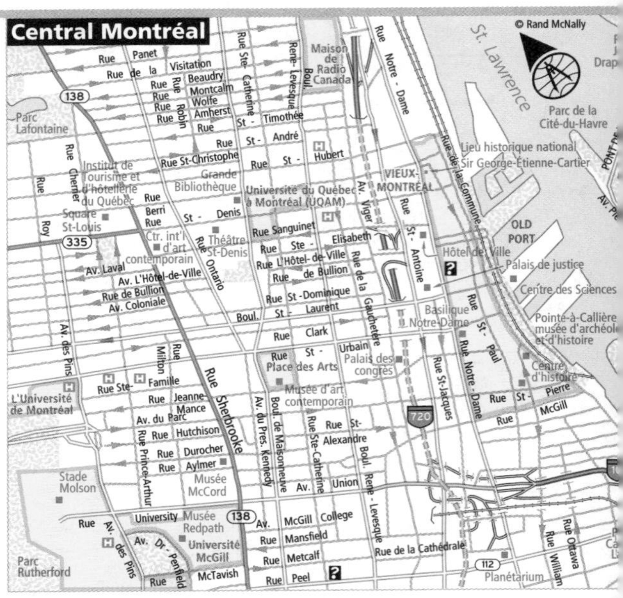

Mileages between cities	Baie-Comeau	Edmundston, NB	Gaspé	Mont-Laurier	Montréal	North Bay, ON	Ottawa, ON	Québec	Rimouski	Rivière-du-Loup	Rouyn-Noranda	Saguenay	Sept-Îles	Sherbrooke	Thetford Mines	Trois-Rivières
Montréal	410	336	566	145		346	124	156	331	266	389	289	534*	93	143	88
Ottawa, ON	533	459	689	122	124	222		279	454	389	323	411	657*	213	266	205
Québec	253	199	429	294	156	501	279		195	129	537	135	397*	146	72	78
Rouyn-Noranda	706	723	953	243	389	181	323	537	719	653		517	921*	481	530	461
Saguenay	196	186*	390*	427	289	634	411	135	156*	108*	517		339	279	205	211
Sept-Îles	143	306*	319*	678*	534*	879*	657*	397*	206*	268*	921*	339		524*	450*	465*
Sherbrooke	400	326	556	237	93	435	213	146	321	256	481	279	524*		65	94
Trois-Rivières	342	268	497	217	89	427	205	78	263	197	461	211	465*	94	88	

*Via ferry

Total mileages through Québec

20 132 937 miles
40 138 765 miles
15 117 412 miles

More mileages at randmcnally.com/MC

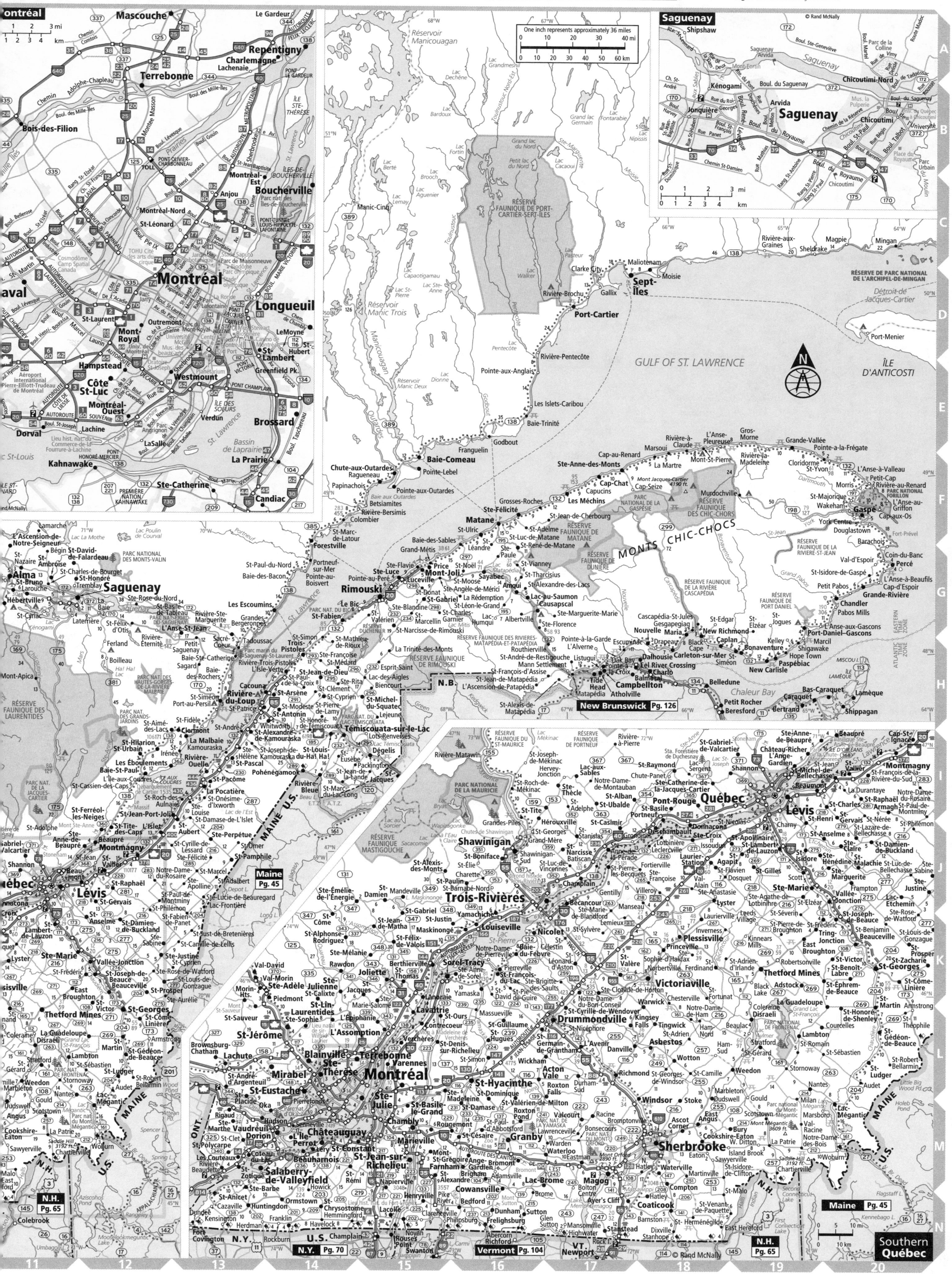

New Brunswick

Capital: Fredericton, H-4
Land area: 27,587 sq. mi. (rank: 11th)
Population: 751,171 (rank: 8th)
Largest city: Saint John, 70,063, J-5

Index of places Pg. 136

Travel planning & on-the-road resources

Tourism Information

Tourism New Brunswick: (800) 561-0123; www.tourismnewbrunswick.ca

Nova Scotia Tourism Agency: (800) 565-0000, (902) 425-5781; www.novascotia.com

Prince Edward Island Tourism: (800) 463-4734; www.tourismpei.com

Newfoundland & Labrador Tourism: (800) 563-6353, (709) 729-2830; www.newfoundlandlabrador.com

Road Conditions & Construction

New Brunswick: 511, (888) 747-7006, (506) 453-3939; www.gnb.ca/roads

Nova Scotia: 511, (902) 424-3933 In Canada: (888) 780-4440; 511.gov.ns.ca/map

Prince Edward Island: 511, (902) 368-4770, In Canada: (855) 241-2680; www.gov.pe.ca/roadconditions

Newfoundland & Labrador: Avalon: (709) 729-2382, Eastern: (709) 466-4120, Central: (709) 292-4300, Western: (709) 635-4217, Labrador: (709) 896-7840; www.roads.gov.nl.ca

Toll Road Information

Strait Crossing Bridge Ltd: (Confederation Bridge) *(StraitPass)*: (888) 437-6565; www.confederationbridge.com

Atlantic Hwy. Management Corp. Ltd. (Cobequid Pass, N.B. (Hwy 104)) *(E-Pass)*: (902) 668-2211; www.cobequidpass.com

Halifax Harbor Bridges (Halifax): *(MACPASS)*: (902) 463-2800; www.hdbc.ca

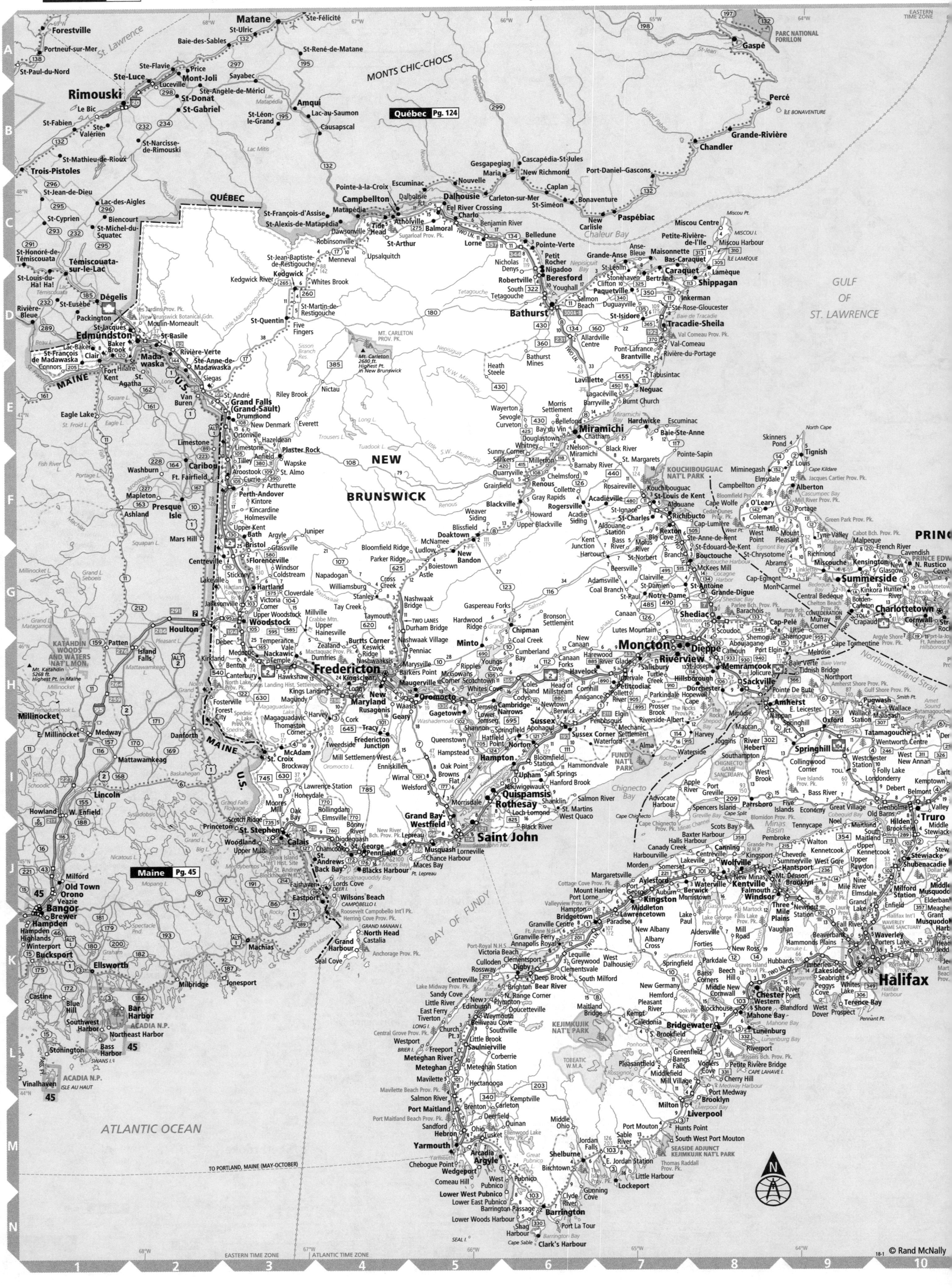

eages ween es	Amherst, NS	Bathurst, NB	Campbellton, NB	Charlottetown, PE	Corner Brook, NL	Edmundston, NB	Fredericton, NB	Grand Falls, NB	Halifax, NS	Moncton, NB	New Glasgow, NS	Saint John, NB	St. John's, NL	St. Stephen, NB	Sydney, NS	Yarmouth, NS
rlottetown, PE	82	214	280		461*	392	222	354	205	112	63	204	888*	274	215	389
undston, NB	319	160	125	392	817*		176	39	442	283	419	239	1244*	215	571	353
ericton, NB	149	160	248	222	647*	176		138	272	113	249	69	1074*	80	401	183
fax, NS	122	286	353	205	496*	442	272	403		162	98	254	923*	323	250	188
cton, NB	39	137	203	112	537*	283	113	244	162		139	95	964*	164	291	346
t John, NB	131	229	295	204	629*	239	69	201	254	95	231		1056*	69	383	114
ohn's, NL	925*	1088*	1155*	888*	433	1244*	1074*	1205*	923*	964*	825*	1056*		1125*	688*	1107*
ney, NS	252	415	482	215	261*	571	401	532	250	291	152	383	688*	452		434

*Via ferry

Mileages © Rand McNally

Nova Scotia
Capital: Halifax, K-9
Land area: 20,594 sq. mi. (rank: 12th)
Population: 921,727 (rank: 7th)
Largest city: Halifax, 390,096, K-9

Prince Edward Island
Capital: Charlottetown, G-10
Land area: 2,185 sq. mi. (rank: 13th)
Population: 140,204 (rank: 10th)
Largest city: Charlottetown, 34,562, G-10

Newfoundland & Labrador
Capital: St. John's, F-20
Land area: 144,353 sq. mi. (rank: 10th)
Population: 514,536 (rank: 9th)
Largest city: St. John's, 106,172, F-20

More mileages at randmcnally.com/MC

Glossary of common French terms found on these maps: pg. 117

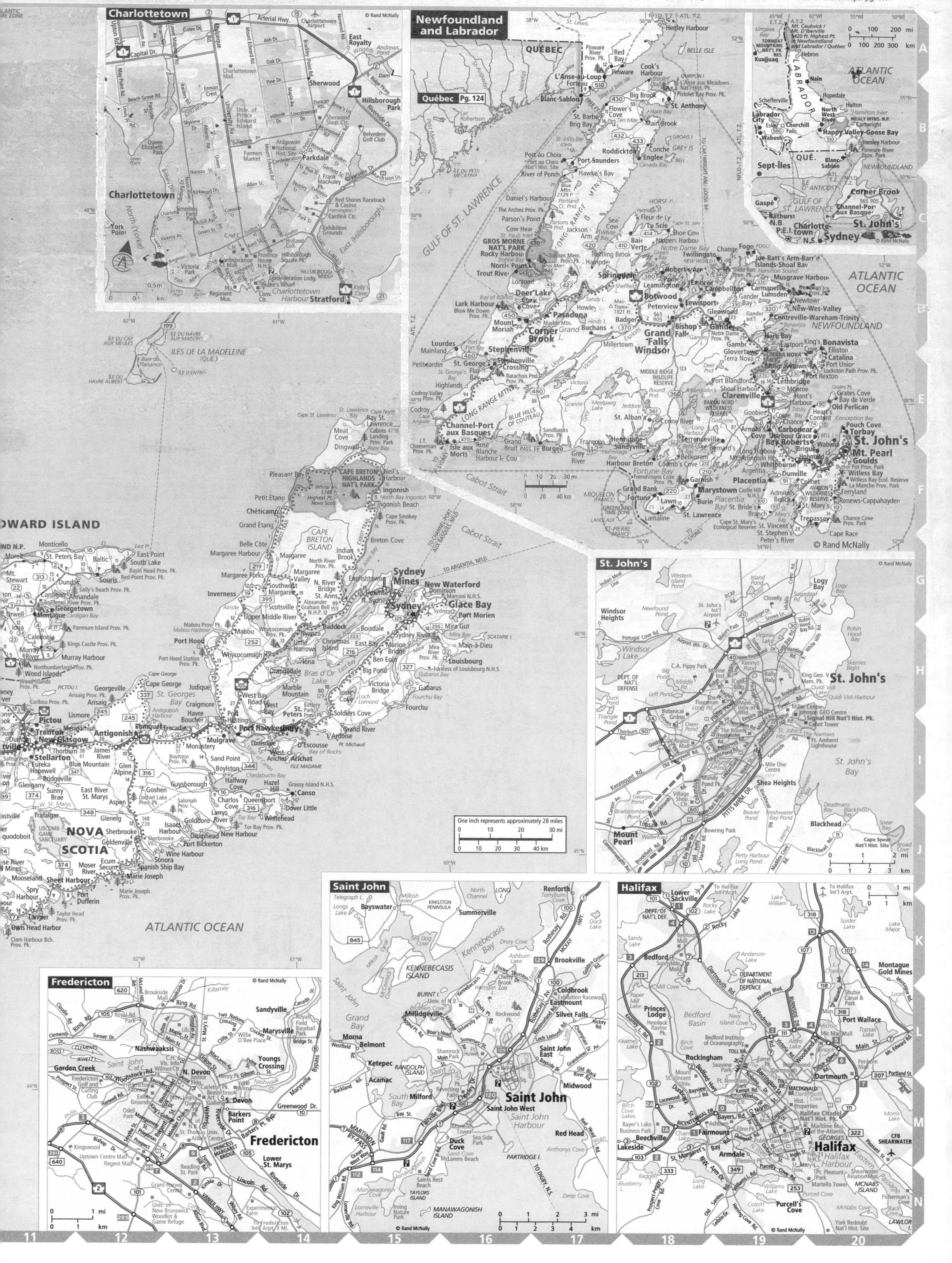

Mexico
Capital: Mexico City, G-8
Land area: 758,450 sq. mi.
Population: 112,336,538
Largest city: Mexico City, 8,851,080, G-8

Puerto Rico (U.S.)
Capital: San Juan, A-13
Land area: 3,425 sq. mi.
Population: 3,725,789
Largest city: San Juan, 381,931, A-13

Index of places Mexico: Pg. 136; Puerto Rico: Pg. 134

Sights to see

Mexico

- Chichen Itza Ruinas G-13
- Barranca del Cobre C-4
- Grutas de Cacahuamilpa H-8
- Parque Ecológico de Xochimilco I-3
- Parque Internacional del Río Bravo C-7
- Plaza de la Constitucion G-2
- Teotihuacán Ruinas G-8
- Tulum Ruinas G-14

Puerto Rico

- Bahía Fosforescente B-10
- Castillo del Morró A-13
- Museo de Arte de Ponce B-11
- Submarine Gardens A-13

On-the-road resources

Mexico Tourism Information
Mexico Tourism Board: (800) 446-3942; www.visitmexico.com/en

Mexico Toll Information, Road Conditions, & Construction
www.gob.mx/carreteras (in Spanish)

Puerto Rico Tourism Information
Tourism Company of Puerto Rico: (800) 866-7827; www.puertorico.com

Puerto Rico Toll Information, Road Conditions, & Construction
(800) 981-3021, (787) 977-2200
www.dtop.gov.pr

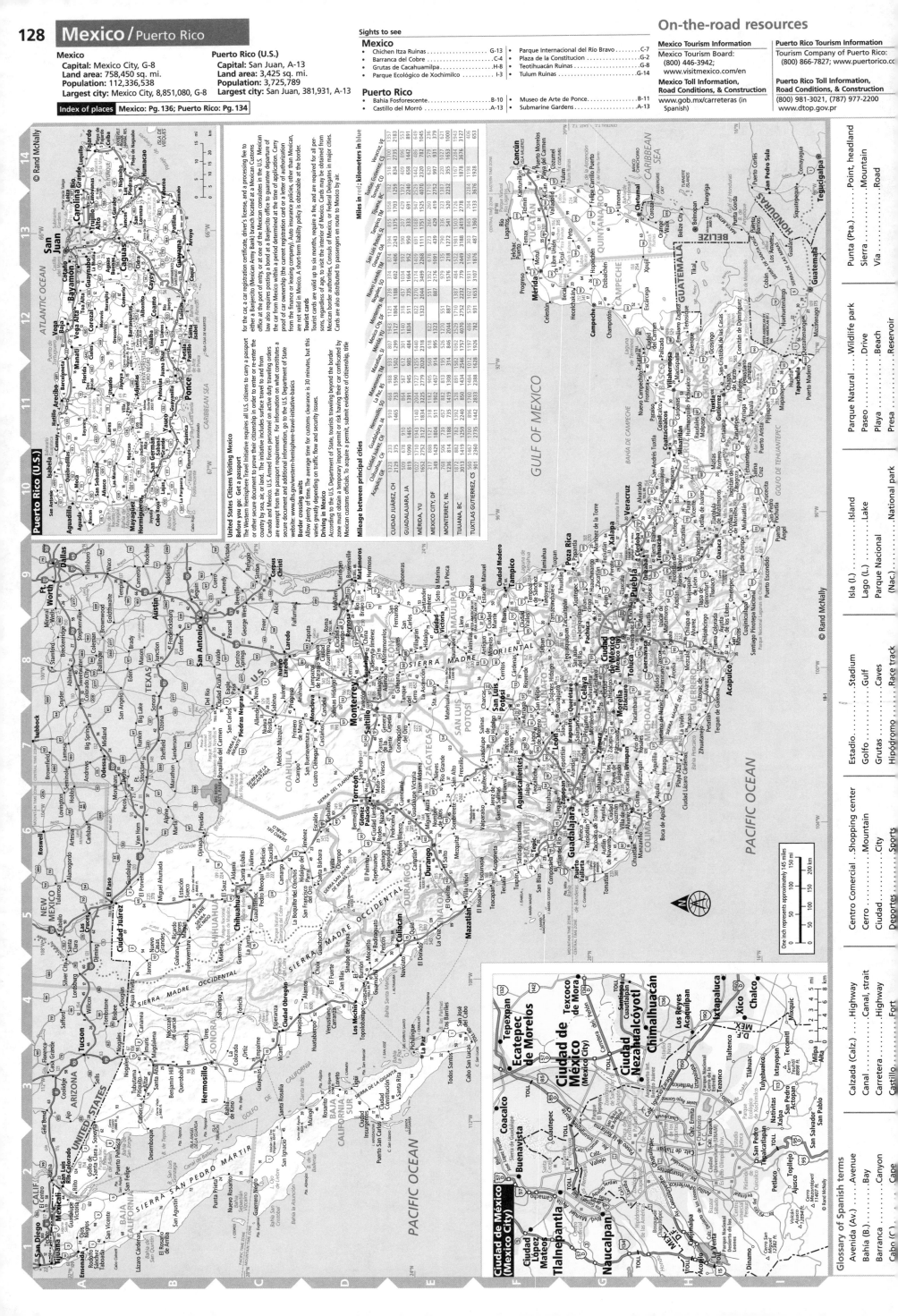

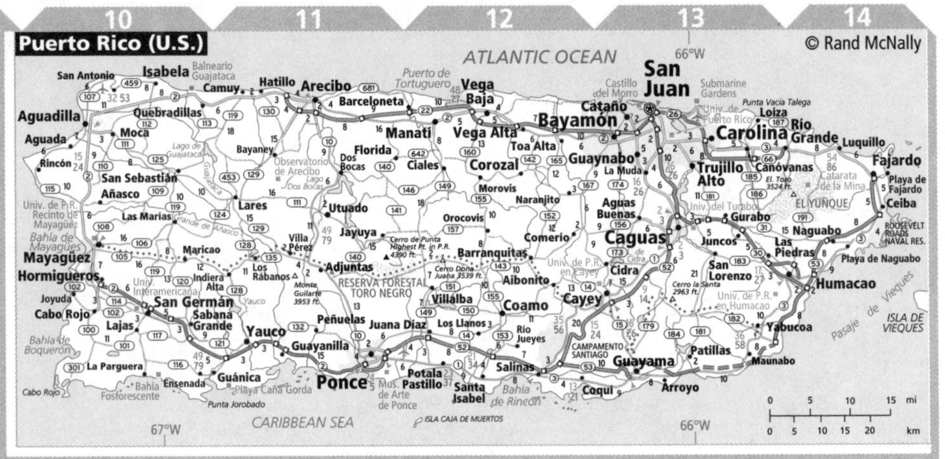

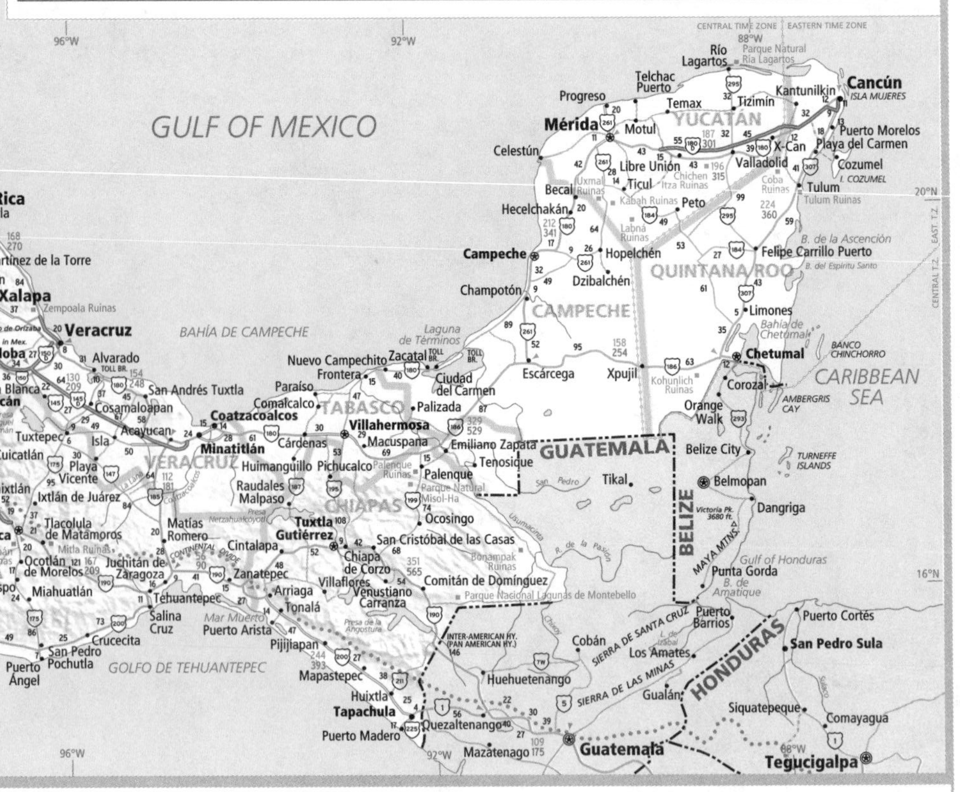

United States Citizens Visiting Mexico

Before you go: Get a passport
The Western Hemisphere Travel Initiative requires all U.S. citizens to carry a passport or other secure document to prove their citizenship in order to enter or re-enter the country by sea, air, or land. The initiative includes surface travel to and from Canada and Mexico. U.S. Armed Forces personnel on active duty traveling orders are exempt from the passport requirement. For information on what constitutes a secure document and additional information, go to the U.S. Department of State website: www.dhs.gov/western-hemisphere-travel-initiative-basics

Border crossing waits
Allow plenty of time. The average time for customs clearance is 30 minutes, but this varies greatly depending on traffic flow and security issues.

Driving in Mexico
According to the U.S. Department of State, tourists traveling beyond the border zone must obtain a temporary import permit or risk having their car confiscated by Mexican customs officials. To acquire a permit, submit evidence of citizenship, title for the car, a car registration certificate, driver's license, and a processing fee to either a Banjercito (Mexican Army Bank) branch located at a Mexican Customs office at the port of entry, or at one of the Mexican consulates in the U.S. Mexican law also requires posting a bond at a Banjercito office to guarantee departure of the car from Mexico within a period determined at the time of application. Carry proof of car ownership (the current registration card or a letter of authorization from the finance or leasing company). Auto insurance policies, other than Mexican, are not valid in Mexico. A short-term liability policy is obtainable at the border.

Tourist cards
Tourist cards are valid up to six months, require a fee, and are required for all persons, regardless of age, to visit the interior of Mexico. Cards may be obtained from Mexican border authorities, Consuls of Mexico, or Federal Delegates in major cities. Cards are also distributed to passengers en route to Mexico by air.

Mileage between principal cities

Miles in red; kilometers in blue

	Acapulco, GR	Chihuahua, CH	Cuidad Juárez, CH	Guadalajara, JA	Hermosillo, SO	La Paz, BS	Matamoros, TM	Mazatlan, SI	Mérida, YU	Mexico City, DF	Monterrey, NL	Nogales, SO	Nuevo Laredo, TM	Oaxaca, OA	San Luis Potosí, SL	Tampico, TM	Tijuana, BC	Torreón, CO	Tuxtlas Gutierrez, CS	Veracruz, VE
CUIDAD JUÁREZ, CH	1323 2129	233 375		910 1465	468 753	988 1590	933 1502	807 1299	1943 3127	1121 1804	739 1188	374 602	874 1406	1394 2243	855 1375	1058 1703	782 1259	518 834	1700 2735	1357 2183
GUADALAJARA, JA	509 819	678 1090	910 1465		864 1391	587 945	612 985	301 484	1140 1834	318 511	457 735	1034 1664	592 952	590 950	207 333	429 691	1392 2240	409 658	896 1442	553 891
MÉRIDA, YU	1027 1652	1710 2752	1943 3127	1140 1834	2004 3225	1727 2779	1255 2020	1440 2318		822 1323	1270 2044	2174 3499	1409 2268	691 1111	1088 1751	947 1525	2529 4070	1442 2320	486 782	649 1045
MEXICO CITY, DF	217 349	888 1429	1121 1804	318 511	1182 1902	905 1457	568 914	618 995	822 1323		551 887	1352 2176	678 1091	273 439	266 429	260 419	1710 2752	620 997	579 931	236 379
MONTERREY, NL	768 1236	506 814	739 1188	457 735	882 1419	813 1308	195 314	526 846	1270 2044	551 887		979 1576	135 218	790 1272	336 541	323 520	1387 2232	220 355	1027 1653	621 1000
TIJUANA, BC	1872 3013	882 1419	782 1259	1392 2240	528 850	891 1434	1582 2546	1092 1757	2529 4070	1710 2752	1387 2232	484 779	1522 2449	1981 3188	1503 2419	1726 2778		1167 1878	2284 3676	1943 3127
TUXTLAS GUTIERREZ, CS	560 901	1467 2360	1700 2735	896 1442	1760 2833	1484 2388	1012 1628	1197 1926	486 782	579 931	1027 1653	1931 3107	1166 1876	303 487	845 1360	704 1133	2284 3676	1198 1928		406 653

Glossary of Spanish terms

- Avenida (Av.) .... Avenue
- Bahía (B.) .... Bay
- Barranca .... Canyon
- Cabo (C.) .... Cape
- Calzada (Calz.) .... Highway
- Canal .... Canal, strait
- Carretera .... Highway
- Castillo .... Fort
- Centro Comercial .... Shopping center
- Cerro .... Mountain
- Ciudad .... City
- Deportes .... Sports
- Estadio .... Stadium
- Golfo .... Gulf
- Grutas .... Caves
- Hipódromo .... Race track
- Isla (I.) .... Island
- Lago (L.) .... Lake
- Parque Nacional (Nac.) .... National park
- Parque Natural .... Wildlife park
- Paseo .... Drive
- Playa .... Beach
- Presa .... Reservoir
- Punta (Pta.) .... Point, headland
- Sierra .... Mountain
- Via .... Road

ndex

nited States Counties, cities, towns & places

ulations are from the 2010 U.S. Census or Rand McNally estimates

ex to Canada and Mexico cities and towns, page 136

Alabama

Map pp. 4 – 5

ville, 2688 M-11
nsville, 4522 F-6
son, 758 D-5
aster, 30352 G-6
tville, 21160 C-8
ander City, 14875 H-9
andria, 3917 E-9
ville, 2486 G-3
na, 933 D-8
lusia, 9015 N-7
ston, 23106 E-9
8050 C-7
ore, 1194 A-6
4071 E-7
n, 764 M-10
ord, 2148 N-11
and, 2037 G-9
lle, 2212 E-8
s, 21897 A-6
re, 10194 O-4
a, 6048 D-9
m, 53380 I-10
UGA CO., 54571 J-7
ugaville, 870 J-7
757 O-3
WIN CO.,
265 O-4
ay, 1580 D-9
OUR CO.,
57 K-11
inette, 8044 O-4
La Batre, 2558 Q-2
Creek, 1070 C-4
1148 E-4
mer, 27456 F-6
CO., 22915 H-6
ngham, 212237 F-7
NT CO., 57322 D-7
tsville, 1684 D-7
9551 D-8
ecour, 900 Q-4
ley, 809 M-8
leyville, 884 G-6
4947 H-5
on, 5408 N-6
eport, 2418 A-10
on, 2945 S-10
nt, 900 D-4
[illegible]
elle, 3905 N-2
n, 8619 H-7
KE CO., 25833 L-3
9708 E-7
CO., 13932 G-9
n, 3008 L-11
RNE CO.,
72 E-10
and, 1303 D-7
399 L-10
g, 1657 G-5
EE CO., 49948 M-9
979 G-4
ERT CO., 54428 B-3
sville, 1983 C-9
biana, 4197 G-7
rd, 1837 F-6
CUH CO., 13228 M-6
A CO., 11539 H-8
da, 1224 J-8
va, 2095 E-5
nwood, 1289 O-11
NGTON CO.,
65 N-7
ts, 1871 N-11
SHAW CO.,
06 L-8
, 1926 O-3
ille, 1862 C-9
ey Chapel, 1630 Q-10
an, 14775 D-6
MAN CO., 80406 D-6
ille, 3230 H-10
CO., 50251 M-10
lle, 5295 N-10
AS CO., 43820 J-5
e, 21570 P-3
in Island, 1238 Q-3
LB CO., 71109 C-9
ille, 1154 I-8
r, 55683 B-6
olis, 7483 I-3
a, 1000 Q-10
2025 E-6
n, 65496 N-11
e Sprs., 1083 D-5
vton, 2478 O-6
n Valley, 2000 T-10
c, 1001 I-9
ater, 883 R-10
940 M-9
, 1498 Q-4
, 1262 I-8
RE CO., 79303 J-9
rise, 26562 N-9
MBIA CO.,
19 N-5
AH CO., 104430 D-9
a, 13137 L-11
, 2934 H-3
een, 3944 M-6
d, 11117 R-10
pe, 15326 P-3
e, 1279 C-6
, 4619 E-3
TE CO., 17241 E-4
eville, 1284 G-8
ton, 1440 O-5
, 1980 O-8
ce, 39319 B-4
14618 Q-4
dale, 10162 F-6
posit, 1344 K-7
chell, 750 J-12
ne, 14012 C-10
KLIN CO., 31704 C-3
City, 1309 M-5
dale, 8380 F-7
1018 C-9
en, 36856 D-9
t, 855 D-8
ndale, 13893 E-6
a, 4452 O-9
VA CO., 26790 O-10
ana, 1738 M-7
ine, 896 C-9
e, 5160 D-9
Hope, 2264 D-6
water, 1475 H-9
, 1750 G-3
Bay, 3672 Q-2
896 B-8
ille, 2165 F-6
NE CO., 9045 H-3
boro, 2497 I-4
ville, 8135 L-7
Hill, 1570 L-4
2376 D-3
nores, 9741 Q-4
sville, 8197 C-8
801 B-8
burg, 1516 C-4
CO., 15760 H-4
ille, 4173 D-4
on, 6885 D-3
ville, 2982 D-7
sville, 1637 G-8
rd, 2624 N-10
lle, 14255 C-6
t, 5281 A-7
ville, 932 K-7
Green, 3630 A-7
nd, 4510 N-11
Heflin, 3480 F-10
Helena, 16793 G-6
Henagar, 2344 B-10
HENRY CO., 17302 M-11
Hillview, 3080 Q-11
Hobson City, 771 F-9
Hokes Bluff, 4286 D-9
Holly Pond, 798 D-7
Hollywood, 1000 B-9
Holt, 3638 G-4
Holtville, 4096 I-8
Homewood, 25167 F-7
Hoover, 81619 F-6
HOUSTON CO., 101547 N-11
Hueytown, 16105 F-6
Huguley, 2540 H-11
Huntsville, 180105 B-7
Indian Sprs. Vil., 2363 G-7
Irondale, 12349 F-7
Irvington, 1000 Q-2
Jackson, 5228 M-3
JACKSON CO., 53227 A-8
Jacksons Gap, 828 H-9
Jacksonville, 12548 E-10
Jasper, 14352 E-5
JEFFERSON CO., 658466 F-5
Jemison, 2585 H-7
Killen, 1108 A-4
Kimberly, 2711 E-6
Kinsey, 2198 N-11
Ladonia, 3142 J-12
LaFayette, 3003 H-11
LAMAR CO., 14564 E-3
Lanett, 6468 H-11
LAUDERDALE CO., 92709 A-4
LAWRENCE CO., 34339 B-5
LEE CO., 140247 I-11
Leeds, 11773 F-7
Leesburg, 1027 D-10
Leroy, 911 M-3
Level Plains, 2085 N-10
Lillian, 900 Q-5
LIMESTONE CO., 82782 A-6
Lincoln, 6266 F-9
Linden, 2123 J-4
Lineville, 2395 G-10
Lipscomb, 2210 F-7
Littleville, 1011 B-3
Livingston, 3485 I-2
Locust Fork, 1186 E-7
LOWNDES CO., 11299 K-6
Loxley, 1632 P-4
Luverne, 2800 L-8
MACON CO., 21452 J-9
Madison, 42938 B-7
MADISON CO., 334811 A-7
Malvern, 1448 N-10
Maplesville, 708 H-6
MARENGO CO., 21027 J-4
Margaret, 4428 F-7
Marion, 3686 I-5
MARION CO., 30776 D-3
MARSHALL CO., 93019 C-7
McCalla, 1000 G-6
McIntosh, 244 N-2
Midfield, 5365 F-6
Midland City, 2344 N-10
Millbrook, 14640 J-8
Millport, 1049 F-3
Mobile, 195111 P-3
MOBILE CO., 412992 P-2
MONROE CO., 23068 M-5
Monroeville, 6519 M-5
Montevallo, 6323 G-6
Montgomery, 205764 J-8
MONTGOMERY CO., 229363 K-8
Moody, 11726 F-7
Moores Mill, 5682 A-7
MORGAN CO., 119490 C-7
Morris, 1859 E-6
Mosses, 1029 K-7
Moulton, 3471 C-5
Moundville, 2427 H-4
Mt. Olive, 4079 E-6
Mt. Vernon, 1574 O-3
Mountain Brook, 20413 R-13
Mulga, 836 Q-9
Munford, 1292 F-9
Muscle Shoals, 13146 B-4
New Brockton, 1146 M-9
New Hope, 2810 B-8
New Market, 1597 A-8
New Site, 773 H-10
Newton, 1511 N-10
Northport, 23330 G-4
Notasulga, 965 I-10
Oakman, 789 E-5
Odenville, 3585 E-8
Ohatchee, 1170 E-9
Oneonta, 6567 D-7
Opelika, 26477 I-11
Opp, 6659 N-8
Orange Bch., 5441 Q-4
Owens Cross Roads, 1521 B-8
Oxford, 21348 F-9
Ozark, 14907 M-10
Parrish, 982 E-5
Pea Ridge, 800 G-6
Pelham, 21352 G-6
Pell City, 12695 F-8
Perdido, 1200 O-4
PERRY CO., 10591 I-5
Peterson, 950 G-5
Petersville, 1400 D-13
Phenix City, 32822 J-12
Phil Campbell, 1148 C-4
PICKENS CO., 19746 G-2
Piedmont, 4878 E-10
PIKE CO., 32899 L-9
Pike Road, 5406 J-9
Pine Hill, 975 K-4
Pinedale Shores, 800 E-8
Pinson, 7163 E-7
Plantersville, 750 I-6
Pleasant Grove, 10110 F-6
Point Clear, 2125 Q-3
Powell, 955 C-9
Prattville, 33960 J-8
Priceville, 2658 B-6
Prichard, 22659 P-3
Ragland, 1639 E-8
Rainbow City, 9602 D-9
Rainsville, 4948 C-9
RANDOLPH CO., 22913 G-10
Red Bay, 3158 C-3
Reform, 1702 F-3
Rehobeth, 1297 N-11
Riverside, 2208 F-8
Roanoke, 6074 G-11
Robertsdale, 5276 P-4
Rockford, 477 H-8
Rogersville, 1257 A-5
RUSSELL CO., 52947 J-11
Russellville, 9830 C-4
ST. CLAIR CO., 83593 E-8
St. Elmo, 1050 Q-2
Saks, 10744 E-9
Samson, 1940 N-9
Saraland, 13405 O-3
Sardis City, 1704 D-9
Satsuma, 6168 O-3
Scottsboro, 14770 B-9
Section, 770 B-9
Selma, 20756 J-6
Semmes, 2350 P-2
Shannon, 1000 T-11
Sheffield, 9039 B-4
Shelby, 1044 G-7
SHELBY CO., 195085 F-7
Skyline, 851 A-8
Slocomb, 1980 N-10
Smiths Sta., 4926 I-12
Snead, 835 D-8
Southside, 8412 E-9
Spanish Fort, 6798 P-3
Springville, 4080 E-7
Stapleton, 1300 P-4
Steele, 1043 E-8
Stevenson, 2046 A-9
Stewartsville, 1767 H-8
Sulligent, 1927 E-3
Sumiton, 2520 E-6
Summerdale, 862 Q-4
SUMTER CO., 13763 I-2
Susan Moore, 763 D-8
Sycamore, 1000 G-8
Sylacauga, 12749 G-8
Sylvan Sprs., 1542 R-9
Sylvania, 1837 B-9
Talladega, 15676 F-9
TALLADEGA CO., 82291 F-8
TALLAPOOSA CO., 41616 I-9
Tallassee, 4819 I-9
Tanner, 750 B-6
Tarrant City, 6397 Q-12
Taylor, 2375 N-11
Theodore, 6130 P-2
Thomasville, 4209 L-4
Thorsby, 1980 H-7
Tillmans Cor., 17398 P-2
Town Creek, 1100 B-5
Trinity, 2095 B-6
Troy, 18033 L-9
Trussville, 19933 F-7
Tuscaloosa, 90468 G-4
TUSCALOOSA CO., 194656 G-4
Tuscumbia, 8423 B-4
Tuskegee, 9865 J-10
Union Sprs., 3980 K-10
Uniontown, 1775 J-4
Valley, 9524 H-11
Valley Grande, 4020 J-6
Vance, 1529 G-5
Vernon, 2000 E-3
Vestavia Hills, 34033 F-7
Vincent, 1988 F-8
Wadley, 751 G-10
WALKER CO., 67023 F-5
Warrior, 3176 E-6
WASHINGTON CO., 17581 N-2
Weaver, 3038 E-9
Webb, 1430 N-11
Wedowee, 823 G-10
W. Blocton, 1240 G-6
W. End Anniston, 2760 F-9
Westover, 1275 G-7
Westwood, 1630 Q-10
Wetumpka, 6528 I-8
White Hall, 858 J-7
White Plains, 811 E-10
WILCOX CO., 11670 L-5
Wilsonville, 1827 G-7
Winfield, 4717 E-4
WINSTON CO., 24484 D-5
Woodstock, 1428 G-5
York, 2538 J-2

Alaska

Map p. 6

Akiachak, 627 G-4
Akutan, 1027 J-1
Alakanuk, 677 F-3
Anchor Pt., 1930 H-7
Anchorage, 291826 G-7
Angoon, 459 I-12
Aniak, 501 G-4
Bethel, 6080 G-4
Big Delta, 591 F-8
Big Lake, 3350 G-7
Chevak, 938 F-3
College, 12964 E-7
Cordova, 2239 G-8
Craig, 1201 J-13
Delta Jct., 958 E-8
Dillingham, 2329 H-4
Emmonak, 762 E-3
Fairbanks, 31535 E-7
Ft. Yukon, 583 D-8
Galena, 470 D-5
Gambell, 681 D-2
Glennallen, 483 F-8
Haines, 1713 H-12
Healy, 1021 F-7
Homer, 5003 H-6
Hoonah, 760 H-12
Hooper Bay, 1093 F-3
Houston, 1912 G-7
Juneau, 31275 H-12
Kake, 557 I-12
Kasigluk, 569 G-4
Kasilof, 549 G-7
Kenai, 7100 G-7
Ketchikan, 8050 J-13
King Cove, 938 J-3
Kipnuk, 639 G-3
Klawock, 755 J-13
Kodiak, 6130 I-6
Kotlik, 577 E-4
Kotzebue, 3201 C-4
Kwethluk, 721 G-4
Metlakatla, 1405 J-13
Mountain Vil., 813 F-3
Naknek, 544 H-5
New Stuyahok, 510 H-5
Nikiski, 4493 G-7
Ninilchik, 883 H-7
Noatak, 514 C-4
Nome, 3598 D-3
Noorvik, 668 C-5
N. Pole, 2117 E-8
Nunapitchuk, 496 G-4
Palmer, 5937 G-7
Petersburg, 2948 I-13
Pilot Station, 568 F-4
Point Hope, 674 B-4
Prudhoe Bay, 2174 A-8
Quinhagak, 669 G-4
St. Marys, 507 F-4
St. Paul, 479 I-10
Sand Pt., 976 J-3
Savoonga, 671 D-2
Scammon Bay, 474 F-3
Selawik, 829 C-5
Seward, 2693 H-7
Shishmaref, 563 C-3
Sitka, 8881 I-12
Skagway, 920 H-12
Soldotna, 4163 G-7
Stebbins, 556 E-4
Sutton, 1447 G-7
Talkeetna, 876 F-7
Thorne Bay, 471 J-13
Togiak, 817 H-4
Tok, 1258 F-9
Toksook Bay, 590 G-3
Trapper Creek, 481 F-7
Unalakleet, 688 E-4
Unalaska, 4376 J-1
Utqiagvik (Barrow), 4212 A-6
Valdez, 3976 G-8
Wainwright, 556 A-5
Wasilla, 7831 G-7
Willow, 2102 G-7
Wrangell, 2369 I-13
Yakutat, 662 H-10

Arizona

Map pp. 8 – 9

* City keyed to p. 7

Aguila, 798 I-5
Ajo, 3304 M-6
Anthem, 21700 I-7
APACHE CO., 71518 D-13
Apache Jct., 35840 J-9
Arivaca, 695 O-9
Arivaca Jct., 1090 N-10
Arizona City, 10475 L-8
Arizona Vil., 946 F-2
Avondale, 76238 J-7
Avra Valley, 6050 M-9
Bagdad, 1876 G-5
Beaver Dam, 1962 *A-3
Benson, 5105 N-11
Bisbee, 5575 O-12
Black Canyon City, 2837 H-7
Bouse, 996 I-3
Buckeye, 50876 J-6
Bullhead City, 39540 F-2
Bylas, 1962 K-12
Cameron, 885 D-9
Camp Verde, 10873 G-8
Carefree, 3363 I-8
Casa Grande, 48571 K-8
Casas Adobes, 66795 O-3
Catalina, 7569 L-10
Cave Creek, 5015 I-8
Central Hts., 2000 J-10
Chandler, 236123 J-8
Chilchinbito, 506 B-12
Chinle, 4518 C-13
Chino Valley, 10817 G-7
Cibecue, 1713 H-11
Citrus Pk., 4028 *H-2
Clarkdale, 4097 G-8
Claypool, 1538 J-10
Clifton, 3311 K-13
COCHISE CO., 131346 M-12
COCONINO CO., 134421 C-8
Colorado City, 4821 A-6
Congress, 1975 H-6
Coolidge, 11825 K-9
Cordes Lakes, 2633 H-7
Cornville, 3280 G-8
Cottonwood, 11265 G-8
Dennehotso, 746 A-12
Desert Hills, 2245 S-10
Dewey-Humboldt, 3894 G-7
Dilkon, 1184 E-11
Dolan Sprs., 2033 D-3
Douglas, 17378 O-13
Dreamland Villa, 4800 *J-8
Drexel Hts., 27749 S-2
Dudleyville, 959 K-10
Duncan, 696 L-14
Eagar, 4885 H-13
E. Fork, 699 I-12
Ehrenberg, 1470 I-2
El Mirage, 31797 *H-3
Eloy, 16631 L-9
Flagstaff, 65870 E-8
Florence, 25536 K-9
Flowing Wells, 16419 P-2
Ft. Defiance, 3624 D-14
Fortuna Foothills, 26265 L-2
Fountain Hills, 22489 J-8
Fredonia, 1314 A-7
Gadsden, 678 L-2
Ganado, 1210 D-13
Gila Bend, 1922 K-6
GILA CO., 53597 I-11
Gila Crossing, 621 *K-4
Gilbert, 208453 *K-8
Gisela, 570 H-9
Glendale, 226721 J-7
Globe, 7532 J-10
Gold Canyon, 10159 J-9
Golden Valley, 8370 E-3
Goodyear, 65275 J-7
GRAHAM CO., 37220 K-12
Grand Canyon Vil., 2004 C-7
Greasewood, 547 E-12
Green Valley, 21391 N-10
GREENLEE CO., 8437 J-13
Guadalupe, 5523 *J-6
Hayden, 662 K-10
Holbrook, 5053 F-11
Hotevilla-Bacavi, 957 D-10
Houck, 1024 E-13
Huachuca City, 1853 O-11
Joseph City, 1386 F-11
Kaibito, 1522 B-10
Kayenta, 5189 B-11
Kearny, 1950 K-10
Kingman, 28068 E-3
Komatke, 821 J-7
Kykotsmovi Vil., 746 D-10
LA PAZ CO., 20489 H-4
L. Havasu City, 52527 G-3
L. Montezuma, 4706 G-8
Leupp, 951 E-10
Linden, 2597 H-12
Litchfield Pk., 5476 *I-3
Lukachukai, 1701 B-13
Mammoth, 1426 L-11
Many Farms, 1348 C-13
Marana, 34961 L-9
Maricopa, 43482 K-8
MARICOPA CO., 3817117 I-6
Martinez Lake, 798 K-2
Mayer, 1497 H-7
McNary, 528 H-12
Meadview, 1224 C-3
Mesa, 439041 J-8
Miami, 1837 J-10
Moenkopi, 964 C-9
MOHAVE CO., 200186 F-4
Morenci, 1489 K-13
Mountainaire, 1119 F-8
Munds Pk., 631 F-8
Naco, 1046 O-12
NAVAJO CO., 107449 E-11
New River, 14952 I-7
Nogales, 20837 O-10
Oracle, 3686 L-10
Oro Valley, 41011 M-10
Page, 7247 A-9
Paradise Valley, 12820 *H-6
Parker, 3083 H-3
Parks, 1188 E-8
Patagonia, 913 O-10
Paulden, 5231 F-7
Payson, 15301 H-9
Peach Sprs., 1090 E-5
Peoria, 154065 J-7
Peridot, 1350 J-11
Phoenix, 1445632 J-7
Picture Rocks, 9563 M-9
Pima, 2387 K-12
PIMA CO., 980263 M-8
PINAL CO., 375770 L-9
Pine, 1963 H-9
Pinetop-Lakeside, 4282 H-12
Pinon, 904 C-11
Pirtleville, 1744 O-13
Plantsite, 600 K-13
Polacca, 700 D-11
Prescott, 39843 G-7
Prescott Valley, 38822 G-7
Quartzsite, 3677 I-3
Queen Creek, 26361 J-8
Queen Valley, 788 J-9
Red Rock, 2169 L-9
Rio Rico, 18962 O-10
Rio Verde, 1811 *G-9
Rock Pt., 642 B-13
Round Rock, 789 B-13
Sacaton, 2672 K-8
Safford, 9566 K-13
Sahuarita, 25259 N-10
St. David, 1699 N-11
St. Johns, 3480 G-13
St. Michaels, 1443 D-14
Salome, 1530 I-4
San Carlos, 4038 J-11
San Luis, 25505 L-2
San Manuel, 3551 L-11
San Tan Valley, 81321 K-9
Sanders, 630 E-13
SANTA CRUZ CO., 47420 O-11
Santa Rosa, 628 M-8
Santan, 650 K-8
Sawmill, 748 D-14
Scottsdale, 217385 J-8
Second Mesa, 962 D-11
Sedona, 10031 F-8
Sells, 2495 N-8
Shongopovi, 831 D-11
Shonto, 591 B-10
Show Low, 10660 H-12
Sierra Vista, 43888 O-11
Snowflake, 5590 G-12
Somerton, 14287 L-2
Sonoita, 818 N-11
S. Tucson, 5652 R-3
Springerville, 1961 H-13
Stanfield, 740 K-8
Star Valley, 2310 H-9
Strawberry, 961 G-9
Summit, 5372 T-3
Sun City, 37499 J-7
Sun City West, 24535 I-7
Sun Lakes, 13975 K-8
Superior, 2837 J-10
Surprise, 117517 I-7
Swift Trail Jct., 2935 L-13
Tacna, 602 L-3
Tanque Verde, 16901 Q-7
Taylor, 4112 G-12
Teec Nos Pos, 730 A-14
Tempe, 161719 J-8
Thatcher, 4865 K-12
Three Points, 5581 M-9
Tolleson, 6545 *J-3
Tombstone, 1380 N-12
Tortolita, 3740 N-2
Tsaile, 1205 C-13
Tuba City, 8611 C-9
Tubac, 1191 O-10
Tucson, 520116 M-10
Tucson Estates, 12192 M-10
Tusayan, 558 D-7
Vail, 10208 M-10
Valle, 832 *E-8
Verde Vil., 11605 G-8
Vicksburg, 597 I-4
Waddell, 500 *H-2
Wellton, 2882 L-3
Wenden, 728 I-4
Whiteriver, 4104 I-12
Wickenburg, 6363 I-6
Wilhoit, 868 G-6
Willcox, 3757 M-12
Williams, 3023 E-7
Window Rock, 2712 D-14
Winslow, 9655 F-10
Wittmann, 763 I-7
Yarnell, 649 H-6
YAVAPAI CO., 211033 F-6
Young, 666 H-10
Youngtown, 6156 *H-3
Yuma, 93064 L-2
YUMA CO., 195751 K-4

Arkansas

Map pp. 10 – 11

Alexander, 2901 H-7
Alma, 5419 E-2
Altheimer, 984 I-9
Altus, 758 E-3
Arkadelphia, 10714 J-5
Arkansas City, 366 K-10
ARKANSAS CO., 19019 I-10
Ash Flat, 1082 B-9
Ashdown, 4723 K-2
ASHLEY CO., 21853 L-9
Atkins, 3016 F-5
Augusta, 2199 E-10
Austin, 2038 G-8
Bald Knob, 2897 E-9
Barling, 4649 E-2
Batesville, 10248 D-9
BAXTER CO., 41513 B-7
Bay, 1801 D-12
Bearden, 966 K-6
Beebe, 7315 F-8
Bella Vista, 26461 A-2
Benton, 30681 H-6
BENTON CO., 221339 B-1
Bentonville, 35301 B-2
Berryville, 5356 B-4
Bethel Hts., 2372 D-20
Blytheville, 15620 C-14
Bono, 2131 C-11
BOONE CO., 36903 B-5
Booneville, 3990 F-3
Bradford, 759 E-10
BRADLEY CO., 11508 L-7
Brinkley, 3188 G-10
Brookland, 1642 C-12
Bryant, 16688 H-7
Bull Shoals, 1950 B-6
Cabot, 23776 G-8
CALHOUN CO., 5368 K-6
Calico Rock, 1545 C-8
Camden, 12183 K-6
Cammack Vil., 768 L-14
Caraway, 1279 D-13
Carlisle, 2214 G-9
CARROLL CO., 27446 B-4
Cave City, 1904 C-9
Cave Sprs., 1729 B-2
Cedarville, 1394 D-1
Centerton, 9515 B-2
Charleston, 2494 E-2
Cherokee Vil., 4671 B-9
CHICOT CO., 11800 M-10
Clarendon, 1664 H-10
CLARK CO., 22995 J-5
Clarksville, 9178 E-4
CLAY CO., 16083 B-12
CLEBURNE CO., 25970 D-8
CLEVELAND CO., 8689 J-7
Clinton, 2602 D-7
Coal Hill, 1012 E-3
COLUMBIA CO., 24552 M-5
Conway, 58908 F-7
CONWAY CO., 21273 F-6
Corning, 3377 B-12
Cotter, 970 B-7
CRAIGHEAD CO., 96443 C-12
CRAWFORD CO., 61948 D-1
CRITTENDEN CO., 50902 F-13
CROSS CO., 17870 E-11
Crossett, 5507 M-8
DALLAS CO., 8116 J-6
Danville, 2409 F-4
Dardanelle, 4745 F-5
De Queen, 6594 J-1
De Valls Bluff, 619 G-10
De Witt, 3292 I-10
Decatur, 1699 B-1
Dermott, 2316 L-10
Des Arc, 1717 G-10
Desha, 750 D-9
DESHA CO., 13008 K-10
Diamond City, 782 A-5
Diaz, 1318 D-10
Dierks, 1133 J-2
Dover, 1378 E-5
DREW CO., 18509 L-9
Dumas, 4706 J-10
Dyer, 876 E-2
Earle, 2414 F-12
E. Camden, 931 K-6
E. End, 6998 H-7
El Dorado, 18884 M-6
Elkins, 2648 C-2
Elm Sprs., 1535 B-2
England, 2825 H-8
Eudora, 2269 M-10
Eureka Sprs., 2073 B-3
Fairfield Bay, 2338 D-7
Farmington, 5974 C-2
FAULKNER CO., 113237 F-7
Fayetteville, 73580 C-2
Flippin, 1355 B-6
Fordyce, 4300 K-7
Foreman, 1011 K-1
Forrest City, 15371 F-12
Ft. Smith, 86209 E-1
Fouke, 859 M-3
FRANKLIN CO., 18125 D-3
FULTON CO., 12245 B-8
GARLAND CO., 96024 G-5
Gassville, 2078 B-7
Gentry, 3158 B-1
Gibson, 3543 J-16
Glenwood, 2228 I-4
Goshen, 1071 C-2
Gosnell, 3548 C-14
Gould, 837 J-9
GRANT CO., 17853 I-7
Gravel Ridge, 3232 J-16
Gravette, 2325 A-1
Green Forest, 2761 B-4
Greenbrier, 4706 F-7
GREENE CO., 42090 C-12
Greenland, 1259 C-2
Greenwood, 8952 F-2
Greers Ferry, 891 E-8
Gurdon, 2212 J-5
Hackett, 812 F-1
Hamburg, 2857 M-9
Hampton, 1324 L-7
Hardy, 772 B-10
Harrisburg, 2288 E-12
Harrison, 12943 B-5
Haskell, 3990 H-6
Hazen, 1468 G-9
Heber Sprs., 7165 E-8
Helena-West Helena, 12282 H-12
HEMPSTEAD CO., 22609 K-3
Hermitage, 830 L-8
Highland, 1045 B-9
Hope, 10095 K-3
Horatio, 1044 J-1
Horseshoe Bend, 2184 B-9
HOT SPRING CO., 32923 I-5
Hot Sprs., 35193 H-5
Hot Sprs. Vil., 12807 H-5
HOWARD CO., 13789 I-2
Hoxie, 2780 C-11
Hughes, 1441 G-12
Huntsville, 2346 C-3
INDEPENDENCE CO., 36647 C-9
IZARD CO., 13696 C-8
JACKSON CO., 17997 E-10
Jacksonville, 28364 G-8
Jasper, 466 C-5
JEFFERSON CO., 77435 I-8
Johnson, 3354 F-19
JOHNSON CO., 25540 E-4
Jonesboro, 67263 D-12
Judsonia, 2019 F-9
Keiser, 759 D-13
Kensett, 1648 F-9
Kibler, 961 E-2
Kirby, 786 I-3
LAFAYETTE CO., 7645 M-3
L. Catherine, 870 H-5
Lake City, 2082 D-13
L. Hamilton, 2135 H-5
Lake Vil., 2575 L-10
Lamar, 1605 E-4
Lavaca, 2289 E-2
LAWRENCE CO., 17415 C-10
Leachville, 1993 C-13
LEE CO., 10424 G-11
Lepanto, 1893 D-13
Lewisville, 1280 L-3
Lincoln, 2249 C-1
LINCOLN CO., 14134 J-9
Little Flock, 2585 B-2
LITTLE RIVER CO., 13171 K-1
Little Rock, 193524 G-7
LOGAN CO., 22353 F-3
London, 1039 E-4
Lonoke, 4245 G-8
LONOKE CO., 68356 G-8
Lowell, 7327 B-2
Luxora, 1178 D-14
Macon, 960 G-8
Madison, 769 F-12
MADISON CO., 15717 C-3
Magazine, 847 F-3
Magnolia, 11577 M-4
Malvern, 10318 I-6
Mammoth Spr., 977 A-9
Manila, 3342 C-13
Mansfield, 1139 F-2
Marianna, 4115 G-12
Marion, 12345 F-13
MARION CO., 16653 B-6
Marked Tree, 2566 E-13
Marmaduke, 1111 B-13
Marshall, 1355 C-6
Marvell, 1186 H-11
Maumelle, 17163 G-7
Mayflower, 2234 G-7
McAlmont, 1873 K-16
McCrory, 1729 F-10
McGehee, 4219 K-10
Melbourne, 1848 C-8
Mena, 5737 H-2
MILLER CO., 43462 L-3
Mineral Sprs., 1208 J-2
MISSISSIPPI CO., 46480 D-13
Monette, 1501 C-13
MONROE CO., 8149 H-10
MONTGOMERY CO., 9487 H-3
Monticello, 9467 K-9
Morrilton, 6767 F-6
Mt. Ida, 1076 H-3
Mountain Home, 12448 B-7
Mountain Pine, 770 H-5
Mountain View, 2748 D-8
Mulberry, 1655 E-2
Murfreesboro, 1641 J-3
Nashville, 4627 J-3
NEVADA CO., 8997 K-4
Newark, 1176 D-10
Newport, 7879 D-10
NEWTON CO., 8330 C-4
Norphlet, 844 L-6
N. Crossett, 3119 M-8
N. Little Rock, 62304 G-7
Oak Grv. Hts., 889 C-12
Ola, 1281 F-5
Oppelo, 781 F-6
Osceola, 7757 D-14
OUACHITA CO., 26120 K-6
Ozark, 3684 E-3
Ozark Acres, 760 B-10
Paragould, 26113 C-12
Paris, 3532 E-3
Parkin, 1105 F-12
Pea Ridge, 4794 A-2
PERRY CO., 10445 G-5
Perryville, 1460 F-6
PHILLIPS CO., 21757 H-11
Piggott, 3849 B-13
PIKE CO., 11291 I-4
Pine Bluff, 49083 I-8
Piney, 4699 E-15
Plumerville, 826 F-6
Pocahontas, 6608 B-11
POINSETT CO., 24583 E-12
POLK CO., 20662 H-2
POPE CO., 61754 E-5
Pottsville, 2838 F-5
PRAIRIE CO., 8715 G-9
Prairie Grv., 4380 C-2
Prescott, 3296 K-4
PULASKI CO., 382748 H-8
Quitman, 762 E-7
RANDOLPH CO., 17969 B-11
Rector, 1977 B-13
Redfield, 1297 H-8
Rison, 1344 J-7
Rogers, 55964 B-2
Russellville, 27920 F-5
ST. FRANCIS CO., 28258 F-11
Salem, 2607 H-6
Salem, 1635 B-9
SALINE CO., 107118 G-6
SCOTT CO., 11233 G-2
Searcy, 22858 F-9
SEARCY CO., 8195 D-6
SEBASTIAN CO., 125744 F-1
SEVIER CO., 17058 J-1
Shannon Hills, 3143 H-7
SHARP CO., 17264 C-9
Sheridan, 4603 I-7
Sherwood, 29523 G-7
Siloam Sprs., 15039 B-1
Smackover, 1865 L-6
Springdale, 69797 B-2
Stamps, 1693 L-4
Star City, 2274 J-9
Stephens, 891 L-5
STONE CO., 12394 D-8
Stuttgart, 9326 H-9
Sulphur Sprs., 1101 I-8
Sweet Home, 849 H-7
Swifton, 798 D-11
Texarkana, 29919 L-2
Tontitown, 2460 B-2
Trumann, 7243 D-12
Tuckerman, 1862 D-10
Tumbling Shoals, 978 E-8
Tyronza, 762 E-13
UNION CO., 41639 M-6
Van Buren, 22791 E-1
VAN BUREN CO., 17295 D-6
Vilonia, 3815 F-8
Waldo, 1372 L-4
Waldron, 3618 G-2
Walnut Ridge, 4890 C-11
Ward, 4067 F-8
Warren, 6003 K-8
WASHINGTON CO., 203065 C-1
W. Crossett, 1256 M-8
W. Fork, 2317 C-2
W. Memphis, 26245 F-13
WHITE CO., 77076 E-8
White Hall, 5526 I-8
Wickes, 754 I-1
Wilson, 903 D-14
WOODRUFF CO., 7260 F-10
Wooster, 860 F-7
Wrightsville, 2114 H-7
Wynne, 8367 F-12
YELL CO., 22185 F-4
Yellville, 1204 B-6

California

Map pp. 12 – 15

Map keys	Atlas pages
NA – NN	12 – 13
SA – SN	14 – 15

* City keyed to p. 16
† City keyed to p. 17
‡ City keyed to pp. 18 – 19

Aberdeen, 100 SJ-4
Acton, 7596 SI-11
Adelanto, 31765 SH-13
Agoura Hills, 20330 SJ-10
Agua Dulce, 3342 ‡N-6
Ahwahnee, 2246 NN-11
Alameda, 73812 NM-5
ALAMEDA CO., 1510271 NM-6
Alamo, 14570 NE-17
Alberhill, 200 ‡J-18
Alhambra, 83089 ‡E-8
Aliso Viejo, 47823 ‡L-13
Allendale, 1506 NK-6
Alpine, 14236 SM-15
ALPINE CO., 1175 NK-11
Alta Sierra, 6911 NI-8
Altadena, 42777 ‡C-9
Alturas, 2827 NC-9
Alum Rock, 15536 NL-20
Amador City, 185 NK-8
AMADOR CO., 38091 NK-10
Ambler Pk., 600 *N-4
American Canyon, 19454 NL-5
Anaheim, 336265 SK-12
Anderson, 9932 NE-5
Angels Camp, 3836 NL-9
Angwin, 3051 NK-5
Antelope, 45770 *F-4
Antioch, 102372 NL-6
Anza, 3014 SK-15
Apple Valley, 69135 SI-13
Aptos, 6220 SB-3
Arbuckle, 3028 NI-6
Arcade, 42000 *G-4
Arcadia, 56364 ‡D-10
Arcata, 17231 ND-2
Arden Town, 55000 *H-4
Armona, 4156 SD-8
Arnold, 3843 NL-9
Arrowhead Highlands, 1900 ‡C-19
Arroyo Grande, 17252 SG-6
Artesia, 16522 ‡H-9
Arvin, 19304 SG-10
Ashland, 21925 NG-16
Atascadero, 28310 SF-6
Atherton, 6914 NK-15
Atwater, 28168 NN-9
Auberry, 2369 SB-8
Auburn, 13330 NJ-8
August, 8390 *L-10
Avalon, 3728 SL-11
Avenal, 15505 SE-7
Avila Bch., 1627 SG-5
Avocado Hts., 15411 ‡E-10
Azusa, 46361 ‡D-11
Bakersfield, 347483 SF-9
Baldwin Pk., 75390 ‡D-10
Banning, 29603 SJ-14
Barstow, 22639 SH-14
Bay Pt., 21349 NC-18
Bayview, 2510 ND-2
Baywood Pk., 6000 SF-5
Beaumont, 36877 SJ-14
Bel Marin Keys, 1650 NB-12
Bell, 35477 ‡F-8
Bell Gdns., 42072 ‡F-8
Bella Vista, 2781 NE-6
Bellflower, 76616 ‡H-9
Belmont, 25835 NJ-14
Belvedere, 2068 NE-12
Ben Lomond, 6234 SA-2
Benicia, 26997 NL-6
Berkeley, 112580 NM-5
Berry Creek, 1424 NH-7
Bethel Island, 2137 NL-7
Beverly Hills, 34109 SJ-11
Big Bear City, 12304 SI-14
Big Bear Lake, 5019 SI-14
Big Pine, 1756 SA-11
Biggs, 1707 NH-7
Biola, 1623 SB-7
Bishop, 3879 NN-14
Black Pt., 470 NA-12
Blackhawk, 9354 NF-19
Bloomington, 23851 ‡E-17
Blue Jay, 700 ‡B-20
Blue Lake, 1253 ND-2
Blythe, 20817 SK-19
Bodfish, 1956 SF-10
Bolinas, 1620 NL-4
Bolsa Knolls, 1950 SB-3
Bonita, 12538 †L-4
Bonsall, 3982 SL-13
Bootjack, 960 NN-1
Boron, 2253 SG-12
Borrego Sprs., 3429 SL-15
Bostonia, 15379 †H-6
Boulder Creek, 4923 SA-2
Boyes Hot Sprs., 6656 NK-5
Bradbury, 1048 ‡D-11
Brawley, 24953 SM-17
Brea, 39282 ‡G-11
Brentwood, 51481 NL-7
Bridgeport, 575 NL-12
Brisbane, 4282 NH-13
Broadmoor, 4176 NG-12
Brockway, 370 *F-9
Brooktrails, 3235 NH-3
Buckhorn, 2429 NK-9
Buellton, 4828 SH-7
Buena Pk., 80530 ‡H-10
Burbank, 103340 SJ-11
Burbank, 4926 NM-19
Burlingame, 28806 NI-14
Burney, 3154 ND-7
BUTTE CO., 220000 NH-7
Buttonwillow, 1508 SF-8
Cabazon, 2535 SJ-14
Calabasas, 23058 ‡D-2
CALAVERAS CO., 45578 NK-10
Calexico, 38572 SN-18
California City, 14120 SG-12
Calimesa, 7879 SJ-14
Calipatria, 7705 SL-17
Calistoga, 5155 NK-5
Camarillo, 65201 SI-9
Cambria, 6032 SF-5
Cambrian Pk., 3282 NN-19
Cameron Pk., 18228 NJ-8
Camino, 1750 NJ-9
Camino Tassajara, 2197 NF-19
Campbell, 39349 SA-3
Campo, 2684 SN-15
Canyon Lake, 10561 SK-13
Carlsbad, 105328 SL-13
Carmel Pt., 500 *N-1
Carmel Valley Vil., 4407 SC-3
Carmel-by-the-Sea, 3722 SC-3
Carmichael, 61762 NK-7
Carpinteria, 13040 SI-8
Carson, 91714 ‡H-7
Caruthers, 2497 SC-7
Casa de Oro, 12000 †J-6
Castaic, 19015 SI-10
Castro Valley, 61388 NM-6
Castroville, 6481 SB-3
Cathedral City, 51200 SK-15
Cayucos, 2592 SF-5
Cedar Glen, 2100 ‡B-20
Cedarpines Pk., 850 ‡B-18
Ceres, 45417 NM-8
Cerritos, 49041 ‡H-9
Charter Oak, 9310 ‡D-12
Chatsworth Lake Manor, 1100 ‡C-2
Cherryland, 14728 NG-17
Chester, 2144 NF-8
Chico, 86187 NG-6
Chino, 77983 ‡F-14
Chino Hills, 74799 SJ-12
Chowchilla, 18720 SA-7
Chula Vista, 243916 SN-14
Citrus, 10866 ‡D-11
Citrus Hts., 83301 NJ-7
Claremont, 34926 ‡D-13
Clayton, 10897 NL-6
Clearlake, 15250 NJ-5
Clearlake Oaks, 2359 NI-5
Cloverdale, 8618 NJ-4
Clovis, 95631 SB-8
Clyde, 678 NC-17
Coachella, 40704 SK-16
Coalinga, 13380 SD-6
Coarsegold, 1840 SA-8
Cobb, 1778 NJ-4
Colfax, 1963 NI-8
Collierville, 1934 NL-7
Colma, 1792 NH-12
Colton, 52154 SJ-13
Columbia, 2297 NL-9
Colusa, 5971 NI-6
COLUSA CO., 21419 NI-5
Commerce, 12823 ‡F-8
Compton, 96455 ‡H-7
Concord, 122067 NL-6
CONTRA COSTA CO., 1049025 NM-6
Copperopolis, 3671 NL-9
Corcoran, 24813 SD-8
Corning, 7663 NG-6
Corona, 152374 SJ-13
Coronado, 18912 SN-14
Coronita, 2608 ‡H-15
Corte Madera, 9253 ND-12
Costa Mesa, 109960 ‡K-11
Cotati, 7265 NK-4
Coto de Caza, 14866 ‡L-15
Cottonwood, 3316 NF-6
Country Club, 9379 *L-9
Covina, 47796 ‡E-12
Cowan Hts., 4000 ‡I-13
Crescent City, 7643 NB-2
Crest Pk., 600 ‡B-20
Crestline, 10770 ‡B-19
Crestmore, 4500 ‡E-17
Crockett, 3094 NB-15
Cudahy, 23805 ‡G-8
Culver City, 38883 ‡F-5
Cupertino, 58302 NM-17
Cutler, 5000 SC-9
Cypress, 47802 ‡I-9
Daly City, 101123 NG-12
Dana Pt., 33351 ‡N-14
Danville, 42039 NM-6
Davis, 65622 NK-7
Del Aire, 10001 ‡G-6
Del Dios, 355 †C-3
Del Mar, 4161 SM-13
Del Monte Forest, 4514 *M-1
DEL NORTE CO., 28610 NB-2
Del Rey, 1639 SC-8
Del Rey Oaks, 1624 SC-3
Delano, 53041 SE-9
Delhi, 10755 NN-8
Denair, 4404 NN-8
Desert Hot Sprs., 25938 SJ-15
Desert View Highlands, 2360 SH-11
Diablo, 1158 NE-18
Diamond Bar, 55544 ‡F-12
Diamond Sprs., 11037 NJ-8
Dinuba, 21453 SC-8
Dixon, 18351 NK-6
Dollar Pt., 1215 *F-8
Dorris, 939 NA-6
Dos Palos, 4950 SB-6
Downey, 111772 SJ-11
Downieville, 282 NH-8
Duarte, 21321 ‡D-11
Dublin, 46036 NM-6
Dunsmuir, 1650 NC-6
Durham, 5518 NH-6
Earlimart, 8537 SE-9
E. Foothills, 8269 NL-20
E. La Mirada, 9757 ‡G-10
E. Los Angeles, 126496 ‡F-8
E. Palo Alto, 28155 NK-16
E. Pasadena, 6144 ‡D-9
E. Quincy, 2489 NG-8
E. Richmond Hts., 3280 ND-14
Easton, 2083 SC-8
El Cajon, 99478 SM-14
El Centro, 42598 SM-17
El Cerrito, 23549 NL-5
El Cerrito, 5100 ‡H-16
EL DORADO CO., 181058 NK-9
El Granada, 5467 NJ-12
El Monte, 113475 ‡E-10
El Rio, 7198 SI-9
El Segundo, 16654 ‡G-5
El Sobrante, 12669 NC-14
El Sueno, 2000 †B-3
Elk Grv., 153015 NK-7
Ellwood, 7800 †B-1
Elverta, 5492 *F-2
Emerald Bay, 1100 ‡L-13
Emerald L. Hills, 4278 NK-15
Emeryville, 10080 NE-14
Empire, 4189 NM-8
Encinitas, 59518 SM-13
Escalon, 7132 NM-8
Escondido, 143911 SL-14
Esparto, 3108 NJ-6
Etna, 737 NC-4
Eucalyptus Hills, 5313 †G-6
Eureka, 27191 ND-2
Exeter, 10334 SD-9
Fair Oaks, 30912 *G-5
Fairbanks Ranch, 3148 †E-2
Fairfax, 7441 NL-5
Fairfax, 991 SM-8
Fairfield, 105321 NL-6
Fairmead, 1447 SB-7
Fairmont Ter., 4000 NG-16
Fairview, 10003 NH-17
Fallbrook, 30534 SL-13
Farmersville, 10588 SD-9
Felton, 4057 SB-3
Ferndale, 1371 NE-1
Fernwood, 500 ‡E-3
Fillmore, 15002 SI-10
Firebaugh, 7549 SB-6
Florence, 25000 ‡G-7
Florin, 47513 *I-3
Folsom, 72203 NJ-8
Fontana, 196069 ‡D-17
Foothill Farms, 33121 *F-4
Ford City, 4278 SG-8
Foresthill, 1483 NI-8
Forestville, 3293 NK-4
Ft. Bragg, 7273 NH-2
Ft. Jones, 839 NB-4
Fortuna, 11926 NE-2
Foster City, 30567 NI-15
Fountain Valley, 55313 ‡J-10
Fowler, 5570 SC-8
Frazier Pk., 2691 SH-9
Freedom, 3070 SB-3
Freeport, 38 *J-2
Fremont, 214089 NM-6
French Camp, 3376 NM-7
Fresno, 494665 SC-8
FRESNO CO., 930450 SC-7
Fullerton, 135161 SJ-12
Galt, 23647 NL-7
Garden Acres, 10648 *L-10
Garden Grv., 170883 SK-12
Gardena, 58829 ‡H-6
Georgetown, 2367 NJ-8
Gilroy, 48821 SB-4
Glendale, 191719 SJ-11
Glendora, 50073 ‡D-12
GLENN CO., 28122 NH-5
Glenview, 160 ‡D-3
Gold River, 7912 *G-5
Golden Hills, 8656 SG-10
Goleta, 29888 SI-7
Gonzales, 8187 SC-4
Goshen, 3006 SD-8
Grand Ter., 12040 ‡E-18
Granite Bay, 20402 *E-6
Granite Hills, 3035 †I-7
Grass Valley, 12860 NI-8
Graton, 1707 NK-4
Green Brae, 3400 ND-12
Greenacres, 5566 SL-5
Greenfield, 16330 SD-4
Gridley, 6584 NH-7
Grover Bch., 13156 SG-6
Guadalupe, 7080 SG-6
Gualala, 1500 NJ-3
Guerneville, 4534 NK-4
Gustine, 5520 SA-5
Hacienda Hts., 54038 ‡F-10
Half Moon Bay, 11324 NN-5
Hamilton City, 1759 NG-6
Hanford, 53967 SD-8
Hawaiian Gdns., 14254 ‡H-9
Hawthorne, 84293 ‡G-6
Hayfork, 2368 NE-4
Hayward, 144186 NM-6
Healdsburg, 11254 NJ-4
Heber, 4275 SM-17
Hemet, 78657 SK-14
Hercules, 24060 NC-15
Hermosa Bch., 19506 ‡H-5
Hesperia, 90173 SI-13
Hidden Hills, 1856 ‡D-2
Hidden Valley Lake, 5579 NJ-5
Highgrove, 3988 ‡F-18
Highland, 53104 SJ-13
Hillsborough, 10825 NI-14
Hollister, 34928 SB-4
Holtville, 5939 SM-18
Home Gdns., 11570 ‡H-16
Hope Ranch, 1600 †B-3
Hughson, 6640 NM-8
HUMBOLDT CO., 134623 NE-2
Humboldt Hill, 3414 NE-2
Huntington Bch., 189992 SK-12
Huntington Pk., 58114 ‡F-7
Huron, 6754 SD-7
Idyllwild, 2200 SK-15
Imperial, 14758 SM-17
Imperial Bch., 26324 SN-14
IMPERIAL CO., 174528 SM-18
Incline, 60 NM-1
Independence, 669 SB-11
Indian Wells, 4958 SK-16
Indio, 76036 SK-16
Indio Hills, 972 SG-2
Industry, 219 ‡F-11
Inglewood, 109673 SJ-11
INYO CO., 18546 SC-13
Ione, 7918 NK-8
Irvine, 212375 SK-12
Irwindale, 1422 ‡D-11
Isla Vista, 23096 SI-7
Isleton, 804 NL-7
Ivanhoe, 4495 SD-9
Jackson, 4651 NK-9
Jamestown, 3433 NL-9
Jamul, 6163 SN-14
Joshua Tree, 7414 SJ-16
Julian, 1502 SM-15
Jurupa Valley, 94235 ‡F-16
Kelseyville, 3353 NI-4
Kennedy, 3254 *M-10
Kensington, 5077 ND-14
Kentfield, 6485 ND-11
Kerman, 13544 SC-7
KERN CO., 839631 SF-10
Kettleman City, 1439 SE-7
Keyes, 5601 NM-8
King City, 12874 SD-5
Kings Bch., 3796 NI-10
KINGS CO., 152982 SD-7
Kingsburg, 11382 SC-8
Knightsen, 1568 NL-7
La Cañada Flintridge, 20246 ‡C-7
La Crescenta, 13000 ‡C-7
La Habra, 60239 ‡G-11
La Habra Hts., 5325 ‡G-11
La Mesa, 57065 †I-5
La Mirada, 48527 ‡G-10
La Palma, 15568 ‡H-10
La Presa, 34169 †J-5
La Puente, 39816 ‡E-10
La Quinta, 37467 SK-16
La Riviera, 10802 *H-4
La Verne, 31063 SJ-12
Ladera, 1426 NL-16
Ladera Hts., 6498 ‡F-6
Ladera Ranch, 350 ‡L-15
Lafayette, 23893 ND-16
Laguna Bch., 22723 SK-12
Laguna Hills, 30344 ‡L-14
Laguna Niguel, 62979 ‡M-14
Laguna Woods, 16192 ‡L-13
L. Arrowhead, 12424 ‡B-20
LAKE CO., 64665 NI-4
L. Elsinore, 51821 SK-13
L. Forest, 77264 SK-12
L. Isabella, 3466 SF-11
L. Los Angeles, 12328 SH-12
L. Nacimiento, 2411 SE-5
Lake of the Pines, 3917 NI-8
L. Wildwood, 4991 NI-8
Lakeland Vil., 11541 ‡K-18
Lakeport, 4753 NI-4
Lakeside, 20648 SM-14
Lakeview, 2104 SJ-14
Lakewood, 80048 ‡H-9
Lamont, 15120 SG-10
Lancaster, 156633 SH-11
Landers, 2300 SI-15
Larkspur, 11926 ND-11
Las Flores, 5971 ‡L-15
LASSEN CO., 34895 NE-9
Lathrop, 18023 NM-7
Laton, 1824 SC-8
Lawndale, 32769 ‡H-5
Le Grand, 1659 SA-7
Lebec, 1468 SH-10
Lemon Grv., 25320 †J-5
Lemon Hts., 2800 ‡I-13
Lemoore, 24531 SD-8
Lennox, 22753 ‡G-6
Lenwood, 3543 SH-14
Leona Valley, 1607 ‡M-6
Lincoln, 42819 NJ-7
Lincoln Acres, 1650 †K-4
Lincoln Vil., 4381 *K-9
Linda, 17773 NI-7
Linden, 1784 NL-8
Lindsay, 11768 SD-9
Live Oak, 8392 NI-7
Livermore, 80968 NM-6
Livingston, 13058 NN-9
Lockeford, 3233 NL-8
Lodi, 62134 NL-7
Loma Linda, 23261 SJ-13
Loma Rica, 2368 NI-7
Lomita, 20256 ‡I-6
Lompoc, 42434 SH-6
London, 1869 SC-8
Lone Pine, 2035 SC-11
Long Bch., 462257 SK-11
Loomis, 6430 NJ-8
Los Alamitos, 11449 ‡I-9
Los Alamos, 1890 SH-6
Los Altos, 28976 NN-6
Los Altos Hills, 7922 NL-16
Los Angeles, 3792621 SJ-11
LOS ANGELES CO., 9818605 SI-12
Los Banos, 35972 SB-5
Los Gatos, 29413 SA-3
Los Molinos, 2037 NG-6
Los Nietos, 8200 ‡F-9
Los Osos, 14276 SF-5
Los Ranchitos, 425 NC-11
Lost Hills, 2412 SF-8
Loyalton, 769 NH-10
Loyola, 3261 NL-17
Lucas Valley, 4000 NC-11
Lucerne, 3067 NI-4
Lucerne Valley, 5811 SI-14
Lynwood, 69772 ‡G-7
Lytle Creek, 701 ‡B-16
Madera, 61416 SB-7
Madera Acres, 9163 SB-7
MADERA CO., 150865 SB-7
Magalia, 11310 NG-7
Malibu, 12645 SJ-10
Mammoth Lakes, 8234 NM-12
Manhattan Bch., 35135 SJ-11
Manteca, 67096 NM-8
Maricopa, 1154 SG-8
Marin City, 2666 NE-12
MARIN CO., 252409 NL-4
Marina, 19718 SC-3
Marina del Rey, 8866 ‡F-5
Marinwood, 2300 NB-11
Mariposa, 2173 NN-10
MARIPOSA CO., 18251 SA-7
Markleeville, 210 NJ-11
Martinez, 35824 NL-6
Marysville, 12072 NI-7
Maywood, 27395 ‡F-8
McFarland, 12707 SE-9
McKinleyville, 15177 ND-2
Mead Valley, 18510 ‡H-19
Meadow Vista, 3217 NI-8
Mecca, 8577 SK-16
Meiners Oaks, 3571 SI-9
MENDOCINO CO., 87841 NH-3
Mendota, 11014 SB-6
Menifee, 77519 SK-14
Menlo Pk., 32026 NN-5
Merced, 78958 SA-6
MERCED CO., 255793 SA-6
Midway City, 8485 ‡J-10
Mill Valley, 13903 NL-5
Millbrae, 21532 NI-13
Milpitas, 66790 NN-6
Mira Monte, 6854 SI-9
Mission Viejo, 93305 SK-12
Modesto, 201165 NM-8
Modjeska, 500 ‡J-15
MODOC CO., 9686 NB-8
Mojave, 4238 SG-11
MONO CO., 14202 NL-13
Monrovia, 36590 ‡D-10
Montague, 1443 NB-5
Montalvin Manor, 2876 NC-14
Montara, 2909 NJ-12
Montclair, 36664 ‡E-14
Monte Nido, 850 ‡E-2
Monte Sereno, 3341 NN-18
Montebello, 62500 ‡F-9
Montecito, 8965 SI-8
Monterey, 27810 SC-3
MONTEREY CO., 415057 SD-4
Monterey Pk., 60269 ‡E-8
Montrose, 4100 ‡C-7
Moorpark, 34421 SI-10
Morada, 3828 *K-10
Moraga, 16016 NE-16
Moreno Valley, 193365 SJ-14
Morgan Hill, 37882 SA-3
Morongo Valley, 3552 SJ-15
Morro Bay, 10234 SF-5
Moss Bch., 3103 NJ-12
Mt. Baldy, 200 ‡B-14
Mt. Helix, 6400 †I-6
Mt. Shasta, 3394 NC-6
Mountain Ranch, 1628 NL-9
Mountain View, 74066 NL-17
Mountain View, 1500 NC-16
Murphys, 2213 NL-9
Murrieta, 103466 SK-14
Murrieta Hot Sprs., 2948 ‡L-20
Muscoy, 10644 ‡D-18
Napa, 76915 NK-5
NAPA CO., 136484 NK-5
National City, 58582 SN-14
Needles, 4844 SH-19
Nevada City, 3068 NI-8
NEVADA CO., 98764 NH-9
Newark, 42573 NM-6
Newberry Sprs., 1500 SH-15
Newman, 10224 SA-5
Newport Bch., 85186 SK-12
Nice, 2731 NI-4
Nipomo, 16714 SG-6
Norco, 27063 SJ-13
N. Fair Oaks, 14687 NK-15
N. Highlands, 42694 *F-4
N. Richmond, 3717 ND-13
N. Shore, 3477 SK-16
N. Tustin, 24044 ‡I-13
Norwalk, 105549 ‡H-9
Novato, 51904 NL-5
Nuevo, 6447 ‡I-20
Nyland, 2200 †B-9
Oak Hills, 8879 SI-13
Oak Pk., 13811 ‡C-1
Oak View, 4066 SI-9
Oakdale, 20675 NM-8
Oakhurst, 2829 NN-11
Oakland, 390724 NM-5
Oakley, 35432 NL-6
Oasis, 6890 SK-16
Oceano, 7286 SG-6
Oceanside, 167086 SL-13
Oildale, 32684 SF-9
Ojai, 7461 SI-9
Olivehurst, 13656 NI-7
Ontario, 163924 SJ-12
Orange, 136416 ‡I-12
ORANGE CO., 3010232 SK-12
Orange Cove, 9078 SC-9
Orangevale, 33960 *F-6
Orcutt, 28905 SH-6
Orinda, 17643 NE-16
Orland, 7291 NG-6
Orosi, 8770 SC-9
Oroville, 15546 NH-7
Oxnard, 197899 SJ-9
Pacheco, 3685 NC-17
Pacific Grv., 15041 SC-3
Pacifica, 37234 NM-5
Pajaro, 3070 SB-3
Palermo, 5382 NH-7
Palm Desert, 48445 SK-15
Palm Sprs., 44552 SJ-15
Palmdale, 152750 SH-11
Palo Alto, 64403 NN-5
Palomar Pk., 530 NJ-15
Palos Verdes Estates, 13438 ‡I-5
Paradise, 26218 NG-7
Paramount, 54098 ‡H-8
Parkway, 14670 *I-2
Parkwood, 2268 SB-7
Parlier, 14494 SC-8
Pasadena, 137122 SJ-11
Paso Robles, 29793 SF-6
Patterson, 20413 NN-8
Penn Valley, 1621 NI-8
Penngrove, 2522 NK-4
Perris, 68386 SK-13
Petaluma, 57941 NL-4
Phelan, 14304 SI-13
Pico Rivera, 62942 ‡F-9
Piedmont, 10667 NE-15
Pine Grv., 2219 NK-9
Pine Hills, 3131 ND-2
Pine Mtn. Club, 2315 SH-9
Pine Valley, 1510 SM-15
Pinole, 18390 NC-14
Piñon Hills, 7272 SI-12
Piru, 2063 SI-10
Pismo Bch., 7655 SG-6
Pittsburg, 63264 NL-6
Pixley, 3310 SE-9
Placentia, 50533 ‡H-12
PLACER CO., 348432 NI-9
Placerville, 10389 NJ-9
Planada, 4584 SA-6
Pleasant Hill, 33152 NL-6
Pleasanton, 70285 NM-6
PLUMAS CO., 20007 NF-9
Plymouth, 1005 NK-8
Point Arena, 449 NJ-2
Pollock Pines, 6871 NJ-9
Pomona, 149058 SJ-12
Port Costa, 190 NB-16
Port Hueneme, 21723 SJ-9
Porterville, 54165 SD-9
Portola, 2104 NG-9
Portola Hills, 6391 ‡K-15
Portola Valley, 4353 NL-15
Poway, 47811 SM-14
Prunedale, 17560 SB-3
Quartz Hill, 10912 SH-11
Quincy, 1728 NG-8
Rainbow, 1832 SL-14
Ramona, 20292 SM-14
Rancho Calaveras, 5325 NL-8
Rancho Cordova, 64776 NK-7
Rancho Cucamonga, 165269 ‡D-15
Rancho Mirage, 17218 SK-15
Rancho Murieta, 5488 NK-8
Rancho Palos Verdes, 41643 ‡J-6
Rancho San Diego, 21208 †J-6
Rancho Santa Fe, 3117 SM-14
Rancho Santa Margarita, 47853 ‡K-16
Red Bluff, 14076 NF-6
Red Hill, 2800 ‡J-13
Redding, 89861 NE-5
Redlands, 68747 SJ-14
Redondo Bch., 66748 SJ-11
Redwood City, 76815 NN-5
Redwood Valley, 1729 NI-3
Reedley, 24194 SC-8
Rialto, 99171 SJ-13
Richgrove, 2882 SE-9
Richmond, 103701 ND-13
Ridgecrest, 27616 SF-12
Rimforest, 700 ‡B-19
Rio del Mar, 9216 SB-3
Rio Dell, 3368 NE-2
Rio Linda, 15106 *F-3
Rio Vista, 7360 NL-7
Ripon, 14297 NM-8
Riverbank, 22678 NM-8
Riverdale, 3153 SC-7
Riverdale Pk., 1128 *J-8
Riverside, 303871 SJ-13
RIVERSIDE CO., 2189641 SJ-16
Rocklin, 56974 NJ-8
Rodeo, 8679 NB-15
Rohnert Pk., 40971 NK-4
Rolling Hills, 1860 ‡I-6
Rolling Hills Estates, 8067 ‡I-6
Rollingwood, 2969 NC-14
Romoland, 1684 ‡I-20
Rosamond, 18150 SH-11
Rosedale, 14058 SF-9
Roseland, 6325 *L-6
Rosemead, 53764 ‡E-9
Rosemont, 22681 *H-4
Rosemont, 800 ‡E-6
Roseville, 118788 NJ-7
Ross, 2415 NC-11
Rossmoor, 10244 ‡I-9
Rowland Hts., 48993 ‡F-11
Running Sprs., 4862 SI-14
Sacramento, 466488 NK-7
SACRAMENTO CO., 1418788 NK-8
St. Helena, 5814 NK-5
Salida, 13722 NM-8
Salinas, 150441 SC-3
Salton City, 3763 SL-16
San Andreas, 2783 NL-9
San Anselmo, 12336 NC-11
San Antonio Hts., 3371 ‡D-14
SAN BENITO CO., 55269 SC-5
San Bernardino, 209924 SJ-13
SAN BERNARDINO CO., 2035210 SG-16
San Bruno, 41114 NM-5
San Carlos, 28406 NN-5
San Clemente, 63522 SL-13
San Diego, 1307402 SN-14
SAN DIEGO CO., 3095313 SM-15
San Dimas, 33371 ‡D-12
San Fernando, 23645 SI-11
San Francisco, 805235 NM-5
SAN FRANCISCO CO., 805235 NE-12
San Gabriel, 39718 ‡E-9
San Jacinto, 44199 SK-14
San Joaquin, 4001 SC-7
SAN JOAQUIN CO., 685306 NL-8
San Jose, 945942 NN-6
San Juan Bautista, 1862 SB-4
San Juan Capistrano, 34593 SK-12
San Leandro, 84950 NM-6
San Lorenzo, 23452 NH-16
San Luis Obispo, 45119 SG-6
SAN LUIS OBISPO CO., 269637 SG-6
San Marcos, 83781 SL-14
San Marino, 13147 ‡D-9
San Martin, 7027 SB-4
San Mateo, 97207 NI-14
SAN MATEO CO., 718451 SA-2
San Miguel, 2336 SE-6
San Pablo, 29139 NL-5
San Quentin, 100 ND-12
San Rafael, 57713 NL-5
San Ramon, 72148 NM-6
Sand City, 334 *M-2
Sanger, 24270 SC-8
Santa Ana, 324528 SK-12
Santa Barbara, 88410 SI-8
SANTA BARBARA CO., 423895 SH-8
Santa Clara, 116468 NL-18
SANTA CLARA CO., 1781642 SA-4
Santa Clarita, 176320 SI-10
Santa Cruz, 59946 SB-3
SANTA CRUZ CO., 262382 SB-3
Santa Fe Sprs., 16223 ‡G-9
Santa Maria, 99553 SG-6
Santa Monica, 89736 SJ-11
Santa Paula, 29321 SI-9
Santa Rosa, 167815 NK-4
Santa Susana, 1037 ‡B-2
Santa Venetia, 4292 NC-12
Santa Ynez, 4418 SH-7
Santee, 53413 SM-14
Saranap, 5202 NE-17
Saratoga, 29926 SA-3
Saticoy, 1029 †A-9
Sausalito, 7061 NE-12
Scotland, 285 ‡B-16
Scotts Valley, 11580 SB-3
Seal Bch., 24168 ‡J-9
Searles Valley, 1739 SE-13
Seaside, 33025 SC-3
Sebastopol, 7379 NK-4
Sedco Hills, 3078 ‡K-19
Seeley, 1739 SM-17
Selma, 23219 SC-8
Shackelford, 3371 *J-9
Shafter, 16988 SF-9
Shasta, 1771 NE-5
SHASTA CO., 177223 NE-6
Shasta Lake, 10164 NE-5
Sherwood Forest, 2600 ND-14
Shingle Sprs., 4432 NJ-8
Shingletown, 2283 NE-6
Shore Acres, 4000 NB-18
SIERRA CO., 3240 NH-9
Sierra Madre, 10917 ‡D-9
Signal Hill, 11016 ‡I-8
Silver Strand, 1200 †C-8
Silverado, 800 ‡J-15
Simi Valley, 124237 SI-10
SISKIYOU CO., 44900 NC-5
Sky Valley, 2406 SG-1
Skyforest, 750 ‡B-20
Solana Bch., 12867 SM-13
SOLANO CO., 413344 NK-6
Soledad, 25738 SC-4
Solvang, 5245 SH-7
Sonoma, 10648 NK-5
SONOMA CO., 483878 NJ-3
Sonora, 4903 NL-9
Soquel, 9644 SB-3
Soulsbyville, 2215 NL-10
S. Dos Palos, 1620 SB-6
S. El Monte, 20116 ‡E-10
S. Gate, 94396 ‡G-8
S. L. Tahoe, 21403 NJ-10
S. Pasadena, 25619 ‡D-8
S. San Francisco, 63632 NM-5
S. San Gabriel, 8070 ‡E-9
S. San Jose Hills, 20551 ‡F-11
S. Taft, 2169 SG-8
S. Whittier, 57156 ‡G-10
Spreckels, 673 *N-5
Spring Valley, 28205 SN-14
Squaw Valley, 3162 SC-9
Stallion Sprs., 2488 SG-10
STANISLAUS CO., 514453 SA-4
Stanton, 38186 ‡I-10
Stockton, 291707 NL-7
Strathmore, 2819 SD-9
Strawberry, 5393 ND-12
Suisun City, 28111 NL-6
Summerland, 1448 SI-8
Sunnyside, 4235 SC-20
Sunnyside, 1000 †K-5
Sunnyvale, 140081 NL-17
Sunol, 913 NI-19
Sunset Bch., 971 ‡J-9
Susanville, 17947 NF-9
Sutter, 2904 NI-6
SUTTER CO., 94737 NI-6
Sutter Creek, 2501 NK-8
Sylvia Pk., 600 ‡D-3
Taft, 9327 SG-8
Taft Hts., 1949 SG-8
Tahoe Vista, 1433 NI-10
Tamalpais Valley, 7000 NE-12
Tara Hills, 5126 NC-14
Tarpey Vil., 3888 SB-20
Tehachapi, 14414 SG-11
Tehama, 418 NG-6
TEHAMA CO., 63463 NG-5
Temecula, 100097 SK-14
Temescal Valley, 22535 ‡I-16
Temple City, 35558 ‡E-9
Templeton, 7674 SF-6
Terra Bella, 3310 SE-9
Thermal, 2865 SK-16
Thermalito, 6646 NH-7
Thousand Oaks, 126683 SJ-10
Thousand Palms, 7715 SJ-15
Three Rivers, 2182 SC-10
Tiburon, 8962 NM-5
Tipton, 2543 SD-9
Topanga, 8289 ‡E-3
Topanga Pk., 600 ‡D-2
Torrance, 145438 SK-11
Trabuco Canyon, 800 ‡K-15
Tracy, 82922 NM-7
Trinidad, 367 ND-2
TRINITY CO., 13786 NE-4
Truckee, 16180 NI-10
Tulare, 59278 SD-9
TULARE CO., 442179 SD-9
Tulelake, 1010 NA-7
Tuolumne, 1779 NL-10
TUOLUMNE CO., 55365 NM-9
Turlock, 68549 NN-8
Tustin, 75540 ‡J-12
Twain Harte, 2226 NL-10
Twentynine Palms, 25048 SJ-16
Twin Peaks, 2100 ‡B-19
Ukiah, 16075 NI-3
Union City, 69516 NI-16
Upland, 73732 SJ-12
Vacaville, 92428 NK-6
Valinda, 22822 ‡E-11
Valle Vista, 14578 SK-14
Vallejo, 115942 NL-5
Valley Ctr., 9277 SL-14
Valley Sprs., 3553 NL-8
Vandenberg Vil., 6497 SH-6
Ventura, 106433 SI-9
VENTURA CO., 823318 SH-9
Vernon, 112 ‡F-7
Victorville, 115903 SI-13
View Pk., 5500 ‡F-6
Villa Pk., 5812 ‡I-12
Vincent, 15922 SI-11
Vine Hill, 3761 NC-16
Vineyard, 24836 *J-4
Visalia, 124442 SD-9
Vista, 93834 SL-13
Walnut, 29172 ‡E-12
Walnut Creek, 64173 NL-6
Walnut Grv., 1542 NL-7
Walnut Pk., 15966 ‡F-7
Wasco, 25545 SF-9
Waterford, 8456 NM-9
Watsonville, 51199 SB-3
Weaverville, 3600 NE-4
Weed, 2967 NC-5
Weldon, 2642 SE-11
W. Athens, 8729 ‡G-7
W. Carson, 21699 ‡I-7
W. Covina, 106098 ‡E-11
W. Hollywood, 34399 ‡E-6
W. Menlo Pk., 3659 NK-15
West Park, 1157 SC-18
W. Puente Valley, 22636 ‡E-11
W. Sacramento, 48744 NK-7
Westlake Vil., 8270 SJ-10
Westminster, 89701 ‡J-10
Westmorland, 2225 SM-17
Westwood, 1647 NF-8
Wheatland, 3456 NI-7
Whittier, 85331 SJ-12
Wildomar, 32176 SK-13
Williams, 5123 NI-6
Willits, 4888 NH-3
Willow Creek, 1710 ND-3
Willows, 6166 NH-6
Wilsonia, 5 SK-1
Wilton, 5363 NK-7
Winchester, 2534 SK-14
Windsor, 26801 NK-4
Windsor Hills, 5000 ‡F-6
Winter Gdns., 20631 †H-6
Winters, 6624 NK-6
Winton, 10613 NN-9
Wofford Hts., 2200 SE-11
Woodcrest, 14347 ‡H-18
Woodlake, 7279 SC-9
Woodland, 55468 NJ-6
Woodside, 5287 NK-15
Woodville, 1740 SD-9
Wrightwood, 4525 SI-12
YOLO CO., 200849 NJ-6
Yorba Linda, 64234 ‡G-13
Yosemite Lakes, 4952 SA-8
Yountville, 2933 NK-5
Yreka, 7765 NB-5
Yuba City, 64925 NI-7
YUBA CO., 72155 NI-7
Yucaipa, 51367 SJ-14
Yucca Valley, 20700 SJ-15

Colorado

Map pp. 20 – 21

* City keyed to p. 22

ADAMS CO., 441603 E-15
Aguilar, 538 L-14
Akron, 1702 D-17
Alamosa, 8780 L-11
ALAMOSA CO., 15445 L-11
Allenspark, 528 D-12
Antonito, 781 M-11
ARAPAHOE CO., 572003 F-14
ARCHULETA CO., 12084 M-8
Arvada, 106433 E-13
Aspen, 6658 G-9
Ault, 1519 C-14
Aurora, 325078 E-14
Avon, 6447 F-10
Avondale, 674 J-15
BACA CO., 3788 L-19
Basalt, 3857 F-8
Bayfield, 2333 M-7
Bennett, 2308 E-15
BENT CO., 6499 K-18
Berthoud, 5105 D-13
Black Forest, 13116 H-14
Blakeland, 700 *L-6
Blende, 878 J-14
Blue River, 849 F-11
Boulder, 97385 D-13
BOULDER CO., 294567 D-12
Bow Mar, 866 *K-6
Breckenridge, 4540 F-11
Brighton, 33352 E-14
Broomfield, 55889 E-13
BROOMFIELD CO., 55889 *E-6
Brush, 5463 D-16
Buena Vista, 2617 H-11
Burlington, 4254 G-20
Byers, 1160 E-15
Calhan, 780 H-15
Campion, 1830 D-13
Cañon City, 16400 I-13
Carbondale, 6427 F-8
Cascade, 500 H-13
Castle Pines North, 12390 *M-8
Castle Rock, 48231 F-14
Cattle Creek, 641 F-8
Cedaredge, 2253 H-6
Centennial, 100377 F-13
Center, 2230 K-11
Central City, 663 E-12
CHAFFEE CO., 17809 I-11
Cherry Creek, 11120 *J-8
Cherry Hills Vil., 5987 *J-7
CHEYENNE CO., 1836 H-19
Cheyenne Wells, 846 H-20
CLEAR CREEK CO., 9088 F-12
Clifton, 19889 G-5
Collbran, 708 G-6
Colorado City, 2193 K-14
Colorado Sprs., 416427 H-14
Columbine Valley, 1256 *K-6
Commerce City, 45913 *H-7
Conejos, 58 M-11
CONEJOS CO., 8256 M-10
Cortez, 8482 L-5
COSTILLA CO., 3524 M-12
Craig, 9464 C-7
Creede, 290 K-9
Crested Butte, 1487 H-8
Cripple Creek, 1189 H-13
CROWLEY CO., 5823 J-16
CUSTER CO., 4255 J-12
Dacono, 4152 D-13
De Beque, 504 F-6
Deer Trail, 546 F-15
Del Norte, 1686 L-10
Delta, 8915 H-6
DELTA CO., 30952 H-6
Denver, 600158 E-13
DENVER CO., 600158 *H-8
Dillon, 904 F-11
Dolores, 936 L-5
DOLORES CO., 2064 K-5
DOUGLAS CO., 285465 G-13
Dove Creek, 735 K-4
Dupont, 3650 *G-7
Durango, 16887 M-6
Eads, 609 I-19
Eagle, 6508 F-9
EAGLE CO., 52197 E-9
Eaton, 4365 C-14
Edgewater, 5170 *I-6
Edwards, 10266 F-9
El Jebel, 3801 F-8
EL PASO CO., 622263 H-14
ELBERT CO., 23086 F-15
Eldorado Sprs., 585 E-13
Elizabeth, 1358 G-14
Ellicott, 1131 H-15
Englewood, 30255 F-13
Erie, 18135 D-13
Estes Pk., 5858 C-12
Evans, 18537 C-14
Evergreen, 9038 F-12
Fairplay, 679 G-11
Federal Hts., 11467 *G-6
Firestone, 10147 D-13
Flagler, 561 G-18
Florence, 3881 J-13
Ft. Carson, 13813 *I-2
Ft. Collins, 143986 C-13
Ft. Lupton, 7377 D-14
Ft. Morgan, 11315 D-16
Fountain, 25846 I-14
Fowler, 1182 J-16
Foxfield, 685 F-14
Fraser, 1224 E-11
Frederick, 8679 D-13
FREMONT CO., 46824 I-12
Frisco, 2683 F-11
Fruita, 12646 G-4
Fruitvale, 7675 G-5
GARFIELD CO., 56389 F-6
Georgetown, 1034 E-12
Gilcrest, 1034 D-14
GILPIN CO., 5441 E-12
Glendale, 4184 *I-7
Glenwood Sprs., 9614 F-8
Golden, 18867 E-13
Goodnight, 1400 I-1
Granada, 517 J-20
Granby, 1864 D-11
GRAND CO., 14843 D-10
Grand Jct., 58566 G-5
Grand View Estates, 528 *L-9
Greeley, 92889 C-14
Green Mtn. Falls, 640 H-13
Greenwood Vil., 13925 *K-7
Gunbarrel, 9263 *A-7
Gunnison, 5854 I-9
GUNNISON CO., 15324 H-8
Gypsum, 6477 F-9
Haxtun, 946 C-19
Hayden, 1810 C-8
Henderson, 600 *F-8
Highlands Ranch, 96713 *L-7
HINSDALE CO., 843 K-7
Holly, 802 J-20
Holyoke, 2313 C-19
Hot Sulphur Sprs., 663 D-11
Hotchkiss, 944 H-7
Howard, 723 I-11
Hudson, 2356 D-14
HUERFANO CO., 6711 L-13
Hugo, 730 G-17
Idaho Sprs., 1717 E-12
Ignacio, 697 M-7
Indian Hills, 1280 F-13
JACKSON CO., 1394 B-10
JEFFERSON CO., 534543 F-12
Johnstown, 9887 D-13
Julesburg, 1225 B-20
Keenesburg, 1127 D-14
Kersey, 1454 C-14
Kiowa, 723 G-14
KIOWA CO., 1398 I-18
KIT CARSON CO., 8270 F-19
Kremmling, 1444 D-10
La Jara, 818 M-11
La Junta, 7077 K-17
LA PLATA CO., 51334 L-6
La Salle, 1955 D-14
La Veta, 800 L-13
Lafayette, 24453 *D-5
Lake City, 408 K-8
LAKE CO., 7310 G-10
Lakewood, 142980 *I-5
Lamar, 7804 J-19
Laporte, 2450 *A-8
LARIMER CO., 299630 C-12
Las Animas, 2410 J-17
LAS ANIMAS CO., 15507 M-15
Leadville, 2602 G-10
Limon, 1880 G-16
LINCOLN CO., 5467 H-17
Lincoln Pk., 3546 I-13
Littleton, 41737 F-13
Lochbuie, 4726 *E-10
Log Lane Vil., 873 D-16
LOGAN CO., 22709 B-17
Loma, 1293 G-4
Lombard Vil., 600 I-2
Lone Tree, 10218 *L-8
Longmont, 86270 D-13
Louisville, 18376 E-13
Loveland, 66859 C-13
Lyons, 2033 D-13
Manassa, 991 M-11
Mancos, 1336 M-5
Manitou Sprs., 4992 H-13
Mead, 3405 D-13
Meeker, 2475 D-6
MESA CO., 146723 H-5
Milliken, 5610 D-14
MINERAL CO., 712 L-8
Minturn, 1027 F-10
MOFFAT CO., 13795 C-6
Monte Vista, 4444 L-10
MONTEZUMA CO., 25535 M-4
Montrose, 19132 I-6
MONTROSE CO., 41276 I-6
Monument, 5530 G-13
MORGAN CO., 28159 D-16
Mt. Crested Butte, 801 H-9
Mountain View, 1700 *B-8
Mountain View, 507 *H-6
Mountain Vil., 1320 K-6
Naturita, 546 J-5
Nederland, 1445 E-12
New Castle, 4518 F-7
Niwot, 4006 D-13
Northglenn, 35789 *F-7
Norwood, 518 J-5
Nucla, 711 J-5
Oak Creek, 884 D-9
Olathe, 1849 I-6
Orchard City, 3119 H-6
Orchard Mesa, 6836 G-5
Ordway, 1080 J-16
OTERO CO., 18831 K-16
Ouray, 1000 K-7
OURAY CO., 4436 J-6
Pagosa Sprs., 1727 M-8
Palisade, 2692 G-5
Palmer Lake, 2420 G-13
Paonia, 1451 H-7
Parachute, 1085 F-6
PARK CO., 16206 G-11
Parker, 45297 F-14
Penrose, 3582 I-13
PHILLIPS CO., 4442 C-19
Pierce, 834 C-14
PITKIN CO., 17148 G-9
Platteville, 2485 D-14
Poncha Sprs., 737 I-11
PROWERS CO., 12551 K-19
Pueblo, 106595 J-14
PUEBLO CO., 159063 J-14
Pueblo West, 29637 J-14
Rangely, 2365 D-4
Redlands, 8685 G-5
Ridgway, 924 J-7
Rifle, 9172 F-7
RIO BLANCO CO., 6666 E-6
RIO GRANDE CO., 11982 L-10
Rocky Ford, 3957 K-16
ROUTT CO., 23509 C-8
Saguache, 485 J-10
SAGUACHE CO., 6108 K-9
Salida, 5236 I-11
Salt Creek, 587 I-2
SAN JUAN CO., 699 L-7
San Luis, 629 M-12
SAN MIGUEL CO., 7359 K-5
Sanford, 879 M-11
Security, 4400 *I-3
SEDGWICK CO., 2379 B-19
Severance, 3165 C-14
Sheridan, 5664 *J-6
Silt, 2930 F-7
Silver Cliff, 587 J-12
Silverthorne, 3887 F-11
Silverton, 637 K-7
Simla, 618 G-15
Snowmass Vil., 2826 G-9
Springfield, 1451 L-19
Steamboat Sprs., 12088 C-9
Sterling, 14777 C-17
Strasburg, 2447 E-15
Stratmoor Hills, 2350 *I-2
Stratton, 658 G-19
SUMMIT CO., 27994 F-11
Superior, 12483 E-13
Swink, 617 K-17
TELLER CO., 23350 H-13
Telluride, 2325 K-6
Thornton, 118772 E-13
Timnath, 625 C-13
Towaoc, 1087 M-4
Trinidad, 9096 M-14
Vail, 5305 F-10
Walden, 608 B-10
Walsenburg, 3068 L-14
Walsh, 546 L-20
WASHINGTON CO., 4814 D-17
Watkins, 653 E-14
Welby, 14846 *G-7
WELD CO., 252825 B-15
Wellington, 6289 B-13
Westcliffe, 568 J-12
Western Hills, 2600 *G-6
Westminster, 106114 E-13
Wheat Ridge, 30166 *H-5
Widefield, 4200 *J-4
Wiggins, 893 D-15
Williamsburg, 662 J-13
Windsor, 18644 C-13
Winter Pk., 999 E-11
Woodland Pk., 7200 H-13
Wray, 2342 D-20
Yuma, 3524 D-19
YUMA CO., 10043 D-19

Connecticut

Map p. 23

Abington, 750 B-13
Addison, 800 C-9
Amston, 780 D-11
Ansonia, 19249 F-6
Attawaugan, 660 B-13
Avon, 1800 C-8
Ball Pond, 2400 E-3
Ballouville, 660 B-14
Baltic, 1250 D-12
Bantam, 759 C-5
Beacon Falls, 1650 E-6
Berlin, 1230 D-8
Bethany, 1280 F-7
Bethel, 9549 F-4
Bethlehem, 2021 D-5
Bloomfield, 7500 B-8
Blue Hills, 2901 H-13
Branford, 5819 G-8
Branford Ctr., 5819 J-11
Bridgeport, 144229 H-5
Bristol, 60477 D-7
Broad Brook, 4069 B-9
Brookfield, 1650 E-4
Brookfield Ctr., 1550 E-4
Brooklyn, 981 C-13
Byram, 4146 I-3
Canaan, 1212 A-5
Candlewood Isle, 1260 E-4
Candlewood Shores, 1800 E-4
Centerbrook, 1000 F-10
Central Vil., 1800 C-13
Cheshire, 5786 E-7
Chester, 1558 F-10
Clinton, 3368 G-10
Colchester, 4781 D-11
Collinsville, 3746 C-7
Columbia, 800 C-11
Cos Cob, 6770 E-1
Cromwell, 2500 D-9
Crystal Lake, 1945 B-10
Danbury, 80893 F-4
Danielson, 4051 C-13
Darien, 20732 H-4
Dayville, 1650 B-13
Deep River, 1700 F-10
Derby, 12902 F-6
Double Bch., 1100 G-8
Durham, 2933 E-9
E. Berlin, 1100 D-8
E. Brooklyn, 1638 C-13
E. Canaan, 1000 A-5
E. Granby, 1300 A-8
E. Haddam, 800 E-10
E. Hampton, 2691 D-10
E. Hartford, 51252 C-9
E. Hartland, 1200 A-7
E. Haven, 29257 G-7
E. River, 3800 G-9
Eastford, 1020 B-12
Ellington, 1700 B-10
Essex, 1270 F-10
Fairfield, 57300 H-5
FAIRFIELD CO., 916829 F-4
Farmington, 3100 C-8
Flanders, 1330 F-11
Gales Ferry, 1162 F-12
Gaylordsville, 730 D-4
Georgetown, 1805 G-4
Giants Neck, 1330 G-11
Glastonbury, 7387 C-9
Goshen, 890 B-5
Granby, 700 A-8
Greenwich, 12942 I-3
Grosvenor Dale, 850 A-13
Groton, 10389 F-12
Guilford, 2597 G-9
Haddam, 1300 E-10
Hamden, 56900 F-7
Hartford, 124775 C-9
HARTFORD CO., 894014 B-7
Hazardville, 4599 A-9
Hebron, 800 D-11
Higganum, 1698 E-9
Honeypot Glen, 1200 E-7
Indian Neck, 2500 G-8
Ivoryton, 2600 F-10
Jewett City, 3487 D-13
Kensington, 8459 D-8
Kent, 1050 C-4
Lakeside, 1340 F-5
Lakeville, 928 A-4
Litchfield, 1258 C-6
LITCHFIELD CO., 189927 A-5
Long Hill, 4205 F-3
Madison, 2290 G-9
Manchester, 30577 C-10
Mansfield Ctr., 947 C-12
Marion, 850 E-7
Meriden, 60868 E-8
Middlebury, 4200 E-6
Middlefield, 1250 E-8
MIDDLESEX CO., 165676 F-9
Middletown, 47648 E-9
Milford, 51271 G-6
Milldale, 900 E-7
Mixville, 1400 E-7
Monroe, 8500 F-5
Moodus, 1413 E-10
Moosup, 3231 C-13
Mystic, 4205 F-13
Naugatuck, 31862 E-6
New Britain, 73206 D-8
New Canaan, 17900 H-4
New Fairfield, 5200 E-4
New Haven, 129779 G-7
NEW HAVEN CO., 862477 E-7
New London, 27620 F-12
NEW LONDON CO., 274055 E-13
New Milford, 6523 D-4
New Preston, 1182 D-5
Newington, 30562 C-8
Newtown, 1941 F-5
Niantic, 3114 F-12
Noank, 1796 F-13
N. Branford, 7400 F-8
N. Granby, 1944 A-8
N. Grosvenor Dale, 1530 A-13
N. Haven, 24093 F-8
N. Windham, 1000 C-12
Northfield, 710 C-6
Northford, 3600 F-8
Norwalk, 85603 H-4
Norwich, 40493 E-12
Oakdale, 910 E-12
Oakville, 9047 D-6
Old Greenwich, 6611 I-3
Old Mystic, 3554 F-13
Old Saybrook, 2039 G-10
Oneco, 750 C-14
Orange, 13956 G-7
Oxford, 2100 F-6
Pawcatuck, 5624 F-14
Pine Br., 1000 F-6
Pine Orchard, 950 G-8
Plainfield, 2557 D-13
Plainville, 17400 D-8
Plantsville, 6000 D-7
Plymouth, 1200 D-6
Point O'Woods, 740 G-11
Pomfret, 670 B-13
Poquonock, 1100 B-9
Poquonock Br., 1727 F-13
Portland, 5862 D-9
Prospect, 7770 E-7
Putnam, 7214 B-13
Quinebaug, 1133 A-13
Redding, 1500 G-4
Ridgefield, 7645 G-4
Riverside, 8416 I-3
Rockfall, 980 E-9
Rockville, 7474 B-10
Rocky Hill, 16500 D-9
Rogers, 660 B-13
Sandy Hook, 1200 F-5
Saybrook Manor, 1052 G-10
Scotland, 900 C-12
Seymour, 14300 F-6
Sharon, 729 B-4
Shelton, 39559 G-6
Simsbury, 5836 B-8
Somers, 1789 A-10
Somersville, 1300 A-10
S. Britain, 1060 E-5
S. Glastonbury, 2000 D-9
S. Windham, 1421 D-12
S. Windsor, 14000 B-9
S. Woodstock, 1291 A-13
Southbury, 3400 E-5
Southport, 1585 H-5
Stafford, 720 A-11
Stafford Sprs., 4988 A-11
Staffordville, 720 A-11
Stamford, 122643 I-3
Stepney, 750 G-5
Sterling, 660 C-14
Stevenson, 1150 F-6
Stonington, 929 F-13
Stony Creek, 830 G-8
Storrs, 15344 C-11
Stratford, 51384 G-6
Suffield Depot, 1325 A-9
Tariffville, 1324 B-8
Terryville, 5387 D-7
Thomaston, 1910 D-6
Thompson, 960 A-14
Thompsonville, 8577 A-9
Tolland, 1350 B-11
TOLLAND CO., 152691 B-10
Torrington, 36383 C-6
Trumbull, 36018 G-5
Uncasville, 1420 F-12
Unionville, 4400 C-7
Upper Stepney, 1000 F-5
Vernon, 28100 B-10
Wallingford, 18209 E-8
Warehouse Pt., 2100 B-9
Washington, 700 D-5
Washington Depot, 700 D-5
Waterbury, 110366 E-6
Watertown, 3574 D-6
Wauregan, 1205 C-13
Wequetequock, 850 F-14
W. Goshen, 700 B-5
W. Granby, 700 A-8
W. Hartford, 63268 C-8
W. Haven, 55564 G-7
W. Simsbury, 2447 B-8
W. Suffield, 860 A-9
Westbrook, 2413 G-10
Weston, 1460 G-4
Westport, 26391 H-4
Wethersfield, 26668 C-9
Willimantic, 17737 C-11
Wilton, 732 G-4
Windham, 1150 C-12
WINDHAM CO., 118428 C-13
Windsor, 18800 B-9
Windsor Locks, 12498 B-9
Winsted, 7712 B-6
Wolcott, 6400 D-7
Woodbridge, 7860 F-7
Woodbury, 1294 E-5
Woodmont, 1488 G-7
Woodtick, 740 D-7

Delaware

Map p. 24

Angola by the Bay, 1200 K-5
Arden, 439 C-3
Bear, 19371 D-2
Bellefonte, 1193 C-3
Bethany Bch., 1060 L-5
Blades, 1241 K-2
Bowers Bch., 335 H-3
Boxwood, 500 C-8
Brandywine, 3600 A-9
Bridgeville, 2048 K-2
Brookside, 14353 D-6
Camden, 3464 H-2
Capitol Pk., 600 G-9
Carpenter, 1300 A-10
Centerville, 500 B-2
Cheswold, 1380 G-2
Christiana, 500 D-2
Claymont, 8253 C-3
Clayton, 2918 F-2
Dagsboro, 805 L-4
Delaware City, 1695 D-2
Delmar, 1597 M-2
Dewey Bch., 341 K-5
Dover, 36047 G-2
Dupont Manor, 300 G-2
Edgemoor, 5677 B-9
Ellendale, 381 J-3
Elsmere, 6131 C-2
Fairfax, 3200 B-9
Fairfield Farms, 700 H-8
Faulkland, 1500 C-7
Felton, 1298 I-2
Fenwick Island, 379 M-5
Frankford, 847 L-4
Frederica, 774 I-3
Georgetown, 6422 K-3
Glasgow, 14303 D-1
Greenville, 2326 C-2
Greenwood, 973 J-2
Harbeson, 400 K-4
Harrington, 3562 I-2
Hockessin, 13527 C-2
Houston, 374 I-3
Iron Hill, 500 E-5
Keen-Wik, 400 M-5
Kent Acres, 1890 H-8
KENT CO., 162310 H-2
Kitts Hummock, 300 H-3
Laurel, 3708 L-2
Lewes, 2747 J-5
Lincoln, 500 J-3
Loveville, 500 B-7
Marshallton, 1800 C-7
Middletown, 18871 E-1
Midway, 600 K-5
Milford, 9559 I-3
Millsboro, 3877 L-4
Milltown, 800 C-7
Millville, 544 L-5
Milton, 2576 J-4
Montchanin, 300 B-8
New Castle, 5285 D-2
NEW CASTLE CO., 538479 E-2
Newark, 31454 C-1
Newport, 1055 C-2
N. Star, 7980 C-1
Oak Orchard, 500 L-5
Ocean View, 1882 L-5
Odessa, 364 E-2
Ogletown, 600 C-2
Pike Creek, 7898 C-6
Pike Creek Valley, 11217 C-6
Rehoboth Bch., 1327 K-5
Riverdale, 500 L-4
Rodney Vil., 1487 H-2
St. Georges, 350 D-2
Seaford, 6928 K-2
Selbyville, 2167 M-4
Shawnee Acres, 450 I-3
Smyrna, 10023 F-2
S. Bethany, 449 L-5
Stanton, 3100 C-7
SUSSEX CO., 197145 K-3
Talleyville, 800 C-2
Townsend, 2049 F-2
Ways Corner, 800 A-9
Wilmington, 70851 C-2
Wilmington Manor, 7889 D-8
Wyoming, 1313 H-2
Yorklyn, 300 C-2

District of Columbia

Map p. 111

Washington, 601723 E-6

Florida

Map pp. 26 – 27

* City keyed to p. 24
† City keyed to p. 25

Alachua, 9059 D-7
ALACHUA CO., 247336 E-7
Alafaya, 78113 H-10
Allentown, 894 Q-3
Altamonte Sprs., 41496 H-10
Alturas, 4185 J-9
Alva, 2596 N-9
Anglers Pk., 980 R-13
Anna Maria, 1503 K-6
Anthony, 1150 F-8
Apalachicola, 2231 T-8
Apopka, 41542 H-10
Arcadia, 7637 L-9
Archer, 1118 E-7
Asbury Lake, 8700 C-9
Astatula, 1810 G-9
Astor, 1556 F-9
Atlantic Bch., 12655 C-10
Atlantis, 2005 N-14
Auburndale, 13507 I-9
Aventura, 35762 P-14
Avon Pk., 8836 K-10
Azalea Pk., 12556 N-4
Babson Pk., 1356 J-10
Bagdad, 3761 R-3
BAKER CO., 27115 B-7
Bal Harbour, 2513 †K-9
Baldwin, 1425 C-8
Balm, 1457 J-8
Barefoot Bay, 3000 J-12
Bartow, 17298 J-9
BAY CO., 168852 S-6
Bay Hbr. Islands, 5628 †K-9
Bay Pines, 2931 †D-1
Bayshore Gdns., 16323 †G-3
Baywood Vil., 1300 †A-1
Bee Ridge, 9598 L-7
Belle Glade, 17467 N-12
Belle Isle, 5988 O-4
Belleair, 3869 J-6
Belleair Bch., 1560 J-6
Belleair Bluffs, 2031 †C-1
Belleview, 4492 F-8
Bellview, 23355 R-2
Beverly Hills, 8445 G-7
Big Coppitt Key, 2458 T-9
Big Pine Key, 4252 T-10
Biscayne Pk., 3055 †K-9
Bithlo, 8268 H-11
Bloomingdale, 22711 †C-5
Blountstown, 2514 R-7
Boca Del Mar, 21800 †F-9
Boca Pointe, 3300 †F-9
Boca Raton, 84392 O-14
Boca West, 2100 †E-9
Bokeelia, 1780 N-8
Bonifay, 2793 Q-6
Bonita Sprs., 43914 O-9
Bowling Green, 2930 K-9
Boyette, 5890 †D-5
Boynton Bch., 68217 N-14
Bradenton, 49546 K-7
Bradenton Bch., 1171 K-6
BRADFORD CO., 28520 D-8
Brandon, 103483 J-7
Brent, 21804 *I-9
BREVARD CO., 543376 J-12
Bristol, 996 R-8
Broadview Pk., 7125 †I-8
Bronson, 1113 E-7
Brookridge, 4420 H-7
Brooksville, 7719 H-7
BROWARD CO., 1748066 O-12
Buckhead Ridge, 1450 L-11
Buckingham, 4036 N-9
Buenaventura Lakes, 26079 I-10
Bunnell, 2676 E-10
Bushnell, 2418 H-8
CALHOUN CO., 14625 S-7
Callahan, 1123 B-9
Callaway, 14405 S-6
Campbell, 2479 I-10
Cantonment, 2800 R-2
Cape Canaveral, 9912 H-12
Cape Coral, 154305 N-8
Carrabelle, 2778 D-1
Carrollwood, 33365 †B-3
Casselberry, 26241 L-4
Cedar Grv., 3397 S-6
Center Hill, 988 H-8
Century, 1698 Q-2
CHARLOTTE CO., 159978 M-9
Charlotte Hbr., 3714 M-8
Chassahowitzka, 850 G-7
Chattahoochee, 3652 R-8
Chiefland, 2245 E-6
Chipley, 3605 Q-6
Christmas, 1146 H-11
Chuluota, 2483 H-11
Chumuckla, 850 Q-2
Citra, 950 E-8
CITRUS CO., 141236 G-7
Citrus Pk., 24252 †B-3
Citrus Ridge, 12015 P-1
Citrus Sprs., 8622 G-7

*, †, ‡, § See explanation under state title in this index. County and parish names are listed in capital letters and in boldface type. Independent cities (not in any county) are shown in italics.

Clair-Mel City, 7500 †C-4
Clarcona, 2990 M-2
CLAY CO., 190865 D-9
Clearwater, 107685 J-6
Clermont, 28742 H-9
Cleveland, 2990 M-8
Clewiston, 7155 M-11
Cocoa, 17140 I-12
Cocoa Bch., 11231 I-12
Coconut Creek, 52909 †F-8
COLLIER CO., 321520 O-10
COLUMBIA CO., 67531 B-7
Conway, 13467 H-10
Cooper City, 28547 †I-8
Coral Cove, 1160 L-7
Coral Gables, 46780 Q-13
Coral Sprs., 121096 O-13
Coral Ter., 24376 †M-7
Cortez, 4241 †G-2
Cottage Hill, 1050 R-2
Cottondale, 933 Q-7
Crawfordville, 3702 C-2
Crescent Bch., 931 D-10
Crescent City, 1577 E-10
Crestview, 20978 Q-4
Cross City, 1728 E-5
Crystal Bch., 1350 †A-1
Crystal River, 3108 G-7
Crystal Sprs., 1327 I-8
Cudjoe Key, 1763 T-10
Curlew, 780 †B-1
Cutler Bay, 40286 Q-13
Cypress Gdns., 8917 †K-5
Cypress Quarters, 1215 L-12
Dade City, 6437 I-8
Dania Bch., 29639 P-13
Davenport, 2888 I-9
Davie, 91992 P-13
Daytona Bch., 61005 F-11
Daytona Bch. Shores, 4247 A-14
De Funiak Sprs., 5177 R-5
De Leon Sprs., 2614 F-10
DE SOTO CO., 34862 L-9
DeBary, 19320 G-10
Deerfield Bch., 75018 O-14
DeLand, 27031 F-10
Delray Bch., 60522 N-14
Deltona, 85182 G-10
Destin, 12305 R-4
DIXIE CO., 16422 E-5
Doctors Inlet, 1800 C-9
Doral, 45704 †L-7
Dover, 3702 J-8
Dundee, 3717 J-9
Dunedin, 35321 J-6
Dunnellon, 1733 F-7
DUVAL CO., 864263 B-8
Eagle Lake, 2255 J-9
E. Naples, 2050 O-9
E. Palatka, 1654 E-9
E. Tampa, 750 †C-4
Eastpoint, 2337 T-8
Eaton Pk., 900 †K-2
Eatonville, 2159 M-3
Edgewater, 20750 G-11
Edgewood, 2503 N-4
Egypt Lake, 3500 †B-3
El Portal, 2325 †K-8
Elfers, 13986 I-6
Ellenton, 4275 K-7
Eloise Woods, 1900 †K-5
Englewood, 14863 M-7
Ensley, 20602 R-2
Enterprise, 2000 G-10
ESCAMBIA CO., 297619 Q-2
Estero, 22612 N-9
Eustis, 18558 G-9
Fairview Shores, 10239 M-3
Fanning Sprs., 764 E-6
Fellsmere, 5197 J-12
Fern Pk., 7704 L-4
Fernandina Bch., 11487 B-10
Ferry Pass, 28921 R-2
Five Points, 1265 C-7
Flagler Bch., 4484 E-11
FLAGLER CO., 95696 E-10
Flamingo Bay, 880 N-8
Floral City, 5217 G-7
Florida City, 11245 Q-13
Florosa, 1000 R-4
Forest City, 13854 L-3
Ft. Lauderdale, 165521 O-13
Ft. Meade, 5626 J-9
Ft. Myers, 62298 N-9
Ft. Myers Bch., 6277 N-8
Ft. Myers Villas, 5600 †N-2
Ft. Pierce, 41590 K-13
Ft. Walton Bch., 19507 R-4
Fountainbleau, 59764 †L-7
FRANKLIN CO., 11549 D-1
Franklin Pk., 2400 †M-2
Freeport, 1787 R-5
Frostproof, 2992 J-10
Fruit Cove, 29362 C-9
Fruitland Pk., 4078 G-8
Fruitville, 13224 L-7
Fuller Hts., 8758 J-8
GADSDEN CO., 46389 B-1
Gainesville, 124354 E-7
Gateway, 8401 N-9
Geneva, 2940 G-11
Gibsonia, 4507 †I-1
Gibsonton, 14234 J-7
Gifford, 9590 K-13
GILCHRIST CO., 16939 E-6
GLADES CO., 12884 M-10
Gladeview, 11535 †L-8
Glenvar Hts., 16898 †M-7
Golden Bch., 919 †J-9
Golden Gate, 23961 O-9
Golden Gate, 2650 L-13
Golden Glades, 33145 †K-8
Goldenrod, 12039 M-4
Gonzalez, 13273 R-2
Gordonville, 1500 †K-4
Gotha, 1915 N-2
Goulding, 4102 *J-9
Graceville, 2278 Q-6
Grand Island, 1200 G-9
Grand Ridge, 892 R-7
Grant-Valkaria, 3850 J-12
Green Cove Sprs., 6908 D-9
Greenacres, 37573 N-13
Greenacres City, 37573 †B-9
Greenville, 843 B-4
Gretna, 1460 B-1
Grove City, 1804 M-7
Groveland, 8729 H-9
Gulf Bch. Hts., 1600 *K-7
Gulf Breeze, 5763 R-3
GULF CO., 15863 T-7
Gulf Harbors, 3300 I-6
Gulf Stream, 786 †D-10
Gulfport, 12029 J-6
Haines City, 20535 I-9
Hallandale Bch., 37113 P-13
HAMILTON CO., 14799 B-6
Hamptons at Boca Raton, 11300 †E-9
Harbinwood Estates, 1900 *L-7
HARDEE CO., 27731 K-8
Harlem, 2658 M-11
Harold, 823 R-3
Havana, 1754 B-2
Haverhill, 1873 †B-9
Hawthorne, 1417 E-8
Heathrow, 5896 G-10
Hedges, 800 B-9
HENDRY CO., 39140 N-10
Hernando, 9054 G-7
HERNANDO CO., 172778 H-7
Hialeah, 224669 P-13
Hialeah Gdns., 21744 †K-7
High Sprs., 5350 D-7
Highland Bch., 3539 N-14
Highland City, 10834 J-9
Highland Lakes, 3700 †A-2
Highland Lakes, 850 K-10
HIGHLANDS CO., 98786 L-10
Highlands Pk. Estates, 1100 L-10
Highpoint, 2300 †C-2
Hilliard, 3086 A-8
Hillsboro Bch., 1875 †F-10
HILLSBOROUGH CO., 1229226 J-8
Hobe Sound, 11521 L-13
Holiday, 22403 I-6
Holley, 1630 R-3
Holly Hill, 11659 F-11
Hollywood, 140768 P-13
Holmes Bch., 3836 K-6
HOLMES CO., 19927 Q-6
Homestead, 60512 Q-13
Homosassa, 2578 G-7
Homosassa Sprs., 13791 G-7
Howey-in-the-Hills, 1098 G-9
Hudson, 12158 I-6
Hypoluxo, 2588 †C-10
Immokalee, 24154 N-10
Indialantic, 2720 I-12
Indian Harbour Bch., 8225 I-12
INDIAN RIVER CO., 138028 K-12
Indian River Shores, 3901 J-13
Indian Rocks Bch., 4113 J-6
Indian Shores, 1420 †C-1
Indiantown, 6083 M-12
Inglis, 1325 G-6
Interlachen, 1403 E-9
Inverness, 7210 G-7
Inwood, 6403 J-9
Islamorada, 6119 S-12
Ives Estates, 19525 †J-9
JACKSON CO., 49746 Q-7
Jacksonville, 821784 C-9
Jacksonville Bch., 21362 C-10
Jan Phyl Vil., 5573 †K-4
Jasper, 4546 B-6
JEFFERSON CO., 14761 C-3
Jennings, 878 B-5
Jensen Bch., 11707 L-13
June Pk., 4094 I-12
Juno Bch., 3176 M-14
Jupiter, 55156 M-14
Jupiter Island, 817 M-14
Kathleen, 6332 I-8
Kendale Lakes, 56148 Q-13
Kendall, 75371 Q-13
Kenneth City, 4980 J-6
Key Biscayne, 12344 Q-13
Key Colony Bch., 797 T-11
Key Haven, 850 T-9
Key Largo, 10433 R-13
Key West, 24649 T-9
Keystone, 24039 †A-2
Keystone Hts., 1350 D-8
Kings Pt., 12200 †D-9
Kissimmee, 59682 I-10
LaBelle, 4640 M-10
Lacoochee, 1714 H-8
Lady Lake, 13926 G-8
LAFAYETTE CO., 8870 D-5
Laguna Bch., 3932 S-5
L. Alfred, 5015 I-9
L. Brantley, 3000 L-3
L. Butler, 1897 D-7
L. Cain Hills, 1600 N-3
Lake City, 12046 C-7
L. Clarke Shores, 3376 †B-10
LAKE CO., 297052 H-9
L. Geneva, 1200 D-8
L. Hamilton, 1231 J-9
L. Helen, 2624 G-10
L. Mary, 13822 G-10
L. Panasoffkee, 3551 G-8
Lake Pk., 8155 M-14
L. Placid, 2223 L-10
L. Suzy, 1040 M-8
L. Wales, 14225 J-9
L. Worth, 34910 N-14
Lakeland, 97422 I-8
Lakewood Pk., 11323 K-13
Land O' Lakes, 31996 I-7
Lantana, 10423 N-14
Largo, 77648 J-6
Lauderdale Lakes, 32593 †H-8
Lauderdale-by-the-Sea, 6056 †G-9
Lauderhill, 66887 †H-8
Laurel, 8171 L-7
Lealman, 19879 †D-2
Lecanto, 5882 G-7
LEE CO., 618754 N-9
Leesburg, 20117 G-9
Lehigh Acres, 86784 N-9
Leisure City, 22655 Q-13
LEON CO., 275487 B-3
LEVY CO., 40801 E-6
LIBERTY CO., 8365 S-8
Lighthouse Pt., 10344 O-14
Live Oak, 6850 C-6
Lochmoor, 1200 †M-1
Lockhart, 13060 M-3
Longboat Key, 6888 K-6
Longwood, 13657 L-4
Loughman, 2680 I-9
Loxahatchee Groves, 3180 N-13
Lutz, 19344 I-7
Lynn Haven, 18493 S-6
Macclenny, 6374 C-8
Madeira Bch., 4263 J-6
Madison, 2843 B-4
MADISON CO., 19224 C-4
Maitland, 15751 M-4
Malabar, 2757 J-12
Malone, 2088 Q-7
MANATEE CO., 322833 K-7
Mango, 11313 †B-5
Mangonia Pk., 1888 †A-10
Marathon, 8297 T-11
Marco Island, 16413 P-9
Margate, 53284 O-13
Marianna, 6102 Q-7
MARION CO., 331298 F-7
Marion Oaks, 4200 G-8
MARTIN CO., 146318 L-13
Mary Esther, 3851 R-4
Masaryktown, 1040 H-7
Mascotte, 5101 H-9
Mayo, 1237 C-5
Medley, 838 †L-7
Medulla, 8892 †K-1
Melbourne, 76068 I-12
Melbourne Bch., 3101 I-12
Melrose, 1100 D-8
Memphis, 7848 †F-3
Merritt Island, 34743 I-12
Mexico Bch., 1072 T-7
Miami, 399457 P-13
Miami Bch., 87779 P-14
Miami Gdns., 107167 P-13
Miami Lakes, 29361 †K-7
Miami Shores, 10493 †K-8
Miami Sprs., 13809 †L-7
MIAMI-DADE CO., 2496435 R-12
Micco, 9052 J-12
Middleburg, 13008 C-9
Midway, 3004 B-2
Midway, 1705 G-10
Millview, 1100 *J-7
Milton, 8826 R-3
Mims, 7058 H-11
Minneola, 9403 H-9
Miramar, 122041 †J-7
Miramar Bch., 6146 R-4
Mission Bay, 2900 †E-8
Mission City, 1700 F-11
Molino, 1277 Q-2
MONROE CO., 73090 Q-11
Monticello, 2506 B-3
Montverde, 1463 M-1
Moore Haven, 1680 M-11
Morse Shores, 3300 †L-3
Mt. Dora, 12370 G-9
Mt. Plymouth, 4011 G-9
Mulberry, 3817 J-8
Myrtle Grv., 15870 R-2
Naples, 19537 O-9
Naples Manor, 5562 P-9
Naples Pk., 5967 O-9
Naranja, 8303 Q-13
NASSAU CO., 73314 B-9
Nassauville, 1900 B-9
Navarre, 31378 R-3
Neptune Bch., 7037 C-10
New Port Richey, 14911 I-6
New Smyrna Bch., 22464 F-11
Newberry, 4950 E-7
Niceville, 12749 R-4
Nocatee, 4524 L-9
Nokomis, 3167 L-7
N. Bay Vil., 7137 †K-9
N. Fort Myers, 39407 N-9
N. Key Largo, 1244 R-13
N. Lauderdale, 41023 †G-8
N. Miami, 58786 P-13
N. Miami Bch., 41523 P-13
N. Palm Bch., 12015 M-14
N. Port, 57357 M-8
N. Redington Bch., 1417 †D-1
N. River Shores, 3079 L-13
Northdale, 22079 I-7
Oak Hill, 1792 G-11
Oakland, 2538 N-1
Oakland Pk., 41363 O-14
Ocala, 56315 F-8
Ocean Ridge, 1786 †C-10
Ocklawaha, 860 F-8
Ocoee, 35579 M-2
Odessa, 7267 I-7
Ojus, 18036 †J-9
OKALOOSA CO., 180822 R-4
Okeechobee, 5621 L-11
OKEECHOBEE CO., 39996 K-11
Oldsmar, 13591 J-6
Olympia Hts., 13488 †M-7
Oneco, 3200 K-7
Opa-locka, 15219 P-13
Orange City, 10599 G-10
ORANGE CO., 1145956 H-11
Orange Pk., 8412 C-9
Orangetree, 4406 O-9
Oriole Bch., 1420 *J-10
Orlando, 238300 H-10
Orlovista, 6123 N-3
Ormond Bch., 38137 F-11
Ormond-By-The-Sea, 7406 F-11
OSCEOLA CO., 268685 I-11
Osprey, 6100 L-7
Oviedo, 33342 H-10
Ozona, 1900 I-6
Pace, 20039 R-3
Pahokee, 5649 M-12
Paisley, 818 G-9
Palatka, 10558 E-9
Palm Bay, 103190 I-12
PALM BEACH CO., 1320134 N-12
Palm Bch., 8348 N-14
Palm Bch. Gdns., 48452 M-13
Palm City, 23120 L-13
Palm Coast, 75180 E-10
Palm Hbr., 57439 I-6
Palm Shores, 900 I-12
Palm Sprs., 18928 †B-10
Palm Sprs. North, 5253 †J-7
Palm Valley, 20019 C-10
Palma Sola, 3100 †F-2
Palmetto, 12606 K-7
Palmetto Bay, 23410 Q-13
Palmetto Estates, 13535 †N-7
Panacea, 816 C-2
Panama City, 36484 S-6
Panama City Bch., 12018 S-5
Parker, 4317 S-6
Parkland, 23962 †F-8
PASCO CO., 464697 I-7
Pebble Creek, 7622 †A-4
Pelican Bay, 6346 O-9
Pembroke Pk., 6102 †J-9
Pembroke Pines, 154750 P-13
Pensacola, 51923 R-2
Pensacola Bch., 1200 R-3
Perry, 7017 C-4
Pierson, 1736 F-10
Pine Castle, 10805 N-4
Pine Forest, 2500 *I-8
Pine Hills, 60076 H-10
Pinecrest, 18223 †N-7
PINELLAS CO., 916542 J-6
Pinellas Pk., 49079 J-6
Pinewood, 16520 †K-8
Plant City, 34721 J-8
Plantation, 84955 †H-8
Pleasant Grv., 1000 *J-8
Plymouth, 1250 L-2
Poinciana, 53193 I-10
Poincianna Pl., 1100 N-13
Polk City, 1562 I-9
POLK CO., 602095 J-9
Pomona Pk., 912 E-9
Pompano Bch., 99845 O-14
Ponce Inlet, 3032 F-11
Ponte Vedra Bch., 3000 C-10
Port Charlotte, 54392 M-8
Port LaBelle, 3530 M-10
Port Orange, 56048 F-11
Port Richey, 2671 I-6
Port St. Joe, 3445 T-7
Port St. John, 12267 E-12
Port St. Lucie, 164603 L-13
Port Salerno, 10091 L-13
Princeton, 22038 Q-13
Progress Vil., 5392 †C-4
Punta Gorda, 16641 M-8
Punta Rassa, 1750 N-8
PUTNAM CO., 74364 E-9
Quincy, 7972 B-1
Rainbow Lakes, 1550 †C-9
Rainbow Lakes Estates, 1050 F-7
Ratliff, 2000 B-9
Redington Bch., 1427 †D-1
Redington Shores, 2121 J-6
Richmond Hts., 8541 Q-13
Ridge Manor, 4513 H-8
River Pk., 5222 L-13
Riverview, 71050 J-7
Riviera Bch., 32488 M-14
Rockledge, 24926 I-12
Roseland, 1472 J-12
Rotonda, 8759 M-8
Royal Palm Bch., 34140 N-13
Royal Palm Estates, 3025 †B-9
Ruskin, 17208 K-7
Safety Hbr., 16884 J-6
St. Augustine, 12975 D-10
St. Augustine Bch., 6176 D-10
St. Augustine Shores, 7359 D-10
St. Cloud, 35183 I-10
St. James City, 3784 N-8
St. Joe Bch., 850 T-7
ST. JOHNS CO., 190039 D-9
St. Leo, 1340 I-8
ST. LUCIE CO., 277789 L-12
St. Pete Bch., 9346 K-6
St. Petersburg, 244769 J-7
Samoset, 3854 K-7
Samsula, 1260 G-11
San Antonio, 1138 I-8
San Carlos Pk., 16824 N-9
San Mateo, 1100 E-9
Sandalfoot Cove, 16600 †F-8
Sanford, 53570 G-10
Sanibel, 6469 N-8
SANTA ROSA CO., 151372 Q-3
Sarasota, 51917 L-7
SARASOTA CO., 379448 L-8
Satellite Bch., 10109 I-12
Satsuma, 1000 E-9
Schall Circle, 1117 †A-9
Scottsmoor, 1340 G-11
Seaglades, 900 *K-7
Sebastian, 21929 J-12
Sebring, 10491 K-10
Seffner, 7579 †B-5
Seminole, 17233 J-6
SEMINOLE CO., 422718 H-11
Seven Sprs., 2000 I-6
Sewall's Pt., 1996 L-13
Shady, 800 F-8
Sharpes, 3411 H-12
Siesta Key, 6565 †H-3
Siesta Lago, 1800 P-3
Silver Sprs., 1050 F-8
Silver Sprs. Shores, 6539 F-8
Sky Lake, 6153 O-3
Slavia, 1000 M-5
Sneads, 1849 R-8
Sorrento, 861 G-9
S. Apopka, 5728 L-2
S. Bay, 4876 N-12
S. Daytona, 12252 F-11
S. Miami, 11657 †M-7
S. Miami Hts., 35696 Q-13
S. Palm Bch., 1171 †C-10
S. Pasadena, 4964 †D-1
S. Punta Gorda Hts., 940 M-8
S. Venice, 13949 M-7
Southport, 1500 S-6
Southwest Ranches, 7345 †I-6
Southwood, 1700 N-3
Spring Hill, 98621 H-7
Spring Lake, 1100 K-10
Springfield, 8903 S-6
Starke, 5449 D-8
Steinhatchee, 1047 E-4
Stuart, 15593 L-13
Summerland Key, 950 T-10
SUMTER CO., 93420 H-8
Sun City Ctr., 19258 K-7
Sun Valley, 1300 †C-9
Sunland Gdns., 1600 K-13
Sunny Isles Bch., 20832 †K-9
Sunrise, 84439 †H-8
Sunset, 16389 †M-7
Surfside, 5744 †K-9
SUWANNEE CO., 41551 C-6
Sweetwater, 13499 P-13
Sweetwater Creek, 6600 †B-3
Sweetwater Oaks, 1100 L-3
Switzerland, 2900 C-9
Taft, 2205 H-10
Tallahassee, 181376 B-2
Tamarac, 60427 O-13
Tampa, 335709 J-7
Tangelo Pk., 2231 O-3
Tangerine, 2865 G-9
Tarpon Lake Villages, 1200 †A-2
Tarpon Sprs., 23484 I-6
Tavares, 13951 G-9
Tavernier, 2136 S-13
TAYLOR CO., 22570 D-3
Temple Ter., 24541 J-7
Tequesta, 5629 M-14
The Villages, 51442 G-8
Thonotosassa, 13014 I-7
Three Lakes, 15047 †N-6
Tice, 4470 N-9
Tierra Verde, 3721 †E-2
Tiger Pt., 3090 R-3
Titusville, 43761 H-11
Treasure Island, 6705 J-6
Trenton, 1999 E-6
Tropical Gulf Acres, 8200 M-8
Uleta, 2300 †J-9
Umatilla, 3456 G-9
UNION CO., 15535 C-7
Union Pk., 9765 M-5
Valparaiso, 5036 R-4
Vamo, 4727 L-7
Venice, 20748 L-7
Venice Gdns., 7104 L-7
Vero Bch., 15220 K-13
Vero Lake Estates, 1600 J-12
Vilano Bch., 2678 D-10
Villas, 11569 N-9
Vineyards, 3375 O-9
Virginia Gdns., 2375 †L-7
VOLUSIA CO., 494593 G-11
Wahneta, 5091 †L-4
WAKULLA CO., 30776 C-1
Waldo, 1015 D-8
Wallace, 1785 R-3
WALTON CO., 55043 R-5
Warm Mineral Sprs., 5061 M-8
Warrington, 14531 R-2
WASHINGTON CO., 24896 R-6
Watertown, 2829 C-7
Wauchula, 5001 K-9
Waverly, 767 J-9
Webster, 785 H-8
Weirsdale, 840 G-8
Wellington, 56508 N-13
Wesley Chapel, 44092 I-7
W. Little River, 34699 †K-8
W. Melbourne, 18355 I-12
W. Miami, 5965 †L-7
W. Palm Bch., 99919 N-14
W. Park, 14156 †J-8
W. Pensacola, 21339 R-2
Westchester, 29862 †M-7
Weston, 65333 O-13
Westview, 9650 †K-8
Westwood Lakes, 11838 †M-7
Wewahitchka, 1981 S-7
Whisper Walk, 5100 †E-9
White City, 3719 K-13
White Sprs., 777 C-6
Wilbur-By-The-Sea, 1300 F-11
Wildwood, 6709 G-8
Williston, 2768 E-7
Williston Highlands, 2275 F-7
Wilton Mnrs., 11632 †H-9
Wimauma, 6373 K-7
Windermere, 2462 H-9
Winston, 9024 †J-1
Winter Bch., 2067 J-13
Winter Gdn., 34568 H-9
Winter Haven, 33874 J-9
Winter Pk., 27852 M-4
Winter Sprs., 33282 G-10
Woodville, 2978 C-2
Wright, 23127 R-4
Yalaha, 1364 G-9
Yulee, 11491 B-9
Zellwood, 2817 G-9
Zephyrhills, 13288 I-8
Zolfo Sprs., 1827 K-9

Georgia

Map pp. 28 – 29

* City keyed to p. 30
† City keyed to p. 95

Abbeville, 2908 K-7
Acworth, 20425 D-3
Adairsville, 4648 C-3
Adel, 5334 N-7
Alamo, 2797 J-8
Albany, 77434 L-5
Alma, 3466 L-9
Alpharetta, 57551 D-5
Alto, 1172 C-6
Americus, 17041 K-5
Appling, 500 F-10
APPLING CO., 18236 K-10
Aragon, 1249 D-3
Arcade, 1786 D-6
Arlington, 1479 M-3
Ashburn, 4152 L-6
Athens, 115452 E-7
ATKINSON CO., 8375 M-8
Atlanta, 420003 E-4
Auburn, 6887 E-6
Augusta, 195844 F-11
Austell, 6581 E-4
Avondale Estates, 2960 *E-5
BACON CO., 11096 L-9
Baconton, 915 M-5
Bainbridge, 12697 N-4
BAKER CO., 3451 M-4
Baldwin, 3279 C-6
BALDWIN CO., 45720 G-7
Ball Ground, 1433 D-4
BANKS CO., 18395 C-6
Barnesville, 6755 H-5
BARROW CO., 69367 D-6
BARTOW CO., 100157 D-3
Baxley, 4400 L-10
Belvedere Pk., 6000 *E-5
BEN HILL CO., 17634 L-7
BERRIEN CO., 19286 M-7
Beverly Hills, 1000 †N-12
BIBB CO., 155547 H-6
Blackshear, 3445 M-10
Blackwells, 5000 E-4
Blairsville, 652 B-5
Blakely, 5068 M-3
BLECKLEY CO., 13063 J-7
Bloomingdale, 2713 J-12
Blue Ridge, 1290 B-4
Bogart, 1034 E-6
Bonaire, 900 I-6
Bonanza, 3135 F-4
Boston, 1315 O-6
Bowdon, 2040 F-2
Bowman, 862 D-8
BRANTLEY CO., 18411 N-10
Braselton, 7511 D-6
Bremen, 6227 E-2
Briar Wood Estates, 750 *A-1
Brookhaven, 7000 E-4
Brooklet, 1395 J-11
BROOKS CO., 16243 N-6
Broxton, 1189 L-8
Brunswick, 15383 N-12
BRYAN CO., 30233 K-12
Buchanan, 1104 E-2
Buena Vista, 2173 J-4
Buford, 12225 D-5
BULLOCH CO., 70217 J-11
BURKE CO., 23316 G-10
Butler, 1972 I-5
BUTTS CO., 23655 G-5
Byron, 4512 I-6
Cairo, 9607 N-5
Calhoun, 15650 C-3
CALHOUN CO., 6694 L-4
CAMDEN CO., 50513 N-12
Camilla, 5360 M-5
CANDLER CO., 10998 J-10
Canon, 804 D-8
Canton, 22958 D-4
Carnesville, 577 C-7
CARROLL CO., 110527 F-3
Carrollton, 24388 F-2
Cartersville, 19731 D-3
CATOOSA CO., 63942 B-2
Cave Spr., 1200 D-2
Cedar Grv., 2000 *G-5
Cedartown, 9750 E-2
Centerville, 7148 I-6
Chamblee, 9892 *B-5
CHARLTON CO., 12171 N-10
CHATHAM CO., 265128 K-13
Chatsworth, 4299 B-3
CHATTAHOOCHEE CO., 11267 J-3
Chattahoochee Hills, 2378 F-3
Chattanooga Valley, 3846 B-2
CHATTOOGA CO., 26015 C-1
CHEROKEE CO., 214346 D-4
Chester, 1596 J-7
Chickamauga, 3101 B-2
Chicopee, 750 D-6
CLARKE CO., 116714 E-7
Clarkesville, 1733 C-7
Clarkston, 7554 *D-6
Claxton, 2746 J-11
CLAY CO., 3183 L-3
Clayton, 2047 B-7
CLAYTON CO., 259424 F-4
Clermont, 875 C-6
Cleveland, 3410 C-6
CLINCH CO., 6798 O-9
COBB CO., 688078 E-4
Cochran, 5150 J-7
COFFEE CO., 42356 M-8
College Pk., 13942 F-4
Colquitt, 1992 N-3
COLQUITT CO., 45498 N-6
COLUMBIA CO., 124053 F-10
Columbus, 189885 I-3
Comer, 1126 D-8
Commerce, 6544 D-7
Conley, 6228 *G-4
Conyers, 15195 F-5
COOK CO., 17212 N-6
Cordele, 11147 K-6
Cornelia, 4160 C-7
Country Club Estates, 8545 R-13
Covington, 13118 F-6
COWETA CO., 127317 G-3
Crawford, 832 E-7
CRAWFORD CO., 12630 I-5
Crawfordville, 534 F-8
CRISP CO., 23439 K-6
Crystal Sprs., 1300 R-7
Cumming, 5430 D-5
Cusseta, 11267 J-3
Cuthbert, 3873 L-3
Dacula, 4442 E-6
DADE CO., 16633 B-1
Dahlonega, 5242 C-5
Dallas, 11544 E-3
Dalton, 33128 B-3
Danielsville, 560 D-7
Darien, 1975 M-12
Dasher, 912 O-7
Davisboro, 2010 H-9
Dawson, 4540 L-4
DAWSON CO., 22330 C-5
Dawsonville, 2536 C-5
DE KALB CO., 691893 F-5
De Soto Pk., 1200 D-2
Decatur, 19335 E-4
DECATUR CO., 27842 N-3
Deenwood, 2146 M-10
Deerwood Pk., 3000 *E-5
Demorest, 1823 C-6
Dock Jct., 7721 R-13
DODGE CO., 21796 J-7
Doerun, 774 M-5
Donalsonville, 2650 N-3
DOOLY CO., 14918 K-5
Doraville, 8330 *B-5
DOUGHERTY CO., 94565 L-4
Douglas, 11589 L-8
DOUGLAS CO., 132403 F-3
Douglasville, 30961 E-3
Druid Hills, 14568 *E-4
Dublin, 16201 I-8
Duluth, 26600 E-5
Dunwoody, 46267 *A-4
Dutch Island, 1257 T-12
EARLY CO., 11008 M-2
E. Dublin, 2441 I-8
E. Newnan, 1321 G-3
East Pt., 33712 F-4
Eastman, 4962 J-7
Eatonton, 6480 G-7
ECHOLS CO., 4034 O-8
Eden, 750 J-12
Edison, 1531 L-3
EFFINGHAM CO., 52250 I-12
ELBERT CO., 20166 D-8
Elberta, 950 I-6
Elberton, 4653 D-8
Ellaville, 1812 J-4
Ellijay, 1619 B-4
EMANUEL CO., 22598 I-10
Embry Hills, 1600 *C-5
Emerson, 1470 D-3
Enigma, 1278 M-7
Eton, 910 B-3
Euharlee, 4136 D-3
Evans, 29011 F-10
EVANS CO., 11000 K-11
Experiment, 2894 G-5
Fair Oaks, 8225 *B-1
Fairburn, 12950 F-4
FANNIN CO., 23682 B-4
FAYETTE CO., 106567 F-4
Fayetteville, 15945 F-4
Fitzgerald, 9053 L-7
Flowery Branch, 5679 D-5
FLOYD CO., 96317 D-2
Folkston, 2502 O-11
Forest Pk., 18468 F-4
Forsyth, 3788 H-6
FORSYTH CO., 175511 D-5
Ft. Gaines, 1107 L-2
Ft. Oglethorpe, 9263 B-2
Ft. Valley, 9815 I-6
Franklin, 993 G-2
FRANKLIN CO., 22084 C-7
Franklin Sprs., 952 D-8
FULTON CO., 920581 D-5
Gainesville, 33804 D-6
Garden City, 8778 K-13
Garden Lakes, 4000 D-2
Georgetown, 11823 T-8
Georgetown, 2513 K-2
Gibson, 663 G-9
GILMER CO., 28292 B-4
GLASCOCK CO., 3082 G-9
Glen Haven, 3000 *E-6
Glennville, 3569 K-11
Glenwood, 1500 D-2
Glenwood Hills, 5200 *E-5
GLYNN CO., 79626 M-11
Gordon, 2017 H-7
GORDON CO., 55186 C-3
GRADY CO., 25011 N-4
Grantville, 3041 G-3
Gray, 3276 H-6
Grayson, 2666 E-5
GREENE CO., 15994 F-7
Greensboro, 3359 F-7
Greenville, 876 H-3
Gresham Pk., 7432 *F-5
Griffin, 23643 G-5
Grovetown, 11216 F-10
Gumlog, 2146 C-8
Guyton, 1684 J-12
GWINNETT CO., 805321 E-5
HABERSHAM CO., 43041 C-6
Haddock, 750 H-7
Hahira, 2737 N-7
HALL CO., 179684 C-5
Hamilton, 1016 H-3
Hampton, 6987 G-5
HANCOCK CO., 9429 G-8
Hannahs Mill, 3298 H-4
Hapeville, 6373 *G-3
HARALSON CO., 28780 E-2
Harlem, 2666 F-10
HARRIS CO., 32024 I-3
HART CO., 25213 D-8
Hartwell, 4469 D-8
Hawkinsville, 4589 J-7
Hazlehurst, 4226 K-9
HEARD CO., 11834 G-2
Helena, 2883 K-8
HENRY CO., 203922 F-5
Hephzibah, 4011 G-10
Hiawassee, 880 B-6
Hinesville, 33437 K-12
Hiram, 3546 E-3
Hogansville, 3060 G-3
Holly Sprs., 9189 D-4
Homeland, 910 O-11
Homer, 1141 D-7
Homerville, 2456 N-9
Honey Creek, 1060 F-5
Hoschton, 1377 D-6
HOUSTON CO., 139900 J-6
Industrial City, 800 C-3
IRWIN CO., 9538 L-7
Irwinton, 589 H-7
Isle of Hope, 2402 K-13
Ivey, 981 H-7
Jackson, 5045 G-5
JACKSON CO., 60485 D-7
Jasper, 3684 C-4
JASPER CO., 13900 G-6
JEFF DAVIS CO., 15068 K-9
Jefferson, 9432 D-6
JEFFERSON CO., 16930 H-9
Jeffersonville, 1035 I-7
JENKINS CO., 8340 H-10
Jesup, 10214 L-11
Johns Creek, 76728 D-5
JOHNSON CO., 9980 I-9
JONES CO., 28669 G-6
Jonesboro, 4724 F-4
Kennesaw, 29783 D-4
Kingsland, 15946 O-11
Knoxville, 69 I-5
La Vista, 5000 *D-4
LaFayette, 7121 B-2
LaGrange, 29588 H-3
Lake City, 2612 *H-4
L. Lucerne, 900 E-5
Lakeland, 3366 N-8
Lakeview, 4839 †N-13
LAMAR CO., 18317 H-5
LANIER CO., 10078 N-8
LAURENS CO., 48434 I-8
Lavonia, 2156 C-8
Lawrenceville, 28546 E-5
LEE CO., 28298 K-5
Leesburg, 2896 L-5
Lenox, 873 M-7
Lexington, 228 E-8
LIBERTY CO., 63453 K-11
Lilburn, 11596 E-5
LINCOLN CO., 7996 E-9
Lincoln Pk., 833 H-4
Lincolnton, 1566 E-9
Lindale, 4191 D-2
Lithia Sprs., 15491 E-4
Lithonia, 1924 E-5
Locust Grv., 5402 G-5
Loganville, 10458 E-6
LONG CO., 14464 L-12
Lookout Mtn., 1602 A-2
Louisville, 2493 H-9
Lovejoy, 6422 F-4
LOWNDES CO., 109233 O-7
Ludowici, 1703 L-11
Lula, 2758 C-6
Lumber City, 1328 K-9
Lumpkin, 2741 K-3
LUMPKIN CO., 29966 C-5
Luthersville, 874 G-3
Lyons, 4367 J-10
Mableton, 37115 E-4
Macon, 91351 H-6
MACON CO., 14740 J-5
Madison, 3979 F-7
MADISON CO., 28120 D-7
Manchester, 4230 H-4
Marietta, 56579 E-4
MARION CO., 8742 J-4
Marlborough, 1600 F-4
Marshallville, 1448 I-5
Martinez, 35795 F-10
Maysville, 1798 D-6
McCaysville, 1056 B-4
McDonough, 22084 F-5
MCDUFFIE CO., 21875 G-9
MCINTOSH CO., 14333 L-12
McRae, 5740 K-8
Mechanicsville, 1600 *A-6
Meigs, 1035 N-5
MERIWETHER CO., 21992 H-3
Metter, 4130 J-10
Midway, 2121 L-12
Milledgeville, 17715 H-7
Millen, 3120 H-11
MILLER CO., 6125 M-3
Milstead, 1500 F-5
Milton, 32661 D-5
MITCHELL CO., 23498 M-5
Monroe, 13234 E-6
MONROE CO., 26424 H-5
Montezuma, 3460 J-5
MONTGOMERY CO., 9123 J-9
Monticello, 2657 G-6
Morgan, 240 L-4
MORGAN CO., 17868 F-7
Morrow, 6445 F-4
Moultrie, 14268 N-6
Mt. Airy, 1284 C-7
Mt. Vernon, 2451 J-9
Mt. Zion, 1696 F-2
Mountain City, 1088 B-7
Mountain View, 1100 *G-3
MURRAY CO., 39628 B-3
Murrayville, 800 C-6
MUSCOGEE CO., 189885 I-3
Nahunta, 1053 M-11
Nashville, 4939 M-7
Nelson, 1314 C-4
New Holland, 1200 D-6
Newnan, 33039 G-3
Newton, 654 M-4
NEWTON CO., 99958 F-6
Nicholls, 2798 L-9
Nicholson, 1696 D-7
Norcross, 9116 E-5
Norman Pk., 972 M-6
N. Atlanta, 40456 *C-4
N. Decatur, 16698 *D-5
N. Druid Hills, 18947 *D-5
Oak Grv., 2850 *D-5
Oakwood, 3970 D-6
Ocilla, 3414 L-7
OCONEE CO., 32808 E-7
Oglethorpe, 1328 J-5
OGLETHORPE CO., 14899 E-7
Omega, 1221 M-6
Oxford, 2134 F-6
Palmetto, 4488 F-3
Panthersville, 9749 F-5
Parkersburg, 1000 T-11
PAULDING CO., 142324 E-3
PEACH CO., 27695 I-6
Peachtree City, 34364 F-4
Pearson, 2117 M-8
Pelham, 3898 N-5
Pembroke, 2196 J-12
Perry, 13839 I-6
PICKENS CO., 29431 C-4
PIERCE CO., 18758 M-10
PIKE CO., 17869 G-4
Pine Mtn., 1304 H-3
Pine Mtn. Valley, 950 H-3
Plains, 776 K-4
POLK CO., 41475 E-2
Pooler, 19140 K-13
Port Wentworth, 5359 J-13
Porterdale, 1429 F-6
Poulan, 851 L-6
Powder Sprs., 13940 E-3
Preston, 2799 K-4
PULASKI CO., 12010 J-7
PUTNAM CO., 21218 G-7
Putney, 2898 M-5
Quitman, 3850 O-6
QUITMAN CO., 2513 K-2
RABUN CO., 16276 B-7
Radium Sprs., 1400 L-5
RANDOLPH CO., 7719 L-3
Raoul, 2558 C-6
Ray City, 1090 N-7
Red Oak, 2800 *H-1
Reed Creek, 2604 C-8
Rehoboth, 1300 *D-5
Reidsville, 4944 K-10
Remerton, 1123 O-7
Reynolds, 1086 I-5
Riceboro, 809 L-12
Richland, 1473 K-3
RICHMOND CO., 200549 G-10
Richmond Hill, 9281 K-12
Rincon, 8836 J-13
Ringgold, 3580 B-2
Riverdale, 15134 F-4
Roberta, 1007 I-5
Rochelle, 1174 K-7
ROCKDALE CO., 85215 F-5
Rockmart, 4199 E-3
Rocky Face, 1000 B-3
Rome, 36303 D-2
Rossville, 4105 A-2
Roswell, 88346 D-4
Royston, 2582 D-8
Russell, 1203 E-6
Rutledge, 781 F-6
St. Marys, 17121 O-12
St. Simons, 12743 N-12
Sandersville, 5912 H-8
Sandfly, 1200 T-11
Sandy Sprs., 93853 E-4
Sardis, 999 H-11
Sargent, 900 F-3
Savannah, 136286 K-13
SCHLEY CO., 5010 J-4
Scottdale, 10631 *D-5
Screven, 766 M-11
SCREVEN CO., 14593 H-11
SEMINOLE CO., 8729 N-3
Senoia, 3307 G-4
Shannon, 1862 C-2
Shellman, 1083 L-4
Skidaway Island, 8341 K-13
Smyrna, 51271 E-4
Snellville, 18242 E-5
Social Circle, 4262 F-6
Soperton, 3115 J-9
SPALDING CO., 64073 G-4
Sparks, 2052 N-7
Sparta, 1400 G-8
Springfield, 2852 J-12
Statenville, 1040 O-8
Statesboro, 28422 I-11
Statham, 2408 E-6
STEPHENS CO., 26175 C-7
STEWART CO., 6058 J-3
Stockbridge, 25636 F-5
Stone Mtn., 5802 E-5
Sugar Hill, 18522 D-5
Summerville, 4534 C-2
SUMTER CO., 32819 K-5
Sunnyside, 1303 M-10
Sunset Vil., 846 H-4
Suwanee, 15355 D-5
Swainsboro, 7277 I-10
Sylvania, 2956 I-12
Sylvester, 6188 L-6
TALBOT CO., 6865 I-4
Talbotton, 970 I-4
TALIAFERRO CO., 1717 F-8
Tallapoosa, 3170 E-2
Tate, 1000 C-4
TATTNALL CO., 25520 J-10
TAYLOR CO., 8906 I-5
TELFAIR CO., 16500 K-8
Temple, 4228 E-3
Tennille, 1539 H-8
TERRELL CO., 9315 K-4
THOMAS CO., 44720 O-5
Thomaston, 7170 H-4
Thomasville, 18413 O-5
Thomson, 6778 F-9
Thunderbolt, 2668 S-11
TIFT CO., 40118 M-6
Tifton, 16350 M-7
Toccoa, 8491 C-7
Toccoa Falls, 900 C-7
TOOMBS CO., 27223 K-10
TOWNS CO., 10471 B-6
Trenton, 2301 B-1
TREUTLEN CO., 6885 J-9
Trion, 1827 C-2
TROUP CO., 67044 G-3
Tucker, 27581 *C-6
Tunnel Hill, 856 B-3
TURNER CO., 8930 L-6
TWIGGS CO., 9023 H-7
Twin City, 1742 I-10
Twin Lakes, 950 O-7
Tybee Island, 2990 K-14
Tyrone, 6879 F-4
Unadilla, 3796 J-6
Union City, 19456 F-4
UNION CO., 21356 B-5
Union Pt., 1617 F-8
Unionville, 1845 M-7
UPSON CO., 27153 H-5
Valdosta, 54518 O-7
Varnell, 1744 B-3
Vidalia, 10473 J-9
Vienna, 4011 K-6
Villa Rica, 13956 E-3
Vinings, 9734 *C-2
Vista Grv., 3000 *D-5
Wadley, 2061 H-9
WALKER CO., 68756 C-2
Walnut Grv., 1330 E-6
Walthourville, 4111 L-12
WALTON CO., 83768 E-6
WARE CO., 36312 N-9
Warner Robins, 66588 I-6
WARREN CO., 5834 G-9
Warrenton, 1937 F-9
Washington, 4134 E-9
WASHINGTON CO., 21187 H-8
Watkinsville, 2832 E-7
Waycross, 14649 M-10
WAYNE CO., 30099 L-10
Waynesboro, 5766 G-11
WEBSTER CO., 2799 K-4
West Pt., 3474 H-2
WHEELER CO., 7421 K-8
WHITE CO., 27144 C-6
WHITFIELD CO., 102599 B-3
WILCOX CO., 9255 K-6
WILKES CO., 10593 E-8
WILKINSON CO., 9563 I-7
Willacoochee, 1391 M-8
Wilmington Island, 15138 K-13
Winder, 14099 E-6
Winterville, 1122 E-7
Woodbine, 1412 N-11
Woodbury, 961 H-4
Woodstock, 23896 D-4
WORTH CO., 21679 M-6
Wrens, 2187 G-10
Wrightsville, 2195 I-9
Young Harris, 899 B-6
Zebulon, 1174 G-4

Hawaii

Map p. 30

'Aiea, 9019 M-4
Anahola, 2223 H-2
Captain Cook, 3429 M-8
'Ewa Bch., 14955 N-3
'Ewa Villages, 6108 M-3
Haiku, 1150 I-9
Hālawa Hts., 4000 M-4
Hale'iwa, 3970 I-4
Hali'imaile, 964 I-9
Hāna, 1235 K-8
Hanamā'ulu, 3835 I-2
Hanapepe, 2638 I-2
Hau'ula, 4148 K-4
Hawai'i Kai, 1150 N-6
HAWAII CO., 185079 L-10
Hāwī, 1081 L-8
Hilo, 43263 M-10
Hōlualoa, 8538 M-8
Honoka'a, 2258 L-9
Honokowai, 2200 K-7
Honolulu, 337256 J-5
HONOLULU CO., 953207 I-5
Honomu, 509 L-9
Honouliuli, 520 M-3
Ka'a'awa, 1379 K-4
Kahala, 800 H-10
Kahalu'u, 4738 L-4
Kahuku, 2614 I-5
Kahului, 26337 K-7
Kailua, 38635 J-5
Kailua, 11975 M-8
Kaimuki, 6800 G-10
Kalāheo, 4595 I-2
Kalihi, 1900 G-7
Kamehameha Hts., 1100 G-8
Kāne'ohe, 34597 J-5
Kapa'a, 10699 I-2
Kapolei, 15186 M-2
KAUAI CO., 67091 I-2
Kaunakakai, 3425 J-6
Kea'au, 2253 M-10
Kealakekua, 2019 M-8
Kekaha, 3537 I-2
Keokea, 1612 K-7
Kīhei, 20881 K-7
Kīlauea, 2803 H-2
Koloa, 2144 I-2
Kualapu'u, 2027 J-6
Kunia Camp, 580 L-2
Kurtistown, 1298 M-10
Lā'ie, 6138 J-4
Lahaina, 11704 K-7
Lāna'i City, 3102 K-6
Laupāhoehoe, 581 L-9
Līhu'e, 6455 I-2
Mā'ili, 9488 M-1
Mākaha, 8278 L-1
Makakilo City, 18248 M-2
Makawao, 7184 I-9
MAUI CO., 154834 J-7
Maunalani Hts., 700 G-10
Maunawili, 2040 M-5
Mililani Town, 27629 L-3
Mountain View, 3924 M-9
Nā'ālehu, 866 N-9
Nānākuli, 12666 J-4
Niu, 570 N-5
Pa'auilo, 595 L-9
Pauwela, 500 K-7
Pacific Hts., 650 F-8
Pacific Palisades, 5600 M-3
Pāhala, 1356 N-9
Pāhoa, 945 M-10
Paia, 2668 I-9
Pāpa'ikou, 1314 M-10
Pearl City, 47698 J-5
Pepe'ekeo, 1789 M-10
Pukalani, 7574 K-7
Punalu'u, 1164 K-4
St. Louis Hts., 1000 G-10
Sunset Bch., 660 J-3
Volcano, 2575 M-9
Wahiawā, 17821 J-5
Wai'anae, 13177 J-4
Waiakoa, 900 J-9
Waialua, 3860 J-7
Waiehu, 600 I-8
Waikapu, 2965 K-7
Waikiki, 3000 H-9
Wailua, 2254 I-2
Wailuku, 15313 K-7
Waimānalo, 5451 J-5
Waimānalo Bch., 4481 M-6
Waimea, 9212 L-9
Waimea, 1855 I-2
Waimea, 650 J-2
Waipahu, 38216 M-3
Whitmore Vil., 4499 L-3
Woodlawn, 1200 F-9

Idaho

Map p. 31

Aberdeen, 1994 L-6
ADA CO., 392365 K-2
ADAMS CO., 3976 H-1
American Falls, 4457 L-6
Ammon, 13816 K-7
Arco, 995 K-6
Ashton, 1127 J-8
BANNOCK CO., 82839 M-7
BEAR LAKE CO., 5986 N-9
Bellevue, 2287 K-4
BENEWAH CO., 9285 E-1
BINGHAM CO., 45607 L-6
Blackfoot, 11899 L-7
BLAINE CO., 21376 K-5
Boise, 205671 K-2
BOISE CO., 7028 J-2
BONNER CO., 40877 C-2
Bonners Ferry, 2543 B-2
BONNEVILLE CO., 104234 K-8
BOUNDARY CO., 10972 B-2
Buhl, 4122 M-4
Burley, 10345 M-5
BUTTE CO., 2891 K-6
Caldwell, 46237 K-1
CAMAS CO., 1117 K-4
CANYON CO., 188923 K-1
CARIBOU CO., 6963 L-7
Cascade, 939 I-2
CASSIA CO., 22952 M-5
Challis, 1081 I-4
Chubbuck, 13922 L-7
CLARK CO., 982 J-7
CLEARWATER CO., 8761 E-3
Coeur d'Alene, 44137 D-1
Cottonwood, 900 G-2
Council, 839 I-2
CUSTER CO., 4368 J-4
Dalton Gdns., 2335 C-1
Driggs, 1660 K-9
Dubois, 677 J-7
Eagle, 19908 K-2
ELMORE CO., 27038 L-3
Emmett, 6557 J-2
Fairfield, 416 K-4
Filer, 2508 M-4
FRANKLIN CO., 12786 M-8
FREMONT CO., 13242 J-8
Fruitland, 4684 J-1
Garden City, 10972 B-6
GEM CO., 16719 J-2
Genesee, 955 F-1
Glenns Ferry, 1319 L-3
Gooding, 3567 L-4
GOODING CO., 15464 L-4
Grace, 915 M-8
Grangeville, 3141 G-2
Greenleaf, 846 K-1
Hagerman, 872 L-4
Hailey, 7960 K-4
Hansen, 1144 M-4
Hayden, 13294 C-1
Hazelton, 753 M-5
Heyburn, 3089 M-5
Homedale, 2633 K-1
Horseshoe Bend, 707 J-2
Idaho City, 485 K-2
IDAHO CO., 16267 G-2
Idaho Falls, 56813 K-7
Inkom, 854 L-7
Iona, 1803 K-7
JEFFERSON CO., 26140 K-7
Jerome, 10890 M-4
JEROME CO., 22374 L-4
Kamiah, 1295 F-2
Kellogg, 2120 D-2
Ketchum, 2689 K-4
Kimberly, 3264 M-4
Kingston, 800 D-2
KOOTENAI CO., 138494 C-1
Kuna, 15210 K-2
Lapwai, 1137 F-1
LATAH CO., 37244 E-2
LEMHI CO., 7936 H-4
LEWIS CO., 3821 F-2
Lewiston, 31894 F-1
Lincoln, 3647 K-7
LINCOLN CO., 5208 L-5
MADISON CO., 37536 K-8
Malad City, 2095 M-7
Marsing, 1031 K-1
McCall, 2991 I-2
McCammon, 809 M-7
Menan, 741 K-7
Meridian, 75092 K-2
Middleton, 5524 K-1
MINIDOKA CO., 20069 L-5
Montpelier, 2597 M-8
Moreland, 1278 L-7
Moscow, 23800 E-1
Mountain Home, 14206 L-3
Moyie Sprs., 718 B-2
Murphy, 97 L-1
Nampa, 81557 K-1
New Plymouth, 1538 J-1
NEZ PERCE CO., 39265 F-1
Nezperce, 466 F-2
Oakley, 763 M-5
ONEIDA CO., 4286 N-6
Orofino, 3142 F-2
Osburn, 1555 D-2
OWYHEE CO., 11526 M-2
Paris, 513 M-8
Parma, 1983 K-1
Paul, 1169 M-5
Payette, 7433 J-1
PAYETTE CO., 22623 J-1
Pinehurst, 1619 D-2
Plummer, 1044 D-1
Pocatello, 54255 L-7
Ponderay, 1137 B-2
Post Falls, 27574 C-1
Potlatch, 804 E-1
POWER CO., 7817 M-6
Preston, 5204 N-8
Priest River, 1751 C-1
Rathdrum, 6826 C-1
Rexburg, 25484 K-8
Rigby, 3945 K-7
Riverside, 838 L-7
Rupert, 5554 M-5
St. Anthony, 3542 J-8
St. Maries, 2402 D-2
Salmon, 3112 H-5
Sandpoint, 7365 C-2
Shelley, 4409 K-7
Shoshone, 1461 L-4
SHOSHONE CO., 12765 D-2
Soda Sprs., 3058 M-8
Spirit Lake, 1945 C-1
Star, 5793 K-2
Sugar City, 1514 J-8
Sun Valley, 1406 K-4
Teton, 735 J-8
TETON CO., 10170 K-8
Troy, 862 E-1
Twin Falls, 44125 M-4
TWIN FALLS CO., 77230 M-4
Tyhee, 1123 L-7
Ucon, 1108 K-7
VALLEY CO., 9862 I-3
Victor, 1928 K-9
Wallace, 784 D-2
WASHINGTON CO., 10198 I-1
Weiser, 5507 J-1
Wendell, 2782 L-4
Wilder, 1533 K-1

Illinois

Map pp. 32 – 33

* City keyed to pp. 34 – 35
† City keyed to p. 57

Abingdon, 3319 G-6
ADAMS CO., 67103 J-3
Addison, 36942 *H-5
Albany, 891 C-6
Albers, 1190 O-8
Albion, 1988 P-12
Aledo, 3640 E-5
ALEXANDER CO., 8238 T-8
Alexis, 831 F-5
Algonquin, 30046 B-11
Alorton, 2002 †I-8
Alsip, 19277 *K-8
Altamont, 2319 M-10
Alton, 27865 N-6
Amboy, 2500 D-9
Andalusia, 1178 E-5
Anna, 4442 S-9
Annawan, 878 E-7
Antioch, 14430 A-12
Arbury Hills, 1770 *M-7
Arcola, 2916 K-11
Argenta, 947 J-10
Arlington Hts., 75101 B-12
Arthur, 2288 K-11
Ashkum, 761 G-12
Ashland, 1333 J-7
Ashmore, 785 K-12
Ashton, 972 C-9
Assumption, 1168 K-9
Astoria, 1141 I-6
Athens, 1988 J-7
Atkinson, 972 E-7
Atlanta, 1692 I-9
Atwood, 1224 J-11
Auburn, 4771 K-7
Aurora, 197899 C-11
Aviston, 1945 O-8
Avon, 799 G-6
Bannockburn, 1583 *D-7
Barrington, 10327 B-12
Barrington Hills, 4209 *E-3
Barry, 1318 K-4
Bartlett, 41208 *G-3
Bartonville, 6471 H-8
Batavia, 26045 C-11
Beach Pk., 13638 A-12
Beardstown, 6123 J-6
Beecher, 4359 E-13
Belleville, 44478 O-7
Bellevue, 1978 G-8
Bellwood, 19071 *H-7
Belvidere, 25585 B-10
Bement, 1730 J-11
Benld, 1556 M-7
Bensenville, 18352 *G-6
Benton, 7087 Q-10
Berkeley, 5209 *H-6
Berwyn, 56657 *I-8
Bethalto, 9521 N-7
Bethany, 1352 K-10
Big Rock, 1126 C-11
Bloomingdale, 22018 C-12
Bloomington, 76610 H-9
Blue Island, 23706 *K-9
Blue Mound, 1158 K-9
Bolingbrook, 73366 D-12
BOND CO., 17768 N-8
BOONE CO., 54165 B-10
Bourbonnais, 18631 F-12
Braceville, 793 E-11
Bradford, 768 F-8
Bradley, 15895 F-13
Braidwood, 6191 E-12
Breese, 4442 O-8
Bridgeport, 1886 N-13
Bridgeview, 16446 *J-7
Brighton, 2254 M-6
Brimfield, 868 G-7
Broadview, 7932 *I-7
Brookfield, 18978 *I-7
Brookport, 984 T-10
BROWN CO., 6937 J-5
Brownstown, 759 M-10
Buffalo Grv., 41496 B-12
Bull Valley, 1077 *B-2
Bunker Hill, 1774 M-7
Burbank, 28925 *J-8
BUREAU CO., 34978 E-8
Burnham, 4206 *L-10
Burr Ridge, 10559 *J-6
Bushnell, 3117 H-5
Butterfield, 3750 *I-5
Byron, 3753 B-9
Cahokia, 15241 O-6
Cairo, 2831 T-9
CALHOUN CO., 5089 L-5
Calumet City, 37042 *L-10
Calumet Pk., 7835 *L-9
Cambria, 1228 R-9
Cambridge, 2160 E-6
Camp Pt., 1132 J-4
Campton Hills, 11131 *H-1
Canton, 14704 H-7
Capron, 1376 A-10
Carbon Cliff, 2134 S-5
Carbondale, 25902 R-9
Carlinville, 5917 L-7
Carlyle, 3281 O-8
Carmi, 5240 Q-12
Carol Stream, 39711 *H-4
Carpentersville, 37691 B-11
Carrier Mills, 1653 R-10
CARROLL CO., 15387 C-7
Carrollton, 2484 L-6
Carterville, 5496 R-9
Carthage, 2605 H-4
Cary, 18271 B-11
Casey, 2769 L-12
Caseyville, 4245 †H-9
CASS CO., 13642 J-6
Catlin, 2040 I-13
Central City, 1172 O-9
Centralia, 13032 O-9
Centreville, 5309 †I-8
Cerro Gordo, 1403 J-10
Champaign, 81055 I-11
CHAMPAIGN CO., 201081 J-12
Channahon, 12560 E-11
Charleston, 21838 L-12
Chatham, 11500 K-7
Chatsworth, 1205 G-11
Chebanse, 1062 F-12
Chenoa, 1785 G-10
Cherry Valley, 3162 B-10
Chester, 8586 Q-7
Chicago, 2695598 C-13
Chicago Hts., 30276 D-13
Chicago Ridge, 14305 *K-8
Chillicothe, 6097 F-8
Chrisman, 1343 J-13
CHRISTIAN CO., 34800 K-8
Christopher, 2382 Q-9
Cicero, 83891 C-13
Cissna Pk., 846 H-12
Clarendon Hills, 8427 *I-6
CLARK CO., 16335 L-13
Clay City, 959 N-11
CLAY CO., 13815 N-11
Clifton, 1468 F-12
Clinton, 7225 I-10
CLINTON CO., 37762 N-8
Coal City, 5587 E-11
Coal Valley, 3743 E-6
Cobden, 1157 S-9
Colchester, 1401 H-5
COLES CO., 53873 K-11
Colfax, 1061 H-10
Collinsville, 25579 N-7
Colona, 5099 T-6
Columbia, 9707 O-6
COOK CO., 5194675 C-13
Cortland, 4270 C-10
Cottage Hills, 980 †D-8
Coulterville, 945 P-8
Country Club Hills, 16541 *M-8
Countryside, 5895 *J-7
CRAWFORD CO., 19817 M-13
Crest Hill, 20837 *M-4
Crestwood, 10950 *L-8
Crete, 8259 E-13
Creve Coeur, 5451 G-8
Crystal Lake, 40743 B-11
Cuba, 1294 H-6
CUMBERLAND CO., 11048 L-11
Dallas City, 945 G-4
Danvers, 1154 H-9
Danville, 33027 I-13
Darien, 22086 *J-5
Davis Jct., 2373 B-9
De Soto, 1590 R-9
DE WITT CO., 16561 I-9
Decatur, 76122 J-10
Deer Pk., 3200 *D-4
Deerfield, 18225 *D-7
DeKalb, 43862 C-10
DEKALB CO., 105160 B-10
Delavan, 1689 H-8
Depue, 1838 E-9
Des Plaines, 58364 B-12
Diamond, 2527 E-11
Diamond Lake, 1500 *C-5
Divernon, 1172 K-8
Dixmoor, 3644 *L-9
Dixon, 15733 C-8
Dolton, 23153 *L-10
DOUGLAS CO., 19980 K-12
Downers Grv., 47833 C-12
Downs, 1005 H-10
Du Quoin, 6109 Q-9
Dunlap, 1386 G-8
DUPAGE CO., 916924 C-12
Dupo, 4138 O-6
Durand, 1443 A-9
Dwight, 4260 F-11
Earlville, 1701 D-10
E. Alton, 6301 N-6
E. Dubuque, 1704 A-5
E. Dundee, 2860 *E-2
E. Galesburg, 812 F-6
E. Hazel Crest, 1543 *M-9
E. Moline, 21302 D-6
E. Peoria, 23402 G-8
E. St. Louis, 27006 O-6
Eastwood Mnr., 950 *A-3
EDGAR CO., 18576 K-13
Edinburg, 1078 K-8
EDWARDS CO., 6721 O-12
Edwardsville, 24293 N-7
Effingham, 12328 M-11
EFFINGHAM CO., 34242 M-11
El Paso, 2810 G-9
Elburn, 5602 C-11
Eldorado, 4122 R-11
Elgin, 108188 B-11
Elizabeth, 761 A-6
Elizabethtown, 299 S-11
Elk Grove Vil., 33127 *F-5
Elkville, 928 Q-9
Elmhurst, 44121 C-12
Elmwood, 2097 G-7
Elmwood Pk., 24883 *H-7
Elwood, 2279 E-12
Energy, 1146 R-9
Erie, 1602 D-7
Essex, 802 F-12
Eureka, 5295 G-9
Evanston, 74486 B-13
Evergreen Pk., 19852 *K-8
Fairbury, 3757 G-11
Fairfield, 5154 P-11
Fairmont, 2459 *M-4
Fairmont City, 2635 †H-8
Fairview Hts., 17078 †I-9
Farmer City, 2037 I-10
Farmington, 2448 G-7
FAYETTE CO., 22140 M-9
Fisher, 1881 I-11
Flanagan, 1110 G-10
Flora, 5070 N-11
Flossmoor, 9464 *M-9
FORD CO., 14081 H-12
Ford Hts., 2763 *N-10
Forest Homes, 1700 †D-8
Forest Lake, 1659 *C-5
Forest Pk., 14167 *I-7
Forrest, 1220 G-11
Forreston, 1446 B-8
Forsyth, 3490 J-10
Fox Lake, 10579 A-12
Fox River Grv., 4854 B-11
Frankfort, 17782 D-12
FRANKLIN CO., 39561 Q-10
Franklin Grv., 1021 C-9
Franklin Pk., 18333 *G-7
Freeburg, 4354 O-7
Freeport, 25638 B-8
Fulton, 3481 C-6
FULTON CO., 37069 H-6
Galatia, 933 Q-11
Galena, 3429 A-6
Galesburg, 32195 F-6
GALLATIN CO., 5589 R-12
Galva, 2589 F-7
Gardner, 1463 F-11
Geneseo, 6586 E-6
Geneva, 21495 C-11
Genoa, 5193 B-10
Georgetown, 3474 J-13
Germantown, 1269 O-8
Germantown Hills, 3438 G-8
Gibson City, 3407 H-11
Gifford, 975 I-12
Gilberts, 6879 *E-1
Gillespie, 3319 M-7
Gilman, 1814 G-12
Girard, 2103 L-7
Glasford, 1022 H-7
Glen Carbon, 12934 †F-9
Glen Ellyn, 27450 *H-5
Glencoe, 8723 B-13
Glendale Hts., 34208 *G-4
Glenview, 44692 *E-7
Glenwood, 8969 *M-9
Godfrey, 17982 M-6
Golconda, 668 S-11
Goodfield, 860 G-9
Goreville, 1049 R-9
Grandview, 1441 *L-17
Granite City, 29849 N-6
Grant Pk., 1331 E-13
Granville, 1427 E-9
Grayslake, 20957 *B-5
Grayville, 1666 P-12
Green Oaks, 3866 *B-6
GREENE CO., 13886 L-5
Greenfield, 1071 L-6
Greenup, 1513 L-12
Greenview, 778 I-7
Greenville, 7000 N-8
Gridley, 1432 G-10
Griggsville, 1226 K-5
GRUNDY CO., 50063 E-11
Gurnee, 31295 *A-6
Hainesville, 3597 *A-5
Hamel, 816 N-7
Hamilton, 2951 H-3
HAMILTON CO., 8457 P-11
Hampshire, 5563 B-11
Hampton, 1863 R-5
HANCOCK CO., 19104 H-3
Hanna City, 1225 G-7
Hanover, 844 B-6
Hanover Pk., 37973 *F-4
Hardin, 967 M-5
HARDIN CO., 4320 S-11
Harrisburg, 9017 R-11
Harristown, 1367 J-9
Hartford, 1429 †E-8
Harvard, 9447 A-10
Harvey, 25282 D-13
Harwood Hts., 8612 *G-7
Havana, 3301 I-7
Hawthorn Woods, 7663 *C-5
Hazel Crest, 14100 *M-9
Hebron, 1216 A-11
Hegeler, 1900 I-13
HENDERSON CO., 7331 G-4
Hennepin, 757 E-9
Henry, 2464 F-8
HENRY CO., 50486 E-6
Herrin, 12501 R-9
Herscher, 1591 F-12
Heyworth, 2841 I-9
Hickory Hills, 14049 *J-7
Highland, 9919 N-8
Highland Pk., 29763 B-13
Highwood, 5405 B-13
Hillcrest, 1326 C-9
Hillsboro, 6207 M-8
Hillside, 8157 *H-6
Hinckley, 2070 C-10
Hinsdale, 16816 *J-6
Hodgkins, 1897 *J-7
Hoffman Estates, 51895 *F-4
Hollywood Hts., 1060 †H-9
Homer, 1193 J-12
Homer Glen, 24220 *L-6
Hometown, 4349 *J-8
Homewood, 19323 *M-9
Hoopeston, 5351 H-13
Hopedale, 865 H-8
Hudson, 1838 H-9
Huntley, 24291 B-11
Hurst, 795 Q-9
Illiopolis, 891 J-9
Ina, 2338 P-10
Indian Head Pk., 3809 *J-6
Ingalls Pk., 3314 *N-5
Ingleside, 1700 *A-4
Inverness, 7399 *E-5
IROQUOIS CO., 29718 G-12
Island Lake, 8080 *B-3
Itasca, 8649 *G-5
JACKSON CO., 60218 Q-8
Jacksonville, 19446 K-6
JASPER CO., 9698 M-12
JEFFERSON CO., 38827 O-10
Jerome, 1656 *M-16
JERSEY CO., 22985 M-6
Jerseyville, 8465 M-6
JO DAVIESS CO., 22678 B-6
JOHNSON CO., 12582 S-10
Johnston City, 3543 R-10
Joliet, 147433 D-12
Jonesboro, 1821 S-9
Justice, 12926 *J-7
KANE CO., 515269 C-11
Kankakee, 27537 F-12
KANKAKEE CO., 113449 F-12
Kansas, 787 K-12
KENDALL CO., 114736 D-11
Kenilworth, 2513 *E-8
Kewanee, 12916 E-7
Kildeer, 3968 *D-5
Kincaid, 1505 K-8
Kingston, 1164 B-10
Kinmundy, 796 N-10
Kirkland, 1744 B-10
Knollwood, 1747 *B-7
KNOX CO., 52919 F-6
Knoxville, 2911 F-6
La Grange, 15550 *I-7
La Grange Highlands, 3650 *J-6
La Grange Pk., 13579 *I-7
La Harpe, 1235 H-4
La Salle, 9609 E-9
LA SALLE CO., 113924 E-10
Lacon, 1937 F-8
Ladd, 1295 E-9
L. Barrington, 4973 *C-4
L. Bluff, 5722 B-12
LAKE CO., 703462 B-12
L. Forest, 19375 B-13
L. Holiday, 4761 D-10
L. in the Hills, 28965 *D-2
L. Mattoon, 1000 L-11
L. Summerset, 2048 A-8
L. Villa, 8741 A-12
L. Zurich, 19631 B-12
Lakemoor, 6017 A-11
Lakewood, 3811 *C-1
Lanark, 1457 B-7
Lansing, 28331 *M-10
LAWRENCE CO., 16833 N-13
Lawrenceville, 4348 N-13
Le Roy, 3560 H-10
Lebanon, 4418 O-7
LEE CO., 36031 D-8
Leland, 977 D-10
Leland Grv., 1503 *M-16
Lemont, 16000 *K-5
Lena, 2912 A-7
Lewistown, 2384 H-6
Lexington, 2060 G-10
Libertyville, 20315 B-12
Lily Lake, 993 C-11
Lincoln, 14504 I-8
Lincolnshire, 7275 *D-6
Lincolnwood, 12590 *F-8
Lindenhurst, 14462 A-12
Lisle, 22390 C-12
Litchfield, 6939 M-8
Livingston, 858 M-7
LIVINGSTON CO., 38950 F-11
Lockport, 24839 D-12
LOGAN CO., 30305 I-8
Lombard, 43165 *H-5
Long Creek, 1328 J-10
Long Grv., 8043 *D-5
Long Lake, 3515 *A-4
Louisville, 1139 N-11
Loves Pk., 23996 A-9
Lovington, 1130 K-10
Lynwood, 9007 *M-10
Lyons, 10729 *I-7
Machesney Pk., 23499 A-9
Mackinaw, 1950 H-8
Macomb, 19288 H-5
Macon, 1138 K-9
MACON CO., 110768 J-9
MACOUPIN CO., 47765 L-7
Madison, 3891 †G-7
MADISON CO., 269282 N-7
Mahomet, 7258 I-11
Malta, 1164 C-10
Manhattan, 7051 E-12
Manito, 1642 H-7
Mansfield, 906 I-11
Manteno, 9204 E-13
Maple Pk., 1310 C-10
Marengo, 7648 B-10
Marine, 960 N-7
Marion, 17193 R-10
MARION CO., 39437 O-10
Marissa, 1979 P-7
Markham, 12508 *L-9
Maroa, 1801 J-10
Marseilles, 5094 E-10
Marshall, 3933 L-13
MARSHALL CO., 12640 F-9
Martinsville, 1167 L-13
Maryville, 7487 †G-10
Mascoutah, 7483 O-7
Mason City, 2343 I-8
MASON CO., 14666 I-7
MASSAC CO., 15429 T-10
Matteson, 19009 *N-8
Mattoon, 18555 L-11
Maywood, 24090 *H-7
Mazon, 1015 E-11
McCullom Lake, 1049 *A-2
MCDONOUGH CO., 32612 I-5
McHenry, 26992 A-11
MCHENRY CO., 308760 A-11
McLean, 830 I-9
MCLEAN CO., 169572 H-10
McLeansboro, 2883 Q-11
Meadowbrook, 1000 †D-9
Melrose Pk., 25411 *H-7
MENARD CO., 12705 I-7
Mendon, 953 I-3
Mendota, 7372 D-9
MERCER CO., 16434 E-5
Meredosia, 1044 J-5
Merrionette Pk., 1900 *K-9
Metamora, 3636 G-8
Metropolis, 6537 T-10
Midlothian, 14819 *L-8
Milan, 5099 T-3
Milford, 1306 G-13
Milledgeville, 1032 C-7
Millstadt, 4011 O-6
Minier, 1252 H-9
Minonk, 2078 G-9
Minooka, 10924 E-11
Mitchell, 1356 †F-8
Mokena, 18740 *M-7
Moline, 43483 D-5
Momence, 3310 F-13
Monee, 5148 E-13
Monmouth, 9444 F-5
MONROE CO., 32957 P-6
Montgomery, 18438 D-11
MONTGOMERY CO., 30104 L-8
Monticello, 5548 J-11
MORGAN CO., 35547 J-6
Morris, 13636 E-11
Morrison, 4188 C-7
Morrisonville, 1056 L-8
Morton, 16267 H-8
Morton Grv., 23270 *F-7
MOULTRIE CO., 14846 K-10
Mound City, 588 T-9
Mounds, 810 T-9
Mt. Carmel, 7284 O-13
Mt. Carroll, 1717 B-7
Mt. Morris, 2998 B-8
Mt. Olive, 2099 M-7
Mt. Prospect, 54167 *E-6
Mt. Pulaski, 1566 J-9
Mt. Sterling, 2025 J-5
Mt. Vernon, 15277 P-10
Mt. Zion, 5833 K-10
Moweaqua, 1831 K-9
Mundelein, 31064 *C-5
Murphysboro, 7970 R-8
Naperville, 141853 C-12
Nashville, 3258 P-8
Nauvoo, 1149 H-3
Neoga, 1636 L-11
New Athens, 2054 P-7
New Baden, 3349 O-7
New Berlin, 1346 K-7
New Lenox, 24394 D-12
Newark, 992 D-11
Newman, 865 J-12
Newton, 2849 M-12
Niles, 29803 *F-7
Nokomis, 2256 L-9
Normal, 52497 H-9
Norridge, 14572 *G-7
Norris City, 1275 Q-11
N. Aurora, 16760 C-11
N. Barrington, 3047 *C-4
N. Chicago, 32574 A-12
N. Dupo, 1380 †J-7
N. Glen Ellyn, 1400 *H-5
N. Riverside, 6672 *I-7
Northbrook, 33170 *E-7
Northfield, 5420 *E-8
Northlake, 12323 *H-6
O'Fallon, 28281 O-7
Oak Brook, 7883 *I-6
Oak Forest, 27962 *L-8
Oak Hills, 1150 †H-9
Oak Lawn, 56690 D-13
Oak Pk., 51878 C-13
Oakbrook Ter., 2134 *I-6
Oakland, 880 K-12
Oakwood, 1595 I-13
Oakwood Hills, 2083 *C-3
Oblong, 1466 M-12
Odell, 1046 F-11
Odin, 1076 O-9
Ogden, 810 I-12
OGLE CO., 53497 B-8
Oglesby, 3791 E-9
Okawville, 1434 O-8
Olive Branch, 864 T-8
Olney, 9115 N-12
Olympia Fields, 4988 *N-9
Onarga, 1368 G-12
Oquawka, 1371 F-4
Orangeville, 793 A-8
Oreana, 875 J-10
Oregon, 3721 C-9
Orion, 1861 E-6
Orland Hills, 7149 *M-7
Orland Pk., 56767 D-12
Oswego, 30355 D-11
Ottawa, 18768 E-10
Palatine, 68557 B-12
Palestine, 1369 M-13
Palos Hts., 12515 *L-8
Palos Hills, 17484 *K-7
Palos Pk., 4847 *K-7
Pana, 5847 L-9
Paris, 8837 K-13
Park City, 7570 *A-7
Park Forest, 21975 D-13
Park Ridge, 37480 *F-7
Paw Paw, 870 D-9
Pawnee, 2739 K-8
Paxton, 4473 H-12
Payson, 1026 J-3
Pearl City, 838 B-7
Pecatonica, 2195 A-8
Pekin, 34094 H-8
Peoria, 115007 G-8
PEORIA CO., 186494 G-7
Peoria Hts., 6156 G-8
Peotone, 4142 E-13
Percy, 970 Q-8
PERRY CO., 22350 P-8
Peru, 10295 E-9
Petersburg, 2260 J-7
Philo, 1466 J-12
Phoenix, 1964 *L-9
PIATT CO., 16729 J-10
PIKE CO., 16430 K-4
Pinckneyville, 5648 Q-8
Pingree Grv., 4532 B-11
Piper City, 826 G-12
Pittsfield, 4576 K-4
Plainfield, 39581 D-12
Plano, 10856 D-11
Pleasant Hill, 966 L-4
Pleasant Plains, 802 J-7
Pocahontas, 784 N-8
Polo, 2355 C-8
Pontiac, 11931 G-10
Pontoon Bch., 5836 †G-8
POPE CO., 4470 S-11
Poplar Grv., 5023 A-10
Port Barrington, 1517 *C-3
Port Byron, 1647 D-6
Posen, 5987 *L-9
Potomac, 750 I-13
Prairie Grv., 1904 *C-3
Preston Hts., 2575 *N-4
Princeton, 7660 E-8
Princeville, 1738 F-7
Prophetstown, 2080 D-7
Prospect Hts., 16256 *E-6
PULASKI CO., 6161 T-9
PUTNAM CO., 6006 E-8
Quincy, 40633 J-3
Ramsey, 1037 M-9
RANDOLPH CO., 33476 Q-7
Rantoul, 12941 I-12
Rapids City, 959 D-6
Raymond, 1006 L-8
Red Bud, 3698 P-7
RICHLAND CO., 16233 N-12
Richmond, 1874 A-11
Richton Pk., 13646 *N-8
Ridge Farm, 882 J-13
Ridgway, 869 R-12
Ringwood, 836 A-11
River Forest, 11172 *H-7
River Grv., 10227 *H-7
Riverdale, 13549 *L-9
Riverside, 8875 *I-7
Riverton, 3455 J-8
Riverwoods, 3660 *D-7
Roanoke, 2065 G-9
Robbins, 5337 *L-9
Robinson, 7713 M-13
Rochelle, 9574 C-9
Rochester, 3689 K-8
Rock Falls, 9266 C-8
Rock Island, 39018 D-5
ROCK ISLAND CO., 147546 E-4
Rockdale, 1976 *N-4
Rockford, 152871 B-9
Rockton, 7685 A-9
Rolling Meadows, 24099 *E-5
Rome, 1738 G-8
Romeoville, 39680 D-12
Roodhouse, 1814 L-6
Roscoe, 10785 A-9
Roselle, 22763 C-12
Rosemont, 4202 *G-7
Roseville, 989 G-5
Rosewood Hts., 4038 †D-8
Rosiclare, 1160 S-11
Rossville, 1331 H-13
Round Lake, 18289 *A-4
Round Lake Bch., 28175 *A-4
Round Lake Hts., 2676 *A-4
Round Lake Pk., 7505 *A-4
Roxana, 1542 N-6
Royalton, 1151 Q-9
Rushville, 3192 I-5
St. Anne, 1257 F-13
St. Charles, 32974 C-11
ST. CLAIR CO., 270056 O-7
St. Elmo, 1426 M-10
St. Jacob, 1098 N-7
St. Joseph, 3967 I-12
Salem, 7485 O-10
SALINE CO., 24913 R-11
Sandoval, 1274 O-9
Sandwich, 7421 D-10
SANGAMON CO., 197465 K-7
Sauk Vil., 10506 *N-10
Savanna, 3062 B-6
Savoy, 7280 J-11
Schaumburg, 74227 B-12
Schiller Pk., 11793 *G-7
SCHUYLER CO., 7544 I-5
SCOTT CO., 5355 K-5
Seneca, 2371 E-10
Sesser, 1931 Q-9
Shabbona, 925 C-10
Shannon, 757 B-7
Shawneetown, 1239 R-12
Sheffield, 926 E-7
SHELBY CO., 22363 K-10
Shelbyville, 4700 L-10
Sheldon, 1070 G-13
Sheridan, 2137 D-10
Sherman, 4148 J-8
Shiloh, 12651 †I-10
Shorewood, 15615 D-12
Sidney, 1233 J-12
Silver Lake, 800 *C-3
Silvis, 7479 S-5
Skokie, 64784 B-13
Sleepy Hollow, 3304 *E-2
Smithton, 3693 O-7
Somonauk, 1893 D-10
S. Barrington, 4565 *E-4
S. Beloit, 7892 A-9
S. Chicago Hts., 4139 *N-9
S. Elgin, 21985 *G-2
S. Holland, 22030 *M-10
S. Jacksonville, 3331 K-6
S. Pekin, 1146 H-8
S. Roxana, 2053 †E-8
Southern View, 1642 *M-16
Sparta, 4302 P-7
Spaulding, 873 J-8
Spring Grv., 5778 A-11
Spring Valley, 5558 E-9
Springfield, 116250 J-8
STARK CO., 5994 F-7
State Park Pl., 2600 †H-9
Staunton, 5139 M-7
Steeleville, 2083 Q-8
Steger, 9570 D-13
STEPHENSON CO., 47711 A-8
Sterling, 15370 C-8
Stickney, 6786 *I-8
Stillman Valley, 1120 B-9
Stockton, 1862 A-7
Stone Pk., 4946 *H-7
Stonington, 932 K-9
Streamwood, 39858 *F-3
Streator, 13710 F-10
Stronghurst, 883 G-4
Sugar Grv., 8997 C-11
Sullivan, 4440 K-10
Summit, 11054 *J-7
Sumner, 3174 N-13
Swansea, 13430 O-7
Sycamore, 17519 C-10
Tampico, 790 D-7
Taylorville, 11246 K-9
TAZEWELL CO., 135394 H-8
Teutopolis, 1530 M-11
Third Lake, 1182 *A-5
Thomasboro, 1126 I-12
Thornton, 2338 *M-10
Tilden, 934 P-7
Tilton, 2724 I-13
Timberlane, 934 A-10
Tinley Pk., 56703 D-13
Tiskilwa, 829 E-8
Toledo, 1238 L-12
Tolono, 3447 J-11
Toluca, 1414 F-9
Tonica, 768 E-9
Toulon, 1292 F-7
Tower Lake, 1283 *C-4
Tremont, 2236 H-8
Trenton, 2715 O-8
Troy, 9888 N-7
Tuscola, 4480 J-11
UNION CO., 17808 S-9
University Pk., 7129 E-13
Urbana, 41250 I-12
Utica, 1352 E-9
Valley View, 2100 *G-2
Valmeyer, 1263 P-6
Vandalia, 7042 M-9
Venice, 1890 †H-7
VERMILION CO., 81625 J-13
Vernon Hills, 25113 *C-6
Vienna, 1434 S-10
Villa Grv., 2537 J-12
Villa Hills, 1410 †J-8
Villa Pk., 21904 *H-5
Viola, 955 E-5
Virden, 3425 L-7
Virginia, 1611 J-6
Volo, 2929 A-12
WABASH CO., 11947 O-13
Wadsworth, 3815 A-12
Walnut, 1416 D-8
Wamac, 1185 O-9
Warren, 1428 A-7
WARREN CO., 17707 G-5
Warrensburg, 1210 J-9
Warrenville, 13140 *I-3
Warsaw, 1607 H-3
Washburn, 1155 F-9
Washington, 15134 G-8
WASHINGTON CO., 14716 P-8
Washington Pk., 4196 †H-8
Wataga, 843 F-6
Waterloo, 9811 P-6
Waterman, 1506 C-10
Watseka, 5255 G-13
Watson, 754 M-11
Wauconda, 13603 B-12
Waukegan, 89078 A-12
Waverly, 1307 K-7
Wayne, 2431 *G-3
Wayne City, 1032 P-11
WAYNE CO., 16760 O-11
Wenona, 1056 F-9
W. Chicago, 27086 *H-3
W. Dundee, 7331 *E-2
W. Frankfort, 8182 Q-10
W. Peoria, 4458 *I-15
W. Salem, 897 O-12
Westchester, 16718 *I-7
Western Sprs., 12975 *I-6
Westmont, 24685 *J-5
Westville, 3202 J-13
Wheaton, 52894 C-12
Wheeling, 37648 *E-6
WHITE CO., 14665 P-11
White Hall, 2520 L-6
WHITESIDE CO., 58498 C-7
WILL CO., 677560 E-12
WILLIAMSON CO., 66357 R-10
Williamsville, 1476 J-8
Willow Sprs., 5524 *J-7
Willowbrook, 8540 *J-6
Wilmette, 27087 B-13
Wilmington, 5724 E-12
Winchester, 1593 K-5
Windsor, 1187 L-11
Winfield, 9080 *H-4
Winnebago, 3101 B-9
WINNEBAGO CO., 295266 A-9
Winnetka, 12187 B-13
Winthrop Hbr., 6742 A-13
Witt, 903 L-8
Wonder Lake, 4026 A-11
Wood Dale, 13770 *G-6
Wood River, 10657 N-6
WOODFORD CO., 38664 G-9
Woodhull, 811 F-6
Woodridge, 32971 *J-5
Woodstock, 24770 A-11
Worden, 1044 N-7
Worth, 10789 *K-8
Wyanet, 991 E-8
Wyoming, 1429 F-7
Yorkville, 16921 D-11
Zeigler, 1801 Q-9
Zion, 24413 A-13

Indiana

Map pp. 36 – 37

* City keyed to p. 35

ADAMS CO., 34387 E-13
Akron, 1167 D-9
Albany, 2165 H-12
Albion, 2349 B-11
Alexandria, 5145 H-10
ALLEN CO., 355329 D-12
Anderson, 56129 I-10
Andrews, 1149 E-11
Angola, 8612 A-13
Arcadia, 1666 H-9
Ardmore, 2200 *I-18
Argos, 1691 C-8
Ashley, 983 B-13
Atlanta, 725 H-9
Attica, 3245 H-5
Auburn, 12731 C-13
Aurora, 3750 N-13
Austin, 4295 O-10
Avilla, 2401 C-12
Avon, 12446 J-8
Bainbridge, 746 J-6
Barbee, 900 C-10
Bargersville, 4013 L-9
BARTHOLOMEW CO., 76794 M-9
Bass Lake, 1195 C-7
Batesville, 6520 M-12
Battle Ground, 1334 G-6
Bedford, 13413 O-7
Beech Grove, 14192 K-9
BENTON CO., 8854 F-4
Berne, 3999 F-13
Bicknell, 2915 O-4
BLACKFORD CO., 12766 G-12
Bloomfield, 2405 N-6
Bloomington, 80405 M-7
Bluffton, 9897 F-12
BOONE CO., 56640 I-8
Boonville, 6246 S-4
Borden, 808 Q-9
Boswell, 778 G-4
Bourbon, 1810 C-9
Brazil, 7912 L-5
Bremen, 4588 B-9
Bright, 5693 M-14
Bristol, 1602 A-10
Brook, 997 E-4
Brooklyn, 1598 L-8
Brookston, 1554 F-6
Brookville, 2596 L-13
BROWN CO., 15242 M-8
Brownsburg, 21285 J-8
Brownstown, 2947 O-9
Buffalo, 692 E-6
Bunker Hill, 888 F-9
Burlington Bch., 900 B-5
Burns Harbor, 1156 A-5
Butler, 2684 B-13
Cambridge City, 1870 J-12
Cannelton, 1563 T-6
Carlisle, 692 N-4
Carmel, 79191 I-9
CARROLL CO., 20155 G-7
Carthage, 927 K-11
CASS CO., 38966 F-8
Cayuga, 1162 J-4
Cedar Lake, 11560 C-4
Centerville, 2552 J-13
Chandler, 2887 S-4
Charlestown, 7585 Q-11
Chesterfield, 2547 I-11
Chesterton, 13068 A-5
Churubusco, 1796 C-12
Cicero, 4812 I-9
CLARK CO., 110232 Q-10
Clarksville, 21724 R-10
Clay City, 861 M-5
CLAY CO., 26890 L-5
Clayton, 972 K-7
Clear Creek, 1200 N-7
Clermont, 1356 J-8
Clinton, 4893 K-4
CLINTON CO., 33224 H-7
Cloverdale, 2172 L-6
Colfax, 691 H-7
Columbia City, 8750 D-11
Columbus, 44061 M-10
Connersville, 13481 K-12
Converse, 1265 F-10
Corydon, 3122 R-9
Country Vil., 1100 H-11
Covington, 2645 I-4
CRAWFORD CO., 10713 Q-7
Crawfordsville, 15915 I-6
Crothersville, 1591 O-10
Crown Pt., 27317 B-4
Culver, 1353 C-8
Cumberland, 5169 J-9
Dale, 1593 R-5
Daleville, 1647 I-11
Danville, 9001 J-7
Darlington, 843 I-6
Darmstadt, 1407 S-3
DAVIESS CO., 31648 O-5
Dayton, 1420 G-6
DE KALB CO., 42223 B-13
DEARBORN CO., 50047 M-13
Decatur, 9405 E-13
DECATUR CO., 25740 M-11
DELAWARE CO., 117671 H-11
Delphi, 2893 F-7
DeMotte, 3814 C-5
Dillsboro, 1327 N-13
Dublin, 790 J-12
DUBOIS CO., 41889 Q-6
Dugger, 920 N-4
Dunkirk, 2362 G-12
Dunlap, 6235 A-10
Dyer, 16390 B-4
E. Chicago, 29698 A-4
Eaton, 1805 H-12
Edgewood, 1913 I-10
Edinburgh, 4480 L-9
Elkhart, 50949 A-9
ELKHART CO., 197559 B-9
Ellettsville, 6378 M-7
Elwood, 8614 H-10
English, 645 Q-7
Evansville, 117429 S-3
Fairmount, 2954 G-11
Fairview Pk., 1386 K-4
Farmersburg, 1118 M-4
Farmland, 1333 H-13
FAYETTE CO., 24277 K-12
Ferdinand, 2157 R-6
Fish Lake, 1016 B-7
Fishers, 76794 J-9
Flora, 2036 G-7
FLOYD CO., 74578 Q-9
Floyds Knobs, 800 Q-10
Ft. Branch, 2771 R-3
Ft. Wayne, 253691 D-12
Fortville, 3929 J-10
Fountain City, 796 J-13
FOUNTAIN CO., 17240 I-4
Fowler, 2317 F-4
Francesville, 879 E-6
Frankfort, 16422 H-7
Franklin, 23712 L-9
FRANKLIN CO., 23087 L-13
Frankton, 1862 H-10
Fremont, 2138 A-13
French Lick, 1807 P-7
FULTON CO., 20836 D-8
Galena, 1818 Q-10
Galveston, 1311 F-9
Garden Vil., 4000 A-10
Garrett, 6286 C-12
Gary, 80294 B-4
Gas City, 5965 G-11
Gaston, 871 H-11
Geneva, 1293 F-13
Georgetown, 2876 R-9
GIBSON CO., 33503 R-3
Goodland, 1043 F-4
Goshen, 31719 B-10
Gosport, 826 L-7
Grabill, 1053 C-13
Grandview, 749 S-5
Granger, 30465 A-9
GRANT CO., 70061 G-10
Greencastle, 10326 K-6
Greendale, 4520 N-14
GREENE CO., 33165 N-6
Greenfield, 20602 J-10
Greensburg, 11492 M-11
Greentown, 2415 G-9
Greenwood, 49791 K-9
Griffith, 16893 B-4
Hagerstown, 1787 J-12
Hamilton, 1532 B-13
HAMILTON CO., 274569 I-9
Hamlet, 800 C-7
Hammond, 80830 A-4
HANCOCK CO., 70002 J-10
Hanover, 3546 P-11
Harlan, 1634 C-13
HARRISON CO., 39364 R-9
Harrodsburg, 691 N-7
Hartford City, 6220 G-12
Hatfield, 813 T-5
Haubstadt, 1577 R-3
Hebron, 3724 C-5
HENDRICKS CO., 145448 K-7
HENRY CO., 49462 J-11
Henryville, 1905 P-10
Heritage Lake, 2880 K-7
Highland, 4489 S-12
Hoagland, 821 E-13
Home Place, 1300 J-9
Hope, 2102 M-10
HOWARD CO., 82752 G-8
Howe, 807 A-11
Hudson Lake, 1297 A-7
Huntertown, 4810 C-12
Huntingburg, 6057 R-6
Huntington, 17391 E-11
HUNTINGTON CO., 37124 E-11
Hymera, 801 M-4
Indian Hts., 3011 G-9
Indianapolis, 820445 J-9
Ingalls, 2394 J-10
JACKSON CO., 42376 O-9
Jamestown, 958 J-7
Jasonville, 2222 M-5
Jasper, 15038 Q-6
JASPER CO., 33478 D-5
JAY CO., 21253 G-13
JEFFERSON CO., 32428 O-11
Jeffersonville, 44953 R-10
JENNINGS CO., 28525 N-10
Jewell Vil., 700 M-10
JOHNSON CO., 139654 L-9
Jonesboro, 1756 G-11
Kendallville, 9862 B-12
Kentland, 1748 F-4
Kingsford Hts., 1435 B-7
Kirklin, 788 H-8
Knightstown, 2182 J-11
Knightsville, 872 L-5
Knox, 3704 C-7
KNOX CO., 38440 P-4
Kokomo, 45468 G-9
Koontz Lake, 1557 B-7
KOSCIUSKO CO., 77358 C-10
Kouts, 1879 C-5
La Fontaine, 875 F-10
La Porte, 22053 A-7
Ladoga, 985 J-6
Lafayette, 67140 G-6
Lagrange, 2625 A-11
LAGRANGE CO., 37128 B-11
LAKE CO., 496005 C-4
L. Dalecarlia, 1355 C-4
L. Holiday, 750 I-6
L. James, 800 A-13
Lake of the Woods, 700 B-8
Lake Village, 765 D-4
Lakes of the Four Seasons, 7033 B-5
Lakeville, 786 B-8
Lapel, 2068 I-10
LAPORTE CO., 111467 B-7
Lawrence, 46001 J-9
LAWRENCE CO., 46134 O-8
Lawrenceburg, 5042 N-14
Lebanon, 15792 I-7
Leo-Cedarville, 3603 C-13
Liberty, 2133 K-13
Ligonier, 4405 B-11
Linden, 759 H-6
Linton, 5413 N-5
Logansport, 18396 F-8
Long Bch., 1179 A-6
Loogootee, 2751 P-6
Lowell, 9276 C-4
Lydick, 800 A-8
Lynn, 1097 I-13
Lynnville, 888 R-4
Lyons, 742 N-5
Madison, 11967 O-12
MADISON CO., 131636 H-10
Marengo, 828 Q-8
Marion, 29948 G-11
MARION CO., 903393 J-9
Markle, 1095 E-12
MARSHALL CO., 47051 C-8
MARTIN CO., 10334 P-6
Martinsville, 11828 L-8
Maryland, 800 M-2
McCordsville, 4797 J-10
Medora, 693 O-9
Melody Hill, 3628 S-13
Mentone, 1001 D-9
Meridian Hills, 1616 *B-18
Merrillville, 35246 B-4
Mexico, 836 E-9
MIAMI CO., 36903 F-9
Michigan City, 31479 A-6
Middlebury, 3420 A-10
Middletown, 2322 I-11
Middletown Pk., 850 J-1
Milan, 1899 N-13
Milford, 1562 B-10
Millersburg, 903 B-10
Milltown, 818 Q-8
Mishawaka, 48252 A-9
Mitchell, 4350 P-7
Monon, 1777 E-6
Monroe, 842 F-13
MONROE CO., 137974 M-7
Monroeville, 1235 E-13
Monrovia, 1063 K-7
Montezuma, 1022 J-4
MONTGOMERY CO., 38124
Monticello, 5378
Montpelier, 1805
Mooresville, 9326
MORGAN CO., 68894
Morgantown, 986
Morocco, 1129
Morristown, 1218
Mt. Vernon, 6687
Mulberry, 1254
Muncie, 70085
Munster, 23603
Nappanee, 6648
Nashville, 803
New Albany, 36372
New Carlisle, 1861
New Castle, 18114
New Harmony, 789
New Haven, 14794
New Palestine, 2055
New Paris, 1494
New Pekin, 1401
New Whiteland, 5472
Newburgh, 3325
Newport, 515
NEWTON CO., 14244
NOBLE CO., 47536
Noblesville, 51969
N. Judson, 1772
N. Liberty, 1896
N. Manchester, 6112
N. Terre Haute, 4305
N. Vernon, 6728
N. Webster, 1146
Notre Dame, 5973
Oakland City, 2429
Odon, 1354
OHIO CO., 6128
Oolitic, 1184
ORANGE CO., 19840
Orleans, 2142
Osceola, 2463
Osgood, 1624
Ossian, 3289
Otterbein, 1262
OWEN CO., 21575
Owensville, 1284
Oxford, 1162
Palmyra, 930
Paoli, 3677
PARKE CO., 17339
Parker City, 1419
Patoka, 735
Pendleton, 4253
Pennville, 701
PERRY CO., 19338
Peru, 11417
Petersburg, 2383
Pheasant Run, 1200
Pierceton, 1015
PIKE CO., 12845
Pine Lake, 1700
Pittsboro, 2928
Plainfield, 27631
Plymouth, 10033
Portage, 36828
Porter, 4858
PORTER CO., 164343
Portland, 6223
POSEY CO., 25910
Poseyville, 1045
Princes Lakes, 1312
Princeton, 8644
PULASKI CO., 13402
PUTNAM CO., 37963
RANDOLPH CO., 26171
Redkey, 1353
Remington, 1185
Rensselaer, 5859
Richmond, 36812
Ridgeville, 803
RIPLEY CO., 28818
Rising Sun, 2304
Roachdale, 926
Roanoke, 1722
Rochester, 6218
Rockport, 2270
Rockville, 2607
Rome City, 1361
Rosedale, 725
Roselawn, 4131
Ross, 1100
Rossville, 1653
Royal Ctr., 861
Royerton, 900
RUSH CO., 17392
Rushville, 6341
Russiaville, 1094
St. John, 14850
ST. JOSEPH CO., 266931
St. Leon, 678
St. Mary-of-the-Woods, 797
St. Meinrad, 706
St. Paul, 1031
Salem, 6319
Santa Claus, 2481
Schererville, 29243
SCOTT CO., 24181
Scottsburg, 6747
Seelyville, 1029
Sellersburg, 6128
Selma, 866
Seymour, 17503
Shadeland, 1610
Shelburn, 1252
SHELBY CO., 44436
Shelbyville, 19191
Sheridan, 2665
Shirley, 830
Shoals, 756
Silver Lake, 915
Simonton Lake, 4678
Smith Valley, 1800
S. Bend, 101168
S. Whitley, 1751
Southport, 1712
Speedway, 11812
Spencer, 2217
SPENCER CO., 20952
Spiceland, 890
STARKE CO., 23363
STEUBEN CO., 34185
Sullivan, 4249
SULLIVAN CO., 21475
Summitville, 967
Sunman, 1049
Swayzee, 981
Sweetser, 1229
SWITZERLAND CO., 10613
Syracuse, 2810
Taylorsville, 919
Tell City, 7272
Terre Haute, 60785
Thorntown, 1520
TIPPECANOE CO., 172780
Tipton, 5106
TIPTON CO., 15936
Topeka, 1153
Town of Pines, 708
Trafalgar, 1101
Trail Creek, 2052
Tri-Lakes, 1421
Union City, 3584
UNION CO., 7516
Upland, 3845
Utica, 776
Valparaiso, 31730
Van Buren, 864
Van Buren Pk., 700
VANDERBURGH CO., 179703
Veedersburg, 2180
VERMILLION CO., 16212
Vernon, 318
Versailles, 2113
Vevay, 1683
VIGO CO., 107848
Vincennes, 18423
Wabash, 10666
WABASH CO., 32888
Wakarusa, 1758
Waldron, 804
Walkerton, 2144
Walton, 1049
Wanatah, 1048
Warren, 1239
WARREN CO., 8508
Warren Pk., 1480
WARRICK CO., 59689
Warsaw, 13559
Washington, 11509
WASHINGTON CO., 28262
Waterloo, 2242
WAYNE CO., 68917
Waynetown, 958
WELLS CO., 27636
W. College Cor., 676
W. Lafayette, 29596
W. Lebanon, 723
W. Terre Haute, 2236
Westfield, 30068
Westlawn, 700
Westport, 1379
Westville, 5853
Wheatfield, 853
WHITE CO., 24643

lland, 4169 I-9
stown, 2867 I-8
LEY CO., 33292 D-11
nsport, 1898 H-4
mac, 2490 D-7
ester, 4935 H-13
all, 708 H-9
ld, 4383 B-5
a Lake, 4908 C-10
w, 864 Q-5
rt, 1000 F-5
ntville, 998 B-12
burn, 1520 H-12
ington, 1463 N-6
wn, 9405 H-11
ville, 14160 I-8

Iowa

Map pp. 38 – 39

keyed to p. 63

1589 E-11
CO., 7682 J-7
CO., 4029 L-6
3682 I-8
845 E-8
1466 K-11
3766 K-12
MAKEE CO.,
30 B-16
1029 D-12
823 B-5
1216 C-3
a, 14541 I-10
58965 G-10
sa, 5533 G-16
972 I-6
y, 45582 H-10
ton, 1128 E-12
IOOSE CO.,
37 M-11
ong, 926 B-7
s Pk., 1126 B-5
4170 E-18
1670 G-15
c, 7112 J-5
on, 2176 H-6
BON CO., 6119 I-6
1036 E-4
1506 I-4
1101 H-11
d, 1440 M-6
laine, 2534 H-13
e, 2191 F-19
d, 2376 D-10
N CO., 26076 G-14
dorf, 33217 I-19
HAWK CO.,
90 F-13
ield, 2640 L-13
rass, 1452 I-18
rant, 3860 I-10
12661 G-9
E CO., 26306 H-9
ER CO., 24276 D-13
069 C-9
n, 1468 H-13
NAN CO.,
8 E-15
VISTA CO.,
0 E-5
1270 I-18
Ctr., 905 B-9
ton, 25663 L-17
R CO., 14867 E-12
UN CO., 9670 F-6
978 C-15
che, 4448 H-19
dge, 827 H-10
Hts., 900 B-20
3876 I-10
10103 G-6
LL CO., 20816 G-6
812 J-4
Lake, 3785 †B-19
e, 2159 F-17
CO., 13956 J-6
CO., 18499 H-17
Falls, 39260 E-13
Rapids, 126326 G-15
Pt., 2421 G-15
ville, 5528 L-12
City, 1257 G-16
GORDO CO.,
1 C-11
n, 4321 K-10
City, 7652 C-12
ee, 5253 D-4
KEE CO., 12072 E-3
ASAW CO.,
9 C-13
e, 974 H-17
a, 5572 L-5
2850 E-9
E CO., 9286 L-9
ille, 1439 D-12
CO., 16667 C-5
ON CO., 18129 D-15
ake, 7777 C-10
26885 H-20
N CO., 49116 H-19
5447 I-9
2093 I-11
76 G-10
us Jct., 1899 J-16
1108 G-12
apids, 1305 H-6
le, 18907 I-15
1635 K-6
ionville, 821 E-3
n, 1585 L-10
Bluffs, 62230 J-3
ORD CO.,
6 G-5
3868 B-14
7834 K-7
City, 843 E-8
Ctr., 1623 I-9
S CO., 66135 I-8
e, 934 L-16
ort, 99685 I-18
CO., 8753 L-13
837 F-8
1050 I-8
5322 H-19
UR CO., 8457 M-9
n, 8127 B-15
ARE CO.,
4 F-16
n, 8298 G-4
1780 E-13
ines, 203433 I-10
OINES CO.,
5 L-16
SON CO.,
7 B-5
209 F-12
son, 912 M-16
e, 57637 E-18
UE CO.,
3 F-17
on, 852 E-14
1042 H-4
1832 I-17
lle, 4058 E-17
1379 G-13
rv., 3583 E-9
1450 I-8
812 E-16
e, 1024 K-12
od, 864 E-16
27 L-14
2732 F-11
5651 I-18
Hts., 1117 F-13
1273 D-16
6 H-15
CO., 10302 B-6
burg, 3904 C-7
1860 F-17
lle, 6360 B-6
ale, 4751 F-13
40 I-6
1113 E-14
2123 H-15
9464 K-14
537 F-17
1338 D-15
E CO., 20880 D-14
CO., 16303 C-12
ity, 4151 B-9
ge, 25206 E-8
ison, 11051 M-16
LIN CO.,
0 E-10
ksburg, 931 D-14
NT CO., 7441 L-4
d, 977 J-17
3129 C-10
1080 B-3
1082 G-9
ok, 945 G-12
od, 5269 K-3
1146 G-6
1037 F-8
ger, 844 C-6
ct., 824 G-8
1244 H-9
1130 D-12
E CO., 9336 H-7
eld, 1982 J-7
8246 I-9

Grinnell, 9218 H-12
Griswold, 1036 J-5
Grundy Ctr., 2706 F-12
GRUNDY CO., 12453 F-12
Guthrie Ctr., 1569 I-7
GUTHRIE CO., 10954 I-6
Guttenberg, 1919 D-17
Hamburg, 1187 M-3
HAMILTON CO., 15673 F-9
Hampton, 4461 E-11
HANCOCK CO., 11341 C-9
HARDIN CO., 17534 F-11
Harlan, 5106 I-5
HARRISON CO.,
14928 H-3
Hartley, 1672 C-4
Hawarden, 2546 C-1
Hazleton, 823 E-14
HENRY CO., 20145 K-16
Hiawatha, 7024 G-15
Hinton, 928 E-2
Holstein, 1396 E-4
HOWARD CO., 9566 B-13
Hubbard, 845 F-10
Hudson, 2282 F-13
Hull, 2175 C-2
Humboldt, 4690 E-8
HUMBOLDT CO., 9815 D-8
Huxley, 3317 H-10
IDA CO., 7089 F-4
Ida Grv., 2142 F-4
Independence, 5966 F-15
Indianola, 14782 I-10
Inwood, 814 B-2
Iowa City, 67862 I-16
IOWA CO., 16355 I-14
Iowa Falls, 5238 E-11
JACKSON CO., 19848 F-18
Janesville, 930 E-13
JASPER CO., 36842 H-11
Jefferson, 4345 G-7
JEFFERSON CO.,
16843 L-14
Jesup, 2520 F-14
Jewell, 1215 F-9
JOHNSON CO.,
130882 I-15
Johnston, 17278 I-9
JONES CO., 20638 G-17
Kalona, 2363 I-15
Keokuk, 10780 N-16
KEOKUK CO., 10511 J-14
Keosauqua, 1006 L-14
Keota, 1009 J-14
Kingsley, 1411 E-3
Knoxville, 7313 J-11
KOSSUTH CO., 15543 C-8
La Porte City, 2285 F-14
Lake City, 1727 F-6
L. Mills, 2100 B-10
Lake Pk., 1105 B-5
L. View, 1142 F-5
Lamoni, 2324 M-9
Lansing, 999 B-16
Larchwood, 866 B-2
Laurens, 1258 D-6
Lawton, 908 E-2
Le Claire, 3765 I-19
Le Grand, 938 G-12
Le Mars, 9826 D-2
LEE CO., 35862 L-16
Lenox, 1407 L-7
Leon, 1977 L-9
LINN CO., 211226 F-16
Lisbon, 2152 H-16
Logan, 1534 I-3
Lone Tree, 1300 I-16
Long Grv., 808 H-18
LOUISA CO., 11387 K-16
LUCAS CO., 8898 K-10
LYON CO., 11581 B-2
MADISON CO., 15679 J-9
Madrid, 2543 H-9
MAHASKA CO.,
22381 J-12
Malvern, 1142 K-4
Manchester, 5179 E-16
Manly, 1323 B-11
Manning, 1500 H-5
Manson, 1690 E-7
Mapleton, 1224 G-3
Maquoketa, 6141 G-18
Marcus, 1117 D-3
Marengo, 2528 H-14
Marion, 34768 G-15
MARION CO., 33309 J-11
MARSHALL CO.,
40648 H-11
Marshalltown, 27552 G-12
Mason City, 28079 C-11
Maxwell, 920 H-10
McGregor, 871 C-17
Mechanicsville, 1146 H-16
Mediapolis, 1560 K-17
Melbourne, 830 H-11
Melcher-Dallas, 1288 J-11
Milford, 2898 B-5
MILLS CO., 15059 K-4
Missouri Valley, 2838 I-3
MITCHELL CO.,
10776 B-12
Mitchellville, 2254 I-10
Monona, 1549 C-16
MONONA CO., 9243 G-3
Monroe, 1830 I-11
MONROE CO., 7970 K-12
Montezuma, 1462 I-13
MONTGOMERY CO.,
10740 K-5
Monticello, 3796 F-17
Montrose, 898 M-16
Morning Sun, 836 K-17
Mt. Ayr, 1691 L-8
Mt. Pleasant, 8668 K-16
Mt. Vernon, 4506 H-16
Moville, 1618 E-2
Muscatine, 22886 J-17
MUSCATINE CO.,
42745 I-17
Nashua, 1663 D-13
Neola, 842 I-4
Nevada, 6798 G-10
New Hampton, 3571 C-13
New London, 1897 L-16
New Sharon, 1293 I-12
Newell, 876 E-6
Newhall, 875 G-14
Newton, 15254 I-11
Nora Sprs., 1431 C-11
N. English, 1041 I-14
N. Liberty, 13374 H-15
Northwood, 1989 B-11
Norwalk, 8945 I-9
Norwoodville, 1200 B-20
O'BRIEN CO., 14398 C-3
Oakland, 1527 J-4
Odebolt, 1013 F-5
Oelwein, 6415 E-14
Ogden, 2044 G-8
Okoboji, 807 B-5
Onawa, 2998 G-2
Orange City, 6004 C-3
Osage, 3619 B-12
Osceola, 4929 K-9
OSCEOLA CO., 6462 B-4
Oskaloosa, 11463 J-12
Ossian, 845 C-15
Ottumwa, 25023 K-13
Oxford, 807 H-15
PAGE CO., 15932 L-5
Palo, 1026 G-15
PALO ALTO CO., 9421 D-7
Panora, 1124 I-7
Park View, 2389 H-19
Parkersburg, 1870 E-12
Paullina, 1056 D-4
Pella, 10352 J-12
Peosta, 1377 F-18
Perry, 7702 H-8
Pleasant Hill, 8785 I-10
Pleasantville, 1694 J-11
PLYMOUTH CO., 24986 E-2
Pocahontas, 1789 E-6
POCAHONTAS CO.,
7310 E-6
Polk City, 3418 H-9
POLK CO., 430640 H-10
Postville, 2227 C-15
POTTAWATTAMIE CO.,
93158 J-4
POWESHIEK CO.,
18914 H-13
Prairie City, 1680 I-11
Preston, 1012 G-19
Primghar, 909 C-4
Princeton, 886 I-19
Readlyn, 808 E-14
Red Oak, 5742 K-5
Redfield, 835 I-8
Reinbeck, 1664 F-13
Remsen, 1663 D-3
RINGGOLD CO., 5131 L-7
Riverside, 993 I-16
Robins, 3142 G-15
Rock Rapids, 2549 B-2
Rock Valley, 3354 C-2
Rockford, 860 C-11
Rockwell, 1039 D-11
Rockwell City, 1709 F-7
Roland, 1284 G-10
Sac City, 2220 F-6
SAC CO., 10350 F-5
St. Ansgar, 1107 B-12
Sanborn, 1404 C-4

Saydel, 3500 A-19
Saylorville, 3301 A-19
Schleswig, 882 G-4
SCOTT CO., 165224 H-19
Sergeant Bluff, 4227 F-2
Sheffield, 1172 D-11
SHELBY CO., 12167 I-4
Sheldon, 5188 C-3
Shell Rock, 1296 E-13
Shellsburg, 983 G-15
Shenandoah, 5150 L-4
Sibley, 2798 B-3
Sidney, 1138 L-3
Sigourney, 2059 J-14
Sioux Ctr., 7048 C-2
Sioux City, 82684 E-2
SIOUX CO., 33704 C-2
Slater, 1489 H-9
Sloan, 973 F-2
Solon, 2037 H-16
Spencer, 11233 C-5
Spirit Lake, 4840 B-5
Springville, 1074 G-16
State Ctr., 1468 G-11
Storm Lake, 10600 E-5
Story City, 3431 G-10
STORY CO., 89542 G-10
Strawberry Pt., 1279 E-16
Stuart, 1648 I-7
Sully, 821 I-12
Sumner, 2028 D-14
Swisher, 879 H-15
Tabor, 1040 L-3
Tama, 2877 H-13
TAMA CO., 17767 G-13
TAYLOR CO., 6317 M-6
Tiffin, 1947 I-15
Tipton, 3221 H-17
Toledo, 2341 G-13
Traer, 1703 G-13
Treynor, 919 J-4
Tripoli, 1313 D-13
Underwood, 917 J-3
UNION CO., 12534 K-7
University Hts., 1051 I-16
Urbana, 1458 G-15
Urbandale, 39463 I-9
VAN BUREN CO.,
7570 L-14
Van Meter, 1016 I-9
Victor, 893 H-13
Villisca, 1252 L-5
Vinton, 5257 G-14
Walcott, 1629 I-18
Walford, 1463 H-15
Wall Lake, 819 F-5
Wapello, 2067 K-17
WAPELLO CO., 35625 L-13
WARREN CO., 46225 J-10
Washburn, 876 F-13
Washington, 7266 J-15
WASHINGTON CO.,
21704 J-15
Waterloo, 68406 E-13
Waukee, 13790 I-9
Waukon, 3897 B-16
Waverly, 9874 E-13
Wayland, 966 K-15
WAYNE CO., 6403 M-10
Webster City, 8070 F-9
WEBSTER CO., 38013 F-8
Wellman, 1408 I-15
W. Branch, 2322 I-16
W. Burlington, 2968 L-17
W. Des Moines, 56609 I-9
W. Liberty, 3736 I-16
West Point, 966 L-16
W. Union, 2486 D-15
Williamsburg, 3068 I-14
Wilton, 2802 I-17
Windsor Hts., 4860 B-18
Winfield, 1134 K-16
WINNEBAGO CO.,
10866 B-9
WINNESHIEK CO.,
21056 B-14
Winterset, 5190 J-8
Winthrop, 850 F-15
Woodbine, 1459 H-3
WOODBURY CO.,
102172 F-3
Woodward, 1024 H-9
WORTH CO., 7598 B-11
WRIGHT CO., 13229 E-9

Kansas

Map pp. 40 – 41

* City keyed to p. 58

Abilene, 6844 E-13
ALLEN CO., 13371 H-17
Alma, 832 D-15
Altamont, 1080 J-18
Americus, 894 F-15
Andale, 928 H-12
ANDERSON CO.,
8102 G-17
Andover, 11791 H-13
Anthony, 2269 J-11
Arkansas City, 12415 J-13
Arma, 1481 I-19
Ashland, 867 J-7
Atchison, 11021 C-18
ATCHISON CO.,
16924 C-17
Atwood, 1194 B-4
Auburn, 1227 E-16
Augusta, 9274 H-13
Baldwin City, 4515 E-18
BARBER CO., 4861 J-9
BARTON CO., 27674 F-9
Basehor, 4613 D-18
Baxter Sprs., 4238 J-19
Bel Aire, 6769 H-13
Belle Plaine, 1681 I-13
Belleville, 1991 B-12
Beloit, 3835 C-11
Benton, 880 H-13
Blue Rapids, 1019 B-14
Bonner Sprs., 7314 D-18
BOURBON CO.,
15173 H-18
BROWN CO., 9984 B-17
Bucklin, 794 I-7
Buhler, 1327 G-12
Burlingame, 934 E-16
Burlington, 2674 G-16
Burrton, 901 G-12
BUTLER CO., 65880 H-14
Caldwell, 1068 J-12
Caney, 2203 J-16
Canton, 748 F-12
Carbondale, 1437 E-16
Chanute, 9119 H-17
Chapman, 1393 E-13
CHASE CO., 2790 G-14
CHAUTAUQUA CO.,
3669 J-15
Cheney, 2094 I-12
Cherokee, 714 I-19
CHEROKEE CO.,
21603 J-18
Cherryvale, 2367 J-17
Chetopa, 1125 J-18
CHEYENNE CO., 2726 B-2
Cimarron, 2184 H-5
CLARK CO., 2215 J-6
Clay Ctr., 4334 C-13
CLAY CO., 8535 D-13
Clearwater, 2481 I-12
CLOUD CO., 9533 C-11
Clyde, 716 C-12
COFFEY CO., 8601 G-16
Coffeyville, 10295 J-17
Colby, 5387 C-4
Coldwater, 828 J-8
Columbus, 3312 J-19
Colwich, 1327 H-12
COMANCHE CO., 1891 J-8
Concordia, 5395 C-12
Conway Sprs., 1272 I-12
Cottonwood Falls, 903 F-15
Council Grv., 2182 E-15
COWLEY CO., 36311 J-14
CRAWFORD CO.,
39134 I-18
De Soto, 5720 D-18
DECATUR CO., 2961 B-5
Deerfield, 700 H-3
Derby, 22158 I-13
DICKINSON CO.,
19754 E-13
Dighton, 1038 F-5
Dodge City, 27340 H-6
DONIPHAN CO., 7945 B-18
DOUGLAS CO.,
110826 E-17
Douglass, 1700 I-13
Downs, 900 C-10
Eastborough, 773 M-9
Edgerton, 1671 E-18
EDWARDS CO., 3037 H-8
Edwardsville, 4340 *I-1
El Dorado, 13021 H-14
ELK CO., 2882 I-15
Elkhart, 2205 J-2
Ellinwood, 2131 F-10
Ellis, 2062 E-7
ELLIS CO., 28452 D-8
Ellsworth, 3120 E-10
ELLSWORTH CO.,
6497 E-11
Elwood, 1224 B-18
Emporia, 24916 F-15
Enterprise, 855 E-13
Erie, 1150 I-18
Eudora, 6136 E-18
Eureka, 2633 H-15
Fairway, 3882 *J-3
FINNEY CO., 36776 G-5
FORD CO., 33848 I-6
Ft. Scott, 8087 H-19
Frankfort, 726 B-15
FRANKLIN CO.,
25992 F-17
Fredonia, 2482 I-16
Frontenac, 3437 I-19
Galena, 3085 J-19
Galva, 870 F-12
Garden City, 26658 H-4
Garden Plain, 849 I-12
Gardner, 19123 E-18
Garnett, 3415 G-18
GEARY CO., 34362 E-14
Girard, 2789 I-19
Goddard, 4344 I-12
Goodland, 4489 C-2
Gove, 80 E-5
GOVE CO., 2695 E-5
GRAHAM CO., 2597 D-6
Grandview Plaza, 1560 D-14
GRANT CO., 7829 I-3
GRAY CO., 6006 H-5
Great Bend, 15995 F-9
GREELEY CO., 1247 F-2
Greensburg, 777 I-8
Greenwich Hts., 960 M-10
GREENWOOD CO.,
6689 H-15
Halstead, 2085 H-12
HAMILTON CO., 2690 G-2
Harper, 1473 J-11
HARPER CO., 6034 J-11
HARVEY CO., 34684 G-12
HASKELL CO., 4256 I-4
Haven, 1237 H-12
Haviland, 701 I-8
Hays, 20510 E-8
Haysville, 10826 I-13
Herington, 2526 E-14
Hesston, 3709 G-12
Hiawatha, 3172 B-17
Highland, 1012 B-17
Hill City, 1474 C-7
Hillsboro, 2993 F-13
HODGEMAN CO.,
1916 G-6
Hoisington, 2706 F-9
Holcomb, 2094 H-4
Holton, 3329 C-16
Horton, 1776 B-17
Howard, 687 I-15
Hoxie, 1201 C-5
Hugoton, 3904 J-3
Humboldt, 1953 H-17
Hutchinson, 42080 G-11
Independence, 9483 J-17
Inman, 1377 G-12
Iola, 5704 H-17
JACKSON CO., 13462 C-16
JEFFERSON CO.,
19126 D-17
Jetmore, 867 G-6
JEWELL CO., 3077 B-11
Johnson, 1495 I-2
JOHNSON CO.,
544179 E-18
Junction City, 23353 D-14
Kansas City, 145786 D-19
KEARNY CO., 3977 G-3
Kingman, 3177 I-11
KINGMAN CO., 7858 I-11
Kinsley, 1457 H-8
Kiowa, 1026 K-10
KIOWA CO., 2553 I-8
La Crosse, 1342 F-8
La Cygne, 1149 F-19
LABETTE CO., 21607 J-18
L. Quivira, 906 *J-1
Lakin, 2216 H-3
LANE CO., 1750 F-5
Lansing, 11265 D-18
Larned, 4054 G-8
Lawrence, 87643 D-18
Leavenworth, 35251 C-18
LEAVENWORTH CO.,
76227 D-18
Leawood, 31867 D-19
Lebo, 940 F-16
Lenexa, 48190 D-19
Leon, 704 H-14
Leoti, 1534 F-3
Liberal, 20525 J-4
Lincoln, 1297 D-11
LINCOLN CO., 3241 D-11
Lindsborg, 3458 F-12
LINN CO., 9656 G-18
Linn Valley, 804 F-19
LOGAN CO., 2756 E-3
Louisburg, 4315 E-19
Lyndon, 1052 F-17
LYON CO., 33690 F-15
Lyons, 3739 G-11
Madison, 701 G-15
Maize, 3420 H-12
Manhattan, 52281 D-14
Mankato, 869 B-10
Marion, 1927 F-13
MARION CO., 12660 G-13
MARSHALL CO.,
10117 B-14
Marysville, 3294 B-14
McLouth, 880 D-18
McPherson, 13155 F-12
MCPHERSON CO.,
29180 F-11
Meade, 1721 J-5
MEADE CO., 4575 J-5
Medicine Lodge, 2009 J-10
Meriden, 813 D-17
Merriam, 11003 *J-2
MIAMI CO., 32787 F-18
Minneapolis, 2032 D-12
Minneola, 745 I-6
Mission, 9323 *J-3
Mission Hills, 3498 *J-3
MITCHELL CO., 6373 D-11
Montezuma, 966 I-5
MONTGOMERY CO.,
35471 I-16
MORRIS CO., 5923 F-14
MORTON CO., 3233 J-2
Mound City, 694 G-19
Moundridge, 1737 G-12
Mt. Hope, 813 H-12
Mulvane, 6111 I-13
NEMAHA CO., 10178 B-16
Neodesha, 2486 I-17
NEOSHO CO., 16512 I-17
Ness City, 1449 F-6
NESS CO., 3107 F-7
Newton, 19132 G-13
Nickerson, 1070 G-11
N. Newton, 1759 G-13
Norton, 2928 B-7
NORTON CO., 5671 B-6
Oaklawn, 3000 N-9
Oakley, 2045 D-4
Oberlin, 1788 B-5
Ogden, 2087 D-14
Olathe, 125872 E-19
Onaga, 702 C-15
Osage City, 2943 F-16
OSAGE CO., 16295 E-16
Osawatomie, 4447 F-18
Osborne, 1431 C-9
OSBORNE CO., 3858 C-9
Oskaloosa, 1113 D-17
Oswego, 1829 J-18
Ottawa, 12649 F-18
OTTAWA CO., 6091 D-12
Overbrook, 1058 E-17
Overland Pk., 173372 D-19
Oxford, 1049 J-13
Paola, 5602 F-18
Park City, 7297 H-13
Parsons, 10500 I-18
PAWNEE CO., 6973 G-7
Peabody, 1210 G-13
Perry, 929 D-17
PHILLIPS CO., 5642 B-8
Phillipsburg, 2581 B-8
Pittsburg, 20233 I-19
Plains, 1146 J-5
Plainville, 1903 D-8
Pleasanton, 1216 G-19
Pomona, 832 F-17
POTTAWATOMIE CO.,
21604 C-15
Prairie Vil., 21447 D-19
Pratt, 6835 I-9
PRATT CO., 9656 I-9
Quinter, 918 D-6
RAWLINS CO., 2519 B-4
RENO CO., 64511 H-11
REPUBLIC CO., 4980 B-12
RICE CO., 10083 F-10
Riley, 939 D-14
RILEY CO., 71115 C-14
Riverton, 929 J-19
Roeland Pk., 6731 *J-3
ROOKS CO., 5181 D-8
Rose Hill, 3931 I-13
Rossville, 1151 D-16
RUSH CO., 3307 F-8
Russell, 4506 E-9
RUSSELL CO., 6970 D-9
Sabetha, 2571 B-16
St. Francis, 1329 B-2
St. John, 1295 H-9
St. Marys, 2627 D-16
Salina, 47707 E-12
SALINE CO., 55606 E-11
Satanta, 1133 I-4
Scott City, 3816 F-4
SCOTT CO., 4936 F-4
Scranton, 710 E-16
Sedan, 1124 J-15
Sedgwick, 1695 H-12
SEDGWICK CO.,
498365 I-12
Seneca, 1991 B-16
SEWARD CO., 22952 J-4
Sharon Sprs., 748 E-2
Shawnee, 62209 D-19
SHAWNEE CO.,
177934 E-16
SHERIDAN CO., 2556 D-5
SHERMAN CO., 6010 C-2
Silver Lake, 1439 D-16
Smith Ctr., 1665 B-9
SMITH CO., 3853 B-9
Solomon, 1095 E-13
S. Hutchinson, 2457 G-11
Spearville, 773 H-7
Spring Hill, 5437 E-19
Stafford, 1042 H-10
STAFFORD CO., 4437 G-9
STANTON CO., 2235 H-1
Sterling, 2328 G-11
STEVENS CO., 5724 J-3
Stockton, 1329 C-8
Sublette, 1453 I-4
SUMNER CO., 24132 J-12
Syracuse, 1812 G-2
THOMAS CO., 7900 C-3
Tonganoxie, 4996 D-18
Topeka, 127473 D-16
Towanda, 1450 H-13
TREGO CO., 3001 E-6
Tribune, 741 F-2
Troy, 1010 B-18
Udall, 746 I-13
Ulysses, 6161 I-3
Valley Ctr., 6822 H-13
Valley Falls, 1192 C-17
Victoria, 1214 E-8
WABAUNSEE CO.,
7053 E-15
WaKeeney, 1862 D-7
Wakefield, 980 D-13
WALLACE CO., 1485 D-2
Wamego, 4372 D-15
Washington, 1131 B-13
WASHINGTON CO.,
5799 B-13
Wathena, 1364 B-18
Wellington, 8172 J-12
Wellsville, 1857 E-18
Westmoreland, 778 C-15
Westwood, 1506 *J-3
Whitewater, 718 H-13
Wichita, 382368 H-13
WICHITA CO., 2234 F-3
Wilson, 781 E-10
WILSON CO., 9409 I-16
Winfield, 12301 J-13
WOODSON CO.,
3309 H-16
WYANDOTTE CO.,
157505 D-19
Yates Ctr., 1417 H-16

Kentucky

Map pp. 42 – 43

† City keyed to p. 112

ADAIR CO., 18656 L-10
Adairville, 852 N-5
Airport Gdns., 700 K-17
Albany, 2033 M-10
Alexandria, 8477 D-13
ALLEN CO., 19956 M-7
Anchorage, 2348 B-10
ANDERSON CO.,
21421 H-11
Annville, 1095 K-14
Ashland, 21684 F-18
Auburn, 1340 M-5
Audubon Pk., 1473 C-7
Augusta, 1190 E-14
BALLARD CO., 8249 E-2
Barbourmeade, 1218 A-9
Barbourville, 3165 M-14
Bardstown, 11700 I-9
Bardwell, 723 F-2
BARREN CO., 42173 M-8
BATH CO., 11591 G-15
Baxter, 800 M-16
Beattyville, 1307 J-15
Beaver Dam, 3409 K-5
Bedford, 599 F-10
Beechwood Vil., 1324 B-8
BELL CO., 28691 M-15
Bellefonte, 888 †B-1
Bellemeade, 865 B-9
Bellevue, 5955 A-20
Benton, 4349 F-4
Berea, 13561 J-13
Bloomfield, 838 I-10
Blue Ridge Mnr., 767 B-9
BOONE CO., 118811 E-11
Booneville, 81 J-15
BOURBON CO.,
19985 H-13
Bowling Green, 58067 L-6
BOYD CO., 49542 G-18
BOYLE CO., 28432 J-11
BRACKEN CO., 8488 F-13
Brandenburg, 2643 H-7
BREATHITT CO.,
13878 J-16
BRECKINRIDGE CO.,
20059 I-6
Brodhead, 1211 K-13
Bromley, 763 B-19
Brooks, 2401 H-9
Brooksville, 642 F-14
Brownsville, 836 K-7
Buckner, 5837 G-9
Buechel, 7272 C-8
BULLITT CO., 74319 H-9
Burgin, 965 I-12
Burkesville, 1521 M-10
Burlington, 15926 D-12
BUTLER CO., 12690 K-6
Cadiz, 2558 M-2
CALDWELL CO.,
12984 K-1
Calhoun, 763 J-4
CALLOWAY CO.,
37191 N-1
Calvert City, 2566 E-4
Camargo, 1081 H-14
CAMPBELL CO.,
90336 E-13
Campbellsburg, 813 F-10
Campbellsville, 9108 K-10
Campton, 441 I-15
Cannonsburg, 856 G-18
Carlisle, 2010 G-14
CARLISLE CO., 5104 F-2
CARROLL CO., 10811 F-11
Carrollton, 3938 F-10
CARTER CO., 27720 G-17
CASEY CO., 15955 K-11
Catlettsburg, 1856 G-18
Cave City, 2240 L-8
Cawood, 731 M-16
Central City, 5978 K-4
CHRISTIAN CO., 73955 L-3
CLARK CO., 35613 I-13
Clarkson, 875 J-7
Clay, 1181 J-2
Clay City, 1077 I-14
CLAY CO., 21730 K-15
Clearfield, 1300 H-16
Clinton, 1388 G-2
CLINTON CO., 10272 N-11
Cloverport, 1152 I-6
Coal Run Vil., 1706 J-19
Cold Spr., 5912 C-20
Coldstream, 1100 A-10
Columbia, 4452 L-10
Combs, 900 K-16
Corbin, 7304 L-14
Corydon, 720 I-2
Covington, 40640 D-12
Crab Orchard, 841 J-12
Crescent Sprs., 3801 B-18
Crestview Hills, 3148 C-18
Crestwood, 4531 G-9
Crittenden, 3815 E-12
CRITTENDEN CO.,
9315 K-1
Crofton, 749 L-3
Cumberland, 2237 L-17
CUMBERLAND CO.,
6856 M-9
Cynthiana, 6402 G-13
Danville, 16218 J-12
DAVIESS CO., 96656 J-4
Dawson Sprs., 2764 L-2
Dayton, 5338 A-20
Dixon, 786 J-2
Douglass Hills, 5484 B-9
Dry Ridge, 2191 F-12
Earlington, 1413 K-3
E. Bernstadt, 716 K-14
Eddyville, 2554 L-1
Edgewood, 8575 C-18
EDMONSON CO.,
12161 K-6
Edmonton, 1595 L-9
Elizabethtown, 28531 I-8
Elkfork, 1539 H-17
Elkhorn City, 982 K-19
Elkton, 2062 M-4
ELLIOTT CO., 7852 H-17
Elsmere, 8451 C-18
Eminence, 2498 G-10
Erlanger, 18082 D-12
ESTILL CO., 14672 I-14
Evarts, 962 M-17
Falmouth, 2169 F-13
FAYETTE CO.,
295803 H-12
Ferguson, 924 L-12
Fern Creek, 17870 D-9
Fincastle, 817 A-10
Flat Lick, 960 M-15
Flatwoods, 7423 F-18
FLEMING CO., 14348 G-14
Fleming-Neon, 770 K-18
Flemingsburg, 2658 G-15
Florence, 29951 D-12
FLOYD CO., 39451 J-18
Ft. Mitchell, 8207 D-12
Ft. Thomas, 16325 D-12
Ft. Wright, 5723 B-19
Frankfort, 25527 G-11
Franklin, 8408 M-6
FRANKLIN CO.,
49285 G-11
Frenchburg, 486 H-15
Fulton, 2445 G-3
FULTON CO., 6813 G-2
GALLATIN CO., 8589 E-11
GARRARD CO.,
16912 J-12
Garrison, 866 F-16
Georgetown, 29098 G-12
Glasgow, 14028 L-8
Goshen, 909 G-9
Graham, 700 K-4
GRANT CO., 24662 F-12
GRAVES CO., 37121 F-4
Gray, 750 L-14
Graymoor-Devondale,
2870 B-9
Grayson, 4217 G-17
GRAYSON CO., 25746 J-7
GREEN CO., 11258 K-9
Green Spr., 715 A-9
Greensburg, 2163 K-9
Greenup, 1188 F-18
GREENUP CO., 36910 F-17
Greenville, 4312 K-4
Guthrie, 1419 N-4
HANCOCK CO., 8565 I-5
Hanson, 742 K-3
HARDIN CO., 105543 I-8
Hardinsburg, 2343 I-6
Harlan, 1745 M-16
HARLAN CO., 29278 L-17
HARRISON CO.,
18846 F-12
Harrodsburg, 8340 I-11
HART CO., 18199 K-8
Hartford, 2672 J-5
Hawesville, 945 I-5
Hazard, 4456 K-17
Hebron, 5929 B-16
Heidrick, 700 M-14
Henderson, 28757 I-3
HENDERSON CO.,
46250 I-2
Hendron, 4687 E-4
HENRY CO., 15416 F-11
Heritage Creek, 1435 D-7
Hickman, 2395 G-2
HICKMAN CO., 4902 G-2
Highland Hts., 6923 C-20
Highview, 15161 D-9
Hillview, 8172 H-9
Hindman, 777 K-17
Hodgenville, 3206 J-8
Hollow Creek, 783 D-8
HOPKINS CO., 46920 K-2
Hopkinsville, 31577 M-3
Horse Cave, 2311 L-8
Hurstbourne, 4216 B-9
Hurstbourne Acres, 1811 C-9
Hyden, 365 L-16
Independence, 24757 E-12
Indian Hills, 2868 B-8
Inez, 717 I-19
Irvine, 2715 I-14
Irvington, 1181 I-7
Jackson, 2231 J-16
JACKSON CO., 13494 J-14
Jamestown, 1794 L-11
JEFFERSON CO.,
741096 H-9
Jeffersontown, 26595 H-9
Jeffersonville, 1506 H-14
Jenkins, 2203 K-18
JESSAMINE CO.,
48586 I-12
JOHNSON CO., 23356 I-17
Junction City, 2241 J-11
KENTON CO., 159720 E-12
KNOTT CO., 16346 J-17
KNOX CO., 31883 L-15
La Center, 1009 E-2
La Grange, 8082 G-10
Lakeside Pk., 2668 C-18
Lancaster, 3442 J-12
LARUE CO., 14193 J-9
LAUREL CO., 58849 L-14
LAWRENCE CO.,
15860 H-18
Lawrenceburg, 10505 H-11
Lebanon, 5539 J-10
Lebanon Jct., 1813 I-8
Ledbetter, 1683 E-4
LEE CO., 7887 J-15
Leitchfield, 6699 J-7
LESLIE CO., 11310 L-16
LETCHER CO., 24519 L-17
LEWIS CO., 13870 F-16
Lewisburg, 810 L-5
Lewisport, 1670 I-5
Lexington, 295803 H-12
Liberty, 2168 K-11
LINCOLN CO., 24742 J-12
Livermore, 1365 J-4
LIVINGSTON CO.,
9519 D-4
Lloyd, 900 F-17
LOGAN CO., 26835 L-5
London, 7993 L-14
Loretto, 713 J-10
Louisa, 2467 H-18
Louisville, 597337 G-8
Lovely, 700 I-19
Loyall, 1461 M-16
Ludlow, 4407 B-19
Lynch, 747 L-17
Lyndon, 11002 B-9
Lynnview, 914 C-7
LYON CO., 8314 L-1
MADISON CO., 82916 I-13
Madisonville, 19591 K-3
MAGOFFIN CO.,
13333 J-17
Manchester, 1255 L-15
Marion, 3039 K-1
MARION CO., 19820 J-10
MARSHALL CO., 31448 F-4
Marshes Siding, 700 M-12
MARTIN CO., 12929 I-19
MASON CO., 17490 F-15
Masonville, 1014 J-4
Massac, 4505 E-3
Mayfield, 10024 F-3
Maysville, 9011 F-15
MCCRACKEN CO.,
65565 E-3
MCCREARY CO.,
18306 N-12
McKee, 800 K-14
MCLEAN CO., 9531 J-3
McRoberts, 784 K-18
MEADE CO., 28602 H-7
Meadow Vale, 736 A-9
MENIFEE CO., 6306 I-15
MERCER CO., 21331 I-11
METCALFE CO., 10099 L-9
Middlesboro, 10334 N-15
Middletown, 7218 G-9
Midway, 1641 H-12
Millersburg, 792 G-13
MONROE CO., 10963 M-9
MONTGOMERY CO.,
26499 H-14
Monticello, 6188 M-11
Morehead, 6845 G-16
MORGAN CO.,
13923 H-16
Morganfield, 3285 I-2
Morgantown, 2394 K-5
Mortons Gap, 863 K-3
Mt. Olivet, 299 F-14
Mt. Sterling, 6895 H-14
Mt. Vernon, 2477 K-13
Mt. Washington, 9117 H-9
MUHLENBERG CO.,
31499 L-4
Muldraugh, 947 I-8
Munfordville, 1615 K-8
Murray, 17741 G-4
NELSON CO., 43437 I-9
New Castle, 912 G-10
New Haven, 855 J-9
Newport, 15273 B-20
NICHOLAS CO., 7135 G-14
Nicholasville, 28015 I-12
N. Corbin, 1773 L-14
Northfield, 1020 B-8
Nortonville, 1204 K-3
Oak Grv., 7489 N-3
Oakdale, 1900 E-4
OHIO CO., 23842 J-5
Okolona, 17807 D-8
OLDHAM CO., 60316 G-10
Olive Hill, 1599 G-16
OWEN CO., 10841 F-11
Owensboro, 57265 I-4
Owenton, 1327 F-11
Owingsville, 1530 H-15
OWSLEY CO., 4755 K-15
Paducah, 25024 E-4
Paintsville, 3459 I-18
Paris, 8553 G-13
Park Hills, 2970 B-19
Pembroke, 869 M-3
PENDLETON CO.,
14877 F-13
PERRY CO., 28712 L-17
Perryville, 751 J-11
Pewee Valley, 1456 G-9
Phelps, 893 J-20
PIKE CO., 65024 J-19
Pikeville, 6903 J-19
Pine Knot, 1621 N-13
Pineville, 1732 M-15
Pioneer Vil., 2030 H-9
Plantation, 832 B-9
Pleasure Ridge Pk.,
25776 D-5
Pleasureville, 834 G-10
Powderly, 745 K-4
POWELL CO., 12613 I-14
Prestonsburg, 3255 I-18
Princeton, 6329 L-2
Prospect, 4698 G-9
Providence, 3193 K-2
PULASKI CO., 63063 L-12
Raceland, 2424 F-18
Radcliff, 21688 I-8
Reidland, 4491 E-4
Revelo, 700 M-13
Richmond, 31364 I-13
ROBERTSON CO.,
2282 F-14
ROCKCASTLE CO.,
17056 K-13
Rolling Hills, 959 B-9
ROWAN CO., 23333 H-16
RUSSELL CO., 17565 L-11
Russell Sprs., 2441 L-11
Russellville, 6960 M-5
St. Dennis, 9177 C-6
St. Matthews, 17472 G-9
St. Regis Pk., 1454 C-9
Salem, 752 K-1
Salyersville, 1883 I-17
Sandy Hook, 675 H-17
Sassafras, 950 K-17
SCOTT CO., 47173 G-12
Scottsville, 4226 M-7
Sebree, 1603 J-3
SHELBY CO., 42074 G-10
Shelbyville, 14045 G-10
Shepherdsville, 11222 H-9
Shively, 15264 G-8
Silver Grv., 1102 D-13
SIMPSON CO., 17327 M-6
Simpsonville, 2484 G-10
Smithland, 301 E-4
Smiths Grv., 714 L-7
Somerset, 11196 L-12
S. Portsmouth, 900 E-17
S. Shore, 1122 E-17
S. Wallins, 859 M-16
Southgate, 3803 B-20
SPENCER CO., 17061 H-10
Springfield, 2519 J-10
Stanford, 3487 J-12
Stanton, 2733 I-14
Stearns, 1416 M-12
Sturgis, 1898 J-1
Sublimity City, 800 L-14
Summit, 900 F-18
TAYLOR CO., 24512 K-10
Taylor Mill, 6604 C-19
Taylorsville, 763 H-10
TODD CO., 12460 M-4
Tompkinsville, 2402 M-9
TRIGG CO., 14339 M-2
TRIMBLE CO., 8809 F-10
Union, 5379 E-12
UNION CO., 15007 I-2
Uniontown, 1002 I-2
Van Lear, 1050 I-18
Vanceburg, 1518 F-16
Verda, 800 M-16
Verona, 1455 E-12
Versailles, 8568 H-12
Villa Hills, 7489 B-18
Vine Grv., 4520 I-8
Walton, 3635 E-12
WARREN CO., 113792 L-7
Warsaw, 1615 E-11
WASHINGTON CO.,
11717 I-10
Watterson Pk., 976 C-8
WAYNE CO., 20813 M-12
WEBSTER CO., 13621 J-2
Weeksbury, 800 K-18
W. Buechel, 1230 C-8
W. Liberty, 3435 I-16
West Point, 797 H-8
Westwood, 4746 †B-1
Wheelwright, 780 K-18
White Plains, 884 K-3
Whitesburg, 2139 L-18
Whitley City, 1170 M-13
WHITLEY CO., 35637 M-13
Wickliffe, 688 F-2
Wilder, 3035 B-20
Williamsburg, 5245 M-14
Williamstown, 3925 F-12
Wilmore, 3686 I-12
Winchester, 18368 H-13
Windy Hills, 2385 B-8
WOLFE CO., 7355 I-15
WOODFORD CO.,
24939 I-11
Woodlawn Pk., 942 B-8
Worthington, 1609 F-18
Worthington Hills,
1446 A-10
Wurtland, 995 F-18

Louisiana

Map p. 44

Abbeville, 12257 H-5
Abita Sprs., 2365 G-9
ACADIA PAR., 61773 G-5
Addis, 3593 G-7
Albany, 1088 G-8
Alexandria, 47723 E-4
ALLEN PAR., 25764 F-4
Amelia, 2459 I-7
Amite, 4141 F-8
Anacoco, 869 E-3
Arabi, 3635 H-9
Arcadia, 2919 B-3
Arnaudville, 1057 G-5
ASCENSION PAR.,
107215 H-7
ASSUMPTION PAR.,
23421 I-7
Avondale, 4954 E-12
AVOYELLES PAR.,
42073 E-5
Baker, 13895 G-7
Baldwin, 2436 I-6
Ball, 4000 E-4
Basile, 1821 G-4
Bastrop, 11365 B-5
Baton Rouge, 229493 G-7
Bawcomville, 3588 B-5
Bayou Blue, 12352 I-8
Bayou Vista, 4652 I-7
BEAUREGARD PAR.,
35654 G-2
Belle Chasse, 12679 I-9
Belle Rose, 1902 H-7
Benton, 1948 B-2
Bernice, 1689 B-4
Berwick, 4946 I-7
BIENVILLE PAR.,
14353 B-3
Blanchard, 2899 B-1
Bogalusa, 12232 F-10
Boothville, 854 J-11
Bossier City, 61315 B-2
BOSSIER PAR.,
116979 A-2
Bourg, 2579 I-8
Boyce, 1004 E-4
Breaux Br., 8139 H-5
Bridge City, 7706 E-12
Broussard, 8197 H-5
Brusly, 2589 G-7
Bunkie, 4171 F-5
Buras, 945 J-10
CADDO PAR., 254969 B-1
Cade, 1723 H-5
CALCASIEU PAR.,
192768 G-2
CALDWELL PAR.,
10132 C-5
Cameron, 406 I-3
CAMERON PAR., 6839 H-2
Campti, 1056 D-3
Carencro, 7526 G-5
Catahoula, 1094 H-6
CATAHOULA PAR.,
10407 D-6
Cecilia, 1980 G-6
Central, 26864 G-7
Chackbay, 5177 I-8
Chalmette, 16751 H-10
Charenton, 1903 I-6
Chauvin, 2912 J-8
Choudrant, 845 B-4
Church Pt., 4560 G-5
Claiborne, 11507 B-5
CLAIBORNE PAR.,
17195 A-3
Clarks, 1017 C-5
Clinton, 1653 F-7
Colfax, 1558 E-4
Columbia, 390 C-5
CONCORDIA PAR.,
20822 E-6
Convent, 711 H-8
Cotton Valley, 1009 B-2
Cottonport, 2006 F-5
Coushatta, 1964 C-3
Covington, 8765 G-9
Crowley, 13265 H-5
Crown Pt., 980 I-9
Crozier, 1250 I-8
Cullen, 1163 A-2
Cut Off, 5976 I-9
DE SOTO PAR., 26656 D-2
Delcambre, 1866 H-5
Delhi, 2919 B-6
Denham Sprs., 10215 G-7
DeQuincy, 3235 G-2
DeRidder, 10578 F-3
Des Allemands, 2505 I-8
Deville, 1764 E-5
Donaldsonville, 7436 H-7
Doyline, 818 B-2
Dubach, 961 B-4
Dulac, 1463 J-8
Duson, 1716 H-5
E. BATON ROUGE PAR.,
440171 G-7
E. CARROLL PAR.,
7759 B-7
E. FELICIANA PAR.,
20267 F-7
Eastwood, 4093 B-2
Edgard, 2441 H-8
Elmwood, 4635 E-12
Elton, 1128 G-4
Empire, 993 J-10
Epps, 854 B-6
Erath, 2114 H-5
Erwinville, 2192 G-7
Estelle, 16377 I-9
Estherwood, 889 H-4
Eunice, 10398 G-4
EVANGELINE PAR.,
33984 G-4
Farmerville, 3860 B-4
Ferriday, 3511 D-6
Fordoche, 928 G-6
Forest Hill, 818 F-4
Franklin, 7660 I-6
FRANKLIN PAR.,
20767 C-6
Franklinton, 3857 F-9
French Settlement, 1116 H-8
Galliano, 7676 J-9
Garyville, 2811 H-8
Gibsland, 979 B-3
Glenmora, 1342 F-4
Golden Meadow, 2101 J-9
Gonzales, 9781 H-8
Grambling, 4949 B-4
Gramercy, 3613 H-8
Grand Coteau, 947 G-5
Grand Isle, 1296 J-10
GRANT PAR., 22309 D-4
Gray, 5584 I-8
Greensburg, 718 F-8
Greenwood, 3219 B-1
Gretna, 17736 H-9
Gueydan, 1398 H-4
Hackberry, 1261 H-2
Hahnville, 3344 H-9
Hammond, 20019 G-8
Harahan, 9277 H-9
Harrisonburg, 348 D-6
Harvey, 20348 F-13
Haughton, 3454 B-2
Haynesville, 2327 A-3
Henderson, 1674 G-6
Hessmer, 802 F-5
Homer, 3237 B-3
Houma, 33727 I-8
IBERIA PAR., 73240 H-6
IBERVILLE PAR.,
33387 G-6
Independence, 1665 G-8
Inniswold, 6180 C-13
Iota, 1500 G-4
Iowa, 2996 H-3
Jackson, 3842 F-7
JACKSON PAR., 16274 C-4
Jean Lafitte, 1903 I-9
Jeanerette, 5530 H-6
Jefferson, 11193 E-12
JEFFERSON DAVIS PAR.,
31594 G-3
JEFFERSON PAR.,
432552 I-9
Jena, 3398 D-5
Jennings, 10383 H-4
Jonesboro, 4704 C-4
Jonesville, 2265 D-6
Kaplan, 4600 H-5
Kenner, 66702 H-9
Kentwood, 2198 F-8
Killian, 1206 G-8
Kinder, 2477 G-4
Kraemer, 934 I-8
Krotz Sprs., 1198 G-6
LA SALLE PAR., 14890 D-5
Labadieville, 1854 I-7
Lacombe, 8679 G-10
Lafayette, 120623 H-5
LAFAYETTE PAR.,
221578 H-5
Lafitte, 972 I-9
LAFOURCHE PAR.,
96318 I-9
L. Arthur, 2738 H-4
L. Charles, 71993 H-3
L. Providence, 3991 B-7
Lakeshore, 1930 B-5
Lakeview, 948 A-8
Laplace, 29872 H-8
Larose, 7400 I-9
Lawtell, 1198 G-5
Lecompte, 1227 F-4
Leesville, 6612 E-3
Leonville, 1084 G-5
LINCOLN PAR., 46735 B-4
Live Oak Mnr., 1900 E-11
Livingston, 1769 G-8
LIVINGSTON PAR.,
128026 G-8
Livonia, 1442 G-6
Lockport, 2578 I-8
Logansport, 1555 C-1
Loreauville, 887 H-6
Luling, 12119 H-9
Lutcher, 3559 H-8
Lydia, 952 H-6
MADISON PAR.,
12093 C-6
Mamou, 3242 G-4
Mandeville, 11560 G-9
Mansfield, 5001 C-2
Mansura, 1419 F-5
Many, 2853 D-2
Maringouin, 1098 G-6
Marksville, 5702 F-5
Marrero, 33141 H-9
Mathews, 2209 I-8
Maurice, 964 H-5
Melville, 1041 G-6
Meraux, 5816 H-10
Merryville, 1103 F-2
Metairie, 138481 H-9
Midway, 1291 D-5
Milton, 3030 H-5
Minden, 13082 B-3
Monroe, 48815 B-5
Montegut, 1540 I-8
Monticello, 5172 A-14
Moreauville, 929 F-5
MOREHOUSE PAR.,
27979 A-6
Morgan City, 12404 I-7
Morse, 812 H-4
Moss Bluff, 11557 G-3
Nairn, 1000 J-10
Napoleonville, 660 H-7
Natchitoches, 18323 D-3
NATCHITOCHES PAR.,
39566 D-3
New Iberia, 30617 H-6
New Llano, 2504 F-3
New Orleans, 343829 H-9
New Roads, 4831 G-6
Newellton, 1187 C-7
Norco, 3074 H-9
Oak Grv., 1727 A-7
Oakdale, 7780 F-4
Oberlin, 1770 G-4
Oil City, 1008 B-1
Old Jefferson, 6980 G-7
Olla, 1385 D-5
Opelousas, 16634 G-5
ORLEANS PAR.,
343829 H-9
OUACHITA PAR.,
153720 C-5
Paincourtville, 911 H-7
Paradis, 1298 I-9
Patterson, 6112 I-7
Pearl River, 2506 G-10
Pierre Part, 3169 H-7
Pine Prairie, 1610 F-4
Pineville, 14555 E-4
Plain Dealing, 1015 A-2
Plaquemine, 7119 H-7
PLAQUEMINES PAR.,
23042 I-10
Pointe a la Hache, 187 I-10
POINTE COUPEE PAR.,
22802 G-6
Ponchatoula, 6559 G-9
Port Allen, 5180 G-7
Port Barre, 2055 G-5
Port Sulphur, 1760 I-10
Prairieville, 26895 H-7
Prien, 7810 H-3
Raceland, 10193 I-8
RAPIDES PAR.,
131613 F-4
Rayne, 7953 H-5
Rayville, 3695 B-6
Red Chute, 6261 B-2
RED RIVER PAR.,
9091 D-3
Reserve, 9766 H-8
RICHLAND PAR.,
20725 C-5
Richwood, 3392 B-5
Ringgold, 1495 C-3
River Ridge, 13494 E-11
Roseland, 1123 F-8
Rosepine, 1692 F-3
Ruston, 21859 B-4
SABINE PAR., 24233 E-2
St. Bernard, 830 I-10
ST. BERNARD PAR.,
35897 H-10
ST. CHARLES PAR.,
52780 I-9
St. Francisville, 1765 F-7
St. Gabriel, 6677 H-7
ST. HELENA PAR.,
11203 F-8
St. James, 828 H-8
ST. JAMES PAR.,
22102 H-8
ST. JOHN THE BAPTIST
PAR., 45924 H-8
St. Joseph, 1176 D-7
ST. LANDRY PAR.,
83384 G-5
ST. MARTIN PAR.,
52160 H-6
St. Martinville, 6114 H-6
ST. MARY PAR., 54650 I-6
ST. TAMMANY PAR.,
233740 G-9
Sarepta, 891 A-2
Schriever, 6853 I-8
Scott, 8614 H-5
Seymourville, 3000 H-7
Sharon Hills, 900 A-13
Shreveport, 199311 B-2
Sibley, 1218 B-3
Simmesport, 2161 F-6
Simsboro, 841 B-4
Slaughter, 997 G-7
Slidell, 27068 H-10
Sorrento, 1401 H-8
Springhill, 5269 A-2
Springville, 840 C-3
Start, 905 B-6
Sterlington, 1594 B-5
Stonewall, 1814 C-2
Sulphur, 20410 H-2
Sunnybrook, 800 A-13
Sunset, 2897 G-5
Swartz, 4536 B-5
Tallulah, 7335 B-7
TANGIPAHOA PAR.,
121097 G-8
TENSAS PAR., 5252 D-6
TERREBONNE PAR.,
111860 I-7
Terrytown, 23319 F-14
Thibodaux, 14566 I-8
Tioga, 1300 E-4
UNION PAR., 22721 A-4
Urania, 1313 D-5
Varnado, 1461 F-10
VERMILION PAR.,
57999 I-4
VERNON PAR., 52334 E-3
Vidalia, 4299 E-6
Ville Platte, 7430 G-5
Vinton, 3212 H-2
Violet, 4973 H-10
Vivian, 3671 A-1
W. BATON ROUGE PAR.,
23788 G-7
W. CARROLL PAR.,
11604 B-6
W. FELICIANA PAR.,
15625 F-6
Waggaman, 10015 E-11
Walker, 6138 G-8
Wardville, 1200 E-4
Washington, 964 G-5
WASHINGTON PAR.,
47168 F-9
Watson, 1047 G-7
WEBSTER PAR.,
41207 A-2
Welcome, 800 H-8
Welsh, 3226 H-4
W. Monroe, 13065 B-5
Westlake, 4568 H-3
Westminster, 3008 C-13
Westwego, 8534 H-9
White Castle, 1883 H-7
WINN PAR., 15313 D-4
Winnfield, 4840 D-4
Winnsboro, 4910 C-6
Wisner, 964 D-6
Woodworth, 1096 F-4
Youngsville, 8105 H-5
Zachary, 14960 G-7
Zwolle, 1759 D-2

Maine

Map p. 45

Alfred, 600 I-2
ANDROSCOGGIN CO.,
107702 G-3
Anson, 752 E-4
AROOSTOOK CO.,
71870 B-8
Ashland, 709 B-13
Auburn, 23055 G-3
Augusta, 19136 F-4
Bailey Island, 650 H-3
Bangor, 33039 E-6
Bar Hbr., 2552 F-8
Bath, 8514 H-4
Belfast, 6668 F-6
Berwick, 2187 J-1
Bethel, 1200 F-2
Biddeford, 21277 I-2
Bingham, 758 D-4
Blue Hill, 943 F-7
Boothbay Hbr., 1086 H-4
Bowdoinham, 722 G-4
Brewer, 9482 E-6
Bridgton, 2071 G-2
Brownville Jct., 800 C-6
Brunswick, 15175 H-4
Bucksport, 2885 F-6
Calais, 3123 C-10
Camden, 3570 G-6
Cape Elizabeth, 8850 I-3
Cape Neddick, 2568 J-2
Caribou, 8189 B-14
Castine, 1029 F-6
Chisholm, 1380 F-3
Clinton, 1419 E-5
Corinna, 1100 D-5
Cumberland Ctr., 2499 H-3
CUMBERLAND CO.,
281674 H-2
Damariscotta, 1142 G-5
Dexter, 2158 D-5
Dixfield, 1076 F-2
Dover-Foxcroft, 2528 D-5
E. Hampden, 1200 J-6
E. Millinocket, 1567 B-7
Eastport, 1331 D-10
Ellsworth, 7741 F-7
Fairfield, 2638 E-4
Falmouth, 7610 G-10
Falmouth Foreside,
1511 G-10
Farmingdale, 1970 G-4
Farmington, 4288 E-3
Ft. Fairfield, 1825 B-14
Ft. Kent, 2488 A-13
FRANKLIN CO., 30768 D-2
Freeport, 1485 H-3
Fryeburg, 1631 G-1
Gardiner, 5800 G-4
Gorham, 6882 H-2
Gray, 884 H-3
Greenville, 1257 C-4
Guilford, 903 D-5
Hallowell, 2381 F-4
Hampden, 4343 E-6
Hampden Highlands,
800 E-6
HANCOCK CO., 54418 D-8
Hartland, 813 E-5
Houlton, 4856 C-14
Howland, 1096 C-7
Jackman, 800 B-3
Jonesport, 1100 F-9
KENNEBEC CO.,
122151 F-4
Kennebunk, 5214 I-2
Kennebunkport, 1238 I-2
Kingfield, 850 D-3
Kittery, 4562 J-2
Kittery Pt., 1012 J-2
KNOX CO., 39736 G-5
Lewiston, 36592 G-3
Limestone, 1075 B-14
Lincoln, 2884 C-7
LINCOLN CO., 34457 G-4
Lisbon, 1400 G-3
Lisbon Falls, 4100 G-3
Livermore Falls, 1594 F-3
Machias, 1274 E-9
Madawaska, 2967 A-13
Madison, 2630 E-4
Manchester, 650 F-4
Mapleton, 683 B-14
Mars Hill, 980 C-14
Mattawamkeag, 650 B-7
Mechanic Falls, 2237 G-3
Medway, 900 B-7
Mexico, 1743 F-2
Milford, 2233 D-7
Millinocket, 4466 B-6
Milo, 1847 C-6
Newcastle, 667 G-5
Newport, 1776 E-5
Norridgewock, 1438 E-4
N. Anson, 750 E-4
N. Berwick, 1615 J-2
N. Vassalboro, 900 F-4
N. Windham, 4904 H-2
Northeast Hbr., 650 F-7
Norway, 2748 G-2
Oak Hill, 700 J-8
Oakland, 2602 F-4
Ogunquit, 892 J-2
Old Orchard Bch., 8624 I-3
Old Town, 7840 D-7
Orono, 9474 E-7
Oxford, 1263 G-2
OXFORD CO., 57833 F-2
Patten, 1000 A-7
PENOBSCOT CO.,
153923 A-7
Phillips, 750 E-3
PISCATAQUIS CO.,
17535 A-5
Pittsfield, 3150 E-5
Pleasant Hill, 900 H-9
Portland, 66194 H-3
Presque Isle, 9692 B-14
Princeton, 750 C-9
Randolph, 1772 G-4
Rangeley, 700 D-2
Richmond, 1760 G-4
Rockland, 7297 G-6
Rockport, 1200 G-6
Rumford, 4218 F-2
Sabattus, 1300 G-3
Saco, 18482 I-2
SAGADAHOC CO.,
35293 G-4
Sanford, 9761 I-2
Sangerville, 650 D-5
Scarborough, 4403 I-3
Searsport, 992 F-6
Skowhegan, 6297 E-4
SOMERSET CO., 52228 B-3
S. Berwick, 3000 J-1
S. Eliot, 3550 J-2
S. Paris, 2267 G-2
S. Portland, 25002 I-3
S. Sanford, 4536 I-2
S. Windham, 1374 H-2
Southwest Hbr., 720 F-7
Springvale, 3292 I-2
Steep Falls, 1139 H-2
Stonington, 800 G-7
Strong, 700 E-3
Thomaston, 1875 G-5
Topsham, 5931 H-4
Van Buren, 1937 A-14
Veazie, 1630 E-6
Vinalhaven, 800 G-6
WALDO CO., 38786 F-5
Waldoboro, 1233 G-5
Washburn, 997 B-14
WASHINGTON CO.,
32856 E-9
Waterboro, 750 I-2
Waterville, 15722 F-4
Wells, 1200 J-2
W. Scarborough, 900 I-3
Westbrook, 17494 H-3
Wilton, 2198 E-3
Winslow, 7794 F-4
Winterport, 1340 E-6
Winthrop, 2650 F-4
Woodland, 952 D-9
Yarmouth, 5869 H-3
York Bch., 900 J-2
YORK CO., 197131 I-1
York Hbr., 3033 J-2
York Vil., 1000 J-2

Maryland

Map pp. 46 – 47

* City keyed to p. 111

Aberdeen, 14959 B-15
Abingdon, 2000 C-15
Accokeek, 10573 G-12
Adamstown, 2372 C-10
Adelphi, 15086 *D-7
ALLEGANY CO., 75087 B-5
Annapolis, 38394 E-14
Annapolis Jct., 800 N-3
ANNE ARUNDEL CO.,
537656 F-13
Aquasco, 981 H-13
Arbutus, 20483 K-4
Arnold, 23106 E-14
Arundel Gdns., 1250 L-6
Arundel on the Bay,
1100 F-14
Arundel Vil., 2700 L-6
Ashton, 1500 D-12
Aspen Hill, 48759 *C-6
Baden, 2128 G-13
Ballenger Creek, 18274 N-19
Baltimore, 620961 C-13
BALTIMORE CO.,
805029 B-13
Baltimore Highlands,
7019 K-5
Barnaby Vil., 5300 *H-7
Bartonsville, 1451 C-10
Bay Ridge, 2200 C-20
Bayside Bch., 950 D-14
Bel Air, 10120 B-15
Bel Air, 1258 B-4
Bel Alton, 1000 H-12
Beltsville, 16772 E-12
Bennsville, 11923 G-12
Berlin, 4485 I-20
Berwyn Hts., 3123 *D-8
Bethesda, 60858 E-11
Bladensburg, 9148 *F-8
Bonnie Brae, 1250 C-12
Boonsboro, 3336 B-9
Bowie, 54727 E-13
Bowleys Qtrs., 6755 C-14
Bowling Green, 1077 B-4
Boyds, 900 D-10
Brandywine, 6719 G-12
Brentwood, 3046 *F-8
Bridgeport, 860 M-17
Brinkleigh Manor, 2500 J-2
Brooklandville, 1700 F-5
Brooklyn Pk., 14373 K-6
Brookmont, 3468 *E-5
Brookwood, 2200 *J-10
Brunswick, 5870 C-9
Bryans Road, 7244 G-11
Buckeystown, 1019 C-10
Burtonsville, 8323 E-12
Cabin John, 2280 *E-4
California, 11857 I-14
Calvert Bch., 808 H-14
CALVERT CO., 88737 H-13
Calverton, 17724 *C-8
Cambridge, 12326 H-16
Camp Sprs., 19096 F-12
Cape Isle of Wight, 750 I-20
Cape St. Claire, 8747 E-14
Capitol Hts., 4337 *G-8
Carney, 29941 G-8
CAROLINE CO.,
33066 F-17
CARROLL CO.,
167134 B-12
Carroll Highlands, 2000 C-12
Cascade, 1000 A-10
Catonsville, 41567 J-4
Catonsville Manor, 2600 J-4
Cavetown, 1473 B-9
CECIL CO., 101108 B-17
Cedar Hts., 1150 *F-8
Centreville, 4285 E-16
Chaptico, 850 I-13
CHARLES CO.,
146551 H-12
Charlestown, 1183 B-16
Charlotte Hall, 1420 H-13
Chase, 920 C-14
Chateau Valley, 1900 K-1
Cheltenham, 950 G-13
Chesapeake Bch., 5753 G-14
Chesapeake Ranch
Estates, 10519 I-14
Chester, 4167 E-15
Chestertown, 5252 D-16
Cheverly, 6173 *F-8
Chevy Chase, 9545 *E-5
Chevy Chase View, 920 *D-5
Chillum, 33513 *E-7
Clarksburg, 13766 D-11
Clarksville, 830 D-12
Clinton, 35970 F-12
Clopper, 1000 *A-3
Clover Hill, 3260 L-19
Cloverly, 15126 *B-7
Cobb Island, 1166 I-12
Cockeysville, 20776 B-13
Colesville, 14647 E-12
College Pk., 30413 *D-8
Colmar Manor, 1404 *F-8
Columbia, 99615 D-12
Columbia Pk., 1000 *F-9
Coral Hills, 9895 *G-8
Cottage City, 1305 *F-8
Cove Pt., 1200 I-14
Cresaptown, 4592 B-4
Crisfield, 2726 K-17
Crofton, 27348 E-13
Croom, 2631 G-13
Crownsville, 1757 E-13
Cumberland, 20859 A-4
Damascus, 15257 D-11
Darnestown, 6802 E-10
Davidsonville, 780 F-13
Dayton, 800 D-12
Deale, 4945 F-14
Defense Hts., 2250 *E-9
Delmar, 3003 H-18
Denton, 4418 F-17
Derwood, 2381 *B-4
Dickerson, 1000 D-10
District Hts., 5837 *G-8
DORCHESTER CO.,
32618 H-16
Dorsey, 1350 M-3
Drum Pt., 2731 I-14
Dundalk, 63597 D-14
Dunkirk, 2520 G-13
E. Riverdale, 15509 *E-8
Easton, 15945 F-16
Eden, 823 I-18
Edgemere, 8669 D-14
Edgewater, 9023 C-18
Edgewood, 25562 C-15
Edmonston, 1445 *E-8
Eldersburg, 30531 C-12
Elkridge, 15593 D-13
Elkton, 15443 B-17
Ellicott City, 65834 D-13
Elmwood, 1650 H-8
Emmitsburg, 2814 A-10
Emmorton, 1400 B-15
Emory Grv., 5300 *A-4
Essex, 39262 C-14
Fairland, 23681 E-12
Fairmount Hts., 1494 *F-8
Fallston, 8958 B-14
Federalsburg, 2739 G-17
Ferndale, 16746 L-5
Finksburg, 1000 B-12
Flohrville, 800 C-12
Font Hill, 890 K-3
Font Hill Manor, 2500 D-12
Forest Glen, 6582 *D-6
Forest Hts., 2447 *H-7
Forest Hill, 900 B-14
Forestville, 12353 F-12
Ft. Foote Vil., 5000 *I-6
Ft. Howard, 890 D-14
Fountain Green, 1400 B-15
Fountain Head, 1350 A-9
Four Cors., 7945 *D-7
Frederick, 65239 C-10
FREDERICK CO.,
233385 B-10
Friendly, 9250 *J-7
Friendship Vil., 4698 *E-5
Frostburg, 9002 A-3
Fruitland, 4866 I-18
Fullerton, 2400 H-8
Fulton, 2049 *A-8
Funkstown, 904 B-9
Gaithersburg, 59933 D-11
Gambrills, 2800 E-13
Garland, 1800 L-6
GARRETT CO., 30097 B-2
Garrett Pk., 992 *D-5
Garrison, 8823 G-3
Germantown, 86395 D-11
Glassmanor, 17295 *H-7
Glen Burnie, 67639 D-13
Glen Hills, 1400 *C-3
Glenarden, 6000 F-12
Glenelg, 1000 D-12
Glenmont, 13529 *C-6
Glenn Dale, 13466 *E-10
Glyndon, 900 B-13
Golden Bch., 3796 H-13
Granite, 950 C-12
Grantsville, 766 A-2
Grasonville, 3425 E-15
Green Valley, 3000 C-10
Greenbelt, 23068 E-12
Greenberry Hills, 1400 N-16
Greensboro, 1931 E-17
Guilford, 1000 D-12
Hagerstown, 39662 B-9
Halethorpe, 2000 K-4
Halfway, 10701 B-8
Hampstead, 6323 B-12
Hampton, 5052 F-6
Hancock, 1545 A-7
Harewood Pk., 1100 C-15
HARFORD CO.,
244826 B-14
Havre de Grace, 12952 B-16
Hebbville, 2500 H-3
Hebron, 1084 H-18
Herald Hbr., 2603 E-14
Hernwood Hts., 960 H-2
High Pt., 3700 M-8
High Ridge, 2500 N-1
Highland, 1034 D-12
Hillandale, 6043 *D-7
Hillcrest Hts., 16469 *H-7
Hillsmere Shores, 2977 C-20
Hollywood, 1000 I-14
HOWARD CO.,
287085 D-12
Hughesville, 2197 H-13
Huntingtown, 3311 G-13
Hurlock, 2092 G-17
Ilchester, 23476 K-3
Indian Head, 3844 G-11
Jarrettsville, 2916 B-14
Jefferson, 2111 C-9
Jessup, 7137 D-13
Johnsville, 1200 C-12
Joppatowne, 12616 C-15
Keedysville, 1152 B-9
Kemp Mill, 12564 *D-6
Kensington, 2213 *D-5
KENT CO., 20197 D-16
Kent Vil., 2700 *F-9
Kenwood, 2500 I-8
Kettering, 12790 F-13
Kings Pk., 3000 H-2
Kingstown, 1733 D-16
Kingsville, 4318 C-14
La Plata, 8753 H-12
La Vale, 3551 D-3
L. Arbor, 9776 *F-10
L. Shore, 19477 E-14
Landover Hills, 1687 *E-9
Langley Pk., 18755 *E-7
Lanham, 10157 *E-9
Lansdowne, 8409 K-5
Largo, 10709 *F-10
Laurel, 25115 E-12
Layhill, 5169 *B-6
Leisure World, 8749 *B-5
Leonardtown, 2930 I-13
Lewisdale, 3100 *E-7
Lexington Pk., 11626 I-14
Liberty Manor, 920 H-3
Libertytown, 950 B-11
Linganore, 8543 C-11
Linhigh, 2100 H-8
Linthicum, 10324 L-5
Lisbon, 1150 C-11
Lochearn, 25333 H-4
Lonaconing, 1214 B-3
Londontowne, 4000 F-14
Long Bch., 1821 H-14
Lusby, 1835 H-14
Lutherville, 6504 F-6
Manchester, 4808 A-12
Maplewood, 1100 I-1
Margate, 1500 M-6
Marion, 1050 K-17
Marley, 1500 M-6
Marlow Hts., 5618 *H-8
Marlton, 9031 F-13
Martins Additions, 933 *E-6
Maryland City, 16093 *B-10
Maugansville, 3071 A-8
Mayo, 8298 F-14
Mays Chapel, 11420 F-6
McAlpine, 4400 K-2
McHenry, 1000 B-1
Meadowood, 1100 *C-7
Mechanicsville, 1508 H-13
Middle River, 25191 I-9
Middletown, 4136 C-9
Milford Mill, 29042 H-3
Millersville, 950 E-13
Mitchellville, 10967 *F-10
Monkton, 800 B-13
MONTGOMERY CO.,
971777 D-11
Montgomery Vil.,
32032 D-11
Montpelier, 3600 *C-9
Morningside, 2015 *H-9
Mt. Airy, 9288 C-11
Mt. Hebron, 2000 I-2
Mt. Pleasant Bch., 2100 M-8
Mt. Rainier, 8080 *F-7
Mt. Savage, 873 A-4
Mt. Vernon, 779 I-17
Mountain Lake Pk., 2092 C-1
Myersville, 1626 B-9
New Carrollton, 12135 E-12
New Windsor, 1396 B-11
N. Beach, 1978 G-14
N. Bethesda, 43828 *C-5
N. East, 3572 B-16
N. Kensington, 9514 *C-5
N. Laurel, 4474 N-1
N. Potomac, 24410 E-11
Oak View, 3400 *D-7
Oakland, 2500 *G-8
Oakland, 1925 C-1
Oaklawn, 1600 *I-8
Ocean City, 7102 I-20
Ocean Pines, 11710 I-20
Odenton, 37132 E-13
Old Farm, 3450 *C-4
Olney, 33844 D-11
Orchard Bch., 2200 M-8
Orchard Hills, 1250 L-16
Overlea, 12275 H-8
Owings, 2149 G-14
Owings Mills, 30622 C-13
Oxon Hill-Glassmanor,
35355 *I-7
Paramount, 1450 L-17
Parkside, 4650 *D-5
Parkville, 30734 C-14
Parole, 15922 B-19
Peppermill Vil., 4895 *G-9
Perry Hall, 28474 C-14
Perryville, 4361 B-16
Pikesville, 30764 H-4
Pinefield, 8800 G-12
Piney Pt., 864 J-14
Pittsville, 1417 I-19
Pleasant Hills, 3379 B-14
Pocomoke City, 4184 J-18
Point of Rocks, 1466 D-9
Point Pleasant, 1000 M-6
Poolesville, 4883 D-10
Potomac, 44965 E-11
Potomac Hts., 1117 G-11
Prince Frederick, 2538 H-14
PRINCE GEORGES CO.,
863420 G-12
Princess Anne, 3290 J-18
Providence, 1400 F-7
Pumphrey, 5317 L-6
QUEEN ANNES CO.,
47798 E-16
Quince Orchard, 5500 E-11
Randallstown, 32430 C-13
Randolph Hills, 6150 *C-5
Redland, 17242 *A-4
Reisterstown, 25968 C-12
Ridge Lake, 1000 J-1
Ridgely, 1639 E-17
Rippling Ridge, 2100 L-6
Rising Sun, 2781 A-16
Riva, 4076 E-14
Riverdale Pk., 6956 *E-8
Riverside, 6425 B-15
Riviera Bch., 12677 M-8
Robinwood, 6918 M-17
Rock Hall, 1310 D-15
Rock Hill Bch., 1350 M-8
Rockdale, 6700 H-3
Rockville, 61209 E-11
Rocky Ridge, 900 B-10
Rosaryville, 10697 *I-10
Rosaryville Estates,
1250 G-13
Rosedale, 19257 I-8
Rossville, 15147 H-9
St. James, 2953 B-8
St. Marys City, 3300 J-14
ST. MARYS CO.,
105151 I-13
St. Michaels, 1029 F-15
Salisbury, 30343 I-18
Sandy Spr., 1200 *A-6
Savage, 7054 N-2
Scientists Cliffs, 750 H-14
Seabrook, 17287 *E-9
Seat Pleasant, 4542 F-12
Severn, 44231 D-13
Severna Pk., 37634 E-14
Shady Side, 5803 F-14
Silver Hill, 5950 *H-8
Silver Spr., 71452 E-12
Smithsburg, 2975 A-9
Snow Hill, 2103 J-19
Solomons, 2368 I-14
Somerset, 1216 *E-5
SOMERSET CO.,
26470 J-17
S. Kensington, 8462 *D-5
S. Laurel, 26112 *C-9
Spencerville, 1594 *B-7
Springbrook, 1100 *C-7
Springdale, 3850 B-13
Springdale, 2994 *F-9
Stevenson, 750 G-4
Stevensville, 6803 E-15
Stonecrest Hill, 1250 K-2
Street, 900 A-14
Suitland, 25825 F-12
Summit Pk., 2900 G-5
Sunnybrook, 980 B-14
Sykesville, 4436 C-12
Takoma Pk., 16715 *E-7
TALBOT CO., 37782 F-16
Taneytown, 6728 A-11
Temple Hills, 7852 *H-8
The Lakes, 9000 C-13
Thurmont, 6170 B-10
Tilghman, 784 G-15
Timonium, 9925 F-6
Towson, 55197 C-13
Trappe, 1077 G-16
Travilah, 12159 *C-2
Union Br., 975 B-11
University Pk., 2548 *E-8
Upper Marlboro, 631 F-13
Urbana, 9175 C-10
Valley Mede, 4700 J-2
Van Bibber, 1000 C-15
Van Lear Manor, 1050 N-15
Villa Nova, 940 H-4
Waldorf, 67752 G-12
Walker Mill, 11302 *G-9
Walkersville, 5800 B-10
Warwick, 850 C-17
WASHINGTON CO.,
147430 A-7
W. Edmondale, 3450 J-4
W. Friendship, 1200 C-12
W. Laurel, 4230 *B-8
W. Ocean City, 4375 I-20
Westernport, 1888 B-3
Westminster, 18590 B-12
Westover, 800 J-18
Wheaton, 48284 E-12
White Marsh, 9513 C-14
White Oak, 17403 *C-7
Whiteford, 750 A-15
WICOMICO CO.,
98733 H-18
Willards, 958 I-19
Williamsport, 2137 B-8
Wilton Farm Acres, 1900 I-2
Woodlawn, 37879 C-13
Woodlawn Hts., 2400 L-5
Woodmoor, 8400 H-4
Woodmore, 3936 *F-10
Woodsboro, 1141 B-10
Woodstock, 850 C-12
WORCESTER CO.,
51454 I-19
Worthington, 2350 K-2

Massachusetts

Map pp. 48 – 49

Abington, 15985 G-15
Acton, 2300 D-12
Acushnet, 3073 J-15
Adams, 5515 C-3
Agawam, 28144 G-5
Amesbury, 12327 A-15
Amherst, 19065 E-6
Andover, 8762 C-14
Arlington, 42844 E-14
Ashburnham, 1500 C-9
Ashby, 700 C-10
Ashfield, 1050 D-4
Ashland, 12100 F-12
Ashley Falls, 850 G-1
Assinippi, 1400 G-15
Assonet, 1300 I-14
Athol, 8265 C-8
Attleboro, 43593 H-13
Auburn, 15000 F-10
Avon, 4300 G-14
Ayer, 2868 D-11
Baldwinville, 2028 C-8
Ballardvale, 1400 C-13
Barnstable, 45193 J-18
BARNSTABLE CO.,
215888 J-17
Barre, 1009 E-8
Bedford, 13300 D-13
Belchertown, 2899 F-7
Bellingham, 4854 G-12
Belmont, 24729 E-13
BERKSHIRE CO.,
131219 E-2
Berlin, 700 E-11
Bernardston, 900 C-6
Beverly, 39502 D-15
Billerica, 6850 D-13
Blackstone, 5000 H-11
Bliss Cor., 5466 F-20
Bondsville, 1850 F-7
Boston, 617594 E-14
Bourne, 1418 J-17
Boxford, 2339 C-14
Boylston Ctr., 950 E-11
Braintree, 33698 F-14
Brant Rock, 1800 G-16
Brewster, 2000 J-20
Bridgewater, 7841 H-15
Brimfield, 800 G-8
BRISTOL CO., 548285 J-14
Brockton, 93810 G-14
Brookfield, 833 F-8
Brookline, 58732 E-14
Bryantville, 1800 G-15
Burlington, 24498 D-13
Buzzards Bay, 3859 J-17
Byfield, 1300 B-15
Cambridge, 105162 E-14
Canton, 18530 G-14
Carlisle, 800 D-12
Carver, 1500 I-16
Cataumet, 1500 J-17
Chaffin, 4000 E-10
Charlemont, 800 C-4
Charlton City, 1400 G-9
Chartley, 750 H-13
Chatham, 1421 J-20
Chelmsford, 33800 C-12
Chelsea, 35177 E-14
Cherry Valley, 1200 F-10
Chester, 627 F-3
Chesterfield, 700 E-4
Chicopee, 55298 G-5
Clark Shores, 700 I-15
Clinton, 7389 E-11
Cochituate, 6569 E-12
Cohasset, 6000 F-16
Concord, 4700 D-12
Congamond, 900 H-4
Conway, 800 D-5
Cordaville, 2650 F-11
Dalton, 6750 D-2
Danvers, 26493 C-15
Dedham, 24729 F-13
Deerfield, 643 D-5
Dennis, 2407 J-19
Dennis Port, 3162 J-19
Dighton, 1100 I-14
Dorothy Pond, 1700 C-20
Dover, 2265 F-13
Dracut, 25600 C-13
Dudley, 3700 G-9
DUKES CO., 16535 L-16
Dunstable, 900 C-12
Duxbury, 1802 G-16
E. Acton, 950 D-12
E. Billerica, 3850 C-13
E. Brewster, 800 I-20
E. Bridgewater, 3400 H-15
E. Brookfield, 1323 F-9
E. Dennis, 2753 J-19
E. Douglas, 2557 G-10
E. Falmouth, 6038 K-17
E. Foxborough, 1000 G-13
E. Freetown, 850 I-15
E. Harwich, 4872 J-20
E. Longmeadow, 13370 G-6
E. Millbury, 1000 F-10
E. Orleans, 1200 I-20
E. Pepperell, 2059 C-11
E. Sandwich, 3940 J-18
E. Sudbury, 800 E-12
E. Sudbury Sta., 800 K-3
E. Templeton, 1350 D-9
E. Walpole, 3800 G-13
E. Wareham, 1500 J-16
Eastham, 1250 I-20
Easthampton, 15994 F-5
Eastondale, 750 H-14
Edgartown, 1500 L-17
Egypt, 900 F-16
Essex, 1471 C-16
ESSEX CO., 743159 C-14
Everett, 41667 E-14
Fairhaven, 15870 J-15
Fall River, 88857 J-14
Falmouth, 3799 K-17
Fayville, 1000 F-12
Fisherville, 2750 F-11
Fiskdale, 2583 G-8
Fitchburg, 40318 C-10
Forestdale, 4099 J-17
Forge Vil., 850 C-12
Foxborough, 5625 G-13
Framingham, 68318 F-12
Franklin, 29560 G-12
FRANKLIN CO., 71372 D-5
Gardner, 20228 C-9
Georgetown, 2200 B-14
Gilbertville, 1050 E-8
Gloucester, 28789 C-16
Grafton, 1650 F-11
Granby, 1368 F-6
Graniteville, 1200 C-12
Great Barrington, 2231 F-1
Green Hbr., 1500 G-16
Greenfield, 13716 C-5
Groton, 1124 C-11
Groveland, 3800 B-14
Hadley, 970 E-6
Halifax, 980 H-15
Hamilton, 1000 C-15
Hampden, 900 G-7
HAMPDEN CO.,
463490 G-4
HAMPSHIRE CO.,
158080 E-4
Hanover, 2500 G-15
Hanover Ctr., 1000 G-15
Hanson, 2118 G-15
Harding, 850 F-13
Harvard, 1200 D-11
Harwich, 1798 J-20
Harwich Port, 1644 J-20
Hatfield, 1318 E-6
Haverhill, 60879 B-14
Head of Westport, 650 K-14
Hingham, 5650 F-15
Hinsdale, 1050 D-3
Holbrook, 10791 G-14
Holden, 4200 E-10
Holland, 1464 G-8
Holliston, 12920 F-12
Holyoke, 39880 F-5
Hopedale, 3753 G-11
Hopkinton, 2550 F-12
Housatonic, 1109 F-1
Hubbardston, 800 D-9
Hudson, 14907 E-11
Hull, 10293 E-15
Huntington, 936 F-4
Indian Mound Bch., 900 J-17
Ipswich, 4222 C-15
Islington, 4800 F-13
Jefferson, 1000 E-9
Kingston, 5591 H-16
Lancaster, 900 D-11
Lanesborough, 1000 D-2
Lawrence, 76377 B-13
Lee, 2051 E-2
Leicester, 3200 F-9
Lenox, 1675 E-2
Leominster, 40759 D-10
Lexington, 31394 D-13
Leyden, 700 C-5
Lincoln, 2850 E-13
Linwood, 750 G-11
Littleton Common,
2789 D-12
Longmeadow, 15784 G-6
Lowell, 106519 C-13
Ludlow, 18820 G-6
Lunenburg, 1760 C-10
Lynn, 90329 D-15
Lynnfield, 11596 D-14
Lyonsville, 650 C-5
Malden, 59450 E-14
Manchaug, 800 G-10
Manchester, 5100 C-16
Manomet, 1600 H-17
Mansfield, 7360 H-13
Marblehead, 19808 D-15
Marion, 1111 J-16
Marlborough, 38499 E-11
Marshfield, 4335 G-16
Marshfield Hills, 2356 G-16
Mashpee, 800 J-17
Matfield, 700 H-14
Mattapoisett, 2915 J-16
Maynard, 10106 E-12
Medfield, 6483 F-13
Medford, 56173 E-14
Medway, 4000 G-12
Melrose, 26983 D-14
Mendon, 1000 G-11
Merrimac, 2200 B-14
Methuen, 47255 B-13
Middleborough, 7319 I-15
MIDDLESEX CO.,
1503085 C-11
Middleton, 4920 C-14
Mileoak Ctr., 2050 G-6
Milford, 25055 G-12
Millbury, 5000 F-10
Millers Falls, 1139 C-6
Millis, 3800 G-12
Millville, 2240 H-11
Milton, 27003 F-14
Monponsett, 730 H-15
Monson, 2107 G-7
Montague, 830 D-6
Monument Bch., 2790 J-17
Morningdale, 1150 E-10
Mt. Hermon, 650 C-6
Nabnasset, 3600 C-12
Nahant, 3410 E-15
Nantucket, 7446 M-20
NANTUCKET CO.,
10172 M-20
Natick, 32200 F-12
Needham, 28886 F-13
New Bedford, 95072 J-15
New Lenox, 800 E-2
New Seabury, 717 K-17
Newburyport, 17416 B-15
Newton, 85146 E-13
NORFOLK CO.,
670850 E-14
N. Acton, 900 D-12
N. Adams, 13708 C-3
N. Amherst, 6819 E-6
N. Andover, 22800 B-14
N. Ashburnham, 800 C-9
N. Attleborough, 16790 H-13
N. Billerica, 5500 C-13
N. Brookfield, 2265 F-8
N. Chatham, 950 J-20
N. Dighton, 1250 I-14
N. Eastham, 1806 I-20
N. Easton, 4500 G-14
N. Falmouth, 3084 J-17
N. Grafton, 3150 F-10
N. Hanover, 980 G-15
N. Oxford, 1200 G-10
N. Pembroke, 3292 G-16
N. Reading, 12000 C-14
N. Scituate, 5077 F-16
N. Seekonk, 2643 *J-10
N. Sudbury, 2600 E-12
N. Swansea, 900 J-13
N. Tewksbury, 1200 C-13
N. Truro, 950 G-20
N. Uxbridge, 1800 G-11
N. Westport, 4571 J-14
Northampton, 28549 E-5
Northborough, 6167 E-11
Northbridge, 3600 G-11
Northfield, 1089 C-6
Norton, 2671 H-13
Norton Grv., 2100 H-13
Norwell, 1200 G-16
Norwood, 28602 F-13
Nutting Lake, 3200 D-13
Oak Bluffs, 2000 L-17
Ocean Bluff, 2500 G-16
Ocean Grv., 2811 J-13
Oldham Vil., 900 G-15
Onset, 1573 J-16
Orange, 4018 C-7
Orleans, 1621 I-20
Otis, 650 F-3
Otter River, 630 C-9
Oxford, 6103 G-10
Palmer, 3900 G-7
Paxton, 1600 E-9
Peabody, 51251 D-15
Pembroke, 2100 G-16
Pepperell, 2504 C-11
Pigeon Cove, 1800 C-16
Pine Lake, 750 E-12
Pine Rest, 750 E-12
Pinehurst, 7152 D-13
Pittsfield, 44737 D-2
Plainville, 6900 H-13
Plymouth, 7494 H-16
PLYMOUTH CO.,
494919 H-15
Pocasset, 2851 J-17
Pt. Independence, 870 J-16
Princeton, 1100 D-10
Provincetown, 2642 G-19
Quincy, 92271 F-14
Randolph, 32112 G-14
Raynham, 2100 H-14
Raynham Ctr., 4100 H-14
Reading, 24747 D-14
Revere, 51755 E-14
River Pines, 3600 D-13
Rochdale, 1150 F-9
Rockland, 16100 G-15
Rockport, 4966 C-16
Rowley, 1416 B-15
Russell, 786 F-4
Rutland, 2111 E-9
Sagamore, 3623 J-17
Sagamore Bch., 1100 I-17
Salem, 41340 D-15
Salisbury, 4869 A-15
Sand Hill, 1800 F-16
Sandwich, 2962 J-17
Saugus, 26628 D-14
Scituate, 5245 F-16
Seekonk, 10400 I-13
Sharon, 5658 G-13
Shawsheen Vil., 2600 C-14
Sheffield, 1150 G-1
Shelburne Falls, 1731 C-5
Sherborn, 1400 F-12
Shirley, 1441 D-11
Shore Acres, 1200 F-16
Shrewsbury, 31600 F-10
Shutesbury, 700 D-7
Silver Bch., 1300 J-16
Silver Lake, 2900 C-13
Sippewisset, 1500 K-17
Smith Mills, 4760 K-15
Somerset, 18165 J-14
Somerville, 75754 E-14
S. Acton, 3200 D-12
S. Amherst, 4994 E-6
S. Ashburnham, 1062 C-9
S. Chatham, 950 J-20
S. Dartmouth, 9800 K-15
S. Deerfield, 1880 D-5
S. Dennis, 3643 J-19
S. Duxbury, 3360 H-16
S. Easton, 1500 G-14
S. Hadley, 5500 F-6
S. Hadley Falls, 5100 F-6
S. Hamilton, 2800 C-15
S. Hanover, 1000 G-15
S. Harwich, 800 J-20
S. Hingham, 4000 F-15
S. Lancaster, 1894 D-11
S. Orleans, 750 J-20
S. Swansea, 1000 J-13
S. Walpole, 1300 G-13
S. Yarmouth, 11092 J-19
Southborough, 1500 F-11
Southbridge, 12878 G-9
Southwick, 1250 G-5
Spencer, 5700 F-9
Springfield, 153060 G-6
Sterling, 1350 E-10
Stockbridge, 1100 F-1
Stoneham, 21437 D-14
Stoughton, 26700 G-14
Stow, 1250 E-12
Sturbridge, 2253 G-8
Sudbury, 1950 E-12
SUFFOLK CO.,
722023 F-14
Sunderland, 1100 D-6
Swampscott, 13787 D-15
Swansea, 900 J-13
Taunton, 55874 I-14
Teaticket, 1692 K-17
Templeton, 1000 D-8
Tewksbury, 11000 C-13
Thorndike, 1150 F-7
Three Rivers, 2900 F-7
Topsfield, 2717 C-15
Touisset, 1500 J-13
Townsend, 1128 C-10
Townsend Hbr., 900 C-11
Turners Falls, 4470 C-6
Upton, 3013 G-11
Uxbridge, 3500 G-11
Vineyard Haven, 2114 L-17
Wakefield, 24932 D-14
Wales, 800 G-8
Walpole, 5918 G-13
Waltham, 60632 E-13
Wamesit, 2700 C-13
Ware, 6170 F-7
Wareham Ctr., 2896 J-16
Warren, 1405 F-8
Watertown, 31915 E-13
Waterville, 800 C-8
Wayland, 2500 E-12
Webster, 11412 G-10
Wellesley, 27982 F-13
Wellfleet, 1200 H-20
Wenham, 4200 C-15
W. Acton, 5200 D-12
W. Andover, 2000 C-13
W. Boxford, 800 B-14
W. Boylston, 3300 E-10
W. Bridgewater, 2100 H-14
W. Brookfield, 1413 F-8
W. Chatham, 1410 J-20
W. Concord, 6028 D-12
W. Dennis, 2242 J-19
W. Falmouth, 1738 K-17
W. Foxborough, 1100 G-13
W. Groton, 900 C-11
W. Hanover, 1700 G-15
W. Harwich, 1500 J-19
W. Mansfield, 650 H-13
W. Medway, 2000 G-12
W. Newbury, 1100 B-14
W. Springfield, 28391 G-5
W. Stockbridge, 850 E-1
W. Townsend, 700 C-10
W. Upton, 1100 G-11
W. Wareham, 2064 I-16
W. Warren, 1300 F-8
W. Yarmouth, 6012 J-19
Westborough, 4045 F-11
Westfield, 41094 G-5
Westford, 1400 C-12
Westminster, 1100 D-9
Weston, 10200 E-13
Westwood, 6500 F-13
Weymouth, 53988 F-15
Whalom, 1400 D-10
Whately, 630 D-5
White Horse Bch.,
1250 H-17
White Island Shores,
2106 I-17
Whitinsville, 6704 G-11
Whitman, 13240 G-15
Wilbraham, 3915 G-6
Wilkinsonville, 900 F-10
Williamsburg, 1200 E-5
Williamstown, 4325 B-2
Wilmington, 22325 D-13
Winchendon, 4213 C-9
Winchester, 21374 D-14
Winthrop, 18303 E-14
Woburn, 38120 D-14
Woods Hole, 781 K-16
Worcester, 181045 F-10
WORCESTER CO.,
798552 D-8
Wrentham, 2250 G-13
Yarmouth, 1300 J-19
Yarmouth Port, 5320 J-19

Michigan

Map pp. 50 – 51

* City keyed to p. 52

Ada, 2300 P-6
Adrian, 21133 S-10
Alanson, 738 G-8
Albion, 8616 R-8
ALCONA CO., 10942 J-11
ALGER CO., 9601 D-5
Algonac, 4110 Q-14
Allegan, 4998 Q-5
ALLEGAN CO.,
111408 Q-5
Allen Pk., 28210 *L-5
Allendale, 17579 P-5
Alma, 9383 N-8
Almont, 2674 P-12
Alpena, 10483 I-11
ALPENA CO., 29598 I-11
Ann Arbor, 113934 R-11
ANTRIM CO., 23580 I-7
ARENAC CO., 15899 L-10
Argentine, 2525 P-10
Armada, 1730 P-13
Athens, 1024 S-7
Atlanta, 827 I-9
Attica, 994 O-12
Au Gres, 889 L-11
Au Sable, 1404 K-12
Auburn, 2087 N-10
Auburn Hills, 21412 *F-5
Augusta, 885 R-7
Backus Bch., 730 J-11
Bad Axe, 3129 M-12
Baldwin, 1208 M-5
Bangor, 1885 R-5
Baraga, 2053 B-13
BARAGA CO., 8860 B-13
Baroda, 873 S-4
Barron Lake, 1570 T-5
BARRY CO., 59173 Q-7
Bath, 2083 P-9
Battle Creek, 52347 R-7
Bay City, 34932 N-10
BAY CO., 107771 M-10
Beadle Lake, 1550 R-7
Beaverton, 1071 M-9
Beecher, 10232 *A-6
Belding, 5757 O-7
Bellaire, 1086 I-7
Belleville, 3991 R-11
Bellevue, 1282 R-8
Belmont, 730 P-6
Benton Hbr., 10038 S-4
Benton Hts., 4084 S-4
BENZIE CO., 17525 J-5
Berkley, 14970 *H-5
BERRIEN CO., 156813 S-4
Berrien Sprs., 1800 S-4
Bertrand, 5500 T-4
Bessemer, 1905 C-10
Beulah, 342 J-5
Beverly Hills, 10267 *H-5
Big Rapids, 10601 M-6
Bingham Farms, 1111 *H-5
Birch Run, 1555 O-11
Birmingham, 20103 *G-5
Blissfield, 3340 T-10
Bloomfield, 41070 *G-4
Bloomfield Hills, 3869 *G-5
Bostwick Lake, 800 O-6
Boyne City, 3735 H-7
BRANCH CO., 45248 T-7
Breckenridge, 1328 N-9
Bridgeport, 6950 N-10
Bridgman, 2291 S-4
Brighton, 7444 Q-11
Bronson, 2349 T-7
Brooklyn, 1206 S-9
Brown City, 1325 O-13
Brownlee Pk., 2108 R-7
Buchanan, 4456 T-4
Bullock Creek, 750 N-9
Burr Oak, 828 T-7
Burton, 29999 P-11
Byron Ctr., 5822 P-6
Cadillac, 10355 K-6
Caledonia, 1511 P-6
CALHOUN CO.,
136146 S-7
Calumet, 726 A-13
Canton, 76366 *K-2
Capac, 1890 P-13
Carleton, 2345 S-12
Caro, 4229 N-11
Carrollton, 6602 N-10
Carson City, 1093 O-8
Caseville, 777 L-12
Caspian, 906 D-12
Cass City, 2428 N-12
CASS CO., 52293 S-5
Cassopolis, 1774 S-5
Cedar Sprs., 3509 O-6
Cedarville, 1070 E-9
Center Line, 8257 *H-7
Central Lake, 952 I-7
Centreville, 1425 S-6
Charlevoix, 2513 H-7
CHARLEVOIX CO.,
25949 H-7
Charlotte, 9074 Q-8
Chassell, 710 A-13
Cheboygan, 4867 G-9
CHEBOYGAN CO.,
26152 H-9
Chelsea, 4944 R-10
Chesaning, 2394 O-10
CHIPPEWA CO.,
38520 D-8
Clare, 3118 M-8
CLARE CO., 30926 M-8
Clarkston, 882 Q-12
Clawson, 11825 *G-6
Climax, 767 R-7
Clinton, 95648 *G-8
Clinton, 2336 S-10
CLINTON CO., 75382 P-8
Clio, 2646 O-11

*, †, ‡, § See explanation under state title in this index. County and parish names are listed in capital letters and in boldface type. Independent cities (not in any county) are shown in italics.

Cloverville, 1950....O-5
Coldwater, 10945....S-8
Coleman, 1243....M-9
Coloma, 1483....S-4
Colon, 1173....S-7
Columbiaville, 787....O-12
Commerce, 5000....Q-11
Comstock, 5600....R-3
Comstock Pk., 10088....P-6
Concord, 1050....R-8
Constantine, 2076....T-6
Coopersville, 4275....P-5
Corunna, 3497....P-10
CRAWFORD CO., 14074....J-8
Croswell, 2447....O-13
Crystal Falls, 1469....D-3
Cutlerville, 14370....*D-2
Davison, 5173....P-11
Dearborn, 98153....R-12
Dearborn Hts., 57774....*J-4
Decatur, 1819....S-5
Deckerville, 830....N-13
Deerfield, 898....S-11
DELTA CO., 37069....F-3
Delton, 872....Q-7
Detroit, 713777....R-12
Detroit Bch., 2087....S-12
DeWitt, 4507....P-9
Dexter, 4067....R-10
DICKINSON CO., 26168....C-13
Dimondale, 1234....Q-8
Dollar Bay, 1082....A-13
Dorr, 1600....Q-6
Douglas, 1232....Q-5
Dowagiac, 5879....S-5
Dryden, 951....P-12
Dundee, 3957....S-11
Durand, 3446....P-10
Eagle Lake, 1160....T-5
Eagle River, 71....A-13
E. Grand Rapids, 10694....*B-3
E. Jordan, 2351....J-7
E. Lansing, 48579....Q-9
E. Tawas, 2808....K-11
Eastpointe, 32442....Q-13
Eastwood, 6340....R-7
EATON CO., 107759....Q-8
Eaton Rapids, 5214....Q-8
Ecorse, 9512....*L-6
Edmore, 1201....N-7
Edwardsburg, 1259....T-5
Elk Rapids, 1642....I-6
Elkton, 808....M-12
Elsie, 966....O-9
EMMET CO., 32694....G-7
Escanaba, 12616....F-2
Essexville, 3478....N-10
Evart, 1903....M-7
Fair Plain, 7631....S-4
Farmington, 10372....*H-3
Farmington Hills, 79740....Q-12

Thorofare, 1700......M-6
Tinton Falls, 17892......I-12
Titusville, 900......I-8
Toms River, 88791......L-12
Totowa, 10804......E-12
Town Bank, 1500......T-7
Trenton, 84913......J-8
Tuckahoe, 800......Q-8
Tuckerton, 3347......O-11
Turnersville, 3742......N-7
Twin Rivers, 7443......J-10
Union, 54405......F-11
Union Bch., 6245......H-12
Union City, 66455......D-5
UNION CO., 536499......G-11
Upper Saddle River, 8208......C-12
Ventnor City, 10650......Q-10
Verga, 800......*G-4
Verona, 13533......B-1
Victory Gdns., 1520......E-10
Vienna, 981......E-8
Villas, 9483......S-7
Vincentown, 900......L-9
Vineland, 60724......P-7
Waldwick, 9622......C-12
Wallington, 11335......B-4
Wanamassa, 4532......I-13
Wanaque, 11116......D-11
Waretown, 1569......M-12
WARREN CO., 108692......E-8
Warrenville, 1000......G-10
Washington, 6461......F-7
Watchung, 5801......G-10
Waterford Works, 1000......N-8
Wayne, 54069......D-11
Wenonah, 2278......N-6
W. Atlantic City, 900......Q-10
W. Cape May, 1024......T-7
W. Collingswood Hts., 1000......*F-5
W. Creek, 800......O-11
W. Freehold, 13613......J-11
W. Keansburg, 1500......H-12
W. Long Branch, 8097......I-13
W. Milford, 26410......C-11
W. New York, 49708......E-13
W. Orange, 44943......F-12
W. Tuckerton, 700......O-11
W. Wildwood, 603......T-8
Westfield, 30316......*J-3
Westville, 4500......*G-5
Westville Grv., 1500......*G-5
Westwood, 10908......*A-9
Wharton, 6522......E-10
White House Sta., 2089......G-8
Whitehouse, 800......G-9
Whitesboro, 1100......T-8
Whiting, 950......L-11
Whitman Sq., 3500......N-7
Wildwood, 5325......T-8
Wildwood Crest, 3270......T-8
Williamstown, 15567......N-7
Winslow, 800......N-8
Wood-Lynne, 2978......*F-5
Wood-Ridge, 7626......B-4
Woodbine, 2716......S-8
Woodbridge, 19265......G-11
Woodbury, 10174......M-6
Woodbury Hts., 3055......M-6
Woodland Park, 10987......A-2
Woodstown, 3505......N-5
Wrightstown, 802......K-9
Wyckoff, 16508......D-12
Yardville, 7186......J-9

New Mexico
Map p. 68
Acomita, 800......E-3
Adobe Acres, 2500......N-8
Agua Fria, 2800......M-4
Alamogordo, 30403......I-6
Albuquerque, 545852......E-4
Algodones, 814......D-5
Alto, 800......H-6
Angel Fire, 1216......B-7
Anthony, 9360......J-5
Arenas Valley, 1522......I-2
Arroyo Seco, 1785......B-6
Artesia, 11301......I-8
Atoka, 1077......I-8
Aztec, 6763......B-3
Bayard, 2328......I-2
Belen, 7269......F-4
Bernalillo, 8320......E-5
BERNALILLO CO., 662564......E-4
Black Rock, 1323......E-1
Bloomfield, 8112......B-3
Bluewater, 628......E-3
Bosque Farms, 3904......F-4
Capitan, 1489......H-6
Carlsbad, 26138......J-8
Carrizozo, 996......G-6
CATRON CO., 3725......G-2
Cedar Crest, 958......E-5
Cedar Hill, 847......A-3
Chama, 1022......A-5
Chamberino, 919......J-4
Chaparral, 14631......J-5
CHAVES CO., 65645......G-9
Chimayo, 3177......C-6
Church Rock, 1128......D-2
CIBOLA CO., 27213......E-2
Cimarron, 1021......B-7
Clayton, 2980......B-10
Cloudcroft, 674......I-6
Clovis, 37775......F-10
COLFAX CO., 13750......B-7
Columbus, 1664......K-3
Corrales, 8329......E-5
Crownpoint, 2278......D-2
Cuba, 731......C-4
CURRY CO., 48376......F-9
DE BACA CO., 2022......F-8
Deming, 14855......J-3
Dexter, 1266......H-8
Dixon, 926......C-6
Doña Ana, 1211......J-4
DOÑA ANA CO., 209233......J-4
Dulce, 2743......A-4
EDDY CO., 53829......J-8
Edgewood, 3735......E-5
El Rito, 808......C-5
Elephant Butte, 1431......H-4
Española, 10224......C-5
Estancia, 1655......E-5
Eunice, 2922......J-10
Fairacres, 824......K-4
Farmington, 45877......B-2
Five Points, 4200......N-8
Flora Vista, 2191......B-2
Ft. Sumner, 1031......F-8
Ft. Wingate, 950......D-2
Gallup, 21678......D-1
GRANT CO., 29514......I-2
Grants, 9182......E-3
GUADALUPE CO., 4687......E-7
Hagerman, 1257......H-8
HARDING CO., 695......D-9
Hatch, 1648......I-4
HIDALGO CO., 4894......K-1
High Rolls, 834......I-6
Hobbs, 34122......I-10
Hurley, 1297......I-2
Jal, 2047......J-10
Jarales, 2475......F-4
Jemez Pueblo, 1788......D-4
Kirtland, 7875......B-2
La Cienega, 3819......D-5
La Luz, 1697......I-6
La Mesa, 728......J-4
La Plata, 612......A-2
La Puebla, 1285......C-5
La Union, 1106......K-4
Laguna, 1241......E-3
Las Cruces, 97618......J-4
Las Vegas, 13753......D-7
LEA CO., 64727......H-9
LINCOLN CO., 20497......G-6
Logan, 1042......D-9
Lordsburg, 2797......J-1
Los Alamos, 12019......C-5
LOS ALAMOS CO., 17950......C-5
Los Chaves, 5446......F-4
Los Lunas, 14835......F-4
Los Padillas, 2500......E-4
Los Ranchos de Albuquerque, 6024......L-8
Loving, 1413......J-9
Lovington, 11009......I-10
LUNA CO., 25095......J-2
Magdalena, 938......G-4
McIntosh, 1484......E-5
McKINLEY CO., 71492......D-3
Melrose, 651......F-9
Mescalero, 1338......H-6
Mesilla, 2196......J-4
Mesquite, 1112......J-4
Midway, 971......I-9
Milan, 3245......E-3
Monterey Park, 2000......N-8
MORA CO., 4881......C-7
Moriarty, 1910......E-5
Mosquero, 93......D-9
Mountainair, 928......F-5
Navajo, 1645......C-1
OTERO CO., 63797......I-6
Paradise Hills, 4256......K-7
Paraje, 777......E-3
Pecos, 1392......D-6
Peña Blanca, 709......D-5
Peralta, 3660......E-4
Placitas, 4977......D-5
Pojoaque Valley, 1907......C-5
Portales, 12280......F-10
QUAY CO., 9041......E-9
Questa, 1770......B-6
Ranchos, 5395......I-9
Ranchos de Taos, 2518......C-6
Raton, 6885......B-8
Reserve, 289......G-1
RIO ARRIBA CO., 40246......B-4
Rio Rancho, 87521......E-4
ROOSEVELT CO., 19846......G-9
Roswell, 48366......H-8
Ruidoso, 8029......H-6
Ruidoso Downs, 2815......H-6
Salem, 942......I-4
San Felipe Pueblo, 2404......D-5
SAN JUAN CO., 130044......B-2
San Juan Pueblo, 1143......C-5
SAN MIGUEL CO., 29393......D-7
San Rafael, 933......E-3
SANDOVAL CO., 131561......C-4
Santa Clara, 1686......I-2
Santa Fe, 67947......D-6
SANTA FE CO., 144170......D-5
Santa Rosa, 2848......E-7
Santa Teresa, 4258......K-4
Santo Domingo Pueblo, 2456......D-5
Shiprock, 8295......B-2
SIERRA CO., 11988......I-4
Silver City, 10315......I-2
Socorro, 9051......G-4
SOCORRO CO., 17866......G-5
Springer, 1047......C-8
Sunland Pk., 14106......K-5
Taos, 5716......B-6
TAOS CO., 32937......B-6
Taos Pueblo, 1135......B-6
Tatum, 798......H-10
Texico, 1130......F-10
Thoreau, 1865......D-2
Tierra Amarilla, 382......B-5
Tohatchi, 808......C-1
Tome, 1867......E-4
TORRANCE CO., 16383......F-6
Truth or Consequences, 6475......H-4
Tucumcari, 5363......E-9
Tularosa, 2842......I-5
Twin Lakes, 1052......D-1
Tyrone, 637......I-2
UNION CO., 4549......B-9
University Pk., 4192......J-4
Vado, 3194......J-5
Valencia, 2192......E-4
VALENCIA CO., 76569......F-4
Waterflow, 1670......B-2
White Rock, 5725......D-5
White Sands, 1651......I-5
Zuni Pueblo, 6302......E-1

New York
Map pp. 69 – 71
Map keys Atlas pages
NA – NN 70 – 71
SA – SJ 69
* City keyed to pp. 72 – 73
Adams, 1775......NF-12
Adams Ctr., 1568......NF-12
Addison, 1763......SJ-8
Afton, 822......NM-14
Akron, 2868......NB-15
Albany, 97856......NK-19
ALBANY CO., 304204......NL-18
Albertson, 5182......*G-17
Albion, 6056......NB-6
Alden, 2605......NJ-5
Alexandria Bay, 1078......ND-11
Alfred, 4174......SH-9
Allegany, 1816......NM-5
ALLEGANY CO., 48946......NL-6
Altamont, 1720......NK-18
Altona, 730......NB-19
Amagansett, 1165......SE-13
Amawalk, 1390......SC-6
Amenia, 955......NN-20
Amherst, 45800......NI-4
Amityville, 9523......SI-8
Amsterdam, 18620......NJ-18
Andover, 1042......NM-7
Angelica, 869......NL-6
Angola, 2127......NK-3
Angola on the Lake, 1675......NK-3
Apalachin, 1131......NM-12
Arcade, 2071......NK-5
Arkport, 844......NL-7
Arlington, 4061......SA-6
Armonk, 4330......SD-6
Arverne, 1750......SI-5
Ashville, 800......NM-2
Athens, 1668......NL-19
Atlantic Bch., 1891......SG-7
Attica, 2547......NJ-5
Auburn, 27687......NI-10
Aurora, 724......NJ-10
Averill Park, 1693......NK-19
Avoca, 946......NL-8
Avon, 3394......NJ-7
Babylon, 12166......SI-9
Bainbridge, 1355......NL-14
Baiting Hollow, 1642......SE-11
Baldwin, 24033......SI-6
Baldwin Hbr., 8102......*D-19
Baldwinsville, 7378......NI-11
Ballston Spa, 5409......NJ-19
Balmville, 3178......SB-5
Batavia, 15465......NI-6
Bath, 5786......NL-8
Baxter Estates, 999......*E-16
Bay Park, 2212......*F-17
Bay Shore, 26337......SI-9
Bayberry, 6200......SH-2
Bayport, 8662......SH-11
Bayville, 6669......SE-7
Beacon, 15541......SB-6
Bedford, 1834......SC-6
Bedford Hills, 3001......SC-7
Belfast, 837......NL-6
Belle Terre, 792......SE-9
Bellerose, 1193......*E-15
Bellerose Terr., 2198......*E-16
Bellmore, 16218......SG-7
Bellport, 2084......SF-10
Belmont, 969......NM-6
Bemus Pt., 1200......NM-3
Berlin, 1200......NK-20
Bethpage, 16429......*H-20
Big Flats, 5277......NM-9
Binghamton, 47376......NM-12
Black River, 1348......NE-13
Blasdell, 2553......NJ-4
Blauvelt, 5689......SD-6
Bloomfield, 1361......NJ-8
Bloomington, 800......SA-5
Blue Pt., 4773......SJ-12
Bohemia, 10180......SI-11
Boiceville, 800......NM-17
Bolivar, 1047......NM-6
Boonville, 2072......NG-14
Brant Lake, 850......NG-19
Brentwood, 60664......SF-9
Brewerton, 4029......NH-11
Brewster, 2390......SC-7
Briarcliff Manor, 7867......SD-6
Bridgehampton, 1756......SE-12
Bridgeport, 1490......NI-12
Brighton, 36609......NI-8
Brightwaters, 3103......SI-10
Broadalbin, 1327......NJ-18
Broadacres, 1280......NJ-17
Brockport, 8366......NI-7
Bronxville, 6543......*A-9
BRONX CO., 1385108......*D-11
Bronxville, 6323......*D-13
Brookhaven, 3451......SF-10
Brookville, 3465......*F-19
BROOME CO., 200600......NM-12
Brownville, 1119......NE-12
Brunswick, 800......NK-19
Buchanan, 2230......SC-6
Buffalo, 292648......NJ-4
Bullville, 900......SB-4
Burnt Hills, 1620......NJ-19
Cadyville, 900......NB-19
Cairo, 1402......NL-18
Calcium, 3491......NE-13
Caledonia, 2201......NJ-7
Calverton, 6510......SE-11
Cambridge, 1870......NI-20
Camden, 2231......NH-13
Camillus, 1213......NI-11
Campbell, 713......NM-9
Canajoharie, 2229......NJ-16
Canandaigua, 10545......NJ-8
Canastota, 4804......NI-13
Candor, 851......NM-11
Canisteo, 2270......NL-7
Canton, 6314......NC-14
Cape Vincent, 726......NE-11
Carle Place, 4981......*G-18
Carmel, 3600......SB-7
Carthage, 3747......NE-13
Castile, 1015......NK-6
Castleton-on-Hudson, 1473......NK-19
Catskill, 4081......NL-19
Cattaraugus, 1002......NL-4
CATTARAUGUS CO., 80317......NL-4
CAYUGA CO., 80026......NI-10
Cayuga Hts., 3729......NL-11
Cazenovia, 2835......NJ-13
Cedarhurst, 6592......*K-16
Celoron, 1112......NM-2
Center Moriches, 7580......SF-11
Centereach, 31578......SE-9
Centerport, 5508......SE-8
Central Islip, 34450......SE-9
Central Sq., 1848......NH-12
Chadwicks, 1506......NI-14
Champlain, 1101......NA-19
Champlain Park, 1200......NB-20
Chappaqua, 1436......SD-7
Chateaugay, 833......NB-18
Chatham, 1770......NL-19
CHAUTAUQUA CO., 134905......NL-2
Cheektowaga, 75178......NE-10
CHEMUNG CO., 88830......NL-9
Chenango Bridge, 2883......NM-12
CHENANGO CO., 50477......NK-13
Chester, 3969......SC-4
Chili Ctr., 4350......SG-1
Chittenango, 5081......NI-13
Churchville, 1961......NI-7
Cicero, 1100......NI-12
Circleville, 1350......SB-4
Clarence, 2646......NI-4
Clarence Ctr., 2257......NI-4
Clark Mills, 1905......NI-14
Clarkson, 4358......NI-6
Clarksville, 800......NK-18
Claverack, 1000......NM-19
Clayton, 1978......ND-12
Cleveland, 750......NH-12
Clifton Park, 1200......NJ-19
Clifton Sprs., 2127......NJ-9
Clinton, 1942......NI-14
CLINTON CO., 82128......NB-19
Clintondale, 1452......SA-5
Clyde, 2093......NI-9
Cobleskill, 4678......NK-17
Cohocton, 838......NK-8
Cohoes, 16168......NJ-19
Cold Spring, 2013......SC-6
Cold Spring Hbr., 5070......SH-8
Colonie, 7793......NJ-19
COLUMBIA CO., 63096......NM-19
Commack, 36124......SE-9
Congers, 8363......SD-6
Conklin, 1800......NM-13
Constantia, 1182......NH-12
Coopers Plains, 1800......NM-8
Cooperstown, 1852......NK-15
Copake, 1200......NM-20
Copenhagen, 801......NF-13
Coram, 39113......SE-10
Corfu, 709......NJ-5
Corinth, 2559......NH-19
Corning, 11183......NM-9
Cornwall-on-Hudson, 3018......SB-5
Cortland, 19204......NK-12
CORTLAND CO., 49336......NK-12
Coxsackie, 2813......NL-19
Cross River, 980......SC-7
Croton Falls, 970......SC-7
Croton-on-Hudson, 8070......SD-6
Crown Pt., 1000......NF-20
Cuba, 1575......NM-5
Cuddebackville, 1100......SB-3
Cutchogue, 3349......SD-13
Dannemora, 3936......NB-19
Dansville, 4719......NK-7
Deer Park, 27745......SF-8
Delevan, 1089......NK-5
Delhi, 3087......NL-16
Delmar, 8300......NK-19
Depew, 15303......NJ-4
Deposit, 1663......NM-14
Derby, 1200......NK-3
Dexter, 1052......NE-12
Dix Hills, 26892......SH-9
Dobbs Ferry, 10875......SE-6
Dolgeville, 2206......NI-16
Dover Plains, 1323......SA-7
Dryden, 1890......NL-11
Dundee, 1725......NK-9
Dunkirk, 12563......NL-2
DUTCHESS CO., 297488......SA-7
Earlville, 872......NK-13
E. Aurora, 6236......NK-4
E. Farmingdale, 6484......SJ-8
E. Glenville, 6616......NJ-18
E. Greenbush, 4487......NK-19
E. Hampton, 1083......SE-13
E. Hills, 6955......*F-19
E. Islip, 14475......SJ-11
E. Marion, 926......SD-12
E. Massapequa, 19069......SJ-8
E. Meadow, 38132......SF-7
E. Northport, 20217......SE-8
E. Norwich, 2709......*E-19
E. Patchogue, 22469......SJ-12
E. Quogue, 4757......SE-12
E. Rochester, 6587......SG-4
E. Rockaway, 9818......*J-17
E. Setauket, 8000......SE-9
E. Shoreham, 6666......SE-10
E. Syracuse, 3084......NI-12
E. Williston, 2556......*G-17
Eastport, 1831......SE-11
Eden, 3516......NK-3
Eggertsville, 15019......NI-11
Elbridge, 1058......NI-11
Eldred, 750......SB-2
Elizabethtown, 754......ND-19
Ellenville, 4135......SA-4
Elma Ctr., 2571......NK-4
Elmira, 29200......NM-10
Elmira Hts., 4097......NM-10
Elmont, 33198......SH-6
Elmsford, 4664......SH-5
Elwood, 11177......SH-9
Endicott, 13392......NM-12
Endwell, 11446......NM-12
ERIE CO., 919040......NK-4
Escarpment, 1200......NA-17
ESSEX CO., 39370......NE-18
Fair Haven, 745......NH-10
Fairmount, 10224......NI-11
Fairport, 5353......NI-8
Fairview, 3099......SB-5
Falconer, 2420......NM-2
Farmingdale, 8189......SJ-8
Farmingville, 16458......SJ-10
Fayetteville, 4373......NI-12
Ferndale, 850......SA-3
Fishers Island, 200......SC-7
Findley Lake, 800......NM-1
Fire Island Pines, 900......SF-10
Fishkill, 2171......SB-6
Flanders, 4472......SE-11
Floral Park, 15967......*F-15
Florida, 2833......SC-5
Flower Hill, 4665......*F-17
Fonda, 795......NJ-17
Forestport, 900......NH-14
Ft. Covington, 1200......NA-16
Ft. Drum, 12955......NE-13
Ft. Edward, 3375......NH-19
Ft. Hunter, 1250......NJ-17
Ft. Plain, 2322......NJ-16
Ft. Salonga, 10008......SE-10
Frankfort, 2598......NJ-15
FRANKLIN CO., 51599......NC-17
Franklin Sq., 29320......*H-17
Franklinville, 1740......NL-5
Fredonia, 11230......NL-2
Freeport, 42860......SG-7
Frewsburg, 1965......NM-3
Friendship, 1218......NM-6
Fulton, 11855......NH-11
FULTON CO., 55531......NI-17
Fultonville, 784......NJ-17
Gainesville, 4617......SF-8
Garden City, 21672......*H-18
Garden City Park, 7806......*H-17
Garden City South, 4024......*H-17
Gardiner, 950......SA-5
Garrison, 800......SC-6
Gasport, 1248......NI-4
Gates Ctr., 4981......*G-18
GENESEE CO., 60079......NJ-6
Geneseo, 8031......NJ-7
Geneva, 13261......NJ-9
Germantown, 845......NM-18
Gerry, 800......NM-2
Getzville, 2300......NC-10
Glasco, 2099......NM-18
Glen Cove, 26964......SE-7
Glen Head, 4697......*E-18
Glenham, 2000......SB-6
Glenmont, 1200......NK-19
Glens Falls, 14700......NH-19
Glenwood Landing, 3779......*E-17
Gloversville, 15665......NI-17
Golden's Bridge, 1630......SC-7
Gordon Hts., 4042......SH-13
Goshen, 5454......SC-4
Gouverneur, 3949......ND-14
Gowanda, 2709......NL-3
Grand Gorge, 1000......NL-17
Grand Island, 800......NJ-3
Grandyle Vil., 4629......NJ-3
Granville, 2543......NH-20
Great Bend, 863......NE-13
Great Neck, 9989......SE-7
Great Neck Estates, 2761......*F-15
Great Neck Plaza, 6707......*F-16
Great River, 1489......SJ-11
Greece, 14519......SG-2
Green Island, 2620......NE-5
Greene, 1580......NL-13
GREENE CO., 49221......NL-18
Greenlawn, 13742......SH-9
Greenport, 2197......SD-12
Greenvale, 1094......*F-18
Greenville, 7116......SJ-5
Greenwich, 1777......NI-20
Greenwood Lake, 3154......SD-4
Groton, 2363......NL-11
Guilderland, 1900......NK-18
Guilderland Ctr., 860......NJ-18
Hadley, 1200......NH-18
Hagaman, 1292......NJ-18
Halesite, 2498......SH-8
Hamburg, 9409......NJ-4
Hamilton, 4239......NJ-13
HAMILTON CO., 4836......NF-16
Hamlin, 5521......NH-6
Hampton Bays, 13603......SE-12
Hampton Manor, 2417......NK-5
Hancock, 1031......NN-14
Hannawa Falls, 1042......NC-15
Harbor Isle, 1301......*K-17
Harriman, 2424......SC-5
Harris Hill, 5508......SE-8
Harrison, 27472......SE-7
Harrison, 13620......*A-16
Hartsdale, 5293......SJ-5
Hauppauge, 20882......SH-11
Haverstraw, 11910......SD-6
Head of the Harbor, 1472......SG-11
Hempstead, 53891......SF-7
Henrietta, 1200......NI-8
Herkimer, 7743......NJ-15
HERKIMER CO., 64519......NH-15
Herricks, 4295......*G-17
Heuvelton, 714......NC-13
Hewlett, 6819......*J-16
Hewlett Hbr., 1263......*K-17
Hicksville, 41547......SF-8
Highland, 5647......SA-5
Highland Falls, 3900......SC-5
Highland Mills, 3468......SC-5
Highland-on-the-Lake, 1800......NK-3
Hillcrest, 7558......SD-6
Hilton, 5886......NH-7
Hinsdale, 900......NM-5
Holbrook, 27195......SI-12
Holland, 1206......NK-5
Holley, 1811......NI-6
Holtsville, 19714......SE-10
Homer, 3291......NK-12
Homewood, 1450......SJ-4
Honeoye Falls, 2674......NJ-7
Hoosick Falls, 3501......NJ-20
Hornell, 8563......NL-7
Horseheads, 6461......NM-10
Houghton, 1693......NL-6
Hudson, 6713......NL-19
Hudson Falls, 7281......NH-19
Hunter, 490......NL-18
Huntington, 18046......SH-8
Huntington Bay, 1425......SE-8
Huntington Sta., 33029......SE-8
Hurley, 3458......NN-18
Hurleyville, 750......SA-3
Hyde Park, 1908......NN-18
Ilion, 8610......NJ-15
Inwood, 9792......SG-7
Irondequoit, 51692......NI-7
Irvington, 6631......SE-6
Island Park, 4655......*K-17
Islandia, 3057......SH-10
Islip, 18689......SJ-9
Islip Terr., 5389......SH-11
Ithaca, 30014......NL-11
Jamesport, 1710......SE-11
Jamestown, 31146......NM-2
JEFFERSON CO., 116229......NE-13
Jefferson Valley, 6700......SC-6
Jericho, 13567......SF-7
Johnson City, 15174......NM-12
Johnstown, 8743......NJ-17
Jordan, 1368......NI-10
Katonah, 1679......SC-7
Keeseville, 1815......NC-19
Kenmore, 15423......NI-8
Kerhonkson, 1684......SA-4
Keuka Park, 1137......NK-9
Kiamesha Lake, 850......SA-3
Kinderhook, 1211......NL-19
KINGS CO., 2504700......SG-5
Kings Park, 17282......SE-9
Kings Pt., 5005......*E-15
Kingston, 23893......NM-18
Kiryas Joel, 20175......SC-5
Lackawanna, 18141......NJ-3
Lacona, 582......NG-12
L. Delta, 2020......NH-14
L. Erie Bch., 3872......NK-2
L. George, 906......NH-19
L. Grove, 11163......SH-13
L. Katrine, 2397......NM-18
L. Luzerne, 1227......NH-19
L. Mohegan, 6010......SC-6
L. Peekskill, 2150......SC-6
L. Placid, 2521......ND-18
L. Pleasant, 350......NH-17
L. Ronkonkoma, 20155......SJ-12
L. Success, 2934......*G-16
Lakeland, 2786......SJ-12
Lakeview, 5615......*J-17
Lakewood, 3002......NM-2
Lancaster, 10352......NJ-4
Lansing, 3529......NL-11
Larchmont, 5864......*A-15
Latham, 4200......NK-19
Lattingtown, 1739......*D-18
Laurel, 1394......SD-12
Laurel Hollow, 1952......*E-20
Le Roy, 4391......NJ-6
Levittown, 51881......SF-8
Lewiston, 2701......NI-3
LEWIS CO., 27087......NG-13
Liberty, 4392......SA-3
Lido Bch., 2897......SH-7
Lima, 2139......NJ-7
Lime Lake, 867......NL-5
Lincoln Park, 2366......NM-18
Lindenhurst, 27253......SJ-9
Little Falls, 4946......NJ-16
Little Valley, 1143......NL-4
Liverpool, 2347......NI-11
LIVINGSTON CO., 65393......NK-7
Livingston Manor, 1221......SA-3
Livonia, 1409......NJ-7
Lloyd Hbr., 3660......SE-8
Lockport, 21165......NI-4
Locust Grove, 9700......*F-20
Locust Valley, 3406......SE-7
Lowville, 3470......NF-14
Lynbrook, 19427......*J-17
Lyndonville, 838......NH-5
Lyons, 3619......NI-9
Macedon, 1523......NI-8
Machias, 1180......NL-5
MADISON CO., 73442......NJ-13
Madrid, 757......NB-15
Mahopac, 8478......SC-7
Malone, 6000......NB-17
Malverne, 8514......*J-17
Mamaroneck, 18929......SE-7
Manchester, 1709......NJ-8
Manhasset, 8080......*F-16
Manlius, 4704......NI-12
Manorhaven, 6556......*E-16
Marathon, 919......NL-12
Marcellus, 1813......NJ-11
Margaretville, 596......NL-17
Marion, 1511......NI-9
Marlboro, 3669......SB-6
Massapequa, 22652......SJ-8
Massapequa Pk., 17008......SJ-8
Massena, 10936......NB-15
Mastic, 15481......SF-10
Mastic Bch., 12930......SF-10
Mattituck, 4219......SE-12
Mattydale, 6446......SJ-3
Maybrook, 2958......SB-5
Mayfield, 832......NI-17
Mayville, 1711......NL-2
Maywood, 3400......NK-3
McGraw, 1053......NK-12
McKownville, 4850......NF-3
Mechanicstown, 6858......SB-4
Mechanicville, 5196......NJ-19
Medford, 24142......SF-10
Medina, 6065......NH-5
Melrose Park, 2294......NJ-11
Melville, 18985......SI-8
Menands, 3990......NK-19
Merrick, 22097......*J-19
Mexico, 1624......NH-11
Middle Hope, 3000......SB-5
Middle Island, 10483......SH-13
Middleburgh, 1500......NK-17
Middleport, 1840......NH-5
Middletown, 28086......SB-4
Middleville, 1400......SD-10
Mill Neck, 997......*D-19
Millbrook, 1452......NN-19
Miller Place, 12339......SE-10
Millerton, 958......NN-20
Milton, 1403......SA-6
Mineola, 18799......SF-7
Minetto, 1069......NH-11
Minoa, 3449......NI-12
Mohawk, 2731......NJ-15
Mohegan Lake, 3600......SC-6
Monroe, 8364......SC-5
Monsey, 15445......SD-5
Montauk, 3326......SD-14
Montgomery, 3814......SB-5
MONTGOMERY CO., 50219......NJ-16
Monticello, 6726......SA-3
Montour Falls, 1711......NL-10
Montrose, 2731......SC-6
Moravia, 1282......NK-11
Moriches, 2838......SF-11
Morrisonville, 1545......NB-19
Morrisville, 2199......NJ-13
Mt. Ivy, 6878......SD-5
Mt. Kisco, 10877......SD-7
Mt. Morris, 2986......NJ-7
Mt. Sinai, 12118......SE-10
Mt. Vernon, 67292......*C-13
Mumford, 800......NI-7
Munsey Park, 2693......*F-16
Munsons Cors., 2728......NI-11
Muttontown, 3497......*E-19
Myers Cor., 6790......SB-6
Nanuet, 17882......SD-6
Naples, 1041......NK-8
NASSAU CO., 1339532......SF-7
Nesconset, 11992......SE-9
New Baltimore, 960......NL-19
New Berlin, 1028......NK-14
New Cassel, 14059......*G-19
New City, 33559......SD-6
New Falconwood, 1200......ND-7
New Hampton, 1200......SC-4
New Hartford, 1847......NI-14
New Hyde Park, 9714......*H-16
New Lebanon, 950......NK-20
New Paltz, 6818......SA-5
New Rochelle, 77062......SE-7
New Windsor, 8922......SB-5
New York, 8175133......SF-6
NEW YORK CO., 1585873......*D-11
Newark, 9145......NI-9
Newark Valley, 997......NM-12
Newburgh, 28866......SB-5
Newfane, 3822......NH-4
Newport, 640......NI-15
Newtonville, 2300......NK-6
NIAGARA CO., 216469......NH-4
Niagara Falls, 50193......NI-3
Nissequogue, 1749......SE-9
Niskayuna, 4859......NJ-19
North Babylon, 17509......SH-9
Nissequogue, 1749......SE-9
Niverville, 1662......NL-19
Norfolk, 1327......NB-15
N. Amityville, 17862......SJ-9
N. Babylon, 17509......SJ-9
N. Bay, 800......NH-10
N. Bellmore, 19941......*J-19
N. Bellport, 11545......SJ-13
N. Bloomfield, 1260......NJ-7
N. Boston, 2521......NK-4
N. Collins, 1200......NI-4
N. Great River, 4001......SI-11
N. Haven, 833......SD-12
N. Hornell, 778......NL-7
N. Lindenhurst, 11652......SJ-9
N. Lynbrook, 793......*J-17
N. Massapequa, 17886......SJ-8
N. Merrick, 12272......*J-19
N. New Hyde Park, 14899......*G-16
N. Patchogue, 7246......SJ-13
N. Salem, 930......SC-7
N. Sea, 4458......SE-12
N. Syracuse, 6800......NI-12
N. Tonawanda, 31568......NI-4
N. Valley Stream, 16628......*J-16
N. Wantagh, 11960......SJ-7
Northport, 7401......SE-9
Northville, 1099......NI-17
Norwich, 7190......NK-14
Norwood, 1657......NB-15
Noyack, 3568......SE-12
Nunda, 1377......NK-6
Nyack, 6737......SD-6
Oakdale, 7974......SH-12
Oakfield, 1813......NI-5
Oceanside, 32109......SG-7
Ogdensburg, 11128......NC-14
Olcott, 1241......NH-4
Old Bethpage, 5523......SJ-8
Old Brookville, 2134......*E-18
Old Field, 918......SE-9
Old Forge, 756......NF-15
Old Westbury, 4671......*F-18
Olean, 14452......NM-5
Oneida, 11393......NI-13
ONEIDA CO., 234878......NH-13
Oneonta, 13901......NL-15
ONONDAGA CO., 467026......NJ-12
Onondaga Hill, 2000......NJ-12
Ontario, 2160......NH-8
ONTARIO CO., 107931......NJ-8
ORANGE CO., 372813......SC-4
Orange Lake, 6982......SB-5
Orchard Park, 3246......NK-4
Orient, 743......SD-13
Oriskany, 1400......NI-14
Oriskany Falls, 732......NJ-13
ORLEANS CO., 42883......NI-6
Ossining, 25060......SD-6
Oswego, 18142......NH-11
OSWEGO CO., 122109......NG-12
Otego, 1010......NL-15
OTSEGO CO., 62259......NK-15
Owego, 3896......NM-11
Oxford, 1450......NL-13
Oyster Bay, 6707......SE-7
Oyster Bay Cove, 2197......*D-20
Painted Post, 1809......NM-9
Palatine Bridge, 737......NJ-16
Palenville, 1037......NM-18
Palmyra, 3536......NI-8
Patchogue, 11798......SF-10
Patterson, 1200......SB-7
Pawling, 2347......SB-7
Pearl River, 15876......SD-5
Peekskill, 22583......SC-6
Pelham, 6910......*C-14
Pelham Manor, 5486......*C-14
Penfield, 6300......NI-8
Penn Yan, 5159......NK-9
Perry, 3673......NK-6
Peru, 1591......NC-19
Phelps, 1989......NJ-9
Philadelphia, 1252......NE-13
Philmont, 1379......NL-19
Phoenix, 2382......NH-11
Pine Bush, 1780......SB-4
Pine Island, 1500......SC-4
Pine Plains, 1353......NM-19
Pine Valley, 813......NM-10
Pinehurst, 1850......NJ-3
Pitcher Hill, 5000......SH-3
Pittsford, 1355......NI-8
Plainedge, 8817......*H-20
Plainview, 26217......SF-8
Plattekill, 1260......SB-5
Plattsburgh, 19989......NB-19
Pleasant Valley, 1145......SA-6
Pleasantdale, 1260......ND-5
Pleasantville, 7019......SD-6
Poestenkill, 1061......NK-19
Point Lookout, 1219......*K-19
Pomona, 3103......SD-5
Poquott, 953......SG-12
Port Byron, 1290......NI-10
Port Chester, 28967......SE-7
Port Dickinson, 1641......NM-12
Port Ewen, 3546......NN-18
Port Henry, 1194......NE-20
Port Jefferson, 7750......SE-9
Port Jefferson Station, 7838......SG-12
Port Jervis, 8828......SC-3
Port Washington, 15846......SF-7
Port Washington North, 3154......*E-16
Portland, 950......NL-2
Portville, 1014......NM-5
Potsdam, 9428......NC-15
Poughkeepsie, 32736......SA-6
Prospect Hill, 900......ND-5
Pulaski, 2365......NG-12
Purdys, 970......SC-7
PUTNAM CO., 99710......SB-7
Putnam Lake, 3844......SB-7
QUEENS CO., 2230722......SF-6
Queensbury, 830......NH-19
Queenstown, 2701......NA-6
Quogue, 967......SF-11
Randolph, 1286......NM-3
Ransomville, 1419......NH-4
Rapids, 1636......NI-4
Ravena, 3268......NK-19
Red Hook, 1961......NM-19
Red Oaks Mill, 3613......SA-6
Remsenburg, 500......SF-11
RENSSELAER CO., 159429......NJ-20
Rhinebeck, 2657......NN-18
Richfield Sprs., 1264......NJ-15
Richmond, 990......NJ-8
RICHMOND CO., 468730......SG-5
Richmondville, 918......NK-16
Ridge, 13336......SE-10
Rifton, 1200......NM-18
Riverhead, 13299......SE-11
Rochdale, 1800......SA-6
Rochester, 210565......NI-7
Rock Hill, 1742......SA-3
ROCKLAND CO., 311687......SD-5
Rockville Centre, 24023......SG-7
Rocky Pt., 14014......SE-10
Rome, 33725......NI-14
Ronkonkoma, 19082......SH-11
Roosevelt, 16258......*I-18
Rosendale Vil., 1349......NN-18
Roslyn, 2770......*F-17
Roslyn Estates, 1251......*F-17
Roslyn Hbr., 1051......*F-17
Roslyn Hts., 6577......*F-17
Rotterdam, 20652......NJ-18
Rotterdam Jct., 1000......NJ-18
Rouses Pt., 2209......NA-20
Rushville, 677......NJ-9
Rye, 15720......SE-7
Rye Brook, 9347......SH-5
Sackets Hbr., 1450......NF-12
Sackets Lake, 800......SB-2
Saddle Rock, 830......*F-15
Sag Harbor, 2169......SE-12
St. James, 13338......SH-11
St. Johnsville, 1732......NJ-16
ST. LAWRENCE CO., 111944......ND-15
Salamanca, 5815......NM-4
Salem, 946......NI-20
Sanborn, 1645......NI-4
Sands Pt., 2675......*D-17
Sandy Bch., 2350......NI-3
Sandy Creek, 771......NG-12
Saranac Lake, 5406......ND-18
Saratoga Sprs., 26586......NI-19
SARATOGA CO., 219607......NI-18
Saugerties, 3971......NM-18
Sauquoit, 930......NI-14
Savona, 827......NL-8
Sayville, 16853......SF-9
Scarsdale, 17166......*A-14
Schenectady, 61821......NJ-18
SCHENECTADY CO., 154727......NJ-18
Schoharie, 922......NK-17
SCHOHARIE CO., 32749......NK-16
Schroon Lake, 833......NF-19
SCHUYLER CO., 18343......NL-10
Schuylerville, 1386......NI-19
Scotia, 7729......NJ-18
Scottsville, 2001......NJ-7
Sea Cliff, 4995......*E-17
Seaford, 15294......*J-20
Searingtown, 4915......*G-17
Selden, 19851......SE-10
SENECA CO., 35251......NK-10
Seneca Falls, 6681......NJ-10
Seneca Knolls, 2011......NI-11
Setauket, 3300......SG-12
Shelter Island, 1333......SD-12
Shelter Island Hts., 1048......SD-12
Sherburne, 1367......NK-14
Sherman, 730......NM-1
Sherrill, 3071......NI-13
Shinnecock Hills, 2188......SE-12
Shirley, 27854......SF-10
Shokan, 1183......NM-18
Shortsville, 1439......NJ-8
Shrub Oak, 2011......SC-6
Sidney, 3900......NL-14
Sidney Ctr., 800......NL-14
Silver Creek, 2656......NK-3
Skaneateles, 2450......NJ-11
Skaneateles Falls, 850......NJ-11
Slate Hill, 800......SC-4
Sleepy Hollow, 9870......SD-6
Slingerlands, 2100......NK-19
Sloan, 3661......NJ-4
Sloatsburg, 3039......SD-5
Smithtown, 26470......SH-11
Sodus, 1819......NH-9
Sodus Pt., 900......NH-9
Solvay, 6584......NI-11
Sound Bch., 7612......SE-10
S. Cairo, 950......NL-18
S. Corning, 1145......NM-9
S. Fallsburg, 2870......SA-3
S. Farmingdale, 14486......SJ-8
S. Floral Park, 1764......*H-16
S. Glens Falls, 3518......NH-19
S. Hempstead, 3243......*I-18
S. Hill, 6673......NL-11
S. Huntington, 9422......SF-8
S. Lockport, 8324......NI-4
S. Salem, 1200......SC-7
S. Valley Stream, 5962......*J-16
Southampton, 3109......SE-12
Southold, 5748......SD-12
Southport, 7238......NM-10
Sparrow Bush, 1200......SC-3
Speigletown, 1200......NK-19
Spencer, 759......NM-11
Spencerport, 3601......NI-7
Spring Valley, 31347......SD-5
Springs, 6592......SE-13
Springville, 4252......NL-4
Staatsburg, 911......NN-19
Stamford, 1119......NL-16
Stanfordville, 1000......NN-19
Stannards, 1000......NN-6
Star Lake, 809......ND-15
Stephentown, 750......NK-20
STEUBEN CO., 98990......NL-8
Stewart Manor, 1896......*H-16
Stillwater, 1738......NI-19
Stone Ridge, 1173......NN-18
Stony Brook, 13740......SE-9
Stony Pt., 12147......SD-6
Stottville, 1375......NL-19
Suffern, 10723......SD-5
SUFFOLK CO., 1493350......SE-10
SULLIVAN CO., 77547......NN-15
Swan Lake, 1200......SA-2
Sycaway, 1950......NE-6
Sylvan Bch., 897......NI-13
Syracuse, 145170......NI-12
Tappan, 6613......SE-6
Tarrytown, 11277......SD-6
Terryville, 11849......SG-12
Theresa, 863......ND-13
Thomaston, 2617......*F-16
Thornwood, 3759......*J-10
Ticonderoga, 3382......NF-20
Tillson, 1586......NN-18
TIOGA CO., 51125......NM-11
Tivoli, 1118......NM-19
Tomkins Cove, 850......SC-6
TOMPKINS CO., 101564......NL-10
Tonawanda, 15130......NC-8
Town Line, 2367......NJ-4
Tribes Hill, 1003......NJ-17
Troy, 50129......NK-19
Trumansburg, 1797......NK-10
Tuckahoe, 6486......*B-13
Tuckahoe, 1373......SE-12
Tully, 873......NK-12
Tupper Lake, 3667......ND-17
Turin, 800......*F-17
Twin Orchards, 1600......SB-10
ULSTER CO., 182493......SA-4
Unadilla, 1128......NL-14
Union Spr., 1197......NJ-10
Uniondale, 24759......*H-18
University Gardens, 4226......*G-16
Upper Brookville, 1698......*E-19
Utica, 62235......NI-14
Vails Gate, 3369......SB-5
Valatie, 1819......NL-19
Valhalla, 3162......SH-6
Valley Cottage, 9107......SD-6
Valley Stream, 37511......SG-7
Verdoy, 1000......NE-3
Vernon, 1172......NI-13
Verona, 852......NI-13
Vestal Ctr., 800......NM-12
Victor, 2696......NJ-8
Village Green, 3891......SH-1
Village of the Branch, 1807......SH-11
Vista, 750......SD-8
Voorheesville, 2789......NK-18
Waddington, 972......NB-14
Wading River, 7719......SE-10
Walden, 6978......SB-5
Wallkill, 2288......SB-5
Walton, 3088......NM-15
Wampsville, 543......NI-13
Wanakah, 3199......NJ-3
Wantagh, 18871......*J-20
Wappingers Falls, 5522......SB-6
Warrensburg, 3103......NG-19
Warsaw, 3473......NJ-6
Warwick, 6731......SC-4
WASHINGTON CO., 63216......NH-20
Washingtonville, 5899......SB-5
Waterford, 1990......NJ-19
Waterloo, 5171......NJ-10
Watertown, 27023......NE-12
Waterville, 1583......NI-14
Watervliet, 10254......NE-5
Watkins Glen, 1859......NL-10
Waverly, 4444......NM-11
Wawarsing, 800......SA-4
WAYNE CO., 93772......NI-9
Webster, 5399......NI-8
Weedsport, 1815......NI-10
Wellsville, 4679......NM-6
W. Babylon, 43213......SF-8
W. Bay Shore, 4648......SJ-10
W. Carthage, 2012......NE-13
W. Corners, 1800......SB-9
W. Elmira, 4967......NM-10
W. Glens Falls, 7071......NH-19
W. Haverstraw, 10165......SD-6
W. Hempstead, 18862......*H-17
W. Hills, 5592......SJ-8
W. Hurley, 1939......NN-18
W. Islip, 28335......SJ-10
W. Point, 6763......SC-5
W. Sand Lake, 2660......NK-19
W. Sayville, 5011......SJ-11
W. Seneca, 44711......NJ-4
W. Webster, 8700......NH-8
W. Winfield, 826......NJ-15
Westbury, 15071......*G-18
Westbury South, 9500......*G-19
WESTCHESTER CO., 949113......SD-7
Westfield, 3224......NL-1
Westhampton, 3079......SF-11
Westhampton Bch., 1721......SF-11
Westmere, 7284......NK-18
Westons Mills, 1472......NM-5
Westvale, 4963......SJ-2
Wheatley Hts., 5130......SJ-8
White Plains, 56853......SE-7
Whitehall, 2614......NG-20
Whitesboro, 3772......SA-12
Whitesville, 800......NM-7
Whitney Pt., 964......NL-12
Williamson, 2495......NH-9
Williamsville, 5300......ND-10
Williston Park, 7287......*G-17
Willow, 1800......NM-18
Willow Ridge Estates, 4800......NC-9
Willsboro, 753......ND-20
Wilmington, 937......ND-19
Wilson, 1264......NH-4
Windsor, 916......NM-13
Wolcott, 1701......NI-10
Woodbury, 8907......SH-8
Woodmere, 17121......*K-17
Woodridge, 847......SA-3
Woodsburgh, 778......*K-17
Woodstock, 2088......NM-18
Worcester, 1113......NK-16
Wurtsboro, 1246......SB-3
Wyandanch, 11647......SH-9
Wynantskill, 3276......NK-19
WYOMING CO., 42155......NJ-5
Yaphank, 5945......SF-10
YATES CO., 25348......NK-9
Yonkers, 195976......SE-6
Yorkshire, 1180......NK-5
Yorktown Hts., 1781......SC-6
Yorkville, 2689......NI-14
Youngstown, 1935......NH-3
Yulan, 750......SB-2

North Carolina
Map pp. 74 – 75
* City keyed to p. 76
Aberdeen, 6350......G-9
Advance, 1138......D-7
Ahoskie, 5039......C-15
Alamance, 951......D-8
ALAMANCE CO., 151131......D-9
Albemarle, 15903......F-7
ALEXANDER CO., 37198......D-4
ALLEGHANY CO., 11155......B-6
Alliance, 776......E-16
Andrews, 1781......M-2
Angier, 4350......E-11
Ansonville, 634......G-8
ANSON CO., 26948......H-7
Apex, 37476......E-11
Arapahoe, 556......F-17
Archdale, 11415......D-8
Arden, 800......F-1
Arlington, 1800......C-6
ASHE CO., 27281......B-3
Asheboro, 25012......E-8
Asheville, 83393......E-1
Atlantic Bch., 1495......H-17
Aulander, 895......C-15
Avery Creek, 1950......F-1
Avon, 776......E-20
AVERY CO., 17797......C-3
Ayden, 4932......F-15
Badin, 1974......F-7
Bakersville, 464......C-3
Banner Elk, 1028......C-3
Bayboro, 1263......G-17
Bayleaf, 800......G-13
Beaufort, 4039......H-17
BEAUFORT CO., 47759......E-16
Belhaven, 1688......E-17
Belmont, 10076......G-5
Belwood, 950......F-4
Benson, 3311......F-12
Bent Creek, 1287......E-1
Bermuda Run, 1725......D-7
BERTIE CO., 21282......D-16
Bessemer City, 5340......F-4
Bethel, 1577......D-15
Bethlehem, 4214......D-5
Beulaville, 1296......H-14
Biltmore Forest, 1343......N-8
Biscoe, 1700......F-8
Black Creek, 769......E-13
Black Mtn., 7848......E-1
BLADEN CO., 35190......I-12
Bladenboro, 1750......I-11
Blounts Creek, 1150......F-16
Blowing Rock, 1241......C-4
Boger City, 3152......F-5
Boiling Spring Lakes, 5372......J-13
Boiling Sprs., 4647......F-3
Bolivia, 143......J-13
Boone, 17122......C-3
Boonville, 1222......C-6
Brevard, 7609......F-1
Broadway, 1229......F-10
Brogden, 2633......F-13
Brunswick, 1119......J-10
BRUNSWICK CO., 107431......J-12
Bryson City, 1424......L-3
Buies Creek, 2942......F-11
BUNCOMBE CO., 238318......E-1
Burgaw, 3872......I-14
BURKE CO., 90912......E-3
Burlington, 49963......D-9
Burnsville, 1693......D-1
Butner, 7591......C-11
Buxton, 1273......F-20
CABARRUS CO., 178011......F-6
Calabash, 1786......K-12
CALDWELL CO., 83029......D-3
Camden, 599......C-18
CAMDEN CO., 9980......B-18
Candler, 1100......L-5
Candor, 840......F-8
Canton, 4227......L-5
Cape Carteret, 1917......H-16
Carolina Bch., 5706......K-14
Carolina Shores, 3048......K-12
Carrboro, 19582......D-10
CARTERET CO., 66469......H-16
Cary, 135234......E-11
Castle Hayne, 1202......I-14
CASWELL CO., 23719......C-9
Catawba, 603......E-5
CATAWBA CO., 154358......E-4
Cedar Pt., 1279......H-16
Chadbourn, 1856......J-11
Chapel Hill, 57233......D-10
Charlotte, 731424......F-5
CHATHAM CO., 63505......E-10
Cherokee, 2138......L-3
CHEROKEE CO., 27444......M-1
Cherryville, 5760......F-4
China Grv., 3563......E-6
Chocowinity, 820......E-15
CHOWAN CO., 14793......C-17
Claremont, 1352......E-5
Clayton, 16116......E-12
Clemmons, 18627......D-7
Cleveland, 871......E-6
CLEVELAND CO., 98078......F-3
Clinton, 8639......G-12
Clyde, 1223......L-4
Coats, 2112......F-11
Colfax, 1050......*B-4
COLUMBUS CO., 58098......J-11
Concord, 79066......E-6
Conover, 8165......E-4
Conway, 836......B-15
Cooleemee, 960......E-6
Cordova, 1775......H-8
Cornelius, 24866......F-5
Cramerton, 4165......G-5
CRAVEN CO., 103505......F-15
Creedmoor, 4124......C-11
Cricket, 1855......C-5
Crouse, 900......F-4
Cullowhee, 6228......L-4
CUMBERLAND CO., 319431......H-11
Cumberland, 800......G-11
CURRITUCK CO., 23547......B-19
Dallas, 4488......G-5
Danbury, 189......C-7
DARE CO., 33920......E-19
Davidson, 10944......F-5
DAVIDSON CO., 162878......E-7
DAVIE CO., 41240......D-6
Denton, 1636......E-7
Denver, 2309......F-5
Dobbins Hts., 866......G-9
Dobson, 1586......C-6
Dortches, 935......D-14
Drexel, 1858......E-3
Dunn, 9263......G-11
DUPLIN CO., 58505......G-13
Durham, 228330......D-11
DURHAM CO., 267587......D-11
E. Flat Rock, 4995......F-1
E. Spencer, 1534......E-7
Eden, 15527......B-8
Edenton, 5004......D-17
EDGECOMBE CO., 56552......D-14
Edneyville, 2367......F-1
Efland, 734......D-10
Elizabeth City, 18683......C-18
Elizabethtown, 3583......I-12
Elkin, 4001......C-6
Ellenboro, 873......F-3
Ellerbe, 1054......G-8
Elm City, 1298......E-14
Elon, 9419......D-9
Elroy, 3869......F-13
Emerald Isle, 3655......H-16
Emma, 1100......M-7
Enfield, 2532......C-14
Enochville, 2925......E-6
Erwin, 4405......F-11
Etowah, 6944......F-1
Eureka Sprs., 2910......K-16
Fair Bluff, 951......J-11
Fairmont, 2663......I-10
Fairplains, 2120......C-5
Fairview, 3324......F-1
Faison, 961......G-13
Faith, 807......E-7
Farmville, 4654......E-14
Fayetteville, 200564......H-11
Fearrington, 903......*J-18
Flat Rock, 3114......F-1
Fleetwood Acres, 920......N-13
Fletcher, 7187......F-1
Forest City, 7476......F-3
FORSYTH CO., 350670......C-7
Four Oaks, 1921......F-12
Foxfire, 902......G-9
Franklin, 3845......M-3
FRANKLIN CO., 60619......C-12
Franklinton, 2023......D-12
Franklinville, 1164......E-9
Fremont, 1255......E-13
Fuquay-Varina, 17937......E-11
Gamewell, 4051......E-4
Garner, 25745......E-12
Gastonia, 71741......F-4
GASTON CO., 206086......F-4
GATES CO., 12197......B-17
Gatesville, 321......C-17
Gibsonville, 6410......D-9
Glen Alpine, 1517......E-3
Goldsboro, 36437......F-13
Gorman, 1011......C-11
Graham, 14153......D-9
GRAHAM CO., 8861......L-2
Granite Falls, 4722......E-4
Granite Quarry, 2930......E-7
GRANVILLE CO., 59916......C-11
Green Level, 2100......D-9
GREENE CO., 21362......F-14
Greensboro, 269666......D-8
Greenville, 84554......E-15
Grifton, 2617......F-15
Grover, 708......G-4
GUILFORD CO., 488406......D-9
Half Moon, 8352......H-15
Halifax, 234......C-14
HALIFAX CO., 54691......C-14
Hamlet, 6495......H-9
Hampstead, 4083......I-14
Harkers Island, 1207......H-17
HARNETT CO., 114678......F-11
Harrisburg, 11526......F-6
Havelock, 20735......H-16
Haw River, 2298......D-10
Hays, 1851......C-5
HAYWOOD CO., 59036......L-5
Hemby Br., 1520......*J-7
Henderson, 15368......C-12
HENDERSON CO., 106740......F-1
Hendersonville, 13137......F-1
Hertford, 2143......C-18
HERTFORD CO., 24669......C-16
Hickory, 40010......E-4
Hickory Grv., 860......G-7
High Pt., 104371......D-8
High Shoals, 696......F-4
Highlands, 924......M-4
Hightsville, 739......I-19
Hildebran, 2023......E-4
Hillsborough, 6087......D-10
HOKE CO., 46952......G-10
Hollister, 674......C-13
Holly Ridge, 1268......I-15
Holly Sprs., 24661......E-11
Hope Mills, 15176......G-11
Hudson, 3776......D-4
Huntersville, 46773......F-5
Hyde Co., 5810......E-18
Indian Trail, 33518......*J-7
Iron Sta., 755......F-5
Jackson, 513......C-15
Jacksonville, 70145......H-15
JACKSON CO., 40271......M-4
James City, 5899......G-16
Jamestown, 3382......D-8
Jefferson, 1611......B-5
JOHNSTON CO., 168878......F-12
JONES CO., 10153......G-15
Jonesville, 2285......C-5
Kannapolis, 42625......F-6
Kenansville, 855......G-13
Kenly, 1339......E-13
Kernersville, 23123......D-8
Kill Devil Hills, 6683......D-20
King, 6904......C-7
Kings Grant, 8113......L-20
Kings Mtn., 10296......G-4
Kingstown, 681......F-3
Kinston, 21677......F-15
Kitty Hawk, 3272......C-20
Knightdale, 11401......E-12
La Grange, 2873......F-14
L. Junaluska, 2734......L-4
L. Lure, 1192......F-2
Lake Pk., 3422......G-6
L. Waccamaw, 1480......J-12
Landis, 3109......E-6
Laurel Hill, 1254......H-9
Laurel Pk., 2180......F-1
Laurinburg, 15962......H-9
LEE CO., 57866......F-10
Leland, 13527......J-13
LENOIR CO., 59495......G-14
Lenoir, 18228......D-4
Lewisville, 12639......D-7
Lexington, 18931......E-7
Liberty, 2656......D-9
Lillington, 3194......F-11
LINCOLN CO., 78265......F-4
Lincolnton, 10486......F-4
Littleton, 674......B-14
Locust, 2930......F-7
Longview, 4871......E-4
Louisburg, 3359......D-12
Lowell, 3526......M-4
Lowesville, 2945......F-5
Lucama, 1108......E-13
Lumberton, 21542......I-11
Maggie Valley, 1150......L-4
Madison, 2246......B-8
MADISON CO., 20764......D-1
Maiden, 3310......E-4
Mamers, 826......F-11
Manteo, 1434......D-20
Marion, 7838......E-2
Mars Hill, 1869......D-1
Marshall, 872......K-5
Marshville, 2402......G-7
MARTIN CO., 24505......E-16
Marvin, 5579......*J-6
Matthews, 27198......G-6
Maury, 1685......F-14
Maxton, 2426......H-10
Mayodan, 2478......B-8
Maysville, 1019......H-16
McAdenville, 651......*G-5
MCDOWELL CO., 44996......E-2
Mebane, 11393......D-10
MECKLENBURG CO., 919628......G-5
Midland, 3073......G-7
Midway, 4679......*D-2
Millers Creek, 2112......C-4
Mills River, 6802......F-1
Mint Hill, 22722......G-6
Misenheimer, 728......F-7
MITCHELL CO., 15579......D-1
Mocksville, 5051......D-6
Moncure, 711......E-10
Monroe, 32797......G-6
MONTGOMERY CO., 27798......F-8
MOORE CO., 88247......F-9
Mooresboro, 311......F-3
Mooresville, 32711......F-5
Moravian Falls, 1901......D-5
Morehead City, 8661......H-17
Morganton, 16918......E-3
Morrisville, 18576......E-11
Mt. Airy, 10388......B-6
Mt. Gilead, 1181......G-8
Mt. Holly, 13656......G-5
Mt. Olive, 4589......G-13
Mt. Pleasant, 1652......F-7
Mountain Home, 3622......F-1
Moyock, 3759......B-18
Mulberry, 2332......C-5
Murfreesboro, 2835......B-16
Murphy, 1627......M-1
Murraysville, 7279......K-20
Myrtle Grv., 8875......J-14
Nags Head, 2757......D-20
NASH CO., 95840......D-13
Nashville, 5352......D-13
Navassa, 1505......J-13
New Bern, 29524......G-16
NEW HANOVER CO., 202667......J-14
Newland, 698......D-2
Newport, 4150......H-17
Newton, 12968......E-4
Newton Grv., 585......F-12
Norlina, 1118......B-13
N. Topsail Bch., 743......I-15
N. Wilkesboro, 4245......C-5
NORTHAMPTON CO., 22099......C-15
Northwest, 735......I-13
Norwood, 2379......G-7
Oak Island, 6783......J-12
Oak Ridge, 6185......C-8
Oakboro, 1859......G-7
Ocracoke, 948......G-19
Ogden, 6766......I-14
Old Fort, 908......E-2
ONSLOW CO., 177772......H-14
ORANGE CO., 133801......C-10
Oriental, 900......G-17
Oxford, 8461......C-12
PAMLICO CO., 13144......G-17
PASQUOTANK CO., 40661......C-18
Pembroke, 2973......H-10
PENDER CO., 52217......I-14
PERQUIMANS CO., 13453......C-17
PERSON CO., 39464......B-11
Pfafftown, 1050......C-7
Pikeville, 678......F-13
Pilot Mtn., 1477......C-6
Pine Knoll Shores, 1339......H-17
Pine Level, 1700......F-13
Pinebluff, 1337......G-9
Pinehurst, 13124......G-9
Pinetops, 1374......E-14
Pineville, 7479......*J-4
Piney Green, 13293......H-15
Pinnacle, 894......C-7
Pisgah Forest, 2150......M-5
PITT CO., 168148......F-15
Pittsboro, 3743......E-10
Pleasant Gdn., 4489......D-8
Plymouth, 3878......D-17
POLK CO., 20510......F-1
Polkton, 3375......G-7
Princeton, 1194......F-13
Princeville, 2082......D-15
Pumpkin Ctr., 2222......D-15
Raeford, 4611......G-10
Raleigh, 403892......E-12
Ramseur, 1692......E-9
Randleman, 4113......E-8
RANDOLPH CO., 141752......E-8
Ranlo, 3434......M-14
Red Cross, 742......F-7
Red Oak, 3430......D-14
Red Sprs., 3428......H-10
Reidsville, 14520......C-9
Rich Sq., 958......C-15
Richlands, 1520......H-15
RICHMOND CO., 46639......G-8
River Bend, 3119......G-16
Roanoke Rapids, 15754......B-14
Robbins, 1097......F-9
Robbinsville, 620......L-2
Robersonville, 1488......D-15
ROBESON CO., 134168......H-10
Rockfish, 3298......G-10
Rockingham, 9558......H-8
ROCKINGHAM CO., 93643......C-8
Rockwell, 2108......E-7
Rocky Mount, 57477......D-14
Rocky Pt., 1602......I-14
Rolesville, 3786......D-12
Rose Hill, 1626......H-13
Roseboro, 1191......G-12
Rosewood, 4300......F-13
Rougemont, 978......C-11
ROWAN CO., 138428......E-6
Rowland, 1037......I-10
Roxboro, 8362......C-11
Royal Pines, 4272......F-1
Rural Hall, 2937......C-7
RUTHERFORD CO., 67810......F-2
Rutherford College, 1341......E-4
Rutherfordton, 4213......F-2
St. James, 3165......K-13
St. Pauls, 2035......H-11
Salem, 2218......E-3
Salisbury, 33662......E-6
Salter Path, 800......H-17
Saluda, 713......F-2
SAMPSON CO., 63431......G-12
Sanford, 28094......F-10
Sawmills, 5240......D-4
Saxapahaw, 1648......D-10
SCOTLAND CO., 36157......H-9
Scotland Neck, 2059......C-15
Seaboard, 632......B-15
Sedgefield, 1000......*C-6
Selma, 6073......E-13
Seven Lakes, 4888......F-9
Shallotte, 3675......K-12
Sharpsburg, 2024......D-14
Shelby, 20323......F-3
Sherrills Ford, 900......E-5
Siler City, 7887......E-9
Silver City, 882......G-10
Silver Lake, 5598......J-14
Skippers Cor., 2785......J-14
Smithfield, 10966......F-12
Sneads Ferry, 2646......I-15
Snow Hill, 1595......F-14
S. Gastonia, 5433......*G-4
Southern Pines, 12334......G-9
Southern Shores, 2714......C-20
Southport, 2833......K-13
Sparta, 1770......B-5
Spencer, 3267......E-7
Spindale, 4321......F-3
Spring Hope, 1320......D-13
Spring Lake, 11964......G-11
Spruce Pine, 2175......D-2
Stallings, 13831......*I-6
Stanfield, 1486......G-7
Stanley, 3556......F-5
STANLY CO., 60585......F-7
Stantonsburg, 784......E-14
Star, 876......F-8
Statesville, 24532......E-5
Stedman, 1028......G-11
STOKES CO., 47401......C-7
Stokesdale, 5047......C-8
Stoneville, 1056......B-8
Stony Pt., 1317......E-5
Summerfield, 10232......C-8
Sunset Bch., 3572......K-12
Surf City, 1853......I-15
SURRY CO., 73673......C-6
SWAIN CO., 13981......L-3
Swannanoa, 4576......E-1
Swanquarter, 324......F-18
Swansboro, 2663......H-16
Sylva, 2588......L-4
Tabor City, 2511......J-11
Tarboro, 11415......D-15
Taylorsville, 2098......D-4
Thomasville, 26757......E-8
Toast, 1450......B-6
Tobaccoville, 2441......C-7
TRANSYLVANIA CO., 33090......M-5
Trent Woods, 4155......G-16
Trenton, 287......G-15
Trinity, 6614......D-8
Troutman, 2383......E-5
Troy, 3189......F-8
Tryon, 1646......F-2
Tuxedo, 1100......F-1
TYRRELL CO., 4407......D-18
UNION CO., 201292......G-6
Unionville, 5929......G-6
Valdese, 4490......E-3
Vanceboro, 1005......F-15
VANCE CO., 45422......C-12
Vandemere, 254......G-17
Wadesboro, 5813......H-8
Wagram, 840......H-10
Wake Forest, 30117......D-12
WAKE CO., 900993......E-12
Walkertown, 4675......C-7
Wallace, 3880......H-13
Walnut Creek, 835......F-13
Wanchese, 1642......D-20
WARREN CO., 20972......C-13
Warrenton, 862......C-13
Warsaw, 3054......G-13
Washington, 9744......E-16
WASHINGTON CO., 13228......D-17
Watauga, 51079......C-4
Waxhaw, 9859......H-6
Waynesville, 9869......L-5
WAYNE CO., 122623......F-13
Weaverville, 3120......E-1
Weddington, 9459......G-6
Weldon, 1655......B-14
Wendell, 5845......E-12
Wentworth, 2807......C-8
Wesley Chapel, 7463......G-6
W. Jefferson, 1299......C-4
Westport, 4026......F-5
Whispering Pines, 2928......F-10
Whitakers, 744......C-14
White Lake, 802......H-12
White Plains, 1074......B-6
Whiteville, 5394......J-11
WILKES CO., 69340......C-5
Wilkesboro, 3413......C-5
Williamston, 5511......D-16
Wilmington, 106476......J-14
Wilson, 49167......E-14
WILSON CO., 81234......E-14
Wilsons Mill, 2277......E-12
Windsor, 3630......C-16
Wingate, 3491......G-6
Winston-Salem, 229617......D-7
Winterville, 9269......E-15
Winton, 769......B-16
Woodfin, 6123......E-1
Woodland, 809......B-15
Wrightsboro, 4896......J-14
Wrightsville Bch., 2477......J-14
Yadkinville, 2959......D-6
YADKIN CO., 38406......C-6
Yanceyville, 2039......C-10
YANCEY CO., 17818......D-1
Youngsville, 1157......D-12
Zebulon, 4433......E-12

North Dakota
Map p. 77
ADAMS CO., 2343......J-4
Amidon, 20......I-3
Ashley, 749......J-9
BARNES CO., 11066......H-11
Beach, 1019......H-2
Belcourt, 2078......B-8
Belfield, 800......H-3
BENSON CO., 6660......E-9
Beulah, 3121......G-5
BILLINGS CO., 783......G-2
Bismarck, 61272......H-7
Bottineau, 2211......D-7
BOTTINEAU CO., 6429......D-7
Bowbells, 336......D-5
Bowman, 1650......J-3
BOWMAN CO., 3151......J-3
BURKE CO., 1968......D-4
BURLEIGH CO., 81308......H-7
Burlington, 1060......E-6
Cando, 1115......D-9
Cannon Ball, 875......J-7
Carrington, 2065......G-9
Carson, 293......I-5
CASS CO., 149778......H-12
Casselton, 2329......H-12
Cavalier, 1302......D-12
CAVALIER CO., 3993......D-10
Center, 571......H-6
Cooperstown, 984......G-11
Crosby, 1070......C-3
Devils Lake, 7141......E-10
DICKEY CO., 5289......J-10
Dickinson, 17787......H-4
DIVIDE CO., 2071......D-3
Drayton, 824......D-12
DUNN CO., 3536......G-4
Dunseith, 773......D-8
EDDY CO., 2385......F-9
Elgin, 642......I-5
Ellendale, 1394......J-10
EMMONS CO., 3550......I-8
Enderlin, 886......I-12
Fargo, 105549......H-13
Fessenden, 479......F-8
Finley, 445......G-11
Forman, 504......J-12
Ft. Totten, 1243......F-9
Ft. Yates, 184......J-7
FOSTER CO., 3343......G-9
Garrison, 1453......F-6
Glen Ullin, 807......H-5
GOLDEN VALLEY CO., 1680......G-2
Grafton, 4284......E-12
Grand Forks, 52838......F-12
GRAND FORKS CO., 66861......F-12
GRANT CO., 2394......I-5
GRIGGS CO., 2420......G-11
Gwinner, 753......J-12
Hankinson, 919......J-13
Harvey, 1783......F-8
Harwood, 718......H-13
Hatton, 777......F-12
Hazen, 2411......G-5
Hebron, 747......H-5
Hettinger, 1226......J-4
HETTINGER CO., 2477......I-4
Hillsboro, 1603......G-13
Horace, 2430......I-13
Jamestown, 15427......H-10
Kenmare, 1096......D-5
KIDDER CO., 2435......G-8
Killdeer, 751......G-4
Kindred, 692......I-13
LA MOURE CO., 4139......I-10
Lakota, 672......E-10
Lamoure, 889......I-11
Langdon, 1878......D-10
Larimore, 1346......F-12
Lidgerwood, 652......J-12
Lincoln, 2406......H-7
Linton, 1097......I-8
Lisbon, 2154......I-12
LOGAN CO., 1990......I-9
Mandan, 18331......H-7
Manning, 74......G-4
Mapleton, 762......H-13
Mayville, 1858......G-12
McCLUSKY, 380......F-7
MCHENRY CO., 5395......E-7
McINTOSH CO., 2809......J-9
MCKENZIE CO., 6360......F-2
MCLEAN CO., 8962......F-6
Medora, 112......H-2
MERCER CO., 8424......G-5
Minot, 40888......E-6
Minto, 604......E-12
Minnewaukan, 224......E-9
Mohall, 783......D-6
MORTON CO., 27471......I-5
Mott, 721......I-4
MOUNTRAIL CO., 7673......E-4
Napoleon, 792......I-8
NELSON CO., 3126......F-11
New England, 600......I-3
New Rockford, 1391......F-9
New Salem, 946......H-6
New Town, 1925......F-4
Northwood, 945......F-12
Oakes, 1856......J-11
OLIVER CO., 1846......G-6
Park River, 1403......E-12
Parshall, 903......F-5
PEMBINA CO., 7413......D-11
PIERCE CO., 4357......E-8
Portland, 606......G-12
RAMSEY CO., 11451......E-10
RANSOM CO., 5457......I-11
RENVILLE CO., 2470......D-5
RICHLAND CO., 16321......J-12
ROLETTE CO., 13937......D-8
Rolla, 1280......D-9
Rugby, 2876......E-8
SARGENT CO., 3829......J-11
SHERIDAN CO., 1321......F-7
SIOUX CO., 4153......J-6
SLOPE CO., 727......I-2
Stanley, 1458......E-4
Stanton, 366......G-6
STARK CO., 24199......H-4
Steele, 715......H-8
STEELE CO., 1975......F-11
STUTSMAN CO., 21100......H-9
Surrey, 934......E-6
Thompson, 986......F-12
Tioga, 1230......E-3
TOWNER CO., 2246......D-9
TRAILL CO., 8121......F-12
Underwood, 778......G-6
Valley City, 6585......H-11
Velva, 1084......E-7
Wahpeton, 7766......J-13
WALSH CO., 11119......E-11
WARD CO., 61675......E-5
Washburn, 1246......G-6
WELLS CO., 4207......G-8
W. Fargo, 25830......H-13
Westhope, 429......C-6
WILLIAMS CO., 22398......D-3
Williston, 14716......E-2
Wilton, 711......G-7
Wishek, 1002......J-9

Ohio
Map pp. 78 – 81
Map keys Atlas pages
NA – NN 78 – 79
SA – SN 80 – 81
* City keyed to p. 112
Aberdeen, 1638......SI-6
Ada, 5952......NI-5
ADAMS CO., 28550......SH-7
Addyston, 938......SJ-1
Adena, 759......NN-19
Akron, 199110......NI-16
Albany, 828......SD-15
Alger, 860......NJ-5
ALLEN CO., 106331......NJ-4
Alliance, 22322......NI-17
Amberley, 3585......*M-4
Amelia, 4801......SG-4
Amherst, 12021......NF-12
Andersonville, 779......SE-6
Andover, 1145......NE-20
Anna, 1567......NM-4
Ansonia, 1174......NN-1
Antwerp, 1736......NF-2
Apple Creek, 1173......NJ-14
Arcanum, 2129......SA-2
Archbold, 4346......NE-3
Arlington, 1455......NI-5
Arlington Hts., 745......*J-4
ASHLAND CO., 53139......NI-12
Ashland, 20362......NI-12
Ashley, 1330......NL-9
Ashtabula, 19124......NC-19
ASHTABULA CO., 101497......NE-18
Ashville, 4097......SC-9
Athens, 23832......SE-13
ATHENS CO., 64757......SF-14
Attica, 899......NH-9
Atwater, 758......NH-17
AUGLAIZE CO., 45949......NK-4
Aurora, 15548......NG-16
Austintown, 29677......NN-19
Avon, 21193......NI-1
Avon Lake, 22581......NF-13
Avondale, 2500......NE-9
Bainbridge, 367......NF-16
Bainbridge, 860......SF-9
Ballville, 2976......NG-8
Baltic, 795......NI-15
Baltimore, 2966......SB-11
Barberton, 26550......NH-15
Barnesville, 4193......SA-17
Batavia, 1509......SG-4
Bay Vil., 15651......NF-14
Beach City, 1033......NK-15
Beachwood, 11953......NF-16
Beavercreek, 45193......SC-4
Bedford, 13074......NF-15
Bedford Hts., 10751......NF-16
Bellaire, 4278......SA-19
Bellbrook, 6943......SD-4
Belle Ctr., 813......NK-6
Bellefontaine, 13370......NL-5
Bellevue, 8202......NG-10
Bellville, 1918......NK-11
BELMONT CO., 70400......NN-17
Belpre, 6441......SF-16
Bentleyville, 864......NE-16
Berea, 19093......NF-14
Berlin, 898......NK-14
Berlin Hts., 714......NH-11
Bethel, 2711......SH-5
Bethesda, 1256......SA-18
Beverly, 1313......SD-15
Bexley, 13057......SB-9
Blacklick Estates, 8682......SI-20
Blanchester, 4243......SF-5
Bloomingburg, 938......SD-7
Bloomville, 956......NH-9
Blue Ash, 12114......SF-3
Bluffton, 4125......NI-5
Boardman, 35376......NH-19
Bolivar, 994......NK-16
Boston Hts., 1300......NG-16
Botkins, 1155......NL-4
Bowling Green, 30028......NF-6
Bradford, 1842......NN-2
Bradner, 985......NG-7
Bratenahl, 1197......SK-18
Brecksville, 13656......NG-15
Bremen, 1425......SC-11
Brentwood, 5500......SK-3
Brewster, 2112......NJ-15
Bridgeport, 1831......NN-19
Bridgetown North, 12569......SJ-1
Brilliant, 1482......NM-20
Brimfield, 3343......NH-16
Broadview Hts., 19400......NG-15
Brook Park, 19212......NF-14
Brookfield Ctr., 1207......NB-14
Brooklyn, 11169......NF-15
Brooklyn Hts., 1543......SM-17
Brookville, 5884......SB-3
BROWN CO., 44846......SH-5
Brunswick, 34255......NG-14
Bryan, 8545......NF-2
Buckeye Lake, 2746......SB-12
Bucyrus, 12362......NJ-9
Burbank, 207......NJ-13
Burton, 1455......NF-17
Butler, 933......NK-11
BUTLER CO., 368130......SE-1
Byesville, 2438......SB-16
Cadiz, 3353......NM-18
Calcutta, 3742......NJ-20
Caldwell, 1748......SC-16
Cambridge, 10635......SA-16
Camden, 2046......SD-1
Campbell, 8235......NH-20
Canal Fulton, 5479......NI-15
Canal Winchester, 7101......SB-10
Canfield, 7515......NH-19
Canton, 73007......NI-16
Cardington, 2047......NL-9
Carey, 3674......NI-7
Carlisle, 4915......SD-3
CARROLL CO., 28836......NK-17
Carrollton, 3241......NK-18
Castalia, 852......NH-10
Cedarville, 4019......SC-6
Celina, 10400......NL-2
Centerburg, 1773......NM-10
Centerville, 23999......SD-4
Chagrin Falls, 4113......NF-16
CHAMPAIGN CO., 40097......NN-5
Champion Hts., 6498......NG-18
Chardon, 5148......NE-17
Chauncey, 1049......SE-13
Cherry Grv., 4378......SM-5
Chesapeake, 745......SK-12
Cheviot, 8375......SL-2
Chillicothe, 21901......SE-9
Chippewa Lake, 711......NH-14
Churchill, 2149......NH-19
Cincinnati, 296943......SG-2
Circleville, 13314......SC-9
CLARK CO., 138333......SB-6
Clarktown, 958......SH-10
Clayton, 13209......SB-3
CLERMONT CO., 197363......SH-4
Cleveland, 396815......NF-15
Cleveland Hts., 46121......NE-15
Cleves, 3234......SG-1
Clinton, 1214......NH-15
CLINTON CO., 42040......SD-6
Clyde, 6325......NG-9
Coal Grv., 2165......SJ-11
Coldwater, 4427......NL-2
Colerain Hts., 2600......SK-2
Columbiana, 6384......NI-19
COLUMBIANA CO., 107841......NJ-19
Columbus, 787033......SB-9
Columbus Grv., 2137......NJ-4
Commercial Pt., 1582......SC-9
Conneaut, 12841......NC-20
Continental, 1153......NH-3
Convoy, 1085......NI-1
Copley, 750......NH-15
Cortland, 7104......NG-19
COSHOCTON CO., 36901......NM-13
Coshocton, 11216......NM-15
Covedale, 6447......SM-2
Covington, 2584......NN-3
Craig Bch., 1180......NH-18
CRAWFORD CO., 43784......NI-9
Crestline, 4630......NI-10
Cridersville, 1852......NJ-4
Crooksville, 2534......SC-13
Crystal Lakes, 1483......SB-5
Curtice, 1526......NE-7
CUYAHOGA CO., 1280122......NG-14
Cuyahoga Falls, 49652......NH-16
Dalton, 1830......NJ-15
Danville, 1044......NL-11
Darbydale, 793......SB-8
DARKE CO., 52959......NM-1
Dayton, 141527......SC-4
De Graff, 1285......NM-5
Deer Park, 5736......SL-5
Defiance, 16494......NG-3
DEFIANCE CO., 39037......NG-2
Deforest, 1150......NE-18
Delaware, 34753......NM-9
DELAWARE CO., 174214......NM-9
Delhi Hills, 20000......SM-2
Delphos, 7101......NI-3
Delta, 3103......NE-4
Dennison, 2655......NL-16
Dent, 10497......SL-1
Deshler, 1799......NG-5
Devola, 2652......SE-16
Dover, 12826......NK-16
Doylestown, 3051......NI-15
Dresden, 1529......SA-13
Dry Run, 750......SJ-4
Dublin, 41751......NN-8
Duncan Falls, 880......SB-14
Dunkirk, 875......NJ-6
E. Canton, 1591......NJ-17
E. Cleveland, 17843......NE-15
E. Liverpool, 11195......NK-20
E. Palestine, 4721......NI-20
E. Sparta, 819......NJ-16
Eastlake, 18577......NE-16
Eaton, 8407......SC-2
Eaton Estates, 1222......NG-13
Edgerton, 2012......NF-1
Edgewater Pk., 700......SB-10
Edgewood, 4432......NC-19
Edon, 834......NE-1
Elida, 1905......NI-4
Elmore, 1410......NF-8
Elmwood Pl., 2188......SL-3
Elyria, 54533......NF-13
Englewood, 13465......SB-3
Enon, 2415......SB-5
ERIE CO., 77079......NF-11
Etna, 1215......SB-11
Euclid, 48920......NE-15
Evendale, 2767......SK-4
Fairborn, 32352......SB-5
Fairfax, 1699......SL-4
Fairfield, 42510......SE-2
FAIRFIELD CO., 146156......SB-11
Fairhope, 1720......NJ-17
Fairlawn, 7437......NH-15
Fairport Hbr., 3109......NE-17
Fairview Lanes, 1000......NG-10
Fairview Pk., 16826......NF-14
Farmersville, 1009......SC-3
Fayette, 1283......NE-3
FAYETTE CO., 29030......SD-8
Felicity, 818......SI-4
Findlay, 41202......NH-6
Finneytown, 12741......SK-3
Five Points, 1824......SD-4
Flushing, 879......NN-18
Forest, 1461......NJ-7
Forest Pk., 18720......SF-2
Forestville, 10532......SG-3
Ft. Jennings, 485......NI-3
Ft. Loramie, 1478......NL-3
Ft. McKinley, 3989......SB-3
Ft. Recovery, 1430......NL-1
Ft. Shawnee, 3726......NJ-4
Fostoria, 13441......NH-7
Frankfort, 1064......SE-8
Franklin, 11771......SD-3
FRANKLIN CO., 1163414......NN-10
Franklin Furnace, 1660......SJ-10
Frazeysburg, 1165......NN-13
Fredericktown, 2493......NL-11
Fremont, 16734......NG-8
Fruit Hill, 3755......SM-5
FULTON CO., 42698......NE-5
Gahanna, 33248......SA-10
Galion, 10512......NJ-10
GALLIA CO., 30934......SH-12
Gallipolis, 3641......SH-13
Gambier, 2391......NL-12
Garfield Hts., 28849......NF-15
Garrettsville, 2325......NG-17
Gates Mills, 2270......NE-16
GEAUGA CO., 93389......NE-17
Geneva, 6215......ND-18
Geneva-on-the-Lake, 1288......NC-18
Georgetown, 4331......SH-5
Germantown, 5547......SD-3
Ghent, 1600......NH-15
Gibsonburg, 2581......NF-7
Girard, 9958......NH-19
Glandorf, 1001......NH-4
Glendale, 2155......SF-3
Glenmoor, 1987......NJ-20
Glouster, 1791......SD-14
Gnadenhutten, 1288......NL-16
Golf Manor, 3611......SL-4
Grafton, 6636......NG-13
Grand Rapids, 965......NF-6
Grandview Hts., 6536......SB-9
Granville, 5646......NN-11
Gratis, 881......SC-2
Green, 25699......NI-16
Green Sprs., 1368......NG-9
GREENE CO., 161573......SC-6
Greenfield, 4639......SF-7
Greenhills, 3615......SJ-3
Greenville, 13227......NN-2
Greenwich, 1476......NH-11
Groesbeck, 6788......SK-2
Grove City, 35575......SB-9
Groveport, 5363......SJ-20
GUERNSEY CO., 40087......NN-16
Hamden, 879......SF-12
Hamilton, 62477......SE-2
HAMILTON CO., 802374......SF-1
Hamilton Meadows, 2100......SB-9
HANCOCK CO., 74782......NH-5
Hanoverton, 403......NJ-19
HARDIN CO., 32058......NK-6
Harrison, 9897......SF-1
HARRISON CO., 15864......NM-17
Hartville, 2944......NI-16
Haskins, 1188......NF-6
Heath, 10310......SA-12
Hebron, 2336......SB-12
HENRY CO., 28215......NG-4
Hicksville, 3581......NG-1
Highland Hts., 8345......SK-20
Highland Hts., 8345......NE-16
HIGHLAND CO., 43589......SF-6
Highpoint, 1503......SJ-4
Hilliard, 28435......SA-8
Hiram, 1406......NG-17
HOCKING CO., 29380......SE-11
Holgate, 1109......NG-4
Holland, 1764......NB-1
HOLMES CO., 42366......NK-13
Hopedale, 950......NM-18
Howland Ctr., 6351......NG-19
Hubbard, 7874......NG-20
Huber Hts., 38101......SB-4
Huber Ridge, 4604......SJ-19
Hudson, 22262......NH-16
Hunting Valley, 705......NE-16
Huron, 7149......NF-11
HURON CO., 59626......NH-11
Independence, 7133......NF-15
Ironton, 11129......SK-11
Jackson, 6397......SG-11
JACKSON CO., 33225......SH-11
Jamestown, 1993......SC-6
Jefferson, 3120......ND-19
JEFFERSON CO., 69709......NK-19
Jeffersonville, 1203......SC-7
Johnstown, 4632......NN-10
Junction City, 819......SC-12
Kalida, 1542......NI-4
Kendall Hts., 850......NB-8
Kent, 28904......NH-16
Kenton, 8262......NK-6
Kenwood, 6981......SK-4
Kettering, 56163......SC-4
Kidron, 944......NJ-15
Killbuck, 817......NL-14
Kings Mills, 1319......SE-3
Kingston, 1032......SE-10
KNOX CO., 60921......NM-12
La Croft, 1144......NK-20
La Rue, 747......NK-7
Lagrange, 2103......NG-13
L. Cable, 2500......NB-9
LAKE CO., 230041......NE-17
L. Milton, 1100......NH-18
Lakemore, 3068......NH-16
Lakeview, 1072......NL-5
Lakewood, 52131......NF-14
Lancaster, 38780......SC-11
Laurel Ridge, 2350......NI-16
LAWRENCE CO., 62450......SJ-11
Leavittsburg, 1973......NG-18
Lebanon, 20033......SE-4
Leesburg, 1314......SE-7
Leetonia, 1959......NI-19
Leipsic, 2093......NH-5
Lewisburg, 1820......SC-1
Lexington, 4822......NK-11
Liberty Ctr., 1180......NF-5
LICKING CO., 166492......NN-11
Lima, 38771......NJ-4
Lincoln Hts., 3286......SK-3
Lincoln Vil., 9032......SB-5
Lisbon, 2821......NJ-19
Lockland, 3449......SK-3
Lodi, 2746......NI-13
Logan, 7152......SD-12
LOGAN CO., 45858......NL-5
Logan Elm Vil., 1118......SD-9
London, 9904......SB-7
Lorain, 64097......NF-13
LORAIN CO., 301356......NG-12
Lordstown, 3417......NN-18
Loudonville, 2641......NK-12
Loveland, 12081......SF-3
Loveland Pk., 1523......SJ-6
Lowellville, 1155......NN-20
LUCAS CO., 441815......NE-5
Lucasville, 2757......SH-9
Luckey, 1012......NF-6
Lynchburg, 1499......SF-6
Lyndhurst, 14001......NE-16
Macedonia, 11188......NG-16
Mack, 11585......SL-1
Madeira, 8726......SF-4
Madison, 3184......ND-18
MADISON CO., 43435......NN-7
Madison-on-the-Lake, 950......ND-18
Magnolia, 978......NK-17
MAHONING CO., 238823......NI-18
Malvern, 1189......NK-17
Manchester, 2023......SI-6
Mansfield, 47821......NJ-11
Mantua, 1043......NG-17
Maple Hts., 23138......NF-15
Marblehead, 903......NG-10
Mariemont, 3403......SL-4
Marietta, 14085......SE-16
Marion, 36837......NK-8
MARION CO., 66501......NK-7
Marne, 783......NN-12
Marshallville, 756......NI-15
Martins Ferry, 6915......NN-19
Marysville, 22094......NM-7
Mason, 30712......SE-3
Massillon, 32149......NI-16
Masury, 2064......NG-20
Maumee, 14286......NE-1
Mayfield, 3460......SK-20
Mayfield Hts., 19155......NE-16
McArthur, 1701......SF-12
McComb, 1648......NH-5
McConnelsville, 1784......SC-14
McDonald, 3263......NH-19
McKinley Hts., 1060......NB-13
Mechanicsburg, 1644......NA-6
Medina, 26678......NH-14
MEDINA CO., 172332......NH-13
Medway, 2000......SB-5
MEIGS CO., 23770......SG-13
Mentor, 47159......NE-16
Mentor-on-the-Lake, 7443......ND-16
MERCER CO., 40814......NK-1
MIAMI CO., 102506......NN-3
Miamisburg, 20181......SD-3
Miamitown, 1259......SJ-1
Middlefield, 2694......NF-17
Middleport, 2530......SG-14
Middletown, 48694......SD-3
Midvale, 754......NK-16
Milan, 1367......NG-11
Milford, 6709......SF-3
Milford Ctr., 792......NN-7
Millbury, 1200......NE-7
Millersburg, 3025......NK-14
Millersport, 1044......SB-11
Millville, 708......SE-2
Mineral City, 727......NK-16
Mineral Ridge, 3892......NH-19
Minerva, 3720......NJ-17
Minerva Pk., 1272......NN-9
Mingo Jct., 3454......NL-20
Minster, 2805......NL-3
Mogadore, 3853......NI-16
Monfort Hts., 11948......SL-2
Monroe, 12442......SE-3
MONROE CO., 14642......SC-18
Monroeville, 1400......NG-11
Montgomery, 10251......SF-3
MONTGOMERY CO., 535153......SC-3
Montpelier, 4072......NE-2
Moraine, 6307......SC-4
Moreland Hills, 3320......SM-20
MORGAN CO., 15054......SC-15
Morrow, 1188......SE-4
MORROW CO., 34827......NK-9
Mt. Carmel, 4741......SM-5
Mt. Carmel Hts., 1200......NH-5
Mt. Gilead, 3660......NK-10
Mt. Healthy, 6098......SK-2
Mt. Orab, 3664......SG-5
Mt. Repose, 4672......SH-4
Mt. Sterling, 1782......SC-8
Mt. Vernon, 16990......NL-11
Mulberry, 3323......SF-4
Munroe Falls, 5012......NA-6
MUSKINGUM CO., 86074......NN-14
Napoleon, 8749......NF-4
Navarre, 1957......NJ-16
Neffs, 993......NN-19
Nelsonville, 5392......SE-13
Nevada, 760......NJ-8
New Albany, 7724......NN-10
New Boston, 2272......SJ-9
New Bremen, 2978......NL-3
New Burlington, 5069......SJ-2
New California, 1411......NN-8
New Carlisle, 5785......SB-5
New Concord, 2491......SA-15
New Holland, 801......SD-8
New Knoxville, 879......NL-3
New Lebanon, 3995......SC-3
New Lexington, 4731......SC-13
New London, 2461......NH-11
New Madison, 892......SB-1
New Matamoras, 896......SD-18
New Miami, 2249......SE-2
New Middletown, 1621......NI-20
New Paris, 1629......SB-1
New Philadelphia, 17288......NL-16
New Richmond, 2582......SH-3
New Straitsville, 722......SD-13
New Vienna, 1224......SE-6
New Washington, 967......NH-10
New Waterford, 1238......NL-20
Newark, 47573......NN-12
Newburgh Hts., 2167......SM-18
Newcomerstown, 3822......NM-15
Newport, 1003......SE-16
Newton Falls, 4795......NG-18
Newtown, 2672......SG-3
Niles, 19266......NG-19
NOBLE CO., 14645......SC-16
N. Baltimore, 3432......NH-6
N. Bend, 857......SF-1
N. Canton, 17488......NI-16
N. College Hill, 9397......SF-2
N. Fairfield, 560......NF-11
N. Industry, 2700......NJ-16
N. Jackson, 900......NH-18
N. Kingsville, 2923......NC-19
N. Lewisburg, 1490......NN-6
N. Madison, 8547......NF-16
N. Olmsted, 32718......NF-14
N. Perry, 893......ND-17
N. Randall, 1027......SM-19
N. Ridgeville, 29465......NF-13
N. Royalton, 30444......NG-15
N. Zanesville, 2816......SB-14
Northbrook, 10668......SK-2
Northfield, 3677......SM-19
Northridge, 8500......SB-4
Northridge, 7572......SB-5
Northwood, 5265......NE-7
Norton, 12085......NH-15
Norwalk, 17012......NH-11
Norwood, 19207......SF-3
Oak Hbr., 2759......NF-8
Oak Hill, 1551......SH-11
Oakwood, 9202......SC-4
Oberlin, 8286......NG-12
Obetz, 4532......SJ-20
Ohio City, 705......NJ-2
Olmsted Falls, 9024......NG-14
Ontario, 6225......NJ-10
Orange, 3323......SM-20
Oregon, 20291......NE-7
Orrville, 8380......NJ-14
Orwell, 1660......NE-19
Ottawa, 4460......NH-4
OTTAWA CO., 41428......NE-7
Ottawa Hills, 4517......NB-1
Ottoville, 976......NI-3
Owensville, 794......SG-4

Column 1 — Ohio (continued)

Oxford, 21321 SD-1
Painesville, 19563 ND-17
Painesville on the Lake, 850 ND-17
Pandora, 1153 NI-5
Parma, 81601 NF-15
Parma Hts., 20718 NF-14
Pataskala, 14962 SA-11
Paulding, 3605 NH-2

PAULDING CO.,
19614 NH-1
Payne, 1194 NH-1
Peebles, 1782 SH-7
Pemberville, 1371 NF-7
Pepper Pike, 5979 NF-15
Perry, 1663 ND-17

PERRY CO.,
36058 SC-12
Perry Hts., 8441 NC-8
Perrysburg, 20623 NE-6
Perrysville, 175 NK-10
Petersburg, 950 NM-16
Philo, 733 SB-14

PICKAWAY CO.,
55696 SD-9
Pickerington, 18291 SA-11

PIKE CO.,
28709 SG-9
Piketon, 2181 SG-9
Pioneer, 1380 ND-2
Piqua, 20738 NM-3
Pitsgah, 1000 SE-3
Plain City, 4225 NM-8
Pleasant Grv., 1742 SB-14
Pleasant Hill, 1200 NM-3
Pleasant Run, 4953 SD-2
Pleasant Run Farm, 4654 SJ-2
Pleasantville, 960 SC-11
Plymouth, 1851 NI-9
Poland, 2555 NH-20
Pomeroy, 1852 SG-14
Port Clinton, 6056 NF-9

PORTAGE CO.,
161419 NH-15
Portage Lakes, 6968 NI-15
Portsmouth, 20226 SI-9
Powell, 11500 NM-9
Powhatan Pt., 1592 SB-19

PREBLE CO.,
42270 SC-1
Prospect, 1112 NL-8

PUTNAM CO.,
34499 NI-4
Quincy, 706 NM-5
Ravenna, 11724 NH-17
Reading, 10385 SI-3
Redbird, 2000 ND-17
Reedurban, 4400 NI-16
Reminderville, 3404 NI-16
Reno, 2993 SE-17
Rensselaer Pk., 850 SI-3
Reynoldsburg, 35893 SB-10
Richfield, 3648 NG-15

RICHLAND CO.,
124475 NI-11
Richmond Hts., 10546 NE-16
Ridgeway, 380 NL-7
Rio Grande, 830 SH-12
Ripley, 1750 SI-5
Rittman, 6491 NI-14
Riverside, 25201 SC-4
Roaming Shores, 1508 NE-19
Rockford, 1120 NJ-2
Rocky River, 20213 NF-14
Rome, 1450 NK-20
Roseland, 2110 NJ-11
Rosemount, 2112 SI-9
Roseville, 1833 SC-13
Ross, 3417 SE-2

ROSS CO.,
78064 SE-9
Rossford, 6293 NF-6
Russells Pt., 1391 NL-5
Sabina, 2564 SD-6
Sagamore Hills, 1930 NG-15
St. Bernard, 4368 SJ-3
St. Clairsville, 5184 NN-18
St. Henry, 2427 NL-2
St. Marys, 8332 NK-3
St. Paris, 2089 NN-5
Salem, 12303 NI-18
Salineville, 1311 NK-19
Salvisa, 2591 SB-14

SANDUSKY CO.,
60944 NF-8
Sardinia, 980 SG-5
Sawyerwood, 1543 NI-16
Schoenbrunn, 700 NL-16
Scio, 763 NL-18

SCIOTO CO.,
79499 SH-9
Sciotodale, 1081 SI-10
Seaman, 944 SH-7
Sebring, 4420 NI-18

SENECA CO.,
56745 NH-8
Seven Hills, 11804 NF-15
Seven Mile, 755 SD-2
Seville, 2296 NI-14
Shadyside, 3785 SA-19
Shaker Hts., 28448 NF-15
Sharonville, 13560 SF-3
Sheffield, 3982 NF-13
Sheffield Lake, 9137 NE-13
Shelby, 9017 NI-10

SHELBY CO.,
49423 NM-3
Sherwood, 827 NG-2
Shiloh, 11000 SB-4
Shreve, 1514 NJ-13
Sidney, 21229 NM-4
Silver Lake, 2519 NH-16
Silverton, 4788 SI-3
Skyline Acres, 1777 SK-2
Smithfield, 869 NM-18
Solon, 23348 NG-16
Somerset, 1481 SC-12
S. Amherst, 1690 NF-12
S. Bloomfield, 1144 SC-10
S. Charleston, 1693 SB-6
S. Euclid, 22295 NF-15
S. Hill Pk., 1040 NB-5
S. Lebanon, 4115 SE-4
South Point, 3958 SJ-12
S. Russell, 3810 NF-16
S. Webster, 860 SH-10
S. Zanesville, 1989 SB-14
Spencer, 753 NH-13
Spencerville, 2243 NK-3
Springboro, 17409 SD-3
Springdale, 11223 SF-3
Springfield, 60608 SB-6

STARK CO.,
375586 NI-17
Steubenville, 18609 NL-19
Stow, 34837 NH-16
Strasburg, 2608 NL-16
Streetsboro, 16028 NG-16
Strongsville, 44750 NG-14
Struthers, 10713 NH-20
Stryker, 1335 NE-3
Sugarcreek, 2220 NL-15
Summerside, 5181 SI-4
Summerside Estates, 1700 SM-6
Summit, 700 SI-9

SUMMIT CO.,
541781 NH-15
Sunbury, 4389 NM-10
Surrey Hill, 700 NB-12
Swanton, 3690 NE-5
Sycamore, 861 NI-8
Sylvania, 18965 ND-5
Syracuse, 826 SG-14
Tallmadge, 17537 NH-16
The Plains, 3080 SE-13
The Vil. of Indian Hill, 5785 SK-5
Thornville, 990 SB-12
Tiffin, 17963 NH-8
Tiltonsville, 1372 NM-19
Tipp City, 9689 NN-3
Toledo, 301285 NE-7
Toronto, 5091 ND-17
Trenton, 11803 SD-3
Trotwood, 24431 SC-3
Troy, 26205 NM-3

TRUMBULL CO.,
210312 NG-18
Turpin Hills, 5099 SK-4
Tuscarawas, 916 NM-16

TUSCARAWAS CO.,
92582 NM-16
Twinsburg, 20629 NG-16
Uhrichsville, 5352 NL-17
Union, 6419 SB-3

UNION CO.,
52300 NL-7
Uniopolis, 231 NK-4
Upper Arlington, 33519 NF-15

Column 2 — Ohio / Oklahoma

Upper Sandusky, 6596 NI-8
Urbana, 11493 NM-6
Urbancrest, 862 SL-10
Utica, 2132 NM-11
Valley View, 2034 NF-15
Van Wert, 10846 NI-2

VAN WERT CO.,
28744 NJ-2
Vandalia, 15246 NB-4

VINTON CO.,
13435 SF-11
Wadsworth, 21567 NH-15
Wakeman, 1047 NG-12
Walbridge, 3019 NC-3
Walnut Creek, 878 NK-15
Walton Hills, 2281 SN-19
Wapakoneta, 9867 NK-4
Warren, 41557 NG-19

WARREN CO.,
212693 SE-4
Warrensville Hts., 13540 NF-15

WASHINGTON CO.,
61778 SD-16
Washington Court House, 14192 SD-7
Washingtonville, 801 NI-19
Waterville, 5523 NF-6
Wauseon, 7332 NE-4
Waverly, 4408 SG-9
Wayne, 887 NG-7

WAYNE CO.,
114520 NI-14
Wayne Lakes Pk., 718 SA-2
Waynesburg, 923 NJ-17
Waynesfield, 847 NK-5
Waynesville, 2834 SD-4
Wellington, 4802 NH-12
Wellston, 5663 SG-11
Wellsville, 3541 NK-19
W. Alexandria, 1340 SC-2
W. Carrollton City, 13818 SC-3
W. Chester, 800 SF-3
W. Hill, 2273 NG-20
W. Jefferson, 4222 SA-8
W. Lafayette, 2321 NM-15
W. Liberty, 1805 NM-5
W. Milton, 4636 SB-3
W. Portsmouth, 3149 SI-9
W. Salem, 1464 NI-13
W. Union, 3241 SI-7
W. Unity, 1671 NE-3
Westerville, 36120 NN-9
Westfield Ctr., 1115 NH-14
Weston, 1590 NF-6
Wheelersburg, 6437 SI-10
White Oak, 19167 SF-2
Whitehall, 18062 SB-10
Whitehouse, 4149 NF-5
Wickliffe, 12750 NE-16
Wilberforce, 2271 SC-5
Wildbrook Acres, 1500 SK-3
Willard, 6236 NH-10
Williamsburg, 2490 SG-4
Williamsport, 1023 SD-9
Willoughby, 22268 NE-16
Willoughby Hills, 9485 NE-16
Willowick, 14171 NE-16
Winchester, 1051 SH-6
Windham, 2209 NG-18
Wintersville, 3924 NL-18
Withamsville, 7021 SG-3

WOOD CO.,
125488 NG-6
Woodbourne, 6050 SB-4
Woodlawn, 3294 SG-3
Woodmere, 884 SL-20
Woodsfield, 2364 SB-18
Woodville, 2055 NF-7
Wooster, 26119 NJ-14
Wooster Hts., 850 NJ-14
Worthington, 13575 NN-9

WYANDOT CO.,
22615 NJ-7
Wyoming, 8428 SI-3
Xenia, 25791 SC-6
Yellow Spgs., 3487 SC-5
Youngstown, 66982 NH-19
Zanesville, 25487 SB-14

Oklahoma
Map pp. 82 – 83

Ada, 16810 H-15
Adair, 790 D-18

ADAIR CO.,
22683 C-19
Afton, 1049 C-19

ALFALFA CO.,
5642 C-11
Allen, 932 H-16
Altus, 19813 I-9
Alva, 4845 C-11
Anadarko, 6762 G-11
Antlers, 2453 I-17
Apache, 1444 H-11
Arapaho, 796 F-10
Ardmore, 24283 J-14
Arkoma, 1989 G-20
Arnett, 524 D-8
Atoka, 3107 I-16

ATOKA CO.,
14182 J-16
Barnsdall, 1243 C-16
Bartlesville, 35750 C-16
Beaver, 1515 B-6

BEAVER CO.,
5636 C-7

BECKHAM CO.,
22119 G-8
Beggs, 1321 F-16
Bethany, 19051 F-13
Bethel Acres, 2895 G-14
Bixby, 20884 E-17
Blackwell, 7051 C-14
Blair, 818 H-9

BLAINE CO.,
11943 F-11
Blair, 818 H-9
Blanchard, 7610 G-13
Mountain View, 796 G-10
Muldrow, 3466 F-20

MURRAY CO.,
13488 I-14
Muskogee, 39223 E-18

MUSKOGEE CO.,
375992 E-17
Mustang, 17395 G-13
Newcastle, 7685 G-13
Newkirk, 2317 B-14
Nichols Hills, 3710 J-14
Nicoma Park, 2424 C-11
Noble, 6481 G-13

NOBLE CO.,
11561 C-14
N. Enid, 860 D-12
Nowata, 3731 C-17

NOWATA CO.,
10536 B-17
Oakhurst, 3183 K-5
Oilton, 1013 E-15
Okarche, 1215 F-12
Okay, 620 F-18
Okeene, 1223 E-11

OKFUSKEE CO.,
12191 F-15
Oklahoma City, 579999 F-13

OKLAHOMA CO.,
718633 F-13
Okmulgee, 12321 F-17

OKMULGEE CO.,
39685 F-16
Ologah, 1146 D-17

OSAGE CO.,
47472 C-15
Ottawa CO, 31848 B-19
Owasso, 28915 D-17
Panama, 1401 G-20
Park Hill, 3909 E-19
Pauls Valley, 6187 H-14
Pawhuska, 3584 C-15
Pawnee, 2230 D-15

PAWNEE CO.,
16577 D-14

PAYNE CO.,
77350 E-14
Perkins, 2831 E-14
Perry, 5126 D-14
Piedmont, 5720 F-12

PITTSBURG CO.,
45837 H-17
Pocola, 4056 G-20
Ponca City, 25387 C-14
Pond Creek, 856 C-12

PONTOTOC CO.,
124098 H-15
Poteau, 8520 G-20

POTTAWATOMIE CO.,
69442 G-14
Prague, 2386 F-15
Pryor, 9539 D-18

PUSHMATAHA CO.,
11572 I-18
Quapaw, 906 B-19

ROGER MILLS CO.,
3647 F-8

ROGERS CO.,
86905 D-17
Rush Spgs., 1231 H-12
Ryan, 816 J-13

SEMINOLE CO.,
25482 H-15
Sentinel, 901 G-9

SEQUOYAH CO.,
42391 F-20
Shady Pt., 1026 G-20
Shattuck, 1356 D-8
Shawnee, 29857 G-14
Skiatook, 7397 D-16
Slaughterville, 4137 G-13
Snyder, 1394 I-10
S. Coffeyville, 785 B-17
Spencer, 3912 J-16
Spiro, 2164 G-20
Sterling, 793 H-11
Stigler, 2685 G-19
Stillwater, 45688 E-14
Stilwell, 3949 E-20
Stratford, 1525 H-14
Stroud, 2690 F-15
Sulphur, 4929 I-14
Tahlequah, 15753 E-19
Talihina, 1114 H-19
Taloga, 299 F-10
Tecumseh, 6457 G-14
Temple, 1002 I-11
Texanna, 2261 G-18
Thomas, 1181 F-10
Tipton, 847 J-9
Tishomingo, 3034 I-15
Tonkawa, 3216 C-13
Tulsa, 391906 D-17

TULSA CO.,
603403 D-17
Tuttle, 6019 G-12
Tyrone, 762 B-6
Union City, 1645 G-12
Valley Brook, 765 L-6
Verdigris, 3993 D-17
Vian, 1466 F-19
Vinita, 5743 C-18
Wagoner, 8323 E-18

WAGONER CO.,
73085 E-18
Walters, 2551 I-11
Warr Acres, 10043 J-13

WASHINGTON CO.,
51225 C-17

WASHITA CO.,
11629 G-9
Watonga, 5111 F-11
Waukomis, 1286 D-12
Waurika, 2064 J-12
Waynoka, 927 D-10
Weatherford, 10833 G-10
Weleetka, 998 G-16
Wellston, 788 F-14
Westville, 1596 E-20
Wetumka, 1282 G-16
Wewoka, 3430 G-15
Wilburton, 3430 H-18
Wister, 1102 H-19

WOODS CO.,
8878 C-10
Woodward, 12051 D-9

WOODWARD CO.,
20081 C-9
Wright City, 762 I-19
Wynnewood, 2212 H-14
Yale, 1227 E-15
Yukon, 22709 F-12

Oregon
Map pp. 84 – 85

Adair Vil., 840 F-4
Albany, 50158 F-4
Aloha, 49425 C-4
Amity, 1614 E-3
Ashland, 20078 M-4
Astoria, 9477 B-3
Athena, 1126 B-13
Aumsville, 3584 F-4
Aurora, 918 D-5

BAKER CO.,
16134 E-15
Baker City, 9828 E-15
Bandon, 3066 J-1
Banks, 1777 C-4
Barview, 1844 I-1
Bay City, 1286 C-3
Beaverton, 89803 C-4
Bend, 76639 F-8
Benton Co., 85579 G-3
Boardman, 3220 B-11
Brookings, 6336 M-1
Brownsville, 1668 G-4
Bunker Hill, 1440 J-1
Burns, 2781 H-11
Canby, 15083 D-5
Cannon Bch., 1690 B-2
Canyon City, 703 G-12
Canyonville, 1588 K-3
Carlton, 2007 D-4
Cave Jct., 1883 M-2
Cedar Hills, 8843 C-4
Cedar Mill, 14646 C-4
Central Point, 17169 M-3
Charleston, 900 J-1
Chenoweth, 1855 C-8
Clackamas, 5177 D-5
Clackamas Co., 375992 E-5
Clatskanie, 1737 B-4
Coburg, 1035 G-4
Columbia City, 1725 B-4

COLUMBIA CO.,
49351 B-4
Condon, 682 D-10
Coos Bay, 15967 J-1

COOS CO.,
63043 J-2
Coquille, 3866 J-1
Corvallis, 49322 F-3
Cottage Grv., 9686 H-4
Crescent, 710 H-7

CROOK CO.,
20978 F-9
Culver, 1357 F-8
Dallas, 14583 E-3
Dayton, 2459 D-4
Depoe Bay, 1398 E-2

DESCHUTES CO.,
157733 F-8
Donald, 979 D-5

DOUGLAS CO.,
107667 J-4
Drain, 1021 H-3
Dufur, 604 D-8
Dundee, 3109 D-4
Dunes City, 1303 H-1
Eagle Point, 8469 L-3
Elgin, 1711 C-14
Enterprise, 1940 C-16
Estacada, 2695 D-6
Eugene, 153690 G-4
Fairview, 8920 C-5
Florence, 8466 H-1
Forest Grv., 21083 C-4
Fossil, 473 D-10
Four Corners, 15947 F-4
Garibaldi, 779 C-3
Gearhart, 1462 B-3
Gervais, 2464 E-4
Gladstone, 12013 K-6
Glendale, 855 K-3
Gold Bch., 2253 L-1
Gold Hill, 1085 L-3
Grand Ronde, 1661 E-3
Gresham, 101058 C-5
Happy Valley, 11903 K-6
Harbor, 2895 M-1

HARNEY CO.,
7422 H-12
Hayesville, 20756 F-4
Hermiston, 15182 B-11
Hillsboro, 91611 C-4
Hines, 1563 I-12
Hood River, 7167 C-7

HOOD RIVER CO.,
22346 C-7
Hubbard, 3173 D-4
Independence, 8590 E-4
Irrigon, 1826 B-11
Island City, 989 D-14

JACKSON CO.,
203206 L-4
Jacksonville, 2795 M-4
Jefferson, 3098 F-4

JEFFERSON CO.,
21726 F-8
John Day, 1744 G-12
Joseph, 1081 D-16

JOSEPHINE CO.,
82713 L-3
Junction City, 5392 G-4
Keizer, 36478 F-4
Keno, 1700 M-6
King City, 3111 M-17

KLAMATH CO.,
66380 L-7
Klamath Falls, 20840 M-6
La Grande, 13082 D-14

LAKE CO.,
7895 K-9
L. Oswego, 36619 K-6
Lakeside, 1699 J-1
Lakeview, 2290 M-10

LANE CO.,
351715 M-4
Lebanon, 15518 F-4
Lincoln Beach, 2065 E-2

LINCOLN CO.,
46034 F-2

LINN CO.,
116672 F-5
Lowell, 1045 H-4
Madras, 6046 F-8

MALHEUR CO.,
31313 I-15
Malin, 805 M-7

MARION CO.,
315335 E-4
Maywood Pk., 752 K-19
McMinnville, 32187 D-4
McNulty, 800 B-4
Medford, 74907 M-3
Melrose, 735 J-3
Merlin, 1615 L-3
Merrill, 864 N-7
Metzger, 3354 M-18
Mill City, 1865 F-5
Milton-Freewater, 7050 B-13
Milwaukie, 20291 K-6
Molalla, 7037 C-13
Monmouth, 9534 E-3
Moro, 324 C-8
Morrow Co., 11173 C-11
Mt. Angel, 3286 E-4
Mulino, 2103 D-5

MULTNOMAH CO.,
735334 C-4
Myrtle Creek, 3439 K-3
Myrtle Pt., 2514 J-1
Netarts, 748 C-3
Newberg, 22068 D-4
Newport, 9989 F-2
N. Bend, 9695 J-1
N. Plains, 1947 C-4
Oakland, 927 J-3
Odell, 2255 C-7
Ontario, 11366 G-17
Oregon City, 31859 D-5
Pacific City, 1035 D-3
Pendleton, 16612 C-13
Philomath, 4682 F-3
Phoenix, 4538 M-4
Pilot Rock, 1502 C-13

POLK CO.,
75403 E-3
Port Orford, 1133 K-1
Portland, 562130 C-5
Powell Butte, 770 F-8
Powers, 689 K-2
Prairie City, 909 G-13
Prineville, 9253 F-8
Rainier, 1895 A-4
Redmond, 23500 F-8
Reedsport, 4154 I-1
Rhododendron, 800 D-6
Riddle, 1185 K-3
Rockaway Bch., 1312 C-2
Rose Lodge, 1894 E-2
Roseburg, 21181 J-3
Rufus, 250 C-9
St. Helens, 12883 B-4
Salem, 154637 E-4
Sandy, 9570 D-6
Scappoose, 6255 B-4
Seal Rock, 600 F-2
Seaside, 6457 B-3
Selma, 695 M-3
Shady Cove, 2944 L-3
Sheridan, 6100 E-3
Silverton, 9222 E-4
Sisters, 1834 F-7
Sodaville, 320 G-4
Springfield, 59403 H-4
Stanfield, 2042 B-12
Stayton, 7644 F-4
Sublimity, 2681 F-4
Sunriver, 1393 H-8
Sutherlin, 7810 J-3
Sweet Home, 9133 G-5
Talent, 6066 M-4
The Dalles, 13620 C-8
Tigard, 48035 C-4
Tillamook, 4935 C-3

TILLAMOOK CO.,
25250 C-3
Toledo, 3596 F-2
Tri-City, 3931 K-3
Troutdale, 15962 C-5
Tualatin, 26054 D-4
Turner, 1852 F-4
Umatilla, 6906 B-12

UMATILLA CO.,
75889 C-13
Union, 2043 D-14

UNION CO.,
25748 D-14
Veneta, 4561 H-3
Vernonia, 2151 B-4
Waldport, 2050 F-2

WALLOWA CO.,
7008 C-16
Warm Spgs., 2431 E-7
Warrenton, 4989 B-3
Wasco, 410 C-9

WASCO CO.,
25213 D-8

WASHINGTON CO.,
529710 C-4
W. Linn, 25109 K-6
W. Slope, 6654 C-17
Wheeler, 391 C-3
White City, 6441 L-3
Willamina, 2064 E-3
Wilsonville, 15509 D-4
Winston, 5379 J-3
Woodburn, 24080 D-4
Yachats, 690 G-1
Yamhill, 1024 D-4

YAMHILL CO.,
99193 D-3
Yoncalla, 1047 J-3

Pennsylvania
Map pp. 86 – 89

Map keys Atlas pages
EA – ET 88 – 89
WA – WT 86 – 87

† City keyed to p. 24
* City keyed to p. 27
‡ City keyed to p. 90

Abbottstown, 1011 WT-13
Abington, 56300 EO-2
Adams CO, 101407 EP-7
Adamsburg, 184 WO-7
Akron, 4046 EO-1
Albion, 1607 WC-2
Aldan, 4152 EO-3
Aliquippa, 10252 WM-2
Allegheny CO, 1281091 WN-4
Allentown, 106992 EM-3
Almedia, 1200 EH-1
Altoona, 48739 WL-12

Column 5 — Pennsylvania

Ambler, 6417 EO-12
Ambridge, 7050 WL-3
Ancient Oaks, 6661 EM-10
Andalusia, 3500 N-8
Annville, 4767 EN-6
Apollo, 1647 WL-6
Archbald, 6984 EG-10
Ardmore, 12655 EP-2
Ardsley, 4500 N-14
Arnold, 5454 WN-7

ARMSTRONG CO.,
68941 WL-5
Arnold, 5157 WN-7
Ashland, 2817 EK-7
Ashley, 2790 EH-8
Aspinwall, 2801 J-7
Athens, 3367 EB-6
Audubon, 8631 EO-11
Avalon, 4705 WN-3
Avoca, 2661 EG-10
Avon, 1661 EN-6
Avondale, 1265 EQ-9
Avonmore, 1011 WM-6
Baden, 4135 WL-3
Bainbridge, 1355 EO-5
Bakerstown, 900 WL-4
Bally, 1090 EM-10
Bangor, 5273 EL-2
Bareville, 1250 EO-8
Beaver, 4621 WM-2

BEAVER CO.,
170539 WK-2
Beaver Falls, 8987 WL-2
Beaver Meadows, 869 EI-9
Beaverdale, 1035 WN-9
Beavertown, 965 EL-1
Bedminster, 942 EN-10
Bedford, 2841 WP-10

BEDFORD CO.,
49762 WO-10
Bellefonte, 6187 EJ-1
Bell Acres, 1388 WL-3
Belle Vernon, 1093 WN-5
Belleville, 1827 WL-14
Bellevue, 8370 J-2
Bellwood, 1828 WL-12
Belmont Hills, 1500 N-5
Ben Avon, 1781 J-4
Bentleyville, 2581 WN-4
Benton, 824 EH-6
Berlin, 2144 WP-8
Bernville, 955 EM-7
Berwick, 10477 EI-7
Berwyn, 3631 EP-11
Bessemer, 1122 WK-1
Bethel Pk., 32313 WN-4
Bethlehem, 74982 EL-11
Big Beaver, 1970 WK-2
Biglerville, 1200 EP-7
Birdsboro, 5289 EN-8
Bishop, 800 WN-4
Black Lick, 1462 WM-7
Blaine Hill, 1100 WO-4

BLAIR CO.,
127089 WN-11
Blakely, 6564 EG-10
Blandon, 7152 EM-8
Blawnox, 1422 WN-4
Bloomingdale, 1709 EH-9
Bloomsburg, 14855 EI-6
Blossburg, 1538 ED-4
Blue Ball, 1031 EO-8
Blue Ridge Summit, 891 ER-1
Boalsburg, 3772 WK-13
Bobtown, 757 WQ-5
Boiling Spgs., 3225 EO-3
Bonneauville, 1800 ER-7
Boothwyn, 4933 A-10
Boswell, 1357 WP-8
Bowmanstown, 937 EK-10
Boyertown, 4005 EN-9
Brackenridge, 3260 WL-5
Braddock, 2682 WN-4
Bradford, 8770 WD-10

BRADFORD CO.,
62622 EE-5
Bradford Woods, 1171 WL-3
Breinigsville, 4138 EM-10
Brentwood, 9643 L-5
Bressler, 1437 ET-4
Brickerville, 1299 EO-7
Bridgeport, 4550 M-3
Bridgeville, 5148 WN-3
Bristol, 9726 EO-14
Brockway, 2072 WH-9
Brodheadsville, 1800 EI-11
Brookhaven, 8100 A-9
Brookville, 3924 WH-9
Broomall, 10789 EP-11
Broughton, 3000 L-6
Brownstown, 1418 EO-1
Brownsville, 2677 WO-5
Bryn Athyn, 1375 N-17
Buck Hill Falls, 800 EH-11
Buckingham, 2000 EN-12

BUCKS CO.,
625249 EM-11
Burgettstown, 1484 WM-2
Burnham, 2065 WL-14
Butler, 14894 WL-5

BUTLER CO.,
183862 WK-4
Buttonwood, 1500 EH-12
California, 6795 WO-4
Caln, 515 EP-10

CAMBRIA CO.,
143679 WN-9

CAMERON CO.,
5395 WF-12
Camp Hill, 7888 ET-2
Campbelltown, 3436 EN-6
Canadensis, 1200 EH-11
Canonsburg, 8982 WN-3
Carbondale, 9057 EG-10

CARBON CO.,
65249 EK-9
Carlisle, 18682 EN-3
Carnegie, 7972 WN-3
Carrolltown, 877 WM-9
Castle Shannon, 8316 K-5
Catasauqua, 6436 EL-11
Catawissa, 1552 EI-6
Centerville, 3266 WO-5
Centerville, 1538 WO-9
Central City, 1185 WO-8
Centre Hall, 1261 WK-14

CENTRE CO.,
153990 EK-1
Chadds Ford, 1200 EQ-10
Chalfont, 4009 EN-12
Chambersburg, 18130 EP-2

Column 6 — Pennsylvania

Coaldale, 2281 EK-9
Coalmont, 1200 WO-12
Coatesville, 11396 WO-4
Cochranton, 1136 WG-3
Coleraine, 2500 EP-2
Collegeville, 5089 EO-11
Collingdale, 8786 B-8
Colmar, 800 EN-12
Colonial Pk., 13229 ET-3
Colonial Pk., 13229 ET-3
Colony, 1076 EO-1

COLUMBIA CO.,
67295 EI-6
Colver, 959 WM-9
Columbia, 10400 EO-5
Colwyn, 2546 B-8
Conestoga, 800 EO-5
Conemaugh, 900 WN-9
Confluence, 780 WP-7
Conneaut Lake, 774 WF-2
Connellsville, 7637 WO-6
Conshohocken, 7833 EO-11
Conway, 2176 WL-3
Conyngham, 1914 EI-8
Coopersburg, 2386 EM-11
Coplay, 3192 EL-11
Coraopolis, 5867 WM-3
Corry, 6605 WE-4
Cornwall, 4110 EN-6
Cornwells Hts., 1391 N-18
Corry, 6605 WE-4
Coudersport, 2546 WE-12
Countryside Pk., 900 EO-14
Crafton, 5951 WN-3

CRAWFORD CO.,
88765 WF-2
Cresson, 1500 WN-10
Cressona, 1651 EL-8
Croydon, 9950 N-19

CUMBERLAND CO.,
235406 EO-3
Curtisville, 1064 WL-4
Curwensville, 2542 WJ-10
Dallas, 2804 EG-8
Dallastown, 4049 EP-5
Danville, 4698 EJ-6
Darby, 10687 B-7
Daubersville, 848 EM-8
Davidsville, 1060 WO-8
Dawson, 600 WO-6
Delano, 965 EK-8

DELAWARE CO.,
565269 EP-11
Delmont, 2686 WM-6
Denver, 3861 EN-8
Derry, 2688 WN-7
Dickson City, 6070 EG-10
Dillsburg, 2563 EO-3
Donora, 5091 WO-4
Dormont, 8541 K-4
Dover, 2007 EO-4
Downingtown, 7891 EP-10
Doylestown, 8380 EN-12
Dravosburg, 1873 WO-4
Dresher, 5610 M-16
Drexel Hill, 28043 P-11
Dublin, 2081 EN-12
Dubois, 7794 WI-10
Dunbar, 1200 WO-6
Duncannon, 1508 EN-3
Duncansville, 1205 WN-11
Dunmore, 14152 EG-10
Dupont, 2711 EG-10
Duquesne, 6772 WN-4
Duryea, 4566 EG-10
E. Bangor, 1006 EL-12
E. Berlin, 1521 EP-6
E. Brady, 942 WK-5
E. Conemaugh, 1220 WN-9
E. Earl, 1144 EO-8
E. Greenville, 3032 EM-10
E. Lansdowne, 2668 B-7
E. McKeesport, 2126 L-7
E. Petersburg, 1822 EO-5
E. Pittsburgh, 1822 L-7
E. Prospect, 905 EP-5
E. Stroudsburg, 9840 EI-12
E. Washington, 2244 WN-3
E. York, 8500 EO-4
Eau Claire, 391 WK-4
Ebensburg, 3351 WN-9
Economy, 8970 WL-3
Eddystone, 2422 A-8
Edgewood, 3192 J-6
Edgeworth, 1619 WL-3
Edinboro, 6100 WE-2
Edwardsville, 4816 EH-7
Effort, 2250 EI-11
Elco, 367 WO-4
Elderton, 369 WL-6
Eldred, 819 WD-11
Elizabeth, 1493 WN-4
Elizabethtown, 11545 EO-6
Elizabethville, 1355 EM-4
Elkland, 1821 EC-4
Elkins Pk., 6500 M-15

ELK CO.,
31946 WG-10
Ellwood City, 8073 WL-2
Elysburg, 2063 EJ-6
Emlenton, 717 WJ-5
Emmaus, 11488 EM-10
Emporium, 2073 WF-12
Emsworth, 2449 J-2
Enola, 5961 ET-1
Ephrata, 13394 EO-7
Erie, 101786 WD-3

ERIE CO.,
280566 WD-3
Etna, 3698 WN-4
Everett, 1905 WP-11
Everson, 859 WO-6
Exeter, 5652 EG-9
Export, 918 WM-6
Exton, 3800 EP-10
Factoryville, 1197 EF-9
Fairchance, 1999 WP-6
Fairdale, 1330 WQ-5

FAYETTE CO.,
146610 WO-5
Fayetteville, 3128 EP-1
Feasterville, 6683 N-17
Fellsburg, 900 WO-4
Ferndale, 1716 WO-9
Fernway, 12141 WL-3
Fleetwood, 4085 EM-8
Flemington, 1279 EH-2

Column 7 — Pennsylvania (continued)

Frisco, 850 WK-3
Fullerton, 14925 EL-10

FULTON CO.,
14845 WP-12
Galeton, 1150 WD-12
Gallitzin, 1668 WM-10
Gap, 1931 EP-8
Garden View, 2503 D-14
Geistown, 2467 WO-9
Georgetown, 1640 EN-7
Germansville, 2818 WN-4
Gettysburg, 7620 EQ-7
Gibsonia, 2733 WL-4
Gilberton, 769 EK-7
Gilbertsville, 6159 EN-9
Girard, 3104 WD-1
Girardville, 1519 EK-7
Gladwyne, 4000 M-3
Glassport, 4483 WN-4
Glen Campbell, 257 WL-9
Glen Rock, 1873 EO-4
Glenolden, 7476 B-7
Glenshaw, 9100 J-5
Glenside, 8881 N-16
Gold Key Lake, 1391 EH-12
Gordon, 763 EK-7
Gouldsboro, 800 EH-10
Graysville, 6000 WQ-4
Grantham, 900 ET-1
Gratz, 765 EL-5
Greencastle, 3995 EQ-2
Greensburg, 15075 WN-7

GREENE CO.,
38686 WQ-3
Greenfields, 1715 EM-8
Greenock, 1035 WN-4
Greensboro, 260 WP-5
Greensburg, 15889 WN-7
Greenville, 5911 WG-2
Grove City, 8322 WJ-3
Halifax, 841 EM-4
Hallam, 2673 EP-5
Hamburg, 4289 EM-8
Hamlin, 2500 EG-11
Hanover, 15289 EQ-6
Harborcreek, 2458 WD-4
Harleigh, 1468 EJ-8
Harleysville, 9286 EN-11
Harmar Hts., 1050 J-8
Harmony, 837 WK-3
Harmonville, 5982 M-2
Harrisburg, 49528 EN-4
Harrison City, 1800 WM-6
Harveys Lake, 2791 EG-8
Hastings, 1278 WM-9
Hatboro, 7360 EO-12
Hatfield, 2926 EN-11
Havertown, 36000 P-11
Hawley, 1302 EF-11
Hazleton, 23300 EJ-8
Hebron, 3000 EN-6
Hegins, 812 EL-6
Hellertown, 5612 EM-11
Hereford, 800 EM-10
Hermitage, 16220 WG-2
Herndon, 356 EL-4
Hershey, 12771 EN-5
Highspire, 2559 ET-5
Hilldale, 1401 H-7
Hollidaysburg, 5791 WM-11
Hollywood, 800 N-17
Holmesburg, 2000 N-18
Homeacre, 1400 WN-5
Homer City, 1707 WM-7
Homestead, 3165 WN-4
Hometown, 1349 EK-8
Honesdale, 4874 EF-11
Honey Brook, 1713 EO-9
Hookstown, 157 WM-2
Hopwood, 2000 WP-6
Horsham, 14842 N-15
Houston, 1319 WN-3
Houtzdale, 917 WK-11
Hudson, 1800 H-7
Hughesville, 2125 EG-5
Hummels Wharf, 1353 EK-4
Hummelstown, 4360 EN-5
Hunlock Creek, 1200 EH-7

HUNTINGDON CO.,
45913 WN-12
Huntingdon Valley, 4000 N-16
Hyde, 1579 WJ-11
Hyde Park, 2528 ES-13
Hyndman, 963 WP-10
Imperial, 3441 WN-3
Indiana, 14895 WM-7

INDIANA CO.,
87963 WL-7
Industry, 1835 WL-2
Ingram, 3300 J-2
Intercourse, 1274 EO-8
Irwin, 3904 WN-6
Ivyland, 650 EN-12
Jacobus, 1841 EP-4

JEFFERSON CO.,
45000 WH-9
Jeannette, 10019 WN-6
Jenkintown, 4422 N-16
Jermyn, 2127 EG-10
Jersey Shore, 4361 EG-3
Jessup, 4642 EG-10
Jim Thorpe, 4804 EK-9
Johnsonburg, 2807 WG-10
Johnstown, 22768 WN-9
Jonestown, 1905 EN-6

JUNIATA CO.,
24636 EM-2
Juniata Terr., 500 WL-14
Kane, 3855 WF-11
Kenhorst, 2834 EN-8
Kennett Sq., 5876 EQ-9
King of Prussia, 18511 EO-11
Kingston, 13182 EH-7
Kittanning, 4417 WL-6
Knox, 1054 WJ-6
Koppel, 809 WL-2
Kulpmont, 2902 EJ-6
Kutztown, 5067 EM-9
Lackawaxen, 800 EF-12

LACKAWANNA CO.,
213646 EG-10
Laflin, 1487 H-8
Lake City, 2989 WD-1
Lampeter, 1800 EO-6

LANCASTER CO.,
494963 EP-7
Lancaster, 55822 EO-6
Landisville, 2502 EO-6
Lanesville, 1033 K-8
Langhorne, 1622 EO-13
Lansdale, 16269 EN-11
Lansdowne, 10620 B-7
Lansford, 4024 EK-9
Laporte, 282 EF-7
Larksville, 4480 H-7
Latrobe, 8777 WN-7
Laureldale, 3855 EN-8
Laurys Sta., 900 EL-10
Lawnton, 3500 ET-5

LAWRENCE CO.,
91108 WJ-2
Leacock, 1200 EO-8
Lebanon, 24461 EN-6

LEBANON CO.,
126900 EN-6
Leechburg, 2268 WL-6
Leeper, 465 WH-7
Leesport, 1918 EM-8

Column 8 — Pennsylvania (continued)

Leesport, 1918 EM-8
New Derry, 800 WN-7
New Eagle, 2184 WO-4
New Freedom, 4464 EQ-5
New Holland, 5378 EO-8
New Hope, 2528 EN-13
New Kensington, 14701 WL-5
New Oxford, 1825 EQ-6
New Stanton, 2083 WN-6
New Wilmington, 2466 WJ-2
Newburg, 2815 WI-5
Newell, 549 WO-4
Newmanstown, 2178 EN-7
Newport, 1574 EM-3
Newton Hamilton, 247 WM-14
Newtown, 2419 EN-13
Newtown Sq., 11300 EP-11
Newville, 1326 EO-2
Nicholson, 767 EF-9
Norristown, 30749 EO-11
Northampton, 9584 EL-10

NORTHAMPTON CO.,
297735 EK-11

NORTHUMBERLAND CO.,
94528 EK-5
Norwood, 5900 B-7
Nuremberg, 937 EK-8
Oak Lane, 1700 M-15
Oakdale, 1558 WN-3
Oakland, 1650 WG-3
Oakland, 1569 WJ-2
Oakmont, 6810 WN-4
Ohiopyle, 72 WP-6
Oil City, 10557 WH-5
Oklahoma, 874 WL-6
Old Forge, 8313 EG-10
Oley, 1282 EN-9
Oliver, 2535 WP-5
Olyphant, 5151 EG-10
Oreland, 5900 M-15
Orwigsburg, 3090 EL-8
Osceola Mills, 1141 WK-11
Oxford, 5077 EQ-8
Palmer Hts., 3762 EL-11
Palmerton, 5414 EK-10
Palmyra, 7320 EN-6
Palo Alto, 1059 EL-8
Paoli, 5575 EP-11
Paradise, 1129 EO-8
Parkesburg, 3420 EP-9
Parkside, 2257 A-9
Patton, 1827 WM-10
Paxtang, 1561 WO-10
Pen Argyl, 3595 EL-12
Penbrook, 3016 ET-4
Penn Hills, 6000 WN-4
Penndel, 2328 O-18
Penns Woods, 2600 M-1
Pennsburg, 4125 EM-10
Pennside, 4215 EN-8
Pennsylvania Furnace, 600 WK-13
Perkasie, 8984 EN-11

PERRY CO.,
45969 EN-3
Perryopolis, 1784 WO-5
Philadelphia, 1526006 EP-12

PHILADELPHIA CO.,
1526006 EP-12
Phoenixville, 14600 EO-11
Picture Rocks, 655 EG-5
Pine Grv., 2182 EL-7
Pine Grv. Mills, 1502 WL-13
Pitcairn, 3294 K-8
Pittsburgh, 305704 WN-4
Pittston, 7739 EG-10
Pleasant Gap, 1800 WK-13
Pleasant Hills, 8161 L-5
Plum, 27126 WN-5
Plumsteadville, 1200 EN-12
Plymouth, 6078 H-7
Plymouth Meeting, 6177 M-2
Pocono Pines, 1409 EH-11
Point Marion, 1159 WP-5
Port Allegany, 2157 WE-11
Port Carbon, 1889 EL-8
Port Trevorton, 762 EL-4
Portage, 2683 WN-10
Pottstown, 21959 EN-9
Pottsville, 14764 EL-7
Punxsutawney, 6271 WI-9

SUSQUEHANNA CO.,
42238 EE-9
Quakertown, 8979 EM-11
Quarryville, 2117 EP-7
Radnor, 1800 P-10
Rankin, 2280 WN-4
Reading, 80855 EN-8
Red Hill, 2347 EM-10
Red Lion, 6227 EP-5
Renovo, 1229 WH-14
Reynoldsville, 2708 WI-9
Rheems, 1258 EO-6
Ridgway, 4078 WG-10
Ridley Park, 7050 B-8
Riegelsville, 868 EM-12

Column 9 — Pennsylvania / South Dakota

Salix, 1149 WN-9
Sanatoga, 8378 EN-10
Sandy, 4960 WI-10
Saxonburg, 1526 WL-5
Sayre, 5587 EB-6
Scalp Level, 778 WN-9
Schaefferstown, 941 EN-7
Schnecksville, 2935 EL-10
Schuylkill Haven, 5437 EL-7

SCHUYLKILL CO.,
148289 EL-7
Schwenksville, 1385 EN-11
Scottdale, 4384 WO-5
Scranton, 76089 EG-10
Selinsgrove, 5654 EK-4
Sellersville, 4249 EN-11
Seven Fields, 2887 WL-4
Sewickley, 3827 WM-3
Shamokin, 7374 EK-6
Sharon, 15100 WG-2
Sharon Hill, 5597 B-7
Sharpsburg, 3446 WN-4
Sharpsville, 4291 WG-2
Shenandoah, 5071 EK-7
Shickshinny, 838 EH-6
Shillington, 5064 EN-8
Shiloh, 11218 EO-4
Shinglehouse, 1127 WD-12
Shippensburg, 5492 EP-1
Shiremanstown, 1378 EM-8
Shoemakersville, 1378 EM-8
Shrewsbury, 3823 EQ-5
Silkworth, 820 H-6
Silverdale, 871 EN-11
Skippack, 3710 EN-11
Slatington, 4464 EL-10
Slippery Rock, 3625 WJ-4
Smethport, 1605 WE-11
Snow Shoe, 765 WJ-13

SNYDER CO.,
39702 EL-4

SOMERSET CO.,
77851 WP-8
Somerset, 6618 WO-8
S. Connellsville, 1970 WP-6
S. Fork, 928 WN-9
S. Greensburg, 2117 WN-7
S. Temple, 1400 EN-8
S. Williamsport, 6379 EG-4
Souderton, 6584 EN-11
Spangler, 2691 WM-10
Spartansburg, 336 WE-4
Speers, 1154 WO-4
Spinnerstown, 1426 EN-11
Spring City, 3323 EO-10
Spring Grove, 2183 EP-4
Spring Mount, 2259 EN-11
Springboro, 488 WF-1
Springdale, 3828 WN-5
Spry, 5000 EP-4
St. Clair, 3004 EL-7
St. Marys, 14502 WG-11
St. Petersburg, 408 WJ-5
Stanton, 4500 EP-11
Steelton, 5990 ET-4
Stewartstown, 2009 EQ-5
Stoneboro, 1051 WH-3
Stony Creek Mills, 1200 EN-8
Stoystown, 378 WO-8
Strabane, 1100 WN-3
Strasburg, 2800 EO-7
Stroudsburg, 5740 EI-12
Sturgeon, 1773 K-1
Sugar Notch, 989 H-7
Summit Hill, 3034 EK-9
Sunbury, 9905 EK-5
Susquehanna Depot, 1660 EE-10
Swarthmore, 6194 B-8
Swissvale, 8983 WN-4
Swoyersville, 5062 H-7
Sykesville, 1163 WI-9
Tamaqua, 7107 EK-8
Tarentum, 4730 WM-5
Tatamy, 1108 EL-11
Taylor, 6475 EG-10
Telford, 4680 EN-11
Temple, 1500 EN-8
Terre Hill, 1282 EO-8
The Hill, 950 EN-8
Thompsonville, 3575 WN-3
Thorndale, 3407 EP-10
Throop, 4010 EG-10
Tidioute, 677 WG-6

TIOGA CO.,
41373 ED-2
Tioga, 638 EC-4
Tionesta, 580 WH-7
Titusville, 5900 WG-5
Topton, 2069 EM-9
Toughkenamon, 1500 EQ-9
Towanda, 2919 ED-6
Tower City, 1380 EL-6
Trafford, 3236 WN-6
Trappe, 3408 EO-11
Tremont, 1714 EL-6
Trevorton, 2058 EK-5
Trevose, 3000 N-18
Troy, 1355 EC-4
Tullytown, 2000 O-18
Tunkhannock, 1911 EF-8
Turtle Creek, 5349 WN-4
Tyrone, 5340 WL-12

UNION CO.,
44947 EK-3
Union City, 3341 WE-3
Uniontown, 11598 WP-6
Upland, 2977 A-9
Upper Darby, 81821 P-11
Ursina, 241 WP-7
Vandergrift, 5097 WL-6
Verona, 2869 WN-4

VENANGO CO.,
56287 WH-5
Versailles, 1526 L-8
Villanova, 800 P-10
Village Green, 1200 A-9
Vinco, 1200 WN-9
Volant, 137 WJ-3
Wampum, 697 WL-2

WARREN CO.,
41815 WE-7
Warren, 9710 WE-7
Warrendale, 1200 WL-3

WASHINGTON CO.,
207820 WN-3
Washington, 15268 WN-3
Waterford, 1553 WE-3
Watsontown, 2144 EH-4
Waymart, 1329 EF-11

WAYNE CO.,
50212 EF-11
Waynesboro, 9614 EQ-2
Waynesburg, 4177 WP-3
Wernersville, 2495 EN-7
Wescosville, 900 EM-10
Wesleyville, 3341 WD-4
W. Bristol, 5000 O-18
W. Brownsville, 992 WP-4
W. Chester, 18461 EP-10
W. Conshohocken, 1500 M-2
W. Easton, 1269 WI-5
W. Elizabeth, 552 L-6
W. Fairview, 1282 ES-2
W. Grove, 2854 EQ-9
W. Hazleton, 4594 EJ-8
W. Homestead, 1985 WN-4
W. Kittanning, 1175 WK-6
W. Lancaster, 800 EO-6
W. Lawn, 1715 EN-8
W. Leechburg, 1294 WL-6
W. Mayfield, 1234 WK-2
W. Mifflin, 20313 WN-4
W. Newton, 2633 WO-5
W. Pittsburg, 1000 WK-2
W. Pittston, 4868 EG-9
W. Reading, 4012 EN-8
W. View, 6834 J-3
W. Wyoming, 2725 H-7
W. York, 4617 EO-4
Westfield, 1064 EE-1

WESTMORELAND CO.,
365169 WM-6
Westwood, 1000 WN-9
Wexford, 1100 WL-3
Whitaker, 1203 L-6
White Haven, 1182 EI-9
White Oak, 7862 WN-5
Whitehall, 13944 WN-4
Wilcox, 801 WF-11
Wilkes-Barre, 41283 EH-7
Wilkinsburg, 15930 WN-4
Williamsburg, 1254 WM-12
Williamsport, 29381 EG-4
Williamstown, 1395 EL-5
Willow Grove, 16000 N-16
Willow Street, 7578 EP-7
Wilmerding, 1940 L-8
Wilson, 7858 EL-11
Wind Gap, 2720 EL-11
Windber, 4138 WO-9
Windsor, 1381 EP-5
Winfield, 900 EK-4
Wolfdale, 2769 WN-3
Womelsdorf, 2810 EN-7
Woodland Hts., 1261 WI-5
Woodland Pk., 950 EJ-3
Woodlyn, 1850 A-8
Wormleysburg, 3019 P-4
Wrightsville, 2310 EP-4
Wyncote, 3044 M-15
Wyndmoor, 5498 M-15
Wyomissing, 10461 EN-8
Yardley, 2413 EN-13
Yeadon, 11762 B-7
Yoe, 1000 EP-4
York, 40862 EP-4

YORK CO.,
434972 EP-4
Yorkshire, 1700 WS-14
Youngsville, 1757 WE-7
Youngwood, 3050 WN-6
Zelienople, 3812 WL-3
Zion, 2030 WK-14

Puerto Rico
Map p. 128

Arecibo, 44191 A-11
Bayamón, 185996 A-13
Caguas, 82243 B-13
Carolina, 157832 A-14
Cayey, 16883 B-13
Guaynabo, 75443 A-13
Humacao, 16829 B-15
Mayagüez, 70463 B-10
Ponce, 132502 C-11
San Germán, 10989 B-10
San Juan, 381931 A-13
Trujillo Alto, 38437 A-13

Rhode Island
Map p. 91

Abbott Run Valley, 1800 B-7
Adamsville, 400 E-8
Allenton, 650 D-6
Anthony, 2400 C-5
Ashaway, 1485 E-3
Ashton, 910 B-7
Barrington, 16819 C-7
Berkeley, 1500 B-7
Bradford, 1406 E-3
Bridgeton, 2200 B-6
Bristol, 22469 D-7
Carolina, 1000 D-4
Central Falls, 18928 B-7
Charlestown, 1000 E-4
Chepachet, 1675 B-5
Common Fence Pt., 900 C-8
Coventry, 8000 C-5
Cranston, 80387 C-6
Cumberland Hill, 7500 B-7
Davisville, 1400 D-6
Diamond Hill, 1000 A-7
E. Greenwich, 12948 C-6
E. Providence, 47037 C-7
Esmond, 3500 B-6
Fiskeville, 1409 C-6
Forestdale, 2000 A-6
Foster Ctr., 300 C-4
Georgiaville, 3500 B-6
Glendale, 800 B-5
Glocester, 9000 B-5
Greene, 500 C-5
Greenville, 8626 B-6
Harmony, 1200 B-6
Harris, 1500 C-5
Harrisville, 1600 B-5
Hope, 1624 C-6
Hope Valley, 1600 E-4
Hopkinton, 8179 E-3
Jamestown, 5622 D-7
Kingston, 6400 E-5
Lincoln, 21105 B-7
Little Compton, 3593 D-8
Manville, 3800 B-7
Mapleville, 1600 B-5
Melville, 1500 C-8
Middletown, 16061 D-8
Mt. View, 1700 C-5
Narragansett Pier, 3409 E-6
N. Kingstown, 26326 D-6
N. Providence, 33510 B-6
N. Scituate, 2500 B-6
N. Smithfield, 11967 A-6
Oakland, 1200 B-5
Pascoag, 4571 B-5
Pawtucket, 71148 B-7
Pawtuxet, 2000 C-6
Peace Dale, 3500 E-6
Portsmouth, 17149 D-7
Primrose, 1000 B-6
Providence, 173618 C-7

PROVIDENCE CO.,
626667 B-6
Quidnessett, 2000 D-6
Quonochontaug, 700 E-4
Riverside, 1000 C-7
Rockville, 600 E-3
Rumford, 6500 C-7
Saunderstown, 1400 D-6
Saylesville, 2000 B-7
Shannock, 700 E-4
Slatersville, 2600 A-6
Slocum, 500 D-5
Smithfield, 21310 B-6
Tiverton, 7282 D-8
Usquepaug, 500 E-5
Valley Falls, 11599 B-7
Wakefield, 8468 E-5
Wallum Lake, 500 A-5
Warren, 11415 C-7
Warwick, 85808 C-6
Washington, 1200 C-6

WASHINGTON CO.,
126979 E-5
W. Barrington, 2000 C-7
W. Greenwich, 2000 D-5
W. Kingston, 1400 E-5
W. Warwick, 29191 C-6
Westerly, 17936 E-3
Wickford, 1400 D-6
Woonsocket, 43224 A-6
Wyoming, 400 E-4

South Carolina
Map p. 92

* City keyed to p. 28

ABBEVILLE CO.,
25417 D-4
Abbeville, 5803 D-4
Aiken, 28232 F-6

AIKEN CO.,
160099 F-6

Column 10 — South Carolina / South Dakota / Tennessee

ALLENDALE CO.,
10419 H-6

ANDERSON CO.,
187126 C-3
Anderson, 26686 C-3
Andrews, 2861 F-12
Arcadia, 3861 B-4
Arial, 2543 B-3
Arthurtown, 1450 H-3
Awendaw, 1294 G-11
Bamberg, 3607 G-7

BAMBERG CO.,
15987 G-7
Barnwell, 4750 G-6

BARNWELL CO.,
22621 G-6
Batesburg-Leesville, 5362 E-6
Beaufort, 12361 I-8

BEAUFORT CO.,
162233 I-8
N. Charleston, 97471 G-10
N. Hartsville, 1200 D-9
N. Myrtle Bch., 13752 E-13
Orangeburg, 13964 F-8

ORANGEBURG CO.,
92501 F-8
Beaufort, 12361 I-8
Belvedere, 5792 F-5
Ben Avon, 1700 C-7
Bennettsville, 9069 C-11

BERKELEY CO.,
177843 G-10
Berea, 14295 B-3
Bishopville, 3471 D-9
Blacksburg, 1848 A-6
Blackville, 2889 G-6
Bluffton, 12530 I-8
Blythewood, 2034 E-8
Boiling Spgs., 8151 B-4
Bonneau, 431 G-10
Branchville, 1004 G-8
Buffalo, 1266 B-5
Burnettown, 2673 F-5
Buxton, 900 F-9

CALHOUN CO.,
15175 F-8
Camden, 7061 E-8
Cane Savannah, 1200 E-8
Catawba, 1300 A-8
Cayce, 12528 F-7
Central, 4514 C-3
Chapin, 1445 E-7
Chapman, 1650 F-4

CHARLESTON CO.,
350209 H-11
Charleston, 106712 H-11
Cheraw, 5851 C-10

CHEROKEE CO.,
55342 A-6
Cherokee Forest, 2100 C-3
Cherokee Village, 1200 A-6
Chester, 5607 B-7

CHESTER CO.,
33140 C-7
Chesterfield, 1472 C-10

CHESTERFIELD CO.,
45148 C-10
Chesnee, 851 A-5
Clearwater, 4390 F-5
Clemson, 13905 C-3
Clinton, 8676 C-5
Clover, 4502 A-7

COLLETON CO.,
38892 H-8
Columbia, 129272 E-7
Conway, 17103 E-12
Cowpens, 2343 A-5
Darlington, 6711 C-9

DARLINGTON CO.,
66881 C-10
Denmark, 3538 G-7
Denny Terr., 1750 G-2

DILLON CO.,
32062 C-12
Dillon, 6781 C-12

DORCHESTER CO.,
136555 G-9
Due West, 1247 D-4
Duncan, 3181 B-5
Early Branch, 1400 H-7
Easley, 19993 B-3
E. Gaffney, 3895 A-5

EDGEFIELD CO.,
26985 E-5
Edgefield, 4750 E-5
Elgin, 2053 E-8
Estill, 2425 H-7

FAIRFIELD CO.,
23956 C-7
Fairforest, 1693 B-4
Florence, 31936 D-11

FLORENCE CO.,
136885 D-10
Folly Bch., 2617 H-10
Forest Acres, 10361 G-3
Fort Mill, 9159 A-8
Fountain Inn, 7799 C-4
Furman, 300 H-7

GEORGETOWN CO.,
60158 F-12
Georgetown, 9163 F-12
Gloverville, 2831 F-5
Golden Grv., 2500 B-3
Goose Creek, 35938 G-10
Graniteville, 2500 F-5
Gray Court, 1000 C-4
Great Falls, 2077 B-8
Greeleyville, 457 E-10

GREENVILLE CO.,
451225 B-3
Greenville, 56002 B-3

GREENWOOD CO.,
69661 D-5
Greenwood, 22638 D-5
Greer, 24096 B-4
Gresham, 1400 F-11
Hampton, 2837 H-7

HAMPTON CO.,
21090 H-7
Hanahan, 17997 H-10
Hardeeville, 2952 I-7
Hartsville, 7556 D-9
Hickory Grv., 400 A-7
Hilton Head Island, 37099 I-8
Hollywood, 4277 H-9
Holly Hill, 1298 G-9
Homeland Pk., 6228 C-3

HORRY CO.,
269291 D-13
Inman, 2369 B-4
Irmo, 11097 E-7
Isle of Palms, 4133 H-11
Iva, 1298 C-4

JASPER CO.,
24777 I-7
Jackson, 1700 F-5
Jefferson, 673 C-9
Joanna, 1600 C-5
Johnsonville, 1457 E-11
Johnston, 2582 E-5
Jonesville, 922 B-5
Kershaw, 1666 D-8

KERSHAW CO.,
61697 E-8
Kiawah Island, 1163 H-10
Kingstree, 3328 E-10
Ladson, 13792 G-10

LANCASTER CO.,
76652 B-8
Lancaster, 8526 B-8
Landrum, 2472 A-4
Langley, 1200 F-5
Latta, 1434 C-11

LAURENS CO.,
70217 C-5
Laurens, 9916 C-5

LEE CO.,
19994 D-9
Lexington, 14227 E-7

LEXINGTON CO.,
262391 E-6
Liberty, 3269 B-3
Little River, 8960 E-13
Loris, 2396 D-13
Lugoff, 6739 E-8
Lyman, 2471 B-4
Mauldin, 22889 B-4

MARION CO.,
33062 D-11
Marion, 6939 D-11

MARLBORO CO.,
28933 C-11
Mayesville, 1005 E-9
Mauldin, 22889 B-4
McBee, 873 D-9
McColl, 2174 B-11

McCORMICK CO.,
9929 E-4
McCormick, 2783 E-4
Meggett, 1226 H-9
Moncks Cor., 7885 G-10
Monetta, 300 E-6
Mt. Pleasant, 63424 H-11
Mullins, 4663 D-12
Murrells Inlet, 7547 F-12
Myrtle Bch., 27976 E-13
New Ellenton, 2052 F-6
Newberry, 10277 D-6

NEWBERRY CO.,
37508 D-5
Ninety Six, 1998 D-5
Norris, 826 B-3
N. Augusta, 21348 F-5
N. Charleston, 97471 G-10

South Dakota
Map p. 93

Aberdeen, 26091 B-10
Alcester, 807 G-13
Arlington, 926 E-12
Armour, 699 F-10
Aurora, 500 E-13
Avon, 549 G-10
Baltic, 1039 F-13
Belle Fourche, 5049 C-1
Beresford, 2005 G-13
Bison, 333 B-4
Box Elder, 2998 D-2
Bowdle, 552 B-8
Brandon, 8785 F-13

BEADLE CO.,
17338 D-9
Bridgewater, 573 F-12

BENNETT CO.,
3431 F-4

BON HOMME CO.,
7124 G-11

BROOKINGS CO.,
29364 E-12
Brookings, 20116 E-12

BROWN CO.,
36531 B-10
Britton, 1261 A-10

BRULE CO.,
5255 F-9

BUFFALO CO.,
1912 E-8

BUTTE CO.,
10110 C-1

CAMPBELL CO.,
1466 B-8
Canton, 3057 G-13
Castlewood, 622 D-12
Centerville, 882 G-13

CHARLES MIX CO.,
9129 G-10
Chamberlain, 2387 F-9

CLARK CO.,
3691 C-10
Clark, 1181 D-11

CLAY CO.,
13631 G-12
Clear Lake, 1235 D-12
Colman, 545 F-12

CODINGTON CO.,
26605 C-11

CORSON CO.,
4050 B-6
Crooks, 1172 F-13

CUSTER CO.,
7473 E-2
Custer, 1906 E-2

DAVISON CO.,
18741 F-10

DAY CO.,
5710 C-10

DEUEL CO.,
4364 D-12
Dell Rapids, 3062 F-13

DEWEY CO.,
5301 C-6
De Smet, 1089 E-11
Dupree, 434 C-6

DOUGLAS CO.,
3002 F-10
Eagle Butte, 625 C-6

EDMUNDS CO.,
4071 B-8
Elk Point, 1963 H-13
Emery, 449 F-11
Estelline, 703 D-12
Eureka, 869 A-8

Tennessee
Map p. 94 – 9

† City keyed to p. 96

Adams, 633 B-8
Adamsville, 2207 E-4
Alamo, 2461 D-3
Alcoa, 8360 C-15
Alexandria, 945 B-10
Algood, 3495 B-11
Allardt, 642 A-12

ANDERSON CO.,
75129 B-14
Apison, 1213 E-12
Ardmore, 1213 F-8
Arlington, 2569 D-2
Ashland City, 4541 B-8
Athens, 13887 D-13
Atoka, 1050 D-1
Atwood, 965 C-4
Baileyton, 431 B-17
Bartlett, 44613 D-2
Baxter, 1365 B-11
Bean Sta., 2826 B-16

BEDFORD CO.,
40271 E-9
Belle Meade, 2912 C-8

BENTON CO.,
16614 C-5
Benton, 1418 D-13
Big Sandy, 514 C-5
Blaine, 1856 B-15

BLEDSOE CO.,
12920 D-11
Blountville, 3074 A-18

BLOUNT CO.,
123010 C-15
Bluff City, 1537 A-18
Bolivar, 5417 E-3
Bradford, 1048 C-4

BRADLEY CO.,
98963 E-12
Brentwood, 35794 C-8
Brighton, 2735 D-2
Bristol, 25406 A-19
Brownsville, 10748 D-3
Bruceton, 1493 C-5
Bulls Gap, 738 B-17
Burns, 1468 C-7
Byrdstown, 903 A-12

CAMPBELL CO.,
40716 B-14

CANNON CO.,
13801 C-10
Carthage, 2251 B-10

CARROLL CO.,
29475 C-4
Carter, Spring, 700 A-18

CARTER CO.,
57424 B-19

, 2297 C-19
495 B-15
ille, 3644 D-9
2279 †M-4
Hill, 1445 E-11
e, 1235 C-10
ooga, 167674 G-16
HAM CO.,
B-10
R CO., 17131 F-6
Hill, 6737 J-17
RNE CO.,
B-20
lle, 132929 B-10
O., 7861 B-14
d, 41285 G-17
2694 F-8
9841 C-19
, 2463 D-18
nt, 841 F-14
CO., 35662 K-16
CO., 52796 E-13
ale, 8282 G-16
lle, 43965 G-3
ood, 982 G-8
Hts., 6934 J-18
a, 34681 E-10
le, 30435 C-15
own, 4278 B-11
ille, 1194 F-11
700 G-7
n, 9038 E-3
1737 G-13
hard, 752 D-17
od Hills, 1600 K-11
TT CO.,
D-4
ains, 1714 B-11
e, 10795 D-16
428 F-7
RLAND CO.,
D-17
e, 2812 K-15
ON CO.,
1 C-11
7191 F-16
B CO., 18723 D-14
1598 E-17
R CO., 11757 E-7
ille, 867 E-7
2361 G-13
14538 C-9
N CO., 49666 C-9
417 B-8
3005 C-6
4815 F-15
1 C-5
O., 38335 C-4
g, 17145 C-4
Vil., 5052 *B-9
20979 G-16
705 G-6
ton, 14176 J-19
od, 1532 F-18
4 C-9
97 K-18
., 2055 F-13
3490 F-18
Glade, 6989 D-17
t, 2825 G-15
7720 D-10
h, 1291 J-17
20676 D-19
CO., 38413 F-3
le, 6827 G-12
S CO.,
B-17
1618 B-19
00 C-3
, 1900 †L-1
ls, 4812 C-11
52487 D-11
N CO.,
G-13
le, 913 E-19
ro, 962 B-14
30278 B-12
, 680 F-3
g, 3944 M-15
wn, 38844 G-2
CO., 49683 D-5
., 29485 F-10
1445 C-6
ville, 15921 C-11
ille, 1213 C-14
ER CO.,
C-20
2 J-18
, 1502 F-16
, 6618 C-12
k, 1064 E-19
r, 6433 B-11
CO., 68831 J-17
le, 15062 K-17
l, 2182 C-5
1167 C-16
ager, 1813 F-15
CO., 13703 F-14
5 D-4
ssroads, 1250 C-19
N CO.,
J-16
N CO.,
F-16
2000 J-19
K CO., 6819 J-15
AN CO.,
G-4
CO., 26026 G-7
6350 D-18
7769 L-14
, 4389 B-20
7870 B-13
S CO., 56833 J-16
D CO., 18787 E-4
d, 865 B-18
n, 6309 F-6
SON CO.,
E-6
nville, 51372 C-12
945 E-3
O., 32330 B-7
I CO., 24690 E-9
ithe, 2600 F-3
d, 3757 E-9
ick, 718 D-7
1874 F-17
I CO., 8426 C-8
, 8452 D-5
EYS CO.,
C-8
54 †M-5
n, 3985 D-6
872 G-13
, 1248 B-18
s., 2200 †J-2
, 2020 B-19
5211 E-5
CO., 11638 C-14
n, 1959 B-17
79 G-15
City, 8047 K-15
N CO.,
C-20
55 B-19
r, 800 I-14
ity, 63152 J-18
I CO., 18244 J-20
ugh, 5051 J-18
281 C-5
395 G-14
Hts., 680 D-20
48205 I-18
5934 D-18
prs., 2756 C-10
Woods, 840 K-11
., 432226 C-20
178874 D-20
32588 D-12
4474 B-13
7456 B-19
7832 C-3
Vil., 3803 D-16
12430 F-2
826 G-16
, 2302 C-12
ALE CO.,
D-3
E CO.,
F-9
urg, 10428 F-10
26190 C-13
, 8642 D-19
., 12161 E-9
, 11100 F-11
7652 E-6
CO., 33361 G-12
8 E-8
, 4058 B-15
897 D-8
tn., 1832 N-11
14 G-9
381 E-18
CO., 48556 E-18
2439 D-19
74 C-20
D-10
6362 F-12
O., 22248 B-14
CO., 98294 E-5
lle, 4577 E-18
r, 10102 F-13
CO., 28237 G-14

MARSHALL CO., 30617 F-11
Martin, 11473 B-5
Maryville, 27465 E-19
Mascot, 2411 C-20
Mason, 1609 F-3
Maury City, 674 D-4
MAURY CO., 80956 E-10
Maynardville, 2413 C-20
McEwen, 1750 C-9
McKenzie, 5310 C-6
MCMINN CO., 52266 F-17
McMinnville, 13605 E-14
MCNAIRY CO., 26075 F-6
Medina, 3479 D-5
MEIGS CO., 11753 F-17
Memphis, 646889 G-2
Middle Valley, 12684 G-16
Middleton, 706 G-5
Midtown, 1360 D-18
Midway, 2491 †N-2
Milan, 7851 D-5
Millersville, 6440 B-11
Millington, 10176 F-2
MONROE CO., 44519 F-19
Monteagle, 1192 F-14
Monterey, 2850 C-16
MONTGOMERY CO., 172331 B-9
MOORE CO., 6362 F-12
Mooresburg, 941 J-16
MORGAN CO., 21987 C-17
Morrison, 694 E-14
Morristown, 29137 K-16
Mosheim, 2362 K-17
Mt. Carmel, 5429 I-17
Mt. Juliet, 23671 C-12
Mt. Olive, 720 K-13
Mt. Pleasant, 4561 E-10
Mountain City, 2531 J-20
Munford, 5927 E-2
Murfreesboro, 108755 D-12
Nashville, 601222 C-11
New Hope, 1082 G-14
New Johnsonville, 1951 D-8
New Market, 1334 C-20
New Tazewell, 3037 B-20
New Union, 1431 E-13
Newbern, 3313 C-4
Newport, 6945 L-16
Niota, 719 E-18
Nolensville, 5861 D-12
Norris, 1491 C-19
Northcott, 800 †J-1
Oak Grove, 4425 J-18
Oak Hill, 4529 C-11
Oak Ridge, 29330 D-19
Oakland, 6623 F-3
Obion, 1119 C-4
OBION CO., 31807 B-4
Oliver Sprs., 3231 D-18
Olivet, 1350 F-7
Oneida, 3752 B-18
Ooltewah, 687 G-16
Orebank, 1300 †J-2
Orlinda, 859 B-11
OVERTON CO., 22083 C-15
Palmer, 672 F-15
Paris, 10156 C-7
Park City, 2442 G-12
Parsons, 2373 E-7
Pegram, 2093 C-10
PERRY CO., 7915 E-8
PICKETT CO., 5077 B-16
Pigeon Forge, 5875 D-20
Pikeville, 1608 E-16
Pine Crest, 2388 J-18
Piperton, 1445 G-3
Plainview, 2125 C-20
Pleasant View, 4149 B-10
POLK CO., 16825 G-18
Portland, 11480 B-12
Powells Crossroads, 1322 G-15
Pulaski, 7870 G-10
Puryear, 671 B-7
PUTNAM CO., 72321 C-15
Ramsey, 700 J-14
Red Bank, 11651 L-12
Red Boiling Sprs., 1112 B-14
RHEA CO., 31809 E-16
Riceville, 670 F-17
Rickman, 750 C-15
Ridgely, 1795 C-3
Ridgetop, 1874 B-11
Ripley, 8445 D-3
Roan Mtn., 1360 K-19
ROANE CO., 54181 E-18
ROBERTSON CO., 66283 B-11
Rockford, 856 D-19
Rockwood, 5562 D-17
Rocky Top, 1781 C-19
Rogersville, 4420 J-16
Russellville, 1200 K-16
Rutherford, 1151 C-5
RUTHERFORD CO., 262604 E-12
Ruthton, 900 I-19
Rutledge, 1122 J-15
St. Joseph, 782 G-9
Sale Creek, 2845 F-16
Savannah, 6982 F-7
SCOTT CO., 22228 B-18
Scotts Hill, 984 E-7
Selmer, 4396 G-6
SEQUATCHIE CO., 14112 F-15
SEVIER CO., 89889 D-20
Sevierville, 14807 D-20
Sewanee, 2311 G-14
Seymour, 10919 D-20
Sharon, 944 C-5
SHELBY CO., 927644 G-2
Shelbyville, 20335 F-12
Shooks Gap, 690 *A-9
Signal Mtn., 7554 G-15
SMITH CO., 19166 B-13
Smithville, 4530 D-14
Smyrna, 39974 D-12
Sneedville, 1387 J-16
Soddy-Daisy, 12714 F-16
Somerville, 3094 F-4
S. Carthage, 1322 C-14
S. Fulton, 2354 B-5
S. Pittsburg, 2992 G-14
Sparta, 4925 D-15
Spencer, 1601 E-15
Spring City, 1981 E-17
Spring Hill, 29036 E-11
Springfield, 16440 B-11
Spurgeon, 3957 J-18
STEWART CO., 13324 B-8
Strawberry Plains, 700 C-20
Suburban Hills, 1500 K-11
SULLIVAN CO., 156823 J-19
Summertown, 866 F-10
SUMNER CO., 160645 B-12
Surgoinsville, 1801 J-17
Sweetwater, 5764 E-18
Tazewell, 2218 B-20
Telford, 921 K-18
Tellico Plains, 880 F-18
Tennessee Ridge, 1368 C-8
Thompson's Sta., 2194 D-11
Three Way, 1709 D-5
TIPTON CO., 61081 E-2
Tiptonville, 4464 B-3
Tracy City, 1481 F-14
Trenton, 4264 D-5
Trezevant, 859 D-6
TROUSDALE CO., 7870 B-13
Troy, 1371 B-4
Tullahoma, 18655 F-13
Tusculum, 2663 K-17
Unicoi, 3632 K-18
UNICOI CO., 18313 K-18
Union City, 10895 B-5
UNION CO., 19109 B-20
Unionville, 1368 E-12
Valley Forge, 2200 †N-5
VAN BUREN CO., 5548 E-15
Vonore, 1474 E-19
Walden, 1898 G-15
Walnut Grove, 864 B-12
Walnut Hill, 2394 †J-4
WARREN CO., 39839 E-14
Wartburg, 918 C-18
WASHINGTON CO., 122979 K-18
Watertown, 1477 C-13
Waverly, 4105 C-8
WAYNE CO., 17021 F-8
Waynesboro, 2449 F-8
WEAKLEY CO., 35021 B-6
Westmoreland, 2206 B-13
White Bluff, 3206 C-10
WHITE CO., 25841 D-15
White House, 10255 B-12
White Pine, 2196 K-16
Whiteville, 4638 F-4
Whitwell, 1699 G-15
Wildwood, 1098 D-20
WILLIAMSON CO., 183182 D-10
WILSON CO., 113993 C-13
Winchester, 8530 G-13
Winfield, 967 B-18
Woodbury, 2680 D-13

Texas

Map pp. 98 – 101

Map keys | Atlas pages
EA – ET | 100 – 101
WA – WT | 98 – 99

* City keyed to p. 96
† City keyed to p. 97

Abernathy, 2805 WG-10
Abilene, 117063 WJ-14
Addison, 13056 †E-10
Agua Dulce, 812 EP-5
Alamo, 18353 WS-10
Alamo Hts., 7031 ER-10
Albany, 2034 EE-2
Aledo, 2716 EE-5
Algoa, 400 *I-7
Alice, 19104 EP-5
Allen, 84246 ED-7
Alpine, 5905 WN-7
Alto, 1225 EG-10
Alton, 12341 WR-9
Alvarado, 3785 EF-6
Alvin, 24236 EL-10
Alvord, 1334 ED-5
Amarillo, 190695 WD-10
Ames, 1003 EK-11
Anahuac, 2243 EK-11
Anderson, 222 EJ-9
ANDERSON CO., 58458 EG-9
Andrews, 11088 WJ-9
ANDREWS CO., 14786 WJ-8
ANGELINA CO., 86771 EI-11
Angleton, 18862 EM-10
Anna, 8249 ED-7
Anson, 2430 WI-14
Anthony, 5011 WK-1
Anton, 1126 WG-10
ARANSAS CO., 23158 EP-7
Aransas Pass, 8204 EP-7
Archer City, 1834 EC-3
ARCHER CO., 9054 EC-3
Arcola, 1642 EL-10
Argyle, 3282 ED-6
Arlington, 365438 EE-6
ARMSTRONG CO., 1901 WE-11
Arp, 970 EF-10
Asherton, 1084 WS-14
Aspermont, 919 WH-13
Atascocita, 65844 *A-7
ATASCOSA CO., 44911 EN-4
Athens, 12710 EF-9
Atlanta, 5675 ED-12
Aubrey, 2595 ED-6
Audobon Pk., 1200 *B-6
Austin, 790390 EK-5
AUSTIN CO., 28417 EK-8
Azle, 10947 EE-6
Bacliff, 8619 *H-9
BAILEY CO., 7165 WF-8
Baird, 1496 EF-2
Balch Sprs., 23728 †H-12
Balcones Hts., 2941 ER-9
Ballinger, 3767 WL-14
Bammel, 600 *A-4
Bandera, 857 EL-3
BANDERA CO., 20485 EL-2
Bangs, 1603 EG-2
Barker *D-1
Barrett, 3199 *C-8
Bartlett, 1623 EI-6
Bartonville, 1469 †C-6
Bastrop, 7218 EK-6
BASTROP CO., 74171 EK-6
Bay City, 17614 EM-9
BAYLOR CO., 3726 EC-2
Bayou Vista, 1537 EM-11
Baytown, 71802 EL-11
Beach City, 2198 EL-11
Beaumont, 118296 EK-12
Beaumont Pl., 8000 *C-7
Beckville, 847 EF-11
Bedford, 46979 †F-6
Bee Cave, 3925 EK-5
BEE CO., 31861 EO-6
Beeville, 12863 EO-5
BELL CO., 310235 EI-6
Bellaire, 16855 EL-10
Bellmead, 9901 EH-6
Bells, 1392 EC-8
Bellville, 4097 EK-8
Belton, 18216 EI-6
Benavides, 1362 EQ-4
Benbrook, 21234 EE-6
Benjamin, 258 WH-14
Berryville, 975 EF-9
Bertram, 1353 EJ-5
Beverly Hills, 1995 WT-7
Bevil Oaks, 1274 EK-12
BEXAR CO., 1714773 EM-4
Big Lake, 2936 WM-11
Big Sandy, 1343 EE-10
Big Spr., 27282 WJ-11
Bisbee †J-6
Bishop, 3134 EQ-5
Blanco, 1739 EK-4
BLANCO CO., 10497 EJ-4
Blooming Grv., 821 EG-7
Blossom, 1494 EC-9
Blue Ridge, 822 ED-8
Boerne, 10471 EL-3
Bogata, 1153 EC-10
Bonham, 10127 EC-8
Booker, 1516 WA-13
BORDEN CO., 641 WI-11
Borderland WQ-1
Borger, 13251 WC-11
BOSQUE CO., 18212 EG-5
Bosqueville WS-6
Bovina, 1868 WE-8
Bowie, 5218 EC-5
BOWIE CO., 92565 EC-11
Boyd, 1207 ED-5
Bracken, 80 EP-12
Brackettville, 1688 WQ-13
Brady, 5528 EI-2
Branch, 400 †B-14
Brazoria, 3019 EM-10
BRAZORIA CO., 313166 EM-10
BRAZOS CO., 194851 EI-8
Breckenridge, 5780 EE-3
Bremond, 929 EI-7
Brenham, 15716 EK-8
BREWSTER CO., 9232 WO-7
Briarcliff, 1438 EJ-5
Bridge City, 7840 EK-13
Bridgeport, 5976 ED-5
BRISCOE CO., 1637 WE-11
Bronte, 999 WK-13
BROOKS CO., 7223 ER-4
Brookshire, 4702 EL-9
Brookside Vil., 1523 *G-5
BROWN CO., 38106 EH-3
Brownfield, 9657 WH-9
Brownsboro, 1039 EF-9
Brownsville, 175023 ET-6
Brownwood, 19288 EG-3
Bruceville-Eddy, 1475 EH-6
Brushy Creek, 21764 WA-5
Bryan, 76201 EJ-8
Buda, 7295 EK-5
Buffalo, 1856 EH-8
Bullard, 2463 EF-10
Bulverde, 4630 EL-4
Bunker Hill Vil., 3633 *D-3
Burkburnett, 10811 EB-3
Burleson, 36690 EF-6
BURLESON CO., 17187 EJ-8
Burnet, 5987 EJ-4
BURNET CO., 42750 EI-4
Cactus, 3179 WB-10
Caddo Mills, 1338 ED-8
Caldwell, 4104 EJ-7
CALDWELL CO., 38066 EL-6
CALHOUN CO., 21381 EO-7
CALLAHAN CO., 13544 EF-2
Calvert, 1192 EI-7
Camelot, 4000 ER-12
Cameron, 5552 EI-7
CAMERON CO., 406220 ET-6
CAMP CO., 12401 EE-10
Campo Alto, 300 WS-10
Canadian, 2649 WB-13
Canton, 3581 EE-9
Canyon, 13303 WD-10
Carrizo Sprs., 5368 WS-14
Carrollton, 119097 EE-7
CARSON CO., 6182 WC-11
Carthage, 6779 EF-12
CASS CO., 30464 ED-11
Castle Hills, 4116 ER-10
CASTRO CO., 8062 WE-9
Castroville, 2680 EM-3
Cedar Hill, 45028 †J-8
Cedar Pk., 48937 EJ-5
Cedar Pt. *F-10
Celeste, 814 ED-8
Celina, 6028 ED-7
Center, 5193 EG-12
Centerville, 892 EH-9
Central Gdns., 4347 ER-13
Cesar Chavez, 1929 WR-11
CHAMBERS CO., 35096 EL-11
Chandler, 2734 EF-9
Channelview, 38289 *D-8
Channing, 363 WC-9
Charlotte, 1715 EN-3
CHEROKEE CO., 50845 EG-10
Chico, 1002 ED-5
Childress, 6105 WF-13
CHILDRESS CO., 7041 WE-13
China, 1160 EK-12
China Grv., 1179 ES-11
Cisco, 3899 EF-3
Clarendon, 2026 WE-12
Clarksville, 3285 EC-10
Claude, 1196 WD-11
CLAY CO., 10752 EC-4
Clear L. Shores, 1063 *G-9
Cleburne, 29337 EF-6
Cleveland, 7675 EJ-10
Cliffside WA-1
Clifton, 3442 EG-5
Clint, 926 WK-2
Cloverleaf, 22942 *D-7
Clute, 11211 EM-10
Clyde, 3713 EF-2
Coahoma, 817 WJ-11
COCHRAN CO., 3127 WG-8
Cockrell Hill, 4193 †H-9
COKE CO., 3320 WK-12
Coldspring, 853 EJ-10
Coleman, 4709 EG-2
COLEMAN CO., 8895 EH-2
College Sta., 93857 EJ-8
Colleyville, 22807 †F-6
COLLIN CO., 782341 ED-7
COLLINGSWORTH CO., 3057 WD-13
Collinsville, 1624 EC-7
Colorado City, 4146 WJ-12
COLORADO CO., 20874 EL-7
Columbus, 3655 EL-8
COMAL CO., 108472 EK-4
Comanche, 4335 EG-4
COMANCHE CO., 13974 EG-4
Combes, 2895 ET-5
Commerce, 8078 ED-8
CONCHO CO., 4087 WM-14
Concord Bridge, 1200 *C-2
Conroe, 56207 EJ-10
Converse, 18198 EL-4
COOKE CO., 38437 EC-6
Coolidge, 955 EG-7
Cooper, 1969 ED-9
Coppell, 38659 †E-8
Copper Canyon, 1334 †C-7
Copperas Cove, 32032 EI-5
Corinth, 19935 ED-6
Corpus Christi, 305215 EP-6
Corral City, 27 †C-5
Corrigan, 1595 EI-11
Corsicana, 23770 EG-8
CORYELL CO., 75388 EH-5
COTTLE CO., 1505 WF-13
Cotton Flat, 250 WH-6
Cotulla, 3603 EO-2
Crabb *G-1
Crandall, 2858 EE-8
Crane, 3353 WL-9
CRANE CO., 4375 WL-9
Crockett, 6950 EH-10
CROCKETT CO., 3719 WN-11
CROSBY CO., 6059 WH-11
Crosbyton, 1741 WG-11
Cross Mtn., 3124 EP-8
Cross Plains, 982 EG-2
Crowell, 948 WG-14
Crowley, 12838 EF-6
Crystal City, 7138 WR-14
Cuero, 6841 EM-6
CULBERSON CO., 2398 WL-5
Culleoka, 250 †B-14
Cumby, 777 ED-9
Cut and Shoot, 1070 EJ-10
Cypress *B-1
Cypress Meadow, 1500 *C-1
Daingerfield, 2560 ED-11
Daisetta, 966 EK-11
Dalhart, 7930 WB-9
DALLAM CO., 6703 WB-9
Dallas, 1197816 EE-7
DALLAS CO., 368139 EF-7
Dalworthington Gdns., 2259 †H-6
Danbury, 1715 EM-10
Dawson, 807 EG-7
DAWSON CO., 13833 WI-10
Dayton, 7242 EK-11
De Kalb, 1699 EC-11
De Leon, 2246 EG-4
DE WITT CO., 20097 EM-6
DEAF SMITH CO., 19372 WD-9
Decatur, 6042 ED-5
DeCordova, 2683 EF-5
Deer Pk., 32010 EL-10
Del Rio, 35591 WQ-12
DELTA CO., 5231 ED-9
Denison, 22682 EC-7
Denton, 113383 ED-6
DENTON CO., 662614 ED-6
Denver City, 4479 WI-8
DeSoto, 49047 EE-7
Devine, 4350 EM-3
Diboll, 4776 EH-11
Dickens, 286 WG-12
DICKENS CO., 2444 WH-12
Dickinson, 18680 EL-11
Dilley, 3894 EN-3
DIMMIT CO., 9996 WS-14
Dimmitt, 4393 WE-9
Dish, 201 †B-4
DONLEY CO., 3677 WD-12
Donna, 15798 WS-11
Double Oak, 2867 †C-7
Dripping Sprs., 1788 EK-5
Dublin, 3654 EG-4
Dumas, 14691 WC-10
Duncanville, 38524 EE-7
DUVAL CO., 11782 EP-4
Eagle Lake, 3639 EL-8
Eagle Pass, 26248 WR-13
Early, 2762 EG-3
Earth, 1065 WF-9
E. Bernard, 2272 EL-9
E. Mountain, 797 EE-11
E. Tawakoni, 883 EE-8
Eastland, 3960 EF-3
EASTLAND CO., 18583 EF-3
ECTOR CO., 137130 WK-8
Eden, 2766 WM-14
Edgecliff Vil., 2776 †I-4
Edgewood, 1441 EE-9
Edinburg, 77100 ES-5
Edna, 5499 EM-7
EDWARDS CO., 2002 WP-13
El Campo, 11602 EM-8
El Cenizo, 3273 EQ-2
El Gato, 200 WT-11
El Lago, 2706 *G-8
El Paso, 649121 WK-1
EL PASO CO., 800647 WK-2
Eldorado, 1951 WM-12
Electra, 2791 EB-3
Elgin, 8135 EJ-6
Elkhart, 1371 EG-9
ELLIS CO., 149610 EF-7
Elmendorf, 1488 EM-4
Elsa, 5660 ET-5
Emory, 1239 EE-9
Ennis, 18513 EF-7
ERATH CO., 37890 EF-5
Escobares, 1188 ES-3
Euless, 51277 †F-7
Eustace, 991 EF-8
Everman, 6108 †I-4
Fair Oaks Ranch, 5986 EL-4
Fairfield, 2951 EG-8
Fairgreen, 2300 *C-5
Fairview, 7248 †B-12
Falfurrias, 4981 EQ-5
Fallbrook, 1500 *B-4
FALLS CO., 17866 EH-7
FANNIN CO., 33915 EC-8
Farmers Branch, 28616 †E-9
Farmersville, 3301 ED-8
Farwell, 1363 WF-8
FAYETTE CO., 24554 EL-7
Ferris, 2436 EF-7
Fifth Street, 2486 *G-3
FISHER CO., 3974 WI-13
Flatonia, 1383 EL-7
Florence, 1136 EI-5
Floresville, 6448 EM-5
Flower Mound, 64669 †D-7
FLOYD CO., 6446 WF-11
Floydada, 3038 WG-11
FOARD CO., 1336 WF-14
Forest Hill, 12355 †I-5
FT. BEND CO., 585375 EL-9
Ft. Davis, 1201 WN-6
Ft. Stockton, 8283 WM-8
Ft. Worth, 741206 EE-6
Four Cors., 12382 *F-1
Franklin, 1564 EI-8
FRANKLIN CO., 10605 ED-10
Frankston, 1229 EG-9
Fredericksburg, 10530 EK-3
Freeport, 12049 EM-10
Freer, 2818 EP-4
FREESTONE CO., 19816 EG-8
Fresno, 19069 *G-4
Friendswood, 35805 EL-10
FRIO CO., 17217 EN-2
Friona, 4123 WE-9
Frisco, 116989 ED-7
Fritch, 2117 WC-11
Fulshear, 1134 EL-9
Fulton, 1358 EP-7
Gail, 231 WI-11
GAINES CO., 17526 WI-9
Gainesville, 16002 EC-6
Galena Pk., 10887 *E-6
Galveston, 47743 EM-11
GALVESTON CO., 291309 EL-11
Ganado, 2003 EM-8
Garden City, 334 WK-11
Garden Ridge, 3259 EP-12
Garland, 226876 EE-7
Garrett, 806 EF-7
Garrison, 895 EG-11
GARZA CO., 6461 WH-11
Gatesville, 15751 EH-5
George West, 2445 EO-5
Georgetown, 47400 EJ-5
Gholson, 1061 EG-6
Giddings, 4881 EK-7
GILLESPIE CO., 24837 EJ-2
Gilmer, 4905 EE-10
Gladewater, 6441 EE-10
GLASSCOCK CO., 1226 WK-11
Glen Rose, 2444 EF-5
Glenn Hts., 11278 †J-10
Godley, 1009 EF-6
Goldthwaite, 1878 EH-4
Goliad, 1908 EN-6
GOLIAD CO., 7210 EO-6
Gonzales, 7237 EL-6
GONZALES CO., 19807 EM-5
Gorman, 1083 EF-3
Graham, 8903 ED-4
Granbury, 7978 EF-5
Grand Prairie, 175396 EE-7
Grand Saline, 3136 EE-9
Grandview, 1561 EF-6
Granger, 1419 EJ-6
Granite Shoals, 4910 EJ-4
Granjeno, 293 WT-9
Grapeland, 1489 EH-9
Grapevine, 46334 †E-6
GRAY CO., 22535 WD-12
GRAYSON CO., 120877 EC-7
Greatwood, 11538 *G-1
Greenville, 25557 ED-8
Greenwood Vil., 4000 *C-5
GREGG CO., 121730 EF-10
Gregory, 1907 EP-6
Grey Forest, 483 EP-8
GRIMES CO., 26604 EJ-8
Groesbeck, 4328 EH-7
Groves, 16144 EK-13
Groveton, 1057 EI-10
Gruver, 1194 WB-11
GUADALUPE CO., 131533 EL-5
Gun Barrel City, 5672 EF-8
Gunter, 1498 ED-7
Guthrie, 160 WG-13
Hackberry, 968 †B-9
Hale Ctr., 2252 WF-10
HALE CO., 36273 WG-10
HALL CO., 3353 WE-12
Hallettsville, 2550 EL-7
Hallsville, 3577 EE-11
Haltom City, 42409 †G-4
Hamilton, 3095 EG-4
HAMILTON CO., 8517 EH-4
Hamlin, 2124 WI-13
HANSFORD CO., 5613 WA-11
HARDEMAN CO., 4139 WF-14
Hardin, 819 EK-11
HARDIN CO., 54635 EJ-12
Harker Hts., 26700 EI-5
Harlingen, 64849 ET-6
HARRIS CO., 4092459 EK-9
HARRISON CO., 65631 EF-12
Hart, 1114 WF-10
HARTLEY CO., 6062 WC-9
Haskell, 3322 WH-14
HASKELL CO., 5899 WH-14
Hawkins, 1278 EE-10
HAYS CO., 157107 EK-4
Hearne, 4459 EI-7
Hebbronville, 4558 EQ-4
Hebron, 415 †D-9
Hedwig Vil., 2557 *D-3
Helotes, 7341 EL-3
Hemphill, 1198 EH-13
HEMPHILL CO., 3807 WC-13
Hempstead, 5770 EK-8
Henderson, 13712 EF-11
HENDERSON CO., 78532 EF-9
Henrietta, 3141 EC-4
Hereford, 15370 WE-9
Hewitt, 13549 EH-6
Hickory Creek, 3247 †B-7
Hico, 1379 EG-5
Hidalgo, 11198 ET-4
HIDALGO CO., 774769 ES-4
Hideaway, 3083 EF-9
Highland Pk., 8564 †F-10
Highland Vil., 15056 †C-7
HILL CO., 35089 EG-7
Hill Country Vil., 985 EQ-10
Hillcrest, 730 *I-6
Hillsboro, 8456 EG-6
Hilshire Vil., 746 *D-3
Hitchcock, 6961 EL-11
HOCKLEY CO., 22935 WH-9
Holland, 1121 EI-6
Holliday, 1758 EC-3
Hollywood Pk., 3062 EQ-10
Hondo, 8803 EM-3
Honey Grv., 1668 EC-8
HOOD CO., 51182 EF-5
Hooks, 2769 EC-11
HOPKINS CO., 35161 ED-9
Horizon City, 16735 WK-2
Houmont Pk., 2500 *C-7
Houston, 2099451 EL-10
HOUSTON CO., 23732 EH-9
HOWARD CO., 35012 WJ-11
Howe, 2600 EC-7
Hubbard, 1423 EG-7
Hudson, 4731 EH-11
HUDSPETH CO., 3476 WL-3
Hughes Sprs., 1760 ED-11
Humble, 15133 EK-10
HUNT CO., 86129 ED-8
Hunters Creek Vil., 4367 *D-3
Huntington, 2118 EH-11
Huntsville, 38548 EI-9
Hurst, 37337 †G-6
Hutchins, 5338 †I-11
HUTCHINSON CO., 22150 WB-11
Hutto, 14698 EJ-6
Idalou, 2250 WG-10
Impact, 35 EA-6
Ingleside, 9387 EP-6
Ingram, 1804 EK-2
Iowa Pk., 6355 EC-3
Iraan, 1229 WM-10
IRION CO., 1599 WL-12
Irving, 216290 EE-7
Italy, 1863 EF-7
Itasca, 1644 EF-6
Jacinto City, 10553 *D-6
JACK CO., 9044 ED-4
Jacksboro, 4511 ED-4
JACKSON CO., 14075 EN-8
Jacksonville, 14544 EG-10
Jamaica Bch., 983 EM-11
Jarrell, 984 EI-5
Jasper, 7590 EI-12
JASPER CO., 35710 EJ-12
Jayton, 534 WH-12
JEFF DAVIS CO., 2342 WM-6
Jefferson, 2106 EE-11
JEFFERSON CO., 252273 EL-12
Jersey Vil., 7620 EK-9
Jewett, 1167 EH-8
JIM HOGG CO., 5300 ER-3
JIM WELLS CO., 40838 EP-4
Joaquin, 824 EG-12
Johnson City, 1656 EK-4
JOHNSON CO., 150934 EF-6
Jollyville, 16151 WB-5
JONES CO., 20202 WI-14
Jones Creek, 2020 EM-10
Jonestown, 1834 EJ-5
Josephine, 812 ED-8
Joshua, 5910 EF-6
Jourdanton, 3871 EN-4
Junction, 2574 WN-14
Justin, 3246 ED-6
Karnes City, 3042 EN-5
KARNES CO., 14824 EN-5
Katy, 14102 EL-9
Kaufman, 6703 EE-8
KAUFMAN CO., 103350 EF-8
Keene, 6106 EF-6
Keller, 39627 †E-5
Kemah, 1773 *G-9
Kemp, 1154 EF-8
Kempner, 1089 EI-5
KENDALL CO., 33410 EK-3
Kenedy, 3296 EN-5
KENEDY CO., 416 ER-6
Kennedale, 6763 †I-5
KENT CO., 808 WI-12
Kerens, 1573 EF-8
Kermit, 5708 WK-8
KERR CO., 49625 EK-2
Kerrville, 22347 EK-3
Kilgore, 12975 EF-10
Killeen, 127921 EI-5
KIMBLE CO., 4607 WN-14
KING CO., 286 WG-13
Kingsville, 26213 EQ-5
KINNEY CO., 3598 WQ-13
Kirby, 8000 EL-4
Kirbyville, 2142 EI-13
KLEBERG CO., 32061 EQ-5
Knox City, 1130 WH-14
KNOX CO., 3719 WG-14
Kohrville, 400 *A-2
Kountze, 2123 EJ-12
Krum, 4157 ED-6
Kyle, 28016 EK-5
La Feria, 7302 ET-5
La Grange, 4641 EK-7
La Grulla, 1622 ET-4
La Homa, 11985 WR-8
La Joya, 3985 ET-4
La Marque, 14509 EL-11
La Porte, 33800 EL-11
LA SALLE CO., 6886 EO-2
La Vernia, 1034 EM-5
La Villa, 1957 ES-5
LaCoste, 1119 EM-3
Lacy-Lakeview, 6489 WR-7
Lago Vista, 6041 EJ-5
Laguna Vista, 3117 ET-6
L. Dallas, 7105 †B-8
L. Jackson, 26849 EM-10
L. Tanglewood, 796 WD-10
L. Worth, 4584 †G-3
Lakeport, 974 EF-11
Lakeside, 1307 †G-2
Lakeside City, 997 EC-4
Lakeway, 11391 EJ-5
Lakewood Vil., 545 †B-8
LAMAR CO., 49793 EC-9
LAMB CO., 13977 WG-9
Lamesa, 9422 WI-10
Lampasas, 6681 EI-4
LAMPASAS CO., 19677 EI-4
Lancaster, 36361 †J-10
Lantana, 6874 †C-6
Laredo, 236091 EQ-2
LAVACA CO., 19263 EM-7
League City, 83560 EL-10
Leakey, 425 WP-14
Leander, 26521 EJ-5
LEE CO., 16612 EJ-6
LEON CO., 16801 EI-8
Leon Valley, 10151 ER-8
Leonard, 1990 ED-8
Levelland, 13542 WG-9
Lewisville, 95290 †C-8
Lexington, 1177 EJ-7
Liberty, 8397 EK-11
LIBERTY CO., 75643 EJ-11
Liberty Grv., 50 †E-14
Liberty Hill, 967 EJ-5
LIMESTONE CO., 23384 EH-7
Lincoln Pk., 308 †A-8
Lindale, 4818 EF-9
Linden, 1988 ED-11
Lindsay, 1018 EC-6
Lipscomb, 37 WB-13
LIPSCOMB CO., 3302 WB-13
Little River-Academy, 1961 EI-6
Littlefield, 6372 WG-9
Live Oak, 13131 EL-4
LIVE OAK CO., 11531 EO-4
Livingston, 5335 EI-11
Llano, 3232 EJ-3
LLANO CO., 19301 EI-3
Lockhart, 12698 EL-5
Lockney, 1842 WF-11
Lometa, 856 EI-4
Lone Star, 1581 EE-11
Longview, 80455 EE-11
Lorena, 1691 EH-6
Lorenzo, 1147 WG-11
Los Fresnos, 5542 ET-6
Los Indios, 1083 ET-5
Lott, 759 EI-7
LOVING CO., 82 WK-7
Lowry Crossing, 1711 †A-13
Lubbock, 229573 WH-10
LUBBOCK CO., 278831 WG-10
Lucas, 5166 †C-13
Lufkin, 35067 EH-11
Luling, 5411 EL-5
Lumberton, 11943 EJ-12
Lyford, 2611 ES-5
LYNN CO., 5915 WH-10
Lytle, 2492 EM-3
Mabank, 3035 EF-8
MADISON CO., 13664 EI-8
Madisonville, 4396 EI-9
Magnolia, 1393 EK-9
Magnolia Gdns. *C-8
Malakoff, 2324 EF-8
Manor, 5037 EJ-6
Mansfield, 56368 EF-6
Manvel, 5179 EL-10
Marble Falls, 6077 EJ-4
Marfa, 1981 WN-6
Marion, 1066 EL-5
MARION CO., 10546 EE-11
Marlin, 5967 EH-7
Marshall, 23523 EE-11
Marshall Creek, 431 †D-5
Mart, 2209 EH-7
MARTIN CO., 4799 WJ-10
Martindale, 1116 EL-5
Martinez ES-12
Mason, 2114 EJ-2
MASON CO., 4012 EJ-2
Matador, 607 WG-12
MATAGORDA CO., 36702 EN-9
Mathis, 4942 EO-5
Maud, 1056 ED-11
MAVERICK CO., 54258 WR-13
Maypearl, 934 EF-6
McAllen, 129877 ET-4
McCamey, 1887 WM-9
MCCULLOCH CO., 8283 EH-2
McGregor, 4987 EH-6
McKinney, 131117 ED-7
McLean, 778 WD-12
MCLENNAN CO., 234906 EH-6
MCMULLEN CO., 707 EO-4
McNair, 1400 *D-9
McNeil, 30 WB-6
Meadows Pl., 4660 *F-2
MEDINA CO., 46006 EM-2
Melissa, 4695 ED-7
Memphis, 2290 WE-13
Menard, 1471 WM-14
MENARD CO., 2242 WN-14
Mentone, 19 WK-7
Mercedes, 15570 ET-5
Meridian, 1493 EG-5
Merkel, 2590 WJ-13
Mertzon, 781 WM-12
Mesquite, 139824 EE-7
Mexia, 7459 EG-8
Miami, 597 WC-12
Midland, 111147 WK-10
MIDLAND CO., 136872 WK-10
Midlothian, 18037 EF-7
Mila Doce, 6222 WS-12
MILAM CO., 24757 EI-7
Miles, 829 WL-13
MILLS CO., 4936 EH-4
Mineola, 4515 EE-9
Mineral Wells, 16788 EE-4
Mission, 77058 ET-4
Mission Bend, 36501 *E-1
Missouri City, 67358 EL-10
MITCHELL CO., 9403 WK-12
Monahans, 6953 WL-8
Mont Belvieu, 3835 EK-11
Montague, 304 EC-5
MONTAGUE CO., 19719 EC-5
MONTGOMERY CO., 455746 EJ-9
Moody, 1371 EH-6
MOORE CO., 21904 WC-10
Morgan's Pt., 339 *F-9
Morgan's Pt. Resort, 4170 EI-6
MORRIS CO., 12934 ED-11
Morton, 2006 WG-9
MOTLEY CO., 1210 WF-12
Moulton, 886 EL-6
Mt. Pleasant, 15564 ED-10
Mt. Vernon, 2662 ED-10
Muenster, 1544 EC-6
Muleshoe, 5158 WF-9
Munday, 1300 WH-14
Muniz, 1370 WR-11
Murphy, 17708 †D-13
Mustang Ridge, 861 EK-5
Nacogdoches, 32996 EG-11
NACOGDOCHES CO., 64524 EH-11
Naples, 1378 ED-11
Nash, 2960 EC-12
Nassau Bay, 4002 *G-8
Natalia, 1431 EM-3
NAVARRO CO., 47735 EG-7
Navasota, 7049 EJ-8
Nederland, 17547 EK-12
Needville, 2823 EL-9
Nevada, 822 ED-8
New Boston, 4550 EC-11
New Braunfels, 57740 EL-5
New Deal, 794 WG-10
New Fairview, 1258 ED-6
New Hope, 614 †A-13
New London, 998 EF-10
New Summerfield, 1111 EG-10
New Territory, 15186 *G-1
New Waverly, 1032 EJ-10
Newark, 1005 EE-6
Newton, 2478 EI-13
NEWTON CO., 14445 EI-13
Nixon, 2385 EM-5
Nocona, 3033 EC-5
NOLAN CO., 15216 WJ-13
Nolanville, 4259 EI-5
Noonday, 777 EF-10
N. Alamo, 3235 WS-10
N. Houston, 2000 *B-3
N. Richland Hills, 63343 EE-6
N. San Antonio Hills, 100 ER-7
Northlake, 1724 †C-5
Northline Ter., 2700 *C-4
NUECES CO., 340223 EP-5
Nurillo, 7344 WR-10
Oak L. Estates, 2000 *F-1
Oak Pt., 2786 †A-8
Oak Ridge N., 3049 EK-10
OCHILTREE CO., 10223 WB-12
Odem, 2389 EP-6
Odessa, 99940 WK-9
O'Donnell, 831 WI-10
Old River-Winfree, 1245 EK-11
OLDHAM CO., 2052 WC-9
Olivarez, 3827 WS-12
Olmos Pk., 2237 ER-10
Olney, 3285 ED-3
Olton, 2215 WF-10
Omaha, 1021 ED-11
Onalaska, 1764 EI-10
Orange, 18595 EK-13
ORANGE CO., 81837 EK-12
Orange Grv., 1318 EP-5
Ore City, 1144 EE-11
Overton, 2554 EF-10
Ovilla, 3492 †J-9
Oyster Creek, 1111 EM-10
Ozona, 3225 WN-11
Paducah, 1186 WG-13
Paint Rock, 273 WL-14
Palacios, 4718 EN-8
Palestine, 18712 EG-9
Palmer, 2000 EF-7
Palmhurst, 2607 WS-9
San Juan, 33856 WS-10
Palo Pinto, 333 EE-4
PALO PINTO CO., 28111 EE-4
Pampa, 17994 WC-12
Panhandle, 2452 WD-11
PANOLA CO., 23796 EF-12
Pantego, 2394 †H-6
Paris, 25171 EC-9
Parker, 3811 †C-13
PARKER CO., 116927 EE-5
PARMER CO., 10269 WE-8
Pasadena, 149043 EL-10
Payne Sprs., 767 EF-8
Pearland, 91252 EL-10
Pearsall, 9146 EN-3
Pecan Grv., 15963 *F-1
Pecos, 8780 WL-7
PECOS CO., 15507 WN-8
Penitas, 4403 ET-4
Perryton, 8802 WA-12
Petersburg, 1202 WG-11
Pflugerville, 46936 EJ-5
Pharr, 70400 ET-5
Pilot Pt., 3856 ED-7
Pine Island, 988 EK-9
Pinehurst, 2097 EK-13
Pineland, 850 EH-12
Piney Pt. Vil., 3125 *D-3
Pittsburg, 4497 ED-10
Plains, 1481 WH-8
Plainview, 22194 WF-10
Plano, 259841 EE-7
Pleak, 1044 EL-9
Pleasanton, 8934 EN-4
Point, 820 EE-9
POLK CO., 45413 EI-11
Ponder, 1395 ED-6
Port Aransas, 3480 EP-7
Port Arthur, 53818 EK-13
Port Isabel, 5006 ET-7
Port Lavaca, 12248 EN-8
Port Neches, 13040 EK-13
Portland, 15099 EP-6
Post, 5376 WH-11
Poteet, 3260 EM-4
Poth, 1908 EM-5
POTTER CO., 121073 WD-10
Pottsboro, 2160 EC-7
Prairie View, 5576 EK-9
Premont, 2653 EQ-5
Presidio, 4426 WP-5
PRESIDIO CO., 7818 WO-5
Princeton, 6807 ED-7
Progreso, 5507 ET-5
Prosper, 9423 ED-7
Providence Vil., 4786 †A-8
Quanah, 2641 WF-14
Queen City, 1476 ED-12
Quinlan, 1394 EE-8
Quitman, 1809 EE-9
RAINS CO., 10914 EE-9
Ralls, 1944 WG-11
Rancho Viejo, 2437 ET-6
RANDALL CO., 120725 WE-10
Ranger, 2468 EF-3
Rankin, 778 WM-10
Ransom Canyon, 1096 WH-10
Raymondville, 11284 ES-5
REAGAN CO., 3367 WL-11
REAL CO., 3309 WP-14
Red Lick, 1008 EC-12
Red Oak, 10769 EF-7
RED RIVER CO., 12860 EC-10
Redwater, 1057 ED-12
REEVES CO., 13783 WL-6
Refugio, 2890 EO-6
REFUGIO CO., 7383 EO-7
Rendon, 12552 †J-5
Reno, 3166 EC-9
Reno, 2494 EE-5
Rhome, 1522 ED-6
Rice, 923 EF-7
Richardson, 99223 †E-11
Richland Hills, 7801 †G-5
Richmond, 11679 EL-9
Richwood, 3510 EM-10
Ridgeheights, 200 WH-6
Riesel, 1007 EH-7
Rio Bravo, 4794 EQ-2
Rio Grande City, 13834 ES-3
Rio Hondo, 2356 ET-6
Rio Vista, 873 EF-6
Rising Star, 835 EG-3
River Oaks, 7427 †G-3
Roanoke, 5962 EE-6
Robert Lee, 1049 WK-13
ROBERTS CO., 929 WC-12
ROBERTSON CO., 16622 EI-7
Robinson, 10509 EH-6
Robstown, 11487 EP-6
Roby, 643 WI-13
Rockdale, 5595 EJ-7
Rockport, 8766 EP-7
Rocksprings, 1182 WO-13
Rockwall, 37490 EE-7
ROCKWALL CO., 78337 EE-8
Rogers, 1218 EI-6
Rolling Hills, 500 WA-2
Rollingwood, 1412 WE-5
Roma, 9765 ES-3
Roscoe, 1322 WJ-13
Rose City, 502 EQ-14
Rosebud, 1412 EI-7
Rosenberg, 30618 EL-9
Rotan, 1508 WI-13
Round Rock, 99887 EJ-5
Rowlett, 56199 †E-13
Royse City, 9349 EE-8
Runaway Bay, 1286 ED-5
Runge, 1031 EN-5
RUNNELS CO., 10501 WK-13
Rushwood, 3600 *B-4
Rusk, 5551 EG-10
RUSK CO., 53330 EG-11
Sabinal, 1695 EM-2
SABINE CO., 10834 EG-12
Sachse, 20329 †D-13
St. Francis Vil., 500 †J-2
St. Hedwig, 2094 EM-4
St. Jo, 1043 EC-5
St. Paul, 1066 †C-13
Salado, 2126 EI-6
San Angelo, 93200 WL-13
San Antonio, 1327407 EM-4
San Augustine, 2108 EH-12
SAN AUGUSTINE CO., 8865 EH-12
San Benito, 24250 ET-6
San Diego, 4488 EP-4
SAN JACINTO CO., 26384 EJ-10
San Juan, 33856 WS-10
San Leon, 4970 *H-10
San Marcos, 44894 EL-5
SAN PATRICIO CO., 64804 EP-6
San Saba, 3099 EI-3
SAN SABA CO., 6131 EI-3
Sanderson, 837 WO-9
Sanger, 6916 ED-6
Sansom Pk., 4686 †G-3
Santa Anna, 1099 EG-2
Santa Fe, 12222 EL-10
Santa Rosa, 2873 ET-5
Sarita, 238 EQ-5
Savoy, 831 EC-8
Sayers, 30 ET-12
Schertz, 31465 EL-4
SCHLEICHER CO., 3461 WM-13
Schulenburg, 2852 EL-7
Scissors, 3186 WT-11
SCURRY CO., 16921 WI-12
Seabrook, 11952 EL-11
Seadrift, 1364 EO-7
Seagoville, 14835 EE-7
Seagraves, 2417 WI-9
Sealy, 6019 EL-8
Seguin, 25175 EL-5
Selma, 5540 EQ-12
Seminole, 6430 WI-9
Seven Pts., 1455 EF-8
Seymour, 2740 EC-2
SHACKELFORD CO., 3378 EE-2
Shady Shores, 2612 †B-7
Shallowater, 2484 WG-10
Shamrock, 1910 WD-13
Shavano Pk., 3035 EQ-9
SHELBY CO., 25448 EG-12
Shenandoah, 2134 EK-10
Shepherd, 2319 EJ-11
Sherman, 38521 EC-7
SHERMAN CO., 3034 WB-10
Shiner, 2069 EL-6
Shoreacres, 1493 *F-9
Sienna Plantation, 13721 *H-3
Sierra Blanca, 553 WL-4
Silsbee, 6611 EJ-12
Silverton, 731 WF-11
Sinton, 5665 EP-6
Slaton, 6121 WH-11
SMITH CO., 209714 EF-9
Smithville, 3817 EK-6
Snyder, 11202 WI-12
Socorro, 32013 WK-2
Somerset, 1631 EM-4
SOMERVELL CO., 8490 EF-5
Somerville, 1376 EJ-8
Sonora, 3027 WN-12
Sour Lake, 1813 EK-12
S. Alamo, 3361 WT-11
S. Houston, 16983 *F-6
S. Padre Island, 2816 ET-7
Southlake, 26575 †E-6
Southmayd, 992 EC-7
Southside Pl., 1715 *E-4
Southton, 100 ET-11
Spearman, 3368 WB-11
Splendora, 1615 EK-10
Spring Valley, 3611 *D-3
Springtown, 2658 EE-5
Spur, 1318 WH-12
Stafford, 17693 *F-3
Stamford, 3124 WI-14
Stanton, 2492 WK-10
STARR CO., 60968 ES-3
STEPHENS CO., 9630 EE-3
Stephenville, 17123 EF-4
Sterling City, 888 WK-12
STERLING CO., 1143 WL-11
Stinnett, 1881 WC-11
Stockdale, 1442 EM-5
STONEWALL CO., 1490 WH-13
Stony, 50 †J-1
Stratford, 2017 WA-10
Sudan, 958 WF-9
Sugar Land, 78817 EL-9
Sullivan City, 4002 ET-4
Sulphur Sprs., 15449 ED-9
Sundown, 1397 WH-9
Sunnyvale, 5130 †G-13
Sunray, 1926 WB-10
Sunset Valley, 749 WF-4
SUTTON CO., 4128 WN-13
Sweeny, 3684 EM-9
Sweetwater, 10906 WJ-13
SWISHER CO., 7854 WE-10
Taft, 3048 EP-6
Tahoka, 2673 WH-10
Tara, 1100 *G-1
TARRANT CO., 1809034 EE-6
Tatum, 1385 EF-11
Taylor, 15191 EJ-6
TAYLOR CO., 131506 WK-14
Taylor Lake Vil., 3544 *G-8
Teague, 3560 EH-8
Temple, 66102 EI-6
Tenaha, 1160 EG-12
Terrell, 15816 EE-8
TERRELL CO., 984 WO-9
Terrell Hills, 4878 ER-10
TERRY CO., 12651 WH-9
Texarkana, 36411 EC-12
Texas City, 45099 EL-11
The Colony, 36328 ED-7
The Hills, 2472 EK-5
Thorndale, 1336 EJ-6
Thrall, 839 EJ-6
Three Rivers, 1848 EO-4
Throckmorton, 828 ED-2
THROCKMORTON CO., 1641 ED-2
Tilden, 261 EO-4
Timpson, 1155 EG-11
Tioga, 803 ED-7
TITUS CO., 32334 ED-10
Tom Bean, 1045 EC-7
TOM GREEN CO., 110224 WM-13
Tomball, 10753 EK-9
Tool, 2240 EF-8
Town West *F-2
TRAVIS CO., 1024266 EJ-5
Trinidad, 886 EF-8
Trinity, 2697 EI-10
TRINITY CO., 14585 EI-10
Trophy Club, 8024 †D-5
Troup, 1869 EF-10
Troy, 1645 EI-6
Tulia, 4967 WE-10
Tye, 1242 WJ-14
Tyler, 96900 EF-10
TYLER CO., 21766 EI-11
Uhland, 1014 EK-5
Universal City, 18530 EQ-12
University Pk., 23068 †F-10
UPSHUR CO., 39309 EE-10
UPTON CO., 3355 WL-10
Uvalde, 15751 WQ-14
UVALDE CO., 26405 WQ-14
VAL VERDE CO., 48879 WO-11
Valley Mills, 1203 EH-6
Valley View, 757 ED-6
Van, 2632 EF-9
Van Alstyne, 3046 ED-7
Van Horn, 2063 WM-4
VAN ZANDT CO., 52579 EE-9
Vega, 884 WD-9
Venus, 2960 EF-6
Vernon, 11002 EB-2
Victoria, 62592 EN-7
VICTORIA CO., 86793 EN-7
Vidor, 10579 EK-12
Village of Tiki Island, 968 *B-8
Vinton, 1971 WK-1
Von Ormy, 1085 EM-4
Waco, 124805 EH-6
Waelder, 1065 EL-6
Wake Vil., 5492 EC-12
WALKER CO., 67861 EI-9
Waller, 2326 EK-9
WALLER CO., 43205 EK-9
Wallis, 1252 EL-9
Walnut Sprs., 827 EG-5
WARD CO., 10658 WL-7
WASHINGTON CO., 33718 EK-7
Waskom, 2160 EE-12
Watauga, 23497 †F-5
Waxahachie, 29621 EF-7
Weatherford, 25250 EE-5
WEBB CO., 250304 WT-14
Webster, 10400 *G-8
Weimar, 2151 EL-7
Wellington, 2189 WE-13
Wells, 790 EH-10
Wells Branch, 12120 WB-6
Weslaco, 35670 ET-5
West, 2807 EG-6
W. Columbia, 3905 EM-9
W. Lake Hills, 3063 WE-4
W. Orange, 3443 EK-13
W. Sharyland, 2309 WR-9
W. Tawakoni, 1576 EE-8
W. University Place, 14787 *E-4
Westfield, 800 *A-4
Westlake, 992 †D-6
Weston Lakes, 2482 EL-9
Westover Hills, 682 †H-3
Westworth Vil., 2472 †H-3
Wharton, 8832 EM-8
WHARTON CO., 41280 EM-8
Wheeler, 1592 WC-13
WHEELER CO., 5410 WD-13
White Deer, 1000 WC-11
White Oak, 6469 EE-10
White Settlement, 16116 †G-2
Whitehouse, 7660 EF-10
Whitesboro, 3793 EC-7
Whitewright, 1604 EC-8
Whitney, 2087 EG-6
WICHITA CO., 131500 EB-3
Wichita Falls, 104553 EC-4
WILBARGER CO., 13535 EC-2
WILLACY CO., 22134 ES-6
WILLIAMSON CO., 422679 EJ-6
Willis, 5662 EJ-10
Wills Pt., 3524 EE-8
Wilmer, 3682 †J-12
WILSON CO., 42918 EN-4
Winchester Country, 2000 *B-2
Windcrest, 5364 ER-11
Windemere, 1037 WB-7
Wink, 940 WK-8
WINKLER CO., 7110 WK-8
Winnsboro, 3434 EE-10
Winters, 2562 WK-14
WISE CO., 59127 ED-5
Wolfe City, 1412 ED-8
Wolfforth, 3670 WH-10
WOOD CO., 41964 EE-9
Woodcreek, 1457 EK-5
Woodlake, 800 ER-11
Woodsboro, 1512 EO-6
Woodville, 2586 EI-12
Woodway, 8452 EH-6
Wortham, 1073 EG-8
Wylie, 41427 EE-7
Yoakum, 5815 EM-6
YOAKUM CO., 7879 WH-8
Yorktown, 2092 EM-6
YOUNG CO., 18550 ED-3
Zapata, 5089 ER-2
ZAPATA CO., 14018 ER-2
ZAVALA CO., 11677 EM-2

Utah

Map pp. 102 – 103

American Fork, 26263 E-9
Annabella, 795 J-8
Apple Valley, 701 N-6
Aurora, 1016 I-8
Ballard, 801 E-12
Bear River City, 853 B-8
Beaver, 3112 K-7
BEAVER CO., 6629 J-6
Blanding, 3375 L-13
Bluffdale, 7598 E-8
Bountiful, 42552 D-8
BOX ELDER CO., 49975 B-5
Brigham City, 17899 B-8
CACHE CO., 112656 B-9
CARBON CO., 21403 G-11
Carbonville, 1567 G-10
Castle Dale, 1630 H-10
Cedar City, 28857 L-6
Centerfield, 1367 H-8
Centerville, 15335 D-8
Central, 613 M-5
Clarkston, 666 A-8
Clearfield, 30112 C-8
Clinton, 20426 C-8
Coalville, 1363 D-9
Copperton, 826 E-8
Corinne, 685 B-8
Cottonwood Hts., 33433 I-19
DAGGETT CO., 1059 D-12
Daniel, 938 E-9
DAVIS CO., 306479 D-7
Delta, 3436 H-7
Draper, 42274 E-8
Duchesne, 1690 F-11
DUCHESNE CO., 18607 E-11
Dugway, 795 F-7
Eagle Mtn., 21415 E-8
E. Carbon City, 1301 G-11
Eden, 600 C-9
Elk Ridge, 2436 F-9
Elsinore, 847 J-8
Elwood, 1034 B-8
EMERY CO., 10976 H-11
Enoch, 5803 L-6
Enterprise, 1711 L-5
Ephraim, 6135 H-9
Erda, 4642 E-8
Escalante, 797 L-9
Eureka, 669 F-8
Fairview, 1247 G-9
Farmington, 18275 D-8
Farr West, 5928 A-2
Ferron, 1626 I-10
Fillmore, 2435 I-7
Ft. Duchesne, 714 E-12
Fountain Green, 1071 G-9
Francis, 1077 E-10
Fruit Hts., 4987 F-3
GARFIELD CO., 5172 L-10
Garland, 2400 B-8
Genola, 1370 F-8
Goshen, 921 F-8
GRAND CO., 9225 I-13
Granite, 1932 J-20
Grantsville, 8893 E-7
Green River, 952 I-12
Gunnison, 3285 H-8
Harrisville, 5567 A-2
Heber City, 11362 E-9
Helper, 2201 G-10
Henefer, 766 D-9
Herriman, 21785 K-17
Hideout, 656 E-9
Hildale, 2726 N-6
Hinckley, 696 H-7
Holladay, 26472 E-8
Honeyville, 1441 B-8
Hooper, 7218 C-8
Huntington, 2129 H-10
Huntsville, 608 C-9
Hurricane, 13748 N-5
Hyde Pk., 3833 L-20
Hyrum, 7609 B-8
IRON CO., 46163 L-5
Ivins, 6753 M-5
JUAB CO., 10246 G-6
Junction, 191 K-8
Kamas, 1811 E-10
Kanab, 4312 N-7
KANE CO., 7125 M-9
Kaysville, 27300 D-8
Kearns, 35731 H-17
La Verkin, 4060 M-5
Layton, 67311 C-8
Leeds, 820 M-5
Lehi, 47407 E-8
Levan, 841 G-8
Lewiston, 1766 A-8
Lindon, 10070 F-1
Loa, 572 J-9
Logan, 48174 B-8
Maeser, 3601 E-13
Magna, 26505 G-16
Manila, 310 D-13
Manti, 3276 H-9
Mantua, 687 B-8
Mapleton, 7979 F-9
Marriott-Slaterville, 1701 B-2
Mendon, 1282 B-8
Midvale, 27964 I-19
Midway, 3845 E-9
Milford, 1409 J-6
MILLARD CO., 12503 H-6
Millcreek, 62139 H-19
Minersville, 907 K-6
Moab, 5046 J-13
Mona, 1547 G-8
Monroe, 2256 J-8
Monticello, 1972 L-14
Morgan, 3687 D-9
MORGAN CO., 9469 C-9
Moroni, 1423 G-9
Mt. Pleasant, 3260 G-9
Murray, 46746 H-19
Naples, 1755 E-13
Nephi, 5389 G-8
Newton, 789 A-8
N. Logan, 8269 M-20
N. Ogden, 17357 C-8
N. Salt Lake, 16322 E-18
Oakley, 1470 D-10
Ogden, 82825 C-8
Orangeville, 1470 H-10
Orem, 88328 E-9
Panguitch, 1520 L-7
Paradise, 904 B-8
Park City, 7558 E-9
Parowan, 2790 L-6
Payson, 18294 F-9
Perry, 4512 B-8
PIUTE CO., 1556 J-8
Plain City, 5476 C-8
Pleasant Grv., 33509 E-9
Price, 8715 G-11
Providence, 7075 B-9
Provo, 112488 F-9
Randolph, 464 B-10
Redmond, 730 I-8
RICH CO., 2264 B-9
Richfield, 7551 I-8
Richmond, 2470 A-9
River Hts., 1734 N-20
Riverdale, 8426 C-2
Riverside, 760 B-8
Riverton, 38753 E-8
Roosevelt, 6046 E-12
Roy, 36884 C-8
St. George, 72897 N-5
Salem, 6423 F-9
Salina, 2489 I-8
Salt Lake City, 186440 D-8
SALT LAKE CO., 1029655 E-19
SAN JUAN CO., 14746 K-13
Sandy, 87461 E-8
SANPETE CO., 27822 H-9
Santa Clara, 6003 N-5
Santaquin, 9128 F-9
SEVIER CO., 20802 I-9
Smithfield, 9495 B-8
S. Jordan, 50418 J-17
S. Ogden, 16532 C-2
S. Salt Lake, 23617 G-19
S. Weber, 6051 D-3
Spanish Fork, 34691 F-9
Spring City, 988 H-9
Spring Glen, 1126 G-10
Springville, 29466 F-9
Stansbury Pk., 5145 E-8
Stockton, 616 E-7
SUMMIT CO., 36324 D-10
Sunset, 5122 D-2
Syracuse, 24331 E-1
Taylorsville, 58652 H-17
Tooele, 31605 E-8
TOOELE CO., 58218 D-6
Toquerville, 1370 M-5
Tremonton, 7647 B-8
Uintah, 1322 C-8
UINTAH CO., 32588 G-13
UTAH CO., 516564 F-8
Vernal, 9089 E-13
WASATCH CO., 23530 F-10
Washington, 18761 N-5
WASHINGTON CO., 138115 M-5
Washington Ter., 9067 C-2
WAYNE CO., 2778 J-10
WEBER CO., 231236 C-9
Wellington, 1676 G-11
Wellsville, 3432 B-8
Wendover, 1400 D-4
W. Bountiful, 5265 D-18
W. Haven, 10272 B-2
W. Jordan, 103712 E-8
West Point, 9511 D-1
W. Valley City, 129480 D-8
Willard, 1772 C-8
Woods Cross, 9761 D-8

Vermont

Map p. 104

ADDISON CO., 36821 F-3
Arlington, 1213 L-2
Barre, 9052 F-5
Barton, 737 C-6
Bellows Falls, 3148 K-5
Bennington, 9074 M-2
BENNINGTON CO., 37125 L-2
Bethel, 569 H-4
Bradford, 788 G-6
Brandon, 1648 H-3
Brattleboro, 7414 M-5
Bristol, 2030 F-3
Burlington, 42417 D-2
CALEDONIA CO., 31227 D-6
Castleton, 1485 I-2
Chelsea, 500 G-5
Chester, 1005 K-5
CHITTENDEN CO., 156545 E-3
Derby Ctr., 597 B-6
Derby Line, 673 A-7
E. Arlington, 620 L-3
E. Barre, 826 F-5
Enosburg Falls, 1329 B-4
Essex Ctr., 850 D-3
ESSEX CO., 6306 C-8
Essex Jct., 9271 D-3
Fair Haven, 2269 I-2
FRANKLIN CO., 47746 C-3
GRAND ISLE CO., 6970 B-2
Graniteville, 784 F-5
Guildhall, 100 D-9
Hardwick, 1345 D-6
Hinesburg, 658 E-3
Hyde Park, 462 C-5
Island Pond, 821 B-7
Jeffersonville, 729 C-4
Jericho, 1329 D-3
Johnson, 1443 C-4
LAMOILLE CO., 24475 D-4
Ludlow, 811 J-4
Lyndonville, 1207 D-7
Manchester, 749 K-3
Manchester Ctr., 2120 K-3
Middlebury, 6588 G-2
Milton, 1861 C-3
Montpelier, 7855 E-5
Morrisville, 1958 D-5
Newfane, 118 L-4
Newport, 4589 B-6
N. Bennington, 1643 L-2
N. Clarendon, 550 I-3
N. Hero, 190 B-2
N. Springfield, 573 J-5
N. Troy, 620 A-5
Northfield, 2101 F-4
Norwich, 878 H-6
ORANGE CO., 28936 F-5
Orleans, 818 B-6
ORLEANS CO., 27231 B-5
Pittsford, 740 H-3
Poultney, 1612 I-2
Proctor, 1740 H-3
Quechee, 656 I-5
Randolph, 1974 G-4
Richford, 1361 A-4
Richmond, 723 D-3
Rutland, 16495 I-3
RUTLAND CO., 61642 I-2
St. Albans, 6918 B-3
St. Johnsbury, 6193 D-7
Saxtons River, 565 K-5
Shelburne, 592 E-2
S. Barre, 1219 F-5
S. Burlington, 17904 D-2
S. Royalton, 694 H-5
S. Shaftsbury, 683 L-2
Springfield, 3979 J-5
Swanton, 2386 B-3
Vergennes, 2588 F-2
Wallingford, 830 I-3
WASHINGTON CO., 59534 D-5
Waterbury, 1763 E-4
Websterville, 550 F-5
W. Brattleboro, 2740 M-5
W. Rutland, 2024 I-3
White River Jct., 2286 H-6
Wilder, 1690 H-6
Williamstown, 1162 F-5
WINDHAM CO., 44513 L-5
Windsor, 2066 I-5
WINDSOR CO., 56670 I-5
Winooski, 7267 D-2
Woodstock, 900 I-5

Virginia

Map pp. 106 – 107

† City keyed to p. 105
‡ City keyed to p. 111

Abingdon, 8191 D-6
Accomac, 519 I-19
ACCOMACK CO., 33164 I-20
Adwolf, 1530 M-1
ALBEMARLE CO., 98970 H-10
Alexandria, 139966 E-15
ALLEGHANY CO., 16250 I-5
Allison Gap, 700 D-7
Altavista, 3450 K-8
AMELIA CO., 12690 J-12
Amelia Court House, 1099 K-12
Amherst, 2231 J-9
AMHERST CO., 32353 I-8
Annalee Hts., 1800 ‡G-4
Annandale, 41008 E-14
Appalachia, 1754 C-4
Appomattox, 1733 K-9
APPOMATTOX CO., 14973 J-9
Aquia Hbr., 6727 F-14
Arlington, 207627 D-15
Arrington, 708 I-9
Arvonia, 750 I-11
Ashburn, 43511 D-14
Ashland, 7225 I-14
Atkins, 1143 L-1
Atlantic, 862 H-20
AUGUSTA CO., 73750 G-9
Austinville, 850 L-3
Bailey's Crossroads, 23643 ‡H-5
Bassett, 1100 M-6
Basye, 1253 E-9
BATH CO., 4731 H-7
Bealeton, 4435 F-13
Bedford, 6222 K-7
BEDFORD CO., 68676 K-7
Bel Air, 1500 ‡G-4
Bellair, 1400 †B-1
Belle Haven, 6518 ‡I-6
Belleview, 2300 ‡E-3
Bellwood, 6352 †E-8
Belvedere, 2200 ‡H-4
Benns Church, 872 L-17
Bensley, 5819 †E-8
Berryville, 4185 C-12
Big Stone Gap, 5614 D-4
Blacksburg, 42620 K-4
Blackstone, 3621 L-12
Blairs, 916 M-8
Bland, 409 K-2
BLAND CO., 6824 K-2
Blevinstown, 800 ‡H-1
Blue Ridge, 3084 J-6
Bluefield, 5444 K-2
Boissevain, 900 K-1
Bon Air, 16366 J-13
BOTETOURT CO., 33148 I-6
Bowling Green, 1111 H-14
Boydton, 431 M-11
Bracey, 1554 M-12
Brambleton, 9845 D-13
Brandermill, 13173 †E-5
Bridgewater, 5644 F-9
Brightwood, 1001 F-11
Bristol, 17835 E-5
Broadway, 3691 E-9
Brookneal, 1112 L-9
Broyhill Pk., 3700 ‡G-3
BRUNSWICK CO., 17434 L-12
Buchanan, 1178 J-7
BUCHANAN CO., 24098 B-6
Buckingham, 350 J-10
Buckingham Cir., 900 †C-1
BUCKINGHAM CO., 17146 I-10
Bucknell Manor, 2350 ‡I-6
Buena Vista, 6650 I-8
Burke, 41055 ‡I-2
CAMPBELL CO., 54842 K-9
Cana, 1254 M-4
Cape Charles, 1009 K-18
Captains Cove, 1042 H-20
CAROLINE CO., 28545 H-14
CARROLL CO., 30042 M-4
Carrollton, 4574 †K-3
Carrsbrook, 950 H-11
Castlewood, 2045 D-5
Cave Spr., 24922 K-6
Cedar Bluff, 1137 C-7
Centreville, 71135 E-14
Chamberlayne, 5456 †B-8
Chantilly, 23039 D-14
Chapel Acres, 1200 ‡J-3
Charles City, 133 J-15
CHARLES CITY CO., 7256 J-15
CHARLOTTE CO., 12586 L-10
Charlotte Court House, 543 L-10
Charlottesville, 43475 H-10
Chase City, 2351 M-11
Chatham, 1269 M-8
Chatmoss, 1698 M-6
Chesapeake, 222209 L-18
Chester, 20987 J-14
Chester Gap, 839 E-12
Chesterbrook, 1600 ‡F-4
Chesterfield, 3560 J-14
CHESTERFIELD CO., 316236 K-13
Chilhowie, 1781 M-1
Chincoteague, 2941 H-20
Christiansburg, 21041 K-4
CLARKE CO., 14034 D-12
Clarksville, 1139 M-10
Claypool Hill, 1776 C-7
Clifton Forge, 3884 I-6
Clintwood, 1414 C-5
Cloverdale, 3119 J-6
Cluster Sprs., 811 M-9
Coeburn, 2139 C-5
Collinsville, 7335 M-6
Colonial Bch., 3542 G-15
Colonial Hts., 17411 K-14
Concord, 1458 K-9
Courtland, 1284 M-15
Covington, 5961 I-6
CRAIG CO., 5190 J-5
Craigsville, 923 H-8
Crewe, 2326 K-12
Crimora, 2209 G-9
Crozet, 5565 H-10
Culmore, 5200 ‡G-4
Culpeper, 16379 F-12
CULPEPER CO., 46689 F-12
Cumberland, 393 J-11
CUMBERLAND CO., 10052 J-11
Dahlgren, 2653 F-15
Dale City, 65969 E-14
Daleville, 2557 J-6
Damascus, 814 E-7
Danville, 43055 N-8
Dare, 1500 †H-4
Dayton, 1530 F-9
Deltaville, 1119 J-17
DICKENSON CO., 15903 C-5
Dinwiddie, 200 L-13
DINWIDDIE CO., 28001 L-13
Dooms, 1327 G-9
Dranesville, 11921 ‡D-1
Dryden, 1208 D-3
Dublin, 2534 K-4
Dumbarton, 7879 †B-7
Dumfries, 4961 F-14
Dunn Loring, 8803 ‡F-3
E. Highland Pk., 14796 †B-8
E. Lexington, 1463 I-8
Eastville, 305 J-19
Edinburg, 1041 E-10
Ednam Forest, 700 †B-1
Elkton, 2726 F-10
Elliston, 902 K-5
Emory, 1251 D-7
Emporia, 5927 M-14
Enon, 3466 K-14
ESSEX CO., 11151 H-15
Ettrick, 6682 K-14
Exmore, 1460 J-19
Fairfax, 22565 D-14
FAIRFAX CO., 1081726 D-14
Fairfax Sta., 12030 ‡I-1
Fairlawn, 2367 K-4
Falls Church, 12332 D-14
Falmouth, 4274 G-14
Farmville, 8216 K-11
FAUQUIER CO., 65203 E-12
Ferrum, 2043 L-6
Ferry Farms, 4000 G-14
Fieldale, 879 M-6
Fincastle, 353 J-6
First Colony, 900 †F-1
Fishersville, 7462 H-9
Five Mile Fork, 700 G-13
Floyd, 425 L-5
FLOYD CO., 15279 L-5
FLUVANNA CO., 25691 I-11
Forest, 9106 J-8
Forksville, 1000 M-12
Ft. Hunt, 16045 ‡J-6
Franconia, 18245 ‡I-4
Franklin, 8582 M-15
FRANKLIN CO., 56159 L-6
Franklin Pk., 1800 ‡F-4
FREDERICK CO., 78305 C-11
Fredericksburg, 24286 G-14
Front Royal, 14440 D-11
Gainesville, 11481 E-13
Galax, 7042 M-3
Gate City, 2034 E-4
GILES CO., 17286 K-3
Glade Spr., 1456 D-7
Glasgow, 1133 I-7
Glen Allen, 14774 †A-7
Glenvar, 976 K-5
Gloucester, 2951 J-17
GLOUCESTER CO., 36858 J-16
Gloucester Pt., 9402 K-17
Goochland, 861 I-12
GOOCHLAND CO., 21717 I-12
Gordonsville, 1496 G-11
Grafton, 1050 †H-4
Gratton, 937 K-1
GRAYSON CO., 15533 M-2
Great Falls, 15427 ‡D-2
GREENE CO., 18403 G-11
GREENSVILLE CO., 12243 M-13
Greenville, 832 H-8
Gretna, 1267 L-8
Grottoes, 2668 G-9
Groveton, 14598 ‡I-5
Grundy, 1021 B-6
Halifax, 1309 M-9
HALIFAX CO., 36241 M-9
Hampden Sydney, 1450 K-11
Hampton, 137436 L-17
Hanover, 252 I-14
HANOVER CO., 99863 I-13
Harrisonburg, 48914 F-9
Harriston, 909 G-9
Hayes, 1000 †F-4
Haymarket, 1782 E-13
Heathsville, 142 H-17
HENRICO CO., 306935 J-14
HENRY CO., 54151 N-6
Henry Fork, 1234 L-6
Herndon, 23292 D-14
HIGHLAND CO., 2321 G-7
Highland Sprs., 15711 J-14
Hillsville, 2681 M-3
Hillwood, 1650 ‡G-4
Hollins, 14673 K-6
Hollymead, 7690 G-11
Holmes Run Acres, 1400 ‡G-3
Honaker, 1449 C-6
Hopewell, 22591 K-14
Horse Pasture, 2227 M-6
Hot Sprs., 738 H-6
Huntington, 11267 ‡I-6
Hurt, 1304 L-8
Hybla Valley, 15801 ‡J-5
Idylwood, 17288 ‡G-3
Independence, 947 M-2
Independent Hill, 7419 E-14
Isle of Wight, 70 L-16
ISLE OF WIGHT CO., 35270 L-16
JAMES CITY CO., 67009 K-16
Jefferson Vil., 2500 ‡G-4
Jolivue, 1129 G-9
Jonesville, 1034 D-2
Kenbridge, 1257 L-12
Keysville, 832 L-11
Kilmarnock, 1487 I-17
KING & QUEEN CO., 6945 I-15
King & Queen Court House, 85 I-16
King George, 4457 G-15
KING GEORGE CO., 23584 G-15
King William, 252 I-15
KING WILLIAM CO., 15935 I-15
Kings Pk., 4333 ‡H-3
L. Monticello, 9920 H-11
Lakeside, 11849 †B-7
Lancaster, 80 I-17
LANCASTER CO., 11391 I-17
Langley, 1450 ‡E-4
Laurel, 16713 I-14
Lawrenceville, 1438 M-13
Lebanon, 3424 D-6
LEE CO., 25587 D-2
Leesburg, 42616 C-13
Lexington, 7042 I-7
Lincolnia, 22855 ‡H-4
Lincolnia Hts., 1800 ‡H-4
Linton Hall, 35725 E-13
Lorton, 18610 E-14
LOUDOUN CO., 312311 D-13
Louisa, 1555 H-12
LOUISA CO., 33153 H-12
Lovettsville, 1613 C-13
Lovingston, 520 I-9
Lunenburg, 165 L-11
LUNENBURG CO., 12914 L-11
Luray, 4895 E-11
Lynchburg, 75568 J-8
Lyndhurst, 1490 H-9
Madison, 229 F-11
MADISON CO., 13308 F-11
Madison Hts., 11285 J-8
Manassas, 37821 E-14
Manassas Pk., 14273 E-14
Mantua, 7135 ‡G-3
Marion, 5968 L-1
Marshall, 1480 D-12
Martinsville, 13821 M-6
Marumsco, 35036 E-14
Mathews, 555 J-17
MATHEWS CO., 8978 J-17
Matoaca, 2403 †H-7
Maurertown, 770 D-11
McLean, 48115 ‡F-4
Meadowview, 967 D-6
Mechanicsville, 36348 I-14
MECKLENBURG CO., 32727 M-11
Merrifield, 15212 ‡G-3
MIDDLESEX CO., 10959 J-17
Middletown, 1265 D-11
Montclair, 19570 E-14
Monterey, 147 F-7
MONTGOMERY CO., 94392 K-4
Montrose, 7993 †D-9
Montross, 384 G-16
Motley, 1015 L-8
Mt. Hermon, 3966 M-8
Mt. Jackson, 1994 E-10
Mt. Vernon, 12416 E-15
Mountain Road, 1100 M-9
Narrows, 2029 K-3
Natural Br., 1500 I-7
Nellysford, 1076 H-9
NELSON CO., 15020 I-9
New Alexandria, 950 ‡I-6
New Baltimore, 8119 E-13
New Castle, 153 J-5
New Hope, 797 G-9
New Kent, 239 J-15
NEW KENT CO., 18429 J-15
New Market, 2146 E-10
Newington, 12943 ‡J-4
Newport News, 180719 L-17
Nokesville, 1354 E-13
Norfolk, 242803 L-18
Norge, 1000 J-16
N. Garden, 900 H-10
N. Shore, 3094 L-7
N. Springfield, 7274 ‡H-3
NORTHAMPTON CO., 12389 J-19
Northfields, 1400 †A-3
NORTHUMBERLAND CO., 12330 H-17
Norton, 3958 C-4
Nottoway, 84 K-12
NOTTOWAY CO., 15853 K-12
Oak Level, 857 M-6
Oakton, 34166 ‡G-2
Occoquan, 934 E-14
Onancock, 1263 I-19
Orange, 4721 G-12
ORANGE CO., 33481 G-12
Ordinary, 1000 †E-4
PAGE CO., 24042 F-10
Palmyra, 104 H-11
Parklawn, 2400 ‡H-4
Parksley, 842 I-19
PATRICK CO., 18490 M-4
Patrick Sprs., 1845 M-5
Pearisburg, 2786 K-3
Pembroke, 1128 K-4
Penhook, 801 L-7
Pennington Gap, 1781 D-3
Petersburg, 32420 K-14
Pimmit Hills, 6094 ‡F-3
PITTSYLVANIA CO., 63506 L-8
Poquoson, 12150 K-17
Portsmouth, 95535 L-17
Pound, 1037 C-4
Powhatan, 700 J-12
POWHATAN CO., 28046 J-12
Prices Fork, 1066 K-4
PRINCE EDWARD CO., 23368 K-10
Prince George, 2066 K-14
PRINCE GEORGE CO., 35725 K-14
PRINCE WILLIAM CO., 402002 E-13
Pulaski, 9086 L-3
PULASKI CO., 34872 K-3
Purcellville, 7727 C-13
Quail Oaks, 1400 †F-8
Queens Lake, 1400 †E-2
Radford, 16408 K-4
RAPPAHANNOCK CO., 7373 E-11
Raven, 2270 C-7
Ravensworth, 2466 ‡H-3
Ravenwood, 2550 ‡G-4
Reston, 58404 D-14
Rich Creek, 774 J-3
Richlands, 5823 C-7
Richmond, 204214 J-14
RICHMOND CO., 9254 H-16
Ridgeway, 742 N-6
Riner, 859 L-4
Roanoke, 97032 K-6
ROANOKE CO., 92376 J-5
ROCKBRIDGE CO., 22307 H-8
ROCKINGHAM CO., 76314 F-9
Rocky Mount, 4799 L-6
Rose Hill, 799 D-2
Ruckersville, 1141 G-11
Rural Retreat, 1483 L-2
Rushmere, 1018 K-16
RUSSELL CO., 28897 C-6
Rustburg, 1431 K-9
St. Paul, 970 C-5
Salem, 24802 K-6
Saltville, 2077 D-7
Saluda, 769 I-16
Sandston, 7571 †C-10
SCOTT CO., 23177 D-4
Seaford, 2700 K-17
Seven Cors., 9255 ‡G-4
Seven Mile Ford, 783 M-1
Shawnee Land, 1873 C-11
Shawsville, 1310 K-5
Shenandoah, 2373 F-10
SHENANDOAH CO., 41993 E-10
Short Pump, 24729 †A-5
Smithfield, 8089 L-16
SMYTH CO., 32208 M-1
S. Boston, 8142 M-9
S. Hill, 4650 M-12
SOUTHAMPTON CO., 18570 L-15
Spotsylvania, 4239 G-13
SPOTSYLVANIA CO., 122397 H-13
Springfield, 30484 ‡I-4
Stafford, 1600 F-14
STAFFORD CO., 128961 F-13
Stanardsville, 367 G-11
Stanley, 1689 F-10
Stanleytown, 1422 M-6
Staunton, 23746 G-9
Stephens City, 1829 D-11
Sterling, 27822 D-14
Strasburg, 6398 D-11
Stuart, 1408 M-5
Stuarts Draft, 9235 H-9
Suffolk, 84585 M-17
Sugar Grv., 758 M-1
Sugar Loaf, 2500 H-1
Sugarland Run, 11799 ‡C-1
Surry, 244 K-16
SURRY CO., 7058 K-15
Sussex, 256 L-14
SUSSEX CO., 12087 L-14
Tabb, 950 K-17
Tangier, 727 H-18
Tappahannock, 2375 H-16
Tazewell, 4627 K-1
TAZEWELL CO., 45078 L-1
Timberlake, 12183 K-8
Timberville, 2522 E-10
Toano, 1200 J-16
Triangle, 8188 F-14
Tuckahoe, 44990 I-13
Tyler Pk., 1250 ‡G-4
Tysons Corner, 19627 ‡F-3
Varina, 3000 †E-9
Verona, 4239 G-9
Victoria, 1725 L-11
Vienna, 15687 D-14
Vinton, 8098 K-6
Virginia Beach, 437994 L-18
Virginia Hills, 2840 ‡I-5
Wakefield, 927 L-15
Warm Sprs., 123 H-6
WARREN CO., 37575 D-12
Warrenton, 9611 E-13
Warsaw, 1512 H-16
Washington, 135 E-11
WASHINGTON CO., 54876 D-7
Waverly, 2149 L-15
Waynesboro, 21006 H-9
Waynewood, 3450 ‡J-6
Weber City, 1327 E-4
Wellington, 1750 ‡J-6
West Point, 3306 J-16
W. Springfield, 22460 ‡I-3
Westmoreland, 900 †A-3
WESTMORELAND CO., 17454 G-15
Weyanoke, 1500 ‡H-4
Weyers Cave, 2473 G-9
Wicomico, 1350 K-17
Williamsburg, 14068 K-16
Wilton Woods, 1400 ‡I-5
Winchester, 26203 C-11
Windsor, 2626 M-16
Wise, 3286 C-4
WISE CO., 41452 C-4
Woodlake, 7319 J-13
Woodlawn, 2343 M-3
Woodstock, 5097 D-10
WYTHE CO., 29235 L-2
Wytheville, 8211 L-2
YORK CO., 65464 J-16
York Ter., 800 †F-2
Yorktown, 195 K-17

Washington

Map pp. 108 – 109

* City keyed to p. 110

Aberdeen, 16896 H-3
ADAMS CO., 18728 I-16
Ahtanum, 3601 J-11
Airway Hts., 6114 F-18
Alderton, 2893 *N-9
Alderwood, 1760 B-7
Algona, 3014 *K-9
Allyn, 1963 G-6
Amboy, 1608 L-7
Anacortes, 15778 C-6
Arlington, 17926 D-8
Asotin, 1251 J-20
ASOTIN CO., 21623 K-19
Auburn, 70180 G-7
Basin City, 1092 J-15
Battle Ground, 17571 M-6
Bayview, 696 C-7
Belfair, 3931 G-6
Bellevue, 122363 *E-9
Bellingham, 80885 B-7
Benton City, 3038 K-14
BENTON CO., 175177 J-13
Big Lake, 1835 C-7
Bingen, 712 M-9
Birch Bay, 8413 A-6
Black Diamond, 4151 G-8
Blaine, 4684 A-6
Bonney Lake, 17374 H-7
Bothell, 33505 *A-9
Bremerton, 37729 F-6
Brewster, 2370 D-13
Bridgeport, 2409 E-13
Brier, 6087 *A-8
Brinnon, 797 F-6
Browns Pt., 1950 *K-6
Bryant, 1870 D-7
Bryn Mawr, 1500 *G-9
Buckley, 4354 H-8
Buena, 990 J-12
Burbank, 3291 K-15
Burien, 33313 G-7
Burlington, 8388 C-7
Camano, 13347 D-7
Camas, 19355 M-7
Carbonado, 610 H-8
Carlsborg, 995 D-5
Carnation, 1786 F-8
Carson, 2279 M-8
Cascade Valley, 2246 H-14
Cascade Vista, 7800 *H-10
Cashmere, 3063 F-11
Castle Rock, 1982 K-5
Cathlamet, 532 K-4
Central Pk., 2685 H-4
Centralia, 16336 I-5
Chehalis, 7259 I-5
Chelan, 3890 E-13
CHELAN CO., 72453 E-11
Cheney, 10590 F-19
Chewelah, 2607 D-18
Chimacum, 800 E-6
CLALLAM CO., 71404 E-4
CLARK CO., 425363 M-7
Clarkston, 7229 J-20
Cle Elum, 1872 G-10
Clear Lake, 1419 H-7
Clear Lake, 1002 C-7
Clearview, 3324 E-8
Clinton, 928 E-7
Clyde Hill, 2984 *D-9
Colfax, 2805 I-19
College Pl., 8765 L-17
COLUMBIA CO., 4078 K-18
Colville, 4673 C-18
Concrete, 705 C-8
Connell, 4209 I-15
Cosmopolis, 1649 H-3
Coulee Dam, 1098 E-15
Country Homes, 5841 *A-2
Coupeville, 1831 D-6
Covington, 17575 G-8
COWLITZ CO., 102410 K-6
Dallesport, 1202 M-10
Darrington, 1347 D-9
Davenport, 1734 F-17
Dayton, 2526 K-18
Deer Pk., 3652 E-19
Des Moines, 29673 G-7
Desert Aire, 1626 I-13
DOUGLAS CO., 38431 F-13
DuPont, 8199 H-6
Duvall, 6695 F-8
E. Wenatchee, 13190 G-12
Eastgate, 4958 *E-10
Eastsound, 1100 B-6
Eatonville, 2758 I-7
Edgewood, 9387 *L-8
Edmonds, 39709 *A-7
Electric City, 968 E-15
Elk Plain, 14205 H-7
Ellensburg, 18174 H-11
Elma, 3107 H-4
Entiat, 1112 F-12
Enumclaw, 10669 G-8
Ephrata, 7664 G-14
Everett, 103019 E-7
Everson, 2481 A-7
Fairfield, 612 G-19
Fairwood, 19102 *H-10
Federal Way, 89306 G-7
Ferndale, 11415 B-6
FERRY CO., 7551 C-16
Fife, 9173 *L-7
Finley, 6012 K-15
Fircrest, 6497 *L-5
Fords Prairie, 1959 I-5
Forks, 3532 E-2
FRANKLIN CO., 78163 J-15
Freeland, 2045 E-7
Friday Hbr., 2162 C-5
GARFIELD CO., 2266 J-18
Garrett, 1419 K-17
Geneva, 2321 *F-3
Gig Hbr., 7126 G-6
Gleed, 2906 I-11
Gold Bar, 2075 E-9
Goldendale, 3407 L-11
Graham, 23491 H-7
Grand Coulee, 988 E-15
Grand Mound, 2981 I-5
Grandview, 10862 K-13
Granger, 3246 K-12
Granite Falls, 3364 D-8
GRANT CO., 89120 G-15
Grapeview, 954 G-6
Grayland, 953 I-3
GRAYS HARBOR CO., 72797 G-3
Hansville, 3091 E-7
Harrah, 625 J-11
Hobart, 6221 G-8
Hollywood, 800 *B-10
Hoquiam, 8726 H-3
Ilwaco, 936 K-3
ISLAND CO., 78506 D-6
Issaquah, 30434 F-8
JEFFERSON CO., 29872 F-4
Kalama, 2344 L-6
Kelso, 11925 K-5
Kenmore, 20460 *A-8
Kennewick, 73917 K-15
Kent, 92411 G-7
Kettle Falls, 1595 B-17
KING CO., 1931249 F-9
Kingsgate, 13065 *B-10
Kingston, 2099 E-7
Kirkland, 48787 *C-9
KITSAP CO., 251133 F-6
Kittitas, 1381 H-12
KITTITAS CO., 40915 H-11
KLICKITAT CO., 20318 L-12
La Center, 2800 L-6
La Conner, 891 C-7
Lacey, 42393 H-6
L. Forest Pk., 12598 *A-8
L. Stevens, 28069 E-8
Lakeland, 12000 *K-8
Lakeview Pk., 915 G-14
Lakewood, 58163 H-7
Leavenworth, 1965 F-11
LEWIS CO., 75455 I-6
Lexington, 800 K-6
LINCOLN CO., 10570 F-16
Lofall, 2289 E-6
Long Bch., 1392 J-3
Longbranch, 3784 G-6
Longview, 36648 K-5
Longview Hts., 3851 K-5
Loon Lake, 783 D-18
Lynden, 11951 A-7
Lynnwood, 35836 E-7
Mabton, 2286 K-13
Manchester, 5413 *F-5
Manson, 1468 E-12
Maple Valley, 22684 G-8
Maplewood Hts., 3300 *H-10
Marysville, 60020 D-7
MASON CO., 60699 H-5
Mattawa, 4437 I-13
McCleary, 1653 H-5
McKenna, 716 H-6
McMillin, 1547 H-7
Mead, 7275 E-19
Medical Lake, 5060 F-18
Medina, 2969 *D-9
Mercer Island, 22699 *E-9
Midland, 8962 *N-6
Mill Creek, 18244 E-7
Millwood, 1786 *B-4
Milton, 6968 *L-8
Monroe, 17304 E-8
Montesano, 3976 H-4
Morgan Acres, 1500 *B-3
Morton, 1126 J-7
Moses Lake, 20366 H-14
Mossyrock, 759 J-7
Mt. Pleasant, 1200 D-5
Mt. Vernon, 31743 C-7
Mountlake Ter., 19909 *A-8
Moxee City, 3308 J-12
Mukilteo, 20254 E-7
Naches, 795 I-11
Napavine, 1766 J-6
Neah Bay, 865 C-2
Newcastle, 10380 *F-10
Newport, 2126 D-20
Nooksack, 1338 A-7
Normandy Pk., 6335 *H-7
N. Bend, 5731 F-8
N. Bonneville, 956 M-8
N. Puyallup, 1743 *M-8
Oak Hbr., 22075 D-6
Oakville, 684 I-5
Ocean Pk., 1573 J-3
Ocean Shores, 5569 H-3
Odessa, 910 G-16
Okanogan, 2552 C-14
OKANOGAN CO., 41120 B-13
Olympia, 46478 H-6
Omak, 4845 C-14
Onalaska, 621 J-6
Orchards, 19556 M-6
Oroville, 1686 A-14
Orting, 6746 H-7
Othello, 7364 I-15
Pacific, 6606 *L-9
PACIFIC CO., 20920 J-4
Palouse, 998 H-20
Parkland, 35803 H-7
Parkwood, 7126 *F-4
Pasadena Pk., 1700 *B-4
Pasco, 59781 K-15
Pateros, 667 D-13
Pe Ell, 632 J-5
PEND OREILLE CO., 13001 B-19
Peshastin, 900 F-11
PIERCE CO., 795225 I-7
Pt. Roberts, 1314 A-5
Pomeroy, 1425 J-19
Port Angeles, 19038 D-4
Port Orchard, 11144 F-6
Port Townsend, 9113 D-6
Poulsbo, 9200 F-6
Prosser, 5714 K-13
Pullman, 29799 I-20
Purdy, 1544 G-6
Puyallup, 37022 H-7
Quincy, 6750 G-13
Rainier, 1794 I-6
Randle, 850 J-8
Ravensdale, 1101 G-8
Raymond, 2882 I-4
Redmond, 54144 *C-10
Renton, 90927 G-7
Republic, 1073 B-16
Richland, 48058 K-14
Ridgefield, 4763 L-6
Ritzville, 1673 H-17
Rochester, 2388 I-5
Rock Island, 788 G-12
Roslyn, 893 G-10
Roy, 793 H-6
Royal City, 2140 I-13
Ruston, 749 *K-5
Salmon Creek, 19686 M-6
Sammamish, 45780 F-8
SAN JUAN CO., 15769 C-5
Satsop, 675 H-4
Satus, 750 K-12
SeaTac, 26909 G-7
Seattle, 608660 F-7
Seaview, 650 J-3
Sedro-Woolley, 10540 C-7
Selah, 7147 I-11
Sequim, 6606 D-5
Shelton, 9834 G-5
Shoreline, 53007 *B-7
Silverdale, 19204 F-6
SKAGIT CO., 116901 C-8
SKAMANIA CO., 11066 L-8
Skokomish, 617 G-5
Skyway, 8500 *G-9
Smokey Pt., 1556 D-7
Snohomish, 9098 E-8
SNOHOMISH CO., 713335 E-9
Snoqualmie, 10670 F-8
Soap Lake, 1514 G-14
S. Bend, 1637 I-3
S. Hill, 52431 *N-8
S. Wenatchee, 1553 G-12
Southworth, 2185 *G-5
Spanaway, 27227 H-7
Spokane, 208916 F-19
SPOKANE CO., 471221 F-19
Spokane Valley, 89755 F-19
Stanwood, 6231 D-7
Steilacoom, 5985 H-6
STEVENS CO., 43531 D-18
Stevenson, 1465 M-8
Sudden Valley, 6441 B-7
Sultan, 4651 E-8
Sumas, 1307 A-7
Summit, 7985 *N-7
Sumner, 9451 G-7
Suncrest, 1500 E-18
Sunnyside, 15858 K-13
Sunnyslope, 3252 G-12
Tacoma, 198397 G-7
Taholah, 840 G-2
Tanglewilde, 5892 L-4
Tanner, 1018 G-8
Tekoa, 778 G-20
Tenino, 1695 I-6
Terrace Hts., 6937 M-16
THURSTON CO., 252264 I-6
Tieton, 1191 I-11
Toledo, 725 J-6
Tonasket, 1032 B-14
Toppenish, 8949 J-12
Town & Country, 4857 *A-2
Tukwila, 19107 *G-8
Tumwater, 17371 H-6
Twisp, 919 C-12
Union, 631 G-5
Union Gap, 6047 J-11
University Pl., 31144 G-7
Vader, 621 J-5
Vancouver, 161791 M-6
Vashon, 10624 G-7
Vashon Hts., 700 *G-6
WAHKIAKUM CO., 3978 J-4
Waitsburg, 1217 K-17
Walla Walla, 31731 K-17
WALLA WALLA CO., 58781 J-16
Wapato, 4997 J-12
Warden, 2692 H-15
Warm Bch., 2437 D-7
Washougal, 14095 M-7
Waterville, 1138 F-12
Wenatchee, 31925 G-12
W. Richland, 11811 K-14
Westport, 2099 H-3
WHATCOM CO., 201140 B-8
White Ctr., 13495 *F-7
White Salmon, 2224 M-9
White Swan, 793 J-11
WHITMAN CO., 44776 H-18
Wilbur, 884 E-16
Winlock, 1339 J-5
Wollochet, 6651 *L-4
Woodinville, 10938 *B-10
Woodland, 5509 L-6
Woodway, 1307 *A-7
Yacolt, 1566 L-7
Yakima, 91067 J-11
YAKIMA CO., 243231 J-12
Yarrow Pt., 1001 *D-9
Yelm, 6848 H-6
Zillah, 2964 J-12

West Virginia

Map p. 112

* City keyed to p. 46

Alderson, 1184 L-6
Alum Creek, 1749 J-3
Anmoore, 770 G-7
Ansted, 1404 J-5
Arthurdale, 1500 F-8
Athens, 1048 M-5
BARBOUR CO., 16589 G-8
Barboursville, 3964 I-2
Barrackville, 1302 F-7
Beaver, 1308 L-5
Beckley, 17614 L-4
Belington, 1921 G-8
Belle, 1260 J-4

Belmont, 903 F-4
Benwood, 1420 D-6
BERKELEY CO., 104169 B-9
Berkeley Sprs., 624 B-9
Bethany, 1036 C-6
Bethlehem, 2499 D-6
Beverly, 702 H-8
Blennerhassett, 3089 G-3
Bluefield, 10447 M-4
Bluewell, 2184 M-4
Boaz, 1297 F-4
Bolivar, 1045 C-10
BOONE CO., 24629 K-3
Bradley, 2040 K-4
BRAXTON CO., 14523 H-5
Bridgeport, 8149 G-7
BROOKE CO., 24069 C-6
Brookhaven, 5171 K-10
Buckhannon, 5639 H-7
Buffalo, 1236 I-2
Buffalo Creek, 900 C-4
Bunker Hill, 700 B-9
CABELL CO., 96319 I-2
CALHOUN CO., 7627 H-4
Cameron, 946 E-6
Cassville, 701 E-7
Cedar Grv., 997 J-4
Ceredo, 1450 C-3
Chapmanville, 1256 K-2
Charles Town, 5259 C-10
Charleston, 51400 J-3
Chattaroy, 756 L-2
Chesapeake, 1554 J-4
Chester, 2585 B-6
Chestnut Ridge, 800 J-10
Clarksburg, 16578 G-7
Clay, 491 I-5
CLAY CO., 9386 I-5
Clendenin, 1227 I-4
Coalwood, 700 M-3
Crab Orchard, 2678 L-4
Craigsville, 2213 J-6
Cross Lanes, 9995 I-3
Culloden, 3061 I-2
Daniels, 1881 L-5
Danville, 691 K-3
Davis, 660 G-9
Despard, 1004 G-7
DODDRIDGE CO., 8202 G-6
Dunbar, 7907 J-3
E. Bank, 959 J-4
Eleanor, 1518 I-3
Elizabeth, 823 G-4
Elkins, 7094 H-8
Elkview, 1222 I-4
Enterprise, 961 F-7
Evans, 700 H-3
Fairlea, 1747 L-6
Fairmont, 18704 F-7
Falling Waters, 876 B-10
FAYETTE CO., 46039 K-5
Fayetteville, 2892 K-5
Follansbee, 2986 C-6
Ft. Ashby, 1380 B-8
Ft. Gay, 705 J-1
Franklin, 721 I-9
Gary, 968 M-3
Gassaway, 908 I-6
GILMER CO., 8693 G-5
Glendale, 1526 D-6
Glenville, 1537 H-5
Grafton, 5164 F-8
GRANT CO., 11937 G-10
Grantsville, 561 H-5
Granville, 781 J-9
GREENBRIER CO., 35480 K-6
Hamlin, 1142 J-2
HAMPSHIRE CO., 23964 C-8
HANCOCK CO., 30676 C-6
HARDY CO., 14025 D-7
HARRISON CO., 69099 F-6
Harrisville, 1876 G-5
Harts, 656 K-2
Hinton, 2676 L-5
Holden, 876 K-2
Hometown, 668 I-3
Hooverson Hts., 2590 C-6
Huntington, 49138 I-1
Hurricane, 6284 I-2
Institute, 1800 J-3
Inwood, 2954 B-9
JACKSON CO., 29211 H-3
JEFFERSON CO., 53498 C-10
KANAWHA CO., 193063 J-4
Kenova, 3216 I-1
Keyser, 5439 B-7
Kingwood, 2939 F-8
Lavalette, 1073 J-1
Lesage, 1358 I-2
LEWIS CO., 16372 G-6
Lewisburg, 3830 L-6
LINCOLN CO., 21720 J-2
Logan, 1779 K-2
LOGAN CO., 36743 L-2
Lubeck, 1311 G-3
Lumberport, 876 F-7
Mabscott, 1408 L-4
Madison, 3076 K-3
Malden, 850 J-3
Mallory, 1654 L-3
Man, 759 L-3
Mannington, 2063 F-7
MARION CO., 56418 F-7
Marlinton, 1054 J-7
Marlowe, 700 B-10
Marmet, 1503 J-3
MARSHALL CO., 33107 E-6
Martinsburg, 17227 B-10
Maryland Jct., 977 *E-3
Mason, 968 G-2
MASON CO., 27324 I-2
MCDOWELL CO., 22113 M-3
McMechen, 1926 D-6
MERCER CO., 62264 M-4
Middlebourne, 815 F-5
Mill Creek, 724 H-8
Milton, 2423 I-2
MINERAL CO., 28212 B-7
MINGO CO., 26839 K-1
Monongah, 1044 F-7
MONONGALIA CO., 96189 E-7
MONROE CO., 13502 L-6
Montcalm, 726 M-4
Montgomery, 1638 J-4
Moorefield, 2544 C-7
MORGAN CO., 17541 B-9
Morgantown, 29660 E-8
Moundsville, 9318 D-6
Mt. Gay, 700 K-2
Mt. Hope, 1414 K-5
Mullens, 1559 L-4
New Cumberland, 1103 B-6
New Haven, 1560 H-2
New Manchester, 700 B-6
New Martinsville, 5366 E-5
Newell, 1376 B-6
NICHOLAS CO., 26233 J-5
Nitro, 7178 I-3
N. Hills, 832 F-4
Nutter Fort, 1593 G-7
Oak Hill, 7730 K-5
Oceana, 1394 L-3
OHIO CO., 44443 D-6
Paden City, 2633 E-5
Parkersburg, 31492 G-4
Parsons, 1485 G-8
PENDLETON CO., 7695 H-9
Pennsboro, 1171 G-5
Petersburg, 2467 H-10
Peterstown, 653 M-5
Philippi, 2966 G-8
Piedmont, 876 F-10
Pinch, 3262 I-4
Pineville, 668 L-3
Piney View, 989 K-5
Pleasant Valley, 3149 F-7
PLEASANTS CO., 7605 F-5
Poca, 974 I-3
POCAHONTAS CO., 8719 J-8
Pocatalico, 1500 I-3
Pt. Pleasant, 4350 H-2
PRESTON CO., 33520 F-8
Princeton, 6432 M-5
Prosperity, 1498 K-4
PUTNAM CO., 55486 I-3
Rainelle, 1505 K-6
RALEIGH CO., 78859 L-4
Rand, 1631 J-3
RANDOLPH CO., 29405 H-8
Ranson, 4440 C-10
Ravenswood, 3876 H-3
Richwood, 2051 J-6
Ridgeley, 675 B-7
Ripley, 3252 H-3
RITCHIE CO., 10449 G-4
Rivesville, 934 F-7
ROANE CO., 14926 H-4
Robinette, 663 L-3
Romney, 1848 B-8
Ronceverte, 1765 L-6
Rupert, 942 K-6
St. Albans, 11044 J-3
St. Marys, 1860 F-4
Salem, 1586 G-6
Scott Depot, 1500 I-3
Seth, 750 K-3
Shady Spr., 2998 L-5
Shepherdstown, 1734 B-10
Shinnston, 2201 F-7
Sissonville, 4028 I-3
Sistersville, 1396 F-5
Smithers, 813 J-4
Sophia, 1344 L-4
S. Charleston, 13450 J-3
Spencer, 2322 H-4
Spring Valley, 900 B-3
Star City, 1825 E-8
Stonewood, 1806 G-7
SUMMERS CO., 13927 L-5
Summersville, 3572 J-5
Sutton, 994 I-6
TAYLOR CO., 16895 F-8
Tennerton, 1800 H-7
Terra Alta, 1477 F-9
TUCKER CO., 7141 G-8
TYLER CO., 9208 F-5
Union, 565 L-6
Upper Falls, 3701 J-3
UPSHUR CO., 24254 H-7
Verdunville, 687 K-2
Vienna, 10749 F-4
War, 862 M-3
Washington, 1175 G-3
Wayne, 1413 J-1
WAYNE CO., 42481 J-1
WEBSTER CO., 9154 I-7
Webster Sprs., 776 I-7
Weirton, 19746 C-6
Welch, 2406 M-3
Wellsburg, 2805 C-6
W. Hamlin, 774 J-2
W. Liberty, 1542 D-6
W. Union, 825 G-6
Weston, 4110 G-6
Westover, 3983 E-8
WETZEL CO., 16583 F-6
Wheeling, 28486 D-6
White Sulphur Sprs., 2444 L-7
Williamson, 3191 L-2
Williamstown, 2908 F-4
Winfield, 2301 I-3
WIRT CO., 5717 G-4
WOOD CO., 86956 G-3
WYOMING CO., 23796 L-4

Wisconsin

Map pp. 114 – 115

† City keyed to p. 113

Abbotsford, 2310 H-7
Adams, 1967 K-8
ADAMS CO., 20875 K-9
Albany, 1018 O-9
Algoma, 3167 D-12
Allenton, 823 M-12
Allouez, 13975 S-3
Alma, 781 J-3
Altoona, 6706 H-5
Amery, 2902 G-2
Amherst, 1035 J-10
Antigo, 8234 G-10
Appleton, 72623 J-12
Arcadia, 2925 J-4
Arena, 834 N-8
Argyle, 857 O-8
Arlington, 819 M-9
Ashland, 8216 C-6
ASHLAND CO., 16157 D-6
Ashwaubenon, 16963 S-3
Athens, 1105 H-8
Augusta, 1550 I-5
Baldwin, 3957 H-2
Balsam Lake, 1009 F-2
Bangor, 1459 K-6
Baraboo, 12048 M-9
Barneveld, 1231 N-8
Barron, 3423 F-4
BARRON CO., 45870 F-3
BAYFIELD CO., 15014 B-5
Bayside, 4389 †C-6
Beaver Dam, 16214 M-11
Belgium, 2245 M-13
Belleville, 2385 O-9
Bellevue, 14570 J-13
Belmont, 986 O-7
Beloit, 36966 P-10
Benton, 973 P-7
Berlin, 5524 K-10
Big Bend, 1290 †I-1
Birnamwood, 818 H-10
Biron, 839 J-8
Black Creek, 1316 J-12
Black Earth, 1338 N-9
Black River Falls, 3622 J-6
Blair, 1366 J-5
Blanchardville, 825 O-8
Bloomer, 3539 G-4
Bloomfield, 3722 P-12
Blue Mounds, 855 N-8
Bonduel, 1478 I-12
Boscobel, 3231 N-6
Boyceville, 1086 H-3
Brandon, 879 L-11
Brillion, 3148 K-13
Bristol, 2584 P-13
Brodhead, 3293 P-9
Brookfield, 37920 N-12
Brooklyn, 1401 O-9
BROWN CO., 248007 D-11
Brown Deer, 11999 N-13
Buffalo City, 1023 J-4
BUFFALO CO., 13587 I-4
Burlington, 10464 O-12
BURNETT CO., 15457 E-2
Butler, 1841 †D-3
Butte des Morts, 962 K-11
Caddy Vista, 900 †J-6
Cadott, 1437 H-5
Caledonia, 24705 O-13
CALUMET CO., 48971 K-12
Cambridge, 1457 N-10
Cameron, 1783 F-4
Campbellsport, 2016 L-12
Cashton, 1102 L-6
Cassville, 947 O-6
Cedar Grv., 2113 M-13
Cedarburg, 11412 M-13
Centuria, 948 F-2
Chetek, 2221 G-4
Chilton, 3933 K-12
CHIPPEWA CO., 62415 G-5
Chippewa Falls, 13661 H-5
CLARK CO., 34690 I-6
Clear Lake, 1070 G-3
Cleveland, 1485 K-13
Clinton, 2154 P-11
Clintonville, 4559 I-11
Colby, 1852 H-7
Colfax, 1158 H-4
COLUMBIA CO., 56833 M-10
Columbus, 4991 M-10
Combined Locks, 3328 O-4
Cornell, 1467 G-5
Cottage Grv., 6192 N-10
Crandon, 1920 F-11
CRAWFORD CO., 16644 N-6
Crestview, 3500 O-13
Crivitz, 984 A-11
Cross Plains, 3538 N-9
Cuba City, 2086 P-7
Cudahy, 18267 O-13
Cumberland, 2170 F-3
Dane, 995 N-9
DANE CO., 488073 O-9
Darien, 1580 P-11
Darlington, 2451 P-8
De Forest, 8936 N-10
De Pere, 23800 J-13
Deerfield, 2319 N-10
Delafield, 7085 N-12
Delavan, 8463 P-11
Denmark, 2123 J-13
Dickeyville, 1061 P-6
DODGE CO., 88759 M-11
Dodgeville, 4693 O-8
DOOR CO., 27785 C-12
Dorchester, 876 H-7
DOUGLAS CO., 44159 C-3
Dousman, 2302 N-12
Dresser, 895 G-2
DUNN CO., 43857 G-4
Durand, 1931 I-3
Eagle, 1950 O-12
Eagle River, 1398 E-10
E. Troy, 4281 O-12
Eau Claire, 65883 H-4
EAU CLAIRE CO., 98736 H-5
Eden, 875 L-12
Edgar, 1479 H-8
Edgerton, 5461 O-10
Elk Mound, 878 H-4
Elkhart Lake, 967 L-13
Elkhorn, 10084 P-12
Ellsworth, 3284 I-2
Elm Grv., 5934 †E-3
Elmwood, 817 I-3
Elroy, 1442 L-7
Evansville, 5012 O-10
Fall Creek, 1315 I-5
Fall River, 1712 M-10
Fennimore, 2497 O-6
Fitchburg, 25260 N-9
Florence, 592 E-12
FLORENCE CO., 4423 E-11
Fond du Lac, 43021 L-12
FOND DU LAC CO., 101633 L-11
Fontana, 1672 P-11
Footville, 808 P-10
FOREST CO., 9304 F-11
Ft. Atkinson, 12368 O-11
Fountain City, 859 K-4
Fox Lake, 1519 M-11
Fox Pt., 6701 †C-6
Franklin, 35451 O-13
Franksville, 1789 †I-8
Frederic, 1137 F-2
Fredonia, 2160 M-13
French Island, 4410 †B-8
Friendship, 725 K-8
Galesville, 1481 K-5
Genoa City, 3042 P-12
Germantown, 19749 N-13
Gillett, 1386 H-12
Glendale, 12872 N-13
Glenwood City, 1242 H-3
Grafton, 11459 M-13
GRANT CO., 51208 O-6
Grantsburg, 1341 E-2
Green Bay, 104057 D-11
GREEN CO., 36842 O-9
Green Lake, 960 L-10
GREEN LAKE CO., 19051 K-10
Greendale, 14046 †G-5
Greenfield, 36720 O-13
Greenwood, 1026 I-7
Hales Cors., 7692 †G-4
Hammond, 1922 H-2
Hartford, 14223 M-12
Hartland, 9110 N-12
Hayward, 2318 D-5
Hazel Green, 1256 P-7
Hewitt, 828 I-8
Highland, 842 N-7
Hilbert, 1132 K-12
Hillsboro, 1417 L-7
Hingham, 886 L-13
Hobart, 6182 S-1
Holmen, 9005 K-5
Horicon, 3655 M-11
Hortonville, 2711 J-11
Howard, 17399 D-11
Howards Grv., 3188 L-13
Hudson, 12719 H-1
Hurley, 1547 C-8
Hustisford, 1123 M-11
Independence, 1336 J-5
Iola, 1301 I-10
IOWA CO., 23687 N-7
IRON CO., 5916 D-7
Iron Ridge, 929 M-11
Ixonia, 1624 N-11
Jackson, 6753 M-12
JACKSON CO., 20449 J-7
Janesville, 63575 P-10
Jefferson, 7973 N-11
JEFFERSON CO., 83686 N-11
Johnson Creek, 2738 N-11
Juneau, 2814 M-11
JUNEAU CO., 26664 K-7
Kaukauna, 15462 J-12
Kenosha, 99218 P-13
KENOSHA CO., 166426 P-13
Keshena, 1262 H-11
Kewaskum, 4004 M-12
Kewaunee, 2952 J-14
KEWAUNEE CO., 20574 C-12
Kiel, 3738 K-13
Kimberly, 6468 J-12
King, 1750 J-10
Kohler, 2120 L-13
Kronenwetter, 7210 H-9
La Crosse, 51320 L-5
LA CROSSE CO., 114638 L-5
Lac du Flambeau, 1969 E-8
Ladysmith, 3414 F-5
LAFAYETTE CO., 16836 P-7
L. Delton, 2914 L-8
L. Geneva, 7651 P-12
L. Mills, 5708 N-11
L. Nebagamon, 1069 C-4
L. Wissota, 2738 H-5
Lancaster, 3868 O-6
LANGLADE CO., 19977 G-10
Lannon, 1107 †C-2
LINCOLN CO., 28743 G-8
Little Chute, 10449 J-12
Lodi, 3050 M-9
Lomira, 2430 L-12
Lone Rock, 888 N-7
Loyal, 1261 I-7
Luck, 1119 F-2
Luxemburg, 2515 D-12
Madison, 233209 N-9
Manawa, 1371 J-11
Manitowoc, 33736 K-14
MANITOWOC CO., 81442 K-13
Maple Bluff, 1313 R-8
Marathon, 1524 H-8
MARATHON CO., 134063 H-9
Marinette, 10968 B-12
MARINETTE CO., 41749 A-11
Marion, 1260 I-11
Markesan, 1476 L-10
MARQUETTE CO., 15404 L-9
Marshall, 3862 N-10
Marshfield, 19118 I-8
Mauston, 4423 L-8
Mayville, 5154 M-11
Mazomanie, 1652 N-8
McFarland, 7808 N-10
Medford, 4326 G-7
Menasha, 17353 J-12
MENOMINEE CO., 4232 H-11
Menomonee Falls, 35626 N-13
Menomonie, 16264 H-3
Mequon, 23132 N-13
Merrill, 9661 G-9
Merton, 3346 N-12
Middleton, 17442 N-9
Milltown, 917 F-2
Milton, 5546 O-11
Milwaukee, 594833 N-13
MILWAUKEE CO., 947735 O-13
Mineral Pt., 2487 O-8
Mishicot, 1442 J-14
Mondovi, 2777 I-4
Monona, 7533 N-10
Monroe, 10827 P-9
MONROE CO., 44673 L-6
Montello, 1495 L-10
Monticello, 1217 O-9
Montreal, 807 C-7
Mosinee, 3988 I-9
Mt. Horeb, 7009 N-9
Mt. Pleasant, 26197 O-13
Mukwonago, 7355 O-12
Muscoda, 1299 N-7
Muskego, 24135 †H-2
Nashotah, 1395 N-12
Necedah, 916 K-8
Neenah, 25501 K-12
Neillsville, 2463 I-7
Nekoosa, 2580 J-8
New Berlin, 39584 N-13
New Glarus, 2172 O-9
New Holstein, 3236 K-13
New Lisbon, 2554 L-8
New London, 7295 J-11
New Richmond, 8375 G-2
Newburg, 1254 M-13
Niagara, 1624 E-13
N. Fond du Lac, 5014 L-12
N. Hudson, 3768 H-1
N. Prairie, 2141 O-12
Oak Creek, 34451 O-13
Oakfield, 1075 L-11
Oconomowoc, 15759 N-12
Oconto, 4513 C-11
OCONTO CO., 37660 B-11
Oconto Falls, 2891 H-12
Omro, 3517 K-11
Onalaska, 17736 L-5
Oneida, 1000 I-12
ONEIDA CO., 35998 E-9
Oostburg, 2887 L-13
Oregon, 9231 O-9
Orfordville, 1442 P-10
Osceola, 2568 G-2
Oshkosh, 66083 K-11
Osseo, 1701 I-5
OUTAGAMIE CO., 176695 J-11
Owen, 940 H-7
OZAUKEE CO., 86395 M-13
Paddock Lake, 2992 P-13
Palmyra, 1781 O-11
Pardeeville, 2115 M-10
Park Falls, 2462 E-7
Pepin, 837 J-3
PEPIN CO., 7469 I-4
Peshtigo, 3502 B-11
Pewaukee, 13195 N-12
Pewaukee, 8166 †D-1
Phelps, 900 D-10
Phillips, 1478 F-7
PIERCE CO., 41019 I-2
Pittsville, 874 J-8
Platteville, 11224 O-7
Pleasant Prairie, 19719 P-13
Plover, 12123 J-9
Plymouth, 8445 L-13
POLK CO., 44205 F-3
Port Edwards, 1818 J-8
Port Washington, 11250 M-13
Portage, 10324 M-9
PORTAGE CO., 70019 J-9
Poynette, 2528 M-9
Prairie du Chien, 5911 N-5
Prairie du Sac, 3972 N-9
Prescott, 4258 I-1
PRICE CO., 14159 F-7
Princeton, 1214 L-10
Pulaski, 3539 I-12
Racine, 78860 O-13
RACINE CO., 195408 O-13
Randolph, 1811 M-10
Random Lake, 1594 M-13
Redgranite, 2149 K-10
Reedsburg, 9200 M-8
Reedsville, 1206 K-13
Rhinelander, 7798 F-9
Rib Lake, 910 G-7
Rice Lake, 8438 F-4
Richfield, 11300 N-12
Richland Ctr., 5184 M-7
RICHLAND CO., 18021 M-7
Rio, 1059 M-10
Ripon, 7733 L-11
River Falls, 15000 H-2
River Hills, 1597 †C-5
Roberts, 1651 H-2
Rochester, 3682 O-12
ROCK CO., 160331 O-10
Rosendale, 1063 L-11
Rothschild, 5269 H-9
RUSK CO., 14755 F-5
ST. CROIX CO., 84345 H-2
St. Croix Falls, 2133 F-2
St. Francis, 9365 N-13
Salem, 1150 P-13
Sauk City, 3410 N-9
SAUK CO., 61976 M-8
Saukville, 4451 M-13
SAWYER CO., 16557 E-6
Schofield, 2169 H-9
Seymour, 3451 I-12
Sharon, 1605 P-11
Shawano, 9305 I-11
SHAWANO CO., 41949 H-10
Sheboygan, 49288 L-13
SHEBOYGAN CO., 115507 L-13
Sheboygan Falls, 7775 L-13
Shell Lake, 1347 E-3
Sherwood, 2713 K-12
Shiocton, 921 J-11
Shorewood, 13162 N-13
Shorewood Hills, 1565 S-7
Shullsburg, 1226 P-7
Silver Lake, 2411 P-12
Siren, 806 E-2
Sister Bay, 876 A-13
Slinger, 5068 M-12
Somerset, 2635 G-2
S. Milwaukee, 21156 O-13
Sparta, 9522 K-6
Spencer, 1925 I-7
Spooner, 2682 E-4
Spring Green, 1628 N-8
Spring Valley, 1352 H-3
Stanley, 3608 H-6
Stevens Pt., 26717 I-9
Stoughton, 12611 O-10
Stratford, 1578 H-8
Strum, 1114 I-5
Sturgeon Bay, 9144 C-13
Sturtevant, 6970 O-13
Suamico, 11346 D-11
Sun Prairie, 29364 N-10
Superior, 27244 B-3
Sussex, 10518 N-12
TAYLOR CO., 20689 G-7
Theresa, 1262 M-12
Thiensville, 3235 †A-5
Thorp, 1621 H-6
Tomah, 9093 K-7
Tomahawk, 3397 F-9
Trempealeau, 1529 K-5
TREMPEALEAU CO., 28816 J-5
Turtle Lake, 1050 F-3
Twin Lakes, 5989 P-12
Two Rivers, 11712 K-14
Union Grv., 4915 O-13
Valders, 962 K-13
VERNON CO., 29773 L-5
Verona, 10619 N-9
VILAS CO., 21430 D-9
Viroqua, 4362 M-6
Wales, 2549 N-12
Walworth, 2816 P-11
WALWORTH CO., 102228 O-11
Washburn, 2117 B-6
WASHBURN CO., 15911 E-4
WASHINGTON CO., 131887 M-12
Waterford, 5368 O-12
Waterloo, 3333 N-10
Watertown, 23861 N-11
Waukesha, 70718 N-12
WAUKESHA CO., 389891 O-12
Waunakee, 12097 N-9
Waupaca, 6069 J-10
WAUPACA CO., 52410 I-10
Waupun, 11340 L-11
Wausau, 39106 H-9
WAUSHARA CO., 24496 K-9
Wautoma, 2218 K-10
Wauwatosa, 46396 †E-4
W. Allis, 60411 †F-4
W. Baraboo, 1414 M-9
W. Bend, 31078 M-12
W. Milwaukee, 4206 †F-5
W. Salem, 4799 K-5
Westby, 2200 L-6
Westfield, 1254 L-9
Weston, 14868 H-9
Weyauwega, 1900 J-10
Whitefish Bay, 14110 N-13
Whitehall, 1558 J-5
Whitewater, 14390 O-11
Whiting, 1724 J-9
Williams Bay, 2564 P-12
Wind Lake, 5342 O-12
Wind Pt., 1723 O-13
Windsor, 3573 N-10
WINNEBAGO CO., 166994 K-11
Winneconne, 2383 K-11
Wisconsin Dells, 2678 L-9
Wisconsin Rapids, 18367 J-8
Wittenberg, 1081 H-10
Wonewoc, 816 L-7
WOOD CO., 74749 J-8
Woodruff, 966 E-9
Woodville, 1344 H-3
Wrightstown, 2827 J-12

Wyoming

Map p. 116

Afton, 1911 J-1
ALBANY CO., 36299 K-8
Alpine, 828 I-1
Arapahoe, 1656 J-4
Bar Nunn, 2213 J-7
Basin, 1285 G-5
BIG HORN CO., 11668 G-4
Buffalo, 4585 G-6
CAMPBELL CO., 46133 H-8
CARBON CO., 15885 L-6
Casper, 55316 J-7
Cheyenne, 59466 M-9
Cody, 9520 G-3
CONVERSE CO., 13833 I-8
CROOK CO., 7083 F-9
Douglas, 6120 J-8
Dubois, 971 I-3
Ethete, 1553 J-4
Evanston, 12359 M-1
Evansville, 2544 A-10
Ft. Washakie, 1759 J-4
FREMONT CO., 40123 J-5
Gillette, 29087 G-8
Glenrock, 2576 J-8
GOSHEN CO., 13249 K-10
Green River, 12515 L-3
Greybull, 1847 G-5
Guernsey, 1147 K-9
Hanna, 841 L-7
Hoback, 1176 I-1
HOT SPRINGS CO., 4812
Jackson, 9577
JOHNSON CO., 8569
Kemmerer, 2656
Lander, 7487
Laramie, 30816
LARAMIE CO., 91738
LINCOLN CO., 18106
Lovell, 2360
Lusk, 1567
Lyman, 2115
Marbleton, 1094
Mills, 3461
Moorcroft, 1009
Moose Wilson Road, 1821
NATRONA CO., 7545[...]
Newcastle, 3532
NIOBRARA CO., 248[...]
Orchard Valley, 800
PARK CO., 28205
Pine Bluffs, 1129
Pinedale, 2030
PLATTE CO., 8667
Powell, 6314
Ranchester, 855
Rawlins, 9259
Riverton, 10615
Rock Sprs., 23036
Saratoga, 1690
Sheridan, 17444
SHERIDAN CO., 291[...]
Sleepy Hollow, 1308
S. Greeley, 4217
S. Laramie, 1560
Star Valley Ranch, 150[...]
Story, 828
SUBLETTE CO., 1024[...]
Sundance, 1182
SWEETWATER CO., 43806
TETON CO., 21294
Thermopolis, 3009
Torrington, 6501
UINTA CO., 21118
Upton, 1100
Vista West, 951
WASHAKIE CO., 853[...]
WESTON CO., 7208
Wheatland, 3627
Wilson, 1482
Worland, 5487
Wright, 1807

Canada Cities and Towns

Populations are from latest available census or are Rand McNally estimates

Alberta

Map pp. 118 – 119

* City keyed to p. 117

Acme, 653 H-16
Airdrie, 42564 H-16
Alberta Bch., 865 E-15
Alix, 830 G-17
Athabasca, 2990 C-16
Banff, 7584 I-15
Barnwell, 771 K-18
Barrhead, 4432 D-15
Bashaw, 873 F-17
Bassano, 1282 I-18
Beaverlodge, 2365 C-11
Beiseker, 785 H-16
Bentley, 1073 G-16
Black Diamond, 2373 I-16
Blackfalds, 6300 G-16
Bon Accord, 1488 E-16
Bonnyville, 6216 D-19
Bow Island, 2025 J-19
Bowden, 1241 G-16
Boyle, 916 C-17
Bragg Creek, 595 I-16
Brooks, 13676 I-18
Bruderheim, 1155 E-17
Calgary, 1096833 I-16
Calmar, 1970 E-16
Camrose, 17286 F-17
Canmore, 12288 I-15
Carbon, 592 H-17
Cardston, 3580 K-17
Caroline, 501 G-15
Carseland, 568 I-17
Carstairs, 3442 H-16
Castor, 932 G-18
Claresholm, 3758 J-17
Clive, 675 G-16
Clyde, 503 D-16
Coaldale, 7493 K-18
Cochrane, 17580 I-16
Cold Lake, 13839 C-19
Consort, 689 G-19
Coronation, 947 G-18
Crossfield, 2853 H-16
Crowsnest Pass, 5565 K-16
Daysland, 807 F-17
Delburne, 830 G-17
Devon, 6510 E-16
Didsbury, 4957 H-16
Drayton Valley, 7049 F-15
Drumheller, 8029 H-17
Duchess, 992 I-18
Dunmore, 502 J-19
Eckville, 1125 G-16
Edmonton, 812201 E-16
Edson, 8475 E-14
Elk Pt., 1412 D-18
Evansburg, 880 E-15
Falher, 1075 B-13
Foremost, 526 K-19
Forestburg, 831 F-18
Ft. Macleod, 3117 K-17
Ft. McMurray, 61374 *E-4
Ft. Saskatchewan, 19051 E-16
Ft. Vermillion, 727 *E-4
Fox Creek, 1969 D-13
Gibbons, 3030 E-16
Gift Lake, 662 B-14
Grande Cache, 4319 E-11
Grande Prairie, 55032 C-11
Grassy Lake, 649 J-18
Hanna, 2673 H-18
Hardisty, 639 F-18
High Level, 3641 *E-4
High Prairie, 2600 B-13
High River, 12920 I-16
Hinton, 9640 E-13
Hythe, 820 C-11
Innisfail, 7876 G-16
Irricana, 1162 H-16
Jasper, 4051 F-12
Kikino, 959 C-17
Killam, 981 F-18
Kitscoty, 846 E-19
Lac La Biche, 2544 C-17
Lacombe, 11707 G-16
L. Louise, 500 H-14
Lamont, 1753 E-17
Leduc, 24279 E-16
Legal, 1225 D-16
Lethbridge, 83517 K-17
Linden, 725 H-16
Lloydminster, 18032 E-19
Magrath, 2217 K-17
Manning, 1164 *E-4
Mannville, 803 E-18
Marwayne, 612 E-19
Mayerthorpe, 1398 D-15
McLennan, 809 B-13
Medicine Hat, 60005 J-19
Milk River, 811 K-18
Millet, 2092 F-16
Morinville, 8569 E-16
Mundare, 855 E-17
Nanton, 2132 J-16
Nobleford, 1000 J-17
Okotoks, 24511 I-16
Olds, 8235 H-16
Onoway, 1039 E-16
Oyen, 973 H-19
Penhold, 2375 G-16
Picture Butte, 1650 J-17
Pincher Creek, 3685 K-16
Ponoka, 6773 F-16
Provost, 2041 F-19
Rainbow Lake, 870 *D-4
Raymond, 3743 K-18
Red Deer, 90564 G-16
Redcliff, 5588 J-19
Redwater, 1915 D-16
Rimbey, 2378 F-16
Rocky Mountain House, 6933 G-15
Rycroft, 628 B-11
St. Albert, 61466 E-16
St. Paul, 5400 D-18
Sedgewick, 857 F-18
Sexsmith, 2418 B-11
Sherwood Pk., 61660 E-16
Slave Lake, 6782 B-15
Smoky Lake, 1022 D-17
Spirit River, 1025 B-11
Spruce Grove, 26171 E-16
Stavely, 505 J-16
Stettler, 5748 G-17
Stirling, 1090 K-18
Stony Plain, 15051 E-16
Strathmore, 12305 I-17
Sundre, 2610 H-15
Swan Hills, 1465 C-14
Sylvan Lake, 12327 G-16
Taber, 8104 J-18
Thorsby, 797 E-16
Three Hills, 3198 H-17
Tofield, 2182 E-17
Trochu, 1072 H-17
Turner Valley, 2167 I-16
Two Hills, 1379 E-18
Valleyview, 1761 C-13
Vauxhall, 1288 J-18
Vegreville, 5717 E-18
Vermilion, 3930 E-19
Viking, 1041 E-18
Vulcan, 1836 J-17
Wabamun, 661 E-15
Wabasca-Desmarais, 1569 A-16
Wainwright, 5925 F-19
Warburg, 789 F-16
Wembley, 1383 C-11
Westlock, 4823 D-16
Wetaskiwin, 12525 F-16
Whitecourt, 9605 D-14

British Columbia

Map pp. 118 – 119

* City keyed to p. 117

100 Mile House, 1886 H-9
150 Mile House, 1172 G-9
Abbotsford, 133497 L-8
Armstrong, 4815 J-11
Ashcroft, 1628 I-9
Barriere, 1773 I-10
Bella Bella, 1095 G-3
Black Creek, 1900 K-5
Bowser, 1613 K-6
Burnaby, 223218 L-3
Burns Lake, 2029 D-5
Cache Creek, 1040 I-9
Campbell River, 31186 J-5
Canal Flats, 685 J-14
Cassidy, 971 L-7
Castlegar, 7816 L-13
Cawston, 1015 L-11
Chase, 2495 I-11
Chemainus, 3035 L-7
Cherryville, 614 J-12
Chetwynd, 2635 B-9
Chilliwack, 77936 L-8
Christina Lake, 1168 L-12
Clearwater, 2331 H-10
Clinton, 636 I-9
Cobble Hill, 637 L-7
Coldstream, 10314 J-11
Comox, 13627 K-5
Coombs, 1547 K-6
Coquitlam, 126456 L-4
Courtenay, 24099 K-5
Cranbrook, 19319 K-15
Creston, 5306 L-14
Crofton, 1092 L-7
Cumberland, 3398 K-6
Dawson Creek, 11583 B-10
Delta, 99863 M-2
Duncan, 4932 L-7
Elkford, 2523 J-15
Enderby, 2932 J-11
Erickson, 520 L-14
Esquimalt, 16209 M-7
Falkland, 805 J-11
Fanny Bay, 815 K-6
Fernie, 4448 K-15
Ft. Nelson, 3902 *D-3
Ft. St. James, 1691 D-7
Fraser Lake, 1167 D-6
Fruitvale, 2016 L-13
Gibsons, 4437 K-7
Gold River, 1267 K-4
Golden, 3701 I-13
Grand Forks, 3985 L-12
Greenwood, 708 L-12
Grindrod, 1453 J-11
Hagensborg, 600 G-4
Harrison Hot Sprs., 1468 L-9
Heriot Bay, 527 J-5
Hope, 5969 K-9
Houston, 3147 D-4
Hudson's Hope, 970 A-9
Invermere, 2955 J-14
Kaleden, 1224 K-11
Kamloops, 85678 J-10
Kaslo, 1026 K-13
Kelowna, 117312 K-11
Keremeos, 1330 L-11
Kimberley, 6652 K-14
Kitimat, 8335 D-3
Ladysmith, 7921 L-7
L. Country, 11708 J-11
L. Cowichan, 2974 L-6
Langley, 25081 L-8
Lantzville, 764 L-6
Lillooet, 2322 I-8
Lions Bay, 1318 K-7
Logan Lake, 2073 J-10
Lower Nicola, 1068 J-10
Lumby, 1731 J-11
Mackenzie, 3507 B-8
Malakwa, 596 I-12
Maple Ridge, 76052 M-5
McBride, 586 F-10
Merritt, 7113 J-10
Midway, 674 L-12
Mission, 36426 L-8
Montrose, 1030 L-13
Mount Currie, 1306 J-8
Nakusp, 1569 J-12
Nanaimo, 83810 L-6
Naramata, 1647 K-11
Nelson, 10230 K-13
New Denver, 504 K-13
New Hazelton, 666 B-4
New Westminster, 65976 M-3
N. Vancouver, 48196 L-7
Oak Bay, 18015 M-7
Okanagan Falls, 1100 L-11
Oliver, 4824 L-11
Osoyoos, 4845 L-11
Parksville, 11977 K-6
Peachland, 5200 K-11
Pemberton, 2369 J-8
Penticton, 32877 K-11
Pitt Meadows, 17736 M-5
Port Alberni, 17743 L-6
Port Alice, 805 J-3
Port Coquitlam, 56342 L-4
Port Edward, 544 D-1
Port Hardy, 4008 I-3
Port McNeill, 2505 I-4
Port Moody, 32975 L-3
Pouce Coupe, 738 B-10
Powell River, 13165 K-6
Prince George, 71974 E-8
Prince Rupert, 12508 C-1
Princeton, 2724 K-10
Qualicum Bch., 8687 K-6
Quesnel, 10007 F-8
Radium Hot Sprs., 777 I-14
Revelstoke, 7139 I-12
Richmond, 190473 L-7
Rossland, 3556 L-13
Royston, 1562 K-6
Saanich, 109752 A-1
Salmo, 1139 L-13
Salmon Arm, 17464 J-11
Savona, 540 I-10
Sechelt, 9291 K-7
Sicamous, 2441 I-11
Sidney, 11178 L-7
Smithers, 5404 C-4
Sointula, 576 I-4
Sooke, 11435 M-7
Sorrento, 1255 I-11
Sparwood, 3667 K-15
Squamish, 17158 K-7
Summerland, 11280 K-11
Surrey, 468251 L-8
Telkwa, 1350 C-4
Terrace, 11486 C-3
Tofino, 1876 L-5
Trail, 7681 L-13
Tumbler Ridge, 2710 C-10
Ucluelet, 1627 L-5
Union Bay, 1156 K-6
Valemount, 1020 F-11
Vancouver, 603502 L-7
Vanderhoof, 4480 D-7
Vernon, 38150 J-11
Victoria, 80017 M-7
W. Vancouver, 42694 K-1
Westbank, 3359 K-11
Whistler, 9824 J-8
White Rock, 19339 L-8
Williams Lake, 10832 G-8
Windermere, 1019 J-14
Wynndel, 870 L-14
Youbou, 966 L-6

Manitoba

Map p. 121

* City keyed to p. 117

Altona, 4088 M-16
Arborg, 1152 J-17
Beausejour, 3126 K-17
Boissevain, 1572 M-13
Brandon, 46061 L-13
Carberry, 1669 L-14
Carman, 3027 L-16
Dauphin, 8251 I-13
Deloraine, 977 M-13
Flin Flon, 5363 C-11
Gilbert Plains, 811 I-13
Gillam, 1281 *F-7
Gimli, 1890 J-17
Gladstone, 879 K-15
Grandview, 859 I-13
Hamiota, 868 K-13
Headingley, 3215 C-16
Ile des Chenes, 1253 L-17
Killarney, 2197 M-14
La Broquerie, 1073 L-18
Lac du Bonnet, 1328 K-18
LaSalle, 1957 L-17
Lockport, 790 K-17
MacGregor, 963 L-15
Manitou, 808 M-15
Melita, 1069 M-12
Minnedosa, 2587 K-14
Morden, 7812 M-16
Morris, 1797 M-17
Neepawa, 3629 K-14
Niverville, 3540 L-17
Pinawa, 1444 K-18
Plum Coulee, 843 M-16
Portage la Prairie, 12996 K-15
Rivers, 1189 K-13
Roblin, 1774 I-12
Russell, 1669 J-12
St. Laurent, 1450 K-16
St. Malo, 1148 M-17
St-Pierre-Jolys, 1099 L-17
Ste. Anne, 1626 L-17
Ste. Rose du Lac, 1023 J-14
Sanford, 852 L-16
Selkirk, 9834 K-17
Snow Lake, 723 C-13
Souris, 1837 L-13
Steinbach, 13524 L-17
Stonewall, 4536 K-16
Stony Mountain, 1696 K-17
Swan River, 3907 H-12
Teulon, 1124 K-17
The Pas, 5513 E-12
Thompson, 12829 A-15
Tyndall, 830 K-17
Virden, 3114 L-12
Warren, 798 K-16
Winkler, 10670 M-16
Winnipeg, 663617 L-17
Winnipeg Bch., 1011 J-17

New Brunswick

Map pp. 126 – 127

Aldouane, 868 F-7
Atholville, 1237 C-4
Baie-Ste-Anne, 1387 E-7
Balmoral, 1719 C-5
Bas-Caraquet, 1380 D-7
Bathurst, 12275 D-6
Belledune, 1548 C-6
Beresford, 4351 D-6
Bertrand, 1137 D-7
Blacks Hbr., 982 J-4
Blackville, 990 F-6
Bouctouche, 2423 G-8
Brantville, 966 E-7
Burtts Corner, 910 H-4
Campbellton, 7385 C-4
Cap-Pelé, 2256 G-8
Caraquet, 4169 D-7
Charlo, 1324 C-5
Chipman, 1236 G-6
Clair, 857 E-1
Dalhousie, 3512 C-5
Dieppe, 23310 H-8
Doaktown, 793 F-5
Dorchester, 1167 H-8
Drummond, 775 E-3
Edmundston, 16032 D-2
Eel River Crossing, 1209 C-5
Florenceville, 860 G-3
Fredericton, 56224 H-4
Fredericton Jct., 752 I-4
Geary, 1080 H-5
Grand Bay-Westfield, 5117 I-5
Grand Falls (Grand-Sault), 5706 E-3
Grande-Digue, 2182 G-8
Hampton, 4292 I-6
Hardwicke, 2329 E-7
Hartland, 947 G-3
Havelock, 1158 H-7
Hillsborough, 1350 H-8
Kedgwick, 993 D-3
Keswick Ridge, 1526 H-4
Kingsclear, 7391 H-4
Lamèque, 1432 D-8
Lepreau, 752 J-4
Maugerville, 1776 H-5
McAdam, 1284 I-3
Memramcook, 4831 H-8
Minto, 2505 H-5
Miramichi, 17811 E-6
Moncton, 69074 H-7
Musquash, 1200 J-5
Nackawic, 1049 H-3
Nauwigewauk, 1539 I-6
Neguac, 1678 E-7
New Bandon, 1195 G-5
New Maryland, 4232 H-4
Nicholas Denys, 873 D-6
Nigadoo, 952 D-6
Norton, 1301 I-6
Notre-Dame, 790 G-8
Oromocto, 8932 H-5
Pennfield, 2218 J-4
Perth-Andover, 1778 F-3
Petit Rocher, 1908 D-6
Petitcodiac, 1429 H-7
Plaster Rock, 1135 F-3
Pointe-Verte, 976 C-6
Quispamsis, 17886 I-5
Rexton, 818 F-7
Richibucto, 1286 F-7
Riverview, 19128 H-7
Robertville, 895 D-6
Rogersville, 1170 F-6
Rothesay, 11947 I-5
Rusagonis, 990 H-4
Sackville, 5558 H-8
St. Andrews, 1889 J-4
St. George, 1543 J-4
Saint John, 70063 J-5
St. Stephen, 4817 J-3
St-Antoine, 1770 G-7
St-Charles, 1982 F-7
St-Jacques, 1599 D-2
St-Joseph, 2171 H-8
St-Louis de Kent, 930 F-7
St-Paul, 866 G-7
St-Quentin, 2095 D-3
Ste-Anne-de-Madawaska, 1002 E-2
Salisbury, 2208 H-7
Scoudoc, 996 H-8
Shediac, 6053 G-8
Shippagan, 5032 D-8
Springfield, 1652 I-6
Sussex, 4312 H-6
Sussex Corner, 1495 I-6
Tabusintac, 833 E-7
Tide Head, 1036 C-4
Tracadie-Sheila, 4933 D-7
Upham, 1306 I-6
Val-Comeau, 800 D-7
Wilsons Bch., 930 J-4
Woodstock, 5254 G-3

Newfoundland & Labrador

Map p. 127

Arnold's Cove, 990 E-19
Badger, 793 D-18
Baie Verte, 1370 C-18
Bay Roberts, 5818 E-20
Bishop's Falls, 3341 D-18
Bonavista, 3589 D-20
Botwood, 3008 D-18
Brigus, 750 F-20
Burgeo, 1464 F-17
Burin, 2424 F-18
Carbonear, 4739 E-20
Carmanville, 737 D-19
Catalina, 990 E-20
Centreville-Wareham-Trinity, 1161 D-19
Channel-Port aux Basques, 4170 F-16
Clarenville, 6036 E-19
Corner Brook, 19886 D-16
Deer Lake, 4995 D-17
Dunville, 2853 F-19
Fortune, 1442 F-18
Gambo, 1984 D-19
Gander, 11054 D-19
Glenwood, 791 D-18
Glovertown, 2122 D-19
Goulds, 4525 F-20
Grand Bank, 2415 F-18
Grand Falls-Windsor, 13725 D-18
Harbour Breton, 1711 F-18
Harbour Grace, 3131 E-20
Hare Bay, 1031 D-19
Holyrood, 1995 F-20
La Scie, 899 C-18
Lewisporte, 3483 D-18
Marystown, 5506 F-18
Mount Moriah, 785 D-16
Mount Pearl, 24284 F-20
Musgrave Hbr., 969 D-19
New-Wes-Valley, 2265 D-19
Pasadena, 3352 D-17
Peterview, 809 D-18
Placentia, 3643 F-19
Port au Choix, 839 B-17
Pouch Cove, 1866 E-20
Robert's Arm, 807 D-18
Rocky Hbr., 979 D-16
Roddickton, 910 B-18
St. Alban's, 1233 E-18
St. Anthony, 2418 B-18
St. George's, 1207 E-16
St. John's, 106172 F-20
St. Lawrence, 1244 F-18
Springdale, 2907 D-18
Stephenville, 6719 E-16
Stephenville Crossing, 1875 E-16
Torbay, 7397 E-20
Twillingate, 2269 C-19
Wabana, 2346 E-20
Whitbourne, 916 F-19
Witless Bay, 1179 F-20

Northwest Territories

Map p. 117

Ft. MacPherson, 792 B-3
Ft. Simpson, 1238 D-4
Ft. Smith, 2093 D-5
Hay River, 3606 D-4
Inuvik, 3463 A-3
Yellowknife, 19234 D-5

Nova Scotia

Map pp. 126 – 127

Amherst, 9717 H-8
Antigonish, 4524 I-12
Arcadia, 770 M-5
Argyle, 8252 M-5
Arichat, 890 I-14
Aylesford, 892 J-7
Baddeck, 769 H-14
Barrington, 6994 N-6
Bear River, 880 K-6
Berwick, 2454 J-7
Bridgetown, 949 K-7
Bridgewater, 8241 L-8
Brookfield, 529 J-10
Brooklyn, 970 M-8
Brooklyn, 970 J-9
Canning, 761 J-8
Canso, 806 I-14
Centreville, 1073 J-8
Chester, 10599 K-8
Chéticamp, 980 F-14
Clark's Harbour, 820 N-6
Digby, 2152 K-6
Donkin, 573 G-16
Fall River, 1887 K-9
Falmouth, 1213 J-8
Glace Bay, 19076 G-16
Halifax, 390096 K-9
Hantsport, 1159 J-8
Hebron, 720 M-5
Hilden, 1720 J-10
Ingonish, 610 F-15
Inverness, 1387 G-13
Kentville, 6094 J-8
Kingston-Greenwood, 6595 J-7
Lakeside, 520 K-9
Lawrencetown, 625 K-7
Liverpool, 2653 M-7
Lockeport, 588 M-7
Louisbourg, 946 H-16
Lower W. Pubnico, 850 N-6
Lunenburg, 2313 L-8
Mahone Bay, 943 L-8
Meteghan, 980 L-5
Meteghan River, 550 L-5
Middle Musquodoboit, 720 J-10
Middleton, 1749 J-7
Milford Sta., 510 J-10
Milton, 1091 M-7
Mulgrave, 794 I-13
Musquodoboit Hbr., 890 K-10
New Glasgow, 9562 I-11
New Waterford, 8942 G-15
Oxford, 1151 I-9
Parrsboro, 1305 I-8
Pictou, 3437 I-11
Pomquet, 510 I-12
Port Hawkesbury, 3366 I-13
Port Hood, 840 H-13
Port Maitland, 500 M-5
Port Morien, 580 G-16
Pugwash, 744 H-9
River Hebert, 545 I-8
St. Peters, 730 I-14
Saulnierville, 540 L-5
Sheet Hbr., 830 J-11
Shelburne, 1686 M-6
Shubenacadie, 780 J-10
Springhill, 3868 I-9
Stellarton, 4485 I-11
Stewiacke, 1438 J-10
Sydney, 97398 G-15
Sydney Mines, 14135 G-15
Tatamagouche, 752 I-10
Terence Bay, 780 L-9
Three Mile Plains, 1300 J-9
Trenton, 2616 I-11
Truro, 12059 I-10
Waterville, 931 J-8
Waverley, 806 K-9
Wedgeport, 1180 M-5
Western Shore, 890 K-8
Westville, 3798 I-11
Windsor, 3785 J-8
Wolfville, 4269 J-8
Yarmouth, 6761 M-5

Nunavut

Map p. 117

Arviat, 2318 E-7
Ikaluktutiak (Cambridge Bay), 1608 B-6
Iqaluit, 6699 C-10
Kangiqsiniq (Rankin Inlet), 2266 D-7
Mittimatalik (Pond Inlet), 1549 B-8
Qamani-tuaq (Baker Lake), 1872 D-7

Ontario

Map pp. 122 – 123

Ailsa Craig, 1070 K-6
Ajax, 109600 I-11
Alban, 919 C-8
Alexandria, 3209 E-19
Alfred, 1530 D-18
Alliston, 15379 H-9
Almonte, 4752 E-16
Alvinston, 1040 K-6
Amherstburg, 21556 M-3
Amherstview, 6100 H-15
Angus, 8603 H-9
Arkona, 579 K-6
Arnprior, 8114 E-16
Arthur, 2421 I-8
Athens, 3118 G-16
Atikokan, 2787 L-14
Atwood, 880 I-7
Aurora, 53203 I-10
Avonmore, 560 E-18
Aylmer, 7151 L-7
Ayr, 4380 J-8
Ayton, 600 H-7
Bancroft, 3880 F-13
Barrie, 135711 H-10
Barry's Bay, 1262 E-13
Bath, 1040 H-15
Bayfield, 1023 J-6
Beachville, 880 D-15
Beaverton, 2915 G-11
Belle River, 4890 M-4
Belleville, 49454 H-14
Belmont, 1849 K-7
Bethany, 600 H-12
Bewdley, 830 H-12
Blenheim, 4563 M-5
Blind River, 3549 C-4
Bloomfield, 597 I-14
Blyth, 1005 I-6
Bobcaygeon, 3533 G-12
Bolton, 25954 I-9
Bonfield, 2016 C-11
Bothwell, 912 L-6
Bourget, 1060 E-18
Bowmanville, 43555 I-11
Bracebridge, 15409 F-10
Bradford, 22378 H-10
Brampton, 523911 I-9
Brantford, 93650 K-9
Breslau, 2415 A-16
Bridgenorth, 2167 H-12
Brighton, 10928 H-13
Brockville, 21870 G-17
Bruce Mines, 566 C-2
Brussels, 1157 I-7
Burford, 1952 K-8
Burk's Falls, 967 D-10
Burlington, 175779 J-9
Cache Bay, 643 C-9
Caesarea, 785 H-11
Caledon, 59460 I-9
Caledonia, 9999 K-9
Callander, 3864 C-10
Cambridge, 126748 J-8
Campbellford, 3493 H-13
Cannington, 1916 H-11
Capreol, 3276 B-7
Cardinal, 1690 F-17
Carleton Place, 9809 F-16
Casselman, 3626 E-18
Cayuga, 1622 K-9
Chalk River, 954 C-14
Chapleau, 2116 M-18
Chatham, 44074 M-5
Chatsworth, 6437 G-7
Chesley, 2015 H-7
Chesterville, 1514 F-18
Clifford, 790 I-7
Clinton, 3114 I-6
Cobalt, 1133 M-20
Cobden, 990 D-15
Cobourg, 18519 I-12
Cochrane, 5340 L-20
Colborne, 2068 I-13
Colchester, 2145 N-4
Coldwater, 1250 G-10
Collingwood, 19241 G-9
Conestogo, 1316 J-8
Cookstown, 1328 H-10
Cornwall, 46340 F-18
Cottam, 720 M-4
Courtland, 920 K-8
Creemore, 1222 H-9
Crysler, 560 E-18
Crystal Bch., 7421 K-11
Deep River, 4193 C-13
Deseronto, 1835 H-14
Drayton, 1880 I-8
Dresden, 2446 L-5
Dryden, 7617 K-13
Dundalk, 1988 H-8
Dunnville, 5789 K-10
Durham, 2823 H-8
Dutton, 1442 L-6
Eganville, 1226 E-14
Elliot Lake, 11348 B-4
Elmira, 9931 J-8
Elmvale, 2369 G-9
Elora, 3800 I-8
Embrun, 6380 E-17
Emo, 1252 L-13
Englehart, 1519 M-20
Enniskillen, 2930 H-11
Erin, 10770 I-9
Espanola, 5364 C-6
Essex, 19600 M-4
Everett, 870 H-9
Exeter, 4785 J-6
Fenelon Falls, 2040 G-11
Fergus, 19126 I-8
Forest, 2876 K-5
Ft. Erie, 29960 K-11
Ft. Frances, 7952 L-13
Foxboro, 1150 H-14
Frankford, 2507 H-13
Fullarton, 1660 J-7
Gananoque, 5194 H-16
Georgetown, 40150 I-9
Geraldton, 1893 K-16
Glencoe, 2086 L-6
Goderich, 7521 I-6
Gooderham, 500 F-12
Gore Bay, 850 D-5
Grafton, 1130 I-13
Grand Bend, 2102 J-6
Grand Valley, 1481 I-8
Gravenhurst, 11640 F-10
Green-bank, 567 H-11
Grimsby, 25325 K-10
Guelph, 121688 J-9
Haileybury, 9988 M-20
Haliburton, 1430 F-12
Hamilton, 519949 J-9
Hampton, 763 I-11
Hanover, 7490 H-7
Harley, 539 K-8
Harriston, 1981 I-7
Harrow, 2713 M-4
Harrowsmith, 700 G-15
Hastings, 1139 H-13
Havelock, 1265 G-13
Hawkesbury, 10551 D-19
Hearst, 5090 K-18
Hensall, 1173 J-6
Hepworth, 530 G-7
Hillsburgh, 1065 I-9
Hornepayne, 1050 L-18
Huntsville, 19056 E-10
Ignace, 1202 L-14
Ilderton, 680 K-6
Ingersoll, 12146 K-7
Ingleside, 1890 F-18
Iron Bridge, 632 C-3
Iroquois, 1139 F-17
Iroquois Falls, 4595 L-20
Kanata, 101760 E-16
Kapuskasing, 8196 L-19
Kearney, 841 E-10
Keene, 550 H-12
Kemptville, 3532 F-17
Kenora, 15348 K-12
Killaloe, 629 E-14
Killarney, 505 D-6
Kincardine, 11174 H-6
Kingston, 123363 H-15
Kingsville, 21362 M-4
Kirkland Lake, 8133 M-20
Kitchener, 219153 J-8
Komoka, 1532 K-6
L'Orignal, 2068 D-18
Lakefield, 2758 G-12
Lanark, 696 F-16
Lancaster, 730 E-19
Lappe, 1360 L-15
Larder Lake, 684 M-20
Leamington, 28403 M-4
Limoges, 1240 E-18
Lindsay, 20354 H-11
Lion's Head, 514 F-7
Listowel, 6867 I-7
Little Current, 1523 D-6
London, 366151 K-7
Long Sault, 1230 F-18
Longlac, 1388 K-17
Lucan, 2076 K-6
Lucknow, 1105 I-6
MacTier, 630 F-9
Madoc, 2197 G-14
Magnetawan, 1454 D-10
Mallorytown, 510 G-16
Manitouwadge, 2105 L-17
Marathon, 3353 L-17
Markdale, 1325 H-8
Markham, 301709 I-10
Marmora, 1483 G-13
Martintown, 530 E-18
Massey, 1040 C-5
Matheson, 980 L-20
Mattawa, 2023 C-11
Mattice, 690 K-18
Maxville, 811 E-18
McKellar, 1144 E-9
Meaford, 11100 G-8
Merlin, 720 M-5
Merrickville, 1030 F-17
Metcalfe, 1763 E-17
Midland, 16572 G-9
Mildmay, 1183 H-7
Millbrook, 1632 H-12
Milton, 84362 J-9
Milverton, 1519 J-7
Minden, 1110 F-11
Mississauga, 713443 J-10
Mitchell, 4448 J-7
Monkton, 540 J-7
Moonbeam, 1101 L-19
Moose Creek, 890 E-18
Morrisburg, 2756 F-18
Mount Albert, 3915 H-10
Mount Brydges, 2332 K-6
Mount Forest, 4757 I-8
Napanee, 15511 H-15
Navan, 760 E-17
Neustadt, 533 H-7
New Dundee, 1219 J-8
New Hamburg, 11953 J-8
New Liskeard, 4910 M-20
Newmarket, 79978 H-10
Newtonville, 549 I-12
Niagara Falls, 82997 K-11
Niagara-on-the-Lake, 15400 J-11
Nipigon, 1631 L-16
Nobleton, 3582 I-10
N. Bay, 53651 C-10
N. Gower, 1250 F-17
Norwich, 10721 K-8
Norwood, 1254 H-13
Nottawa, 530 G-9
Oakville, 182520 J-10
Oakwood, 740 H-11
Odessa, 1160 H-15
Oil Sprs., 704 L-5
Omemee, 1247 H-12
Orangeville, 27975 I-9
Orillia, 30586 G-10
Oshawa, 149607 I-11
Ottawa, 883391 E-17
Otterville, 820 K-8
Owen Sound, 21688 G-7
Paisley, 1003 H-7
Palmerston, 2599 I-7
Paris, 11763 K-8
Parkhill, 1885 K-6
Parry Sound, 6191 E-9
Pembroke, 14360 D-14
Penetanguishene, 9111 G-9
Perth, 5840 F-16
Petawawa, 15988 D-14
Peterborough, 78698 H-12
Petrolia, 5528 K-5
Pickering, 88721 I-11
Picton, 4487 H-14
Plantagenet, 1055 D-18
Port Burwell, 860 L-8
Port Colborne, 18424 K-10
Port Elgin, 7555 G-7
Port Hope, 16214 I-12
Port Lambton, 1350 L-4
Port McNicoll, 1790 G-9
Port Perry, 8981 H-11
Port Rowan, 850 L-8
Port Stanley, 2229 L-7
Powassan, 3378 C-10
Prescott, 4284 G-17
Queensville, 640 H-10
Rainy River, 842 L-12
Red Rock, 942 L-16
Renfrew, 8218 E-15
Richmond, 3797 E-16
Richmond Hill, 185541 I-10
Ridgetown, 3117 L-5
Ripley, 640 H-6
Rockland, 11099 E-17
Rockwood, 3869 J-9
Rodney, 1023 L-6
Russell, 15247 E-17
St. Catharines, 131400 K-10
St. Clements, 1261 J-8
St. George, 3124 J-9
St. Isidore, 752 E-18
St. Jacobs, 1891 J-8
St. Joseph, 1201 J-6
St. Marys, 6655 J-7
St. Thomas, 37905 L-7
Sarnia, 72366 K-5
Sault Ste. Marie, 75141 B-1
Schomberg, 590 I-10
Schreiber, 1126 L-16
Scotland, 600 K-8
Seaforth, 2627 J-6
Sebringville, 690 J-7
Seeleys Bay, 550 G-16
Sharbot Lake, 530 G-15
Shelburne, 5846 H-9
Simcoe, 14777 K-8
Smiths Falls, 8978 F-16
Smooth Rock Falls, 1376 L-19
Sombra, 710 L-4
S. River, 1049 D-10
Southampton, 3440 G-7
Spanish, 696 C-5
Spencerville, 550 F-17
Springfield, 763 K-7
Stayner, 4126 G-9
Stoney Pt., 1424 M-4
Stouffville, 24886 I-10
Straffordville, 910 L-8
Stratford, 30886 J-7
Strathroy, 14221 K-6
Sturgeon Falls, 6672 C-9
Sudbury, 160274 B-7
Sunderland, 1110 H-11
Sundridge, 985 D-10
Sutton, 5938 H-10
Sydenham, 900 G-15
Tamworth, 730 G-14
Tara, 1037 G-7
Tavistock, 2784 J-7
Tecumseh, 23610 M-4
Teeswater, 1011 I-7
Temagami, 820 M-20
Terrace Bay, 1471 L-16
Thamesford, 1990 K-7
Thamesville, 928 L-5
Thedford, 804 K-6
Thessalon, 1279 C-3
Thornbury, 2253 G-8
Thornton, 1001 H-10
Thorold, 17931 K-11
Thunder Bay, 108359 L-15
Tilbury, 4700 M-4
Tillsonburg, 15301 K-8
Timmins, 43165 L-19
Tiverton, 705 H-6
Toronto, 2615060 I-10
Trenton, 19370 H-13
Trout Creek, 552 D-10
Tweed, 6057 G-14
Uxbridge, 20623 H-11
Vankleek Hill, 1833 D-19
Vaughan, 288301 E-2
Vermilion Bay, 560 K-13
Verner, 1080 B-9
Verona, 1120 G-15
Victoria Hbr., 1550 G-9
Vienna, 733 L-8
Virginiatown, 780 M-20
Wainfleet, 6356 K-10
Walkerton, 4967 H-7
Wallaceburg, 10163 L-5
Warkworth, 640 H-13
Warwick, 3717 K-5
Wasaga Bch., 17537 G-9
Waterloo, 98780 J-8
Watford, 1592 K-6
Wawa, 2975 M-18
Welland, 50631 K-10
Wellesley, 10713 J-8
Wellington, 1860 I-14
W. Lorne, 1415 L-6
Westport, 628 G-16
Wheatley, 2925 M-4
Whitby, 122022 I-11
White River, 607 L-17
Whitestone, 918 D-9
Whitney, 770 E-12
Wiarton, 2291 G-7
Williamsburg, 550 F-18
Winchester, 2482 F-17
Windsor, 210891 M-3
Wingham, 2875 I-7
Woodstock, 37754 K-8
Woodville, 857 H-11
Wyoming, 2333 K-5
Yarker, 580 H-15
Zurich, 865 J-6

Prince Edward Island

Map pp. 126 – 127

Alberton, 1135 F-9
Borden-Carleton, 750 G-9
Charlottetown, 34562 G-10
Cornwall, 5162 G-10
Georgetown, 675 G-11
Kensington, 1496 G-9
Miscouche, 869 G-9
Montague, 1895 G-11
N. Rustico, 583 G-10
O'Leary, 812 F-8
Souris, 1173 G-12
Stratford, 8574 G-10
Summerside, 14751 G-9
Tignish, 779 F-9

Québec

Map pp. 124 – 125

* City keyed to p. 117

Acton Vale, 7664 L-9
Albanel, 2293 F-10
Alma, 30904 G-11
Amos, 12671 F-2
Amqui, 6322 G-16
Arundel, 604 L-7
Asbestos, 7096 L-10
Audet, 724 L-12
Aumond, 725 K-5
Baie-Comeau, 22113 F-15
Baie-des-Sables, 609 G-16
Baie-St-Paul, 7332 I-12
Barraute, 1980 G-3
Beauceville, 6354 K-12
Beaumont, 2420 J-12
Beaupré, 3439 J-12
Bécancour, 12438 K-10
Bedford, 2684 M-9
Bégin, 868 G-11
Berry, 625 F-2
Blainville, 53510 L-8
Blue Sea, 674 K-5
Bois-des-Filion, 9485 B-11
Bonaventure, 2775 H-19
Boucherville, 40753 C-14
Bromont, 7649 M-9
Brossard, 79273 E-14
Bryson, 647 L-4
Cacouna, 1939 H-13
Calumet, 551 L-7
Campbell's Bay, 775 L-4
Candiac, 19876 F-13
Cap-Chat, 2623 F-17
Caplan, 2039 H-18
Carignan, 7966 I-9
Carleton-sur-Mer, 3991 H-18
Cascapédia-St-Jules, 741 G-18
Causapscal, 2458 G-16
Chambord, 1773 G-10
Chandler, 7703 G-20
Chapais, 1610 D-7
Charlemagne, 5853 A-14
Chénéville, 792 L-6
Chibougamau, 7541 D-7
Chisasibi, 2659 *F-9
Chute-aux-Outardes, 1644 F-15
Chute-St-Philippe, 892 J-6
Châteauguay, 45904 M-8
Clermont, 3118 F-1
Cloridorme, 743 F-19
Coaticook, 9255 M-10
Colombier, 747 F-14
Contrecoeur, 6252 L-9
Cookshire-Eaton, 5171 M-11
Cowansville, 12489 M-9
Dégelis, 3051 I-15
Desbiens, 1053 G-10
Disraeli, 2502 L-11
Dolbeau-Mistassini, 14384 F-10
Donnacona, 6283 J-11
Dorval, 18208 E-11
Dosquet, 887 K-11
Drummondville, 71852 L-10
Dudswell, 1771 M-11
Dunham, 3471 M-9
Duparquet, 657 F-1
Dupuy, 930 F-1
E. Angus, 3741 M-11
E. Broughton, 2229 K-11
Escuminac, 588 H-17
Ferme-Neuve, 2822 J-6
Fermont, 2874 *F-11
Forestville, 3270 F-14
Fort-Coulonge, 1377 L-4
Frelighsburg, 1094 N-9
Gaspé, 15163 F-20
Gatineau, 265349 M-5
Gesgapegiag, 688 G-18
Girardville, 1100 F-10
Gracefield, 2355 K-5
Granby, 63433 M-9
Grand-Remous, 1168 J-5
Grande-Rivière, 3456 G-20
Grande-Vallée, 1137 E-19
Grenville-sur-la-Rouge, 2746 L-7
Ham-Nord, 832 L-11
Hampstead, 7153 E-12
Havre-St-Pierre, 3418 *F-12
Hébertville, 2441 G-11
Huntingdon, 2457 M-7
Joliette, 19621 L-8
Kamouraska, 589 I-13
Kazabazua, 847 L-5
Kiamika, 772 K-6
L'Ancienne-Lorette, 16745 B-4
L'Anse-St-Jean, 1208 G-13
L'Ascension, 844 K-6
L'Ascension-de-Notre-Seigneur, 1983 G-11
L'Isle-Verte, 1469 H-14
L'Islet, 3999 J-12
La Conception, 1287 K-7
La Doré, 1453 G-9
La Guadeloupe, 1787 L-12
La Macaza, 1053 K-7
La Malbaie, 8862 I-13
La Patrie, 749 M-11
La Pocatière, 4266 I-13
La Prairie, 23357 F-14
La Sarre, 7719 F-1
La Tuque, 11227 I-9
Labelle, 2445 K-7
Lac-au-Saumon, 1453 G-16
Lac-aux-Sables, 1373 J-10
Lac-Bouchette, 1174 G-10
Lac-Brome, 5609 M-9
Lac-des-Écorces, 2713 K-6
Lac-des-Aigles, 551 H-15
Lac-Mégantic, 5932 M-12
Lachute, 12551 L-7
Lamarche, 557 F-11
Lambton, 1584 L-11
Larouche, 1277 G-11
Laval, 401553 D-11
Le Bic, 1286 G-14
Lebel-sur-Quévillon, 2159 F-4
Les Éboulements, 1328 I-12
Les Escoumins, 2000 G-14
Les Méchins, 1107 F-17
Lévis, 138769 J-11
Longueuil, 231409 D-14
Lorrainville, 1272 I-1
Louiseville, 7517 K-9
Low, 920 L-5
Luceville, 1362 G-15
Lyster, 1628 K-11
Macamic, 2734 F-1
Magog, 25358 M-10
Malartic, 3449 G-2
Maliotenam, 1316 D-18
Maniwaki, 3930 K-5
Maria, 2536 G-18
Mascouche, 42491 A-12
Matagami, 1526 D-3
Matane, 14462 F-16
Matapédia, 664 H-17
Messines, 1608 K-5
Métabetchouan-Lac-à-la-Croix, 4097 G-10
Moisie, 930 D-18
Mont-Joli, 6665 G-15
Mont-Laurier, 13779 K-6
Mont-Royal, 19503 D-12
Mont-St-Michel, 633 J-6
Mont-Tremblant, 9494 K-7
Montebello, 978 L-6
Montmagny, 11491 J-12
Montréal, 1649519 M-8
Montréal-Ouest, 5085 E-12
Morin-Heights, 3925 L-7
Murdochville, 764 F-19
Namur, 596 L-6
Nantes, 1374 L-11
New Carlisle, 1358 H-19
New Richmond, 3810 G-18
Nicolet, 7828 K-9
Nominingue, 2019 K-6
Normandin, 3137 F-10
Normétal, 856 E-1
Notre-Dame-de-la-Merci, 978 K-7
Notre-Dame-de-la-Paix, 718 L-6
Notre-Dame-de-la-Salette, 757 L-5
Notre-Dame-du-Laus, 1518 K-5
Notre-Dame-du-Nord, 1075 H-1
Nouvelle, 1689 H-18
Ormstown, 3595 M-7
Otter Lake, 1109 L-4
Packington, 595 I-14
Palmarolle, 1465 F-1
Papineauville, 2165 L-6
Paspébiac, 3198 H-19
Percé, 3312 G-20
Petit-Saguenay, 727 H-13
Pierreville, 2176 L-9
Plaisance, 1103 L-6
Plessisville, 6688 K-10
Pohénégamook, 2770 I-14
Pointe-aux-Outardes, 1330 F-15
Pointe-Lebel, 1973 F-15
Pointe-à-la-Croix, 1472 H-17
Port-Cartier, 6651 D-17
Port-Daniel-Gascons, 2453 G-19
Portneuf, 3107 J-10
Portneuf-sur-Mer, 761 G-14
Price, 1673 G-15
Princeville, 5693 K-10
Québec, 516622 J-11
Quyon, 790 L-4
Racine, 1252 M-10
Ragueneau, 1405 F-15
Repentigny, 82000 A-14
Richmond, 3275 L-10
Rimouski, 46860 G-15
Ripon, 1522 L-6
Rivière-Beaudette, 1885 M-7
Rivière-Bleue, 1299 I-14
Rivière-du-Loup, 19447 H-13
Rivière-Héva, 1433 G-2
Rivière-Ouelle, 1058 I-13
Rivière-Pentecôte, 620 D-16
Rivière-Rouge, 4645 K-6
Rivière-à-Pierre, 671 J-10
Roberval, 10227 G-10
Rock Island, 901 N-10
Rouyn-Noranda, 41012 G-1
Sacré-Coeur, 1881 H-13
Saguenay, 144746 G-11
St-Aimé-des-Lacs, 1073 I-12
St-Alexandre-de-Kamouraska, 2050 I-13
St-Alexis-de-Matapédia, 548 H-17
St-Alexis-des-Monts, 3046 K-9
St-Alphonse-Rodriguez, 3134 K-8
St-Ambroise, 3546 G-11
St-André, 651 I-13
St-Anselme, 3458 K-12
St-Antonin, 4027 H-14
St-Arsène, 1253 H-14
St-Aubert, 1409 J-13
St-Bruno, 2636 G-11
St-Côme, 2198 K-8
St-Côme-Linière, 3274 L-12
St-Camille-de-Lellis, 844 K-13
St-Casimir, 1500 J-10
St-Charles-de-Bourget, 690 G-11
St-Clet, 1738 M-7
St-Cyprien, 1163 H-14
St-Cyprien, 548 K-13
St-Cyrille-de-Lessard, 753 J-12
St-Damase-de-L'Islet, 591 I-13
St-Damien, 2020 K-8
St-Damien-de-Buckland, 2071 K-12
St-David, 832 L-9
St-David-de-Falardeau, 2657 G-11
St-Donat, 4130 K-7
St-Donat, 890 G-15
St-Eustache, 44154 M-8
St-Eusèbe, 614 I-14
St-Fabien, 1906 G-14
St-Fabien-de-Panet, 992 K-13
St-Faustin-Lac-Carré, 3467 K-7
St-Félicien, 10278 G-10
St-Félix-d'Otis, 801 G-12
St-Ferdinand, 2067 L-11
St-Ferréol-les-Neiges, 2964 J-12
St-Fidèle, 920 H-13
St-François-d'Assise, 706 H-17
St-François-de-Sales, 654 G-10
St-Frédéric, 1085 K-12
St-Gabriel, 2844 K-8
St-Gabriel, 1180 G-15
St-Gabriel-de-Valcartier, 2933 J-11
St-Gédéon, 2001 G-11
St-Gédéon-de-Beauce, 2277 L-12
St-Georges, 31173 L-12
St-Gervais, 2058 J-12
St-Hilarion, 1181 I-12
St-Honoré, 5257 G-11
St-Honoré-de-Témiscouata, 780 I-14
St-Hyacinthe, 53236 L-9
St-Irénée, 674 I-13
St-Jacques, 4021 L-8
St-Jean-de-Dieu, 1606 H-14
St-Jean-Port-Joli, 3304 I-13
St-Jean-sur-Richelieu, 92394 M-8
St-Jérôme, 68456 L-7
St-Joseph-de-Beauce, 4722 K-12
St-Jovite, 4869 K-7
St-Just-de-Bretenières, 709 K-13
St-Lambert, 21555 E-1
St-Lambert-de-Lauzon, 6177 K-11
St-Léon-le-Grand, 992 G-16
St-Louis-de-Gonzague, 1389 K-12
St-Louis-du-Ha! Ha!, 1318 I-14
St-Ludger, 1255 L-12
St-Marc-de-Figuery, 771 G-3
St-Martin, 2462 L-12
St-Mathieu-de-Rioux, 678 H-14
St-Michel-des-Saints, 2201 J-8
St-Michel-du-Squatec, 1171 H-15
St-Modeste, 1128 H-14
St-Narcisse-de-Rimouski, 1017 G-15
St-Nazaire, 2114 G-11
St-Onésime-d'Ixworth, 559 I-13
St-Pacôme, 1658 I-13
St-Pamphile, 2685 J-13
St-Pascal, 3490 I-13
St-Paul-de-Montminy, 824 J-12
St-Paul-du-Nord, 710 G-14
St-Philémon, 742 J-12
St-Prime, 2758 G-10
St-Prosper, 3605 K-12
St-Raphaël, 2463 J-12
St-Raymond, 9615 J-10
St-Rémi, 7265 M-8
St-René-de-Matane, 1089 G-16
St-Robert-Bellarmin, 676 L-12
St-Roch-des-Aulnaies, 967 I-13
St-Sébastien, 697 L-12
St-Siméon, 1300 H-19
St-Siméon, 1179 H-13
St-Thomas-Didyme, 677 F-9
St-Tite, 3880 J-9
St-Tite-des-Caps, 1506 J-12
St-Ulric, 1642 F-16
St-Urbain, 1474 I-12
St-Valérien, 893 G-15
St-Vallier, 1046 J-12
St-Victor, 2451 K-12
St-Zénon, 1115 K-8
Ste-Agathe-des-Monts, 10115 L-7
Ste-Angèle-de-Mérici, 999 G-15
Ste-Anne-de-Beaupré, 2854 J-12
Ste-Anne-des-Monts, 6933 F-17
Ste-Anne-du-Lac, 619 J-6
Ste-Aurélie, 910 K-12
Ste-Barbe, 1403 M-7
Ste-Catherine, 16762 F-13
Ste-Croix, 2352 K-11
Ste-Émélie-de-l'Énergie, 1644 K-8
Ste-Félicité, 1175 F-16
Ste-Flavie, 919 G-15
Ste-Hedwidge, 824 G-10
Ste-Hélène, 911 I-13
Ste-Jeanne-d'Arc, 1089 F-10
Ste-Justine, 1845 K-12
Ste-Louise, 704 I-13
Ste-Luce, 2851 G-15
Ste-Marie, 12889 K-11
Ste-Monique, 865 F-10
Ste-Perpétue, 1774 J-13
Ste-Pétronille, 1041 B-6
Ste-Rose-de-Watford, 787 K-12
Ste-Sabine, 1120 K-12
Ste-Sophie, 13375 L-8
Salaberry-de-Valleyfield, 40077 M-7
Sawyerville, 805 M-11
Sayabec, 1864 G-16
Senneterre, 2953 G-4
Sept-Îles, 25686 D-17
Shannon, 5086 J-11
Shawinigan, 50060 K-9
Shawville, 1664 L-4
Sherbrooke, 154601 M-10
Sorel-Tracy, 34600 L-9
Stanstead, 2857 N-10
Stornoway, 559 L-11
Stratford, 1062 L-11
Tadoussac, 813 H-13
Taschereau, 981 F-2
Témiscaming, 2385 J-1
Témiscouata-sur-le-Lac, 5096 I-14
Terrebonne, 106322 B-12
Thetford Mines, 25709 L-11
Thurso, 2455 L-6
Trois-Pistoles, 3456 H-14
Trois-Rivières, 131338 K-9
Val-Barrette, 588 K-6
Val-d'Or, 31862 G-3
Val-des-Bois, 938 L-5
Vallée-Jonction, 1940 K-12
Varennes, 20994 L-8
Victoriaville, 43462 L-10
Ville-Marie, 2595 I-1
Wakefield, 610 L-5
Warwick, 4766 L-10
Waskaganish, 1955 *G-10
Waswanipi, 1777 D-5
Waterloo, 4330 M-9
Weedon, 2683 L-11
Wemindji, 1378 *G-9
Westmount, 19931 E-12
Windsor, 5367 M-10
Wotton, 1453 L-10

Saskatchewan

Map pp. 120 – [...]

* City keyed to p. 117

Assiniboia, 2418
Balgonie, 1625
Battleford, 4065
Beauval, 756
Bienfait, 780
Biggar, 2161
Birch Hills, 1064
Buffalo Narrows, 1153
Candle Lake, 765
Canora, 2219
Carlyle, 1441
Carnduff, 1126
Caronport, 1068
Carrot River, 1000
Creighton, 1498
Cudworth, 770
Cumberland House, 772
Dalmeny, 1702
Davidson, 1025
Delisle, 975
Deschambault Lake, 900
Esterhazy, 2472
Estevan, 11054
Eston, 1031
Foam Lake, 1148
Ft. Qu'Appelle, 2034
Gravelbourg, 1116
Grenfell, 1049
Gull Lake, 989
Hague, 878
Herbert, 759
Hudson Bay, 1477
Humboldt, 5678
Indian Head, 1815
Kamsack, 1825
Kelvington, 864
Kerrobert, 1061
Kindersley, 4678
Kipling, 1051
La Loche, 2611
La Ronge, 2304
Langenburg, 1148
Langham, 1290
Lanigan, 1390
Lashburn, 967
Leader, 821
Lloydminster, 9772
Lumsden, 1631
Macklin, 1415
Maidstone, 1156
Maple Creek, 2176
Martensville, 7716
Meadow Lake, 5045
Melfort, 5576
Melville, 4517
Moose Jaw, 33274
Moosomin, 2485
Nipawin, 4265
N. Battleford, 13888
Osler, 1088
Outlook, 2204
Oxbow, 1285
Pelican Narrows, 790
Pilot Butte, 1848
Porcupine Plain, 855
Preeceville, 1070
Prince Albert, 35129
Radville, 860
Redvers, 975
Regina, 193100
Regina Bch., 1081
Rocanville, 857
Rosetown, 2317
Rosthern, 1572
Sandy Bay, 1233
Saskatoon, 222189
Shaunavon, 1756
Shellbrook, 1433
Southey, 778
Spiritwood, 916
Swift Current, 15503
Tisdale, 3180
Unity, 2389
Wadena, 1306
Wakaw, 985
Waldheim, 1035
Warman, 7084
Watrous, 1857
Watson, 777
Weyburn, 10484
White City, 1894
Whitewood, 950
Wilkie, 1301
Wolseley, 864
Wynyard, 1767
Yorkton, 15669

Yukon

Map p. 117

Carmacks, 503
Dawson, 1319
Haines Jct., 593
Watson Lake, 802
Whitehorse, 23272

Mexico Cities and Towns (map p. 128)

Populations are from 2010 Mexican Census or are Rand McNally estimates

Aguascalientes

Aguascalientes, 722250 F-7
Rincón de Romos, 27988 F-7

Baja California

Ensenada, 279765 A-1
Lázaro Cárdenas, 16294 B-1
Mexicali, 689775 A-2
Rosarito, 65278 C-2
San Felipe, 16702 A-2
Tecate, 64764 A-1
Tijuana, 1300983 A-1

Baja California Sur

Cabo San Lucas, 68463 E-3
Guerrero Negro, 13054 C-2
La Paz, 215178 E-3
San Jose del Cabo, 69788 E-4

Campeche

Campeche, 220389 G-12
Champotón, 30881 G-12
Ciudad del Carmen, 169466 H-12
Escárcega, 29477 G-12

Chiapas

Chiapa de Corzo, 45077 H-11
Cintalapa, 42467 H-11
Comitán de Domínguez, 97537 I-12
Huixtla, 32033 I-11
Ocosingo, 41878 H-12
Palenque, 42947 H-12
San Cristóbal de las Casas, 158027 H-11
Tapachula, 202672 I-11
Tonalá, 35322 I-11
Villaflores, 39180 I-11
Tuxtla Gutiérrez, 537102 H-11

Chihuahua

Chihuahua, 809232 C-5
Ciudad Juárez, 1321004 A-5
Cuauhtémoc, 114007 C-5
Delicias, 118071 C-6
Hidalgo del Parral, 104836 D-5
Jiménez, 34281 D-6
Madera, 15447 C-4
Nuevo Casas Grandes, 55553 B-5
Ojinaga, 22744 B-6
Santa Rosalía de Camargo, 40221 C-6

Coahuila

Ciudad Acuña, 134233 C-7
Matamoros, 52233 D-6
Melchor Múzquiz, 35060 C-7
Monclova, 215271 D-7
Nueva Rosita, 38158 C-7
Piedras Negras, 150178 C-8
Sabinas, 54905 C-7
Saltillo, 709671 D-7
San Pedro, 48746 D-7
Torreón, 608836 D-6

Colima

Colima, 137383 G-6
Manzanillo, 130035 G-6
Tecomán, 85689 H-6
Villa de Álvarez, 117600 G-6

Distrito Federal

Ciudad de México (Mexico City), 8851080 G-8
Mexico City, 8851080 G-8

Durango

Ciudad Lerdo, 79669 D-6
Durango, 518709 E-6
El Salto, 24241 E-6
Gómez Palacio, 257352 D-6
Santiago Papasquiaro, 26121 E-6

Guanajuato

Acámbaro, 57972 G-8
Celaya, 340387 G-8
Dolores Hidalgo, 59240 F-7
Guanajuato, 72237 F-7
Irapuato, 380941 G-7
León, 1238962 F-7
Moroleón, 43200 G-7
Pénjamo, 40070 G-7
Salamanca, 160169 G-7
Salvatierra, 37203 G-7
San Felipe, 28452 F-7
Silao, 74242 G-7

Guerrero

Acapulco, 673479 H-8
Chilapa de Álvarez, 31157 H-8
Chilpancingo, 187251 H-8
Ciudad Altamirano, 25168 H-8
Iguala, 118468 H-8
Ometepec, 24120 I-9
Petatlán, 21659 H-7
Taxco, 52217 H-8
Tlapa de Comonfort, 46975 H-9
Zihuatanejo, 67408 H-7

Hidalgo

Apan, 26642 G-9
Ixmiquilpan, 34814 G-8
Pachuca, 256584 G-8
Tulancingo, 102406 G-9
Zacualtipán, 23125 G-8

Jalisco

Ameca, 36150 G-6
Arandas, 52175 G-7
Autlán, 45382 G-6
Cihuatlán, 18164 G-6
Ciudad Guzmán, 97750 G-6
Guadalajara, 1495182 G-6
Lagos de Moreno, 98206 F-7
Ocotlán, 83769 G-7
Puerto Vallarta, 203342 G-6
Sayula, 26789 G-6
Tecalitlán, 12411 G-6
Teocaltiche, 23726 F-7
Tepatitlán, 91959 G-7
Tequila, 29203 G-6
Zapopan, 1142483 G-6

México

Amecameca, 31687 G-8
Buenavista, 206081 F-2
Chalco, 168720 I-4
Chimalhuacán, 612383 G-4
Ciudad López Mateos, 489160 F-1
Ciudad Nezahualcóyotl, 1024585 G-3
Coacalco, 277959 F-2
Ecatepec de Morelos, 1655015 F-3
Ixtapaluca, 322271 H-4
Los Reyes Acaquilpan, 85359 H-4
Naucalpan, 792211 G-1
Tepexpan, 102667 F-4
Texcoco, 105165 G-4
Tlalnepantla, 653410 F-2
Toluca, 489333 G-8
Xico, 356352 I-4

Michoacán

Apatzingán de la Constitución, 99010 G-7
Ciudad Hidalgo, 60542 G-8
Ciudad Lázaro Cárdenas, 79200 H-7
La Piedad de Cabadas, 83323 G-7
Los Reyes de Salgado, 39209 G-7
Morelia, 597511 G-7
Pátzcuaro, 52298 G-7
Sahuayo, 64431 G-7
Tacámbaro, 25665 G-7
Uruapan, 264439 G-7
Zacapu, 52806 G-7
Zamora, 141627 G-7
Zitácuaro, 84307 G-8

Morelos

Cuautla, 154358 H-8
Cuernavaca, 338650 G-8

Nayarit

Acaponeta, 19140 F-5
Compostela, 17573 F-6
Ixtlán del Río, 23303 F-6
Tepic, 332863 F-6
Tuxpan, 21709 F-5

Nuevo León

Allende, 26065 D-8
Anáhuac, 16628 D-8
Cadereyta Jiménez, 68111 D-8
Cerralvo, 7169 D-8
China, 8997 D-8
Guadalupe, 673616 D-8
Linares, 63104 E-8
Montemorelos, 45108 D-8
Monterrey, 1135512 D-8
Sabinas Hidalgo, 33068 D-8
Santiago, 36840 D-8

Oaxaca

Huajuapan de León, 53043 H-9
Juchitán de Zaragoza, 74825 I-10
Matías Romero, 18944 H-10
Miahuatlán de Porfirio Diaz, 23940 I-9
Oaxaca, 255029 H-9
Puerto Escondido, 25902 I-9
Salina Cruz, 76596 I-10
San Pedro Pochutla, 13685 I-10
Santiago Pinotepa Nacional, 29604 I-9
Santo Domingo Tehuantepec, 42082 I-10
Tlaxiaco, 17543 H-9
Tuxtepec, 101810 H-10

Puebla

Acatlán de Osorio, 16307 H-9
Atlixco, 86690 G-9
Cholula, 127861 G-9
Huauchinango, 56206 G-9
Izúcar de Matamoros, 43006 H-9
Puebla, 1434062 G-9
Tehuacán, 248716 H-9
Tepeaca, 27449 G-9
Teziutlán, 58699 G-9
Xicotepec, 39803 G-9

Querétaro

Jalpan, 11010 F-8
Querétaro, 626495 G-8
San Juan del Río, 138878 G-8
Tequisquiapan, 29799 G-8

Quintana Roo

Cancún, 628306 F-14
Chetumal, 151243 G-13
Cozumel, 77236 F-14
Felipe Carrillo Puerto, 25744 G-13
Playa del Carmen, 149923 F-14
Tulum, 18233 G-14

San Luis Potosí

Cárdenas, 15469 F-8
Cerritos, 14804 F-8
Ciudad Valles, 124644 F-8
Ébano, 24296 F-9
Matehuala, 77328 E-8
Rioverde, 53128 F-8
San Luis Potosí, 722772 F-7
Tamazunchale, 24562 F-8

Sinaloa

Culiacán, 675773 E-5
El Rosario, 16001 F-5
El Dorado, 13197 E-5
Escuinapa, 30790 F-5
Guamúchil, 63743 D-4
Guasave, 71196 D-4
Los Mochis, 256613 D-4
Mazatlán, 381583 E-5
Navolato, 29153 E-4

Sonora

Agua Prieta, 77254 A-4
Caborca, 59922 B-3
Cananea, 31560 B-4
Ciudad Obregón, 298625 C-4
Empalme, 42516 C-3
Guaymas, 113082 C-3
Hermosillo, 715061 B-3
Navojoa, 113836 C-4
Nogales, 212513 A-3
Puerto Peñasco, 56756 A-2
San Luis Río Colorado, 158089 A-2

Tabasco

Cárdenas, 91558 H-11
Comalcalco, 41458 H-11
Huimanguillo, 27344 H-11
Macuspana, 32225 H-11
Paraíso, 25186 H-11
Tenosique, 32579 H-12
Villahermosa, 353577 H-11

Tamaulipas

Ciudad Madero, 197216 F-9
Ciudad Mante, 84787 F-8
Ciudad Victoria, 305155 E-8
Matamoros, 449815 D-9
Nuevo Laredo, 373725 C-8
Reynosa, 589466 D-9
Río Bravo, 95647 D-9
San Fernando, 29665 E-9
Tampico, 297284 F-9
Valle Hermoso, 48918 D-9

Tlaxcala

Tlaxcala, 14689 G-9

Veracruz

Acayucan, 50934 H-10
Alvarado, 23128 G-10
Coatzacoalcos, 235938 H-10
Córdoba, 140896 G-9
Cosamaloapan, 30577 H-10
Martínez de la Torre, 60074 G-9
Minatitlán, 112046 H-10
Orizaba, 120844
Papantla, 53546
Poza Rica, 1852242
San Andrés Tuxtla, 61769
Tuxpan, 84750
Veracruz, 428323
Xalapa, 424755

Yucatán

Mérida, 777615
Motul, 23240
Progreso, 37369
Ticul, 32796
Tizimín, 46971
Valladolid, 48973

Zacatecas

Fresnillo, 120944
Guadalupe, 124623
Jerez de García Salinas, 43064
Río Grande, 32944
Zacatecas, 129011

*, †, ‡, § See explanation under state title in this index. County and parish names are listed in capital letters and in boldface type. Independent cities (not in any county) are shown in italics.